WITHDRAWN

D1071650

Weimar Prussia, 1925–1933

Dietrich Orlow

943.085
Or5we

WEIMAR PRUSSIA
1925–1933
The Illusion of Strength

UNIVERSITY OF PITTSBURGH PRESS

Published by the University of Pittsburgh Press, Pittsburgh, Pa. 15260

Copyright © 1991, University of Pittsburgh Press
All rights reserved
Eurospan, London
Manufactured in the United States of America

Library of Congress Cataloging in Publication Data

Orlow, Dietrich.
    Weimar Prussia, 1925–1933 : the illusion of strength / Dietrich
Orlow.
    p. cm.
    Includes bibliographical references and index.
    ISBN 0-8229-3684-4 (cloth)
    1. Prussia (Germany)—History—1918–1933. I. Title.
DD453.076 1991
943.085—dc20   91-8117
                                         CIP

A CIP catalogue record for this book is available from the British
Library.

For my parents

4-22-92 mls 47.15 CAT Jun 29 '92

ALLEGHENY COLLEGE LIBRARY

91-6080

Contents

Acknowledgments

The debts of gratitude accumulated in the course of researching a work of scholarship are numerous, and it is a pleasant duty to acknowledge the many forms of aid and encouragement that facilitated the emergence of this study.

Above all, I am grateful to the Alexander von Humboldt Foundation for its lengthy and generous fellowship support of my research. My tenure as a Humboldt Fellow for more than two years enabled me to carry out the bulk of the necessary archival researches. The Historische Kommission zu Berlin also provided much appreciated grants-in-aid.

Because of the upheavals of twentieth-century German history, primary source material is located in a variety of institutions in several countries. This requires a considerable amount of travel. Research is also more difficult because of the dispersal of what were once single sets of papers: the Otto Braun papers, for example, now reside in three different archives. I would like to express my gratitude to the numerous institutions I visited in the course of researching this study. The staffs of all of them were unfailingly helpful and generous in making the materials in their custody available to me.

Every research project benefits immensely from discussions with colleagues in the field. Some of the cross-fertilization may be so subtle as to remain almost unnoticed, but in this case two colleagues deserve very specific and public acknowledgement. They are Hans Mommsen of Bochum, who originally suggested the topic of this study, and Werner Jochmann of Hamburg. Professor Jochmann's constructive criticism was instrumental in shaping the organizational format of the study, and his generosity in sharing his unrivaled knowledge of the period in numerous conversations with me greatly facilitated the work's progress. I would also like to thank Hagen Schulze, Berlin, for giving me copies of some interviews he had conducted in researching his biography of Otto Braun.

Finally, this book, more than most perhaps, has been a family affair. My wife labored long and arduously with me on the various drafts of this book. I gratefully acknowledge her help at every stage of the project.

Needless to say, whatever errors and shortcomings that remain are my responsibility.

Weimar Prussia, 1925–1933

Introduction

"Prussia is in again," observed the German historian Hans-Ulrich Wehler a few years ago as he surveyed the "Prussian wave," that sudden flood of publications and exhibitions during the 1970s and 1980s focusing on the state and its history.[1] Wehler saw the sudden revival of interest in Prussia's history and legacy as a mixed blessing. He was not alone. Other prominent historians also complained that there was altogether too much nostalgia in the "Prussian wave"; too many publications presented a decidedly one-sided view of the state's society and history.

Short on new archival research,[2] the picture of Prussian history presented in many of the "wave" publications was both politically and methodologically simplistic. Concentrating their interest on Prussia before 1918, the authors portrayed life in the state before World War I as something close to a social and political idyll. Prussia, it appeared, was a politically stable, corruption-free land in which a well-contented populace was glad to be governed by enlightened rulers. Critics pointed to the "other," the real Prussia: The state that had exercized predominant influence in Germany since the mid-nineteenth century was controlled by a narrow-minded group of professional military and civil administrators still largely drawn from the state's traditional premodern ruling class, the Junkers, who imposed a thoroughly undemocratic political and socially repressive system on the state. As for enlightened rulers, Frederick the Great might deserve that label, but his successors, men like Frederick William IV or William II, were hardly of the same caliber as the great king. In fact, these rulers and their administrative elite worked hard to prevent the evolution of a modern political system in Prussia. After all, the refusal by the Prussian elite to permit changes in the state's undemocratic electoral system was a major factor in precipitating the revolution of 1918 that finally brought down the "old," and suddenly idolized, Prussia.[3]

Much of the criticism by Wehler and other "progressive" historians was well directed, although some of it was clearly overstated and polemical. Like the state's colors, Prussian history seemed to be either black or white. Curiously, both sides in the debate ignored that Prussian history did not end in 1918. The self-imposed chronological limitations by the creators of the "Prussian wave" is perhaps understandable; fixated on the glories of the Prussian monarchy, they found it difficult to feel nostalgia for the Weimar era. But that does not explain the critics' decision to ignore the last fifteen years of Prussia's history. With a few exceptions, for the most part even the

3

critics' interest in Weimar Prussia is limited to discussing the proper date for the final demise of the state (1918, 1932, 1933, and 1947 have all been suggested) and debating the extent to which the leaders of the "old" Prussia were responsible for helping the Nazis come to power.[4]

The seeming lack of concern for the history of Prussia during the Weimar era is unfortunate. Weimar Prussia presents an important counterweight to the state's prevailing image as a stronghold of authoritarianism. If Prussia prior to 1918 symbolized the dominance of political and social authoritarianism in Germany, the state after 1918 was synonymous with the country's first attempt to build a parliamentary democracy. In fact, parliamentary democracy in Weimar Germany for all practical purposes succeeded only in Prussia. Without Prussia, in other words, not only would the Weimar experiment have ended much sooner, but also there would have been far less of a democratic legacy to build upon during the years of political reconstruction of Germany after World War II.[5]

This volume, like its predecessor,[6] is an attempt to present some aspects of the "third," the democratic Prussia. The earlier treatment, which brought the story to 1925, sought to answer the question of why parliamentary democracy succeeded in the state—which made up three-fifths of Germany's territory and population—while it failed in the Reich as a whole. For the years covered in this book, 1925 to 1933, other issues come to the fore. Having succeeded in firmly establishing parliamentary democracy as the state's political system, how did the Prussian leaders use this system to advance their political program and why did they fail to defend their creation in the crisis years after 1930? In short, how close the state came to realizing its goal of paving the way for democracy in Germany and why it ultimately failed is the subject of this book.

The time span covered in this book encompasses both Prussia's political triumphs during the "golden years" of the Weimar era and the period of the state's declining influence that culminated in the federal takeover in July 1932 and the Nazi *Machtergreifung* a few months later. Covering both the zenith and the nadir of Prussia's history during the Weimar years is in itself unusual. Most treatments of the period see the years after 1925 (or in some cases from 1930) as little more than a prelude to Papen's coup of July 1932.[7]

In the last quarter century, functionalism has been the dominant school among historians of recent German history, and this approach has left its mark on the history of Weimar Prussia as well. In the case of Prussia, turning away from an emphasis on leaders and personalities and concentrating on the effect of "functional" causes to explain the state's political successes and failures has meant focusing on Prussia's constitutional system and the interaction of its political parties. It has become almost axiomatic to blame the shortcomings of the Reich constitution and the ineptitude of Germany's national parties for the failure of modern democratic politics at the Reich level. In contrast, historians pointed to the positive features of the Prussian constitutional system and the pragmatism of the state's democratic parties as decisive for Prussia's success as a stable parliamentary democracy.[8]

Yet functionalism has never dominated the historiography of Weimar Prussia's political history in the same way as it permeated accounts of the national scene. Personalism, particularly political biographies, has been important in accounts of the state's republican era. This is not surprising. In contrast to the lackluster leaders in the Reich, Weimar Prussia produced a number of powerful and singularly effective political leaders. Particularly the state's longtime prime minister, Otto Braun, has fascinated historians. Braun was something of a legend even in his own time. The story of his rise from the obscurity of a working-class family in East Prussia to become prime minister of Germany's largest state symbolized Prussia's "democratic mission" in the Weimar years. Much the same can be said about Ernst Heilmann, the longtime chairman of the Prussian legislature's Social Democratic caucus. Here, too, the contrast between the old, authoritarian and the new, democratic Prussia was striking. In the state's pre-1914 political system, Jews were systematically prevented from achieving real power. Only democracy permitted a man like Heilmann, who was Jewish, to become the most powerful man in the legislature.[9]

This volume attempts to strike a balance between the pitfalls of excessive personalism, overstated functionalism, and political necrophilia. If there is a leitmotiv running through the political history of Weimar Prussia, it is the interaction of the state's leading political figures, the pragmatism of its Weimar coalition parties—the Social Democrats, the Center party, and the left-wing Liberals—and what might perhaps best be described as the Prussian *mentalité*. The last factor was the often voiced conviction that Prussia was destined to lead, indeed to dominate, the Reich and its political future.

There is no doubt that Prussia possessed political leaders who were far better at making a parliamentary democracy work than were their counterparts in the Reich. But it was not leaders alone that set Reich and state apart. In Prussia the political parties, which in the Reich seemed singularly ineffective at parliamentary politics, did not show a penchant for creating political gridlock that so often paralyzed democracy at the Reich level. A major reason for this development was that the state's political life was permeated by the Prussian *mentalité*. The Weimar coalition parties were convinced that in the interest of state and nation their parochial interests had to be subordinated to those of the state as a whole. This was not an appeal to altruism, but to the identification of national and particular interests. The state's leading parties were convinced it was Prussia's destiny to create a politically viable system that could stabilize the Reich as a whole. In this sense, there was a remarkable continuity from the prewar era to the Weimar era. Prussia had imposed its political system on Germany in the nineteenth century, and it continued to do so in the twentieth. The only difference was that until 1918 the system had been Bismarckian and Wilhelminian authoritarianism, while after 1918 it would be parliamentary democracy. "Prussianism," Otto Braun quoted a newspaper editorial approvingly, meant "pursuing the goal of democracy and serving the interests of the whole state without reservation [*völlige Hingabe an das Staatsganze*]." [10] Except for the change in constitutional system, Bismarck would have agreed with the sentiment.

All through the Weimar Republic's "golden years," Prussia's leaders insisted that this "Prussian consciousness" *(Preussenbewusstsein)* was a formula for political success. Working together in the executive and the legislature, the Weimar coalition parties cooperated with remarkably little friction and spared Prussia the numerous cabinet crises that characterized parliamentary democracy in the Reich. "A new, democratic [and] Republican Prussia was growing *(war im Werden)* and would have come to fruition *(Vollendung)*, if its evolution had not been prevented by the power of the Reich," wrote Otto Braun wistfully in his memoirs. [11]

But was it just the Reich's action that led to the crumbling of the "rock of democracy"? There is no doubt, of course, that the presidential Reich chancellors who dominated federal politics after March 1930 deliberately set out to weaken parliamentary democracy in the state. But were there not other factors leading to the downfall of the Prussian bastion as well? The rise of the Nazis, and, to a lesser extent, the Communists, neither of whom subscribed to the values of the Prussian *mentalité,* undermined the state's strong political position. The growing power of the extremists undoubtedly contributed to a massive feeling of political burnout among the state's leaders after 1930, rendering them increasingly fatalistic about the future. In the final analysis, however, the Prussian *mentalité* itself undermined the foundations of Prussia's seemingly successful democratic system. Convinced that the success of the constitutional and political system in Prussia alone was sufficient to guarantee the survival of political democracy in the Reich as a whole, the state's political leaders concentrated on perfecting their cooperation in the state and attempting to isolate Prussia from the effect of developments in the Reich as a whole. In the end, Prussia suffered from a kind of political hybris. With a long history of national crises during which the state had controlled the flow of events behind them, Prussia's dominant leaders and parties were convinced that "fortress Prussia" would always be able to ward off attacks from any quarter. It was a serious and ultimately fatal miscalculation, but it was one based upon a record of political success that was unequaled in the history of Weimar Germany.

CHAPTER 1

Prussia and the German Political Parties, 1925–1930

In the short history of the Weimar Republic, the years from the election of Paul von Hindenburg as Reich president in April 1925 to the resignation of the last parliamentary Reich cabinet in March 1930 are full of paradoxes. Supporters of the republic apparently had reason to congratulate themselves. There was evidence of a return to political stability; in the 1928 Reichstag election, the moderate parties won back many of the votes they had lost four years earlier. Putsch attempts by left and right extremists vanished from the headlines.[1]

The situation seemed even more promising in Prussia. In the 1928 Landtag election (which was held simultaneously with the Reichstag contest) the prorepublican parties not only regained the ground lost in 1924, but actually won a majority in the state parliament. (In the Reichstag elections the three parties of the Weimar coalition—the Social Democrats, German Democrats, and the Center Party—together received only 46.8 percent of the vote.) Frequent cabinet crises and rapid personnel shifts continued to be the rule in the Reich, but in the state Otto Braun, the "red czar of Prussia," presided over a stable government that would remain in office until 1933.[2]

But there was another side to the republic's "golden years." With the benefit of hindsight, it is not difficult to discern the portents of future problems. Much of the electoral support for the Weimar parties was "soft," it was a reflection of the economic upturn, rather than an expression of deep-seated commitment to parliamentary democracy. In other words, the republic still lacked consensual support. There were a number of reasons for the voters' continuing alienation from the Weimar constitutional system, but many supporters of the republic were convinced that the problems were primarily structural: Only a complete overhaul of the German parties and the country's federal structure could bring political stability to the Reich.

Among the moderate groups, the Liberal parties faced the most formidable difficulties. Deeply divided among themselves, their share of the popular vote in Prussia dropped from 21.9 percent in the 1919 election to 13.0 percent in 1928. Political leaders and pundits alike recognized that something had to be done. The magic words seemed to be *unity* and *mergers*. Consequently, the

7

second half of the decade was marked by a succession of self-important movements, associations, clubs, and circles, all determined to unite all or parts of an elusive "republican center." An obvious first step was a reunion of the left- and right-wing Liberals (DDP and DVP), but there were more ambitious schemes as well. There were several initiatives to create a "large national republican party"; its backers hoped the new formation would include the Social Democrats, the DDP, and "very large parts of the Center party." Something called the "republican cartel" concentrated its efforts on persuading the right-wing paramilitary Young German Order (Jungdeutscher Orden) to become a prorepublican group.[3]

In addition to these transparent and largely self-serving schemes to halt the decline of liberalism, there were also efforts to cure the country's political malaise by large-scale structural reforms. Many analysts saw Germany's federal structure as a crucial weakness of the Weimar Republic, and attempted to launch grass-roots initiatives to develop public support for the elusive *Reichsreform*. In 1926 several prominent Social Democrats and German Democrats created the German Republican Reich Association. The new organization set out to mobilize public opinion in favor of replacing the Reich's federal structure with a unitary, centralized form, such as existed in France or Great Britain. A larger and more influential group was the Association for the Rejuvenation of the Reich. Established in 1928 and headed by a former Reich chancellor, Hans Luther, it received genuine multipartisan support from across the political spectrum. The group's proposals for reforming Germany's federal structure lacked specificity, but Luther and his associates generated a great deal of publicity and convinced many that reforming the federal structure was the key to Germany's political future.[4]

Although such groups undoubtedly meant well, their collective efforts were actually politically counterproductive. By giving credence to the notion that Germany's problems were structural, not political, they discredited the established parties as inadequate to accomplish the needed reforms in Weimar Germany. In doing so, the advocates of structural reforms helped to undermine the political system they were attempting to perfect.

This was also true of the extraparliamentary, paramilitary pressure groups. To be sure, most of the significant military organizations that operated after 1925 were left- and right-wing pressure groups whose avowed aim was to use their paramilitary organization and trappings to attack Weimar Germany's parliamentary democracy.[5] But groups advocating politics beyond the parties were not limited to political extremists, or restricted to the far right. The Reichsbanner Schwarz-Rot-Gold (Reich Banner Black-Red-Gold) took a leaf from the extreme right's book. Equipped with rudimentary uniforms, bands, and a semblance of paramilitary discipline, the Reichsbanner saw itself as a multipartisan organization whose members were committed to supporting parliamentary democracy and German nationalism. Although the Reichsbanner was a nationwide organization, it had a specific Prussian connection. Its national leader and driving force was Otto Hörsing, the controversial governor of the Prussian province of Saxony.[6]

The Reichsbanner was not an unmitigated success. The organization had been founded by a group of SPD and socialist union leaders, and its affiliation with the Social Democrats remained strong throughout its existence. Efforts to overcome its image as a socialist or "Marxist" organization failed. Initially a number of prominent DDP and Center party members joined the organization,[7] but leaders of the bourgeois parties soon became uneasy over their association with a "Marxist" paramilitary organization. By the end of 1926, most of the bourgeois leaders had resigned from the Reichsbanner. One of the few who remained active was Joseph Wirth, another former Reich chancellor and later Reich minister of the interior. Wirth, a prominent leader of the Center party's left wing, fervently supported the Reichsbanner as a means of overcoming the class divisions among the supporters of the prorepublican parties. Unfortunately, Wirth's point of view was not shared by most leaders of his own party, and his position in the party became increasingly isolated.[8]

Prussia's political leaders were less concerned about the Reichbanner's socialist image than about the personality of its leader and the group's self-proclaimed status as a democratic paramilitary organization. Otto Hörsing had been a controversial figure since his days as state commissioner in Silesia in late 1918, and he remained a gadfly among Prussia's territorial administrators. His eccentricities and chronic insubordination eventually led the Prussian interior minister to ask for his resignation.[9] An even more central problem was the question if a prorepublican paramilitary organization properly belonged in a parliamentary democracy. As far as the Reichsbanner was concerned, its function was to "wrest control of the street from the extremists." But as Carl Severing, Prussia's minister of the interior, asked pointedly, was it not contradictory to use paramilitary organizations to combat the evils of paramilitarism? The very presence of an organization like the Reichsbanner supported the argument that a parliamentary system, which depended on political parties to function, had failed. Like the structural reform groups, organizations like the Reichsbanner unwittingly shook confidence in a political system that at least in Prussia was functioning quite well.

Systemic contradictions were not a concern for the paramilitary organizations affiliated with the left- and right-wing extremist parties. For them, the "politics of the streets" was a natural arena of activity. In 1924, the same year in which the Reichsbanner was founded, the Communists created their own paramilitary group, Roter Frontkämpferbund (Red Front Fighters' Association, RFB). Its founders hoped to lure members from the Reichsbanner to the Communist camp, but in this they were singularly unsuccessful. RFB members were recruited almost entirely from those already committed to the Communist cause. Instead of becoming a serious rival to the Reichsbanner, the RFB remained a fringe organization on the political landscape. When the Prussian government ordered its dissolution in 1929, the action was more of a coup de grace than a death blow. Despite its structural weakness and lack of mass membership, the RFB also contributed to the instability of the Weimar Republic. It not only shared the far right's penchant for street violence, but its very existence permitted the right-wing extremists to claim that the danger of a Communist revolution continued to be real and that the republican governments were unable or unwilling to take decisive measures against the Bolshevik subversives. From this it followed that only the paramilitary groups on the far right could save Germany from Communism.[10]

Most of the traditional paramilitary rightist groups had passed their prime. After 1925 they had neither large memberships nor much political influence. However, there was one exception: the Stahlhelm—Bund der Frontsoldaten (Steel Helmet—Association of Battlefront Veterans). Founded by Franz Seldte, a Saxon soft drink manufacturer, by 1926 the Stahlhelm boasted a membership of more than 5 million, a figure that far eclipsed all other paramilitary groups. Despite its name, the Stahlhelm did not actually insist that its members be veterans; in reality anyone could join the organization. Ostensibly, the Stahlhelm was a nonpartisan organization that "stood above the parties," but in practice the group maintained close political and organizational ties to the right-wing parties. Dual memberships among the DNVP and the Stahlhelm were common, and several provincial chairmen of the DNVP were also regional leaders of the Stahlhelm.[11]

The Stahlhelm adopted different political tactics from rival paramilitary organizations. Unlike other such organizations, which were generally contemptuous of all political parties, Seldte offered to cooperate with the antirepublican parliamentary groups. Working together with some right-wing Liberals, the German Nationalists, and later the Nazis, the Stahlhelm launched a variety of antirepublican initiatives, including several efforts intended to remove the "Marxist" government in Prussia from office.

Prussia's unique position in the German political and federal system meant that both the Weimar coalition parties and opposition groups never saw Prussian politics as isolated from developments in the Reich. In view of this linkage and the continuing absence of political consensus in Germany as a whole, it was both remarkable and unexpected that Prussia remained an island of relative political stability. Much of the explanation lay in the peculiar Prussian consciousness *(Preussenbewusstsein)* shared by all of the major political parties, except for the Nazis and the Communists. Both the government coalition and the traditional rightists were convinced that as a state and as an idea, Prussia would continue to play a decisive role in German political history. A broad spectrum of parties ranging from the SPD to the DNVP accepted as a political axiom that the state would always be the cornerstone of Germany's national unity and the guarantor of whatever political system prevailed in Germany as a whole.

The Weimar Coalition Parties: The Social Democrats

The Prussian SPD was a key factor in the success of parliamentary democracy in the state. The Social Democrats obtained the largest number of popular votes in every state election from February 1919 through May 1928. It was only in the last Landtag election of the Weimar years, in April 1932, that the party dropped to second place behind the Nazis. The SPD also dominated the cabinet. Between April 1925 and July 1932 the two most important ministerial posts, those of prime minister and minister of the interior, were always occupied by a Social Democrat.

The Prussian SPD wrote its own success story. The Prussian SPD was strong and united, the national party was weak and vacillating.[12] The party's Prussian leaders—Otto Braun, the longtime prime minister; Ernst Heilmann, the equally perennial leader of the SPD's Landtag delegation; and Albert Grzesinski, the state's minister of the interior for most of the second half of the decade—were strong personalities and skillful politicians. In contrast, at the Reich level the SPD had long lacked a really effective national leader, and the situation did not improve after 1925. Hermann Müller and Otto Wels, the two national co-chairmen, were honorable *apparatchiks,* but they lacked charisma and willpower. The troika that headed the Reichstag caucus (Rudolf Breitscheid, Wilhelm Dittmann, and Wels) satisfied the demands of the party's ideological wings for access to leadership positions, but collectivity could not compensate for a lack of ideas and clear direction. As a result of these difficulties at the national level, the party was beset by increasingly severe morale problems.[13]

The national SPD and its Reichstag delegation were torn by chronic factional disputes. The national party was divided on some fundamental questions of policy and ideology. Coalition politics and the party's attitude toward the "formal" democracy of the Weimar Republic—the key to the political success of the Prussian SPD—ranked high as sources of dispute. The left wing blamed the party's coalition with the bourgeois parties for the SPD's loss of votes and members to the KPD, while some among the militant right urged the party to shed much of its Marxist ideology and become part of the "republican center." The aging national leadership sympathized with the right wing, but, aware of the emotional appeal of the left wing's position among the party's rank and file, equivocated and treaded water.[14]

The primary arena for intraparty battles was the party's annual national

congress. Since the party identified itself as Marxist, the formal programs the
congresses adopted or amended were not seen as tactical platforms designed
to attract voter support, but as integral steps in an ongoing revelation of
Marxist scientific truth.[15] The myth that programmatic debates concerned
interpretations of a body of truth lent a curiously ritualistic air to the congresses. Although the delegates knew that the controversies really concerned
problems of daily politics, such as whether to join coalition governments or
how to target new voter groups, speakers at the annual congresses cast their
contributions in terms of abstract ideological points about the definition of
socialism, democracy, the class struggle, or the proletariat.[16]

The party's right wing, which included the SPD's leaders in Prussia,
argued that at Germany's present stage of economic development, advanced
capitalism, parliamentary democracy, and coalitions between the SPD and the
moderate bourgeois parties were effective ways of advancing the further
transformation of the society from capitalism to socialism. The left wing
strongly disagreed. It did not dispute the benefits of parliamentarism, but it
regarded bourgeois–Social Democratic coalitions as a mixture of fire and
water that served only to confuse the SPD's membership about the nature of
the class struggle. When the right wing pointed to the SPD's successful
coalition with the Center party in Prussia as confirmation of its views, the left
countered by urging the SPD to look upon the Center party as the Social
Democrats' most dangerous adversary. Supporters of the left argued the
Catholic party, unlike other bourgeois groups, would lure proletarian members and voters away from the SPD and Marxism. As a consequence, the left
wing demanded an end to coalitions with the Center party and a vigorous
anticlerical stand by the SPD.

The results of the often impassioned debates at party congresses were
mixed. Resolutions calling for an end to coalitions with the Center party and
other bourgeois groups were defeated by heavy majorities,[17] but the demands
of the left wing also tended to put the Prussian SPD on the defensive. This
stand in turn aroused the suspicions of the Center party's right wing, which,
for different reasons, was equally opposed to cooperation with the Social
Democrats.

Just as the question of coalitions with bourgeois parties was linked to the
discussion of the nature of the class struggle, debates over national defense
evoked bitter discussions about the SPD's attitude toward nationalism as a
factor of modern political life. Socialist leaders from Karl Kautsky to Otto
Braun recognized the pervasive force of modern mass nationalism, but the
sense that the link between nationalistic passions and militarism was part of
the ideological superstructure of capitalism also remained strong. Indeed, the
Social Democrats were justified in their fear and distrust of the German
military establishment; the antidemocratic and antisocialist sentiments of most

Reichswehr leaders were all too well known. But the party's right wing argued that the left wing was again throwing out the baby with the bath water. The concepts of *nation* and *national defense* should not be a monopoly of the capitalists. Raising doubts about the party's patriotism in the eyes of the SPD's potential bourgeois coalition partners actually gave additional credence to the antidemocratic voices in the Reichswehr.[18]

The debates during the SPD's 1929 congress on appropriations for the navy in the defense budget provided a good example of the strength of anti-Reichswehr feelings among the party's rank and file. Initially, the question seemed simple and straightforward: should the Reich cabinet and the Reichstag approve outlays for a new class of naval ships, the so-called battle cruisers? The legality of the appropriation was not in doubt; such vessels were clearly permitted under the Versailles Treaty.[19]

Serious questions remained, however, about the military value of the shipbuilding program, its consequences for Germany's foreign relations, and the domestic political implications of voting for these defense outlays. In concrete terms: should the Social Democrats agree to vote money for a controversial piece of hardware that would strengthen the most reactionary branch of the Reichswehr, and contribute to the international arms race? The Prussian SPD sought to defuse the issue by rejecting the navy's proposals on pragmatic grounds. The state's Social Democratic leaders, as well as the spokesmen of the other Weimar coalition parties, decided the battle cruiser was militarily useless and politically provocative. The cabinet instructed the Reichsrat delegates under its control to support an amendment eliminating the proposed appropriation for the battle cruiser from the 1928 Reich budget. The Reichsrat agreed, and in December 1927 the issue seemed dead.[20]

But pressure for renewing the navy's request quickly mounted in the Reich. The DVP, the Reich president, and the navy all insisted on the construction program, and in March 1928 the issue again came before the Reichsrat. This time Prussia, in an obvious effort to avoid open conflict, muted its opposition. It did not oppose the construction program on substantive grounds, but merely argued that further financial feasibility studies were needed.[21]

This may have been a tactical mistake, because the Reich cabinet eventually voted for the appropriation, and the debate now shifted to a larger political arena. The Social Democrats managed to fall between all stools. After the 1928 Reichstag election, the SPD joined the Reich cabinet, and in order not to endanger the federal coalition, the Social Democratic ministers approved the measure along with their bourgeois colleagues. That decision raised a storm of protest among rank-and-file SPD members and the party's Reichstag delegation. A majority of the SPD's Reichstag caucus not only opposed the outlays, but also voted to cast the SPD delegation's ballots as a unit, so that the Social Democratic ministers (as Reichstag members) were subjected to the humiliation of having to vote against a measure on the floor of the Reichstag which in their capacity as Reich ministers they had proposed to the legislature.[22]

The SPD failed to stop the appropriation, but the intraparty recriminations did not end there. Pressure from the rank and file led the SPD leadership to sponsor a national initiative and referendum campaign jointly with the Communists to reverse the Reichstag's decision. This action also failed, but campaigning side by side with the KPD was hardly less embarrassing to SPD leaders than the original vote for the appropriations had been. And as a final blow, the 1929 national convention, with massive support from back-bench delegates, passed a resolution that amounted to a vote of censure for Reich chancellor Hermann Müller and the other Social Democratic ministers.[23]

The position of the Prussian SPD throughout the controversy was a model of political astuteness. As we saw, the Prussian SPD along with the state cabinet had opposed the naval project from the beginning. Otto Braun, for one, was outraged that Hermann Müller and the SPD's national leaders had allowed themselves to be drawn into the ideological quagmire.[24] In contrast, the Prussians felt the issue should be debated on pragmatic, not ideological grounds. As a result, the Prussian SPD itself was not adversely affected by the continuing furor within the party, but in fact, reaped a number of political rewards from the affair. Its stand pleased the SPD's left wing,[25] while the pragmatic reasons advanced by the Prussian SPD leaders prevented an ideological confrontation with the party's bourgeois coalition partners in the state.

For the most part, the state's party remained an island of calm in the swirls of controversy that troubled the national party. The Prussian party leaders deliberately avoided the limelight, generally speaking out only on issues that concerned Prussian politics directly. No leading Prussians were members of the commission that drafted the SPD's defense plank in the 1929 program, and the party's parliamentary leader in Prussia, Ernst Heilmann, was not even a delegate to the 1929 conclave.[26] With the exception of Braun and Severing, prominent Prussian politicians seldom took the floor at the national congresses. When they did, it was to defend actions, such as the concordat with the Catholic church, which aroused the particular ire of the left wing, but which the Prussian SPD regarded as central to maintaining the party's position in Prussia.[27]

A major reason for the Prussians' lack of prominence in national party affairs was their disinclination to become involved in what they regarded as fruitless ideological debates. In the Prussian SPD ideological positions and practical politics went hand in hand. The party's activities in the state were focused on the Landtag caucus and the party's ministers in the state cabinet.

The state's leaders opposed a statewide party organization separate from the Landtag caucus as redundant. Only once in this period did the SPD hold a Prussian state convention and that was for a very circumscribed purpose, to organize the campaign for the 1928 state elections. (The Prussian congress that year took the place of the SPD's national convention.)[28]

Throughout the second half of the decade, the Prussian party's leadership was characterized by relative harmony of purpose, as well as personal and institutional continuity. Otto Braun's dominant position in the Prussian SPD was unquestioned.[29] Never a modest man, Braun left no doubt that his leadership of the state's SPD was the key to the party's political success in Prussia. Even after he was forced into exile, Braun tended to minimize the contributions of his associates. The cult of personality around the prime minister was the target of some intraparty criticism—especially from outside Prussia—but for the most part Braun remained above criticism. This was not all to the good. In retrospect it is clear that Braun's untouchable position made it difficult for younger members of the party to gain political stature. This was true, for example, of Kurt Schumacher, in the last years of the Weimar Republic one of the SPD's rising stars and after 1945 the leader of the party in West Germany. Braun held Schumacher back simply because he disliked the young Landtag delegate.[30]

Braun was particularly unfair to Ernst Heilmann, the SPD's legislative leader. The original draft of the prime ministers's memoirs did not even include a specific reference to Heilmann's role in Prussia; Braun added some laudatory remarks only in a revision. Yet in many ways, it was Heilmann who made Braun's successes as prime minister possible. Braun's judgment was colored by his aversion to Heilmann's life style. The legislative leader was extroverted, while Braun had a pronounced dislike of idle socializing. Heilmann liked women and gambling, Braun was a puritan and a homebody. Nevertheless, the two men complemented each other politically, and Heilmann was superb at his job.[31]

Although all ideological wings of the party were represented in the hundred-member Landtag caucus, the political center of gravity in the Prussian group was considerably further to the right than was true for the party's Reichstag delegation. The majority of the SPD's Landtag delegation, which, like the Reichstag caucus, was composed primarily of provincial party bureaucrats and union officials, agreed with Braun's judgment that the formula, "The road to power lies in the application of scientific Marxism," was not a very useful guide to practical politics.[32] Among the state's district organizations only Berlin and the two Silesian districts were dominated by leftists, and left-wing criticism of the state's SPD leaders had far less impact on the party's policies in Prussia than in the Reich. The caucus chairman, Ernst Heilmann, was himself part of the extreme right wing of the party. The journal he edited,

ALLEGHENY COLLEGE LIBRARY

Das Freie Wort, became one of the leading mouthpieces for the SPD's right wing in the republic's last years.

Pragmatism and quality of leadership were the keys to the Prussian SPD's political success between 1925 to 1930. The Prussian leaders' common-sense attitudes toward state and national politics kept intraparty strife to a minimum, while facilitating continued cooperation with the other parties in the Weimar coalition. The voters, too, approved of the party's stand. The Social Democrats' showing in the Prussian state elections of May 1928 confounded the conventional wisdom that the SPD's share of the vote declined whenever the party shared governmental responsibility: the Prussian party achieved its best results since 1919.

The Weimar Coalition Parties: The Center Party

The history of the Prussian Center party after 1925 was strikingly parallel to that of the SPD. The state leaders of both parties worked hard to isolate the Prussian parties from developments at the national level. In the process they succeeded in converging their parties to form the backbone of Prussia's political stability. If the Prussian SPD had to defend itself against attacks from the party's left wing, the Center party was concerned with the growing strength of the Catholic's right wing. The Reichstag election of December 1924 had demonstrated the resurgence of Catholic conservatism, convincing the party's right-wing leaders that political Catholicism needed to align itself more closely with the right. Coalitions with the SPD were not part of the new image. Some of the Center party's left-wing leaders, such as ex-chancellor Joseph Wirth, vigorously opposed the Center party's turn to the right, but at the Reich level the right wing steadily increased its influence over the national party.[33]

Signs of the Center party's increasing alignment with the right were not difficult to discern. In July 1927, amid much media coverage, the party's national leader, Wilhelm Marx, resigned his membership in the Reichsbanner Schwarz-Rot-Gold, thereby severing an important symbolic link between political Catholicism and Social Democracy. But the most dramatic evidence came a year later with the election of Monsignor Ludwig Kaas as the Center party's new national leader, the first cleric to head the national organization.

Kaas's election surprised even his supporters. The leading candidates at the party's 1928 convention were two men closely identified with the Catholic labor and lay movements: Joseph Joos, a leader of the organized Catholic laity, and Adam Stegerwald, the former Prussian prime minister and leader of the Catholic unions. Both men, no doubt sensing the new mood in the party, had drawn away from the SPD by 1928, but the defeat of both front-runners was nevertheless a sharp rebuff to the left wing. Joseph Hess, chairman of the

Center party's caucus in the Prussian Landtag and an enthusiastic supporter of Joseph Joos, was deeply disappointed.[34]

Kaas quickly put his stamp on the national Center party. Shortly after he became national leader, his longtime protegé Heinrich Brüning was elected chairman of the party's Reichstag delegation. This development signaled a further turn to the right, since it was no secret that Brüning favored greater cooperation between his party and the German Nationalists. Equally well known was Brüning's distrust and dislike of the Social Democrats.[35]

The shifts of the Center party's political fulcrum were of considerable concern to the party's coalition partners in Prussia. As early as July 1925, the SPD feared the Center party's rightward shift would make cooperation with the Catholics in Prussia more difficult. The election of Kaas, whom Otto Braun characterized as a "representative of . . . authoritarian clericalism,"[36] heightened the concerns. Actually, the SPD's worries were misplaced or at any rate very premature. The Prussian Center party and its Landtag delegation remained largely isolated from national-level developments. The influence of the conservative wing in Prussia remained quite limited. The longtime nominal leader of the Prussian Center party's Landtag delegation, Carl Herold, died in 1930, but the right wing was unable to elect a successor from its ranks. Brüning, in some ways the natural choice as the new leader, resigned his Landtag seat in October 1929, in order to devote his full attention to his position as leader of the Center party in the Reichstag. Franz von Papen, a strong advocate of the party's opening to the right and a leader with a major regional base of support in the Westphalian farmers' organization, was handicapped by the memory of his divisive escapades during the 1925 cabinet crisis.[37]

In contrast, a number of circumstances contributed to strengthening the Center party's traditional left-of-center stance in Prussia. Some of the party's best organized districts in the Catholic diaspora—Berlin, Potsdam, and Niederbarmin—were dominated by particularly enthusiastic prorepublican leaders.[38] Above all, the party's leaders in the legislature and the cabinet remained firmly committed to the left-of-center course. In the Landtag Joseph Hess, an enthusiastic supporter of democracy and for many years the de facto leader of the Landtag delegation, formally succeeded to Herold's position as caucus chairman. Unfortunately, he died only two years later. Particularly noteworthy was the prorepublican attitude of some prominent clerics among the Center party's Landtag delegates. In contrast to Kaas, who favored cooperation with the "Christian" DNVP and rejected the "atheistic" SPD, men like Albert Lauscher, professor of Catholic theology at the University of Bonn, and Johannes Linneborn, dean of the cathedral chapter at Aachen, remained deeply suspicious of the DNVP's traditional anti-Catholicism. Far from rejecting cooperation with the SPD, they pointed to the benefits which the

Catholic minority in Prussia had derived from its long years of cooperation with the Weimar coalition parties.

Among the Center party members of the cabinet, Heinrich Hirtsiefer, the minister of welfare, was an especially loyal supporter of the republic and the Weimar coalition. A locksmith by training and a longtime Catholic union official with decidedly left-wing views, Hirtsiefer felt very comfortable alongside his Social Democratic colleagues. He was also one of a handful of Center party leaders who was sharply critical of Wilhelm Marx's decision to resign from the Reichsbanner.[39]

Supported by his colleagues in the Landtag and the cabinet, Joseph Hess was able to isolate the state's Center party from the effects of the right-wing policies pursued by the party's national leaders. But, as with the SPD, there were limitations on the influence of the Prussian Catholics. Although the Prussian Center party had the potential of acting as a major power block in the Center party as a whole, Hess, much like Braun and Heilmann, never openly opposed his party's national leadership. It was a policy that served the Prussian Catholics' purpose well as long as the national leadership did not attempt to interfere in Prussian affairs. However, that would be true only as long as parliamentary democracy was still functioning at both the state and Reich levels, a situation that ended abruptly in March 1930.[40]

The Weimar Coalition Parties: German Democratic Party (DDP)

The third and smallest of the Prussian coalition parties confronted difficult times after 1925. The gap between the party's self-image and its actual political influence and voter appeal became ever wider. The German Democratic party still saw itself as the bridge between the progressive parts of the middle class and the cooperative elements among the working classes. This self-image succeeded at first, but since 1920 the German Democrats' share of the popular vote in the Reich and the state had been declining steadily. Major segments of the left-wing Liberals' traditional constituency turned away from the party. Low-level civil servants deserted to the SPD, small businessmen turned to the DVP, and urban landlords to the Economics party. Even professionals, once the most solid nucleus of support for left-wing liberalism, became vulnerable to the appeal of the emerging single-issue parties. Various attempts to recapture voters and members from the right wing of the SPD or the left wing of the DVP failed. The DDP was increasingly a group of contentious leaders without followers.[41]

In its effort to recapture fleeing voters, the party was in almost continuous crisis from 1924 until its demise six years later. Each new election brought the loss of yet more voters and members as well as wrenching intraparty conflicts over who was to blame. The feuding factions agreed only that the German Democrats needed to end their isolation. As a result, the leaders of left-wing liberalism took the initiative in a dizzying variety of efforts to overcome the divisions and to restore the political strength of German liberalism. Eugen Schiffer, a former deputy Reich chancellor, and the industrialist Carl Friedrich von Siemens, for example, hoped to collect all moderates beneath the umbrella of a Liberal Association. That project was a utopian hope from the start, but chances for a union of the two liberal parties, the DDP and the DVP, seemed more propitious, especially toward the end of the decade. The DVP's difficulty in retaining voters and members was only slightly less severe than that of the DDP. The question of who would head the united party, which had prevented a union in 1918 and 1919, now appeared to present few problems. The DVP's national leader, Gustav Stresemann, was everybody's natural choice. He stood at the zenith of his political influence and popularity, and the DDP had no leader of comparable stature.[42]

Nevertheless, a union between the two parties remained beyond reach. A major reason was the widening ideological and political split in the liberal camp along the Reich-Prussian axis. Even before Stresemann's death in October 1929, powerful influences in the DVP preferred cooperation with the German Nationalists to a union with the left-wing Liberals, and under Stresemann's successors the DVP accelerated its move to the right. Some of the DDP's national leaders were willing to pursue union with the DVP along this road, but the Prussian DDP, like the state's Center party, remained staunchly left of center.[43]

The Prussian DDP's stand brought both rewards and frustrations. The party's loyalty to the Weimar coalition gave it far more political influence in the state than was warranted by the size of its popular vote. The DDP with sixteen seats in the legislature had two ministers in the government, while the Social Democrats, whose 136 delegates in the Landtag constituted the largest group in the legislature, were content with three cabinet seats. But the perennial crises in the party also made it difficult to develop clear political directions. The party was simply too small to contain side-by-side leaders like Hermann Höpker-Aschoff, the able but also extremely ambitious Prussian minister of finance, who wanted the DDP to become a more conservative "Republican Center" party, and Otto Nuschke, whose views were already far closer to Social Democracy than traditional liberalism. (Nuschke would continue to move to the left; after the Second World War he became head of the fellow-traveling Liberal Democratic party in the former German Democratic Republic.) These divisions, coupled with persistent attempts by the DDP's leaders in the Reich to interfere in state affairs, did not make the task of leading the Prussian left Liberals an easy one. Bernhard Falk, chairman of the party's Landtag delegation throughout these years, had the respect of all factions, but he complained bitterly of the problems inherent in leading his small and dwindling band.[44]

The Moderate Opposition Parties:
The German People's Party (DVP)

It was one of the paradoxes of Prussian political life that the second Braun cabinet, which took office in the spring of 1925, was for more than three years a minority government. Until May 1928, when the Weimar coalition parties received a clear mandate from the voters, the strength of the combined opposition parties in the Landtag was larger than that of the coalition. The cabinet remained in office because it had a "majority minus one plus the opposition's fear of new elections," as Braun quipped.[45] There was something to the prime minister's analysis, but a more important factor in the opposition's weakness was the political division within its ranks. The opposition parties seldom acted in concert. Their ranks ranged from the DVP, which was negotiating almost constantly to join the government, to the Nazis and Communists, whose sole aim was to destabilize parliamentary democracy and German society in general.

To be sure, the DVP was certainly one of the parties that feared new elections. Like its left Liberal rival, the German People's party suffered from declining voter appeal and a shrinking membership. After 1930 the DVP was for all practical purposes destroyed by the Nazis' electoral successes, but until then it occupied a strange position on the political spectrum. The DVP was in decline, but it was also a key to the future success of parliamentary democracy in the Reich and in Prussia. If the right-wing Liberals opted for cooperation with the moderate left and center, the coalition of the Weimar parties gained strength and stability. If, on the other hand, the DVP aligned itself alongside the DNVP and the antirepublican right, the chances for an authoritarian *Bürgerblock* were markedly enhanced.[46]

The party needed to decide whether to turn left or right. Unfortunately, the DVP did everything but come to a clear decision. The utopians in the party dreamed of becoming the nucleus of a large, new grouping that would encompass the present People's party, the "reasonable" elements in the DDP, and the left wing of the DNVP, but the chances for such an entity were even more remote than a simple merger with the DDP.[47] Unable to gain strength through mergers and unwilling to opt for either left or right, the right-wing Liberals between 1925 and 1930 were torn between sympathizers of the left and right. Gustav Stresemann succeeded in keeping the Reichstag delegation and the party as a whole on a moderate, slightly left-of-center path. He did not want his party to become a satellite of the German Nationalists, and while he was often highly critical of Social Democracy, he always kept the lines of communication to the SPD open. For both domestic and foreign policy reasons (Stresemann served as Reich minister of foreign affairs from 1923 to 1929), the DVP leader favored grand coalition governments in Prussia and the Reich. After Stresemann's death, the DVP, under its new leader, Eduard Dingeldey, veered sharply to the right, drawing closer to the DNVP and away from the Weimar coalition parties.

The DVP's ideological divisions at the national level had their parallels in the Prussian party. The Landtag delegation was no less split than its counterpart in the Reichstag, although most members of the Prussian legislature criticized the irresponsible demagogues on the far right, and worked for cooperation with the Weimar parties including resurrection of the grand coalition. But some rejected both the parliamentary system and any coalition with the SPD. When these delegates had their way, the DVP could be found at the side of the DNVP, the Nazis, and the KPD enthusiastically voting for resolutions of no confidence against the government.[48]

Neither the right nor the left wing was able to dominate the Landtag delegation consistently for any length of time, largely because the DVP in Prussia lacked a strong leader. In May 1925, Rudolf von Campe, who had steered the Landtag delegation through the years of the grand coalition, stepped down as chairman. He accepted the consequences of the failure of his convoluted strategy for continuing the grand coalition with some personnel changes. His successor was Ernst Stendel, a stolid district judge from East Frisia, whose political views, despite his disclaimers, tilted more to the right than Campe's. The new leader also had some anti-Semitic prejudices, which certainly strained his relations with his Jewish counterpart in the SPD, Ernst Heilmann.[49]

Stendel's lack of leadership often allowed the right-wingers in the Landtag considerable autonomy to pursue their own plans, but the situation was even more complicated in the second house of the Prussian parliament, the Staatsrat. Here the right-wingers did control the party caucus. Their leader, Karl Jarres, once mayor of Duisburg and in 1925 the joint Reich presidential candidate of the DVP and the DNVP, attempted to align the right-wing Liberals with the German Nationalists in a permanent parliamentary pact. Jarres was convinced that while it might be possible to work with the Social Democrats at the local level, "in the long run" the SPD and DVP could not be coalition partners at the state and Reich levels. In contrast, Jarres felt the DVP, the Center party, and the DNVP were compatible: the Center party was turning to the right, and the Conservatives after 1925 had become a moderate party that had abandoned its earlier extremist stands.[50]

In September 1926 Jarres proposed that the DVP and DNVP delegations in the Staatsrat unite to form a single parliamentary group. This scheme, which Jarres saw as the first step in the formation of a Prussian *Bürgerblock* to replace the Weimar coalition, was enthusiastically supported by Baron Wilhelm von Gayl, the DNVP's virulently antirepublican and antidemocratic leader in the Staatsrat. Jarres and Gayl laid their plans in secret (Stresemann had not been consulted), but the project was leaked to the press, and the moderate wing of the DVP raised a storm of protest. Stresemann vigorously criticized what he regarded as yet another scheme to reduce the DVP to the status of a junior partner of the German Nationalists. Members of the national executive committee and the Landtag delegation pointed to important differences between the DVP as a liberal and the DNVP as a conservative party. They also cited numerous instances of bad faith by the Conservatives' regional leaders in dealing with the DVP.[51]

The combined opposition from Stresemann, members of the Landtag delegation, and several provincial leaders succeeded in derailing the projected parliamentary union of the DVP and the DNVP in the Staatsrat. The realignment of the two parties did not go beyond arrangements for informal cooperation that had been in effect for some years. Nevertheless, the episode left a poor impression of the DVP's Prussian leader. The one politician who seems to have had very little part in managing the affair was Ernst Stendel.

Another problem confronting the DVP and its Prussian leader was the thorny issue of the party's relations with the Stahlhelm. The paramilitary group worked hard to establish closer relations with the right-wing Liberals, having already succeeded in forging an alliance with the DNVP. The right wing of the People's party favored close relations with the Stahlhelm as a way of underscoring the DVP's image as a party of the right. The left wing, on the other hand, opposed ties to the Stahlhelm precisely because an alliance of the DVP and the antirepublican paramilitary organization would certainly make further cooperation with the Weimar coalition parties more difficult. Stendel and a majority of the Landtag delegation (as well as Stresemann) sided with the left wing. In 1929 the Prussian DVP took the unusual step of prohibiting joint memberships between the party and the Stahlhelm, a gesture of good will that was warmly applauded by the Weimar coalition parties.

But the vacillations and internal conflicts, as well as Stendel's seeming inability to control the Prussian party, left its potential partners among the Weimar coalition parties uneasy. A majority of the DVP's Landtag delegation undoubtedly hoped for cooperation with the left Liberals as well as a revival of the grand coalition, but many in the DDP and especially among the Social Democrats (including Otto Braun) never quite trusted that the DVP's left wing would prevail against the forces working to align the party with the antirepublican right.

Relations between the DVP and the Center party had their own problems. On some economic issues and on questions involving civil liberties, the two parties were in agreement, but church-state relations constituted a major stumbling block to mutual good will and cooperation. A largely Protestant party, the DVP retained much of the anticlericalism and especially anti-Catholicism common to the European liberal parties before World War II. It was unfortunate for the future dealings between the DVP and the Center party that the Prussian concordat with the Holy See became a central issue in coalition politics in the second half of the decade. This meant that the latent antagonism between right-wing Liberalism and political Catholicism repeatedly burst into the open, souring relations between the Center party and the DVP.[52]

The Moderate Opposition Parties:
The Economics Party (WiP)

Despite its imposing subtitle—"Reich party of the German *Mittelstand*"—the Economics party was actually an "insignificant, if noisy splinter group" that never achieved the status of a major political party.[53] However, the precarious balance of power in the Prussian Landtag from 1925 to 1928 gave the WiP far more political influence than was warranted by the number of its members and supporters. Indeed, the Economics party was less a *Weltanschauung* party in the traditional German sense than the first and most successful of the special interest parties that became a characteristic feature of the German political landscape in the latter years of the Weimar Republic. Its founders claimed that the WiP fell somewhere between the DVP, the DDP, and the DNVP in the German party spectrum, but for all practical purposes the Economics party was no more than a lobbying group for small business interests and especially urban landlords.

Both of these groups were traditionally liberal, and the WiP above all represented a direct challenge to the two classic liberal parties, especially the DDP. In response, the DDP attempted to appease the WiP. Pressured by the German Democrats, the Weimar coalition parties repeatedly attempted to seduce the WiP into joining the cabinet. Once they claimed that agreement on the WiP's joining the coalition was close at hand, but this was vigorously denied by the Economics party.[54]

The right-wing opposition, for its part, devoted just as much energy to luring the WiP into its camp, with much more success. In fact, the hopes and expectations of the Weimar coalition parties that the WiP would join the government coalition always involved considerable wishful thinking on their part. Especially in Prussia the policies of the Economics party were virtually indistinguishable from those of the DNVP; the WiP was little more than a group of Conservative fellow travelers. It is true that the WiP, which drew most of its support from urban voters, sometimes criticized the excessive subsidies for agricultural interests advocated by the DNVP, but the Economics party shared the DNVP's dislike of parliamentary democracy in general and the Prussian cabinet in particular. Unlike the DVP, the Prussian WiP had a strong leader: Carl Ladendorff, an effective demagogue whose specialties were Socialist- and Catholic-baiting. His characterization of the Weimar parties' coalition as a "dictatorship of Social Democracy assisted by the Center party" was a succinct statement of his political beliefs.[55]

The Moderate Opposition Parties:
The German Nationalist People's Party (DNVP)

Until the 1932 Landtag elections, the German Nationalists constituted the largest opposition party in Prussia. The DNVP, too, was beset by sharp internal conflicts that eventually led to a complete split of the party. In 1929 members of the defeated left-wing minority left the DNVP and founded a new, more moderate conservative group, the People's Conservative party (Volkskonservative Partei, VKP).[56]

The formal division of the DNVP was foreshadowed by sharp differences within the party over its policies and tactics in the Reich and in Prussia. For some years after 1925, the German Nationalists in the Reich were dominated by moderate forces who led the party to become "practically a constitutional party." The DNVP was a member of several federal *Bürgerblock* coalitions. The party's national leaders hoped that their cooperative stance in the Reich would have repercussions in Prussia as well. By demonstrating the party's willingness to accept parliamentarism at the Reich level, the moderate wing of the DNVP hoped to persuade its potential partners among the bourgeois parties in Prussia—notably, the DDP, the DVP, and the Center party—to agree to a *Bürgerblock* coalition there as well. However, the moderates were never able to capture control of the Prussian DNVP, in which the party majority remained unremittingly obstructionist, rejecting all aspects of the Weimar "system." For the party's Prussian leaders, "constitutional reform began with limitations on parliamentarism."[57] As if to underscore the party's defiance of modernity, the chairman of the DNVP's Landtag delegation, Friedrich von Winterfeld, proudly described himself as the "owner of a knightly estate *(Rittergutsbesitzer)*" and listed his profession as "director of the knights of Kurmark."

Until the simultaneous Reichstag and Landtag elections in May 1928, the contradictions between the DNVP's Reich and Prussian strategies did not matter much. The Prussians could wallow in useless demagoguery, while the party's national leadership concentrated on gaining a share of power at the Reich level. But the DNVP's poor showing in both the Reichstag and Landtag elections brought the party's crisis to a head. Left- and right-wing leaders blamed each other for the debacle at the polls. Walther Lambach, the leader of the DNVP's small labor wing, and one of the most outspoken critics of the DNVP's Prussian course, argued forcefully that the election outcome demonstrated that the German Nationalists were in danger of becoming a party of the East Elbian agricultural backwater.[58] For his open criticism, Lambach was promptly expelled from the party.

Lambach's expulsion was the signal for the final struggle over the future direction of the DNVP. There is no doubt that most of the DNVP's rank and file, and especially the party's regional chairmen, had long disliked the moderate course pursued by the DNVP's national chairman, Count Kuno Westarp. Increasingly, their spokesman was Alfred Hugenberg, the owner of a media empire and a man with close ties to the Pan German Association and the Stahlhelm.[59] The DNVP's poor showing in the elections of May 1928 allowed Hugenberg to make his move. By July, he had already secured the allegiance of more than a third of the party's provincial leaders in his quest to replace Westarp. At the end of August he published his famous article "Block statt Brei" ("A Rock Instead of Putty"), a call to the party to remain true to its antirepublican stand even if that meant the loss of voters.[60] At its national congress in October of that year, the DNVP elected Alfred Hugenberg as its new national chairman.

Hugenberg was convinced his election meant a new dawn for the party. Vastly overestimating his abilities, Hugenberg and his followers saw him leading a huge anti-Marxist front of all German nonsocialist parties. A curious *Führer* cult developed around the essentially uncharismatic and unprepossessing new German Nationalist leader. As far as Prussia was concerned, Hugenberg continued the DNVP's antisystemic policies. He was convinced he could force the Center party to abandon its coalition with the Social Democrats, and join an antidemocratic *Bürgerblock* cabinet in Prussia dominated by the DNVP.[61]

The Prussian DNVP enthusiastically welcomed Hugenberg's election and supported his policies. In late 1929, after the new leader's obstructionist tactics had led to the split of the DNVP, only three members (out of seventy-three) of the Landtag delegation left the party to join Westarp and Heinrich Brüning's friend Gottfried Treviranus in forming the more moderate VKP. (The moderate minority in the Reichstag was considerably larger. Out of the total of eighty-two members of the party's Reichstag delegation twelve left the DNVP and joined the VKP.) Interestingly, however, the dissidents included Ernst von Schlange-Schöningen, the Prussian DNVP's best orator and until then one of its most radical spokesmen.[62]

Hugenberg's tactics further isolated the party in Prussia and increased its political impotence. Attacks upon the SPD as the party of the "stab-in-the-back," as well as demagogic explanations that the "Galician Jew Hilferding" had caused the German hyperinflation of 1923 had always been part and parcel of the DNVP's arsenal of smear tactics,[63] but under Hugenberg the Prussian DNVP also seemed to go out of its way to alienate the party's potential *Bürgerblock* partners. The new leader aligned the DNVP more closely with the interests of heavy industry, a decision that displeased not only the labor wing of his own party but also the Center party; the DNVP's labor organization had traditionally maintained close ties with Stegerwald's Catholic unions. And even if it could be argued that such a policy was calculated to please the right wing of the Center party, Hugenberg's anti-Catholic stand negated whatever benefits his economic policies might bring to the DNVP. The insistence by the DNVP's Landtag delegation that its members cast a block vote against the concordat between Prussia and the Catholic church was a direct affront to the Center party. In the view of the Prussian Catholics, the DNVP under Hugenberg had become a tactical partner of the Communists and the Nazis, rather than a potential ally of the moderate bourgeois parties.[64]

The Prussian Liberals echoed this criticism. Both the DVP and the DDP complained—quite correctly—that in joining the Communists in voting for resolutions of no confidence against the government, the DNVP under its new leader had adopted what was essentially a nihilist position.[65] In the long run, however, it was the German Nationalists' increasingly close relations with the Nazis that had the most disastrous consequences. True, in parliamentary terms the Nazi-DNVP alliance mattered little for the moment. Until their landslide victory of April 1932, the Prussian Nazis were a negligible political force in the state; their eight Landtag delegates were a nuisance, not a political factor. Nevertheless, there is no doubt that the DNVP's and the Stahlhelm's willingness to give the Nazis respectablility and publicity helped Hitler's movement to gain political stature even before the onset of the Depression.

Between 1925 and 1930, the DNVP's Prussian strategy remained a failure. The party exhausted itself in sterile opposition, alienating the moderate bourgeois parties whose cooperation the DNVP needed if a *Bürgerblock* was to take the place of the Weimar coalition under the rules of parliamentary democracy. Even the alliance with the Nazis proved destructive. Otto Nuschke, one of the leaders of the DDP's left wing, predicted quite accurately as early as October 1929 that the relationship between the NSDAP and the DNVP would soon be reversed: at the moment the DNVP might be nurturing the Nazis, but as soon as the latter gained sufficient strength, they would devour the German Nationalists. But the Prussian DNVP remained blind. Its hatred of parliamentary democracy was so intense that even when it had become obvious that Hugenberg's Prussian course had failed, the state's German Nationalists retained unlimited faith in their *Führer* and his strategy.[66]

The Extremists: The National Socialist German Workers' Party (NSDAP) and German *Völkisch* Freedom Party (DVFP)

Confronted with the NSDAP's explosive rise to popularity after 1929, historians tend to exaggerate the Nazis' significance before the onset of the Depression. Certainly in Prussia during most of the second half of the decade, the Hitler movement was a minuscule political group. These were years of painfully slow growth and ineffective political strategies for the NSDAP. The party's electoral campaigns emphasized, in addition to constant anti-Semitic demagoguery, a radical pseudo-socialism, which included calls for trust-busting, aid to small business, and legislation to curb the activities of department stores and consumer cooperatives. Except for their attacks upon the Jews, the Nazis essentially combined the appeals of the Economics party and the Communists.

This strategy, the so-called urban plan, was a failure.[67] In September 1927, the NSDAP obtained 1.8 percent of the popular vote in the municipal elections in Altona, one of Prussia's most industrialized cities, and the results for the 1928 Landtag elections were not much better: in the state as a whole the Nazis received 2.9 percent of the popular vote.[68] Such figures led the party's opponents to conclude as late as December 1929 (when the Nazis had already scored major gains in the Prussian local elections) that the NSDAP would never be more than a second-rate party in the state.[69]

Despite its unimpressive showing at the ballot box, these were important years in the history of the NSDAP; the Nazis evolved from being one of many groups on the extreme right to become the dominant force in the *völkische* camp. The Nazis also expanded their organization throughout Prussia. Prior to Hitler's Beer Hall putsch in 1923, the party had virtually no organization in most areas of the state. The major *völkisch* force in Prussia was the DVFP, a group that had split from the DNVP in 1922 and later merged with the northern remnants of the NSDAP when Hitler was sent to jail in the wake of the failed putsch. After the Nazi leader was released from prison at the beginning of 1925, the aggressive organizing efforts of the revitalized NSDAP quickly eclipsed the DVFP. The latter continued to exist, but it had no leader to match Hitler's charisma and organizational ability.

Hitler's triumph over his *völkisch* rivals did not mean that the NSDAP's impact on Prussian politics increased significantly. Until 1929 the party was isolated from any other power bloc except, paradoxically, the Communists. Indeed, the extremists of the right and left had much in common. Both were determined to make the parliamentary system unworkable, and to this end they often supported each other's frivolous votes of no confidence against the government. They also shared a penchant for initiating violence to disrupt the

Landtag sessions. In a sense, the small band of eight Nazis that was elected to the Landtag in May 1928 was isolated within the NSDAP as well. Products of the "urban plan," the eight delegates belonged to the party's left wing, insofar as that label applied to politicians whose primary ideology was loyalty to Hitler. The Prussian representatives tended to look to Gregor Strasser for their programmatic inspiration, and the delegation's chairman, the "Prussian *Führer*" Wilhelm Kube, delighted in a particularly virulent antibourgeois rhetoric.

This was increasingly at variance with Hitler's new game plan for the party. After May 1928, the Nazi leader abruptly abandoned the urban plan and sought to give the NSDAP an image of middle-class respectability. Wilhelm Kube and his band were odd men out. Already suspect because of his former membership in the DVFP, Kube further raised eyebrows as a follower of Artur Dinter, proponent of a Germanic religious cult and a fierce anti-Catholic. When Hitler expelled Dinter from the party in 1928, Kube broke with Dinter as well, but he retained a penchant for "Wotan mongering." (After 1933 Kube was instrumental in an abortive attempt to replace traditional Protestantism with a Nazi-sponsored "German Christian" church.)[70] The other members of the Landtag delegation were less interested in religious questions, but their radical rhetoric on economic and social issues did not mark them as potential partners of any of the bourgeois parties.

In principle, the party's prospects for increased influence in Prussia as well as in the Reich improved with Hugenberg's takeover of the DNVP. Since the German Nationalists' new leader planned to forge what was virtually an alliance between the two parties, the Nazis could expect to travel on the coattails of the still far larger DNVP. But in practice Hugenberg's hand of friendship was extended to Hitler, not Kube. The DNVP leader valued Hitler's seeming turn to the right, but he and his followers in Prussia remained suspicious of Kube and his band of "socialist" radicals. The political prospects for the Prussian Nazis continued to look bleak.

The Extremists: The Communist Party of Germany (KPD)

The German extreme left went through particularly turbulent times in the second half of the decade. The KPD's internal developments were directly linked to the struggle for power in the Soviet Union. Paralleling the conflicts among Stalin and his rivals in Russia, left, ultraleft, centrist, and right factions competed for control of the KPD, but by 1929 the party's stalinization was complete: Led by a "centrist," the former Hamburg dock worker Ernst Thälmann, the German Communist party became a reliable instrument in Stalin's hands.

Thälmann was precisely the sort of leader that Stalin preferred as chairman of the Communist parties in Western Europe. Unburdened by intellectual ambitions, Thälmann was loyal, and, if need be, susceptible to political blackmail. In 1927–28 an embezzlement affair shook the KPD's Hamburg district. Thälmann, district chairman at the time, at first tried to cover up the scandal, particularly since one of his closest associates was at the center of the affair. When this proved impossible, a majority of the national KPD's central committee wanted to force Thälmann out as district chairman. It required Stalin's personal intervention to prevent Thälmann's dismissal. The later national chairman of the KPD thus owed the salvation of his political career quite literally to Stalin.[71]

Unlike their Social Democratic or Catholic counterparts, the Prussian Communists had no political line of their own, although the KPD's leaders in the state tended to sympathize with the ultra-left faction of the national party. They welcomed the Comintern's condemnation in 1928 of any conciliatory stance toward the SPD as "right deviationism," and enthusiastically supported the doctrine of "social fascism." According to this theory—which the Comintern did not formally abandon until 1935—the Social Democrats rather than the Nazis or the reactionary paramilitary groups constituted the primary fascist danger in Germany. As a result of this doctrine, the KPD's political venom was almost entirely directed against the Social Democrats. The Nazis were practically regarded as allies: "Until he gets on his anti-Semitic kick, Mr. Kube's ideas are really quite reasonable," argued a KPD Landtag member in late 1928.[72]

Quite aside from the doctrine of social fascism, the relations between the two Marxist parties in Prussia were also particularly bitter because of their peculiarly juxtaposed roles. The Social Democrats occupied key positions of executive power; the Communists felt themselves the primary victims of the exercise of that power. In day-to-day Prussian politics, the KPD's social fascism concept meant incessant and vehement personal attacks upon the state's leading Social Democrats. According to the KPD, it was they who were blocking the advance of the Communists' second revolution. The KPD called upon the SPD's rank and file to forge proletarian "unity from below" with the Communists by overthrowing their leaders. The effort failed, and the ultraleft elements in the state's KPD convinced themselves that only the desperate efforts of the Social Democratic leaders—Carl Severing, Albert Grzesinski, and Otto Braun—prevented Germany's proletarian masses from unleashing the forces of revolution. The KPD's rhetoric featured frequent references to revolutionary martyrdom for the workers and promises of the hangman's noose for the "social fascist" leaders.[73]

In reality, such verbal grandstanding did little more than hide the KPD's political ineffectiveness. Repeated purges of the national leadership prevented the formulation of any long-term strategies, while the street violence initiated by the radical wing of the KPD alienated even those Social Democrats who were dissatisfied with what they felt to be an excessively moderate course of their own party. Like the Nazis, the Communists from 1925 to 1930 became an increasingly isolated, violence-prone political sect that played no major role in Prussian politics.[74]

Election Results

The federal structure of Weimar Germany subjected the country to almost constant campaigning.[75] The national contests were clearly the most important, but Prussian elections were watched almost as closely. Prussia was the largest and most populous German *Land*, its electoral districts for the most part were identical with those used for national elections, and there were no specifically Prussian parties. Consequently, the German political organizations essentially treated Prussian campaigns as national contests in a slightly reduced geographic area. In the second half of the decade, Prussia was subjected to five statewide campaigns: provincial and county elections in late 1925 and early 1926, Reichstag and Landtag contests in May 1928, and local, county and provincial elections in November 1929.

Provincial and county elections traditionally did not attract as much attention as Landtag elections, but their outcome had a direct bearing on the state's political balance of power. Since the provincial legislatures selected one half of Prussia's delegates to the Reichsrat, the results had a significant impact on the political decisions at both the state and national levels.

The 1925–26 contests were held while Germany was in the midst of a severe recession following the currency stabilization of a year earlier. Not surprisingly, the results did not augur well for the future strength of the Weimar coalition parties, while they brought major gains for the opposition parties. For example, in the province of East Prussia, where the recession had aggravated an already chronically depressed economic situation, the DNVP virtually dominated the new provincial diet.[76]

The county and local elections demonstrated another weakness of the Weimar coalition parties: they lacked vertical depth. In both provincial and local elections, candidates frequently ran not on individual party labels, but as representatives of larger, often ostensibly nonpartisan coalitions. Actually, these "nonpartisan" lists were little more than thinly veiled combinations of various bourgeois parties. For example, in the 1925 county elections in the province of Schleswig-Holstein a "bourgeois list" *(Bürgerliche Liste)*, representing the DNVP, DVP, and Center party, easily won in most areas. In effect, then, the *Bürgerblock* that eluded the rightist forces at the state level became reality in many localities and provinces. The SPD, the major pillar of the Weimar coalition, was forced back into isolation at the local level.[77]

Still, the counties did not run the state, and the Landtag elections presented a far different picture of Prussia's political landscape. In May 1928 the voters elected both a new Landtag and a new Reichstag. The decision to stage the contests simultaneously was controversial. The parties tended to favor simultaneous elections for several legislative bodies to save costs and increase voter turnout, but this decision also made it more difficult for the Weimar coalition parties in Prussia to highlight their accomplishments. Otto Braun, for one, was convinced the May 1928 results in Prussia would have been even more favorable to the government coalition if the elections had not been held at the same time as the Reich balloting.[78] Table 1 shows a comparison of the results.

The similarity of the results is not surprising. The parties made little effort to differentiate between their state and national campaigns, so that most voters cast their ballots for the same party in the Reichstag and Landtag elections. It is interesting, however, that the parallel showings were based upon quite different premises. Among the government parties, the SPD's results confounded the traditional wisdom that the party did better when out of power than when part of the government coalition. The SPD's Prussian voters certainly did not punish the party for its long years of governmental responsibility. In the Reich, where the Social Democrats had been in the opposition since 1923, the SPD did only marginally better. Similarly, the big success story among the Weimar parties was the Center party. Prussia's Catholic voters obviously gave a resounding vote of confidence to the party's left-of-center orientation. In the Reich, where the Center party had been part of a right-of-

Table 1. Reichstag and Landtag Elections, May 1928

	Reichstag		Landtag	
	Popular Vote (in millions)	*% of Popular Vote*	*Popular Vote (in millions)*	*% of Popular Vote*
SPD	9.2	29.8	5.5	29.0
DDP	1.5	4.9	0.8	4.5
Center party	3.7	12.1	2.7	14.5
WiP	1.4	4.5	0.9	4.5
DVP	2.7	8.7	1.6	8.5
DNVP	4.4	14.2	3.3	17.4
NSDAP	0.8	2.6	0.3	2.9
DVFP	—	—	0.2	1.1
KPD	3.3	10.6	2.2	11.9

Sources: Statistisches Jahrbuch des Deutschen Reiches (Berlin, 1928), p. 25; Statistisches Jahrbuch für den Freistaat Preussen (Berlin, 1928), pp. 320–25.

center coalition for the last five years, the Catholics did considerably less well. The only disappointment among the Weimar coalition parties was the DDP. The left-wing Liberals were unable effectively to resist either the declining appeal of liberalism or the competition from the Economics party and the DVP.

The effects of the "governmental bonus" are even more apparent when the results of the 1928 Landtag elections and those held four years earlier are compared. (See table 2.) The SPD increased its share of the popular vote from 24.9 percent to 29 percent. While the percentages for the Center party and the DDP both declined, the major opposition party, the DNVP, suffered a far more dramatic setback: it lost more than a million votes and dropped from 23.7 to 17.4 percent of the popular vote. (Ironically, Hugenberg used the DNVP's marginally better 1928 showing in Prussia as compared to the Reich to argue that Conservative voters preferred the party's Prussian obstructionism to the moderate policies of Count Westarp.)

The 1928 elections also demonstrated the Prussian parties' lack of geographic breadth and demographic depth. None of the state's political groups were *Volksparteien* in the modern sense. The SPD had a strong showing among the state's industrial workers, but it did very poorly in rural areas. The Center party, of course, obtained virtually no support from Protestant voters. The DDP simply lacked depth altogether. The left-wing Liberals were able to elect delegates in only fourteen of the twenty-three electoral districts. And only in the area around Berlin (the city itself and Potsdam II) were they sufficiently strong to send two delegates to the Landtag.

Table 2. Landtag Elections of December 1924 and May 1928

	December 1924		May 1928	
	Popular Vote (in millions)	% of Popular Vote	Popular Vote (in millions)	% of Popular Vote
SPD	4.6	24.9	5.5	29.0
DDP	1.1	5.9	0.8	4.5
Center party	3.2	17.6	2.9	14.6
WiP	0.5	2.5	0.9	4.5
DVP	1.8	9.8	1.6	8.5
DNVP	4.4	23.7	3.3	17.4
NSDAP	0.5	2.5	0.6	2.9
DVFP	—	—	—	—
KPD	1.8	9.6	2.2	11.9

Source: Horst Möller, *Parlamentarismus in Preussen, 1919–1932* (Düsseldorf, 1985), p. 601.

The same pattern held true for the opposition. More than 10 percent of the DNVP's strength (nine out of eighty-two Landtag delegates) came from one district, Frankfurt a.O., a traditional stronghold of Prussian conservatism. The Nazis were sufficiently strong to elect delegates directly (which required at least 60,000 popular votes in any one district) in only three districts, all agriculturally depressed areas in 1928: Schleswig-Holstein, Hanover-South, and Hessen-Nassau. The Communists presented a picture of similarly uneven strength. About 20 percent of their delegates in the Landtag came from one district, the city of Berlin. This area, the district of Berlin-Brandenburg in the party's organizational parlance, was not only the party's largest district, but also a major stronghold of the "ultraleftists."[79]

The parties' inability to attract voters outside a fairly narrow geographic area and demographic pool meant that "coalition arithmetic" was the key to Prussia's political stability as a parliamentary democracy. Table 3 shows the relative delegate strength in the new legislature.

Table 3. Delegate Strength in the Prussian Landtag, May 1928

	No. of Delegates	% of Total
SPD	136	30.4
DDP	21	4.7
Center party	71	15.1
WiP	21	4.7
DVP	40	8.9
DNVP	82	18.2
NSDAP	8	1.3
DVFP	2	0.4
KPD	56	12.4

Source: *Statistisches Jahrbuch für den Freistaat Preussen* (Berlin, 1928), pp. 25, 320–25.

As a result of the modified proportional representation system used for awarding seats in the Landtag, the May 1928 elections gave the Weimar parties a narrow but clear parliamentary majority of 50.2 percent. (The actual combined popular vote of the SPD, the DDP, and the Center party was 48 percent.) A potential grand coalition—which meant that the DVP would join the Weimar parties to form a new government—would have had a comfortable majority of 59.1 percent of the Landtag seats. However, a *Bürgerblock* coalition composed of the DNVP, the DDP, the Center party, and the DVP could count upon the support of only 46.9 percent of the delegates, and needed the Economics party as a partner in order to attain a majority. In view of the sharp antagonism between the WiP and the Center party, chances of a

Bürgerblock cabinet were remote even before Hugenberg aligned the DNVP alongside the Nazis.

There were no further statewide elections until April 1932, but the balloting for municipal, county, and provincial legislative bodies on November 17, 1929, provided a major test for the parties' electoral strength just when the first effects of the Depression were beginning to be felt. The results foreshadowed the collapse of the moderate parties and the rise of the Nazis that became a nationwide shock in the Reichstag elections a year later. Among the Weimar coalition parties the two liberal parties—DVP and DDP—suffered the highest losses. The Center party and the SPD held their own, although the Social Democrats were badly hurt by a corruption scandal in Berlin involving a number of SPD city administrators.[80]

Among the opposition groups, both the Communists' and Hugenberg's strategy backfired. Despite the growing number of unemployed blue-collar workers, the KPD did not significantly erode the SPD's strength.[81] The rightist parties benefited disproportionately from the onset of the Depression, but the major victor was not the DNVP but the NSDAP. Compared to their statewide average in May 1928, the Nazis increased their vote by almost 100 percent, from 2.9 to 5.1 percent. Some of the Nazis' support came from the collapse of the liberal parties and special interest groups, but the bulk of their new strength resulted from disaffected DNVP voters: Hitler's movement did best in the old Conservative strongholds of East Elbia. In East Prussia the Nazi vote increased by 600 percent.[82]

While the results of the November 1929 contests appear in retrospect like the beginning of the end of the Weimar Republic, the numbers should not be overdramatized. The early effects of the Depression had relatively little influence on the stability of the parliamentary form of government in Prussia. Among the Weimar parties, the DDP was the primary loser, but the Democrats were already the smallest of the three coalition parties, and they had little option or inclination to desert the government coalition. Both the SPD and the Center party held onto the bulk of their voters, and there is every reason to assume that if the economic downturn had been limited to a recession along the lines that the country experienced in 1925 and 1926, parliamentary democracy in Prussia would have remained strong and viable. At the beginning of 1930, at any rate, news of the death of parliamentary democracy in Weimar Prussia was decidedly premature.

CHAPTER 2

Coalitions and Cabinets, 1925–1930

In the winter of 1924–25 the relatively smooth course of Prussian political life had been interrupted for several months by a severe government crisis.[1] Following the Landtag elections in December 1924, the cabinet of the grand coalition (SPD, Center party, DDP, and DVP) resigned, and the legislature was unable to agree on a new government until April 1925. Even then, few political observers predicted a long life for the new cabinet, another coalition of the three Weimar parties (SPD, Center party, and DDP). The coalition partners did not have a parliamentary majority in the legislature, and most contemporaries predicted new Landtag elections soon, perhaps as early as the following summer.[2]

Such fears (or hopes) were premature. The Prussian legislature sat for a full four-year term, and the government coalition proved to be even more durable; it remained in office for more than seven years—the longest tenure for any government in the Weimar era. It is true, however, that throughout this time the cabinet seemed constantly on the verge of being restructured. The primary reason was, as so often before, various attempts to restore a Reich-Prussian linkage by creating politically homogenous cabinets at the Reich and state levels. Most of the Reich cabinets in the second half of the decade were *Bürgerblock* governments. The German Nationalists sat in several Reich governments after 1925, and the DVP was a member of all Reich cabinets in this period. Both parties were anxious to achieve power in Prussia as well. As it turned out, the obstructionist stance of the Prussian DNVP prevented any *Bürgerblock* coalition in the state, but a revival of the grand coalition seemed a genuine possibility. The Weimar coalition parties and the right-wing Liberals engaged in almost continuous talks on restructuring the Prussian coalition, and on several occasions appeared close to agreement on enlarging the coalition.

Despite apparent good will on all sides, agreement on a grand coalition cabinet eluded the potential partners. In time, what had looked like at best an interim solution in the spring of 1925 assumed paradigmatic significance for the Weimar coalition parties. In 1927 the speaker of the Reichstag, Paul Löbe, praised the Weimar coalition government in Prussia as a "model of a successful coalition." This feeling of *felix Borussia* became stronger as the decade continued. In the spring of 1929, during yet another cabinet crisis in

35

the Reich, a Prussian Social Democrat noted proudly that in contrast to the situation in the Reich, "nowhere is it less appropriate to speak of a parliamentary or government crisis than in Prussia."[3]

The reasons for the unexpected success of the Weimar coalition in Prussia were complex and not entirely the result of the Weimar parties' skillful handling of the situation. The political and parliamentary ineptitude of the opposition also helped the Weimar coalition stay in power. The German Nationalists as well as the Communists and the DVP had a habit of shooting themselves in the foot and sabotaging viable alternatives to the Weimar coalition. But the coalition parties did some things right. Bernhard Falk, chairman of the DDP delegation in the Landtag, pointed to the "firm and efficient cooperation among the government parties."[4] Falk referred particularly to the relationship among the Weimar coalition party leaders. As we saw earlier, these politicians were willing to deal with each other in a spirit of pragmatic cooperation, searching for viable solutions and compromises. This attitude brought short-term advantages and some long-term problems. On more than one occasion, a successful compromise meant the coalition partners had merely agreed to delay tackling a particular problem or to ignore it altogether.[5]

At the same time, political pragmatism assured a high degree of team spirit among the cabinet ministers and legislative leaders of the coalition parties. Collegial decision making, especially at the cabinet level, had a long tradition in the state. Since the days of the grand elector in the seventeenth century, Prussian cabinets were governed by a "collegial constitution" *(Kollegialverfassung)*. In practice this meant that matters affecting more than one ministry were decided on the basis of discussions among all cabinet members. Consensus was reached either in the course of full-scale cabinet meetings (each minister had the right to propose items for the agenda) or by "commenting" (actually, voting), upon position papers circulated by one or more ministers *(Umlaufverfahren)*. The latter method was also used to clarify positions prior to cabinet meetings. Before the revolution of 1918, the Prussian collegial constitution had not been tested in the context of parliamentary democracy. Until then, Prussian governments were responsible to the king, not the Landtag, and the cabinet ministers all shared a fundamental commitment to the political principles of Prussian conservatism.[6]

Both before and after 1918, the prime minister played a crucial role in the workings of the *Kollegialverfassung,* and Otto Braun was an acknowledged master at playing the role of primus inter pares among his cabinet colleagues. Braun's role is probably best described as participant honest broker. As we shall see, Braun was perhaps too much of a team player. Although he did not hesitate to mold and influence the views of his cabinet colleagues, he often preferred to table an issue rather than risk a fight in the cabinet or the coalition. He took great care to underscore the cabinet's unity toward outsiders, keeping his often quite critical views of his cabinet colleagues to himself. The prime minister's office was a notably poor source for press leaks—unless they were intentional and had the approval of the full cabinet.[7] Braun also prevailed upon his colleagues to do the same. At the beginning of 1927, in response to complaints by the minister of finance that his colleagues were subtly undermining the collegial contract, the cabinet reaffirmed its determination to present the image of a united government both to the Landtag and to the public at large.[8]

Braun's effectiveness as prime minister was undoubtedly enhanced by his willingness to share the political limelight. The prime minister had never enjoyed the role of political glad-hander, and in the second half of the decade, as his wife became chronically ill, requiring a great deal of bed rest and almost constant care, he reduced his public appearances even further. (She died in exile in 1934.) The prime minister severely limited his public and social activities, leaving this aspect of modern politics to his cabinet colleagues.[9]

Political and personal continuity characterized Prussia's cabinets in the second half of the decade. Albert Grzesinski, a gruff and strong-willed labor leader, served as minister of the interior from 1926 to 1930. Hermann Höpker-Aschoff, minister of finance for the entire five-year span, was regarded as an able but abrasive minister with political ambitions that considerably exceeded his power base in the small and shrinking DDP. The ministers of agriculture and commerce, Heinrich Steiger (Center party) and Hermann Schreiber (DDP) also had long terms of office, but their political horizon did not extend much beyond the affairs of their departments. There were two ministers of justice, both from the Center party. Hugo am Zehnhoff, who retired in March 1927, was known more for his durability than his qualities of leadership. When he left office, he had been minister in Prussia longer than any other cabinet member in the republican era, but his tenure was singularly undistinguished. Hermann Schmidt, am Zehnhoff's successor, was a considerably more energetic official. The minister of education until January 1930, Carl Heinrich Becker, was perhaps the most distinguished figure in the government and another veteran of previous cabinets. A well-known scholar of oriental languages as well as an able administrator, Becker never joined a political party, although he was usually described as a left-wing Liberal, and in the coalition mix he counted as close to the DDP. The minister for welfare and social services was a special case. Heinrich Hirtsiefer (Center party) was usually a man of easygoing habits who did not head one of the heavyweight ministries. After am Zehnhoff's retirement, he was the most senior member of the cabinet. More important, he was an influential voice on the left wing of the Center party, and, as we have seen, instrumental in keeping political Catholicism on its left-of-center course.

While cabinet collegiality was undoubtedly an important factor in Prussia's political system, in the final analysis, the success of the state's parliamentary democracy depended on the interaction of executive and legislature. In the state the relationship of the leaders of the two branches of government for the most part functioned well, far better than in the Reich. Rather than reducing the cabinet members to the status of handmaidens of the parliamentary caucuses, leaders of the Weimar coalition parties in the Landtag acted as a "protective barrier," enabling the cabinet to govern effectively.[10]

This did not mean, of course, that the Prussian coalition always sailed smoothly. The coalition partners remained *Weltanschauungsparteien* (ideological parties), anxious to maintain political profiles of their own. They were certainly not above more or less subtle political blackmail. Since the Weimar coalition would collapse if any of its three members resigned from the government, each partner could, and often did, exercise a sort of negative veto in the cabinet or in the Landtag whenever the party felt a proposed course of action would substantially reduce its voter appeal or threaten part of its ideological bedrock. The Catholic delegates in the Landtag, for example, prevented reforms in the allocation of Reichsrat votes, even though Center pary members in the cabinet agreed with their colleagues from the other coalition parties that the present system unduly restricted Prussia's influence in the second chamber of the national legislature.[11]

The centrifugal tendencies among the coalition parties were particularly pronounced before and during election campaigns. The Prussian coalition partners made no commitments to continue their cooperation after the elections. Consequently, each simultaneously defended the government's record and criticized his former (and, as it turned out, future) coalition partners in his battle for popular votes.

Since the coalition parties entered state election campaigns with a pronouncement that "all options are open," intense discussions about changing or enlarging the coalition invariably followed the election of a new Landtag. Resignations or retirements from the cabinet also provided opportunities for negotiating new coalition terms as well as reshuffling cabinet seats. So did the numerous national cabinet crises. Each time a Reich government fell (a frequent occurrence in the Weimar era) the potential partners negotiating the terms of a new national cabinet also tried to play their "Prussian card" at the federal level. As an opening gambit, a party would insist it could join the Reich government only if its partners also accepted it as a member of the Prussian coalition.

The period from 1925 to 1930, then, was a stable but hardly calm time in

Prussia's political history. Negotiations to enlarge or change the government coalition seemed to go on constantly, but with the benefit of hindsight we can divide the history of Prussia's coalition politics into four fairly distinct segments. From April 1925 to May 1926, the Weimar coalition government in Prussia appeared particularly weak, and the *Bürgerblock* parties, which formed the Reich cabinet at this time, hoped to persuade the two bourgeois parties in Prussia to break off their alliance with the SPD and join the German Nationalists and the DVP to form a parallel *Bürgerblock* government in the state. This ploy failed, leaving the Prussian coalition in a considerably stronger position than before. During the second phase, pressure from the *Bürgerblock* parties in the Reich lessened, since a series of short-lived bourgeois cabinets needed the parliamentary support of the SPD in the Reichstag to stay in office. The Social Democrats used their pivotal position in the Reich to pressure their coalition partners in Prussia to forego consideration of a *Bürgerblock* coalition in the state.

The simultaneous Reichstag and Landtag elections in May 1928 inaugurated the third phase. Negotiations between the Weimar parties and the DVP to form parallel grand coalitions in the Reich and Prussia began almost immediately after the election results were in, and continued with varying levels of intensity until Gustav Stresemann's death in October 1929. The fourth phase, in some ways the most crucial period in Weimar Prussia's political history, began with the foreign minister's death and ended with the fall of the Müller government in the Reich in March 1930. During this time the Weimar coalition parties in Prussia could (and probably should) have agreed to a grand coalition in the state as a way of supporting the faltering grand coalition in the Reich and consequently shoring up the Weimar constitutional system as a whole. The rapidly worsening economic situation in Germany and the resignation of two Prussian ministers in early 1930 certainly presented a favorable opportunity to recreate a grand coalition cabinet in Prussia. The DVP was a member of the Reich cabinet, and it was well known that the right-wing Liberals were anxious to become part of a grand coalition in Prussia as well. Such a course of action would perhaps have been the best way of preventing the German People's party under its new leader, Eduard Dingeldey, from following the path of Hugenberg's DNVP. But Otto Braun and the leaders of the Weimar coalition parties in Prussia felt the political price for reestablishing the Reich-Prussian linkage was too high; the negotiations ended in failure and mutual recriminations.

from Luther to Marx: April 1925–May 1926

The Prussian cabinet that took office in April 1925 seemed to owe its election more to default than to design. For months the Landtag, with the

Weimar coalition parties and the opposition groups at equal strength, had been deadlocked and unable to elect a new prime minister. With its vote of confidence for the new cabinet, the Landtag underscored that once again Prussia was out of step with the rest of the country; its government's political composition ran counter to Germany's general rightward trend. While Prussia's Catholics and left-wing Liberals joined the Social Democrats to continue the coalition of the Weimar parties, at the federal level the Center party and the DDP had just agreed to join the DVP and the DNVP in a *Bürgerblock* coalition under the new Reich chancellor Hans Luther. Not surprisingly, the Prussian Social Democrats were pessimistic about the long-term chances of the Prussian coalition. The SPD expected the Weimar coalition in Prussia to fall victim to a sort of negative Reich-Prussian linkage: they expected that under the pressures of cooperating with the DNVP in the Reich and the SPD in the state, the Social Democrats' bourgeois partners would find it impossible to keep the Prussian coalition intact.

The SPD was especially fearful that the Center party's national leadership would persuade Prussia's Catholics to leave the Social Democrats and form a parallel *Bürgerblock* cabinet with the right-wing parties in Prussia. The times were changing. It was an open secret that some leaders of the Center party's Reichstag delegation, Heinrich Brüning, for example, hoped that the Catholic-DNVP coalition in the Reich would soon be followed by a parallel coalition in Prussia.[12]

Such a course of action had its supporters in the Center party's Landtag delegation as well. A number of them ostentatiously cast their ballots with the opposition against the new government on some issues. They were relatively unimportant questions, and the votes did not endanger the government, but such symbolic actions could be seen as portents of an opening to the right. Confidential contacts between the Center party and the DNVP in Prussia, which were quickly leaked to the press, seemed to provide additional evidence that a "blue-black" deal was in the making. One DNVP delegate later recalled that his party had been willing to "make far-reaching concessions in order to reach agreement with the Catholics."[13] As a result, few SPD leaders initially expected the Braun government to survive later than the fall of 1925.[14]

The politicians and pundits were wrong. In fact, the difficulties of the Prussian coalition turned out to be minor compared to the conflicts that beset the Luther cabinet in the Reich. The federal government's foreign policy quickly ran into fierce opposition from one of the coalition parties, the DNVP. Although the German Nationalist leaders had agreed to support the basic concept of Stresemann's foreign policy—revisionism of the Versailles settlement on the basis of reconciliation with the Western allies—as part of the coalition agreement that formed the basis of the *Bürgerblock,* the DNVP's provincial chairmen opposed the national leaders' commitments. Certain of rank-and-file support, the DNVP's regional chieftains forced the party's spokesman in the Reichstag and its ministers in the cabinet to launch vicious attacks against the fruits of Stresemann's foreign policy, the treaties of Locarno and Germany's membership in the League of Nations.

Disagreements on how to deal with the severe recession of 1925–26 added further problems. The DNVP insisted on agricultural and industrial subsidies as well as reduced expenditures for social services. The moderate bourgeois parties wanted to avoid a confrontation with organized labor—the inevitable result of the DNVP's domestic policies.[15]

With his astute sense of politics, Otto Braun was one of the first to realize that the *Bürgerblock* cabinet in the Reich was a house divided against itself. He saw that especially foreign policy issues would split the *Bürgerblock* coalition. For this reason he advised the Social Democrats in the Reichstag to continue supporting Stresemann's foreign relations objectives, leaving the German Nationalists to attack their cabinet colleagues' policies. Braun confidently predicted such a strategy would lead to the fall of the Luther cabinet and pave the way for a grand coalition in the Reich.[16]

The prime minister also realized that the Prussian Center party was far less receptive to German Nationalist overtures than many Social Democrats feared. Prussia's Catholics and the state's DNVP distrusted each other.[17] The two parties were far apart on many issues, including such fundamental questions as the form of government—the DNVP continued to reject parliamentary democracy as "un-Prussian"—and church-state relations. On a more emotional level, many in the Center party accused the German Nationalists of continuing to harbor anti-Catholic sentiments. Prussian DNVP members retaliated by accusing Catholic politicians in the Rhineland of being "pro-French." The Center party looked upon such attacks as dirty politics and took them quite seriously. Hess was convinced the accusations of unpatriotic activities were not personal vendettas of DNVP backbenchers, but part of a deliberate policy endorsed by the DNVP's leaders. Needless to say, such mutual recriminations reduced the chances of "blue-black" cooperation.[18]

The SPD's fear of potential cooperation between Catholics and Conservatives in the state led the Social Democrats to ignore the far more realistic possibility for enlarging the current minority coalition into a cabinet of the grand coalition in Prussia. Paradoxically, all of the potential partners favored this alternative. It was well known that Gustav Stresemann, the DVP's national chairman, had opposed breaking up the Prussian coalition in early 1925. Even then the DVP's national leader had been skeptical about a coalition with the German Nationalists. The Conservatives' sabotage of his Locarno policy confirmed Stresemann's belief, and persuaded him and a number of other DVP leaders that the party had been duped by the DNVP. In the Prussian German People's party, too, both leaders and backbenchers came to regret the party's January 1925 decision to leave the state's government. One backbencher expressed the party's feeling some years later: breaking up the grand coalition had been a "grave mistake" with increasingly unfortunate consequences.[19] The Center party was informally negotiating with the DVP as early as May 1925; among the SPD's leaders, Severing later recalled, "I wanted the grand coalition."[20] Other Social Democrats, such as Heilmann, were more restrained in their enthusiasm, but most SPD delegates in the Landtag would certainly have accepted a return of the grand coalition once the party's leaders presented concrete proposals.[21]

But the leaders took their time. Despite protestations of good will on all sides, personal and political reasons prevented a quick revival of the grand coalition. At this time, only the Center party seemed to welcome the DVP's participation in an enlarged Prussian cabinet without reservations. The Social Democrats equivocated. Severing was an enthusiastic advocate of enlarging the coalition. Otto Braun admired Gustav Stresemann, but still resented what he regarded as the DVP's game of duplicity in breaking up the old government. Ernst Heilmann, too, blamed the DVP's right-wingers for the January decision, so that relations between the DVP's right wing and the Social Democrats in the Landtag remained strained. Tactical considerations also influenced the SPD's thinking. Seemingly oblivious to the argument that the grand coalition itself would make new elections unnecessary, the SPD feared an agreement with the DVP would put the Social Democrats in a bad light for the expected new state elections. The party's campaign strategists warned that a revival of the grand coalition would drive some potential Social Democratic voters to the KPD or prevent Communist voters from returning to the SPD's fold.

The vacillations of the Prussian DVP seemed to confirm Otto Braun's fears that the state's right-wing Liberals could not be trusted to follow a clear, prorepublican line. Within the DVP, the discussion over reviving the grand coalition in Prussia quickly became a debate on the party's larger political future. The party's right wing feared that a vote for the grand coalition in Prussia would permanently align the party with the Weimar coalition parties and block cooperation with the DNVP and an eventual *Bürgerblock* in Prussia.[22] The consequences of the DVP's internal conflicts were political paralysis. A revealing indication of the party's internal dilemma came in mid-October 1925 when one of many Communist-sponsored motions of no confidence against the minister of the interior came up for a vote in the Landtag. After the DNVP had announced that, as expected, it would support the KPD's motion, Eugen Leidig, leader of the DVP's right wing in the Landtag, rose to explain that the DVP, too, would vote "man for man and woman for woman" against Carl Severing. But Leidig's forecast of a united party was wishful thinking. In the final roll-call vote, most of the DVP's delegates abstained, simultaneously exposing the party's internal division, saving the government, and, not incidentally, leaving the door open for future negotiations on restructuring the cabinet.[23]

Tactics were also a concern of the German Democrats. On the one hand, the DDP was particularly anxious not to face new elections, a consideration that facilitated the DVP's return to the cabinet. On the other hand, the DDP feared for its privileged position on the ministerial bench. The party was currently represented by two ministers. If the DVP returned to the coalition, the DDP would certainly have to yield one of its cabinet seats to the stronger right-wing Liberal rival.

After a few months, the hectic pace of rumors and negotiations subsided, and it became clear that while the government might lack a parliamentary majority, the opposition presented no realistic alternative to the Weimar coalition. The calm did not last, however; developments in the Reich again cast their shadow on the political constellation in Prussia. In January 1926 the *Bürgerblock* coalition in the Reich fell. The DNVP's rank and file, and especially the party's provincial leaders, had succeeded in forcing the party to withdraw from the cabinet. The move was vigorously opposed by the DNVP's national leaders, Kuno von Westarp and Martin Schiele, but resentment of Stresemann's Locarno policy was so intense in the DNVP that the leaders were unable to prevent the breakup of the coalition.[24]

For many political observers, this seemed a perfect opportunity to form parallel grand coalition cabinets in the Reich and in Prussia. Confronted by the recession of 1925–26, both the Reich and its largest state needed strong cabinets with a broad parliamentary base to support the tough decisions that were needed to combat the country's economic and social woes. Once again the Social Democrats held the key to the Reich's and the state's political future, and once again the party's leaders were divided. The Prussian spokesmen urged their Reichstag colleagues to agree to a grand coalition, but were reluctant to follow suit in Prussia.[25]

Were the Prussian Social Democrats unduly cautious? As the cabinet crisis in the Reich reached its climax, there were clear signs that in reaction to the DNVP's attacks on Stresemann, both the federal and the state DVP were moving to the left. In a major policy address, Rudolph von Campe, Stendel's predecessor as head of the Prussian DVP and still an influential member of the Landtag, attacked the DNVP's sabotage of Stresemann's foreign policy, while portraying the right-wing Liberals as responsible partners of the Weimar parties.[26] An editorial in the party's Cologne newspaper suggested the DVP was going out of its way to show appreciation for the SPD's point of view on the longstanding controversy over compensation for the property of the former Prussian royal family. The prime minister interpreted the article as signaling a larger change of the DVP's strategy. He commented, "Very important! Seems to prepare a shift for the People's party."[27]

Despite the signs of good will and the generally improved atmosphere, the negotiations again failed. In Prussia the DVP aroused the suspicions of its potential partners by insisting that, contrary to previous practice, the parties agree on a detailed, full-scale government program rather than a statement of principles before signing a coalition pact.[28] This demand would not only prolong the negotiations since the four coalition parties were far apart on many substantive issues, but possibly cause them acute political embarrassment as well. The unsuccessful discussions in the summer of 1921 had demonstrated that well-placed leaks about policy positions could be effectively used to stir up controversy in a rival party.[29]

Decisive for the failure of the Prussian negotiations, however, was the right-wing Liberals' insistence on a firm link between the Reich and Prussian coalitions.[30] The Prussian SPD had always rejected such a condition, fearing the simultaneous births of two coalitions would also mean their simultaneous deaths since the linkage would subject Prussia to the political fallout from every government crisis in the Reich. The DVP's revival of the linkage demand also raised suspicions about the party's genuine interest in resurrecting the grand coalition in the state. As the People's party well knew, the 1921 agreement on the Prussian grand coalition had come about only after the DVP dropped its insistence on the Reich-Prussian linkage. In the end, no grand coalition cabinet took office either in the state or the Reich. The Prussian SPD leaders rejected the Reich-Prussian linkage, and the DVP refused to drop it. The state's Social Democrats continued to urge their colleagues in the Reichstag to join a grand coalition at the federal level, but the party's national leaders countered that agreement on foreign policy issues was too narrow a base for cooperation with the DVP. In addition, the SPD's national leaders held fast to their maxim that the party benefited politically from being in the opposition.[31]

Ironically, the Social Democrats were not alone in rejecting participation in the federal government. For entirely different reasons, the conservative Reich president and his entourage also opposed a Reich cabinet that included the SPD. They were relieved when Hans Luther's second cabinet turned out to be another *Bürgerblock*, this time without the DNVP. The new government had no majority in the Reichstag, and no one expected it to last long. The pundits were right; the cabinet was in office less than six months. It stumbled over one of the most emotional and divisive issues in Weimar politics, the question of the national colors.[32]

Pressured by his advisors, Reich president von Hindenburg suggested to the chancellor in May 1926 that German government institutions abroad (embassies, consulates, and so forth) fly the Reich's commercial flag alongside the national colors. The innocent-sounding request contained political dynamite. The German national colors were black, red, and gold, but in the commercial flag the national colors were indicated only by a small black, red, and gold inset. Dominating the commercial flag were the old imperial colors of black, white, and red. Luther, who may not have recognized the volatility of the president's suggestion, issued an executive order implementing Hindenburg's request—and raised a storm of protest from prorepublican forces. Supporters of the Weimar Republic interpreted the new flag directive as the Reich president and his advisors had undoubtedly intended it: an attempt to give additional legitimacy to the imperial, antirepublican colors. The DDP, the party that was particularly identified with the colors black, red, and gold, resigned from the Reich cabinet, thereby bringing down the entire government. In addition, a particularly vigorous protest came from the Prussian government. The state's cabinet objected to the flag decree not only on political grounds, but also because Luther had issued the directive without consulting the states. Prussia complained the Reich chancellor had violated its state's rights.[33]

From Marx to Müller, May 1926–May 1928

After the fall of the Luther government, the familiar "chancellor carousel" once again began turning in the Reich. Press and politicians considered and rejected various candidates for Germany's most difficult and least secure job. The circle of candidates was severely limited. The Reich president (who had the constitutional duty of nominating the chancellor for confirmation by the Reichstag) wanted someone who was willing to head a *Bürgerblock* cabinet that included the DNVP. But Hindenburg and his advisors also knew that unless the German Nationalists agreed to support Stresemann's foreign policy no moderate bourgeois party leader would agree to head such a cabinet.[34]

Among the names that surfaced early on was that of Otto Gessler, the present Reich minister of defense. Gessler was nominally a German Democrat, but he was usually classified as a right-winger who favored cooperation with the German Nationalists. Gessler's candidacy was brief. The left wing of his own party rejected him primarily because he was willing to work with the DNVP, while the German Nationalists distrusted Gessler because of his membership in the DDP. The Reich president then turned to another dark horse, Konrad Adenauer, the lord mayor of Cologne and president of the Prussian Staatsrat. Adenauer was a right-wing member of the Center party; he was known to look with disfavor upon long-term coalition agreements between his party and the Social Democrats. At the same time, Adenauer's fervent Catholicism did not endear him either to the anticlerical elements in the two liberal parties or the militant Protestants in the DNVP.[35]

Prussia was not directly involved in the search for a Reich chancellor, but every federal cabinet crisis raised the specter of the Reich-Prussian linkage. Especially the prime minister was determined to avoid parallel discussions of the Prussian and Reich coalitions. For that reason Braun asked Severing, who wanted to resign as minister of the interior for reasons of health, to stay in office until the fall, when the cabinet crisis in the Reich was expected to have been solved. Neither of the early candidates aroused much enthusiasm among the state's leaders. Gessler's announced intent to persuade the DNVP to rejoin the coalition in the Reich naturally raised fears, especially among the Prussian SPD, that the German Nationalists would insist on a parallel *Bürgerblock* cabinet in the state as their price for joining the federal government. In addition, Gessler and the Prussians had often feuded in the past. The Prussian minister of the interior had frequently clashed with the Reich defense minister over the latter's unwillingness to curb the flirtations of some Reichswehr commanders with the extreme right.[36] As for Adenauer, Otto Braun and the president of the Staatsrat were not only far apart politically, but also had widely differing ideas on the constitutional powers of the cabinet and the state's second legislative chamber.

After Gessler failed to put together the *Bürgerblock* coalition preferred by the Reich president, Adenauer did not even pursue this dead end street. Instead he tried to put together a cabinet of the grand coalition. The SPD's leaders were divided over the prospect of a grand coalition in the Reich. Many of the party's parliamentary leaders still regarded the DVP as politically "unreliable," but initially the Social Democrats did not reject Adenauer's proposals. They merely wanted to delay the inauguration of the cabinet until after the June 20 national referendum (which SPD and the KPD were sponsoring jointly) calling for expropriation without compensation of the property of Germany's former royal houses. But Adenauer's feelers were firmly rebuffed by the DVP. The right-wing Liberals emphasized their irreconcilable differences with the Social Democrats in a number of areas, including the "flag directive" and the question of compensation for formerly royal property. Far from agreeing to join the SPD in a national coalition, the DVP's negotiators suggested rather naively that ways had to be found to turn the SPD's voting constituency away from the party. Once again there would be no grand coalition in the Reich.[37]

When both Gessler and Adenauer failed to create cabinets that had the support of a majority of the Reichstag and the Reich president, Hindenburg turned next to a familiar figure: Wilhelm Marx. Practiced at this sort of thing, the former Reich chancellor was able to form a minority cabinet with ministers from the moderate bourgeois parties, the DDP, the Center party, the

DVP, and the Bavarian People's party. The DNVP headed the opposition to the new coalition, and Marx's cabinet needed the "toleration" of the SPD to stay in office. The solution to the latest government crisis in the Reich was another weak federal cabinet with a short life expectancy.

Paradoxically, the bourgeois parties' inability to form a strong *Bürgerblock* coalition in the Reich actually seemed to increase the chances for reestablishing the grand coalition in the state. The failure of the June referendum on the expropriation of princely property removed a major stumbling block standing in the way of SPD-DVP cooperation in Prussia. Severing resigned his post in October, providing the traditional opportunity for reshuffling and restructuring the cabinet.

Spokesmen for the SPD's right wing called publicly for a return of the grand coalition in the state; so did Albert Grzesinski, Severing's more left-leaning successor at the interior ministry.[38] On the DVP's side, disillusionment with the DNVP seemed to draw the right-wing Liberals closer to the Weimar parties. Stresemann supported the grand coalition in Prussia, while attacking the "stubbornness and lack of political understanding" among the German Nationalists. For several months at least a part of the DVP's Landtag delegation abstained from voting on various KPD-sponsored (and DNVP-supported) motions of no confidence against the government, enabling the Weimar coalition to stay in power. At the beginning of October, Eugen Leidig and Joseph Hess met personally to take stock of the situation.[39]

Still, like the royal children in the fairy tale, the sides could not come together. Otto Braun's prediction in August that a grand coalition was "unlikely" was right on the mark.[40] This time, the fault lay primarily with the DVP and the Center party. Stresemann and the party's Reichstag leaders concentrated their attention on the coalition in the Reich and all but ignored Prussia. As a result, the right-wing Liberals missed obvious opportunities, such as Severing's resignation from the cabinet, to take the initiative. For reasons of personal pique, von Campe deliberately leaked news of the contacts between Leidig and Hess. The premature exposure ended the secret talks before concrete agreements could be reached. Finally, Karl Jarres's and Friedrich von Gayl's behind-the-scenes maneuver to create a joint DVP-DNVP parliamentary group in the Staatsrat fueled new suspicions among all of the Weimar coalition parties.[41]

These developments certainly confirmed the untrustworthy character of the German People's party for many Social Democrats (including Otto Braun), but it was the Center party, not the Social Democrats, that finally blocked the road to a new grand coalition in Prussia. Intentionally or not, the Jarres-Gayl pact revived unpleasant memories in the ranks of the Center party that before 1918 the right-wing Liberals and the Conservatives had systematically excluded Catholics from a share of political power in Prussia.

Stresemann was well aware of the mood among the Center party's Landtag delegation after the Jarres-Gayl plan became known: he commented bitterly that in all likelihood not one Catholic delegate would now vote for opening the present Prussian coalition to the right.[42]

The Center party also had specific concerns about future policy issues. In the summer of 1926 negotiations began between the state of Prussia and the Holy See on a concordat between Prussia and the papacy.[43] The Center party was vitally interested in the success of these negotiations, and the Catholics were not at all certain that the DVP's presence in the cabinet would help the talks—certainly not if the right-wing Liberals, already suspect because of their anticlerical and anti-Catholic heritage, continued to pursue the goal of forging a permanent alliance with the DNVP, the self-proclaimed spokesperson for militant Protestantism. Finally, the leaders of the Prussian Center party were determined to counter their national party's drift to the right. While Reichstag leaders like Heinrich Brüning continued to criticize the Prussian Catholics for their alliance with the SPD,[44] the state's Catholics saw the Weimar coalition in Prussia as an effective way of preventing the Center party as a whole from being captured by its militant right wing. Both Joseph Hess and Hermann Schmidt joined Braun and the SPD in rejecting the grand coalition in the fall of 1926.[45]

Publicly the potential partners now pretended that a grand coalition had never been their goal, but signs of failure and disappointment were unmistakable. Recriminations and mutual attacks filled the pages of the press. In late October, Grzesinski dismissed the state secretary in the ministry of the interior, Friedrich Meister. This official was generally regarded as a political ally of the right-wing Liberals and the DVP-owned *Deutsche Allgemeine Zeitung* saw the decision (correctly) as a deliberate affront to the German People's party. The DVP, for its part, dropped its tactic of "saving" the government. At the beginning of November the Landtag delegation cast a unanimous vote for a DNVP-sponsored motion of no confidence against the government. This time the cabinet survived because the Communists decided to abstain.[46]

In December Ernst Scholz, the head of the DVP's Reichstag delegation and Philipp Scheidemann, his counterpart in the SPD, widened the gap between their two parties. Speaking at party meetings in the East Prussian cities of Königsberg and Insterburg, Scholz opposed any coalitions between SPD and DVP, while underscoring that on most issues the right-wing Liberals agreed with the German Nationalists. Scheidemann answered in kind. In a major address to the Reichstag, he exposed some of the Reichswehr's secret rearmament activities and announced the end of the SPD's "toleration" of the Reich government. Still, many responsible leaders in the DVP and the SPD regretted the open battle between the two parties. The DVP's Reichstag delegation in effect disavowed its chairman by agreeing to enter into negotiations on a grand coalition in the Reich without preconditions only three days after Scholz made his public remarks. On the SPD's side, a majority of the party's national executive committee counseled Scheidemann aganst attacking the Reichswehr, and Otto Braun privately advised his party against introducing a motion of no confidence to bring down the federal government.[47] For the moment, however, mutual distrust and recriminations dominated the political scene. The SPD's Reichstag delegation introduced a resolution of no confidence against the federal cabinet that had been in office for less than six months. As expected, the motion was supported by both the KPD and the DNVP, and it passed easily. At the end of the year the Reich had another "Christmas crisis." The chancellor carousel had to begin turning again.[48]

The search for a new Reich leader was especially difficult this time. The uncertain parliamentary majorities in the Reichstag meant that Reich president von Hindenburg and his advisors (among whom the Reichswehr's chief political lobbyist, General Kurt von Schleicher, was an increasingly influential voice) would again play a major role in selecting potential candidates to form a new government. They preferred a nonparty man or a member of the DVP. Among those mentioned were former chancellor Hans Luther and Robert Curtius, the number two man in the DVP's Reichstag delegation.[49]

Luther had no interest in returning to national office, but Curtius did attempt to form a *Bürgerblock* cabinet. It was a short-lived quest. The Center party, without whom no bourgeois cabinet was possible, rejected Curtius or any other chancellor from the ranks of the DVP. It was difficult not to sympathize with the Catholics' attitude. Since the fall of the latest Marx cabinet, the German People's party seemed to change its position on the future Reich coalition almost daily. Seemingly flying in the face of its recent altercations with the SPD, the DVP all but endorsed a grand coalition in principle on December 15. Two days later the party favored a "prepact" with the Conservatives, but after another twenty-four hours the right-wing Liberals declared they were free to negotiate with all sides.[50] In addition, the Center party continued to distrust the right-wing Liberals' position on educational and religious issues, which were particularly important concerns in 1927 since the new cabinet would be guiding the long-delayed Reich education law through the Reichstag and the Reichsrat.

Seemingly demonstrating the truth of the adage *plus ça change* . . . in politics, the new Reich cabinet was another *Bürgerblock*, again headed by Wilhelm Marx. But there was a new twist. Surprising most political observers,[51] the Catholics accepted the DNVP as part of the coalition. For the Center party, an agreement with the German Nationalists on the terms of the proposed Reich education law was the heart of the coalition pact. Constituting a self-proclaimed "Christian majority" in the cabinet, the two parties agreed to incorporate provisions for confessionally segregated public schools into the proposed Reich education law, even though article 146 of the Weimar constitution specifically gave preference to nonsectarian public schools.[52] For this reason both liberal parties had difficulties with the "Christian" pact on the schools. The DVP reluctantly joined the coalition (mostly because Stresemann, who remained Reich foreign minister in the new cabinet, wanted to ensure the continuity of his foreign policy), but the left-wing Liberals regarded the terms of the proposed education legislation as unconstitutional and refused to become part of the cabinet.[53]

As always, negotiations on the federal coalition raised the issue of the Reich-Prussian linkage. At first glance, the DNVP had apparently learned its lesson from previous negotiations with the Center party: when the Catholics strongly objected to including discussions of Prussia's political future as part of the federal agreement, the DNVP dropped its traditional demand that the coalition pact contain a reference to the desirability of a Prussian *Bürgerblock*. In reality, however, a primary reason for the DNVP's willingness to rejoin the Reich cabinet was the party's hope that an agreement with the Center party at the federal level would pry the Catholics loose from their alliance with the Social Democrats in Prussia and prepare the way for a *Bürgerblock* cabinet in the state. The German Nationalists' goal, said Kuno von Westarp at a meeting of the DNVP's national executive committee in June 1927, "is to strengthen the national coalition and to conquer Prussia."[54]

The Social Democrats, the Catholics, and the left-wing Liberals all rejected changing the Prussian coalition as a consequence of the formation of the new Marx cabinet. The SPD seemed to have a new appreciation of Prussia's importance. Unafraid of hyperbole, Rudolf Hilferding underscored the European and global significance of continuing the Weimar coalition in the state.[55] The Prussian Catholics, too, had no intention of abandoning their left-of-center position; in fact, Hess noted the *Bürgerblock* in the Reich was possible only because the Center party in Prussia remained firmly anchored in the Weimar coalition. The Center party had tactical reasons for its decision, but the Prussian Catholics' stand also reflected the differing political outlooks of the Prussian and Reich wings of the Center party. In the Reich, the DNVP and Center party had agreed on the terms of the proposed federal education law, but on the most burning, specifically Prussian, issue, the concordat between the state and the Catholic church, the German Nationalists and the state's Catholics were very far apart. The DNVP was on record as opposing any treaty with the Holy See, while in cooperation with the Prussian SPD, the negotiations between the state and the papal negotiators were going well. As for the DDP, its primary goal at the moment was to prevent the proposed Reich education legislation from becoming law, and that could be done most effectively by influencing the votes of the Prussian delegates in the Reichsrat. The left-wing Liberals, that is to say, had every reason for preserving the Weimar coalition in Prussia. The successful creation of the federal *Bürgerblock* cabinet, then, indirectly strengthened the Weimar coalition in the state.[56]

Despite apparently strong support in the Reichstag, Marx's fourth cabinet was a decidedly weak affair. The DNVP remained a house divided against itself. While the party's leaders counseled caution and moderation, its right wing saw few benefits in joining a government that forced the German Nationalists to recognize the legitimacy of the republic and to support Stresemann's foreign policy. The right-wing zealots insisted not only on a linkage of the Reich and Prussian coalitions, but demanded changes in the Reich constitution enabling the Reich president and the chancellor to serve as Prussian state president and prime minister, respectively.[57]

As for the DVP, it soon developed doubts about the agreement on the education law worked out between the DNVP and the Center party. Having long championed nonsectarian public schools, the right-wing Liberals came to see the "Christian" public schools favored by the Center party and the German Nationalists as a major step backward in the evolution of Germany's system of public education. In May 1927, the Prussian German People's party provided a foretaste of the party's future bitter opposition to the Reich education law. The state's DVP introduced a nonbinding resolution in the Landtag asking the state's cabinet to support an amendment restoring preferential treatment for nonsectarian public elementary schools when the Reich education bill came before the Reichsrat. The motion, which passed 177 to 107, created some remarkable parliamentary bedfellows in Prussia. The SPD, DDP, and DVP voted for the resolution; the Center party and the Communists opposed it; the DNVP abstained.[58]

The Landtag recessed in June and did not return to Berlin until October. By that time, a new national cabinet crisis was already visible on the horizon. The coalition partners had come close to the breaking point on a number of economic and fiscal issues. A salary reform for federal civil servants had caused bitter animosity between the Center party and the DNVP ministers.[59] As for the keystone of the coalition agreement, the Reich education law, fierce opposition from both the left- and right-wing Liberals and the Social Democrats succeeded in derailing the measure; the bill died in a Reichstag committee. By October, the coalition was effectively dead, and the parties were already maneuvering for their place on the next turn of the chancellor carousel. Ironically, only the DNVP was interested in keeping the coalition alive in order to reach the party's "final goal, Prussia."[60]

Prussia and the Müller Era, May 1928–March 1930

The impending fall of the second experiment with a right-of-center *Bürgerblock* cabinet in the Reich seemed to benefit all the moderate parties in

Prussia. Despite the approaching elections (national and state elections had to be scheduled before the fall of 1928 and were expected in the spring), the potential partners of a grand coalition in Prussia seemed ready to cooperate. Otto Braun again authorized Robert Weismann, the prime minister's chief aide and confidant, to begin preliminary negotiations with the DVP. Weismann was not an accidental choice as go-between; he was known to favor a return of the grand coalition.[61] The initiative was not mere pre-election jostling. Supported by the Weimar coalition parties, the prime minister publicly asked the right-wing Liberals to "quit sulking" and rejoin the coalition.

Other parties seemed equally enthusiastic. Among the right-wing Liberals Stresemann had consistently worked for a grand coalition in Prussia, but this time even the party's Prussian spokesmen sounded like converts. The Catholics, too, indicated that they looked forward to discussing an expansion of the present coalition.[62] On the eve of the 1928 Landtag election it certainly appeared that the major obstacles to the grand coalition in Prussia had been removed and that the potential partners were only awaiting the election returns to formalize their agreement.

Like so much else in the history of Weimar Germany, the Müller era in federal politics presents a picture of paradoxes. Between the May 1928 elections and the appointment of the first presidential Reich government in March 1930, parliamentary democracy really seemed to work both at the national and state levels. The Reich government had the support of a majority of the Reichstag, and Chancellor Hermann Müller was the leader of the largest party in the national legislature. The federal government, the last parliamentary cabinet in the Reich, also enjoyed one of the longest tenures among the usually short-lived Reich governments. Although it underwent several changes of personnel and labels, the Müller cabinet remained in office for almost two years. However, while the politicians were finally able to form a grand coalition at the federal level, in Prussia that combination eluded them yet again.

Most observers and political leaders expected that after the elections the long-sought goal of parallel grand coalitions in the Reich and in Prussia would finally be realized. The voters seemed to agree. The parties of the grand coalition enjoyed majorities in both the Reichstag and the Landtag. The Prussian voters, however, added a complication. In the state legislature both the Weimar and the grand coalitions could count on the support of a majority of the delegates.

After the election, the Prussian government, contrary to expectations and against the advice from some quarters, decided not to resign to make way for a new cabinet. This decision did not preclude a grand coalition once the new Landtag had constituted itself, but Otto Braun and the Weimar coalition parties argued that to create an artificial cabinet crisis immediately after the voters had just endorsed the government's composition and policies would negate the electoral mandate.[63]

The Weimar parties' triumphant attitude was understandable in the first flush of victory, but the coalition was far less united than it appeared. The cabinet was beset by internal problems. The SPD's left wing demanded once again that the party sever its alliance with the bourgeois parties. Its spokesmen argued that the party in Prussia had fulfilled its "historic mission" of securing the state against counterrevolution, and that it should now return to leading the opposition against capitalism.[64] Relations between the SPD and the DDP grew increasingly acrimonious. The Social Democrats demanded a redistribution of cabinet seats to reflect the SPD's triumph and the DDP's continuing decline at the polls.

Specifically, the SPD Landtag delegation wanted one of their own in place of the incumbent minister of education, C. H. Becker, who was regarded as a fellow traveler of the DDP. Becker, a fervent supporter of the republic and a distinguished scholar, enjoyed Braun's respect, but the prime minister's party colleagues in the Landtag were less enchanted. The party's legislative leaders felt Becker paid too little attention to the needs of party patronage in his personnel appointments. Personality clashes between Albert Grzesinski and Hermann Höpker-Aschoff added to the friction between SPD and DDP. Shortly before the elections, Grzesinski described his cabinet colleague as lacking "the most elementary qualifications for political leadership." Privately, many of the state's political leaders hoped that expanding the coalition after the election would solve what might be described as a sort of political midlife crisis in the coalition.[65]

Following custom, the parties turned their attention first to the makeup of the Reich coalition, although, as always, the problem of the Reich-Prussian linkage hovered over the federal negotiations. In fact, in June 1928 the linkage issue was raised in a double form. Not only did the DVP insist on simultaneous grand coalitions in the Reich and in Prussia, but the idea of combining the offices of Reich chancellor and Prussian prime minister was seriously considered as well.[66]

A return to the prewar practice of having the same man head the top offices at the federal and state levels seemed to offer a number of advantages. It went a long way in solving the "Prussian problem" in the context of German federalism by facilitating effective coordination between the cabinets in the Reich and the country's largest state. Under a strong leader, parallel grand coalition governments, backed by solid parliamentary majorities in both legislatures, held out the promise of long-term stability. There was even an obvious candidate for the superpost: Otto Braun. The Prussian prime minister stood at the zenith of his political influence and popularity, and he was not unwilling to try the experiment. Braun felt that he was better qualified to be Reich chancellor than Hermann Müller, the man who was eventually chosen to head the new Reich cabinet. Ironically, Müller himself agreed.[67]

Would the history of the Weimar Republic have been markedly different if Braun rather than Müller had attempted to steer Reich and state through the crises that lay ahead? Some contemporaries were convinced a major chance was lost in mid-1928,[68] but the trial balloon proposing Braun as simultaneous Reich chancellor and Prussian prime minister was quickly punctured. A number of personal and political considerations rendered the plan unrealistic. Both the Reich president and the Center party objected to going back to the prewar practice—Hindenburg for political reasons, the Catholics on constitutional grounds. Still, as the prime minister noted, these factors might have been overcome. Decisive for Braun's failure was the unwillingness of the SPD's national leadership to give strong backing to his candidacy. Instead of the Prussian prime minister, the Social Democrats' executive supported the party's national co-chairman, Hermann Müller, as the SPD's candidate for Reich chancellor. The failure to obtain his party's backing was a great personal disappointment to the prime minister; he especially resented that Müller was unwilling to step back.[69]

The end of Braun's candidacy as Reich chancellor—if the episode can be called that—also ended speculation about placing authority for two of the highest political offices in Germany in the hands of one leader, but the problem of the political linkage between state and Reich coalition remained. It was raised repeatedly in the negotiations on the future of the Reich coalition. Since the SPD had been the clear winner in the elections, the Reich president, in strict accordance with the rules of parliamentary democracy, asked Hermann Müller as the leader of the strongest party in the Reichstag to form a new national government. Müller hoped to put together a grand coalition, and he expected that the formation of a similar government in Prussia would help him in his quest.

The three Weimar coalition parties had already agreed in principle to invite the DVP to join a grand coalition cabinet in the Reich, but the right-wing Liberals now saw themselves in a strong bargaining position and initially demanded a very high price for agreeing to join the Müller cabinet. Specifically, the DVP stipulated three prior conditions: the SPD would have to agree to the navy's request for appropriations to construct the battle cruiser A, the new Reich government was to oppose a Prussian proposal in the Reichsrat making August 11 (the day on which the Weimar constitution was adopted in 1919) a national holiday, and, most important, the Weimar coalition parties in Prussia would include both the DVP and the Economics party in a new state cabinet.

These conditions were put forward by the DVP's right-wing intransigents, and were clearly unacceptable to the Weimar coalition parties. This was not surprising. The demands were really an attempt by the DVP's right wing to sabotage the grand coalition, not facilitate its formation. Having permitted the obstructionists their day of grandstanding, the DVP's Reichstag delegation and especially the national leadership soon drew up more realistic terms. Scholz, the head of the party's Reichstag delegation, "clarified" the DVP's position on Prussia by noting that taking the WiP into the Prussian cabinet was "highly desirable," but not a sine qua non. Even the insistence by the DVP's Reichstag delegates that agreement on the terms of a Prussian grand coalition was necessary before the party would sign on in the Reich seemed less firm. Von Campe attempted to obtain a resolution to this effect in a joint meeting of the Reichstag and Landtag delegations, but the best he could get was a statement by Scholz, couched in carefully subjunctive terms, that it was the sense of the meeting that the delegates felt such a chronological linkage should occur.[70]

In the meantime, the leaders of the Weimar coalition parties in Prussia seemed to be preparing the way for the grand coalition in the state. Albert Grzesinski noted that this was an "opportune time for a gesture toward the DVP." Braun agreed. Both the Reichstag and Landtag delegations of the Center party stated that grand coalitions at the federal and state levels were desirable. Three weeks after the election, the Weimar parties issued a joint statement formally announcing their readiness to "enter into discussions about enlarging the parliamentary base of the government . . . at an appropriate time and with proper regard for the conditions laid down by the cabinet."[71]

The cabinet's "conditions" were not precisely spelled out, and the phrase "appropriate time" would turn out to be a sticking point as well. Nevertheless, in retrospect the differences between the potential partners appeared more tactical than substantive. The Weimar parties in Prussia had no objections to parallel grand coalitions in the Reich and the state as such; they merely insisted the DVP drop its demand for a formal linkage between the Reich and Prussian coalitions. The DVP, recognizing that it was in a strong bargaining position in Prussia only as long as the chancellor-designate needed the party to put together the Reich coalition, refused to drop its demands. The right-wing Liberals also knew that Hermann Müller was willing to accept the DVP's linkage demands. The chancellor-designate even appeared in person at a meeting of the newly elected SPD caucus in the Prussian Landtag in order to plead the case for linkage. However, led by Otto Braun and Ernst Heilmann, a majority of the delegation rejected the party chairman's pleas. Stresemann, too, failed to persuade Braun to change his mind.[72]

Braun and the leaders of the Prussian Weimar coalition parties who supported his stand acted from a variety of motives. Personal pique and the rivalry between Braun and Müller undoubtedly played a role. So did selfishness and lack of vision. The Prussians had a misguided sense in 1928 and in later years that Prussia could be isolated from the tumults of Reich politics, much as it had been in the early years of the republic. Braun and the leaders of the Weimar parties in Prussia saw no need to use their political capital to rescue the Reich coalition. After all, the Weimar parties had a majority in the Landtag; they did not need the DVP to form a stable government. In addition, a number of specifically Prussian political problems stood in the way of a grand coalition. The leaders of the Weimar parties were concerned about what Braun later rather vaguely called "the stagnating influence" of the DVP.[73] One item on the cabinet's agenda that would become more difficult to deal with if the DVP were a member of the coalition was the concordat between the Prussian cabinet and the Vatican. By June 1928 it was becoming clear that agreement on the terms of the treaty with the papacy was likely among the Weimar parties in Prussia; whether the compromises would hold if the DVP were included in the cabinet was by no means certain.[74]

The DDP presented another problem. The left-wing Liberals had been notably reticent in their comments on enlarging the Prussian coalition. The realization that the German Democrats would have to yield one of their cabinet seats to the DVP certainly dampened the DDP's welcome to the new partner, particularly since the small DDP recognized that as part of the Weimar coalition it occupied a pivotal parliamentary position. Without the DDP's support, the Weimar coalition parties lost their majority in the Landtag; if the DVP was part of the coalition, the DDP's dropping out of the cabinet would have no parliamentary consequences.

By late June the coalition talks in the Reich had deadlocked, while the discussions in Prussia had not gotten beyond preliminary soundings. Repeated telephone appeals from Müller to Braun and other SPD leaders on the linkage issue could not budge the Prussians.[75] At this point, Gustav Stresemann took matters in hand in order to end the impasse in the Reich at least. On June 23 the DVP leader sent Hermann Müller a long telegram from Bühlerhöhe in the Black Forest, where Stresemann was then convalescing from an illness. In his missive the foreign minister reiterated his support for parallel grand coalitions in Prussia and the Reich, but also indicated that as an interim solution he would be willing to remain Reich foreign minister in a "cabinet of personalities." Such a government could take office without fulfilling a set of prior conditions and would not require formal agreement on a grand coalition.[76]

Stresemann had not cleared his initiative with the other members of the DVP's executive committee, and his telegram caused considerable consternation among the party's parliamentary leaders in the Reich and in Prussia. Stresemann acted out of concern for the continuity of his foreign policy. So as not to jeopardize the process of peaceful revision of the Versailles system that had begun with the treaties of Locarno, he was willing to sacrifice his party's short-term tactical advantages. His colleagues in the Reichstag and Landtag took a less statesmanlike view. Especially the DVP's Landtag delegation felt, as the *Deutsche Tageszeitung* noted, that Stresemann had treated it "pretty much as though it were so much air."[77]

The federal "cabinet of personalities" was a strange entity, to say the least. The parties backing the "personalities" seemed to stress their aloofness from the government rather than their support of the cabinet. The DVP's Reichstag delegates made it clear that there would be no formal federal grand coalition before a Prussian grand coalition had been "safeguarded." The SPD's caucus did not give Müller and the Social Democratic Reich ministers a mandate to govern, but merely agreed that as individuals the Social Democrats might become members of the cabinet if they wished to. The Center party did not even go this far. Its representative in the government, the minister of transport, Theodor von Guérard, was officially just the party's "observer" in the cabinet. The new government did not seem destined for a long life.[78]

The consequences of the "cabinet of personalities" for the still unsolved coalition question in Prussia were unclear. On the one hand, the DVP's anger might increase its intransigence. On the other hand, the agreement in the Reich removed the threat of political blackmail from the Prussian negotiations. The potential coalition partners could now turn to specifically Prussian problems. At least in the past, the partners had drawn closer together once the Reich-Prussian linkage was not part of the bargaining agenda.

There was reason for both pessimism and optimism regarding the future of Prussian coalition politics.[79] Various developments seemed to drive the potential partners further apart. The suggestion by some DVP leaders that the party hold talks with the DDP and the Center party separate from those with the SPD raised the Social Democrats' fears that the right-wing Liberals were attempting to lure the bourgeois parties into a *Bürgerblock*. (Such a combination, of course, needed the support of the DNVP to have a majority in the Landtag.) The DVP in turn was concerned that the SPD's cooperation with the Communists in opposing the construction of the battle cruiser demonstrated the Social Democrats' continuing lack of patriotism and untrustworthiness on questions of national defense. Yet the DVP's Landtag delegation also voted unanimously to join the Prussian coalition if the terms were acceptable. Moreover, if there were differences between the SPD and the DVP, all was not well among the bourgeois parties either. Right-wing Liberals and Catholics seemed to draw further apart on the concordat question. The Center party became increasingly concerned about the strident anticlericalism of some DVP spokesmen. Nevertheless, the potential partners remained in contact, and political observers expected a new set of initiatives in Prussia after the legislature returned from its summer recess.[80]

The Prussian negotiations took a back seat while Müller attempted to convert his "cabinet of personalities" into a formal grand coalition. As its price for agreeing to Müller's proposal, the DVP's Reichstag delegation voted unanimously, although "probably not without serious reservations," to continue insisting on the Reich-Prussian linkage. The leaders of the Weimar coalition parties in Prussia still resisted this demand. Braun, for one, seriously doubted that Stresemann would be able to keep his party on a center-left course.[81] Nevertheless, even the prime minister softened his opposition to the Reich-Prussian linkage by assuring the DVP's leaders in the Landtag that once negotiations were successfully concluded in the Reich, it would take only three days to put together a parallel coalition in Prussia. Weismann added that the prime minister not only assumed that there would be a grand coalition in Prussia, but also that the DVP would again control two of the six cabinet seats—the same number the party held from 1921 to 1924. In fact, some Social Democrats, assuming that a DVP minister of education would take office in the near future, were already making plans to safeguard patronage appointments in the provinces.[82]

Despite the indications of mutual good will, the concrete talks made little headway. The prime minister, in poor health, removed himself from the scene; he was taking the waters at Bad Gastein from the middle of August to the end of September. He left no doubt, however, that he still rejected any attempt to shore up or create a grand coalition in the Reich with the formal promise of a similarly constituted cabinet in Prussia. Braun does not seem to have considered that his attitude was making Stresemann's task of keeping the DVP left of center and helping Hermann Müller put together a grand coalition in the Reich more difficult.

Formal negotiations on enlarging the coalition in Prussia began when the Landtag reconvened on October 2. All parties seemed intent on reaching an early agreement. Robert Curtius, the deputy chairman of the DVP's Reichstag delegation, quoted Braun as saying, "I want a grand coalition in Prussia." As gestures of good will toward the Weimar parties, the DVP not only dropped its demand that the Economics party be included in the coalition, but prohibited dual memberships in the German People's party and the Stahlhelm.[83]

Nevertheless, the negotiations immediately ran into difficulties. A number of substantive issues remained to be cleared away before an agreement on a Prussian grand coalition could be formalized. They included economic and tax policies, the concordat, as well as the distribution of ministerial seats in the cabinet. In addition, the ongoing problems with the Reich coalition and the DVP's insistence on the linkage question provided disturbing background noises.

On the matter of assigning seats in the Prussian cabinet, the DVP proposed returning to the practice that had prevailed from 1921 to 1924: three SPD ministers, one from the DDP, and two each from the Center party and the DVP. The German People's party was to hold the finance and education portfolios, as it had during the last grand coalition. The DVP's plan had tradition on its side, but in 1928 it raised a number of political difficulties. Since 1924 the DVP's strength in the Landtag had declined drastically, and the Center party, now much stronger than the right-wing Liberals, was unwilling to yield one of its cabinet positions to the DVP. In addition, the strong-willed DDP finance minister Höpker-Aschoff balked at sacrificing his post in the interest of coalition arithmetic.

But it was the ministry of education that proved to be the largest stumbling block. This ministry was in charge of the day-to-day negotiations on the concordat with the Holy See, and the Center party adamantly opposed placing a militant Protestant, which a DVP appointee was likely to be, at its head. A change in the education ministry also presented difficulties for the Social Democrats. Backbenchers and leaders of the Prussian SPD had long insisted that a new education minister must be a Social Democrat.

To get around the problems with the ministries of finance and education, the Weimar coalition parties offered the DVP the ministries of commerce and agriculture. But that offer—two of the least prestigious cabinet posts— seemed almost calculated to insult the DVP. The right-wing Liberals also suspected the Weimar coalition parties were playing games with their potential partner. When Joseph Hess hinted that the Center party might give up one minister, thereby raising the DVP's hopes, Ernst Heilmann immediately claimed the post for the SPD. An atmosphere of mutual suspicion remained.

At the end of January 1929, after a number of inconclusive if amiable conversations, Otto Braun, acting as a sort of participant mediator, delivered to DVP negotiators what he described as the Center party's bottom-line negotiating stand. The Catholics offered to link parallel grand coalitions in Reich and state, but in return they demanded a "satisfactory declaration" by the DVP on the concordat, and agreement by the People's party that the Center party would retain two cabinet seats. Commenting upon the message, the prime minister endorsed the linkage offer. Braun also suggested that without knowing the terms of the concordat, the DVP could not commit itself to the treaty with the Holy See, and he had "no comment" on the third demand. The DVP refused the conditions.[84]

It may seem surprising that both Braun and the Center party suddenly became enthusiastic supporters of the Reich-Prussian linkage, but there was a good reason for this. The particularly severe winter of 1928–29 brought a sharp decline in business activity and high unemployment. The result was a financial crisis in the Reich, and the likelihood of rising social tensions in the states. Hermann Müller and Otto Braun were anxious to create broadly based cabinets. Now it was the DVP's turn to balk. The right-wing Liberals, until now the foremost champions of the Reich-Prussian linkage, suddenly seemed to lose interest. In view of the growing fiscal problems at the federal level, it now appeared more important to the party's leaders to insist on their tax reform and economic goals in the present Reich cabinet, even if it meant delaying the formation of the formal grand coalition in the Reich or Prussia.[85]

As for the other two demands, it is difficult to tell the prime minister's true feelings about the Center party's tough negotiating stance. Was he unwilling to criticize the Catholics, or was he using his coalition partners' seeming intransigence as a way of sabotaging the negotiations without becoming directly involved? After the talks failed, Braun recalled that he never had much hope for their success, but it is not clear that the Center party was to blame. Catholic observers did lament the growing anticlerical sentiment among the right-wing Liberals, but according to sources in the DVP, the Center party also hinted broadly that it would be willing to give up one of its two cabinet posts if the German People's party promised to support the concordat. Specifically, the Catholics hoped for DVP support to force the current minister of finance, the most outspoken opponent of concessions to the Catholic church, out of the cabinet.[86] Whatever his actual intent, Braun succeeded in shifting the blame for the failure to resurrect the grand coalition in Prussia from the SPD to the Center party. When the DVP's national executive committee met at the end of February to assess the situation, Stresemann acknowledged the Social Democrats' reasonableness, but he sharply criticized the Center party's "brutal will to power."[87]

Despite the unpromising January negotiations, on February 20 Braun submitted a firm offer on behalf of the Weimar coalition parties to the DVP. Actually, two offers: the right-wing Liberals would be alloted one minister (commerce) in a restructured Prussian cabinet and one state secretary (deputy minister) in another ministry; or alternatively, the DVP could have two ministers, but no state secetary. Under the second scenario, the Reich minister for economics, Robert Curtius, would join the Prussian cabinet as minister without portfolio or salary, but with a vote. Curtius would also have been Prussia's liaison minister to the Reich government. This time Braun insisted he needed the DVP's answer within three days. Moreover, the prime minister communicated his proposal directly to Stresemann, not to the leaders of the Prussian DVP. The Reich foreign minister and a majority of the DVP's Reichstag delegation seemed "delighted" to accept the offer of two ministers, but there were problems with the Prussian DVP. The party's Landtag delegation rejected the second offer outright and was willing to consider the first only if the DVP were assigned the ministry of education, a demand the Center party and DDP continued to resist. The latest effort to form a grand coalition in Prussia had failed. Braun announced the end of "his mission."[88]

After the collapse of the talks came the postmortem and mutual assignments of blame. Had "the Weimar coalition parties conducted the negotiations in an incredibly cynical manner," [89] and practically set up the DVP's rejection of what was never a serious offer? Or should the state's right-wing Liberals have accepted Braun's second offer, as Stresemann urged them to do, and continued the conversations with a view toward eventually "winning" the ministry of education for the DVP? Stresemann, for one, felt Braun had made a show of good will and had not closed the door on putting a right-wing Liberal at the head of the ministry of education. [90]

Both sides were partially right. In spite of their public pronouncements, the Weimar coalition parties were not particularly anxious to resurrect the Prussian grand coalition at this time. As we have seen, the DVP held the Catholics primarily responsible, but actually, as Braun wrote in his memoirs, the Center party acted in close conjunction with the prime minister and the Social Democrats. Their motives were different, but their goals coincided. In the face of increasing pressure from the SPD's Landtag delegation to appoint Christoph König, a former elementary schoolteacher and the caucus' spokesman on education affairs, as the new minister of education, Braun was unwilling to discuss personnel changes at the head of the ministry. The Catholics agreed. They wanted neither König, a well-known agnostic, nor a militant Protestant right-wing Liberal heading the ministry that had primary responsibility for conducting the concordat negotiations for the state. In addition, the continuing difficulties in forging a coalition in the Reich eventually reinforced Braun's conviction that Prussia had to be isolated from the "wheeling and dealing in the Reich." In hindsight, this standpoint seems short-sighted. In view of Germany's difficult economic and financial situation, establishing a *Personalunion* between the Reich and Prussian ministries of economics made sense; such a move would certainly have facilitated policy decision making and implementation at the two levels of government. Moreover, Hermann Müller was quite right in observing that the Prussians' attitude was endangering the future of parliamentary government in Germany as a whole, and that *"in the long run"* Prussia could not isolate itself from the consequences. [91]

The Weimar coalition parties' fears that by taking the DVP into the cabinet they would be bringing a Trojan horse into the government had their basis in the Prussian DVP's attitude toward the coalition negotiations. In rejecting Braun's offer, the party's Prussian leaders emphasized that they wanted positions of real power in the cabinet to "restore health" to the Prussian state—a code phrase the German Nationalists routinely employed to denounce the state's parliamentary democracy. Equally dismaying, especially to the Center party, was the impression that many in the Prussian DVP wanted the party to join the government so that the right-wing Liberals could sabotage the concordat negotiations. Despite Stresemann's admonition not simply to reject the treaty with the papacy, a number of right-wing Liberals made it clear that in cooperation with the DDP they hoped to accomplish just that. The fears of the Weimar coalition parties that by accepting the DVP into the cabinet they would lay the groundwork for the next cabinet crisis were not entirely groundless.[92]

The failure of the negotiations in the winter of 1928–29 effectively ended what was probably the only realistic chance for a grand coalition in Prussia. The Weimar coalition parties congratulated themselves on their success in isolating the state from the *quérelles fédérales*. Nevertheless, like opposing forces in a magnetic field, the potential partners continued to be drawn toward one another. In June the prime minister renewed his offer to the DVP of two ministerial posts, a liaison minister to the Reich cabinet and the minister of commerce. Although there were some indications that the Prussian right-wing Liberals had developed second thoughts about their precipitous rejection of Braun's offer, the party again refused the proposal when it was broached in June. And, as if to widen the chasm between itself and the Weimar coalition parties, the DVP vehemently attacked and eventually voted against the draft concordat which the cabinet sent to parliament for ratification in July.[93]

When the Landtag returned in mid-October from a long recess, the political situation had changed considerably. Signs of an economic downturn precipitated the growth of left and right extremists groups. The Nazis and the Stahlhelm, at odds earlier in the spring, together with the DNVP now formed a united front against the Reich and Prussian coalitions.[94] The DVP as part of the Reich cabinet was certainly included among the targets of the extremists' campaigns. At the same time, the Weimar coalition in Prussia was subjected to serious strains. A number of prominent Social Democrats were involved in a massive corruption scandal that shook the municipal finance administration of Berlin. In February 1930, the minister of the interior Albert Grzesinski was forced to resign when it became public knowledge that for some years he had been living with a woman who was not his wife. Both SPD and the Center party backbenchers demanded the resignation of C. H. Becker as minister of education.

Family squabbles among the Weimar coalition parties was one reason for reconsidering the question of taking in a new partner. There were other reasons as well. A major stumbling block in the earlier rounds of talks, the concordat, was no longer at issue; the treaty with the Holy See had in the meantime been ratified by the Landtag. On the whole, the times seemed propitious for the moderate groups to unite in defense of pluralism and parliamentary democracy.[95] Nevertheless, although one DVP Landtag member later claimed "it was close," success again eluded the potential partners. The distribution of ministerial seats remained a problem, but a more important barrier was the national DVP's sharp turn to the right. The right-wing Liberals and the Weimar coalition parties were no longer on the same side of the political spectrum. For some years Stresemann had labored tirelessly to keep the right-wing Liberals in the moderate camp. When he died in October 1929 after a long illness and a series of strokes, the party's new national leaders decided the DVP's political future and fortune lay on the side of the self-styled "national opposition." In other words, the right-wing Liberals would become the allies of the DNVP, the Stahlhelm, and, with some reservations, the Nazis. As far as Prussia was concerned, a majority of the DVP's Landtag delegation still supported the grand coalition, but the party's rank and file for the most part enthusiastically welcomed the shift to the right.[96]

The DVP's precipitous turn to the right became a self-fulfilling prophesy for the Weimar coalition parties. Both the Social Democrats and the Center party concluded that the DVP's opening to the right proved that the right-wing Liberals were not a reliable partner for a grand coalition in Prussia. At the end of January, Otto Braun effectively cut off further negotiations by moving on his own to reshuffle the cabinet. Yielding to pressure from Ernst Heilmann and the SPD's Landtag caucus, the prime minister asked C. H. Becker, the minister of education, to resign "for reasons of political necessity." Braun had insisted that Becker was indispensable for the negotiations with the Holy See, but once the concordat had been ratified with the help of the SPD, the party demanded its pound of flesh.[97]

The dismissal of Becker, one of republican Prussia's longest serving and most distinguished cabinet members, was a particularly unfortunate and narrow-minded decision by the state's Social Democrats. To a large extent it was a political power play by Ernst Heilmann, designed primarily to demonstrate the aging leader's remaining political prowess. There is no doubt that the minister's dismissal alienated many of the great names of "Weimar culture." Among those protesting the firing of the man who had "transformed the Prussian ministry of education from a government agency into a factor in Germany's cultural life" were Heinrich and Thomas Mann, Max Liebermann, Käthe Kollwitz, and Albert Einstein.[98] The SPD's accusations against Becker were also blatantly unfair. The minister was neither a tool of his reactionary advisors, nor blind to the dangers emanating from the antirepublican right.

Perhaps the only positive aspect of the shabby Becker affair was the person of his successor, Adolf Grimme. Otto Braun knew that the vendetta of his colleagues in the Landtag had both negative and positive aims. Heilmann and the SPD's Landtag leaders wanted Becker out and Christoph König, a former schoolteacher and the party's education spokesman, in. For both personal and political reasons, Braun rejected König. The prime minister had little regard for König's professional qualifications, and he knew that as a former Catholic, but now militant agnostic, König would sour relations with the Center party. Instead of König, the prime minister turned to the man

Becker himself had recommended as his successor. Within a half hour of Becker's resignation, Braun informed the Landtag that he had asked Grimme to become minister of education. Otto Braun based his decision on Becker's suggestion and a personal meeting with Grimme; he did not consult either the SPD's Landtag caucus or its leader.[99]

The new minister, who was to have a distinguished career after World War II as minister of education in the state of Lower Saxony and head of the Northwest German Radio, was one of those rare politicians who combined absolute personal integrity with high professional qualifications and political effectiveness. It was difficult to find anyone who did not think highly of Adolf Grimme. He was a friend of Becker's, but Heilmann and König also valued him as a person. Even the Nazis lauded his "Germanic enhusiasm" and complained only of his philo-Semitism.[100]

Highly praised by intellectuals like Heinrich Mann, Grimme was indeed an unusual Social Democrat. In contrast to most of his colleagues, the SPD was not Grimme's first political home. He had originally joined the left-wing Liberals, but switched his affiliation after the assassination of Walther Rathenau because he felt he could do more for the republic and democracy in the SPD than as a member of the DDP. Even so, he remained something of an outsider in his new party. He was particularly active in the Association of Religious Socialists, a Social Democratic affiliate dedicated to breaking down the barriers between Social Democracy and the Christian churches.[101]

Although the new minister was personally and politically popular, his appointment had the (perhaps unintended) effect of finally shutting the door on further discussions with the right-wing Liberals. Blocked from attaining one of its major goals, the ministry of education, the DVP had little interest in exploring the grand coalition further. This development, too, did not lack irony and paradox. Unlike Becker, whose left-wing Liberal sympathies made him suspect in the eyes of many DVP members, Grimme actually had a good relationship to right-wing Liberals like von Campe and Stendel.

Conclusion: Prussia and the End of Parliamentary Government in Weimar Germany

The simultaneous occurrence of the final failure of efforts to form a grand coalition in Prussia and the fall of the Müller cabinet in March 1930 has led to a long debate about the causal link (if any) between developments in Prussia and in the Reich at the beginning of 1930. There is little doubt that the resignation of Hermann Müller's cabinet marked the end of an era. Despite some similarities in the policies of the Müller and Brüning cabinets, the new chancellor and the men who had put him in office (notably Kurt von Schleicher) hoped a government responsible to the Reich president and independent of the Reichstag would begin the process of returning Germany to an authoritarian constitutional system.

When the Müller cabinet resigned (ostensibly because the government parties could not agree on the amounts employers and employees should contribute to the national unemployment insurance system) the coalition had been incapable of vigorous action for more than six months. Müller himself blamed Prussia for part of his difficulties. Seriously ill at the time, the chancellor repeatedly attempted to use Prussia as a rivet to hold the Reich coalition together. Prussia's unwillingness to exercise its influence on the feuding parties in the Reich, Müller was convinced, contributed significantly to his cabinet's inability to survive.[102]

Personally, both Braun and the SPD's Landtag delegation opposed their colleagues' eventual decision to leave the Reich cabinet. In a rare move, the Social Democratic Landtag delegates actually passed a resolution criticizing the action of their Reichstag colleagues. But Otto Braun and his coalition partners also refused to throw Prussia into the fray as a stabilizing factor. Specifically, the Prussian leaders were not willing to accept the DVP as a coalition partner as a way of aiding Müller's efforts to keep the Reich coalition together. The prime minister remained convinced that Prussia could be isolated from the aftershocks of any Reich crisis. More than that: as had been true in the first five years of the Weimar Republic's history, a politically stable Prussia was the best foundation for the return of stability in the Reich.[103]

The Prussian leaders' unwillingness to use their reservoir of political influence to shore up parliamentary democracy at the federal level was a serious error of political judgment. The view that the transition from Müller to Brüning was another example of the principle of *plus ça change . . .* in the history of Weimar politics recognized neither the fundamental character of the shift from Müller to Brüning, nor the growing weakness of the Prussian coalition's own position.[104]

Whether the DVP's rightward drift could have been prevented if the party had been a member of the Prussian coalition is an open question, but the haughty Prussian leaders might have remembered that earlier they had pointed proudly to the stabilizing effect that the grand coalition in Prussia had had upon the attitude of the DVP in the Reich. Braun's slight-of-hand in replacing Becker with Grimme as minister of education sacrificed long-term strategic gain for short-term tactical advantages. For a man of Braun's stature it showed a singular lack of vision regarding the larger political picture. The prime minister demonstrated that he could impose his will on the SPD's Landtag delegation—but he also effectively ended what turned out to be the last chance for the grand coalition in Prussia.

Welcoming the DVP at the beginning of 1930 might have prevented the fall of the last parliamentary government in the Reich and increased the political defense against extremism in Prussia. After all, Prussia was clearly not isolated from the rise of political extremism. The Weimar coalition's mandate was rapidly eroding; the DDP had all but disappeared as a political force. Prussia, no less than the Reich, was ill prepared for the crises that lay ahead.

Innenpolitik: Security Matters, Personnel Policies, Administration, and Church-State Relations

"**D**omestic policies" *(Innenpolitik)* in German bureaucratic parlance is the collective label for that vast complex of policy making and implementation involving internal security, personnel appointments, local and regional administration, as well as educational matters and church-state relations. *Innenpolitik* is the nexus of interaction between government and citizens in a modern, complex society. In many ways the handling of domestic policy was also decisive for determining the success or failure of the constitutional system of parliamentary democracy in Germany's largest state.[1]

When the second Braun cabinet took office in April 1925, it confronted a number of familiar and increasingly pressing *innenpolitische* concerns. Police and security matters remained high on the agenda. The continued presence of a large number of paramilitary groups and the likelihood that their activities would erupt into political violence made a reliable security force indispensable. Salary reform for the state's civil servants—a group of officials, it will be recalled, that included university professors and public schoolteachers—moved to the foreground. Personnel costs were the largest item in the state budget, and the budget cuts that were part of the currency stabilization efforts following the hyperinflation of 1923 had severely eroded the standard of living of the state's civil servants. The debate over the professional and political dimensions of personnel appointments raged on; slogans like *democratization, republicanization* and *professionalization* were all shorthand descriptions of political programs for restructuring the state's appointment priorities for its corps of civil servants.

Administrative reforms, an issue that had been too long on the back burner, became a top concern for Prussia in the second half of the decade. A new minister of the interior attempted to steer a full-scale reform package through the cabinet and the Landtag, but, like his predecessors, he was thwarted by lack of interest on the part of the prime minister and active opposition by his cabinet colleagues and special interest groups in the legislature. In the end, the government settled for a decidedly more limited package of reforms. On the other hand, the cabinet and the Landtag succeeded in putting church-state relations on a new footing. After years of negotiations, Prussia and the Holy See concluded a concordat, and a few months later a similar agreement was signed with the Protestant churches.[2]

In the second half of the decade, three men served as Prussian ministers of the interior: Carl Severing, Albert Grzesinski, and Hermann Waentig. All were Social Democrats, but they had decidedly different personalities and styles of administration. Two were well-known public figures; since the revolution Severing and Grzesinski had played leading roles in the the state's political life. Hermann Waentig, however, was virtually unknown when he joined the cabinet. One of a handful of academics in a party dominated by men with a working-class background, Waentig had been an outsider in the SPD and a backbencher in the Landtag before his appointment as minister.

When Carl Severing took his seat as a member of the Braun cabinet, he was returning to an office he had occupied virtually without interruption since March 1920. His name and program evoked strong reactions. The minister who had inaugurated the systematic infusion of republican sympathizers into the Prussian civil service—the "System Severing"—was admired by the supporters of parliamentary democracy and hated by those who longed for a return to conservative, authoritarian rule.[3]

After more than five years in office, subjected to constant abuse from his opponents, Severing was suffering from political burnout. He had lost his reputation as the strong man in the cabinet; increasingly the senior officials in the ministry acted on their own. The death of the union leader Ernst Mehlich, one of his closest personal friends, in the spring of 1926 plunged Severing into a deep depression. He took an extended sick leave. He returned to his desk in the summer, but both he and Braun recognized that Severing needed a rest to restore his health. In the fall Severing submitted his resignation.[4]

Severing's successor faced a formidable task. The job required someone with a forceful personality, considerable administrative skills, and experience as an effective political in-fighter. The prime minister's first choice (or at least thought) as Severing's successor seems to have been Gustav Noske, the former Reich defense minister and present governor of the province of Hanover. (It was a foregone conclusion that the new minister would again be a Social Democrat, since under the coalition agreement the ministry was assigned to the SPD.) A trial balloon was quickly deflated, however, when it became obvious that a majority of the SPD's Landtag caucus vigorously opposed Noske's appointment.[5]

At the suggestion of Ernst Heilmann, Braun turned to Albert Grzesinski. Coming from a working-class background (he had been a machinist before becoming active in the Metalworkers' Union and the Social Democratic party), Grzesinski quickly rose to prominence during the 1918 revolution. He was elected as a member of the Central Council of the Workers' and Soldiers' Councils, and after the establishment of parliamentary democracy became a leading figure in the SPD's Landtag caucus. In April 1925, Severing appointed him chief of police in Berlin.

The new minister was not reluctant to shoulder the burden of office. Grzesinski quite openly enjoyed the exercise of political power. Nor did he lack self-confidence. In his reminiscences he wrote of his becoming chairman of the workers' and soldiers' council in Kassel in November 1918: "I 'governed' [*regierte*] as though I had never done anything else in my life." His political friends agreed. When Grzesinski resigned as police chief in the capital to become minister of the interior, the Center party's Berlin paper showered him with editorial praise.[6]

There were profound differences between Severing's and Grzesinski's personalities and styles of administration. Grzesinski was blunt and abrasive, while Severing was proud of his conciliatory manner. Grzesinski privately criticized his predecessor for being weak and excessively conciliatory. The new minister relished his reputation as a tough boss. When a German Nationalist heckler shouted that "autocracy" reigned in the ministry, Grzesinski replied, "Yes, sir, autocracy! Indeed! The chief of the ministry is responsible to parliament, and within the ministry the others have to obey."[7]

Grzesinski quickly installed his own team of top officials to replace Severing's longtime associates. Wilhelm Abegg, a young and ambitious career civil servant with left-of-center political views, became state secretary (or deputy minister), replacing Wilhelm Meister, an old-line bureaucrat with close ties to the DVP. Grzesinski's choice to head the police desk in the ministry was Erich Klausener, a member of the Center party and another official with strong democratic convictions. As the commander of the uniformed Prussian police, the minister selected Colonel Magnus Heimannsberg. Here, too, his choice was a man who had a reputation for loyalty to parliamentary democracy and republicanism.

The new minister enjoyed a warm relationship with his close associates in the ministry,[8] but his abrasive personality did not make life easy for the territorial administrators and the political leaders of the coalition parties. Severing had always gone out of his way to cooperate with both the German Democrats and the Center party, but Grzesinski was far less inclined to appease the SPD's bourgeois partners. He was particularly unwilling to accept the German Democrats as equals. The minister felt the DDP's continuing decline at the polls did not justify that party's claim to a near equal share of political influence in the cabinet.[9] Among the territorial administrators, Otto Hörsing, the *Oberpräsident* of the Prussian province of Saxony (who was also head of the Reichsbanner Schwarz-Rot-Gold and a member of the SPD's national executive committee) was a particularly severe critic of the minister. Grzesinski responded by accusing Hörsing of insubordination.

Albert Grzesinski soon gained a reputation as the ablest and most successful minister of the interior since the establishment of the Weimar Republic. His record of accomplishments and his vigorous defense of the ideals of parliamentary democracy made him the personification of republican strength.[10] Unlike Severing, Grzesinski thrived on political controversy. Constant and increasingly vicious attacks from the extreme left and right did not seem to affect either his health or his energy. The minister was not at all anxious to be relieved of the burdens of office, and he was angered and severely disappointed when revelations about his private life forced him to resign after little more than three years in office.

The affair that ended Grzesinski's ministerial career sounds rather tame by today's standards, but in 1930 expectations of morality for public officials were considerably stricter. When Grzesinski took office he had been separated from his wife for several years, but was not formally divorced; the parties did not agree on a financial settlement until May 1930. In the meantime, Grzesinski had been living with an American actress, Daisy Torrens, whom he married as soon as his first wife agreed to a divorce. Grzesinski's living arrangements were well known to insiders, but—standards were different in this regard as well—the press did not "expose" the minister's private life. Few members of the Landtag and virtually no one in the wider public knew that Grzesinski was "living in sin."[11]

The minister's private affairs became a political scandal in February 1930, when Walther Grützner, a provincial official with a rather checkered past whom Grzesinski had dismissed as district director of Merseburg in 1929, sent identical open letters to all members of the coalition parties in the Prussian Landtag detailing Grzesinski's living arrangements and accusing the coalition legislators of tolerating a public scandal. For good measure, Grützner also communicated "details" of the minister's "mismanagement" to the Nazis.[12]

Otto Braun and the leaders of the coalition parties at first hoped to ignore Grützner's accusations and ride out the political storm, but this proved impossible. It soon became clear that if Grzesinski remained in office the Weimar coalition itself would be in danger. A number of backbenchers in the Center party threatened to support a vote of no confidence against the minister who had, according to the precepts of the Catholic church, committed two mortal sins: seeking a divorce and living in adultery. (That Grzesinski was not a Catholic made little difference.) On February 28, 1930, the minister resigned—officially for health reasons. He returned to his former post as chief of police in Berlin and held this crucial position until the federal takeover of Prussia in July 1932. Shortly after the Nazis came to power, they forced him into exile, and Grzesinski spent the last years of his life in straitened circumstances, working as a machinist in New York.[13]

Grzesinski's immediate successor was Hermann Waentig, then virtually unknown. Like his predecessors, Waentig was an old-line Social Democrat and a member of the Landtag, but his expertise was in finance, not public administration. Waentig's appointment seems to have been the result of several miscalculations. When Grzesinski resigned, he fully expected to return to his post after the political storm had blown itself out. For this reason, he suggested Waentig to Braun as a sort of weak, interim minister who could head the ministry for a few weeks or months. The prime minister accepted the nomination partly because he, too, wanted to keep the position open for Grzesinski, but also because Braun wanted to move quickly and create a fait accompli before backbenchers in the SPD's Landtag delegation or the party's national leadership interfered in what the prime minister regarded as a question of executive privilege.[14]

Braun, Grzesinski, and Ernst Heilmann (who had also approved of Waentig's appointment), soon regretted their choice. The new minister, an arrogant, suspicious man who lacked political experience, judgment, and determination, proved to be singularly incompetent. Above all, he was the wrong man for the times. The rapid increase in political violence by left- and right-wing extremists required a strong-willed minister of the interior to keep law and order in the state. Waentig's tenure in office was brief. Increasingly dissatisfied by his performance, Braun asked him to resign in October 1930. The final straw was Waentig's inability to prevent anti-Semitic riots staged by the Nazis to mark the first meeting of the Reichstag elected in September 1930. Waentig seems to have been as surprised by his dismissal as he had been by his appointment. The quip by a DNVP Landtag member that Waentig "came, saw, and went" was not an inaccurate summary of his tenure.[15]

Before the new cabinet could turn to its own *innenpolitische* agenda, a piece of unfinished business remained. The problem of compensating the members of the former Prussian royal family (as well as the former ruling houses of the other German states) for their "lost" property had aroused political tempers ever since the revolution. Ostensibly, for Prussia the question involved paying the House of Hohenzollern for property—such as the royal art collections, palaces, and theaters—that was now controlled by the state, but underlying the battle over specific objects was a more fundamental controversy. Essentially the issue pitted the bourgeois parties and their concept of the sanctity of private property against the notion supported by the Marxist groups that the Hohenzollerns' "private" property had in reality been stolen from "the people." The controversy had already created tensions among the Weimar coalition partners in the Reich and the state on earlier occasions.[16]

By 1925 the state government and the Hohenzollerns were deadlocked; a variety of proposals for a comprehensive, negotiated settlement had been rejected by the Hohenzollern family as providing inadequate compensation. The former royal house was in no hurry to settle the issue; the courts were on their side. The family brought a number of civil suits against the Prussian government demanding money for specific properties, and the resulting court judgments routinely condemned the state to pay what the cabinet regarded as excessive compensation. Within the cabinet the new minister of finance, Hermann Höpker-Aschoff, continued to press for a comprehensive, out-of-court settlement, but his ministerial colleagues, and especially the Social Democratic Landtag leaders, handled his proposal in a rather dilatory manner.[17]

A bold political maneuver by the Communists forced the Social Democrats to suspend their participation in the search for a compromise settlement. In November 1925, the KPD began a campaign for a national referendum to force the Reichstag to pass a law expropriating the property of all the former ruling houses without compensation. The Social Democrats were caught in a dilemma. While they did not support the demogogic intentions of the KPD's initiative, they also felt they had to cooperate with the Communists' campaign in order not to create confusion among the SPD's rank-and-file members. That decision was not without its critics. Although the opposition to the referendum was led by the Reichsbürgerrat—the same organization that had successfully engineered the election of Reich president von Hindenburg—Otto Braun, for one, did not feel that the referendum was "really a plebiscite on the choice between republic or monarchy." He was convinced that the SPD had allowed itself to be manipulated by the KPD.[18]

The outcome of the referendum was neither as surprising nor as dramatic as supporters and opponents of the effort had anticipated. A majority of German voters rejected the principle of expropriation without compensation, but the relatively large number of yes votes—some 15 million—also indicated that many Germans wanted to express their opposition to the former rulers' excessive demands. The size of the affirmative vote indicated that not only the traditional supporters of the two working-class parties had supported the referendum, but also a substantial number of voters who traditionally supported one of the bourgeois parties had joined them.

After the referendum both sides went back to the bargaining table to negotiate in better faith. Höpker-Aschoff again took the lead, steering a bill through the Reich and state legislatures that was acceptable to both sides. The settlement was more favorable to the Hohenzollerns than Braun and the Prussian Social Democrats had wished, but the financial costs to the state were actually less than they would have been if any of the previous comprehensive proposals had become law. Even so, much bitterness remained. In the Reichstag the SPD rejected the final compromise, and only with difficulty could Braun convince his party colleagues in the Landtag to at least abstain from voting when the proposal came before the Prussian legislature. [19]

The most important result of the Hohenzollern compromise was to clear the atmosphere for the work ahead. Until this divisive and emotional issue had been settled, the cabinet could not make progress on a whole host of other pressing reforms and policy decisions.[20]

Security Matters

For most of its short history, the Weimar Republic suffered from a lack of political consensus. Politics during the republican years was highly polarized, and violence by extremist groups a constant threat. Security in its most rudimentary sense—maintaining law and order—as well as preserving the constitutional system were major concerns for all Prussian cabinets. In the second half of the decade, the danger of actual attempts to overthrow the Reich and Prussian governments by military or paramilitary force receded. There were no more Kapp and Hitler putsches, and the Communists also abandoned attempts to stage their "second revolution." The republic "had prevailed" (sich durchgesetzt) as Grzesinski noted, not without pride, at the beginning of 1927.[21]

The major problem after 1925 was political violence directed at ordinary citizens and altercations between rival paramilitary organizations. The task of the state's security forces was complicated by serious disagreements among the Reich and Prussian ministries of the interior on how to handle political violence. In the federal Bürgerblock cabinets that held office in 1925 and 1927, the ministry of the interior was assigned to a German Nationalist, Walter von Keudell, while his counterpart in Prussia was a Social Democrat. Keudell was an engaging, urbane man, but his political sympathies lay far to the right. In fact, his political views abbreviated his earlier administrative career in Prussia. In 1920 Severing had dismissed Keudell from his post as Landrat because of his involvement with the Kapp putschists.[22]

Not surprisingly, the Reich ministry of the interior saw only the Communists as a danger to law and order. Keudell regarded the paramilitary maneuvers and demonstrations of the "patriotic" organizations of the extreme right as harmless, or even beneficial activities. After all, they combatted the evils of Communism. The Prussian authorities, however, were more even-handed. They looked upon the Communists and the extreme right as equally dangerous and urged similar treatment for all antiparliamentary forces.[23]

The differences between Reich and state were not merely theoretical; the two levels of government clashed repeatedly over both legislative approaches and specific administrative measures. A particularly sensitive legislative issue was the Reich Law for the Protection of the Republic. The law was passed in 1922 in the wake of the wave of right-wing terrorism that culminated in the assassination of Walther Rathenau, the Reich foreign minister, in June of that year. The legislation specifically prohibited various activities intended to undermine or insult republican symbols, institutions, and officials. The law also contained provisions prohibiting the return of the former emperor to Germany, a clause the SPD's left wing regarded as particularly important.[24]

Unless renewed by the Reichstag, the Law for the Protection of the Republic would expire after five years, so it had to be reconsidered in 1927. Led by Keudell, the Reich interior ministry proposed that the law should either be permitted to lapse, or, failing that, be amended to strengthen its anti-Communist provisions and relax those dealing with right-wing activities. The Prussian government argued forcefully for a simple renewal of the law, but was unable to prevail against the *Bürgerblock* majority in the Reich cabinet and the Reichstag. For about eighteen months—fortunately, it was a time of relatively little political violence—there was no specific legislative weapon to combat political extremism. Not until 1929, when a cabinet of the grand coalition had replaced the *Bürgerblock* government in the Reich (and Carl Severing had succeeded von Keudell at the head of the Reich ministry of the interior) could Prussian leaders persuade the federal cabinet and the Reichstag to pass a new, weakened version of the law.[25]

The differences in the assessment of the security problem between Reich and state meant that the Prussian authorities for much of the period covered here were essentially on their own in confronting right-wing political extremism. This was a severe disappointment to the Prussian security experts, since they were convinced that the federal authorities' attitude of benevolent neutrality toward the activities of the extreme right had a doubly unfortunate effect. Not only did the friendly attitude by the Reich officials encourage right-wing extremists, but also the activism of the right in turn stirred up their Communist opponents.[26]

The state was determined to create a police force that could deal effectively with outbreaks of political violence by all antirepublican forces. Prussia's goal was a well-organized, well-paid, and politically reliable police force that would also be kept free of interference by the Reich. The state's municipal police chiefs were the only group of top officials in Prussia that contained a large number of *Aussenseiter* (literally "outsiders"; the American technical term is "lateral entries"), which did not sit well with some of the champions of "professionalism" among the state's leaders.[27] ("Outsiders" were officials who lacked the administrative law degree that was the traditional prerequisite for a high-level civil service career in Prussia.) Ten of the thirteen municipal police chiefs appointed after August 1925 were *Aussenseiter*, for the most part former labor union officials. Prussia also kept ties between its police forces and the Reichswehr to a minimum. Prussian police legislation precluded the routine transfer of army veterans to positions in the state police, a practice that had been traditional in Prussia before 1914 and continued to a lesser extent even after the revolution. Similarly, the state resisted any efforts by the Reich authorities to subject the state's police forces to the control of the Reichswehr during times of declared states of emergency.[28] It was not surprising that the state's personnel policies for its police forces evoked a cry of indignation from the German Nationalists.[29]

Although the Reich authorities would later charge that Prussia's concern with right-wing extremism and the state's unwillingness to cooperate with the Reichswehr in internal security matters meant that the state's security experts were blind to the Communist danger, the Prussian authorities for a long time actually underrated the fascist threat, and overestimated the Communists' strength.

Both Prussian and Reich officials gave excessive credence to the Communists' own boasts. As we saw, in the years after 1925 the KPD underwent massive internal upheavals. The final result was the party's subjugation to Stalin and the Comintern, but before the party's stalinization was complete, left, right, and center factions attempted to prove to the KPD's Russian masters as well as to the party's rank-and-file members that their particular strategies could bring about the long-delayed Communist revolution in Germany.[30]

A key factor in evaluating the danger of a Communist coup was assessing the strength of the KPD's own paramilitary organization, the Rote Frontkämpferbund (RFB). Founded in 1925, the RFB had a membership of several thousand, but opinions differed widely about its discipline and combat readiness. The Reich government argued that the RFB was a genuine threat to law and order, while the Prussian authorities regarded it as a blustering, but not acutely dangerous organization. Almost as soon as the RFB was founded, the Reich minister of the interior demanded that Prussia prohibit the RFB throughout the state, but Severing and Grzesinski both felt it was sufficient to keep a close watch on the organization. They only moved against individual locals when, as was true in Dortmund, the police found that the RFB maintained stores of illegal weapons.[31]

However, by 1928 there was increasing evidence that ultraleftist elements in the KPD were using the RFB as a part of their strategy of provoking street violence to create what they regarded as a protorevolutionary situation. The Prussian interior ministry planned to restrain the RFB's activities in the spring of 1928. However, tactical considerations delayed action: the Prussians felt that moving against the RFB just before the upcoming national and state elections would give the Communists an additional campaign issue.

In view of what was to come, the delay was unfortunate. In the fall and winter of 1928–29, the KPD's ultraleft wing, disappointed by the failure of the strategy of "union from below" to weaken the SPD, felt that spectacular action was needed both to impress the Comintern councils and to demonstrate to the Social Democrats that the German Communists were still a force to be reckoned with. Communist violence culminated in a series of riots in Berlin in May 1929. The KPD had applied for permission to stage one of their traditional May Day demonstrations in the capital. The Berlin chief of police at the time, Karl Zörgiebel (SPD) feared the demonstrations would lead to violence and prohibited the march. The Communists deliberately and openly ignored the ban. The police chief was determined to meet what he regarded as a direct challenge to law and order. Fully supported by the Prussian ministry of the interior, Zörgiebel ordered the police to use massive force in breaking up the Communist demonstrations. The result was a bloody altercation between the police and the demonstrators in which more than a dozen people lost their lives. Immediately afterwards the ministry ordered the dissolution of the RFB throughout Prussia.[32]

The political wisdom and long-range consequences of these events are not easy to assess. The Berlin police and the Prussian ministry of the interior assumed that the Communists planned the riots as a direct provocation of the Prussian government, and the Communists' open talk about the final armed battle with capitalism seemed to support such an interpretation.[33] On the other hand, verbal posturing was a familiar KPD propaganda tactic. It was often intended more for intraparty consumption than to launch concrete activities. It is also true that after the prohibition of the RFB there was a decline in the level of large-scale Communist violence in Prussia, but it remains unclear if the state's decree was cause or coincidence. The KPD's ultraleft phase had probably reached its end in any case. Recent research has demonstrated that the Prussian authorities and especially Zörgiebel as police chief were not without blame in creating the situation; the Berlin police's handling of the May Day demonstrations showed all the classic symptoms of overreaction and unnecessary violence.[34]

There is no doubt, however, that Zörgiebel's and Grzesinski's reaction to the May demonstrations plunged relations between the Communists and the Social Democrats to new levels of bitterness and animosity. While the Social Democrats professed to have a "clear conscience" about the May Day actions, for the Communists these events became the "bloody May." The Communists described Zörgiebel as the "Mussolini of Berlin" and Grzesinski as the "murderer of the workers."[35] On the eve of new challenges from the extreme right, the left was more divided than ever.

In their handling of the right-wing extremists the Prussian authorities concentrated far too long on the danger of a new putsch. The ministry of the interior was convinced that various groups were planning a new coup, although the officials also recognized that dissension and ineffective leadership prevented any of the pseudo-military formations from launching another putsch, at least for the moment.[36] Nevertheless, Prussia remained vigilant. The state's authorities were especially nervous since they were convinced that in the battle against right-wing extremism they were essentially on their own. Little help could be expected from either the civilian or the military agencies in the Reich. On the contrary, the Reich interior ministry all but sabotaged Prussia's efforts to suppress the activities of the antirepublican right.

The divergent views between Prussia and the Reich on the danger from the extreme right became glaringly apparent in the handling of one of the most active and ambitious of the right-wing paramilitary organizations, the Wikingbund. This group, composed mostly of former army officers, openly advocated the violent overthrow of parliamentary democracy. In May 1926, the state's ministry of the interior ordered the dissolution of the organization throughout Prussia. The Wikingbund challenged the order on constitutional grounds, but the Staatsgerichthof, the court established to try offenses against the Law for the Protection of the Republic, upheld the constitutionality of the Prussian action. The Reich interior minister, however, flatly rejected the state's request that he urge other *Länder* to follow Prussia's example and prohibit the Wikingbund.[37]

Although the dissolution of the Wikingbund was a largely symbolic act— the organization was too small to be a real danger—the disagreement between the Reich and Prussia in this relatively unimportant case did not augur well for cooperation between federal and state authorities in handling more significant issues. Relations between the Prussian government and the Reichswehr remained strained. With the approval of the Reich cabinet, the military engaged in some admittedly small-scale clandestine rearmament activities. Prussia (and the leaders of the SPD's Reichstag delegation) openly criticized such activities as a waste of money, a liability for the Reich's foreign policy, and a danger to German parliamentary democracy.[38] The Prussians also opposed the decision, taken "for reasons of economy," to abolish the office of civilian state secretary in the Reich ministry of defense. The agency was replaced by a "ministerial liaison office," headed by a military officer. The Reichswehr countered with complaints about the Prussians. As Colonel Kurt von Schleicher, the first head of the new "ministerial liaison office" told Otto Braun, the army was tired of the nosings around *(Schnüffeleien)* by the Prussian government into matters the army regarded as its internal affairs.[39]

Actually, the Reichswehr's secret and not-so-secret rearmament plans were not Prussia's major worry: it was far more concerned about the army's role in domestic politics. Fixated on the danger of another Kapp-style putsch, the officials responsible for Prussia's internal security were deeply suspicious of the widespread contacts between the Reichswehr and various paramilitary organizations. It was an open secret that some regional Reichswehr commanders maintained friendly contacts with the right-wing paramilitary organizations in their areas of command. Prussia was unconvinced by the argument that such organizations constituted a potential reserve force in case of domestic or foreign "trouble."[40]

Another difference of long standing concerned the so-called Black Reichswehr. These "self-defense" *(Selbstschutz)* organizations were a sort of clandestine army reserve. Equipped and led by Reichswehr officers, the secret units were garrisoned in eastern Germany. During Severing's term of office, Prussia had tolerated their existence, accepting the Reichswehr's argument that they were needed to discourage a potential Polish attack on the eastern border provinces. Grzesinski, on the other hand, feared the dangerous domestic activities of the Black Reichswehr, whose members were recruited almost exclusively from right-wing paramilitary organizations. Prussia noted that some Black Reichswehr units had participated in the so-called Küstriner putsch, a small, unsuccessful uprising in September 1923. Members of the Black Reichswehr were also involved in the infamous *Femegerichte,* the terrorist killings of individuals suspected of revealing German violations of the Treaty of Versailles to Allied authorities. For these reasons, the Prussian authorities demanded that the Reichswehr dissolve the bulk of the *Selbstschutz* organizations; the interior ministry agreed only that a few units might be needed as an auxiliary force to defend Germany's eastern borders.[41]

The contest between Prussia and the Reichswehr on the army's relations with paramilitary groups ended in a draw, but in reality Prussia won. The state authorities were unable to obtain an official order severing all ties between active officers and extreme rightist organizations, but the political consequences of such contacts became less important as the paramilitary groups that wanted to mount a new putsch declined in both membership and influence. Moreover, in the wake of the Küstriner putsch and revelations about the *Femegerichte* (which an investigating committee of the Prussian Landtag helped bring to light), the Reich authorities, including senior Reichswehr commanders, lost most of the enthusiasm for clandestine activities. More far-sighted officers like Kurt von Schleicher pursued more subtle approaches to weaken republicanism in Prussia and the Reich. Instead of using military force to destroy the German constitutional system, the senior leaders of the armed forces envisioned the Reichswehr's gaining increasing influence over the federal cabinet to advance the cause of neoauthoritarianism.[42]

The Reichswehr may have abandoned its Putsch plans, but this was certainly not true of another organization, the Pan-German Association. In May 1926 the Prussian government announced that it had uncovered a plot by the Pan-Germans to seize power in the Reich and the state, and establish a military dictatorship. The announcement did not come as a surprise. Rumors of a coup by the Pan-Germans had circulated for some time. Since February an investigating committee of the Prussian Landtag had detailed the Pan-Germans' involvement in the conspiratorial secrets of the *Femegerichte*. It was also known that Heinrich Class, the leader of the Pan-Germans, saw himself as Germany's future dictator. His plans revolved around a "cold coup": using the danger of a Communist uprising as a pretense, Reich president Hindenburg would declare a national state of emergency under Article 48 of the Reich constitution. The Reich president would then dissolve the Reichstag and the state parliaments, and appoint a new Reich government composed of men sympathetic to the German Nationalists and the Pan-Germans. Law and order would be maintained by the Reichswehr and members of the far-right paramilitary organizations. Eventually, Hindenburg would resign, allowing Class (or in some other versions, Hugenberg) to become Reich protector.[43] Prime minister Braun, temporarily in charge of the interior ministry while Severing was on sick leave, ordered the Prussian police to search the offices of Class and a number of his close associates.

Supported by the coalition parties, the prime minister announced with considerable fanfare that only swift action by the Prussian police had prevented a Pan-German putsch.[44] This was an exaggeration, to put it mildly. The Prussian government and Class himself vastly overestimated the ability of the leader of the Pan-Germans to influence the course of events. Hindenburg certainly had no intention in 1926 of taking part in a coup organized by the Pan-Germans. Hugenberg's part in the planning of the conspiracy is also doubtful. Even Class himself, after consulting with a number of leaders from various paramilitary organizations at the end of 1925, seems to have concluded that these groups were too weak to carry out the planned coup.[45]

In the final analysis, the whole affair proved rather embarrassing to the Prussian authorities. Several prominent individuals were caught in the government's wide-ranging investigative net. They included the industrialist Adelbert Vögler, a close associate of the Reich foreign minister, Gustav Stresemann. His office was searched, but nothing incriminating was found. In fact, the amount of incriminating material uncovered by the police proved to be quite meager. The Reich solicitor general, to whom the Prussian government turned over its findings, refused to indict anyone but Class, and that action was settled out of court. The Prussian government eventually had to apologize to several of those who had been subjected to the police search.[46]

Like Class himself, the Prussian government realized rather late that the focus of activity of the extreme right was switching from coups to mass mobilization. The new threat was first personified by the Stahlhelm, which by the late 1920s had become the largest paramilitary organization in Germany. Legal and respectable—Reich president Hindenburg was honorary president— the Stahlhelm was nonetheless a dangerous foe of parliamentary democracy. The Prussian government had some difficulty coping with the new danger. The cabinet soon prohibited the state's civil servants from joining the Stahlhelm or giving political support to its positions, but the state's security experts re- mained convinced the Stahlhelm's primary danger was its potential ability to organize a new coup, rather than its skill in mobilizing public opinion.

The result was another instance of apparently precipitous and counter- productive action on the government's part. In September 1929, Grzesinski ordered the dissolution of the Stahlhelm's Westphalian regional organiza- tion. This group had been organizing military maneuvers—nighttime marches and training in hand-to-hand combat—activities that the minister felt were strongly reminiscent of actions taken by Italian fascists shortly before the March on Rome. In Prussia the coalition parties loyally supported the minis- ter, although some Landtag delegates in the Weimar coalition parties ob- jected mildly that the government should have provided more evidence to justify its action. Still, the cabinet easily survived a DNVP-sponsored reso- lution of no confidence.[47]

The federal authorities, however, sharply criticized the Prussian move, and Hindenburg looked upon Grzesinski's order as a personal affront and insult to his organization. In the Reichstag the leaders of the Center party and the DDP described Grzesinski's moves as Socialist grandstanding. Even Carl Severing, Reich minister of the interior at the time, called the Prussian action unnecessary and excessive.[48] In retrospect, Severing was right. While the Prussian leaders insisted that "the responsible guardians of the democratic state have to be vigilant and investigate all elements *(Erscheinungen)* that appear to be in touch with sympathizers of a putsch," they lost sight of other, far more dangerous manifestations of extraparliamentary political activity among the extreme right. Convinced that "the overwhelming majority of the German people supports democracy,"[49] they felt the constitutional system could be toppled only by a violent coup.

One of the themes running through the literature on the Weimar years is that the republic's political leaders recognized the new form of the Nazi danger far too late. This is certainly true, although hindsight tends to blind us somewhat to the Nazis' failures in the mid-1920s. If the danger of a Stahlhelm putsch was negligible, the threat of another Nazi coup was even more so. Not only had Hitler learned his lesson from the failed Beer Hall putsch of 1923, but also his party was a very minor player on the far-right stage. Prussia lifted its prohibition on public appearances by Hitler (which the state had imposed in 1925) in March 1927 precisely because at this time no responsible political leader regarded Hitler and his movement as a major force, let alone a serious threat to parliamentary democracy. For many contemporary observers, the Nazis were simply a much smaller if somewhat noisier version of the DNVP.

The Prussian analysis of Hitler's movement may have lacked sophistication, but the state's security apparatus could legitimately point out that it had taken firm steps against the Nazis long before the party came to national attention. Grzesinski and later Waentig continued to keep a close watch on Nazi activities, and as early as October 1928 they considered prohibiting the NSDAP in the state. Nevertheless, the Prussians were still primarily concerned about the Nazi party's penchant for violence, not its potential for undermining parliamentary democracy through the ballot box and extraparliamentary mobilization techniques. The state's security experts looked upon the Nazis and especially the storm troopers as a sort of fascist version of the RFB.[50]

In March 1930, after the Nazis had scored spectacular gains in the local elections of the previous November, Grzesinski, now police chief of Berlin, again proposed prohibiting the NSDAP. (For reasons of symmetry, he wanted to include the KPD as well.) Waentig refused on political and legal grounds. The minister feared—quite correctly—that not only would such a move have led to another conflict with the Reich, but also the Prussian initiative would probably have been thrown out by the courts on constitutional grounds.[51]

Prussia's record on security matters in the years between the cabinet crisis of 1925 and the end of parliamentary government in the Reich in March 1930 is mixed. Firmly committed to defending parliamentary democracy in the state, the cabinet with the full support of the Weimar coalition parties was especially alert to the danger of further coups by either the extreme left or right. Measures by the interior ministry certainly succeeded in preventing another Kapp or Beer Hall putsch, but the likelihood of such an event was remote in any case. In the contest for the "hearts and minds of the people," the state's authorities were rather less successful. They recognized the destructive power of the extraparliamentary politics practiced by the Stahlhelm and the Nazis, but by continuing to insist that these organizations were planning a coup and moving against them on these grounds, the Prussian security officials actually gave them something of a martyr image. At the same time, actions like Zörgiebel's "bloody May" of 1929 exacerbated the tensions between Social Democrats and Communists and lessened the possibility of a united front of the left-wing parties against the growing threat from the extreme right.

Personnel Policies

Security and personnel policies were corollary and complementary aspects of Prussia's *Innenpolitik*. While reliable security forces dealt with acute dangers to the state's democratic system, appointments to the Prussian civil service looked to the future. The 60,000 men and women who staffed Prussia's administrative and technical offices, as well as the 80,000 police officers and the 110,000 public schoolteachers could either be a living backbone of the state's young democracy or an element that undermined Prussia's constitutional system from within.

There is little disagreement among historians that ineffective personnel policies of the Reich and Prussian governments contributed to the failure of the Weimar Republic. The thousands of civil servants whom the republic inherited from the monarchical era, so the argument goes, maintained their political loyalty to the emperor and king, sabotaged republican policies, and—not incidentally—prevented the appointment of new prorepublican officials to the corps of civil servants.[52]

Before analyzing this hypothesis in more detail regarding Prussia, it must be emphasized that most discussions of Prussia's personnel policies—both before and after 1918—concerned not the entire body of civil servants, but the 500 or so appointments to the "political" civil service. These included the top officials in the ministries, the governors (Oberpräsidenten) of Prussia's twelve provinces, the 32 district directors, and the almost 400 county executives (Landräte). These appointees were "political" in the sense that they were not permanent members of the corps of civil servants. Unlike "nonpolitical" civil servants, who attained career-length tenure after a probationary period, political officials served at the pleasure of each cabinet. They could be temporarily retired (in den einstweiligen Ruhestand versetzt) at any time and without cause.

When the second Braun cabinet took office, the System Severing of appointments to the political civil service had been in effect for more than five years. The avowed aim of the System Severing was the democratization or "republicanization" of Prussia's political civil service. Despite claims to the contrary by the opposition,[53] by 1925 the results were noticeable but not dramatic. The overwhelming number of political appointees was still "professionally qualified," which meant that they had an administrative law degree from one of the state's notoriously conservative faculties of law. Aussenseiter who might be expected to bring new ideas to their positions remained a small minority. Protestants still predominated, although the number of Catholic appointments had increased. Politically, all of the Oberpräsidenten and most of the district directors were members of, or at least sympathetic to, one of the Weimar coalition parties, but fewer than half of the county executives were regarded as stalwart supporters of the republic. In the ministries the situation varied considerably. In most departments, the senior officials were at least republican loyalists, if not enthusiasts; but some, like the ministry of justice, had a reputation for particularly low levels of republicanism among its senior officials.[54]

The new Braun government, then, faced formidable challenges. These included agreeing on new rules for the appointment process. In the wake of the currency stabilization that followed the hyperinflation of 1923, the state had dismissed some 15,000 state employees (more than two-thirds of them public schoolteachers) in order to reduce Prussia's personnel costs, always the largest item in the state budget. During the emergency the minister of finance had been given a virtual veto power over all new appointments, but by 1925 the cabinet and Landtag agreed that Prussia's finances had been stabilized sufficiently to reinstitute normal appointment procedures.[55]

At the same time, the government wanted to continue some sort of mechanism to keep the number of Prussian bureaucrats from exploding as it had during and just after World War I. However, agreeing on the specifics of such a program proved difficult. The minister of finance proposed continuing his veto power over all new line appointments, but that suggestion was understandably rejected by his colleagues. Instead, the cabinet went back to collegial decision making. The minister of finance, as the keeper of the purse, was merely assigned a consulting role, along with the ministers holding the other portfolios, in determining the number of line appointments for each ministry. The cabinet also stipulated that the entire effort to control the size of the Prussian civil service should be handled in a "flexible" manner.[56]

Chronic friction between the minister of finance and his cabinet colleagues over personnel appointments involved the problematic relationship between the need to provide government services and the desire to maintain fiscal responsibility as ways of bolstering support for the political system. Höpker-Aschoff's concern was the state's rising personnel costs; his colleagues argued that the state's need to provide services was equally important. From their different points of view, both sides felt they were supporting Prussia's parliamentary democracy. The finance minister insisted that fiscal responsibility would earn voters' support, while his colleagues stressed services as a way to create a positive image among citizens.[57]

Höpker-Aschoff's concerns were aggravated by the 1927 salary reform. This project was a Reich initiative. Federal employees, too, had been forced to accept massive salary and wage cuts during the years of retrenchment. By 1927, German civil servants were generally underpaid, and the entire civil service suffered from low morale. Since the 1927 federal budget was expected to show a sizable surplus, the Reich cabinet proposed using some of the extra money to finance an upward adjustment of civil servants' salaries.

The Reich cabinet at this time was a *Bürgerblock* coalition; the minister of the interior a German Nationalist, Walter von Keudell. He proposed that the bulk of the salary increase should go to the higher ranks of the civil service, a group that included many sympathizers of the DNVP. The Reich minister of finance, Heinrich Köhler, warned against excessive outlays in general, while his Center party colleague, Minister of Labor Adam Stegerwald, wanted to give most of the salary increases to the lower civil service ranks. In the end, the Reich cabinet agreed on a program of increases (between 17 and 25 percent) for all ranks. Unfortunately, the joy that spread through all civil service levels was shortlived. The costs went far beyond the financial resources of the Reich. The budget surplus of 1927 turned out to be a brief windfall. Within two years, the Reich budget was again in the red.[58]

Legally, the Reich Salary Reform Act of 1927 affected only federal employees, but both political and fairness considerations dictated that the states and localities had to follow suit and raise their civil servants' compensation. But the states, including Prussia, encountered a far different situation. Budgetary surpluses in the states and especially the municipalities were much smaller than in the Reich, and local financial experts generally agreed that the increases allotted to federal civil servants were beyond their financial resources. Moreover, the long-term costs of any salary reform would be especially high in a state like Prussia, whose corps of public employees included more tenured civil servants *(Beamten)* and fewer nontenured white-collar employees *(Angestellten)* and blue-collar workers *(Arbeiter)* than was true for the Reich. Finally, a significant percentage of the Reich employees' increases would be passed on to the states; many of the Reich's civil servants were paid at least in part from state funds.[59]

These considerations should have persuaded the Prussian cabinet to be conservative in adapting the 1927 salary reforms to the state. Actually, this was not the case. Höpker-Aschoff later claimed that he persistently tried to hold back the percentages of increase, but when the Reich reforms were proposed and discussed in the Reich cabinet, the Prussian finance minister, who was present for most of these discussions, raised no objections. Höpker-Aschoff was as optimistic about the Reich's and the state's economic and fiscal future as were his counterparts in the Reich. As a result, Prussia's civil servants received salary increases that were essentially the same as those awarded to their federal colleagues.[60]

The consequences were soon apparent. Despite official disclaimers, the 1927 salary reform became a major factor in producing deficits in 1928 and 1929. By 1929 Höpker-Aschoff pleaded that the salary movement must come to an end.[61] But the damage was done. The salary reforms of 1927 raised expectations that could not be met, especially among municipal employees, traditionally the lowest-paid German officials, local government being the financially weakest level of government. Local officials' resentment because of the cuts that began in 1930 was one of the reasons for the high proportion of Nazi sympathizers among municipal employees.

Still, the salary reforms of 1927 contributed to the favorable atmosphere in which the continuing democratization of the Prussian political civil service took place. The new minister of the interior, Albert Grzesinski, was determined to force the pace of democratization among Prussia's civil servants, especially political appointees. While Severing had been content as long as the political administrators no longer openly supported monarchical or antirepublican ideas and symbols, Grzesinski insisted on evidence of open and public support for the republic and its symbols. This meant that Prussia's political civil servants were not only encouraged to join prorepublican political and social organizations, but also required to display the black, red, and gold colors from their office buildings and homes on national and state holidays.[62] (To demonstrate their dislike of the republican symbols, those sympathetic to prewar Prussian authoritarianism liked to restrict their flag displays to the black and white colors of the state flag; these colors were also the emblem of the House of Hohenzollern.)

Undoubtedly, the most controversial aspect of Grzesinski's republicanization program was his insistence that the state's territorial administrators—the provincial governors, district directors, and county executives—should not remain politically neutral at election time. They were ordered to use their offices to give open support to the coalition parties and publicly respond to the opposition's attacks on the coalition. Not surprisingly, Grzesinski's contention that political civil servants were not free in their political activities except in the secrecy of the ballot box, was sharply criticized by the antirepublican right and even many traditionalists in the civil service. They argued that as long as the political appointees did not back political groups that advocated illegal actions, they were free to support opposition parties and their initiatives. Prussian civil servants should be permitted, for example, to support initiatives to force the government out of office, or even to join the Nazi or Communist parties.[63]

Grzesinski's concern about civil servants' election-time activities was part of the minister's media consciousness. A steady stream of plans for press campaigns, newsreels, and documentary films to propagandize the successes of the Prussian government emanated from his office. Later analyses and the Nazis' success demonstrated that this was an area of politics which the republican governments tended to neglect to their peril, but at the time Grzesinski's efforts met with little success. His proposals were enthusiastically supported by the chief of the Prussian state press office, but the finance minister rejected virtually all of the plans as too expensive.[64]

The right of political civil servants to oppose the government became a bitterly debated issue in the last years of the Weimar Republic. In the fall of 1929 the Stahlhelm, in cooperation with the Nazis and DNVP, organized a nationwide initiative campaign against the Young Plan, the recently negotiated international agreement on the modalities of Germany's future reparation payments. The Prussian cabinet mobilized its resources to urge a no vote on the initiative. Braun addressed the Prussian people on radio urging the voters not to support the Stahlhelm's action. All political appointees were ordered not only to withhold support, but also to sign petitions opposing the initiative. The Weimar coalition parties, in this case joined by the DVP, supported the government's effort to prevent civil servants from engaging in antirepublican activities.[65]

Most of the state's political civil servants followed the cabinet's lead and worked hard to defeat the Stahlhelm's initiative at the ballot box, but a small number of officials defied the cabinet's instructions. Grzesinski at first intended to suspend the recalcitrants (most of whom were county executives) immediately, but dropped his plan when it became clear that the Reich authorities would refuse to take parallel punitive action against federal employees. In the end, only two political appointees in Prussia were dismissed in connection with the Stahlhelm initiative. On the other hand, a DNVP-sponsored resolution urging the cabinet not to discipline civil servants who supported the Stahlhelm initiative was easily defeated in the Landtag by the combined vote of the Weimar coalition parties and the DVP.[66]

Obviously, the best way to avoid conflicts with civil servants was to create a corps of political appointees that was actively committed to the republican constitution and did not secretly hope for the return of authoritarianism. This had been the goal of the System Severing. Severing's personnel policies had two priorities. To begin with, except for some aggressive moves immediately after the Kapp putsch, the minister relied on natural attrition to change the character of the political civil service; prorepublican appointees replaced traditionalists as the latter retired. Second, the minister was concerned that personnel appointments should solidify the cohesion and cooperation of the Weimar coalition parties, that is to say, all coalition parties had to benefit equitably from the system of appointment patronage.[67]

When Severing left office, the decidedly slow process of the "republicanization" of the political civil service was clearly apparent. The "system's" success was greatest in the top ranks of the territorial administrators. Of the 12 *Oberpräsidenten,* 4 were members of the SPD, 3 each belonged to the DDP and the Center party, one to the DVP, and the political affiliation of another was "unknown." ("Unknown" was usually a code word for antirepublican sympathies.) The corresponding figures for the 32 district directors were 6 SPD, 10 DDP, 7 Center party, 4 DVP, and 4 "unknown." But among the 398 county executives there were 239 "unknowns." The Weimar coalition parties were represented by a total of 151: 58 from the SPD, 22 from the DDP, and 71 from the Center party. There were also 7 members of the DVP, and a single *Landrat* who gave his party affiliation as DNVP. Among the 23 municipal chiefs of police, 11 belonged to the SPD, 2 each to the DDP and the Center party, one to the DVP and the political affiliation of 7 was "unknown."[68]

By the fall of 1926, Severing's "system" had come to a virtual halt. During the years of the budget crisis, retiring civil servants were simply not replaced, and when the hiring stop ended, Severing's poor health prevented him from acting with renewed vigor. The situation, then, was ripe for a man of Grzesinski's activist temperament.

The new minister left little doubt about his priorities. He wanted to increase the number of sincere republicans—*Herzensrepublikaner*—in top ministry positions and in the politically sensitive posts of the territorial administration. He also wanted to accelerate the pace of new appointments. To this end, Grzesinski immediately after coming into office replaced Wilhelm Meister, a DVP member who had served as state secretary (deputy minister) in the ministry under Severing, with the energetic and passionately pro-republican Wilhelm Abegg. The minister also abolished the traditional requirement that all candidates for appointment to high-level civil service positions serve a probationary period as administrative lawyers *(Referendarzeit)*. Grzesinski believed that the number of *Aussenseiter* among political appointees needed to be significantly augmented to hasten the democratization of the civil service.[69]

The minister may have been determined to sweep with new brooms, but Grzesinski, too, was hampered by a number of constraints. His difficulties began in the cabinet. Grzesinski worked well with Braun's chief of staff, Robert Weismann, who handled personnel matters in the prime minister's office, but his relations with the finance minister, Hermann Höpker-Aschoff, were often acrimonious. Coalition politics added to the difficulties. Political logic dictated that political civil service appointments be allocated in proportion to the electoral success of the coalition parties, but this proved impossible. In the past, the two largest coalition partners, the SPD and the Center party, were underrepresented among the state's political civil servants, since relatively few of their members and sympathizers had the requisite formal educational requirements. In contrast, the DDP, although politically the weakest of the three Weimar coalition parties, had a disproportionately large reservoir of members and sympathizers with administrative law degrees. As a result, the number of "DDP-men" among the political civil servants was considerably larger than the party's success at the ballot box warranted. Finally, there was the issue of the relationship between personnel appointments and pressure groups sympathetic to the larger coalition parties, such as the Catholic and Socialist unions, as well as members of the Center and Social Democratic parties in the Landtag. Under Severing, the interior ministry had been relatively open to outside pressure.[70]

Did Grzesinski finally introduce personnel policies such as "the SPD had hoped for since 1919"? Not really. Despite a good public relations image, he, too, handled personnel appointments in line with the constraints of coalition politics. He severely criticized the DDP's pretensions,[71] but in general political appointments continued to be made under Grzesinski much as they were during Severing's administration. Grzesinski's goal of increasing the number of *Aussenseiter* in the political civil service had some success, especially among the provincial governors, but he also admitted that "outsiders" would always remain a small minority in the political civil service. The overwhelming number of district directors and especially county executives would continue to be drawn from candidates with administrative law degrees.[72]

Still, the minister left behind an important legacy of new appointments, particularly in the ranks of the *Oberpräsidenten*. Grzesinski quickly and forcefully removed a number of entrenched provincial governors, some of whom had been in office since the days of the revolution. In removing incumbents he considered unsatisfactory, Grzesinski did not spare members of his own party. He retired Bartels in Frankfurt a.O. as well as Kürbis in Kiel—both prominent Social Democrats. Most important, however, Grzesinski finally confronted head-on the "Hörsing problem." Hörsing, the head of the Reichsbanner Schwarz-Rot-Gold, had been *Oberpräsident* of the Prussian province of Saxony since 1919. Almost from the day of his appointment, Hörsing had been an administrative gadfly who brought sleepless nights to Grzesinski's predecessors. Severing had been unwilling to confront and restrain the politically powerful Social Democrat, but the new minister did not lack the courage. In July 1927, he asked for Hörsing's resignation, citing the governor's chronic insubordination. With ill grace, the provincial head left office.[73]

Hörsing's removal was symptomatic of the impact of Grzesinski's personnel policies, which was most noticeable among provincial governors: at the end of 1928 eleven of the twelve *Oberpräsidenten* were *Aussenseiter*. At this level of administration, Grzesinski actually preferred *Aussenseiter*, because the minister regarded their political qualifications and life experience as more important than experience in public administration. For example, Hermann Lüdemann, the head of a white-collar union and for a few months in 1920 Prussian minister of finance, became governor of Lower Silesia. Lüdemann had been district director of Lüneburg (in the province of Hanover) for less than a year before his new appointment. Grzesinski's choice for Upper Silesia was Hans Lukaschek, whose only administrative experience had been service as mayor of the medium-sized town of Hindenburg in the same province.

Incidentally, not all of Grzesinski's searches were successful. Both Severing and Otto Landsberg turned down the minister's request to succeed Hörsing in Saxony.[74]

Grzesinski also set new accents in the districts. In the course of a state-wide inspection tour, he became convinced that the number of *Herzensrepublikaner* in the ranks of the district administrators was painfully small. In most areas only the directors themselves were enthusiastic about parliamentary democracy; other high-ranking officials were at best *Vernunftrepublikaner*. As a result, although Grzesinski generally restricted his district appointments to career civil servants, he attempted to select enthusiastic republicans as district directors and their deputies. In March 1928, the cabinet retired six deputy district directors. All were career officials without party affiliation, which in the Prussian parlance usually meant sympathizers of the pre-1918 regime. Their successors were also career officials, but their political sympathies clearly lay with one of the coalition parties. Moreover, although Grzesinski agreed that the job of district director required more technical administrative skills than that of *Oberpräsident,* at the end of 1928 eighteen of the thirty-two district directors were *Aussenseiter.*[75]

The county executives *(Landräte)* were a perennial problem child of the political civil service. It was difficult to find more than 400 qualified local administrators who were politically acceptable to the cabinet, to the leaders of the coalition parties in the Landtag, and, last but not least, to the voters and local party organizations in the county. Consequently, the corps of county executives inherited by the republican regime from the Hohenzollern era remained pretty much intact. Especially in East Elbia many opponents of parliamentary democracy retained a tight hold on county offices. They could even claim a democratic mandate of sorts, since many DNVP sympathizers were very popular among the traditionally conservative population in Germany's eastern provinces. Despite much talk about wholesale purges in the ranks of the *Landräte* between 1919 and Grzesinski's appointment, only one-third of the East Elbian *Landräte* (forty-one in all) had been replaced over the previous six years.[76]

The situation again seemed ripe for a man of Grzesinski's activst temperament, especially since there was no lack of replacement candidates. The county organizations of the coalition parties and the local Landtag delegates (if they belonged to one of the coalition parties) sent Grzesinski a steady stream of suggestions for appointments. However, despite his firebrand reputation and his criticism of his predecessor's lackluster record, the new minister, too, rejected any suggestions of republicanizing the county executives by wholesale dismissals. He cautioned even (or especially) members of his own party that the wishes of the local party organization or Landtag delegates were only one factor in the appointment of county executives, and that in any case the cabinet, not the legislators, decided personnel appointments. In a number of instances, Grzesinski's choices were opposed by the local party organizations of one or more of the coalition parties, and it required considerable "jawboning" to overcome these objections.[77]

The concrete result of Grzesinski's personnel appointments in the counties was a significant, though still not dramatic, change in the makeup of the *Landräte*. Both the number of *Aussenseiter* and the percentage of county executives who were members or sympathizers of one of the coalition parties increased. At the end of 1926 the percentage of career officials among the county executives had been 94 percent; a year later, the figure had dropped to 83 percent. More significantly, by May 1928, 183 of the 416 county executives (43 percent) belonged to one of the coalition parties: 55 were members of the SPD, 81 belonged to the Center party, and 47 to the DDP. This meant, of course, that almost two-thirds continued to have little sympathy for the republic, but Grzesinski did appoint more *Herzensrepublikaner* as county executives than Severing had been able to do.[78]

Grzesinski's efforts to add outsiders to the political civil service were perhaps most successful in the ranks of Prussia's mayors. Under the Prussian constitution, mayors were selected by the city councils, although the interior ministry set minimum standards of qualification, and all mayors had to be confirmed by the ministry. Since the SPD was the dominant party in a number of the state's municipalities, and few of its members and sympathizers had university law degrees, the city councils frequently elected *Aussenseiter* as mayors. Under Grzesinski these nominees had good chances of being confirmed. In setting the minimum standards of qualification for mayor, the ministry specifically determined that a law degree was not a prerequisite.[79]

Did the overall results of Grzesinski's personnel policies justify his retrospective boast that he had appointed "several hundred high officials . . . with strong democratic leanings"?[80] Vehement attacks by the right-wing opposition in the Landtag seemed to support this claim. Especially the DNVP never tired of protesting that Grzesinski, even more than Severing, had destroyed the professionalism of the Prussian civil service and turned it into a pork barrel institution to benefit the Weimar coalition parties. On the other hand, Gustav Noske, the right-wing Social Democratic *Oberpräsident* of Hanover, complained that the ministry had been very remiss in sending "real" republicans to his province.[81]

A more balanced assessment of Grzesinski's record certainly does not support the DNVP's claim that the minister "destroyed" the Prussian civil service. Grzesinski's admonition to the district directors to "be especially careful to nominate only persons whose qualifications cannot be doubted" was a time-honored formula used by all interior ministers.[82] The overwhelming number of political appointees still had formal training in administrative law. The percentage of *Aussenseiter* among the county executives, for example, never exceeded 17 percent, and at the end of 1929 over half of the *Landräte* still belonged to or "leaned" toward one of the opposition parties. Grzesinski had made progress in creating a corps of loyal administrators, but had yet to transform the political civil service into a group of solid *Herzensrepublikaner.*[83]

However, Grzesinski succeeded in breaking up the social and religious homogeneity especially of the higher civil service ranks. When he left office, the civil service included an increased sprinkling of men from middle- and lower middle-class backgrounds, diluting a corps that was traditionally dominated by scions of aristocratic or upper middle-class families. Moreover, past political appointees had been overwhelmingly Protestant. Under Grzesinski, the number of Catholics (as well as a few Jewish appointees) increased significantly.[84]

Administrative Reforms

The need for a comprehensive reform of the territorial administration, Weimar Prussia's most vexing political issue, had been articulated by royal commissions as far back as the mid-nineteenth century. "Constant demands" for comprehensive reforms continued in the republican era; politicians from every camp and public administration specialists agreed that reforms at all levels—local, county, district, province, and central agencies—were long overdue. Reforms, acording to their proponents, would produce immense benefits, ranging from financial savings to the creation of a proper climate for the even more elusive full-scale Reichsreform.[85]

There was no shortage of proposals. Shortly after coming to power, the new revolutionary Prussian government asked the last royal minister of the interior, Bill Drews, to submit proposals for comprehensive administrative reforms. The ex-minister immediately took off the shelf legislation he had proposed earlier in the decade. Drew's submissions included draft legislation for redrawing the provincial boundaries, clearer definitions of the rights and duties of local government bodies, and ideas for solving the most difficult part of any reform: delineating the relationship between *Oberpräsidenten* and district directors.

Since the establishment of both offices at the beginning of the nineteenth century, the functions of the *Oberpräsidenten* and district directors had become hopelessly interwoven, creating much inefficiency and duplication of effort. Drews argued for increased autonomy and rights of self-government at the provincial level, and proposed abolishing the office of *Oberpräsident*. The chief executive officer in the provinces would have been a *Landeshauptmann* (provincial chief), to be elected for a twelve year term by the provincial diet.

The *Landeshauptmann* would not, however, administer directly. Drews proposed that the cabinet maintain control over the appointment of district directors and county executives, who would report to both the *Landeshauptmann* and the minister of the interior.[86]

Like all earlier plans, Drews's proposals aroused a storm of controversy. In the cabinet the opposition was led by Ernst von Richter, the finance minister from 1921 to 1924. Richter, a former *Oberpräsident* himself, vigorously objected to Drews's suggestion that the office of *Oberpräsident* be abolished. The finance minister was a centralist who insisted that a simple head of administration, responsible to the cabinet, had to be maintained in the provinces.[87]

In the face of unbridgeable differences between the centralists and the autonomists in the cabinet, Severing, although he generally agreed with the basic tenor of Drews's ideas, soon decided to abandon any attempt to submit a comprehensive reform package of his own to the Landtag. The Ruhr crisis forced further delays, but in November 1923 the cabinet agreed "to begin work speedily on the organic reconstruction of the internal administration." The ministers first considered using their decree powers to institute reforms (until the end of 1923 a state of emergency was still in effect), but eventually decided to employ regular legislative processes.[88]

This decision reflected the democratic convictions of the Prussian ministers, but it probably also doomed any comprehensive reform package. In meetings with the legislative leaders of the coalition parties, Severing found very little agreement on any body of comprehensive reforms in the Landtag. For that reason he proposed falling back on a so-called little reform bill, an effort to introduce some minor changes at the county level and tinker with the system of agricultural and school administration at the provincial level. The problem of delineating the duties of the *Oberpräsidenten* and the district directors was not addressed. Faced with strong opposition in the Landtag, Severing gave up his efforts to abolish either of these offices.[89]

Even the "little reform" failed, ironically because the draft bill was both too much and too little. The act of submitting any reform legislation at all enabled the autonomists and centralists in the Landtag to reopen the debate on the positions of the *Oberpräsident* and district directors. At the same time, for those who felt only a comprehensive reform package could address the problem, the bill did not go far enough. The result was a deadlock in the Landtag. In the spring of 1925, administrative reforms had gone no further than when the republican era began seven years earlier.[90]

When Carl Severing returned to his old position as minister of the interior in the second Braun cabinet, he made another attempt to get the administrative reform project moving, this time acting on his own. At the end of 1925 he submitted a comprehensive reform package to the cabinet and the Landtag.

Although the minister had earlier sided with the provincial autonomists, under Severing's new plan the focal points of the Prussian territorial administration would have been the counties, the cities, and the provinces. Severing proposed the abolition of the district directors as a separate level of administration; their functions would be taken over by provincial governors.[91]

The minister argued that these changes would streamline and rationalize the administrative structure, but he was unable to convince either his cabinet colleagues or the leaders of the Center party in the Landtag. Both objected to increased powers for the *Oberpräsidenten*. The cabinet argued that such a change would have unduly increased the authority of the interior minister, to whom the governors would have reported. (At present the provincial governors oversaw a hodge-podge of offices ranging from provincial school committees to agricultural extension bureaus. For their various supervising functions they reported to the appropriate cabinet member.) The Center party objected to any strengthening of the position of the *Oberpräsidenten*, who were cabinet appointees, as a blow to the principle of provincial autonomy, one of the bedrock fundamentals of the Catholic concept of federalism. The Center party succeeded in "burying the comprehensive reform package," as a leading Social Democrat put it.[92]

The issue of defining the role of Prussia's governors and district directors was so divisive because it touched upon points crucial not only for Prussia's political future, but also for the evolution of German federalism. Those who favored strengthening the position of the *Oberpräsidenten* argued that such a step would ensure Prussia's traditional role as the guarantor of national unity and Germany's constitutional system. As we have seen, the ranks of the *Oberpräsidenten* contained the largest number of *Aussenseiter* and *Herzensrepublikaner*, and they in turn strengthened the case for preserving Prussia itself as Germany's largest federal unit. Those favoring strong district directors saw themselves as innovators and modernizers. They regarded the *Oberpräsidenten* as anachronistic viceroys, obsolete in the twentieth century. Weakening or even abolishing their functions would not only make the Prussian administration more efficient and bring it "closer to the people," but also facilitate redrawing provincial and state boundaries as part of an overall *Reichsreform*.

Severing's initiative remained stillborn, and Grzesinski did not attempt to revive his predecessor's reform proposals. Although the Landtag's Ways and Means Committee asked the cabinet in March 1927 to submit proposals for a comprehensive administrative reform, Grzesinski concluded that any effort to tackle the problem before the elections scheduled for May 1928 would be futile. Ernst von Richter derisively summed up the history of administrative reforms in Prussia after almost ten years of planning and debate: "Administrative reform—people start laughing as soon as you mention it."[93]

While Grzesinski saw no hope of getting his proposals passed by the sitting Landtag, he was not idle. By the end of July, the minister had drafted a thirty-six-page position paper outlining a series of reforms at all administrative levels. On the crucial point of the *Oberpräsidenten* and district directors, Grzesinski took a middle position: he rejected abolishing either office, and pleaded instead for a rational division of labor. The governors would become the "eyes and ears" of the cabinet in the provinces, assuring that the government's directives were carried out throughout the state. The *Oberpräsidenten* would also supervise the district directors. At the same time, the governors would be freed of detailed administrative duties; that was to be the task of the district directors.[94]

The minister intended to obtain the cabinet's agreement before May 1928 so that the relevant bills could be presented to the new Landtag as soon as it met, but Grzesinski underestimated his ministerial colleagues' ability to procrastinate. The cabinet planning stage was an uphill struggle. Several times discussions were taken off the cabinet agenda because the ministers were not ready to debate Grzesinski's proposals or, after objecting, had not submitted alternative plans. It was not until November 1928 that the government formally voted that both the offices of *Oberpräsident* and district director were to be retained in any reform package.[95]

Despite the slow progress, the cabinet's unanimous agreement in principle was a triumph for the interior minister. Although most cabinet members, including the prime minister, agreed with the basic tenor of Grzesinski's proposals, there were major obstacles to overcome. For fiscal reasons the finance minister, Höpker-Aschoff, originally wanted to reduce the administrative functions of the governors even further, but the minister of education was the major holdout. He wanted the *Oberpräsidenten* as the focal point of Prussia's territorial administration. The administration of the Prussian public school system was centered in autonomous provincial school committees; the minister of education had little institutional leverage in the districts. Still, in the end he joined his colleagues in endorsing the central concept of Grzesinski's proposals.[96]

While Grzesinski waited until the new Landtag had been elected before submitting his comprehensive reform proposals to the legislature, he was unwilling to defer the problem of local and county government. Here, too, the central aim was increased efficiency and rationalization. In 1927 the minister proposed far-reaching territorial changes in Prussia's local administration. These included incorporating a number of formerly rural, but now clearly suburban areas, as part of larger cities in Western Prussia, and, in East Elbia, abolishing altogether a unique Prussian institution, the *Gutsbezirke* (literally "estate districts"). These were local administrative units that lay entirely within a private estate, so that the estate's owner exercised governmental power over what was actually part of his private land. Virtually all of these *Gutsbezirke*—there were some 12,000 left by 1928—were located in East Elbia. About a quarter of them were uninhabited, but those who lived in the remainder were little more than human chattel, subject to the whims of encrusted and often reactionary East Elbian Junkers, who exercised governmental control under the auspices of a democratic republic.

In the cabinet, the ministers of finance and agriculture raised some objections, but Braun and Grzesinski quickly overcame them.[97] The real problems came in the legislature and with public opinion in the affected regions. The territorial reforms in the West opened a Pandora's box of clashing local interests, and the plan to abolish the *Gutsbezirke* brought the defenders of Prussian traditionalism to the fore.

Virtually all experts in public administration looked upon the *Gutsbezirke* as a relic of feudal times; Drews had already proposed their abolition in his plans for comprehensive administrative reforms. Grzesinski and the Social Democrats regarded their continued existence as an insult to a modern democracy.[98] The Weimar coalition parties agreed. Even the DVP sided with the government. Only the German Nationalists fought a losing, bitter rear-guard action to preserve the *Gutsbezirke* as symbols of the old and "greater" Prussia. The Communists, who had long assailed the *Gutsbezirke,* paradoxically formed a de facto alliance with the German Nationalists. The KPD opposed the government's proposals because the cabinet's plans allowed brief delays in implementation by permitting consideration of special local circumstances before abolishing a few of the *Gutsbezirke*.[99]

The government's victory was a foregone conclusion. The opposition delayed a final vote in the Landtag by a variety of parliamentary maneuvers, but in December 1927 the legislature passed the bill by a voice vote. Nine months later, 10,500 of the 11,900 estate districts had been dissolved and incorporated into neighboring counties. Grzesinski promised to finish the job by the end of the year.[100]

The abolition of the *Gutsbezirke* turned out to be the government's only unmitigated triumph. Neither the proposed comprehensive municipal reform act nor the bill to redefine the functions of the governors and district directors passed the Landtag. Reform of local government faltered on two counts: the relationship between state control and local autonomy and redrawing local boundaries.[101] Both had political implications. Many small localities in the western part of the state and along the Main River and in some areas of Silesia were under the political domination of the bourgeois parties, while the neighboring larger cities were usually led by Social Democratic administrations. Local administrators mobilized their friends in the legislature—and these often included members of the DDP and the Center party—and among the provincial administrators to prevent being incorporated into neighboring cities.[102] The differences cut across party lines as well. The interests of one local party organization were pitted against those of the same party in a neighboring locality. All of these conflicts made it impossible to keep the Landtag delegation of any one party, much less the coalition as a whole, in line.

As a result, the full-scale territorial reform that Grzesinski had envisioned remained on the drawing boards. Aside from some amendments to the Greater Berlin Law, Grzesinski's most significant accomplishment was the enactment of a comprehensive territorial reform in the Ruhr industrial area. Building upon the earlier Ruhr Settlement Pact *(Ruhrsiedlungsverband),* the minister overcame massive opposition from entrenched local interests and succeeded in persuading the Landtag to change the crazy-quilt pattern of municipal boundaries into a few urban concentrations. The minister, never a modest man, called the Ruhr communal reforms "the most important and most extensive municipal reform act ever accomplished in Prussia."[103]

Grzesinski was particularly disappointed by his failure to steer a comprehensive package of administrative reforms through the Landtag.[104] Some of the reasons were personal. Grzesinski's forced resignation came at a particularly unfortunate time. The cabinet sent the reform package to the Landtag at the end of 1928, and the legislature spent much of 1929 examining the various bills in committee. In fact, the process was still going on when Grzesinski left office in February 1930. Hermann Waentig, a much weaker personality, proved unable to keep up the pressure on the legislators.

The real problems, however, were political. The slow progress of the committee hearings gave cabinet members who had never been enthusiastic about Grzesinski's proposals an opportunity to press their parochial interests before the legislators. But perhaps the most important factor in the unraveling of the cabinet compromise was the role played—or rather not played—by the prime minister. Otto Braun did not assert his power to force the cabinet to present a united front in the Landtag. The result was a debate without progress on the reforms themselves. The prime minister was deliberately sacrificing a short-term goal to preserve what he saw as a larger political strategy: to keep the Weimar coalition together. During the crucial year of 1929, when the weakness of the grand coalition in the Reich was becoming increasingly apparent and the concordat with the Catholic church moved to the forefront of the cabinet agenda, Braun felt he could not endanger the stability of the Prussian coalition by insisting on the enactment of a comprehensive reform package. And once Braun's priorities became obvious, neither the ministers nor the parties in the Landtag could be held in line. In the end the coalition survived, but the price was the failure of a reform project that all agreed was a crucial step in Prussia's evolution as a modern society.[105]

Church-State Relations

The German system of federalism assigned the Länder virtually exclusive jurisdiction over two major areas of public policy: education and church-state relations. True, the Reich as always retained a *Kompetenzkompetenz,* as German bureaucratese put it (literally, "the competency to determine the competency"), the power to delineate the parameters of Reich-state power relations, but in practice the Reich constitution and federal legislation were silent on most aspects of educational policies and church-state relations.

The church-state issue was especially complicated in Prussia. Unlike some of the other *Länder*—such as Bavaria—the state was religiously heterogeneous. About two-thirds of the Prussian population was Protestant, and most of the remainder Catholic. However, in view of the size of Prussia's population, this meant that although Catholics formed a religious minority in the state, in absolute numbers most of Germany's Catholics lived in Prussia.

Church-state relations in Prussia were determined not only by the religious mix of the population; there was also a historical mortgage. Before 1918 church-state relations and politics in Prussia had been closely intertwined. But it was a one-sided relationship, uniting only the Protestant churches and the state's political leaders. The king served, much as in England today, as *summus episcopus* of the Protestant churches, personifying the union of throne and altar. The alliance was also important in the countryside. In East Elbia the close relationship of Junker landlords and Protestant pastors formed a central pillar of prewar Prussian authoritarianism.

In contrast, the state's relations with the Catholic church were weak and irregular. They were regulated not by a series of intra-Prussian agreements, as was true for the Protestant churches, but unilaterally by a papal bull, *De salute anima* of 1825. Legally, then, the rights of the Catholic church in Prussia were not secured under either state or international law. In part because they lacked legal protection, Catholics in pre-1918 Prussia were also subjected to various social and political discriminations.

After the revolution, the new democratic leaders of Prussia recognized that church-state relations needed to be put on a new footing. There were radical plans advanced by left-wing Socialists and Communists for a total separation of church and state, but it quickly became clear that public opinion would not support such a step. Church and state remained institutionally, although not politically, intertwined. The state still collected church taxes and passed them on to the denominations, and virtually all public elementary schools remained segregated by confession. Even the institution of the *summus episcopus* continued, albeit in a rather novel form. In 1920 a troika of three Protestant ministers in the Prussian cabinet replaced the king as *summus episcopus.*

For Catholics, the new era was a decided improvement: parliamentary democracy ended all discriminatory legislation. But there was no change in the formal relations between the state and its Catholic minority; these were still inadequately governed by the bull of 1825. There were recurrent suggestions, especially from the Center party, that a concordat between the papacy and the state should replace *De salute anima,* but both political and constitutional considerations blocked the way. The SPD's left wing argued that a concordat was incompatible with the party's avowed goal of complete separation of church and state. The Reich cabinet raised constitutional objections. Since a concordat was a treaty with a foreign power—the Holy See— such an agreement constituted part of the Reich's foreign relations, which the Weimar constitution assigned to the federal government. Prussia insisted on equally clear constitutional provisions for states' rights in church-state relations. Nothing was done before 1925; both Prussia and the Reich wanted to avoid a constitutional confrontation.[106]

The situation had changed dramatically by the time the second Braun government took office. In October 1924, Bavaria signed a concordat with the papacy, setting a precedent for *Länder* agreements with the Holy See. The Reich government raised no objections. The Bavarian agreement also provided one model for settling what was to become one of the most controversial issues in the negotiations for a Prussian treaty with the papacy. The Bavarian concordat provided for an institutional role of the Catholic clergy in the state's system of public education. In Bavaria, where the population was overwhelmingly Catholic, and virtually all public schools were de facto Catholic institutions, such a provision presented few difficulties. But the situation was entirely different in Prussia, where most of the population, and thus the public schools, were Protestant. A mandated institutional role for the Catholic clergy would offend the Protestant majority, but it was equally obvious that Catholic church representatives would insist that the Bavarian concordat form the basis for any future agreement with any other German *Land.*

After the Bavarian treaty had been concluded, the Reich government agreed that Prussia, too, could begin negotiations with the Holy See.[107] Both sides anticipated long and difficult discussions. Not only were church and state far apart on a number of issues, but the concordat involved an intricate set of Prussian political problems as well, including disagreements among the coalition partners: the Center party enthusiastically supported a concordat, but the German Democrats, traditionally anticlerical and anti-Catholic, remained wary of formal ties between the state and the Catholic church. The Social Democrats, as noted earlier, were committed to total separation of church and state, so that programmatically at least they had to oppose any contractual link between Prussia and the pope. The Prussian Protestant churches were unabashedly hostile to any agreement with the Catholic church, and they wielded considerable influence in the bourgeois opposition parties, especially the DNVP and the DVP.

The agreement with the Catholic church was also an important factor in the continuing discussions about enlarging the Prussian government coalition. The votes of the right-wing Liberals might be necessary to obtain parliamentary approval for any agreement, and for the DVP this knowledge was a major bargaining chip in the coalition talks. In view of the probable opposition of the German Nationalists to any concordat and the SPD's unclear stand, the DVP's decision to approve or reject any concordat might become crucial.[108] Despite the potential problems, Otto Braun believed it politically necessary to begin talks with the papacy. A concordat was the best means of tying the Center party to the Weimar coalition and making it immune to the siren calls of the bourgeois opposition.

To a large extent, success or failure of the concordat talks would depend on the personalities and skills of the negotiators. On the Prussian side, three men played crucial roles: Carl Becker, the minister of education; Friedrich Trendelenburg, the head of the ministry's division of church affairs, who handled the day-to-day negotiations with the papal representatives; and the prime minister himself. Ironically, none was a Catholic. Becker and Trendelenburg were Protestants, and Otto Braun had no church affiliation. Politically, Becker and Trendelenburg were not members of any party, although the minister was usually regarded as an ally of the DDP, while Trendelenburg probably sympathized with the left wing of the DVP.

The chief negotiator for the Holy See was Eugenio Pacelli, the papal nuncio in Bavaria and one of Pope Pius XI's closest advisors. He had also headed the church's negotiating team for the concordat with Bavaria. Pacelli, who would later become Pope Pius XII, was well acquainted with Germany and German church affairs. He had lived in the country since 1912, and spoke and wrote German fluently. Despite his delicate appearance, Pacelli was a tough and skillful negotiator. In the spring of 1925, fresh from his success in negotiating the Bavarian concordat, he transferred his residence from Munich to Berlin.

In negotiating the Prussian concordat, Pacelli was aided by a number of German clerics. They included Ludwig Kaas, a papal house prelate and after the fall of 1928 the head of the Center party; Johannes Linneborn, the head of the cathedral chapter at Aachen, and Albert Lauscher, professor of Catholic theology at the University of Bonn and the Prussian Center party's spokesman on religious affairs. Although both Linneborn and Lauscher were Center party members of the Prussian Landtag, throughout the negotiations there was never a suggestion that confidential aspects of the negotiations were leaked to other members of the party delegation.

Negotiations began in response to a formal request by one of the Weimar coalition parties. On July 1, 1925, Felix Porsch, the head of the Center party's Landtag delegation,[109] wrote the prime minister asking that talks on a Prussian concordat begin as soon as possible. Serious bargaining, however, did not begin until almost a year later, and it took more than two years to reach an agreement. The main points of controversy emerged quite early: the modalities of episcopal appointments, public financial aid for church activities, and, above all, the church's institutional role in public elementary education.[110]

The negotiations dragged on through much of 1926 and 1927. The papal side had originally expected that the terms of the Bavarian concordat, with some modifications, could become the basis for the Prussian treaty, but Pacelli and his aides soon recognized that this would be impossible. Not only were the issues far more complicated in Prussia, but also the Prussian government was unwilling to sign any concordat before the May 1928 Landtag elections. As noted earlier, the 1928 elections gave the Weimar coalition parties a majority in the Landtag, but they also shifted the balance of power within the Weimar coalition. The SPD registered the largest gains, and since the party's rank and file was for the most part opposed to any concordat, the SPD's leaders were adamant that an agreement with the Catholic church contain no mention of the school issue. The church, in contrast, always insisted that a "school clause" was a sine qua non for the treaty.[111]

To improve the atmosphere, Braun and Pacelli held a face-to-face meeting in July 1928. The talks between the two leaders went surprisingly well; Braun's chief of staff, Robert Weismann, anticipated a treaty would be ready for cabinet consideration in October.[112] However, despite the cordial atmosphere, the two sides were still far apart on some crucial and emotion-laden details. One was the establishment of a Catholic diocese in Berlin. The church argued the number of Catholics in the city justified such a step, but the Protestant churches fiercely opposed a Catholic "bridgehead" in what they regarded as a traditional seat of German Protestantism. Surprisingly, political and financial issues were not insurmountable stumbling blocks. The state's generosity facilitated an accord on public financial support for church activities (which included everything from the maintenance of "cultural monuments" like major cathedrals to support for Catholic welfare organizations). Prussia's coffers were relatively full, and with only the minister of finance objecting, the cabinet agreed to double the state's level of support for the church's activities.

On the political side, the state insisted on a "political clause" for all episcopal appointments. That is to say, before a bishop could be invested in Prussia, the ministry of education had to certify that the candidate was not an opponent of the republican form of government. The state's negotiators were especially insistent on this provision because it set a precedent for any future agreement with the Protestant churches, many of whose leaders were open enemies of parliamentary democracy. This, too, proved to be no problem in the negotiations. The Catholic church raised no fundamental objections to the political clause, confirming institutional Catholic support for Prussia's new system of government.[113]

The school problem presented the largest hurdle. For a long time the outcome of this issue and the entire concordat was in doubt. As late as May 1929, it was not certain that the parties would agree. The DDP and most SPD members, including the prime minister, insisted that educational questions were matters of Prussian domestic policy that did not belong in an international treaty. In sharp contrast, for Pope Pius XI, the primary significance of the Bavarian concordat and any subsequent treaties was that they settled the school issue to the satisfaction of the Holy See.

Pacelli insisted that he would have to offer Rome "something" on the school issue, but in the face of the state's absolute refusal and developments in the Reichstag, the church's position became progressively weaker. Especially the Reichstag's failure to pass a national education law in 1927 despite strong support from the Center party and the DNVP convinced the leaders of the Prussian Center party that the papacy's demand for institutionalized church influence in the public elementary schools would doom any agreement. Pacelli long resisted dropping the school clause, but eventually even the papal nuncio acknowledged that its inclusion would defeat any concordat in the Landtag. There would be either a concordat without a school clause or none at all.[114] On the other hand, the state yielded on the question of establishing a Catholic diocese in Berlin.

Much as the face-to-face meeting between the papal nuncio and the prime minister had established a generally cooperative atmosphere for the negotiations, a lengthy bargaining session between Pacelli and Minister of Education Carl Becker broke the deadlock over specific issues.[115] It took another six months to tie up the remaining loose ends, but on June 14, 1929, the Prussian concordat was formally signed.[116] Cabinet approval was a foregone conclusion. The minister of finance, Höpker-Aschoff, adopted a hard line on many items (and later gave himself credit for preventing even more "giveaways" to the church), but the cabinet easily overruled his objections to the financial settlement and the planned bishopric in Berlin.[117]

The concordat faced a far less certain future in the Landtag. The SPD, the largest party in the legislature, found itself on the horns of a dilemma. The Prussian Social Democrats did not wish to endanger the coalition, but the concordat also ran directly counter to one of the party's oldest ideological precepts. In fact, many rank-and-file members had close ties to the Association of German Atheists (*Freidenkerverein*)—as the Communists gleefully reminded their former comrades. The KPD itself, of course, was absolutely opposed to any agreement with the Catholic church. The Communists used the concordat issue to embarrass the right-wing Social Democrats for their potential support of what the KPD's speakers described as the alliance of religion and capitalism.[118]

Among the bourgeois parties in the Weimar coalition, only the Catholic Center party could be expected to provide solid parliamentary support for any agreement that had the papacy's approval. Many in the DDP were opposed to a formal agreement with the Catholic church. Distrust of the Catholic clergy and especially the papacy still ran strong in the ranks of the left-wing Liberals. Moreover, the party feared it would suffer politically in the competition for liberal voters if it were seen as "soft on clericalism." To safeguard its liberal image, the DDP insisted that only its strong opposition had prevented the state's negotiators from yielding on the church's demands for control of the public elementary schools. At the same time, like the SPD, the Prussian left-wing Liberals did not want the controversy over the concordat to endanger the government coalition in the state.[119]

The DDP's right-wing Liberal rivals found themselves in a similar quandary. In their ranks, too, anticlericalism ran high, and, like the DDP, the People's party wanted to be able to claim that it had prevented "giveaways" to the Catholic church. In addition, even more than the DDP, the People's party insisted on equal treatment for the Protestant churches. The Prussian DVP, however, was also anxious to rejoin the government coalition, and a positive vote on the concordat would certainly facilitate such a development.

The DNVP's position seemed similarly equivocal. The German Nationalists traditionally had close ties to the Protestant churches, and a number of virulently anti-Catholic Protestant church leaders were active in the party. Yet there were countervailing political considerations. Since the DNVP's hope of establishing a *Bürgerblock* coalition in Prussia needed the cooperation of the Center party, the moderate forces in the DNVP had been wooing Catholic conservatives. Political and tactical reasons, then, seemed to dictate an accommodating stance by the DNVP on an issue as important to Catholics as the concordat.[120]

Faced with such difficulties in the Landtag, the cabinet had anticipated that an ad hoc majority in the legislature would approve the concordat. Positive votes from the Center party, the DVP, and the DNVP would offset negative votes or abstentions by the SPD, the DDP, and the Communists. This would require some appeasing gesture, especially toward the DVP and the Protestant churches, but there was also an expected political benefit: the gesture would ease a return of the grand coalition. However, such a plan meant that the government was dependent on the votes of the opposition to obtain parliamentary approval for a major cabinet proposal.

Eventually, Otto Braun decided against creating an ad hoc majority for the concordat. Instead of attempting to buy bourgeois votes by concessions, the prime minister planned to obtain approval for the concordat with the votes of all of the Weimar coalition parties, including those of the SPD. Braun still hoped for some DVP votes, but he wanted to avoid a situation in which the DVP, by threatening to withhold its votes for the concordat, could dictate the terms of any agreement on a return of the grand coalition in Prussia.

Braun's plan, whose "boldness was impressive," was first tested when the second house of the state legislature, the Staatsrat, considered the concordat. (The political risks were considerably lower in the Staatsrat than in the Landtag. The second chamber's vote was advisory, not binding on either the cabinet or the Landtag.) Somewhat surprisingly, by a vote of forty-four to thirty-six the delegates of the Weimar coalition parties easily defeated the opposition, consisting of the KPD, the DVP, and the DNVP. The Staatsrat also rejected an amendment to the treaty making approval of the concordat dependent upon reaching a satisfactory agreement with the Protestant churches.[121]

Throughout the ratification process, the cabinet maintained a deliberately conciliatory stance. Before the treaty went to the legislature, Braun met separately with the leaders of all parties except for the KPD and the NSDAP. The Landtag referred the measure to the legislature's Ways and Means Committee. Although the cabinet had hoped that the treaty would be reported out without amendments, a majority of the committee succeeded in attaching a rider to the concordat obligating the cabinet to initiate immediate negotiations for a parallel agreement with the Protestant churches.[122]

The concordat went to the full Landtag on July 1. In introducing the treaty, the minister of education portrayed it as the capstone of developments that put an end to the long and sometimes bitter relations between Prussia and the Catholic church. During the subsequent debate in the full Landtag, the Center party predictably and enthusiastically supported the concordat. In remarks clearly addressed to his Weimar coalition partners, Joseph Hess combined praise for the agreement with enthusiastic endorsement of Prussia's parliamentary democracy: in contrast to their authoritarian predecessors, the state's republican leaders had put into practice the ideal of religious toleration for Catholics. The German Democrats announced that despite some misgivings they, too, would vote for ratification; they argued the concordat promoted interconfessional peace and would prevent a new *Kulturkampf*.

That left the SPD among the Weimar coalition parties. The Social Democrats held the balance for defeat or approval of the concordat. It was no secret that the party remained deeply divided on the issue, and for this reason most of the Landtag delegation had originally favored abstaining from the vote. However, Braun, ably supported by Heilmann, created a political "masterpiece." "By utilizing all of [his] authority," he convinced his party colleagues that abstention would result in a serious and probably irreparable coalition crisis. With the SPD's virtually unanimous vote for ratification, the Weimar coalition parties passed the treaty without making any concessions to the opposition.[123]

Among the opposition parties, the attitude of the radical left and right, the KPD and the Nazis, was a foregone conclusion. The leader of the small Nazi delegation, Wilhelm Kube, in addition to rejecting anything supported by the government, made a specialty out of Catholic-baiting. As noted earlier, the Communists used the concordat to attack the Catholic church for its alleged role in the system of capitalist exploitation and to expose the SPD as an ally of the forces of reaction and superstition. The Economics party, on the other hand, provided a small political sensation. Following a meeting between Braun and the WiP's national leader, Victor Bredt, the Economics party decided to vote for the treaty—the first government-sponsored measure ever supported by the party.[124]

If Economics party support was a surprise, so was the DVP's virulent and unanimous opposition to the treaty. The right-wing Liberals directed sharp attacks on the treaty during the hearings in the Ways and Means Committee, and the party's representatives continued their demagoguery in the plenary debates. During the final roll call, all of the DVP delegates voted against the concordat. The reasons were both political and ideological. As noted earlier, the proposed treaty with the Catholic church stirred deep-seated liberal feelings of anticlericalism and anti-Catholicism. More important, perhaps, the DVP was angered by Braun's success. Instead of being able to use the concordat issue to force concessions from the Weimar parties and pave the way for a grand coalition, the DVP found that the prime minister was using the concordat in order to solidify the cooperation of the Weimar parties and effectively block a return of the grand coalition.[125]

The DNVP, the party that regarded itself as the spokesman for German Protestantism, had succeeded in linking the concordat to a treaty with the Protestant churches in the Ways and Means Committee, but its larger strategy of luring the Center party into a *Bürgerblock* coalition failed. The SPD's decision to support the concordat kept the government coalition intact and made the DNVP's vote irrelevant to the fate of the agreement. In the face of this tactical defeat, the radicals had their own way in the DNVP's Landtag delegation. In a move that deliberately offended Catolic sensibilities, a majority of the DNVP's Landtag caucus succeeded in passing a resolution forcing all members, including the Catholic delegates, to vote against the concordat. One Catholic Landtag delegate who refused to follow his party's dictates was expelled from the DNVP.[126]

Neither the DVP's not the DNVP's stand influenced the final outcome, and the concordat passed easily. The real significance of the parliamentary debate and the vote was political: it deepened the chasm between the Weimar parties on the one hand and the DVP on the other, thereby making the enlargement of the Prussian coalition on the eve of the republic's worst crisis virtually impossible.[127]

The cabinet repeatedly refused to accept any formal linkage between the concordat and parallel agreements with the Protestant churches, and the concordat was ratified without the rider attached by the Ways and Means Committee. Nevertheless, to be even-handed, the state had to begin work on similar accords with the Protestant churches. Not only the bourgeois opposition parties, but also the DDP demanded immediate negotiations. Otto Braun, too, wanted an agreement, if only to remove yet another issue that might become the basis for a *Bürgerblock* agreement among the bourgeois parties.[128]

But any agreement with the Protestant churches also faced serious political obstacles. The SPD, for good reasons, was deeply suspicious of the politics of the Protestant church establishment. Before the revolution, Protestant pastors routinely used their pulpits to preach against the evils of Social Democracy, and the situation did not improve significantly in the republican era. Many a Sunday sermon gave pastoral endorsement to the stab-in-the-back legend: the SPD, the "party without a fatherland" had betrayed the nation in the First World War. For the Prussian local elections in December 1929, the Protestant churches urged their members not to vote for either the Social Democrats or the Communists; they did not issue a similar admonition for the Nazis. Leading Protestant clergymen also maintained close ties to the DNVP. Heinrich Winckler, one of the members of the churches' negotiating team, was also a leader of the DNVP's Landtag delegation. As far as the SPD was concerned, then, any agreement with the Protestant churches had to contain an iron-clad "political clause" to assure that the churches were not free to engage in antirepublican political activities.

The government had initiated negotiations with the Protestant churches in 1926, but talks did not begin in earnest until after the concordat with the papacy had been ratified. The talks were further delayed by the resignation of Carl Becker, the state's longtime minister of education, in January 1930. Finances were not a major issue; the Protestants accepted the terms worked out with the Catholics. There was also little discussion of the school question. While the Catholic church, representing a minority of the population, feared encroachments by the Protestant majority, the Protestants had no such fears. Non-Catholic schools were almost by definition Protestant schools. (The number of "biconfessional" and "secular" public elementary schools in Prussia was very small.)[129]

As expected, the most controversial issue in the negotiations was the "political clause" for major ecclesiastical appointments. The negotiations on this point proved long and arduous. Although the state's negotiators soon made it clear that without a satisfactory "political clause" there would be no agreement, the church leaders fought a rear-guard action against the "political clause" for a long time. The government insisted on cabinet approval of all nominees for high church positions before nominees could be invested. In contrast to the Catholics, Protestant church leaders rejected such a procedure, arguing rather disingenuously that it was incompatible with the concept of separation of church and state and the Weimar constitution's guarantees of freedom of speech. Not until May 1931 was the final agreement signed.[130]

The ratification debate in the Landtag provided some ironic twists. The agreement was guided through the legislative hearings by the new minister of education, Adolf Grimme, a Social Democrat, but the minister's own party did not support the accord. Except for Social Democratic cabinet members, the SPD delegates acted as they had been expected to do in the case of the concordat: they abstained. The SPD could afford the luxury of abstaining because it (and the cabinet) knew that the bourgeois opposition parties, which had so bitterly opposed the concordat, would support the agreement with the Protestant churches. Together with the votes of the DDP and the Center party, supporters of the pact had a comfortable majority. Both the Nazis and the Communists continued to object to any church-state pacts, but their opposition did not matter; the agreement passed easily by a vote of 200 to 56.[131]

Conclusion

Were Prussia's "domestic policies" from 1925 to 1930 a success? At first glance the answer seems clearly, no. The republican governments failed to produce a comprehensive administrative reform, and the personnel changes did not prevent the neoconservatives and later the Nazis from using the bulk of the Prussian civil service for their own ends. Regarding church-state relations, the Prussian concordat was in effect for less than four years. In 1933 it was replaced by a Reich concordat, negotiated by the new Hitler government. Ironically, Eugenio Pacelli represented the Holy See in these negotiations as well. And the "political clause" in the agreement with the Protestant churches did not prevent many church leaders from enthusiastically welcoming Adolf Hitler's appointment as Reich chancellor.

However, there is also an element of reductionism in these criticisms: 1930 or even 1931 was not 1933. Before the onset of the Weimar Republic's final crisis, the democratic government in Prussia was able to solve some longstanding problems. There was no comprehensive administrative reform, but the important changes in urban and rural local government, which included the dissolution of the anachronistic *Gutsbezirke*, were not small matters. By the end of the decade, no one doubted the loyalty of the state's internal security forces. The cabinet's personnel policies were—

slowly—increasing the number of loyal republicans in the corps of political administrators.[132]

Even the short-lived agreements with the Catholic and Protestant churches were politically significant. Catholics, as Joseph Hess noted, gratefully acknowledged that Prussia's political democracy had given them full and equal rights. The Protestant churches, too, recognized the reality and strength of Prussia's political democracy: even in 1931, more than a year after parliamentary democracy had ceased to function at the Reich level, the churches were convinced they had no choice but to reach a modus vivendi with this constitutional system in Prussia. On the whole, then, Prussia's *innenpolitische* record did not show an unimpressive balance sheet for the young parliamentary democracy in the state.

CHAPTER 4

The "Prussian Problem": State and Reich, 1925–1930

Since before the founding of the German empire in 1871, the discussion of Prussia's relationship to the rest of the country had supported a minor literary industry. The debate did not end with unification; it merely shifted to new ground. Bismarck had provided a privileged position for the state in the federal constitution of 1871, but before long it was clear that the role Bismarck had intended for Prussia was incompatible with Germany's evolving modern society. The new Reich constitution of 1919 abolished Prussia's constitutionally unique position among the German *Länder*, but it did not solve other aspects of the "Prussian problem." Making up three-fifths of the Reich's territory and population, Prussia by its very existence created an unbalanced federal structure.

Most political observers and constitutional experts agreed that in the long run the only solution to Germany's federal problem was a package of comprehensive territorial and political reforms. Prussia's leaders were not in principle opposed to a comprehensive *Reichsreform*, but they argued that dissolving Prussia—which many analysts saw as the starting point of any meaningful solution to the problem—was the wrong way to begin.

First, the state argued, Prussia's size was not a problem, but part of the solution. As a large-scale, centralized entity, Prussia represented a major step on the road to a more efficient federal structure. The state's experienced administrative apparatus already provided many needed services for most of the Reich. Creating new Reich offices, which would become necessary if Prussia were dissolved, or "coddling" the smaller *Länder* at Prussia's expense was a step backward, not forward.[1] Second, there was the political dimension of the "Prussian problem." Since unification Prussia had exercised political hegemony in Germany—that is, the state had sufficient influence in the country to assure that Prussia's political system also prevailed in the rest of the Reich.

According to the state's political leaders, that situation had not changed after 1918: during the empire Prussia had guaranteed the survival of political authoritarianism; in the Weimar Republic, the state assured that democracy was Germany's dominant political system. These considerations acquired increased significance when the political center of gravity in the Reich moved to the right. Observing this process, the state's leaders became deeply suspicious of any solution to the "Prussian problem" that involved weakening Prussia's position among the German *Länder*.

Reich-Prussian Relations: Some Case Studies

In a variety of formal and informal ways Prussia's position as primus inter pares of the German states had always included a special relationship to the federal government. In the first half of the decade, Prussia was pleased with the symbiotic relationship between Reich and state. In return for effective and vocal support of the often weak Reich cabinets, the state's leaders were able to exercise considerable influence over the determination of the Reich's policies.[2] The Reich, for its part, was less pleased; federal authorities had resented Prussian tutelage all along. Friction between the two jurisdictions increased noticeably after the DNVP became part of the federal coalition. The outspoken state secretary in the Prussian ministry of the interior, Wilhelm Abegg, assessed the situation from Prussia's point of view in 1927: "It is an undeniable fact . . . that Prussia wholeheartedly supports the Reich, while the federal government works against Prussia in almost all areas."[3]

Nevertheless, controversies between Reich and state had not yet escalated to the level of constitutional altercations, but remained differences of opinion on specific policy and administrative questions. Under the German federal system the Reich did not administer most domestic federal legislation directly, but assigned the implementation to the states. In practice this meant that Prussia became the largest "subcontractor" *(Auftragsverwalter)* for the administration of federal legislation. The state regarded this state of affairs, a tradition going back to imperial times, as efficient and effective, but in the republican era the Reich was increasingly determined to create its own administrative offices for the areas of jurisdiction which the Weimar constitution assigned to the federal government.

An early difference of opinion concerned the administration of Germany's inland waterways. The bulk of the Reich's river and canal system was located inside Prussia, although the waterways obviously carried interstate and international commerce as well. In the 1920s a foreign policy dimension was added to the administration of the waterways. Under the Dawes Plan, Germany's foreign creditors were entitled to be represented on the management boards of the waterways. The Reich argued that since it had jurisdiction over interstate commerce, and a constitutional monopoly for dealing with foreign powers, the management of the waterways should be federalized. Consequently, the Reich began to establish its own administrative machinery for managing the waterways when the Dawes Plan went into effect at the end of 1924.

Supported by a number of other *Länder*, as well as the overwhelming majority of the Landtag (including the DNVP), the Prussian government objected on constitutional and practical grounds. The state brought a case before the State Court for the Reich *(Staatsgerichtshof)*, arguing that a separate Reich administration was superfluous since the state already had personnel with long years of experience in administering virtually all of Germany's waterways. The Reich was equally adamant that the traditional *Auftragsverwaltung* was insufficient; making and implementing foreign policy decisions required continuous, direct federal control. The federal government should administer its own legislation with its own personnel. The Reich won its case. The court ruled that the Reich had the authority to establish its own administrative offices for the waterways.[4]

Since Prussia had sold its railroads to the Reich in 1920, disputes over the composition of the board of directors of the German Federal Railroads (Deutsche Reichsbahn) did not involve a claim to administrative jurisdiction. The problem here was, rather, Prussia's claim that the Reich was deliberately attempting to reduce the state's influence on federal agencies. When a vacancy on the Reichsbahn board of directors occurred in 1926, the Prussian government, again supported by a large majority of the Landtag, insisted on the appointment of a high official from the state's ministry of commerce. Otto Braun complained that the Reich cabinet, following the advice of Hjalmar Schacht, the president of the Reich bank, refused to appoint the Prussian nominee. The state sued again, and this time Prussia won; however, the federal authorities still refused to yield. It took more than another year for the two parties to reach a compromise of sorts. They eventually agreed on the selection of Hans Luther, a former chancellor and at the time mayor of Essen. Nevertheless, the dispute smoldered on. It flared up again in 1928, when, at the time of another vacancy, Prussia claimed the Reich had given precedence to a Bavarian candidate over the Prussian nominee.[5]

Matters like the administration of the inland waterways and the German Federal Railroads involved questions of prestige and influence on what were essentially technical administrative bodies. They did not really concern political differences. In contrast, another dispute that erupted in 1926, the so-called flag decree, led to a direct political clash between Reich and state. As we saw, in May 1926 Reich president von Hindenburg asked chancellor Hans Luther, then head of a right-of-center *Bürgerblock* cabinet, to require all German diplomatic establishments abroad to fly the Reich's commercial flag alongside the national flag. The decree touched upon one of the most divisive issues in Weimar politics, the controversy over the national colors.

Since the founding of the republic, supporters of parliamentary democracy had rallied around a black, red, and gold flag, while the old imperial colors of black, white, and red symbolized the bygone era of Germany's greatness for the opponents of the republic. (In an allusion to the "stab-in-the-back" legend, the German Nationalists routinely insulted the national colors as "black, red, and yellow.") Emotions were already high at the time of the constitutional convention. In an attempt to satisfy both sides, the Weimar assembly had decided upon a curious and not very satisfactory compromise described earlier: the German national colors were black, red, and gold, but the imperial black, white, and red dominated the country's commercial flag. Until the 1926 flag decree, the commercial flag was hoisted only by German ships sailing to foreign ports. Luther's order, then, was a not very subtle attempt to raise the status of the antirepublican colors of black, white, and red to a position of near equality with black, red, and gold.[6]

The political intent of the decree was not lost on the prorepublican forces either, and they raised a storm of protest. Leading the forces rallying to the defense of black, red, and gold was the Prussian state government. The state recognized the decree as a conservative, antirepublican maneuver, although formally the cabinet based its objections to Luther's decree on constitutional grounds. The prime minister accused the Reich government of violating the federal contract since Luther had not sought the approval of the Reichsrat, the representative body of the *Länder,* before issuing his decree. The Reich government rejected the protest.[7]

When Prussia failed to have Luther's decree withdrawn, the state's cabinet attempted to contain the political damage with a decree of its own. In October 1927, Prussian officials were ordered to make sure that the national colors of black, red, and gold (and not just the black-and-white state colors) were prominently displayed before they agreed to participate in official ceremonies or public gatherings. The conservative opposition immediately recognized the intent of this decree as well, and protested what it saw as a Prussian attempt to undermine Luther's action, but the coalition parties fully supported the cabinet's prorepublican action. Not so the Staatsgerichtshof, which in the fall of 1928 ruled the Prussian decree unconstitutional. It was not until 1929 that the Reich cabinet, in the face of increasing attacks from right- and left-wing extremists, issued a parallel decree to protect the republican symbols.[8]

Undoubtedly, the most dramatic (and ironic) battle between Reich and state involved their conflict over the proposed Reich Education Law—another issue left over from the Weimar constitutional convention. Article 146 of the Reich constitution provided that "as a rule" there should not be separate public elementary schools for children of different religious denominations. Protestant, Catholic, and Jewish students should be "simultaneously" educated *(Simultanschule),* except for courses in religious instruction traditionally a part of the German public school curriculum. The details of this constitutional provision were to be spelled out by subsequent federal legislation. Until the federal law went into effect, the status quo would prevail. Since virtually all public elementary students in 1919 attended schools of their own religious affiliation (*Konfessionsschulen*) and there were virtually no *Simultanschulen,* the anticipated Reich Education Law was indispensable for implementing Article 146.

Between 1920 and 1927, several Reich governments introduced education bills, but the Reichstag could never agree on a federal education law. By default, German public schools remained religiously segregated, a situation that was on the face of it unconstitutional. In 1926 the Reich minister of the interior, Wilhelm Külz, again attempted to revive the stalled federal education legislation. Külz was a member of the DDP, which had traditionally championed the *Simultanschule,* and his bill was intended to make such schools the rule, as Article 146 intended.[9]

Külz's draft legislation was ready just in time for the next federal cabinet crisis. In May 1927, the third Marx cabinet fell, and Külz had to resign from the government. The following (fourth) Marx cabinet was dominated by the DNVP and the Center party; the DDP was not part of the coalition. The most aggressive personalities in the cabinet were two German Nationalists, the minister of the interior, Walther von Keudell, and the minister for agriculture, Martin Schiele. With their Center party colleagues, they initiated a plan that had been in the works since 1925. Under the guidance of Catholic and Protestant conservatives, the new Reich cabinet turned Külz's draft on its head. Instead of making the *Simultanschule* the "regular" public school, the new bill proposed to permit the states to retain parochial schools as the "rule" if this had been past practice.[10]

The new Reich Education Law contained political dynamite. Not only did it falsify the intent of the constitution, but also its implementation in Prussia would require a reversal of political alliances. It was clear to its framers that in Prussia only a *Bürgerblock* cabinet dominated by the two self-styled Christian parties would support legislation continuing parochial schools as the "normal" type of public school. In effect, the new Reich Education Law was designed to break up the Weimar coalition in Prussia, and drive the Center party into the arms of the DNVP. Precisely for this reason, the Reich government had not, contrary to the usual practice when major pieces of legislation were under consideration, involved the Prussian cabinet in drafting the Reich Education Law.[11]

Although the Social Democrats early recognized the political intent of the new law, the party was tactically rather inept in meeting the challenge. As the public debate became more heated, the party's longtime moderate and respected spokesman on education affairs in the Reichstag, Heinrich Schulz, moved into the background while Kurt Löwenstein, a fervent atheist and champion of a third type of school, the secular school *(weltliche Schule)*, which would remove religion from the curriculum, became the party's chief spokesman.[12]

The Prussian SPD never adopted the strident tones of the national party. Throughout the controversy it underscored the common ground of the Weimar coalition parties in Prussia, not their differences. This was also true for the Prussian DDP. Even the Center party, while publicly supporting the draft Reich law, was uneasy about the legislation's political intent and implication. The Center party was aware that in Prussia any effort to put up legal barriers against the establishment of the *Simultanschule* would be unpopular. Despite Center party opposition, on May 20 the Landtag voted 177 to 107 in support of a resolution (introduced by the DVP) asking the cabinet to support multi-confessional schools in Prussia.[13]

Confronted by a clear vote in the Landtag, fissures in the coalition, and the Reich government's attempt to use the school issue to change Germany's political landscape, the Prussian cabinet found itself in a difficult position. In reacting to the proposed legislation, the Prussian cabinet was determined to preserve the state's coalition. But this could be achieved only if none of the Weimar coalition parties lost face or felt itself on the defensive. At the same time, the cabinet was also convinced that the key passage of the law, mandating religiously segregated public elementary schools as a "rule," was unconstitutional.

Coordinated by Carl H. Becker, the minister of education, Prussia's handling of the potential crisis was a masterful combination of conciliation and opposition. At the end of August he sent a "carefully considered *(wohldurchdacht)*" position paper to Marx and Keudell. The paper became the basis for the Prussian stand on the Reich Education Law. The state argued that it could not support the legislation in its present form, but would work together with the Reich authorities to find a way that ensured both the *Simultanschule* as the "normal" school type and retained denominationally segregated religious education courses in German public schools.

After some arm twisting by the prime minister, not only the cabinet but also Joseph Hess and the Center party supported Becker's stand. To avoid exposing the differences between the Reich and the state, the position paper and the cabinet decision were not made public. However, to pressure the Reich government, Becker and the Prussian finance minister, Höpker-Aschoff, agreed that the latter would take the low road in public. Without claiming to speak for the cabinet or the coalition, Höpker-Aschoff sharply criticized the Reich Education Law in a series of speeches and interviews.[14]

The Reich government rejected the Prussian proposals. Otto Braun later blamed the chancellor's "clerical intransigence and . . . narrowness of heart [*Engherzigkeit*]" for the Reich cabinet's lack of cooperation. (Wilhelm Marx was also national chairman of the Catholic School Association.) Nevertheless, the state seemed well on its way to winning the political battle when the Reichsrat decided to use the Prussian counterproposals rather than the Reich government's draft legislation as the basis for discussions when the issue came before the second chamber of the national legislature. But it was a short-lived victory. On October 14 the Reichsrat defeated the Prussian substitute by a vote of thirty-seven to thirty-one. Coordinated by Gürich, the head of the education office in the Reich ministry of the interior, the opposition in the Reichsrat was made up of delegates from the Catholic states of southern Germany and a number of Prussian provinces.

The defeat of the Prussian cabinet's position in the Reichsrat demonstrated once again the crucial significance of the provisions in the Weimar constitution that gave control of half of the Prussian Reichsrat votes to the cabinet and the other half to the provincial legislatures. The cabinet instructed its thirteen Reichsrat delegates to vote unanimously for the substitute legislation, but eleven of the provinces ordered their delegates to vote against the cabinet's position. The reasons were political and religious. Catholic provinces favored Catholic parochial schools, and a number of Protestant provinces were dominated by the DNVP. Their delegates voted no in order to support the German Nationalists in the Reich government and to embarrass the hated Weimar coalition cabinet in the state.[15]

But in the end the Conservatives' triumph was equally short-lived. Unable to break up the Prussian coalition[16] and angered by Stresemann's Locarno policy, the DNVP withdrew from the Reich cabinet. The DVP belatedly remembered its liberal and anticlerical heritage, and in February 1928 the Reichstag defeated the government's education bill. Another attempt to implement the constitutional mandate had failed. As far as the "Prussian problem" and Reich-state relations were concerned, the legacy of the Reich Education law was mixed. Reich and state remained deadlocked. The Reich was unable to carry through on its initiative, but Prussia's alternative proposals were also defeated. The only real beneficiary was the Weimar coalition in the state. It came out of the controversy strengthened and more determined than ever to continue its cooperation.[17]

While the battle over the Reich Education Law involved primarily political and ideological issues, some of the longest standing conflicts between Reich and state raged over money, not politics. The Reich Finance Act of 1919 had reversed the financial relationship between the German states and the Reich that had prevailed during the Bismarck and Wilhelminian eras. After 1919 the federal government, rather than the states, collected most of the direct taxes. The *Länder* complained that the shift in fiscal power put them at a severe disadvantage. Their resources were now insufficient to provide needed services, while the Reich was routinely using its *Kompetenzkompetenz* to impose administrative tasks on the states without additional allocations from the federal treasury.

Prussia joined the other *Länder* in the chorus of general complaints, but the state also felt that it labored under some unique handicaps. Most of the direct taxes collected by the Reich were returned to the states under a revenue-sharing system, the *Reichsfinanzausgleich,* but the state's leaders insisted the distribution key consistently favored the southern and smaller states at Prussia's expense. The Prussians argued that both the German federal structure itself and the political constellation of the Reich government worked against the interests of Germany's largest state. Prussia contended that many of the small *Länder* in northern Germany were viable only because they received infusions of federal money out of all proportion to their own tax contributions. In other words, Prussia's efficient administration was indirectly subsidizing the inefficiency of its smaller neighbors. Prussia also complained about the leverage which the Bavarian People's party (BVP), the dominant political force in Germany's second largest state, exercised at the Reich level. The BVP was a member of several Reich *Bürgerblock* cabinets, and the Bavarians used this position, the Prussians argued, to institute a distribution key for revenue sharing that deliberately favored the southern states.

The frictions smoldered until 1927 when the Reich cabinet (which at the time included a BVP minister) proposed that Bavaria and Württemberg should be given a special federal subsidy to compensate them for the lack of income from a state beer tax. Unlike most German states, Bavaria and Württemberg, for political reasons of their own, had no beer tax, and consequently forfeited this source of revenue. Prussia protested vehemently, but the state lost its case in the Reichstag and the Reichsrat. The federal government's proposals were enacted into law. Prussia's attempts to change the distribution key after the grand coalition cabinet took office were similarly unsuccessful.[18]

It was fashionable in Weimar Germany to blame most of the country's economic and financial problems on the Treaty of Versailles. Here, too, the Prussians joined in the chorus, but once again they felt they had a right to sing louder than other *Länder* because of the disproportionately onerous financial losses the state suffered as a result of the treaty. Prussia especially blamed the peace treaty for many of the chronic economic problems of the East Elbian areas. Particularly the province of East Prussia, cut off from the Reich and the rest of Prussia by the Polish Corridor, was, according to the Prussians, a victim of Versailles. The state demanded help from the Reich for all of East Elbia and especially for East Prussia.[19]

Reich and state agreed that a program of subsidies for the impoverished East was needed, but the intended beneficiaries and officials from the two levels of government were far apart on how much money was needed, how it should be allocated, and who should determine how the funds should be spent. Prussia argued that while the resources had to come from the Reich, Prussian rather than federal officials were best qualified to administer the *Osthilfe*, or eastern aid program. The federal *Bürgerblock* cabinets in the second half of the decade, particularly when the DNVP was a member of the government, took an entirely different point of view. The German Nationalists accused the Prussians of using the *Osthilfe* for partisan political purposes, specifically to advance the "bolshevization" of the East. According to the DNVP, the state's officials by refusing to allocate *Osthilfe* funds to save the often hopelessly debt-ridden Junker estates, was attempting to drive the Junkers off their ancestral lands. The two sides came to no agreement, and the *Osthilfe* dispute remained unresolved when the presidential cabinets took office in March 1930.[20]

These cases, and others that could be cited, demonstrated that in the face of determined Reich cabinets, the state's influence in the dynamics of the German federal system was far less than its size and political stability would seem to warrant. In contrast, the potential power of the Reich's financial leverage was immense. Prussia could contain the political damage of some substantive decisions by the Reich government—the flag decree, or the Reich Education Law—but in its financial demands Prussia was unable to prevail against the Reich. For the moment, Prussia's financial weakness did not undermine the stability of parliamentary democracy in Prussia, but the realities of the Reich-state relationship did not augur well for a time when the Reich government might decide to use its financial lever as part of a concerted effort to change Prussia's political system rather than merely limiting the state's influence in the Reich's affairs.

The Search for a Comprehensive Solution to the Reich-Prussian Dualism

There was widespread agreement that Prussia's position in Germany's federal structure was anomalous. But agreement in principle that reforms of the federal structure were needed left a large number of specific questions unanswered. Above all, there was no agreement on the eventual nature of the German federal structure. Assuming, as many did, that Prussia had to disappear as part of a comprehensive *Reichsreform*, would the state's provinces become embryonic new *Länder* (this is the case in present-day Germany), or should the districts that made up the *Länder* be turned into something like the French *départements* in a future unitary Reich?[21]

Such questions, of course, had a direct bearing on the parallel discussions about intra-Prussian administrative reforms. Strengthening the position of the *Oberpräsidenten* was a step toward seeing them as proto-governors of new *Länder*, while increasing the power of the district directors might begin to elevate the districts to the status of *départements*. The position of the *Oberpräsidenten* and district directors was in turn linked to the future role of the Prussian Staatsrat. Weakening the position of the provinces would make the Staatsrat largely superfluous, while strengthening them would also increase the importance of the state's second legislative chamber.

The role of the Prussian Staatsrat had always been controversial. The fathers of Prussia's republican constitution of 1920 had envisioned an institution that would provide a voice for regional concerns, especially on matters before the Landtag that had fiscal implications for the provinces. Particularly the Center party had been (and continued to be) a champion of the Staatsrat as a voice for the provinces. In contrast, the Social Democrats and the German Democrats, who favored a unicameral legislature in principle, during the constitutional deliberations had sought to reduce the powers of the Staatsrat. They regarded this chamber as an essentially anachronistic institution that weakened the power of the directly and democratically elected Landtag. The conservative opposition parties, for their part, wanted a strong Staatsrat, both as a voice of the provinces and a substitute for the old Prussian House of Lords.

The majority of the constitutional convention rejected both a unicameral legislature and the concept of the Conservatives. Consequently, by 1925 the Staatsrat occupied an uncertain status in the state's political life. The bourgeois parties controlled the chamber, and they worked hard to increase its influence. This was particularly true for the Staatsrat's energetic president, Konrad Adenauer. As a leader of the Prussian Center party, the president was a political ally of the Weimar coalition parties, but he was also an eloquent and tenacious proponent of provincial autonomy. When defending the powers of the Staatsrat and the provinces, Adenauer did not hesitate to oppose party colleagues in the cabinet and the Landtag.

The aims of Baron Friedrich von Gayl, the energetic leader of the DNVP caucus who in 1932 became Reich minister of the interior in the cabinet of Franz von Papen, were more blatantly political. He wanted to build the Staatsrat into an institution that could effectively sabotage policies of the Weimar coalition parties in the cabinet and the Landtag. As we saw earlier, Gayl had dreams of using the DNVP-DVP caucus in the Staatsrat as a crucible for forging a *Bürgerblock* coalition to replace the Weimar coalition government in the state.

Conflicts between Landtag, cabinet, and Staatsrat flared up repeatedly in the second half of the decade, but neither Gayl's intrigues nor the ambitions of Konrad Adenauer could transform the Staatsrat into a second chamber of the legislature. Both the Prussian constitution and the cooperation of the Weimar coalition parties in the cabinet and the Landtag proved insurmountable barriers. Cabinet and Landtag energetically opposed the Staatsrat's claims to be recognized as a coequal legislative body with the Landtag.[22]

Another perennial controversy that directly affected the triangular relationship between the Prussian government, the state's provinces, and the role of both in the German federal structure was the composition of the state's representation in the Reichsrat. Until the Weimar era, Prussia had dominated the Reichsrat. The state had the largest block of delegates in the second chamber, and all of Prussia's representatives voted according to instructions from the state's cabinet. In an effort to reduce Prussia's powerful position in the Reichsrat, Article 63 of the Weimar constitution limited Prussia's votes in the Reichsrat to two-fifths of the total (although the state still made up almost three-fifths of the Reich's territory and population) and divided the state's Reichstag delegates into two groups. Half of Prussia's twenty-six delegates represented the cabinet and their votes according to instructions from the state government, and the other thirteen represented Prussia's provinces and voted as instructed by their provincial diets.

Article 63 was born of the fear among the Weimar constitutional convention delegates that a reborn, authoritarian Prussia might undermine Germany's fledgling democracy. In practice the provision achieved the opposite. The main problem was the potentially paralyzing effect of dividing the Prussian Reichstag votes between the state's cabinet and the provinces. The DNVP, which controlled several Prussian provincial diets, elected delegates to the Reichsrat who routinely used the second national legislative chamber to block prorepublican initiatives of the Prussian cabinet. The ubiquitous Baron von Gayl, for example, represented East Prussia in the Reichsrat from 1920 to 1932. In contrast, Social Democratic and left-wing Liberal delegates were rare among the provincial representatives. Of the thirteen provincial delegates serving in the Reichsrat at the beginning of 1926, only three were members of the SPD or the DDP.

In cooperation with their political allies from other *Länder,* the Conservative provincial delegates more than once were able to defeat motions and policies supported by their own state governments. In the second half of the decade, the fragmentation of the Prussian votes became an increasingly vexing problem. Blocked by the provincial votes, the state government found its influence in the Reichsrat all but eliminated on some key issues, a development that had certainly not been intended by the authors of the Weimar constitution. Political observers complained that Bavaria, whose ten Reichsrat delegates were all instructed by that state's cabinet, increasingly controlled the second chamber.[23]

There was widespread agreement within Prussia that this state of affairs was unsatisfactory, but no consensus on causes and remedies. The provincial delegates blamed the cabinet's chief Reichsrat delegate (until 1927 the prime minister's chief of staff, Robert Weismann) for failing to coordinate "his" votes with those of the provinces. The cabinet and the leaders of the Weimar coalition parties in the Landtag in turn accused the provincial delegates of putting politics ahead of their provinces' and the state's interests. Complicating the situation was the curious position of the Center party. Critics noted that the Catholics were playing a double game. As a member of the government coalition, the party agreed the division of votes undermined Prussia's influence in the Reichsrat, but behind the scenes it was equally concerned with preserving and increasing provincial autonomy, and consequently quietly determined to defeat any proposals for alleviating the fragmented vote problem if it involved reducing the provinces' influence in the Reichsrat.[24]

Political commentators saw a connection between the Center party's lack of concern about the problem and the coalition parties' noticeable reluctance to attempt to solve it. The DVP had to take the initiative in trying to cut the Gordian knot of Prussia's Reichsrat votes. In 1925 the right-wing Liberals introduced legislation to ensure that the Prussian Reichsrat votes, like those of other *Länder,* would be cast as a bloc. How the state's twenty-six votes would be cast on any issue was to be decided by majority vote. To determine majority sentiment, the law provided for a complicated system of internal consultations and weighted ballots among the government-instructed and provincial delegates.[25]

Support for the legislation seemed to be widespread. The legislation was endorsed by the Weimar coalition parties and the DVP; the DNVP, the WiP, the KPD, and the *Völkische* rejected the measure. In January 1926 the Landtag by a vote of 211 to 176 passed the DVP-sponsored bill. The cabinet supported the legislation during the committee hearings, and the influential newspaper *Berliner Tageblatt* called it "one of the most important laws passed by the Landtag in the last years." It came as a surprise, then, that the law was stillborn. A few weeks after the Landtag passed the bill, the cabinet informed the legislature that it was unable to implement the legislation. The cabinet noted that the Staatsrat, which had to be consulted because the law infringed upon the constitutional rights of the provinces, rejected the law by a virtually unanimous vote. In addition, constitutional experts in the ministry of justice questioned whether the Prussian Landtag had the power to pass legislation that might affect provisions of the Reich constitution.[26]

Although these reasons were significant barriers to the implementation of the law, they were not the decisive factors. The cabinet and particularly the prime minister all but sabotaged the legislation for short-term and narrowly political considerations. The Center party had voted for it in the Landtag, but Braun feared that in practice the law would increase tensions among Catholics and consequently among the coalition parties. Not only did many rank-and-file members in the Center party oppose the leadership's decision to support the law in the Landtag, but the prime minister anticipated problems within the cabinet as well. Center party ministers might now be tempted to take advantage of the complicated intradelegation voting system to side with their political allies among the provinces' delegates. Above all, however, the prime minister did not want to be indebted to the DVP at a time when the People's party was pushing hard to reestablish the grand coalition in the state.[27]

Hiding behind the objections of the Staatsrat solved Otto Braun's immediate political problem, but the failure to implement the law on Prussia's Reichsrat votes left the original difficulty unresolved. In fact, the difficulties became worse in 1926 and 1927 as the *Bürgerblock* cabinet in the Reich sent a stream of conservative proposals to the Reichsrat. As we saw, on some important pieces of legislation, such as the Reich education law and the beer tax subsidy, the position of the Prussian cabinet was defeated by the combined votes of other *Länder* and some of the state's provincial delegates.[28]

Ironically, within a year the prime minister's and the DVP's positions on the 1926 legislation were reversed. At the end of 1927 the minister of the interior, Albert Grzesinski, compiled yet another set of statistics to show that a way had to be found to assure that Prussia's Reichsrat votes were cast as a unit. Otto Braun was now convinced that the 1926 law was not incompatible with the Weimar and Prussian constitutions. On the other hand, some members of the People's party, angered by what they saw as sabotage of their efforts to help the government, now voiced doubts about the constitutionality of the proposal. Others, however, including the author of the legislation, Rudolf von Campe, continued to argue that the 1926 law was constitutional. But all this was political shadowboxing. At this time, neither the prime minister nor the leaders of the Weimar coalition parties were willing to risk sufficient political capital to make reform of the method of casting Prussia's Reichsrat votes a priority item on their political agenda. The controversy became another unsolved issue for the remainder of the Weimar years. There remained only the (illusory) hope that an overall and comprehensive *Reichsreform* would include a satisfactory amendment of Article 63 of the Weimar constitution.[29]

Any discussion of a comprehensive *Reichsreform* had to address what was perhaps the most basic problem of the German federal structure: Prussia's future as a state and its relationship to the smaller *Länder* in northern Germany. Not surprisingly, given the fierce historic particularism of all the German *Länder*, Prussia and its neighbors had rather different ideas on the territorial restructuring of the Reich. Prussia looked upon many of its smaller neighbors as anachronistic entities that should be incorporated into Prussia in the interest of administrative efficiency. Such a development would complete the historic process of Prussification of Germany north of the Main River, and at the same time constitute a major step toward a full-scale territorial *Reichsreform*. Prussia's plan had support from across virtually the entire political spectrum in the state. On issues that concerned Prussia's self-proclaimed role as magnet for northern Germany and rivet of the Reich, the cabinet could count on the wholehearted agreement not only of the coalition parties, but of the right-wing opposition as well.[30]

Feelings were rather different among the potential candidates for annexation. Enthusiasm for incorporation into Prussia was decidedly lacking when the state's leaders raised the territorial issue with one of Germany's smallest states, Schaumburg-Lippe. A remnant of long-forgotten feudal divisions, Schaumburg-Lippe had a population in 1926 of less than 50,000. Schaumburg-Lippe's annexation by Prussia had been under discussion since 1921, and the Prussian leaders fully expected a favorable vote by the inhabitants of the tiny state when a plebiscite on the question was held in June 1926. However, the voters of Schaumburg-Lippe confounded the experts and decided against formal annexation. Reacting angrily to the vote, Prussia announced that in the future the state would refuse to perform a variety of administrative services for Schaumburg-Lippe which Prussia had provided since the nineteenth century. Prussia was more successful in its dealings with another dwarf state, Waldeck. The two state governments negotiated a treaty of union that was overwhelmingly approved by the legislatures of both states. At the beginning of 1929, Waldeck became a part of Prussia.[31]

Two other cases of potential union between Prussia and smaller states in northern Germany, Brunswick and Thuringia, revolved primarily around political considerations. In 1929 discussions had reached the stage of considering concrete agreements, but by this time the Nazis were gaining ground in both *Länder,* and the Prussian government had to decide whether merging the two territories with the state would help defuse the danger of the extreme right, or, conversely, help this political bacillus to grow inside Prussia itself. Ironically, Brunswick and Thuringia were governed by *Bürgerblock* coalitions at this time that were sympathetic to a union with Prussia. In the end, Prussia gave up pursuing the union; a short time later, both states came under the control of a political coalitions that included the Nazis.[32]

Brunswick, Schaumburg-Lippe, and Waldeck (Thuringia was a somewhat different case) were entities whose future as separate *Länder* in a modern Germany was questionable to all but the most vociferous particularists. The situation was far different for the city-state of Hamburg. With a population of more than one million and a centuries-old tradition as a free city, Germany's largest port was a viable entity whose citizens had no desire to be annexed by Prussia. Hamburg was completely surrounded by Prussian territory, the province of Schleswig-Holstein in the north and west, Hanover to the south and east. Tensions and mutual suspicions had long characterized relations between Hamburg and Prussia. Hamburg not only rejected incorporation into Prussia, but also argued that the Prussian territories immediately adjacent to the city—notably, the industrial centers of Altona and Harburg—should be joined to Hamburg, since they were in fact suburbs of the city, economically and socially part of the larger metropolis.[33] The Prussian cabinet and legislature vigorously opposed Hamburg's ambitions. At one point, Otto Braun traveled to Altona and publicly praised the mayor's successful efforts to resist Hamburg's encroachments.[34]

The controversy was decades old, and by 1925 it had generated small libraries full of statistic-laden memoranda and mutual accusations of obstinacy. The antagonists were not divided along political lines. The Hamburg Social Democrats supported the city's point of view, their Prussian comrades the state's arguments. It was something of a testimony to the success of parliamentary democracy that Hamburg and Prussia were able to negotiate at least a partial solution to their rivalry during the Weimar era. Prussia continued to refuse Hamburg's demands for territorial expansion, fearing that any territorial changes would set in motion "premature" and more wide-ranging efforts to cut off parts of Prussia in the name of the *Reichsreform*. The territorial aspect of the problem was not settled to Hamburg's satisfaction until 1937, but in 1929 Prussia did agree to join the city in establishing a Port of Hamburg Authority. In creating this agency, which Hamburg dominated administratively, Prussia finally gave up its fruitless attempts to build up the Prussian port of Altona, located just west of Hamburg on the Elbe, as a rival to its larger neighbor.[35]

As these examples demonstrate, the piecemeal approach to the comprehensive *Reichsreform* was not promising. Increasingly, political leaders and constitutional experts insisted the only answer was a full-scale federal reform package that addressed all aspects of the problem—political, territorial, and economic—in a single blueprint for an overall *Reichsreform*.

By 1927 four options for a comprehensive *Reichsreform* had crystallized out of the discussions. The first involved the reestablishment of Prussia's hegemony in the Reich, much as during the Bismarck and Wilhelmenian eras. A second proposal envisioned the abolition of the German federal structure altogether; the *Länder* would be replaced by a centralized state with administrative subdivisions on the French model. Under a third set of plans just Prussia would disappear, with most of the state's twelve provinces becoming separate *Länder*, the smaller northern states joined to them. On the other hand, the middle-sized southern German states, such as Bavaria and Württemberg, would remain intact. And finally, there was the suggestion that Prussia should be federalized—that is to say, converted from a *Land* into a federal district governed directly by the Reich cabinet.[36]

The difficulties facing any comprehensive *Reichsreform* were daunting on several accounts. Creating new *Länder* or, alternatively, territorial subdivisions of a centralized Reich administration that were more or less equal in size, population, and economic resources was a monumental task. Perhaps even more intractable were the political aspects of the problem. As we saw, Reich and state were suspicious of each other's motives. The Weimar coalition parties in Prussia feared that the *Bürgerblock* governments in the Reich intended to use the *Reichsreform* to curtail Prussia's states' rights as a first step in paving the way for the return of Hohenzollern authoritarianism. The Prussian government was thus reluctant to support any efforts at comprehensive reforms that were initiated by the federal *Bürgerblock* coalition cabinets.[37]

Within the individual parties, parochial interests caused further divisions on the best way to achieve the *Reichsreform*. The Social Democrats, for example, were traditionally and programmatically committed to abolishing the *Länder* and creating a unitary state. The party's congresses regularly passed resolutions affirming this goal as the basis for any comprehensive *Reichsreform*. However, as we just saw, the Hamburg SPD fully identified itself with the proud tradition of their city-state, while Prussia's Social Democrats were equally adamant that the first step toward realizing the future unitary state should not be the destruction of Prussia. They argued instead that the existence of Prussia in its present form—large, viable, dynamic, and democratic—was essential to achieving the goal. After all, three-fifths of the Reich was already governed as a centralized, unitary state.[38]

Similar disagreements divided the Reich and Prussian wings of the other two Weimar coalition parties as well. Among the German Democrats, Hugo Preuss, the "father" of the Weimar constitution, continued to press for the dissolution of Prussia. Preuss argued that the existence of large *Länder* and especially the Prussian superstate made any balanced federal structure impossible. As he had in 1918, the DDP leader wanted to reduce the power of the *Länder* and instead create a strong Reich administration that simultaneously permitted far-ranging rights of local self-government. German Democratic leaders in the southern states, such as the former Reich minister of defense, Otto Gessler, agreed with Preuss on the dissolution of Prussia, but they insisted the medium-sized states like Bavaria had to remain intact. Most Prussian DDP leaders rejected Preuss's ideas as far as Prussia was concerned. They agreed with their colleagues in the SPD that preserving Prussia was the indispensable beginning of a meaningful *Reichsreform*.[39]

The stand of the national Center party on the *Reichsreform* was determined by the interests of Germany's Catholics. The party's leaders favored a decentralized federal structure with wide-ranging autonomy for the *Länder* if the majority of the population was Catholic (as in Bavaria) or for the provinces, if (as in Prussia) Catholics formed a minority of the population.

National party leaders were not committed to the preservation of Prussia. But, as was true for the SPD, the Prussian wing of the Center party had serious reservations about the national party's position. The leaders of the Prussian Center party were concerned about the political consequences of destroying Prussia. While endorsing the concept of provincial autonomy, Prussia's Catholics also wanted to preserve the state as a whole as a bastion of parliamentary democracy. This political system had assured Prussia's Catholics a larger portion of political influence than had ever been possible during the long years of authoritarian rule. An equitable federal system, Joseph Hess concluded, meant preserving the status quo.[40]

Most members of the Prussian cabinet were equally wary of any plans for a full-scale *Reichsreform* that began with Prussia's destruction. Otto Braun and Albert Grzesinski, for example, noted that plans for Prussia's dissolution or its transformation into a federal district were often advanced by those who wanted to weaken democracy in Germany. Braun's answer to such proposals was the restoration of the prewar practice of appointing a single incumbent to head the various Reich and Prussian cabinet positions. Given the political strength of the state's leaders, this meant Prussia's hegemony would be restored in the Reich, assuring the continued stability of parliamentary democracy at both the Reich and state levels. The prime minister recognized that his proposals were unlikely to be supported by the *Bürgerblock* leaders in the Reich, and for that reason he preferred the status quo to any risky experiments.[41]

The only prominent members of the state's executive who supported reform plans that envisioned the dissolution of Prussia were Hermann Höpker-Aschoff, the finance minister, and Arnold Brecht, from 1927 to 1933 Prussia's chief Reichsrat delegate. Höpker-Aschoff was a fervent unitarist who was willing to sacrifice Prussia in order to create a centralized Reich. In the 1920s he submitted a whole series of very detailed proposals for a comprehensive *Reichsreform*. Brecht, for his part, followed Preuss's ideas and advocated the eventual dissolution of Prussia to make way for a decentralized federal structure. While he recognized the importance of Prussia as a bulwark of political democracy in Germany, he was also convinced that in the long run the existence of a Prussian superstate was incompatible with the evolution of a healthy democracy in the Reich as a whole.[42]

Except for these two officials, however, the three Prussian coalition partners were not very far apart on the question of a comprehensive *Reichsreform*. They might harbor rather different ideas on a future ideal structure of the Reich, but the Weimar coalition parties in Prussia preferred maintaining the status quo with all of its readily apparent problems to embarking on an untrodden path with unforeseeable and potentially dangerous political and territorial consequences.

Among the Prussian opposition parties, the DVP took the most interest in the *Reichsreform*, but the People's party national leadership was primarily concerned about the constitutional aspects of the problem. Gustav Stresemann and other DVP leaders introduced a bill in the Reichstag amending articles 54 and 55 of the Weimar constitution to make votes of no confidence against the federal cabinet more difficult. The Prussian DVP endorsed these proposals, which did not directly touch on the future of Prussia, but the state's right-wing Liberals were also concerned about opening the Pandora's box of constitutional amendments. Like the Weimar coalition parties, the Prussian DVP was opposed to weakening the state's territorial integrity or political influence as the prerequisite for any comprehensive federal reform package.[43]

While the DVP attempted to remove constitutional difficulties at the Reich level with its reform proposals, the German Nationalists were interested only in the political consequences of the *Reichsreform* . As far as the DNVP was concerned, the primary purpose of any reform was to weaken or destroy Prussia as a pillar of parliamentary democracy. As early as October 1926, Alfred Hugenberg proposed amending the Reich constitution to increase the power of the Reich president, while reducing the influence of the Reich and Prussian legislatures. Under the plans of the German Nationalists, the Reich president was to serve as both national and Prussian head of state. In this dual capacity he would have had the power to appoint and dismiss cabinet ministers in both jurisdictions. A strong Reich president was the DNVP's answer to the Reich-Prussian dualism; with the chief executive acting as surrogate emperor and king, Prussia would become little more than a federal district. At the same time, the German Nationalists, like the Weimar coalition parties, held fast to the concept of Prussia as guarantor of Germany's political system. With power in Prussia exercised by the conservative Reich president, the state could return to its traditional function of guaranteeing the viability of an authoritarian political structure throughout Germany.[44]

In January 1928, the national government invited representatives from the states to a federal conference *(Reichskonferenz),* a sort of summit meeting of state leaders. The decisions of such conferences, a tradition in German constitutional history, were often of crucial importance. A similar meeting in January 1919, for example, had determined to keep the German *Länder* intact, rather than redraw the Reich's administrative boundaries in line with Hugo Preuss's proposals. The plan for the 1928 conference envisioned three days of meetings attended by the leaders of the *Länder* and members of the Reich cabinet. The delegates would agree on an agenda for the future *Reichsreform* and set up several expert commissions, staffed with lower-level officials, that would subsequently draft specific proposals to deal with the problems identified during the plenary meetings.[45]

Prussia's stand during the federal conference was consistent with the state's views on the overall problem of federal reform and its suspicions of the Reich cabinet's motives. But as critics pointed out, Prussia's attitude hardly helped to make the summit meeting a success. In fact, observers concluded that the Prussian executive was deliberately dragging its feet on the *Reichsreform*. Recognizing that for many of the delegates from states outside of Prussia, the existence of Germany's largest state was the major barrier to a *Reichsreform*, Prussia went out of its way to dampen expectations of a breakthrough on the reform problem. Even before the conference met, Braun emphasized that, as far as Prussia was concerned, the purpose of the meeting was not to make decisions, but to air views and exchange opinions.[46]

Prussia's selection of a chief delegate to the *Reichskonferenz* underscored the cabinet's ambivalence, if not disdain, for the summit. While most of the other *Länder* were represented by their prime ministers, Prussia's chief delegate was Arnold Brecht, a department head *(Ministerialdirektor)* in the Prussian ministry of the interior. Brecht was an acknowledged expert on constitutional questions and a fervent republican, but his relatively low rank meant that his views certainly did not commit the Prussian cabinet as a whole. There were also some political problems. Brecht had not been a Prussian civil servant for long. Until 1927, when the German Nationalist Reich minister, Walther von Keudell, dismissed him for his prorepublican views, Brecht headed the office for constitutional affairs in the Reich Interior Ministry. Immediately after leaving the Reich civil service, Grzesinski appointed Brecht to a similar position in Prussia. Prussia's chief delegate, then, was very much persona non grata among the Conservatives.[47]

Despite his controversial politics and relatively junior status, Brecht advanced the boldest plan for territorial reform: the Prussian provinces should become separate states. At the same time, the powers of the Reich government would be strengthened at the expense of all states, both old and newly established.[48]

Similar ideas had been voiced earlier by a multipartisan lobbying group chiefly comprised of leading businessmen, the Bund zur Erneuerung des Reiches (Association for the Rejuvenation of the Reich). The brainchild of Hans Luther, the former chancellor (as well as the future president of the Reich Bank and German ambassador to Washington), the Luther Bund, as the organization was usually called, launched a massive public relations campaign in support of its own *Reichsreform* plans. Luther and his associates suggested that in the interest of administrative efficiency Prussia should absorb most of the smaller states in northern Germany. However, the superstate would exist only on paper, since the enlarged Prussia would itself become a federal district, a centrally administered *Reichsland*. To compensate for the loss of the state's autonomy, the Luther Bund suggested substantially increased rights of self-government for the Prussian provinces, virtually raising them to the status of *Länder*.[49]

Neither Brecht's enthusiasm nor the lobbying efforts of the Luther Bund were able to advance the cause of the *Reichsreform*. After their plenary session, the conference delegates issued a catalog of platitudes and declarations of good will.[50] The committee deliberations had no better luck; at the end of 1929 Braun indicated that the experts were far from reaching any conclusions. For all practical purposes, the *Reichsreform* under democratic auspices had failed. The Prussian prime minister himself seems to have concluded that eventually the Reich president, acting under the authority of Article 48 of the constitution, would need to cut through the thicket of conflicting interests and issue the necessary reforms "from above" in the form of an executive order.[51]

The *Reichsreform* failed for a number of reasons. A major difficulty was the lack of leadership provided by the Reich cabinet. It was symptomatic that the Reich government presented no concrete proposals to the 1928 federal conference, but merely listened to the discussions. Fear by the southern German states that they would lose some of their states' rights was another constant factor; in particular, Bavaria was extremely sensitive to any threat to its historic rights. In addition, as we saw, the political parties were deeply divided on how to achieve the needed reforms. In his memoirs Otto Braun lay much of the blame for the failure of the *Reichsreform* on the Center party. With feet firmly planted in simultaneous left-of-center and right-of-center coalitions in the Reich and Prussia, respectively, the Catholics, he argued, prevented Prussia from taking the initiative in the *Reichsreform* discussion.[52]

However, here as on other occasions, Braun exhibited a tendency to blame others for his own shortcomings. A major if not decisive cause for the failure of the *Reichsreform* was the prime minister's conviction—shared by other political leaders in Prussia—that the "Prussian problem" should not be the primary focus of federal reform plans. In fact, from the Prussians' point of view the Reich-Prussian dualism was part of the solution: a strong, democratic Prussia guaranteed national unity and political stability in the Reich. Prussia could fulfill its role only if the Weimar coalition parties in the state continued to cooperate. For this reason Braun was not willing to see the coalition torn apart as the partners went after individual and contradictory goals in pursuit of an elusive *Reichsreform*. The prime minister hastened to disavow the state's chief delegate to the federal conference: Brecht's proposals represented his private opinion; they had not been discussed, much less approved by the Prussian cabinet. Braun reiterated Prussia's well-known position. The state favored a total reorganization of the Reich, including increasing the powers of the Reich cabinet, but not at the price of Prussia's dissolution, while Bavaria and other southern states maintained their territorial integrity and political autonomy.[53]

In the short run, the strategy was highly successful. Prussia remained a bulwark of democracy for the remainder of the decade; the *Reichsreform* did not drive the Weimar coalition apart. But the failure to move federal reforms along under democratic auspices also gave neoauthoritarians who dominated the Reich cabinets after March 1930 yet another opportunity to claim that democracy had failed to serve Germany's national interests and that the destruction of parliamentary democracy was a prerequisite for the *Reichsreform*.[54]

CHAPTER 5

The German Parties and Prussia, 1930–1933

During the last three years of the Weimar era, most of the traditional German parties confronted severe difficulties. Partly cause, partly consequence of a general constitutional and economic crisis, particularly the moderate parties were in the midst of a profound systemic malaise. The prestige of the constitutional system had sunk to new lows. All too many Germans agreed with the conclusions of the neoconservative publicist Heinz O. Ziegler: the constitutional alternatives for Germany's future were authoritarianism or totalitarianism. There was no place for parliamentary democracy.[1] In desperate moves to retain their appeal for members and voters, the moderate groups searched for new leaders, new programs, and ways to merge with each other—to no avail. Increasingly, they lost their character as broadly based ideological parties and became instead political lobbies for specific interest groups.[2]

There was a need, many agreed, for a restructuring of the entire party system. Paradoxically, the remedy most often advocated was to create political parties that stood above parties. As if to demonstrate the depth of the systemic malaise, the traditional parties attempted to borrow a concept from the increasingly successful movements of the extreme left and right: they, too, sought to convert themselves into movements *(Bewegungen),* dropping the seemingly unpopular party label. Plans for moderate superparties abounded. Among the Weimar coalition parties, the elusive "party of the center" that would encompass the Social Democrats, the Catholics, and the German Democrats in one political entity dominated the discussions. On the right side of the political spectrum the German Nationalists and the right-wing Liberals hoped to counter their decline at the polls by coopting new "nonpartisan" groups for their own purposes.[3]

The position of the Prussian parties in this swirl of activity was paradoxical. Outwardly the state remained a viable parliamentary democracy throughout most of the crisis years. On the other hand, Prussia obviously could not be isolated from developments in the Reich. The rising tide of Nazism was obvious to all.[4] An even more immediate threat came from the presidential cabinets in the Reich. In a very real sense, the original justification for

131

Prussia's existence as a parliamentary democracy in the Weimar era—the self-proclaimed rock of democracy to which the Reich clung—became reversed with the inauguration of the first presidential cabinets in the Reich.

But Prussia remained true to its self-appointed function. Convinced that the Reich needed the state's support to cope with Germany's constitutional and economic crisis, the Weimar coalition parties in Prussia aided the neoconservative Reich chancellors even when evidence mounted that the systematic erosion of the state's parliamentary democracy was high on the presidential cabinets' agendas. The Prussian government parties did little more than react to initiatives from the Reich. Prussia was on the way to becoming a sandcastle instead of a rock of democracy. This was a welcome development for the Prussian opposition parties. Blocked from achieving their ends by parliamentary means, they set out to paralyze parliamentary democracy in order either to further the neoauthoritarian constitutional goals of the Reich cabinets or, in the case of the Nazis and Communists, to hasten the collapse of any constitutional system as a prelude to realizing their own totalitarian ends. In the last years of the Weimar Republic, the Prussian Landtag all but abandoned its function as a legislative assembly for the state. It became instead a forum for bitter and fruitless debates about the future of the Reich.

Yet it would be a distortion to paint too pessimistic a picture of the state during these crisis-laden years. Despite rising Nazi votes, increasing political violence in the streets, and systematic attempts by the presidential cabinets in the Reich to turn the constitutional clock back to 1914, until almost the end of the Weimar era Prussia remained a political domain of the Weimar coalition parties. The founding parties of the republic—the Social Democrats, the German Democrats, and the Center party—did not lose their comfortable Landtag majority until April 1932, and even then the Weimar coalition cabinet remained in office as a caretaker government.

SPD, DDP, and Center party continued to work together. It is true that with Franz von Papen's Prussian coup of July 1932,[5] parliamentary and coalition politics had little effect upon political decision making in the state—that power had been usurped by the Reich government—but until then, and to some extent even after the state had been federalized, the history of the SPD, the DDP, and the Center party in Prussia was significantly different from their evolution at the national level and in other German states.

The Weimar Coalition Parties: The Social Democrats (SPD)

Until the April 1932, Landtag elections, the SPD remained the strongest party in Prussia, even though the national party's decline became painfully apparent after the September 1930 Reichstag elections. The Prussian party, wrote Hermann Müller, was the SPD's largest storehouse of reserve power;

many on the right saw Otto Braun as the republican strongman, a sort of democratic Mussolini.[6]

Actually, Prussian Social Democracy was not without its problems. Braun might be the "red czar of Prussia" and Ernst Heilmann, the SPD's legislative leader, the "real ruler of the state," but their positions were strong only as long as Prussia exercised a disproportionately large influence in national party affairs. As the state's significance as the stabilizing factor for Germany's constitutional system declined, so did the power of its Social Democratic leaders. And there were personnel problems as well. Braun and Heilmann were exhausted from long years of political struggle and abuse. Heilmann wanted to retire as the SPD's parliamentary leader in Prussia and was grooming a successor, Ernst Hamburger, a young Silesian Landtag delegate. The SPD leader's attempt to pass the torch to the younger generation was laudable, but the knowledge of Heilmann's impending retirement also made him something of a lame duck. With the politician's unerring instinct for who (if not what) mattered, Heilmann's political associates were beginning to isolate and ignore the outwardly still powerful leader.[7]

Whatever the policy differences among party leaders, the Prussian SPD had no doubts about its loyalty to the constitutional system. The party's leaders were the strongest supporters of parliamentary democracy in Germany. In defense of the constitutional system and the Weimar coalition, the state's Social Democrats even suspended their personal convictions. As we saw, although many of the delegates were members of the German Association of Atheists (Freidenkerverband), the party voted for the concordat with the Catholic church to preserve its coalition with the Center party.[8]

The stature of Prussia's SPD and its undisputed leader loomed so large in part because its stable direction and political purposefulness seemed to contrast vividly with the situation in the national party. At the Reich level, the Social Democrats were in the throes of a deep and growing crisis. Perhaps the most obvious problem was a paucity of real leaders. Hermann Müller, the party's national chairman, died unexpectedly in the summer of 1930. His successor, Otto Wels, a longtime and rather colorless party functionary, lacked Müller's skills as an intraparty mediator. Wels's election also personified the party's much criticized "calcification" (Verkalkung). The new Reichstag leader was of the same generation as Ebert, Haase, and Hermann Müller himself. More important, despite his nickname "our dictator," Wels was unable to control the growing division of the party or the increasing autonomy of its prominent Reichstag leaders.[9]

The problems were not new. All through the 1920s the German Social Democrats were an institutional contradiction: on the one hand the SPD projected the image of a revolutionary party with a Marxist program and the values and behavior patterns of a proletarian class movement. Yet in terms of practical politics the party was a left-of-center reformist group that had long ago abandoned its revolutionary goals. However, during the crisis years the SPD as a whole could no longer ignore its internal problems. Stagnating membership statistics and declining votes made the leadership crisis and political malaise of the national SPD obvious to all. At stake were not only personal careers, but also the party's future political direction.

Not surprisingly, there was no agreement on remedies for the party's difficulties. Right-wingers complained that the left-wing minority's fixation on attracting the support of blue-collar workers alienated the party from important sources of voters, like the new *Mittelstand*. These groups, the right wing argued, rejected a proletarian image for themselves and could be attracted to the SPD only if the party emphasized its reformist character. In addition, left-wing rhetoric made it more difficult for the party to form coalitions with the moderate bourgeois parties. The left wing countered that it was precisely the party's association with the moderate, bourgeois parties that had diluted and distorted the true character of the SPD. The left-wing supporters noted that especially in a time of deepening economic crisis, the SPD needed to emphasize its character as a single class party offering clear alternatives to the crisis-ridden capitalist system. Without such a clear, antibourgeois stand, the party's traditional supporters would desert the SPD for the Communists.[10]

The Prussian leaders had little sympathy for these arguments. In their view the SPD had a future only as a democratic, parliamentary, reformist party.[11] The party's national leadership, however, wavered between appeasement, equivocation, and passivity. The national executive rejected the path advocated by the left wing, but the leaders of Germany's largest party saw no alternative but to watch the country's economic and political crisis work itself out. As Rudolf Hilferding put it, the party had no way of bringing about a socialist solution to the Depression, and a capitalist one depended on the actions of America and England. To make the best of a bad situation, the national SPD "tolerated" Brüning's presidential regime, a decision that made the party as a whole uneasy and led a small group of left-wingers to leave the SPD altogether.[12]

In the fall of 1931, disappointed by the rejection of their position at the SPD's 1931 national congress, a group of left-wing leaders seceded from the party and formed the Sozialistische Arbeiterpartei Deutschlands (Socialist Workers' Party of Germany; SAPD). It was hardly a venture of young radicals; many of the activists, like Heinrich Ströbel and Max Seydewitz, had been founding members of the USPD in 1917. The SAPD was also a stillborn enterprise, with organizational strength primarily in the state of Saxony. (Appropriately, the party's founding convention was held in Dresden.) The leaders' hope of attracting large numbers of left-wing Social Democratic and right-wing Communist members and voters proved futile. In Prussia only three of the 136 members of the Social Democratic Landtag caucus joined the SAPD. The three defectors did include one of the best-known left-wingers in the caucus, Hans Marckwald (Frankfurt a.M.), but the new party had no real influence in the legislature. The primary activity of the three dissidents was to act as political gadflies, attacking their erstwhile colleagues in the SPD, to the amusement of the Communists and the bourgeois opposition parties.[13]

If the SAPD was a failure, the attempt by the Reichsbanner Schwarz-Rot-Gold leader and ex-governor of the province of Saxony, Otto Hörsing, to rally the dissatisfied right wing of the SPD under the banner of yet another new party, the Sozialrepublikanische Partei (Social Republican party, SRP) was ludicrous. Founded in June 1932 after Hörsing was expelled from the SPD and the *Reichsbanner* for violating party discipline, the SRP had no significant following, and both the party and its leader quickly disappeared from public view.[14]

The attempts to carve new parties out of the SPD bloc failed, but it was clear to the socialist leaders that they could not continue doing business as usual. The spectacular rise of the Stahlhelm and the Nazi storm troopers had already demonstrated the important role of extraparliamentary organizations in the political dynamics of Weimar Germany. Still, for a long time the Social Democrats misinterpreted and underestimated particularly the Nazis' character and significance. Until the September 1930 Reichstag elections, most Social Democrats looked upon Hitler's movement as a slightly more radical version of the DNVP, rather than as a new and uniquely dangerous threat to the Weimar Republic's constitutional system. Typical was Heilmann's quip, "Frick [the Nazis' Reichstag leader] is just a front for Flick [one of Germany's leading industrial magnates]." But increasing political violence and the Nazis' spectacular victory at the polls in September 1930 forced the SPD to confront the new challenge of right-wing extremism in both its parliamentary and extraparliamentary forms.[15]

One response was the founding of the Iron front, a somewhat paradoxical effort to defeat the extremists with their own weapons. The Iron Front was intended as the prorepublican counterpart of the Harzburger Front, the informal alliance which the Nazis, the Stahlhelm, and the DNVP had created at the end of 1931. The Iron Front was ostensibly a multipartisan, extraparliamentary organization founded to protect the republic from its enemies on the left and right. Its organizers intended to supply extraparliamentary aid to the Weimar coalition parties during the undoubtedly bitter presidential, Reichstag, and Landtag elections that lay ahead in 1932.

The founders had hoped to attract support from a variety of prorepublican groups, but in reality, the new organization was never more than an SPD front organization. Since the Iron Front's active supporters were limited almost entirely to members of the SPD, the Reichsbanner, and the socialist unions, its significance was primarily to give a psychological boost to the supporters of the SPD. At least it suggested that the party was doing something other than politics as usual. Even so, the psychological uplift was limited. Leaders and rank-and-file members of the SPD and the Iron front spent much of the crisis years oscillating between extreme pessimism and equally unrealistic illusions—chief among the latter was that the Nazis were a sort of political nightmare from which Germany would soon awaken to resume its rational parliamentary processes.[16]

The attitude of the Prussian SPD leaders toward the Iron Front was guarded. Several leading Prussian Social Democrats, including Braun, Severing, and Grzesinski, were on its executive committee, but they remained skeptical of any group that sought to support parliamentary democracy by extraparliamentary means. They agreed with those in the national leadership, like Hilferding and Breitscheid, who argued that trying to copy the Nazis' methods would in the long run inevitably benefit the enemies of the republic.[17]

Suspicious of the national leadership's "new politics," the state's Social Democrats attempted to isolate themselves from the developments in the party as a whole. They relied instead on the inner cohesion and firm leadership of the Prussian SPD to preserve the party's parliamentary and governmental influence in the state. For a time the strategy seemed eminently successful: the party remained strong in the state legislature and executive for most of the crisis years. But the future looked dark. Political extremism was gaining on all fronts, and under dispirited leaders, the SPD was not in a favorable position to face the voters in the April 1932 Landtag elections.

The Weimar Coalition Parties: The German Democratic Party (DDP) and the German State Party (DStP)

The smallest of the three Weimar coalition parties, the German Democrats, had every reason to be pessimistic about its political future; it was in danger of extinction. Since its one spectacular performance at the polls in the 1919 Reichstag elections, the DDP had been in a steady decline. The consequences were chronic and bitter debates among the leaders about the party's future direction: left-of-center, as its founders had intended, or right-of-center, where what was left of the reservoir of liberal voters seemed to be. The two wings were about evenly divided, and since the DDP, even more than the SPD, lacked a strong national leader, these disputes essentially paralyzed the party.

In 1930 the decline of left-wing voters and members led the DDP's leaders to conclude that on its own left-wing Liberalism had no political future. Only a fusion with another political party or extraparliamentary group could save the party. The most logical fusion candidate, of course, was the DVP. The right-wing Liberals were experiencing similar problems—an alarming decline in members and voters. Other possibilities were an amalgamation with the Liberal Association (Liberale Vereinigung), a left-of-center group that had split off from the DVP, and the People's Conservative party (Volkskonservative Partei, VKP), the group that, as we saw, broke off from the German Nationalists.[18]

For a variety of reasons, mostly having to do with the longstanding personal rivalries among party leaders, the German Democrats and the German People's party were unable to reach agreement on reuniting the forces of liberalism. The Liberal Association was too small to matter, and the VKP's attempt to rally the anti-Hugenberg elements in the DNVP was a failure; most DNVP members followed Hugenberg on his disastrous path. Instead, the DDP, to the surprise of many observers, joined with one of the smaller extraparliamentary groups, the Jungdeutscher Orden (Young German Order), to form a new party, the Deutsche Staatspartei (German State party, DStP).

The new entity was a strange political marriage, to say the least. Very much the creation of its *Hochmeister* (grand master) Arthur Mahraun, the Jungdeutscher Orden had been founded in the early 1920s as a quasi-fascist organization. Its members looked upon themselves as a self-selected elite that would lead Germany to new heights of glory. The Jungdeutscher Orden originally opposed democracy and parliamentary politics as unworthy of its elite members, but by 1930 Mahraun had abandoned his antidemocratic stand. Frightened by the rise of the Nazis and mounting political violence, he now supported Germany's constitutional system. Nevertheless, the fusion of Mahraun's order of self-proclaimed elitists with the DDP, whose founders had envisioned the party as the embodiment of German Liberalism's commitment to mass politics, was likely to be explosive.[19]

The Prussian left-wing Liberals were divided on the creation of the DStP. The state's finance minister, Hermann Höpker-Aschoff, was one of its initiators and undoubtedly saw himself as the new group's future national leader. However, the chairman of the DDP's Landtag caucus, Bernhard Falk, vigorously opposed both the concept of the new party and the DDP's association with Mahraun. In practical terms, their disagreement did not matter much, since the creation of the DStP did not solve the DDP's problems. Mahraun's organization had no electoral or parliamentary experience, and the founding of the DStP did nothing to halt the further decline of the left-wing Liberals. In any case, Mahraun and his organization soon lost interest in parliamentary politics and withdrew from the whole enterprise.

After the severance of the brief relationship with the Jungdeutscher Orden, the DStP was little more than the old DDP under another name, subject to the same rivalries that had characterized the left-wing Liberals for a decade. Höpker-Aschoff and the DDP's Reichstag leader, Erich Koch-Weser, fought for control of what was left of the party organization. Although both men saw the DStP as a right-of-center party seeking its political partners among the moderate bourgeois groups rather than in alliance with Social Democracy, they differed on how far to the right the party should go. Koch-Weser, who in 1926 had labeled Mahraun "a *condotierre*" with whom the DDP should under no circumstances associate, accused his rival of wanting to turn the DStP into a purely "rightist party." Höpker-Aschoff countered by charging Koch-Weser with harboring sympathies for Marxism. Actually, there were few substantive differences between them.

Höpker-Aschoff's determination to steer the DStP to the right did have an impact on Prussian politics, however. It led to a noticeable cooling of relations between the ambitious finance minister and his few colleagues in the Landtag. The Prussian legislators were unwilling to follow Höpker-Aschoff's leadership; they continued to back Falk's efforts to keep the party on a left-of-center course. Lack of support from his Prussian party comrades undoubtedly contributed to Höpker-Aschoff's decision to resign from the cabinet in October 1931. But isolated as he was, his decision had no effect on the Prussian coalition itself.[20]

The Weimar Coalition Parties: The Center Party

The dichotomy between the Center party's left-of-center course in Prussia and the party's pronounced right-of-center orientation in the Reich became even more pronounced in the last years of the Weimar Republic. While the Prussian Center party remained true to its traditional leftist course, the party's national leaders deliberately and systematically steered political Catholicism toward the right.

Two men largely determined the Center party's politics in the Reich: Monsignor Ludwig Kaas, the cleric who was elected national chairman of the Center party at its 1928 national congress, and Heinrich Brüning, until his appointment as Reich chancellor in March 1930 the head of the Center party's Reichstag delegation. Kaas and Brüning intended to steer political Catholicism to what they regarded as its true calling—that is to say, as a right-wing and nationalistic party whose natural allies were the DNVP and the DVP rather than the left-wing Liberals and Social Democrats. The Center party's national leaders rejected alliances with "Marxists" of any color. They cited political, theological, and moral reasons that precluded political partnerships with both the Social Democrats and the Communists. In contrast, the party's national leaders did not a priori exclude forming coalitions with the Nazis. Such a combination, it appeared, would depend on Hitler's future actions.[21]

The Kaas-Brüning line was not popular among most Prussian Center party leaders. Although in public the state's Catholic spokemen refrained from criticizing the national leadership, only a few, like Franz von Papen, were decidedly enthusiastic about the party's national course. Papen was not a member of the Landtag between 1928 and 1930, but he remained an influential voice in Catholic agrarian circles. He had worked hard for Kaas's election because of what he called the cleric's "basically conservative convictions." When he returned to the Landtag in 1930, Papen continued his maverick ways. He was often ostentatiously absent when his party voted in support of the Weimar coalition government, thereby aiding indirectly the cause of the opposition. However, Papen did not represent the majority sentiment in the Prussian Center party. The right wing's influence was primarily restricted to local politics; the Prussian Catholics kept Papen out of any leadership position at the state level.[22]

The state's leaders held fast to their coalition with the Social Democrats, while Heinrich Brüning gladly acceded to the Reich president's insistence that the Catholic leader form a Reich cabinet "free of socialists" *(sozialistenrein)* as a prerequisite for his nomination as Reich chancellor. Personnel decisions underscored the Prussian center party's determination to retain its relative autonomy from national executive decisions. In May 1930, Joseph Hess, who had been for many years the head of the Prussian center party in all but name, was formally elected head of the Landtag delegation. Hess, who had been instrumental in keeping the state's Center party left-of-center ever since the end of World War I, remained convinced that the state's Catholics could protect their ideals and interests most effectively by cooperating with the Prussian Social Democrats. He pointed not only to the Concordat of 1929, but also to parliamentary democracy itself. Only the present constitutional system had made it possible for Prussia's Catholics to gain a proportional share of influence in the state. As Hess put it, "To belong to the Center party means to serve the German democratic republic."[23]

Hess's convictions were shared by the overwhelming majority of the Center party's Landtag delegation, including its clerical members. Unlike Kaas, men like Alber Lauscher and Johannes Linneborn did not reject co-operation with the SPD. They were also far more suspicious of the Nazis and Hugenberg's DNVP than the Center party's national leaders. In a much noted Landtag speech, Linneborn sharply criticized the Nazis' anti-Semitism and any attempts to link the Center party to such sentiments.[24]

It was a heavy blow for Prussia's Catholics and the future of the state's democracy that Hess was unable to lead the Prussian Center party through all of the crisis years. He became ill in the fall of 1931 and died in February 1932. His death removed the strongest personality in the Prussia Center party at a time when his judgment and political skills were desperately needed. Especially the Social Democrats recognized the significance of

Hess's loss. Otto Braun, growing increasingly pessimistic about the political future, claimed that after Hess's death Brüning and Kaas took control of the Landtag delegation. This was certainly not the case, but the lack of Hess's firm hand left the Prussian Center party in a weakened and wavering position that contrasted sharply with its earlier image as a tower of prorepublican strength.[25]

Hess's nominal successor as caucus chairman was Fritz Grass, but the real leader of the Center party after Hess died was a cabinet member, the minister for social services, Heinrich Hirtsiefer. Like Hess, Hirtsiefer was a prominent "leftist." He also got along well with the Social Democrats, and was one of the few nonsocialists on the executive committee of the Iron Front. At the same time, his abrasive personality differed strikingly from his predecessor's conciliatory manner. In addition, as a full-time member of the cabinet, Hirtsiefer had neither the time nor the legislative experience to provide steady and effective leadership for the state's Catholics.[26]

The task guiding the Prussian center party became especially difficult after the April 1932 Landtag elections, when the Weimar coalition parties lost their majority in the legislature and the Center party was in a position to determine whether or not the Nazis would become part of a new parliamentary cabinet. Hirtsiefer firmly opposed any deal with the Nazis, but some prominent members of the Center party Landtag delegation had different ideas. Faced with their own version of the *Verfassungsnotstand*—a deadlocked legislature—and pressure from their party's national leaders, they began to toy with the idea of "taming" the Nazis by making them part of a *Bürgerblock* coalition in Prussia. For a variety of reasons, the effort failed, but that the attempt was made at all was symptomatic of the lack of direction and unity in the party no longer under Joseph Hess's strong hand.[27]

The Opposition Parties

Before 1930 it was possible to divide the Prussian opposition groups into moderates and extremists, but after the advent of the presidential cabinets in the Reich, that distinction became increasingly meaningless. Spanning a spectrum from the right-wing Liberals to the Communists, the Prussian opposition parties did not constitute a "loyal opposition." Except for the small Economics party, a few anti-Hugenberg Conservatives, and some DVP members, the opposition parties now shared a fundamental objection to the system of parliamentary democracy itself. Their common aim was not so much to replace the present cabinet with another coalition, but to introduce a new political and constitutional system, although they differed completely on what it should be. DVP and DNVP had visions of restoring a form of Bismarck authoritarianism, the Nazis wanted a *"völkisch* totalitarianism," whatever that might be, and the Communists demanded a dictatorship of the proletariat. Their tactics also varied; only the Nazis and Communists engaged in large-scale street violence as a form of political expression. But for the moment the profound ideological differences mattered little. All the opposition parties worked together to hasten the destruction of Prussia's parliamentary democracy. In the Landtag it was not at all unusual to find right-wing Liberals lustily voting for Communist resolutions of no confidence against the government.

German People's Party (DVP)

The right-wing Liberals underwent perhaps the most complete self-transformation among the opposition groups. A few short months after the death of Gustav Stresemann, the DVP—which had been a partner of the Weimar coalition parties in a cabinet of the grand coalition for almost three years in the early 1920s, and which had spent much of the second half of the decade negotiating with the Weimar coalition parties to regain a seat at the cabinet table—joined the obstructionists. During the crisis years, the right-wing Liberals became tactical, if uneasy, allies of the German Nationalists, the Communists, and the Nazis.

The reasons were fear and lack of leadership. Like the DDP, the DVP was a party confronting possible extinction, and without Stresemann's firm hand there was no one to show the party a way out of its dilemma. Since 1920 the DVP's national leader had not only skillfully kept the divergent wings of the party together, but also had almost single-handedly steered the party on a moderate course that had made the DVP acceptable as a member of both *Bürgerblock* and grand coalitions in the Reich and Prussia.

Stresemann was succeeded by Eduard Dingeldey, until then the leader of the party's state organization in Württemberg. Unfortunately, the new chairman had a number of illusions about himself and the DVP. To begin with, he saw himself as a strong, integrative force. Adopting the increasingly popular *Führer* jargon, he spoke of the party's need for firm, centralized leadership. In fact, Dingeldey was never a strong leader. In the national party, all important decisions were made by the Reichstag delegation, not the party's executive office. Dingeldey also vastly overestimated the political attractiveness of right-wing liberalism during the crisis years. His call for the DVP to become a "vital [*zündende*] mass movement" reflected an astounding lack of political realism.[28]

Far from being firmly led, united, or a mass movement, the DVP was a dwindling group of activists deeply divided over the future course of the party. Like the DDP, it was torn between a left and a right wing, both claiming to represent the spirit of Stresemann. The leftists insisted that the DVP cooperate with the moderate forces and take a clear stand against the Nazis and Hugenberg's DNVP. This group was also inclined to cooperate with the DStP, noting that just before his death Stresemann had contacted Arthur Mahraun and the *Jungdeutscher Orden* in an effort to begin to reunite all liberal elements in Germany. The right wing pinned its hopes on neoconservatism and the Reich president. Insisting the DVP needed to become an integral part of the "Hindenburg Front," the right wing was also willing to associate itself with the Harzburg Front, the loose alliance of Nazis, Stahlhelm, and DNVP, although it was unwilling to enter into a full-fledged partnership with the Nazis. In the Reich the "leftists" won out, at least for the moment. Despite Dingeldey's objections, the DVP became a part of the "Brüning coalition." [29]

The Prussian DVP had operated in the shadow of the Reich party in Stresemann's last years, and that relationship became more pronounced under Dingeldey. Seemingly, part of the new centralized leadership style was to ignore the Prussian wing of the party even more. This left the state's DVP buffeted between its competing right and left wings. While the leftists in the national party urged the Prussians to continue negotiating to reestablish the grand coalition in the state, Dingeldey and the right wing recommended closer cooperation with the opposition parties. (One concrete result of the latter policy was a cooperation agreement for the 1932 Landtag election campaign between the DNVP and the DVP in some areas of Prussia.) The factions were united only in their opposition to making common cause with the left-wing Liberals in Prussia. [30]

The intraparty squabbling left the German People's party floundering on all fronts. The DVP's attitude toward the 1931 plebiscite to force early Prussian Landtag elections exemplified the party's ineffectiveness during the crisis years. The aim of the plebiscite, sponsored by the Harzburg Front, was to force the Weimar coalition out of office as a first step toward ending democracy in Prussia. The DVP's right wing persuaded the national leadership to commit the entire party to support the plebiscite. The move put the Prussian DVP in an extremely embarrassing position. Still engaged in coalition talks with the Weimar parties, the DVP also campaigned to bring down the government the party was trying to join. [31]

This sort of tightrope-walking produced few positive results for the DVP. The Prussian DVP leaders' claim that despite their support of the plebiscite they were not really part of the Harzburg Front, did not allay the Weimar coalition parties' suspicions of their former and potential future coalition partner. They had good reason for their distrust: it was becoming increasingly difficult to distinguish the DVP's rhetoric and tactics from that of the "national opposition." The party's speakers in the Landtag even tried to join the anti-Semitic bandwagon—albeit in a somewhat subtle and refined way. It was all in vain. Carving out a position on the right side of the political spectrum was a forlorn hope. By 1930 that position had been preempted by far more skillful demagogues than the DVP could muster.[32]

The Economics Party (WiP)

Since there were no Landtag elections in Prussia during most of the crisis years, the state was largely spared another characteristic of late Weimar politics—the rise of a multiplicity of small, special interest parties. (In the July 1932 Reichstag elections, German voters had a choice of twenty-six parties on the ballot.) The major parties dominated Prussian politics through virtually all of the Weimar era, and the special interest groups were never able to tip the balance in the legislature or the cabinet. Without a statewide contest, the small parties did not succeed in moving into the Landtag, and by the spring of 1932 most of them had ceased to exist; they had been swallowed by the Nazi juggernaut.

One notable exception was the Economics party, a product of the hyperinflation of the early 1920s. The WiP also followed an exceptional path among the opposition groups. Never a major force in the state, the WiP nevertheless was the only special interest group to be represented in the Landtag. Until 1930 the party functioned primarily as a "me-too" support group for the German Nationalists. The party's leader in Prussia, Carl Ladendorff, was one of the most effective, antirepublican demagogues in the Landtag.

The WiP did an abrupt about-face after the September 1930 Reichstag elections. Although the party held onto its voting constituency remarkably well, both the party's national chairman, Victor Bredt, and, surprisingly, Ladendorff himself were shocked by the symptoms of social disintegration and determined to help in stabilizing the republic. Bredt joined the Brüning cabinet as Reich minister of justice, and Ladendorff used his polemical talents to denounce the DNVP's turn toward the extreme right.

Remarkably, the Prussian Economics party regarded the German Nationalists, not the Nazis, as the villains in the Weimar Republic's final years. Like many others, the WiP saw the Nazis as the champions of the little guy. Ladendorff had a good personal relationship with Wilhelm Kube, the head of the small Nazi delegation in the Landtag. Kube was known as a supporter of Gregor Strasser, the NSDAP's leading "leftist," and Ladendorff interpreted Kube's anticapitalist rhetoric as evidence that the Nazis, like the WiP, supported the interests of small entrepreneurs, while the DNVP under Hugenberg acted as political spokesmen for large-scale business and agriculture.

Unfortunately, the WiP's belated turn to the left came just as severe personnel and financial problems were undermining the party's chances for survival. After the fall of 1930, one disaster after the other hit the WiP.

Within the national leadership, massive disagreements over the party's relationship to Brüning's austerity program eventually led to the party's split. In the fall of 1931 two members of the small WiP delegation in the Prussian Landtag left the party to form their own—unsuccessful—group, the radical *Mittelstand*. The collapse of the Deutsche Mittelstandsbank, a financial insitution with close ties with the party's own house bank, the Berliner Bank für Handel und Grundbesitz, brought financial ruin to the WiP. In the meantime the Nazis were steadily eroding the party's voting strength. In the 1932 Landtag elections the WiP was unable to obtain 50,000 votes in any single district, and consequently there were no WiP delegates in the state's last republican legislature. The Economics party had ceased to be a force in Prussian politics.[33]

The German Nationalist People's Party (DNVP) and Conservative Splinter Groups

The largest of the Prussian opposition parties, the DNVP, had consistently rejected parliamentary democracy as a constitutional system ever since the revolution of 1918. Despite mounting evidence that its obstructionist policies hurt the party, the DNVP blindly followed this course to the end, resolutely refusing to function as a loyal opposition. Rejecting the advice of some moderates in its ranks, they continued to pursue the dream of restoring Prussian authoritarianism.

For a time, this obstructionist course brought the state group into open conflict with the party's national leaders. Recognizing the futility of hoping for a coup by the Reichswehr sanctioned by the Reich president—on which Prussian radicals had pinned their hopes—Kuno von Westarp, Oscar Hergt, and Gottfried Treviranus broke with the radical course. After 1925 they steered the national DNVP on a more moderate path and encouraged the German Nationalists to work politically with the middle-of-the-road bourgeois parties. As we saw, in one sense the strategy worked. The DNVP became a member of several *Bürgerblock* Reich cabinets in the mid-1920s, with German Nationalists heading important ministries such as interior and agriculture.

But "coalition politics" was never popular with many of the party's rank and file, and the strategy was strongly opposed by the party's Prussian provincial and Landtag leaders. Alfred Hugenberg's election as national DNVP chairman at the end of 1928 was enthusiastically welcomed by the DNVP's Prussian wing, since it meant that the party's Prussian and Reich strategies would once again move along parallel lines. But Hugenberg's election signaled more than a return to obstructionism for the party as a whole; it meant not only increased influence by the antiparliamentary radicals in the DNVP, but also the end of intraparty democracy and the virtual expulsion of the party's labor wing.[34] The Deutschnationale Handlungsgehilfenverband (German National Association of Retail Clerks), a white-collar union that had been closely allied with the DNVP since 1918, essentially severed relations with the party.[35]

Hugenberg insisted that under his firm leadership—the personally unprepossessing national chairman also liked to have himself referred to as *Führer*—the DNVP had become a *Block anstatt Brei* ("a solid block instead of mush"), but while the metaphor was supposed to describe the party's compact strength, it also pointed to another development: the DNVP was losing voters. In addition, the hopes that the DNVP could absorb some of the smaller, special interest parties did not materialize. It is true that these groups disappeared, but they were absorbed by the Nazis, not the German Nationalists. In fact, under Hugenberg's "firm" leadership the DNVP was transformed from a large and influential opposition party into little more than an appendage of the Nazis.

Some far-sighted Conservatives recognized that since the DNVP's Prussian strategy had been singularly ineffective in the past,[36] following Hugenberg's lead in continuing and intensifying the party's past mistakes would be disastrous. Among the state's German Nationalists the band of dissidents was extremely small, although it included a few well-known figures, such as the party's constitutional expert, Otto Hoetzsch, and above all its best orator, Ernst von Schlange-Schöningen. The Hugenberg loyalists in Prussia resented particularly Schlange-Schöningen's change of heart. An old-line Pommeranian Junker, Schlange-Schöningen had been one of the Prussian DNVP's most radical opponents of parliamentary democracy in the early 1920s. He rose quickly through the party's leadership ranks and in March 1926 was elected one of the DNVP's deputy national chairmen. However, he bitterly opposed Hugenberg's election as national chairman and the new leader's nihilistic course. Socially and politically ostracized in the DNVP, Schlange-Schöningen resigned from the party. By 1931 he was determined to work for his conservative principles in the context of parliamentary democracy, rather than attempt to destroy the constitutional system. For his former colleagues, Schlange-Schöningen had become a traitor and a Bolshevik.[37]

In the Reich the dissidents, led by Gottfried Treviranus, formed the Volkskonservative Partei (People's Conservative party, VKP). The new group never attracted any significant following, but for a time it exercised considerable national influence. Not only was the party's leader a personal friend of Brüning, but also the VKP provided crucial parliamentary support for his minority government. In Prussia the VKP had neither an effective leader nor a pivotal position in the Landtag. Schlange-Schöningen, the natural rallying point for any new conservative formation in the state, left Prussian politics and joined the Reich cabinet as Brüning's commissioner for the *Osthilfe*. His political confederates were singularly unsuccessful in establishing anti-Hugenberg conservatism on the political landscape. The VKP rejected cooperation with the Nazis, but endorsed the initiative, launched by the DNVP, the Nazis, and the Stahlhelm, to force an early dissolution of the Landtag. The VKP claimed that while it rejected the sponsors' antiparliamentary motivation, a victory for the plebiscite would advance a comprehensive *Reichsreform*. Standing on an irrelevant political platform in the midst of the republic's worst crisis, the VKP sank into oblivion. Plans to fuse the VKP with the two liberal parties and the Economics party did not get beyond the discussion stage.[38]

Kuno von Westarp did not join the VKP, and his own effort to draw Conservatives away from Hugenberg's disastrous course, the Christlich-Soziale Volksdienst (Christian Social People's Service, CSVD), was equally unsuccessful. Inspired by Adolf Stöcker and his program of paternalistic Christian socialism, the CSVD saw itself as the embodiment of traditional, responsible German and Prussian conservatism. The CSVD's attempt to restore fairness and rationality to politics in the crisis years was futile. The party had only four delegates in the Landtag before 1932 and none after the April elections. It remained a rather wistful reminder of what German and Prussian Conservatism might have been if the German Nationalists had decided to abandon their obstructionist policies and become a "loyal opposition."[39]

The Hugenberg radicals quickly tightened their grip on the Prussian DNVP. Moderate leaders like Wolfgang von Kries and Friedrich von Winterfeld were eclipsed by a new group of radical and ruthless spokesmen. The DNVP Landtag delegation was now dominated by Lothar Steuer and Hans-Joachim von Rohr-Demmin, two of Hugenberg's most loyal lieutenants in the state. Especially Steuer, a former policeman, was an early and enthusiastic supporter of the DNVP's alliance with the Nazis. He had established close personal relations with Hitler's men in the Landtag long before such arrangements became institutionalized between the national leaders of the two parties. Von Rohr, for his part, had been Hugenberg's agent in the Landbund (Farmers' Union). Together the new leaders purged the Prussian DNVP of "moderate" and "leftist" elements. By controlling the candidate lists for the 1932 Landtag elections, the radicals made sure that the Prussian DNVP became a homogeneous group of Hugenberg followers.[40]

The DNVP's goal in Prussia was straightforward and counterproductive. The German Nationalists insisted on dividing the state's political parties into the "enemies of the nation," the groups that supported political democracy, and the parties of the "national right" that would restore authoritarianism to

Prussia. This goal could be accomplished only by a new constitutional system, one that would permanently destroy the political power of the Weimar coalition parties. In practice the DNVP's program was to restore the political conditions that had prevailed in Prussia before 1918. Any other course, the DNVP claimed, would result in "Bolshevik chaos."[41]

Increasingly sharp attacks on Prussia's Catholic politicians were one manifestation of Hugenberg's control of the Prussian party. Descriptions of the SPD as "the party of treason" and "the stab-in-the-back" had long been part of the Conservatives' standard demagogic repertoire, but in their attempt to forge an alliance of Conservatives and Catholics as the basis for a state *Bürgerblock* coalition, the DNVP moderates had in the past concentrated their efforts on driving a wedge between the Catholic Center party and its allies in the Weimar coalition. The DNVP's decision (with Hugenberg's wholehearted approval) to vote against the treaty with the papacy had already soured the atmosphere, and the German Nationalists' "new course" drove the Center party even more firmly into the arms of the Weimar coalition. The "new" DNVP accused the Catholics of sympathizing with Marxism, and bringing to Prussia the "evils" of "socialism" after 1918.[42]

In contrast, the DNVP accepted the Nazis as full-fledged partners of the "national right." Although some DNVP members told Otto Braun privately of their misgivings about the emerging partnership, it became increasingly difficult to distinguish the programmatic positions, parliamentary tactics, or political rhetoric of the two parties. Not even anti-Semitism distinguished them as the DNVP's speakers in the Landtag became increasingly open in their attacks on Jews.[43]

Uninterested in an alliance with the moderate bourgeois parties, the DNVP in the last years of the republican era largely limited its parliamentary activities in Prussia to demagogic speeches and supporting and sponsoring motions of no confidence against the government. (Between May 1928 and October 1931, the DNVP sponsored twenty-one such resolutions against the Prussian cabinet.) For the DNVP's leaders, what really mattered were politics in the streets and in the Reich president's office, not the work of the Landtag. In Prussia, the party endorsed the political violence of the extraparliamentary "national opposition" and helped to organize the initiative to force an early dissolution of the Landtag so that new state elections could be held. Some DNVP locals were decidedly lukewarm toward the plebiscite effort largely because local contests in Prussia and other *Länder* clearly demonstrated that the Nazis rather than the DNVP would benefit. Nevertheless, the DNVP's national and state leaders in close cooperation with the Stahlhelm spearheaded the drive to force early elections. The state's German Nationalists would serve as junior partners of the Nazis in order to see the hated system of political democracy destroyed.[44]

National Socialist German Worker's Party (NSDAP)

There is no doubt that the Nazis were the real success story of the Weimar Republic's last years. The 1928 Landtag elections were held when the NSDAP's political fortunes were at their nadir. The Nazis' vote for the state as a whole was 2.9 percent. The NSDAP was able to send only eight delegates to the Landtag, seven fewer than the number required for formal caucus status. Four years later, at the time of the April 1932 state elections, the NSDAP stood virtually at the apex of its growth. This time the voters sent 162 Nazis to the Landtag; Hitler's men had become the largest delegation in the legislature.[45]

Before 1930 the Prussian Nazis occupied a position not unlike that of the Prussian Social Democrats before 1918: they operated in the political backwaters, both in the state and in their own party. The Nazis' national leaders and especially Hitler himself had little interest in Prussian politics at this time; the strength of the Weimar coalition in Prussia discouraged the NSDAP from attempting major initiatives there. After the disastrous results of the 1928 Reichstag election, the party as a whole emphasized its middle-class respectability in line with Hitler's changed strategy, but under the leadership of the eccentric Wilhelm Kube the Nazis in the Prussian Landtag continued to follow a decidedly leftist and anticapitalist line. The NSDAP competed with the KPD for leadership of the "revolutionary opposition." To be sure, such revolutionary rhetoric did not prevent the Nazis from also demanding a *Bürgerblock* coalition in the state, or glorifying the state's Hohenzollern past. The Nazis were never afraid of contradicting themselves.[46]

Although signs of the Nazis' corrosive effect on some segments of German society had been evident for some time (the explosive growth of the Nazi student movement, for example, clearly indicated the movement's inroads among middle-class Germans),[47] for most Prussians the NSDAP emerged from the fringes of state politics on November 17, 1929. After the statewide local elections, the Nazis were no longer a laughable political sect, but a force that obviously was going to play a significant role in local and state politics. Overnight the NSDAP had become the state's fifth largest party. Moreover, they had a broad base of support. Because of the continuing agricultural crisis as well as emerging difficulties in the cities, the Nazis did well in both urban and rural areas; in some city districts their vote exceeded 20 percent.

The size of the party's victory came as a shock for most political observers (including the Nazis themselves), but the party adjusted quickly to its newfound popularity, and frustration turned to megalomania. Kube's first address to the Landtag after the November elections left no doubt that the Prussian Nazis saw the reigns of power within his grasp.[48] The Nazis envisioned one of two possibilities: either the frightened bourgeois parties would offer to form a

Bürgerblock coalition with the Nazis in Prussia, or in cooperation with the "national opposition" the Nazis would win a majority of the popular vote after the parties of the Harzburg Front had forced an early dissolution of the Landtag.

Neither scenario worked. Instead, the NSDAP experienced a series of frustrating setbacks on their road to power in Prussia. Throughout 1930 and 1931 the party's organization and preparedness left much to be desired. Joseph Goebbels, the Nazi leader in Berlin, complained about the party's lack of "tight concentration," and wondered if Kube was the right leader: "He is very nice to me. But he is pretty bombastic [*polterig*] and uneven [*unbeständig*]." The bourgeois parties—which really meant the Center party, since the DNVP had already agreed to work with the Nazis and the other groups were too small to matter—refused to form a government with the Nazis. Finally, the failure of the October 1931 referendum to force early Landtag elections blocked the way through the ballot box, at least until scheduled elections were held in April 1932.[49]

Since parliamentary democracy did not work for them, the Prussian Nazis lost interest in parliament. For several months the small band of Nazis boycotted the Landtag sessions altogether, while Nazi-generated street violence rose unabated throughout 1931 and 1932. Nevertheless, Kube and his colleagues confidently expected to win a majority of Landtag seats in the April 1932 elections. After all, the series of local, state, and national elections in 1931 and 1932 demonstrated the rising appeal of the Nazis in all parts of Germany.

For Nazi strategists, the April elections were a severe disappointment. As expected, the party registered spectacular gains, but even in conjunction with the DNVP the "national opposition" did not control the Landtag. The party also faced increasing financial problems and friction between the storm troopers and the political cadres.[50] Frustrated party leaders now began to pursue two increasingly divergent paths to power in Prussia. The growing split over a Prussian strategy had been apparent for some time, but only after the failure to win a parliamentary majority did bitter intraparty conflict emerge into the open. In theory the two strategies were complementary, but their proponents made little effort to coordinate their actions.[51]

Put briefly, the faction led by Kube and Strasser, which had expected a parliamentary majority, now abandoned hope of achieving power on their own in Prussia. Following the adage that whoever controlled Prussia would dominate the Reich, they began to concentrate on forming a *Bürgerblock* coalition with the Center party and the DNVP. They expected that once the Nazis had their hands on the levers of power, the bourgeois partners could be pushed aside. To prepare the NSDAP for handling governmental tasks, Gregor Strasser in his capacity as the party's Reich organizational leader built up an elaborate hierarchy of planning and shadow-government offices.[52]

This, of course, was the strategy Hitler successfully employed in January 1933. It is true that the Nazi *Machtergreifung* seemingly reversed the Reich-Prussian relationship, but it must be remembered that the Reich government had by then taken control of the state.[53]

An alternative, primarily extraparliamentary strategy, was developed by the Gauleiter of Berlin, Joseph Goebbels, and the state's storm troop leaders. (Goebbels was a member of the Prussian Landtag after April 1932, but he valued his parliamentary immunity only as a way to avoid prosecution for libel and slander.) Under this plan, increasingly bitter and bloody clashes between the Nazis and their political opponents would lead to one of two "chaos" scenarios. In the first, Nazi violence would provoke a Communist putsch attempt with the result that the Reich president would give the Nazis plenipotentiary power as the only force capable of restoring law and order and preventing a Bolshevik coup. In the second, the Communists would avoid a putsch of their own, but the increasingly uncontrollable political violence in Germany—in which the storm troopers again played a major part—would bring the nation to the brink of anarchy so that the Reich's leaders had no choice but to hand dictatorial power over to the Nazis.[54]

Although tactical and personal differences among the Nazi party leaders would get increasingly bitter, it is incorrect to describe the Strasser-Kube wing as "moderate" or the Goebbels group as "radical." The aim of all Nazis was total power. The differences concerned tactics, personal influence, and timing. Goebbels' extraparliamentary strategy aimed at total power immediately, while Kube and Strasser envisioned a relatively peaceful transition period of cooperation with the bourgeois parties.[55]

In the meantime, the two scenarios worked against each other. None of the Nazis rejected violence inside and outside of parliament as a form of "political" activity (to Goebbels' delight, in late May Nazi and Communist delegates fought a pitched battle in the halls of the Landtag),[56] but political violence worked against the parliamentary strategy. As we shall see, the Prussian Center party essentially refused to be bullied into a coalition with the NSDAP. Moreover, despite mounting street violence, the Prussian police did not lose control of the situation, so that the Nazis' planned "chaos" never materialized. In fact, in August 1932 the Reich president pointedly refused to give Hitler dictatorial power.

By mid-1932 all of the Nazis' Prussian strategies had failed, and Goebbels and Hitler, although not Kube or Strasser, had lost interest in coming to power by the Prussian route. Until the federal takeover of July 1932 the Prussian bastion stood firm against the Nazi onslaught. After the federal takeover, the Nazi leader in Berlin and his *Führer* pinned their hopes on coming to power in the Reich. Strasser continued to pursue a dual strategy. Time, as we now know, was not on the Nazis' side. Over the course of 1932 internal antagonisms in the party mounted as the *Machtergreifung* repeatedly eluded the Nazis. At the end of the year the NSDAP's appeal to the voters was declining rapidly and, in addition, the party was experiencing increasingly severe financial problems. It is indeed ironic that just before their coming to power in January 1933 the Nazis themselves saw little cause for optimism about their political future.[57]

The Communist Party of Germany (KPD)

In many ways, the Nazis and the Communists were mirror images. The KPD could not match the NSDAP's membership numbers or voter appeal, but the history of the party in the crisis years was nevertheless another success story. Its penchant for street violence equaled that of the Nazis. Both the KPD and the NSDAP saw themselves as "antiparties," and in a very real sense each justified its own self-image by referring to the actions and ideology of the other. The Nazis' claimed that only they could save Germany from the Bolshevik revolution, while the KPD looked upon the Nazis as evidence that the last crisis of German capitalism was at hand and the proletarian revolution just around the corner.

But there were also profound differences between the two extremist parties. The intraparty struggles in the NSDAP concerned only German issues, while those among the Communists were closely related to the battles for power in the Soviet Union and control of the Comintern among Lenin's successors. The Nazis had a surfeit of Prussian strategies, but the Communists never developed a separate strategy for getting to power in the state. The correct party line in Prussia was merely one of the issues that fueled the chronic intraparty factional disputes rocking the KPD.[58]

Despite some significant tactical shifts between 1929 and 1933, the KPD generally followed a leftist or ultraleftist course. In both leaders and strategy, the German Communists were closely allied with the Zinoviev faction within the Comintern leadership in Moscow. Heavily dependent on the Comintern for both ideological guidance and financial support, the KPD faithfully followed the Comintern's "social fascism" line. According to this concept, some of whose most enthusiastic proponents were Communist members of the Prussian Landtag, the KPD identified the SPD rather than the Nazis or the DNVP as the spearhead of fascism and capitalist reaction in Germany. The communists were slow to recognize the Nazi danger, arguing well into the 1930s that the NSDAP was less dangerous than the "social fascist" SPD and the Prussian government that party dominated. Consequently, Communist theoreticians argued that the destruction of the SPD as the last real pillar of capitalism was a prerequisite for the collapse of the capitalist system as a whole and inauguration of the Communist revolution that would inevitably follow. It is ironic that after months of intraparty wrangling (which concerned personality clashes more than disagreements over strategy) the victory of the ultraleftists and their doctrine of social fascism was complete just a few weeks before Hitler became chancellor.[59]

Although the doctrine of social fascism was in no sense a strategy for revolution, the KPD's ultraleft line did gain the party members and voters during the years of acute economic crisis. But the support was one-dimensional and soft. The KPD became *the* political organization of unskilled and especially unemployed blue-collar workers; it was unable to make significant inroads into the bulk of organized, skilled labor. What supporters it did have were kept in line more by unrealistic, short-term illusions generated by the party's verbal radicalism than by any real, ideological commitments to the KPD.[60]

Prussian issues had little to do with determining the KPD's social fascism line, but relations between the state's Social Democrats and the Communists bolstered the arguments of the ultraleft faction in the battle for leadership of the KPD. Again and again the leftists cited the May 1929 riots in Berlin and their suppression by the Prussian police as proof that the Prussian Social Democrats had established a reactionary, fascist regime in the state. During the crisis years, efforts by the Prussian police to suppress political violence by the communists (as well as other extremists) convinced the KPD that the "social fascist" rulers of Prussia remained the primary barrier to the coming proletarian revolution. Removing the SPD from power in Prussia would deal a death blow to capitalism and fascism in Germany. As a result, the Communists concentrated their venom on the Prussian SPD and especially the Social Democrats in the cabinet. In an unending series of attacks in and out of the Landtag, the KPD accused the Prussian government of everything from causing the economic and social problems resulting from the depression to obeying the orders of its fascist-capitalist masters in violently suppressing the coming proletarian revolution.[61]

During the crisis years, the KPD in the Reich and in Prussia was led by a tightly knit group of activists who coopted each other into leading positions within the party. After 1930 the most prominent spokesmen of the Prussian Communists were leftists. They included Wilhelm Pieck and Walter Ulbricht. Pieck headed the party's Landtag delegation in the last years of the Weimar Republic, and Ulbricht was chairman of the party's largest district organization, that of Berlin-Brandenburg. After 1945 both men played prominent roles in the former German Democratic Republic.

The KPD's conviction that the Weimar coalition government in Prussia had to be brought down at all costs led the party to form limited tactical alliances with the Nazis and the other right-wing opposition parties. Perhaps the most famous instances were the Communists' support of the October 1931 referendum to force early Landtag elections and the strike of Berlin's transport workers which the KPD and the NSDAP organized jointly a year later. In both cases, the object was to embarrass and weaken the Social Democrats. Through the referendum, the KPD hoped to force the Weimar coalition government out of office, while the strike was directed against the capital's SPD-dominated municipal government.

As the party ruefully admitted later, the KPD's decision to support the Stahlhelm initiative and referendum was a mistake. The party had "lost sight of its main task," concluded one East German historian later.[62] Moreover, the KPD more or less backed into the decision. When the possibility of the referendum first surfaced, party leaders unanimously rejected cooperating with its extreme right-wing sponsors. It was only a combination of pressure from Moscow and the illusion that the referendum might succeed in bringing down the hated "social fascist" enemy that persuaded them reluctantly to enter into this strange partnership.[63]

The KPD leaders may have been convinced that the referendum effort was a clever tactical move, but their followers were not. Many Communist voters refused to follow their party's directives to support the October 1931 referendum. The KPD's explanation that Communist support for the referendum transformed it from a reactionary move into a progressive action was unconvincing.[64]

At the beginning of 1932, the party was in the midst of a major crisis. The KPD came under the control of increasingly opportunistic and "infantile" elements. Incapable of launching a revolution, unable to persuade most German workers to desert their traditional allegiances, and blind to the real menace of the Nazis, the KPD wallowed in verbal radicalism. It suffered severe setbacks at the polls. In the Reich presidential and Landtag elections of April 1932, the KPD did far less well than either the Nazis or the Social Democrats.[65]

After the party's poor showing in the Landtag elections, there were signs of somewhat greater flexibility in the KPD's line. In Berlin, Communist and Socialist unions organized joint May Day demonstrations, and in several other cities the Communists suggested a truce with the Social Democrats. In the spring of 1932, two of the KPD's Landtag delegates, Ernst Torgler and Wilhelm Kasper, approached Prussian SPD leaders to test the possibility of a statewide truce or even cooperation with the Social Democrats as part of a united front against the Nazis. But relations between the two labor parties were so bitter that the Social Democrats did not trust the KPD's intentions. In addition, Kasper had earlier been particularly vicious in his attacks on the SPD.[66]

Above all, however, the Social Democrats knew that Kasper and Torgler did not speak for either the KPD's national leadership or the Comintern. And in a sense events proved them right. Bolstered by what the party's national leaders regarded as success in the July Reichstag elections, the KPD leaders ordered all activists to concentrate their main attack *(Hauptschlag)* once again on the SPD. Both the spokesmen for the Communist International and the KPD's national leaders continued to oppose all attempts to soften the doctrine of social fascism. Instances of spontaneous cooperation between KPD and SPD activists in various cities, which some authors have interpreted as evidence of a changing attitude on the part of both parties, came to nothing. Until the end of the Weimar Republic, the KPD's leaders insisted that Braun and Heilmann were the real enemies, Papen and Hitler only paper tigers.[67]

Election Results

The last years of the Weimar Republic might well be described as the endless campaign. National, state, and local elections followed each other in quick succession. Moreover, in the absence of any real consensus on the constitutional system itself, campaigning for all levels of government was highly emotional, abusive, slanderous, and almost always accompanied by political violence. Prussia stood at the center of the political battles. As had been true since the founding of the Reich, the issues in Prussian elections were virtually indistinguishable from those in national contests. And now, with the constitutional system itself a campaign issue, the parties used the Reich and Prussian forums interchangeably in their clashes over the democratic system.

Early in the republican era, the stability of Prussia's parliamentary democracy had been the major reason for the survival of democracy in Germany as a whole. The situation was fundamentally different after the last parliamentary government in the Reich collapsed in March 1930. The presidential cabinets in the Reich proudly claimed that they acted independently of the vagaries of voter sentiment. Nevertheless, the question of the residual strength of democracy in Prussia as compared to the whole Reich remains an important consideration for assessing the fate of Weimar Germany. Granted that the democrats were losing their appeal for voters in all parts of Germany, was the erosion process slower and recovery quicker in Prussia than in the nation as a whole?

The Nazis burst upon the national scene as a result of their spectacular victories in the Reichstag elections of September 1930. There were no parallel Landtag elections, but the "national opposition" parties, and especially the Nazis, attempted to translate their strong showing in the Reich into greater influence at the state level. They insisted that the results in Prussia demonstrated that the Weimar coalition parties had lost their mandate to govern the state. The right-wing opposition parties quoted figures to show that if Prussian voters had been asked to elect a new Landtag as well as a new Reichstag, the opposition would have obtained a majority of eighty-six seats in the Prussian legislature.[68]

This was shadow-boxing, of course. Past elections provided no evidence for such mechanical transfers between voting patterns in the Reich and the state. In earlier contests, such as the December 1924 and May 1928 elections, Prussian voters had shown significantly more confidence in the parties of the Weimar coalition than did voters in the Reich. It should also be noted that Prussian voters overwhelmingly rejected the initiative for an early dissolution of the Landtag in October 1931. Whatever their political sentiments, voters were content to let the legislature serve out its term. Moreover, the "opposition" was a parliamentarily meaningless concept. Even if the "opposition" had obtained a majority in the mythical Landtag, it was a force united only in support of a negative goal; the opposition parties would certainly not cooperate in forming an alternative government. In contrast, the Weimar coalition parties in Prussia, contrary to what had happened in the Reich, continued to cooperate in the cabinet and the Landtag.

Nevertheless, the national elections of 1930 undeniably pointed to serious problems for the Weimar coalition parties and the stability of parliamentary democracy in the state. The real winners in the Reichstag elections were the Nazis;[69] Hugenberg's appeasement of Hitler benefited them, not the German Nationalists. The most dramatic losers were the Liberals. The voters clearly had no faith in the DDP and the DVP—or, for that matter, in any of the numerous efforts to form a new "party of the center." The Center party and SPD held their own, but the Social Democrats confronted a special dilemma. While gaining some votes from sections of the new *Mittelstand,* they were also losing part of their blue-collar constituency to the Communists. For a party that saw itself primarily as a class-specific interest group, this was an ominous sign. Not surprisingly, some party leaders and pundits wanted to abandon all efforts to become a modern *Volkspartei* and concentrate instead on maintaining the allegiance of Germany's industrial proletariat. But that meant "talking out of the left side of the mouth," a tactical course that would inevitably produce further friction in the Weimar coalition.[70]

If the results of the September 1930 contest spread clouds of doom among the supporters of the republic, the outcome of the two initiatives and referenda sponsored by the opposition parties over the following year gave rise to somewhat more optimism. Under the hyperdemocratic provisions of the Weimar and Prussian constitutions, an initiative campaign was successful if 10 percent of the eligible voters signed the necessary petitions. A referendum, however, required the approval of a majority to be successful. In March 1931 the right-wing opposition parties attempted to use the plebiscitary provisions of the constitution to defeat the Young Plan. In October the opposition tried to force an early dissolution of the Landtag to pave the way for new state elections before the regularly scheduled date of April 1932.

In both cases, the results were a severe disappointment to the sponsors. Although the combined forces of the far right (Stahlhelm, DNVP, and Nazis) campaigned for the Young Plan referendum, and the Communists joined them for the Landtag plebiscite, the referenda received far fewer votes than the same parties garnered in the September 1930 Reichstag election. In several districts, the vote was less than half of the total obtained during the Reichstag elections. The DNVP's contention that the campaign rather than the results was important for advancing the right-wing opposition's cause was lame at best.[71]

The primary reason was the nature of the plebiscite process itself. Voters who did not bother to go to the polls were counted as opposing the referendum, since only yes votes determined the success of the plebiscite. As far as Prussia was concerned, there was an important political lesson here as well. The number of ballots cast in favor of the Landtag referendum was deceptively low (37 percent). While the results obviously did not mean that 63 percent of the voters were satisfied with the political situation in the fall of 1931, clearly a large majority of Prussia's voters were not yet willing to follow the left- and right-wing radicals. In addition, especially in the case of the Landtag initiative and referendum, the government's clear opposition to the plebiscite, communicated through territorial administrators, seems to have helped to convince many voters that the cabinet remained in control of the situation.[72]

The first true statewide election was the Reich presidential contest in the spring of 1932. President Hindenburg's term of office expired in April. To prevent a divisive and bitter national campaign at the height of the Depression (as well as to keep himself in power), Chancellor Brüning had proposed that the Reichstag extend Hindenburg's term by acclamation, but that plan was rejected by the Communists and the Nazis. Instead, four candidates—Hindenburg, Hitler, the Communist leader Thälmann, and Theodor Düsterberg, a prominent Stahlhelm leader supported by the DNVP—competed for the office. The Weimar constitution provided that if no candidate obtained a majority of votes, a runoff election was required. The second time, a plurality sufficed for victory. Hindenburg barely missed obtaining an absolute majority in the first contest on March 13, 1932, but he easily won the runoff a month later.

The Prussian results for the two presidential contests, the second of which was held just two weeks before the Landtag elections in April 1932, generally paralleled those in the Reich. (See tables 4 and 5, below.) Neither Thälmann nor Düsterberg had a realistic chance of being elected, so their showing was of interest primarily for assessing the strength of their nominating organizations, the Communists in the case of Thälmann, and DNVP and the Stahlhelm for Düsterberg. Düsterberg's results were extremely disappointing to his backers. His national average was 6.8 percent, far behind Hindenburg and Hitler. The figure was both a reflection of the candidate's lack of charisma and a symptom of the German Nationalists' decline and a portent for the future. Düsterberg's share of the vote in Prussia was about one-third of the DNVP's popular vote in 1928 (17.4 percent), but his support almost exactly paralleled the vote for the German Nationalists in the April 1932 Landtag election (6.9 percent). Düsterberg experienced personally the consequences of Hugenberg's alliance with Hitler. Thälmann, on the other hand, simply continued the KPD's role as outsider and spoiler. The share of his popular vote in the presidential contest for the Reich (13.3 percent) came close to the Communist candidates' showing in the 1928 (11.9 percent) and 1932 (12.8 percent) Landtag elections.

The real contest, of course, was between Hitler and Hindenburg. Hitler's share of the popular vote in Prussia in the first contest was very close to his national average: 30.4 percent in Prussia, 30.1 percent for the Reich. Hindenburg's share was somewhat lower: 47.6 percent in Prussia, 49.6 percent in the Reich as a whole. The relationship between the two men did not significantly change in the runoff election. With Düsterberg now out of the way (unlike Thälmann, Düsterberg decided not to take part in the runoff), Hindenburg obtained a majority of the votes in Prussia (51.9 percent) and in the Reich (53 percent). Hitler's share of the vote also increased: 37.9 percent in Prussia, 36.8 percent in the Reich.[73]

The conclusion was inescapable: In the runoff election most of Düsterberg's support in the first contest went to Hitler, not to Hindenburg. The Nazi leader was able to make heavy inroads into the DNVP's traditional voter reservoirs in the Prussian heartland. A few examples from the East Elbian districts will illustrate the ominous development. (See table 4.)

All three Weimar coalition parties had supported Hindenburg in both contests, and the Reich president's relatively poor showing coupled with Hitler's popularity in the Prussian electoral districts left little ground for optimism among the democratic parties as they faced the most important Prussian contest, the April 1932 Landtag elections. The fateful date was April 24, virtually another national election day; in addition to Prussia, state legislatures were also elected in Bavaria, Württemberg, Anhalt, and Hamburg. Anticipating the inevitable rise of the extremist vote, the Weimar coalition parties had taken a number of controversial steps. Using their majority in the old Landtag, the SPD, Center party, and DStP had forced through a change in the rules of procedure to make the election of a prime minister who did not have majority support in the legislature more difficult.[74] To discourage voters from wasting their ballots on small, parochial interest parties, the number of popular votes necessary for a Landtag seat was raised from 40,000 to 50,000.

Table 4. Presidential Election, 1932
(Percent of popular vote)

Election District	Hindenburg	Düsterberg	Hitler
East Prussia			
1st contest	43.8	11.5	34.5
2d contest	48.6	—	43.8
Frankfurt a.O			
1st contest	42.9	12.9	35.4
2d contest	48.1	—	45.7
Pommerania			
1st contest	34.4	18.9	37.4
2d contest	40.7	—	52.6
Breslau			
1st contest	48.1	7.3	35.8
2d contest	51.7	—	42.0
Liegnitz			
1st contest	46.6	8.7	37.9
2d contest	50.8	—	44.4
Oppeln			
1st contest	51.8	7.7	25.9
2d contest	57.2	—	30.7
Magdeburg			
1st contest	45.7	9.6	34.1
2d contest	49.9	—	41.9

Source: Statistisches Jahrbuch für das Deutsche Reich 1932 (Berlin, 1932), pp. 546–47.

(Plans to set the number at 60,000 were dropped when it appeared that the DStP would not be able to surmount this hurdle.) An attempt by the WiP to raise the voting age from twenty to twenty-five was rejected by the other major parties as unconstitutional and blatantly partisan.[75]

At first glance, these efforts to contain the radicals were of no avail. By any measure, the results of the 1932 Landtag elections were disastrous for the democratic parties. This was especially obvious when the 1932 outcome is compared with the elections of four years earlier. (See table 5.)

The voters turned to the radicals; Communists and Nazis together now controlled 52 percent of the Landtag seats. Among the Weimar coalition parties, the Center party held its own, the SPD suffered some losses, and the DStP all but disappeared. Together, the three Weimar coalition parties obtained only slightly more votes than the Nazis alone. On the other hand, the extreme right fell far short of obtaining a majority in the new Landtag. The NSDAP and DNVP together did not control the legislature.

The strength of the parties varied considerably across the state. With the exception of the Nazis, none of the Prussian political groups could claim to be

Table 5.   Prussian Landtag Elections, 1928 and 1932

	1928		1932	
	Popular Vote (in millions)	% of Popular Vote	Popular Vote (in millions)	% of Popular Vote
SPD	5.5	29.0	4.7	21.2
DStP (DDP)	0.84	4.5	0.3	1.5
Center party	2.9	14.5	3.4	15.3
DNVP	3.3	17.4	1.5	6.9
DVP	1.6	8.5	0.3	1.5
WiP	0.86	4.5	0.06	0.8
NSDAP	0.6	2.9	8.0	36.6
KPD	2.2	11.9	2.8	12.9

Total Votes Cast
   1928: 18.9 million
   1932: 22.1 million

Source: Horst Möller, Parlamentarismus in Preussen, 1919–1932 (Düsseldorf, 1985), p. 601.

genuine *Volksparteien*. The SPD, which held on to the bulk of its voters, did best in heavily industrialized and urban areas (30 percent in Berlin, 28 percent in Potsdam I and II, and 34 percent in Magdeburg), surprisingly well in some of the rural districts (22 percent in East Prussia, 26.2 percent in Schleswig-Holstein), and very poorly in heavily Catholic areas (6.3 percent in Koblenz-Trier, 9.5 percent in Düsseldorf-West).

A look at the Center party's regional strength demonstrated why the coalition of Center party and Social Democrats had been able to assure Prussia's political stability for so many years. Voters of the Center party complemented those of the SPD. Generally, the Catholics did poorly in areas that were focal points of Social Democratic strength (4 percent in Berlin, 2 percent in Magdeburg, 6 percent in South Hanover) and well in districts that produced few votes for the SPD (36 percent in Oppeln, 35 percent in North Westphalia, 42 percent in Cologne-Aachen, and 47 percent in Koblenz-Trier).

While the Center party and the SPD held their own in most areas, the left-wing Liberals, the third partner in the Weimar coalition, was decimated. The DStP's highest share of the vote in any district was 4 percent; this was the case in Potsdam II, a district that included some of the wealthier suburbs of Berlin. Nowhere else did the party gain more than 2 percent of the vote, and in eight of the state's twenty-three electoral districts the party's vote was statistically insignificant.

The DNVP did somewhat better in absolute numbers than the left-wing Liberals, but in relative terms the April elections were almost as much of a disaster for the German Nationalists as for the DStP. The DNVP's highest share of the vote in any district was 17 percent (Pommerania); nowhere else did the party achieve more than 10 percent of the popular vote. In several of the East Elbian districts in which the party used to dominate (East Prussia, Potsdam I and II, Frankfurt a.O.), the DNVP was reduced to an insignificant minority.

It is true that the April contest was a triumph for the extremists, but is was a one-sided victory. For all their bluster, the Communists were neither absolute nor relative winners. The KPD was unable to reach 30 percent in any district, and it came close in only one (29 percent in Berlin). In fact, the Communists gained more than 20 percent of the popular vote in only three districts (in addition to Berlin, 22 percent in Merseburg, and 23 percent in Düsseldorf-East). Equally important, in view of the party's perennial attempt to forge "union from below" with the Social Democratic workers, was the KPD's failure to surpass the SPD. The KPD significantly outstripped the Social Democrats only in Düsseldorf-East, an area that included much of the Ruhr industrial region, where the KPD obtained 23 percent of the popular vote to the SPD's 11.8 percent. In addition, the KPD did somewhat better than the SPD in Merseburg (22 to 18.9 percent), and the two were close in Berlin (29 percent for the KPD, 30 percent for the SPD). In all other districts, the SPD did considerably better.

The Nazis were the real victors in the April elections. The NSDAP was the only party to obtain more than 20 percent of the popular vote in all districts and the only group to achieve an absolute majority in any district (51 percent in Schleswig- Holstein). Hitler's movement was a clear beneficiary of the Depression misery, and unlike the Communists the NSDAP was able to win the support of both rural and urban voters (46 percent in East Prussia, 45 percent in Frankfurt a.O, 44 percent in Pommerania, 47 percent in East Hanover, 45 percent in Liegnitz). The party did least well—in relative terms—in areas that remained strongholds of the SPD and the Center party (24 percent in Berlin, 22 percent in Cologne-Aachen, 28 percent in Koblenz-Trier).[76]

In terms of parliamentary politics, these figures were meaningless. The April election resulted in a deadlocked Landtag. The opposition parties had a majority in the legislature, but they were divided among themselves and unable to produce a parliamentary alternative to the Weimar coalition government. As a result, the Braun cabinet remained in control of the executive as a caretaker government.

If the April elections paralyzed the legislature in Prussia, the takeover of the state by the federal government in July 1932 ended its influence altogether. Elections in Prussia in the second half of 1932 merely helped to answer the question whether Prussian voters would recover from the "Nazi madness," as Ernst Heilmann called it, sooner than voters in the Reich. The answer was no.

In the July and November 1932 Reichstag elections, the Nazis, as had been true for the Reich presidential elections, did marginally better in Prussian districts than in the Reich as a whole. Yet the Nazis' popularity fell significantly in the November elections, and continued to fall in the remaining months of the Weimar era. (See tables 6 and 7.) In local elections in November and December they suffered losses of 40 percent and more. Some observers were convinced that the Braun government was beginning to regain control of the situation.[77]

But, of course, after July 1932, the influence of Prussia's voters on the state's political decision making was negligible. Prussia was under the control of Franz von Papen and the Reich government, who answered only to the Reich president, not to the voters of either Germany or Prussia. Still, a survey

Table 6. Votes in Reichstag Election, July 1932: Prussian Electoral Districts (percent of popular vote)

	SPD	DNVP	Center Party	KPD	DStP	NSDAP
East Prussia	19.7	9.5	7.7	12.9	0.6	47.1
Berlin	27.9	6.7	4.6	33.4	1.1	24.6
Potsdam II	26.3	10.9	5.2	20.3	2.1	33.0
Potsdam I	26.7	9.0	3.0	20.1	1.1	38.1
Frankfurt a.O.	23.5	9.2	6.3	9.6	0.7	48.1
Pommerania	20.9	15.8	1.5	10.7	0.8	47.9
Breslau	24.4	5.6	14.7	8.8	0.5	43.5
Liegnitz	26.3	6.9	7.2	7.6	1.0	48.0
Oppeln	8.7	6.9	34.6	17.0	0.2	29.3
Magdeburg	32.3	7.5	2.0	11.1	1.1	43.8
Merseburg	19.8	8.1	1.6	24.3	1.0	42.6
Schleswig-Holstein	26.2	6.5	1.2	10.7	1.4	51.0
Weser-Ems	22.4	7.9	18.2	7.9	1.2	38.4
East Hanover	24.5	8.4	1.4	8.2	1.0	49.5
South Hanover	31.5	5.1	4.9	8.2	0.8	46.1
Westphalia North	18.0	5.7	32.9	13.0	0.3	25.7
Westphalia South	18.7	4.7	23.6	20.6	0.6	27.2
Hessen-Nassau	22.3	4.0	15.0	10.5	0.7	43.6
Cologne-Aachen	14.6	3.7	40.5	17.5	0.3	17.4
Koblenz-Trier	8.8	4.7	46.2	8.6	0.2	28.8
Düsseldorf East	12.2	4.9	20.6	26.3	0.3	31.6
Düsseldorf West	10.2	5.9	34.0	19.8	0.2	27.0
Average						
Prussia	21.5	7.2	14.9	14.7	0.8	37.7
Reich	21.6	5.9	15.7	14.3	0.95	37.3

Source: Based on Wilhelm Dittmann, Das politische Deutschland vor Hitler (Zurich, 1945).

Table 7. Votes in Reichstag Election, November 1932: Prussian
Electoral Districts (percent of popular vote)

	SPD	DNVP	Center Party	KPD	DStP	NSDAP
East Prussia	20.0	14.4	7.5	13.9	0.5	39.7
Berlin	23.7	6.7	4.6	37.7	1.1	24.6
Potsdam II	22.7	15.5	4.6	23.1	1.9	29.1
Potsdam I	23.5	12.8	2.7	23.6	1.1	34.0
Frankfurt a.O.	22.7	13.3	6.2	11.4	0.6	42.6
Pommerania	19.8	20.6	1.2	12.1	0.5	43.1
Breslau	23.1	7.7	14.1	10.5	0.5	40.4
Liegnitz	26.3	9.9	7.1	9.9	0.8	42.1
Oppeln	9.1	8.0	35.8	16.9	0.2	26.8
Magdeburg	31.0	10.6	1.9	13.4	0.8	39.0
Merseburg	19.3	12.4	1.5	27.1	0.8	34.4
Schleswig-Holstein	24.7	10.2	1.0	13.3	1.2	45.7
Weser-Ems	21.3	10.8	17.9	10.3	1.1	31.9
East Hanover	23.3	12.1	1.3	10.3	0.7	42.8
South Hanover	31.0	7.4	4.7	10.7	0.7	46.5
Westphalia North	17.0	7.1	31.9	15.8	0.2	22.3
Westphalia South	16.6	6.2	23.1	23.2	0.4	24.8
Hessen-Nassau	21.6	5.0	14.0	13.4	0.9	41.2
Cologne-Aachen	14.7	5.2	39.3	19.3	0.3	17.4
Koblenz-Trier	9.5	5.9	45.8	9.6	0.2	26.1
Düsseldorf East	11.5	7.1	20.5	28.3	0.3	26.9
Düsseldorf West	24.2	7.0	32.8	22.5	0.2	24.2
Average						
Prussia	20.8	9.8	14.5	17.1	0.7	33.8
Reich	20.4	8.5	15.0	16.9	0.95	33.1

Source: Based on Wilhelm Dittmann, *Das politische Deutschland vor Hitler* (Zurich, 1945).

of election results in Prussia during the crisis years reveals something about the state's reputation as a rock of pluralism in extreme times. It was at best a brittle rock. Until the fall of 1932 Prussia was no more immune from the fever of political radicalization than the rest of Germany. In April 1932, the Prussian people essentially voted parliamentary democracy out of office. But after the high point of radicalization had been reached in the spring and summer of 1932, Prussia's voters turned away from the extremist parties. Unfortunately, elections at the end of 1932 were a "pale sequel to a sequel," to use Golo Mann's phrase. They ended the state's Weimar era on a positive, if ultimately meaningless, note.[78]

Prussia and the Depression: *Innenpolitik* During the Republic's Final Years, 1930–1933

The fall of the Müller cabinet in March 1930 marked the beginning of the Weimar Republic's last and fatal crisis. Formally, the Reich cabinet resigned for lack of agreement on how to cope with the unemployment problem. However, this inability to deal with the country's economic difficulties was not so much cause as effect of larger systemic problems, and a catalyst for worse ones in the future. As Werner Conze has noted, the Depression transformed the republic's chronic political malaise into a political emergency. During that emergency the problems that had plagued Reich-level politics for most of the Weimar Republic's history developed into a full-scale constitutional and systemic crisis. Leadership of the Reich passed from the Reichstag and the federal cabinet to the Reich president, his entourage, and the chancellors they selected. Simultaneously, steadily worsening economic and social conditions made it possible for political extremists to destroy any vestiges of democratic consensus, eventually enabling Hitler to come to power.[1]

While the literature on the period called the *Staats- und Wirtschaftskrise* (constitutional and economic crisis), is voluminous, Prussia's part in the unfolding of events has been curiously neglected. Germany's largest state is mostly ignored entirely or treated as an object of the power struggles in the Reich. This is unfortunate because it distorts the picture of the Weimar Republic's demise. To begin with, there was no political crisis in Prussia before April 1932. Until then Prussia, like the rest of Germany, suffered severe economic and fiscal problems, but there was no systemic crisis, no *Staatskrise*. The state government, unlike the Reich cabinet, had the confidence of the legislature, and parliamentary democracy remained functional. It was not until the spring of 1932 that the political paralysis that had characterized the crisis in the Reich since March 1930, destroyed parliamentary democracy in Prussia as well. Moreover, the politicians recognized that Prussia's role in implementing the policies of the Reich president and the federal chancellor was crucial for the success of the neoconservatives' political and economic program.[2]

163

Prussia's handling of the *innenpolitische* crisis facing Reich and state was complicated by the interlaced political and economic goals pursued by Heinrich Brüning and his successors in the Reich chancellor's office. The neoconservatives' policies had far-reaching foreign and domestic goals: rather than focusing on social misery at home and preserving parliamentary democracy, they were intended to use the country's economic problems and systemic crisis to forge a new constitution that would redefine the Reich-Prussian dualism and restore the Reich's full sovereignty in international relations by ending the reparations. With parliamentary democracy already in de facto suspension in the Reich, the presidential chancellors also planned to destroy, or at least substantially weaken, political democracy in Prussia so as to help restore a neoauthoritarian, monarchical political system in Germany.

Brüning reached an important interim goal in his program of "constitutional reforms" with the *Dietramszeller Notverordnung* (Dietramszell emergency decree, DNV) of August 1931. This executive order suspended the provisions of the Reich and *Länder* constitutions requiring parliamentary approval for state and federal budgets. Under the guise of coping with an emergency, the Reich president's decree abolished one of the foundations of parliamentary democracy.[3]

Against this background a number of questions arise. Was the Prussian leaders' analysis of the causes and consequences of the Depression more sophisticated than that of the federal cabinets? And, more important, did leaders attempt to use the strength of Prussia's democratic system to counter the federal efforts to weaken parliamentary democracy in all of Weimar Germany? In other words, did Prussia's leaders continue to hold fast to the state's self-conception as the "rock of democracy in Germany"?

Answers to these questions are dificult, largely because pragmatic, day-to-day decisions tended to obscure the underlying fundamental political differences between Reich and state. For example, virtually everyone agreed on the desperate need for law and order as well as cuts in government expenditures. To this end, federalizing the states' police forces or various economic aid programs, notably the *Osthilfe,* might well increase efficiency and save money. Heinrich Brüning and succeeding chancellors certainly advanced such pragmatic arguments in talks with Prussian officials. The state's representatives seemed to accept that the central issue was indeed to find ways to coordinate services at the two levels of government in the most cost-effective manner. Unfortunately, the Prussian leaders failed to see that for the neoconservatives the quest for efficiency was a smoke screen. Brüning, Franz von Papen, and Kurt von Schleicher never lost sight of their larger political agenda: to use the "fortuitous" economic crisis to restore neoauthoritarianism in Germany. A major obstacle in their path was what they saw as the "Prussian problem," a functioning parliamentary democracy in the state.

Fiscal Policies

The answer to an earlier question, whether the Prussian leaders viewed the causes of and remedies for the Depression differently from their Reich colleagues, is no. Like virtually all German politicians, economists, businessmen, and labor leaders, the state's political leaders were convinced the Depression was above all a problem of public finances that required hardheaded fiscal solutions. They willingly if unenthusiastically followed Brüning on his path of extreme deflation: the key to any economic upturn lay in stimulating private investment, and that could be done only if investors were convinced government spending on social programs and, equally important, reparations payments would not lead to inflation. Following this reasoning, balanced budgets at all levels of government were absolutely essential. In practice this meant that as the Depression worsened, continually declining government receipts had to be matched by ever increasing cuts in expenditures and, eventually, raised taxes. Inevitably, there were fierce struggles over specific budget cuts, and, much as had been the case during the years of hyperinflation, the Reich and state finance ministers became key officials during the Depression years.

Prussia had two ministers of finance in the Depression era. Both were fiscal conservatives, but here the similarities ended. Hermann Höpker-Aschoff, a familiar figure, had been in office since 1925. In the last five years he had acquired a formidable reputation both as an expert in public finance and a political strongman. Höpker-Aschoff's influence was far larger than his immediate political base—the small DDP and later the even less important DStP—because over the years he had attained the confidence of his Weimar coalition partners. Men like Otto Braun and Carl Severing respected the minister's democratic convictions as well as his professional competence.[4]

To be sure, Höpker-Aschoff was not without his critics. His well-known national ambitions and his abrasive personality had long made him a difficult colleague. His fiscal philosophy was another point of controversy. Like Brüning, the Prussian finance minister had always been an extreme monetarist. Even before the crisis years the former minister of the interior and later chief of police in Berlin, Albert Grzesinski, accused Höpker-Aschoff of sacrificing the republic on the altar of monetarism. As the crisis reached catastrophic dimensions, Höpker-Aschoff's failure to see the political consequences of his seemingly unending proposals for further budget cuts and heavier taxes aroused increasingly bitter criticism.[5]

Although he continued to enjoy the prime minister's confidence, Höpker-Aschoff resented his mounting isolation within the cabinet and within the coalition parties in the Landtag. He also saw the post of Prussian finance minister as a political dead end. Increasingly dependent upon subsidies from the Reich, the state's finance ministry was becoming little more than a disbursement agency for the Reich chancellor and the federal minister of finance. These considerations help to explain the minister's sudden resignation from the Prussian government in October 1931. A few months later Brüning offered Höpker-Aschoff the post of Reich minister of finance, but, embittered by his recent experiences with the Prussian cabinet and his party colleagues, he preferred to leave active politics altogether. He served as head of the Prussian general accounting office (Oberrechnungshof) until the Nazis forced him into retirement. After 1949 he ended his distinguished public career as a member of the West German Federal Constitutional Court.[6]

The prime minister, frequently plagued by health problems during these years, was recuperating in Ascona, Switzerland, at the time of Höpker-Aschoff's sudden resignation. He later wrote that he had been "left holding the bag" *(im Stiche gelassen)*. More important, the lack of advance notice made it impossible for the prime minister to follow his "beautiful principle" of having a successor ready. After consulting with the leaders of the coalition parties, he appointed Otto Klepper, not a particularly felicitous choice.[7]

There was no doubt about Klepper's feistiness or his commitment to the republican cause. Since his appointment in 1928 as the head of the state's largest public institution for agricultural credit, the Preussische Zentralgenossenschaftskasse (Prussian Central Bank of Agricultural Cooperatives)—or Preussenkasse as it was generally known—Klepper had become a frequent target for right-wing attacks. He agreed with those who argued that many of the large East Elbian estates were so hopelessly indebted that all efforts to salvage them with new credits were useless. Acting on this principle, the *Preussenkasse,* which held a sizable portfolio of agricultural mortgages in East Elbia, restricted credit in an effort to force owners to sell their bankrupt estates and permit their conversion into family farms. For these owners, many of them Junkers with close political ties to the antirepublican right, Klepper became the personification of Prussia's "Bolshevik agrarian policies." Of course, Klepper's appointment as minister of finance was greeted with a howl of indignation by the political right.[8]

Despite his reputation as an energetic administrator and *Herzensrepublikaner,* Klepper was not the equal of Höpker-Aschoff, having neither the fiscal experience nor the political presence of his predecessor. An indifferent public speaker, Klepper cut a poor figure in a legislature eventually dominated by jeering delegates from the extremist parties. Perhaps to compensate for his shortcomings, the new minister liked to exaggerate his personal role in the flow of events. Given to intrigues, he imagined himself at the center of things, pulling strings behind the scenes. Moreover, his appointment was of little consequence. Höpker-Aschoff had been right: by Klepper's time, the Reich government's systematic efforts to erode the financial autonomy of the states had stripped real decision-making power from the Prussian finance ministry. Prussia's chief financial officer was little more than an errand boy carrying out in the name of the state decrees issued by the Reich chancellor under the authority of the Reich president. It was not a job that satisfied the restless Klepper, particularly since his cabinet colleagues also refused to give him financial veto powers over what remained of the Prussian budget.[9]

But that is getting ahead of the story. In the spring of 1930 the effective end of the state's fiscal autonomy was neither imminent nor expected. Höpker-Aschoff was proud that since becoming finance minister in 1925 he had eliminated Prussia's chronic budget deficits, a problem since 1918. Despite Prussia's constant complaints about the unfair allocation of federal revenue sharing programs, the budgets submitted to the Landtag for the fiscal years 1925, 1926, and 1927 were balanced. The 1928 budget showed a small deficit—a consequence of the 1927 salary increases for the state's civil servants—but the cabinet and the finance minister were confident anticipated economic growth would wipe out the deficit in 1929.

The economic downturn caused by the particularly severe winter of 1928–29 ended that illusion, and by the end of the year the onset of the Depression had caused a "virtually threatening" situation, as Höpker-Aschoff put it. The 1930 budget he submitted to the Landtag showed a deficit of 88 million Reichsmarks (RM), but in internal documents Höpker-Aschoff had earlier estimated that without cuts in expenditures the deficit would run to 245 million RM. (The total state budget was 1.8 billion RM.) Still, Höpker-Aschoff remained optimistic about the future. He pointed out that Prussia's total public indebtedness was less than 10 percent of the state's gross annual product, and he was hopeful that there would be no further downturn in the economy.[10]

These economic and fiscal forecasts were of course unrealistic, and public finances at both the Reich and state levels were soon in a catastrophic state. The problems were particularly severe for the *Länder*. As noted earlier, the Weimar Republic's tax system left the states with very limited powers. The most lucrative forms of revenue, like the personal and corporate income taxes, were collected by the Reich, which returned a portion of the receipts to the states—too little, as the *Länder* never tired of complaining. Prussia (and the other states) were essentially restricted to raising or lowering indirect and consumer taxes, whose maximum rates were determined by the Reichstag. In fact, the only direct tax the states could control was a Weimar anomaly, the *Hauszinssteuer*, or building interest tax (BIT). Originally authorized by the Reichstag in 1926, the BIT demanded that owners of real property, whose assets had retained their value during the inflation years, should compensate society for their unearned good fortune. Owners of liquid property had seen their assets disappear as a result of runaway inflation. To this end, the state taxed the presumed inflation-related profits of real estate owners and used the tax receipts to finance public housing.

The BIT, always unpopular with landlords, was a political football. Led by the Economics party, the right-wing parties attacked the tax as an unfair levy on a single group of property holders, and public housing as a form of socialism. Its critics called the BIT a typical "socialist" tax that punished those who had worked hard and benefited those who had not done as well. Controversy over the BIT was particularly bitter in Prussia. The minister for social services, who administered the state's public housing program, was Heinrich Hirtsiefer, a leader of the Center party's left wing and a former Catholic union leader who sincerely believed that constructing affordable public housing was a major ethical duty of the state.

As we have seen, the Prussians were eager to blame their financial problems on the unfair distribution of federal revenues and other Reich decisions. These included not only the distribution key for federal revenue sharing, but also the Reich cabinet's handling of the perennial reparations controversy. Prussia was particularly critical of the Müller government for accepting the Young Plan, arguing that restructuring the reparation payments imposed too heavy a burden on Germany's public finances.[11] However, the state also contributed to its own difficulties. Prussia's personnel expenditures, always the largest single item in the budget, remained excessively high. Government and opposition, of course, disagreed on the causes. The cabinet pointed to legislative spending sprees, new administrative tasks mandated by federal legislation, and the expense of the 1927 salary reform. The opposition parties blamed the growth of big government after 1918. All agreed that the state needed to reduce the number of its civil servants and streamline the delivery of services, but virtually nothing was done before the Depression. During the "good" years, Prussia lived at the limits of its resources, and sometimes even beyond; in 1929 the Preussenkasse had to borrow 100 million RM from the Reich.[12] The state's personnel policies certainly had to change because of the Depression, but even then the cabinet was reluctant to take immediate and drastic action. The government waited until May 1930 to impose a hiring freeze.[13]

Prussia's fiscal policies during the Depression years were a failure on all counts. They constituted deficit spending without either the economic or political benefits of Keynesianism. Despite a flurry of cost-cutting measures (discussed below), the state was unable to balance its budget. In December 1929 Höpker-Aschoff estimated the 1930 shortfall at 88 million RM; by May 1930 it had grown to over 100 million RM. For the fiscal year 1931, the shortfall had more than doubled to 230 million RM. Höpker-Aschoff described the situation as catastrophic. But there was worse to come. Klepper's first budget presentation to the Landtag, in March 1932, included the admission that in the last four years the state budget had accumulated a deficit of 928 million RM. By the summer of 1932, receipts were barely sufficient to pay the already drastically cut civil servants' salaries. The 1932 budget showed a deficit of 511 million RM, and of this amount 100 million RM could not be covered by any effort on Prussia's part. Without help from the Reich, the state was bankrupt.[14]

The financial situation in the cities was even worse. German cities had taken advantage of the easy credit situation after 1925 and quietly accumulated municipal debts that often far exceeded their tax base. (Much of Germany's short-term foreign debt in 1930 was in the form of municipal bonds.) The loans paid for worthy expenditures—mostly improvements in the cities' social infrastructure like swimming pools, parks, and communal athletic fields—but the fiscal consequence was that during the Depression years many of Prussia's cities were unable to service their debts and had to declare bankruptcy.

The situation in the cities brought fiscal consequences for the state as well. Under Prussian law the state not only had to approve the cities' floating of bond issues, but also guaranteed the cities' debts. Hence, the municipalities' problems meant a lowered credit rating for the state and the loss of local self-government in many areas. For some of Prussia's largest cities—such as Cologne—the interior minister suspended self-government and appointed state commissioners with extraordinary powers to bring order to local finances. In March 1931 more than 500 Prussian municipalities had gone into receivership.[15]

As state and localities exhausted their own resources, they turned for support to the Reich. But the federal authorities had their own problems and agendas. For both financial and political reasons, Brüning and the other presidential chancellors saw balancing the federal budget as their top priority, particularly to maintain the trust of potential foreign investors. This was the financial justification. Politically, all presidential chancellors wanted to use the financial problems of the *Länder*, and especially Prussia's, to reduce the German states' autonomy. In other words, Brüning and his successors deliberately exploited the fiscal crisis to change the balance of power in favor of the Reich.[16]

Pressure from the Reich as well as the state's financial problems severely strained parliamentary democracy within the state. The parliamentary budget approval process broke down; the 1931 budget was the last to be approved in plenary session by the Landtag. Subsequent budget bills could not muster a quorum in the legislature because both the opposition parties and some backbenchers among the coalition parties refused to attend the Landtag sessions, protesting the government's budget-cutting policies. In mid-July 1932, less than a week before the Reich Government took control of the state, for the first and only time the Prussian cabinet was even forced to use its authority under the *Dietramszeller Notverordnung* to provide the state with a budget.[17]

Although the crisis increasingly strained the solidarity of the Weimar coalition parties in Prussia, party leaders remained firm in their support of long-term cooperation. In contrast to the situation in the Reich, for more than two years the leaders of the Weimar coalition parties resisted pressures from constituent groups within the parties that would have led to the breakup of the Prussian partnership. Parliamentary democracy in Prussia was destroyed by forces outside of parliament; the system itself did not commit political suicide.

Prussian leaders showed considerable strength of purpose in maintaining their coalition in the face of mounting fiscal and political pressures, but they failed to use this successful political cohesion to develop imaginative, realistic solutions to economic and social problems. Maintaining the coalition became an end in itself. Like their counterparts in the Reich, Prussian leaders ignored the few voices who warned that it was more important to look at the political consequences than at the fiscal causes of the crisis.[18]

Instead, the state implemented orthodox, monetarist policies. Reducing the salaries of state civil servants constituted Prussia's first and foremost weapon in the battle to cut the budget. Matching similar cuts in the Reich, the salaries of Prussia's civil servants, the largest single item in the state's budget, were reduced by more than one-third between 1930 and 1932. Arnold Brecht, the state's chief *Reichsrat* delegate, noted with a sort of perverse pride that in terms of percentages the Prussian budget cuts in personnel costs went even further than those of the Reich. Unfortunately, such fiscal soundness was politically counterproductive. Fiscal conservatism eroded the civil servants' loyalty to political democracy. There was no doubt that the cuts were unpopular. Unable to obtain a majority in the Landtag, the cabinet had to use its decree-invoking authority to implement necessary legislation. Across-the-board cuts also significantly reduced their standard of living, making civil servants easy prey for extremist propaganda, notably from the Nazis.[19]

Much like Brüning (or for that matter Herbert Hoover), Prussia's political leaders had no real appreciation of the depth and severity of the Depression. They expected that each new budget cut or tax adjustment would, finally, achieve a balanced budget. Since cuts were not enough, Prussia, again following the Reich's lead, reallocated tax revenues and eventually raised taxes. Almost inevitably, one of the first revenue reallocations was a decision to use the proceeds of the BIT, specifically earmarked for public housing construction, for general revenue purposes. Again, the move made fiscal sense: it helped fill a large hole in the state budget without actually raising taxes. However, this step destroyed what might have become a significant pump-priming device—subsidies for the construction industry to soften the impact of the Depression. In addition, it alienated the primary beneficiaries of public housing, which included a large block of supporters of two major Weimar coalition parties, the SPD and the Center party. The importance attached by the parties' rank and file to the public housing issue can be gauged from Hirtsiefer's passionate objection to diverting the BIT to the general budget, and from a resolution adopted at the 1925 SPD party congress specifically opposing the use of the building interest tax for general revenue purposes.[20]

Needless to say, neither massive salary cuts nor reassigning the interest tax for general expenditures were sufficient. To continue their deflationary policies, both the Reich and Prussia raised taxes. In Prussia these came in the form of indirect and consumer levies, since Prussia had no constitutional authority to impose new direct levies. In addition, Höpker-Aschoff fully agreed with his Reich colleague, Paul Moldenhauer, that the key to economic recovery lay in reducing direct taxes on individuals and especially businesses.[21]

In retrospect, the policy of increasing indirect and particularly consumer taxes in the midst of the Depression was clearly procyclical. Such levies reduced demand and consequently hampered commercial and business activity even further. Prussian tax increases were all retrogressive and nuisance taxes. The state increased the property tax by 100 percent (a measure that further depressed the housing market), and raised the levies on local commerce and trade *(Gewerbesteuer)*. There were also higher taxes on beer and soft drinks. A particularly onerous revenue for psychological reasons was a head tax *(Bürgersteuer)* imposed upon everyone regardless of income. Finally, in the summer of 1932 Prussia levied an animal slaughter tax *(Schlachtsteuer)*, which angered both consumers and producers: it increased the cost of meat and reduced meat consumption. This last tax, it must be noted, was something of a desperation effort to avoid declaring bankruptcy and thereby give the Reich an excuse to take the Prussian government into federal receivership.[22]

Reich and state agreed on fiscal aims, but they differed on how to implement them. Brüning preferred to use the president's decree powers and seldom consulted with the Reichstag and its committees. The Prussian government, on the other hand, attempting to uphold the spirit of parliamentary democracy as long as possible, sought the Landtag's approval for its fiscal policies. Even after the *Dietramszeller Notverordnung* authorized the state government to issue decrees with the force of law, the cabinet usually presented its fiscal measures for legislative approval. Only when the Landtag with increasing frequency failed to muster a quorum did the government begin to resort to the DNV.[23]

Although leaders like Otto Braun and Heinrich Hirtsiefer recognized better than Brüning the sociopolitical consequences of the chancellor's deflationary course, Germany's largest state was very reluctant to criticize the Reich's fiscal policies. Prussia consistently argued against further cuts in unemployment compensation or in civil servants' salaries, but not until far too late did Prussia endorse a public works program that involved deficit financing or a major shift of priorities in the Reich budget. When the federal budget came before the Reichsrat, Prussia's delegates objected mildly to the Reich's defense outlays, but did not challenge such fundamental economic decisions as the Reich's excessive agricultural tariffs or question the subsidies paid to the farmers of East Elbia. Not until April 1932 did the Prussian cabinet urge that the Reich institute a massive jobs program for the 6 million unemployed. However, even then the demand was not actually sent, presumably because Otto Braun decided it would create further difficulties for Brüning when the chancellor was already in deep political trouble.[24]

On the other hand, there was much criticism of the grapeshot approach to fiscal policy. Within their own areas of responsibility, the cabinet members bitterly resented the state's fiscal measures. Höpker-Aschoff recognized that using the building interest tax for general revenue purposes would hurt the housing industry, but insisted that there was no alternative. The minister of commerce refused to support the slaughter tax and the minister of the interior opposed salary cuts for civil servants, but neither was willing to risk a cabinet crisis to press his point. Prussia's leaders argued that the state's fiscal woes would be solved only by a thorough reform of the system of federal-state revenue sharing and an upturn in the economy. Until then, the state's government had to bow before the altar of fiscal orthodoxy. Neither the cabinet nor the coalition parties realized that it was precisely the policy of fiscal orthodoxy that undermined confidence in the democratic system. The "rock of democracy" was being eroded by the waves of discontent created by fiscal fatalism.[25]

Prussia's leaders avoided the political consequences of their disastrous fiscal policies for as long as they did because the opposition offered no alternatives. The left- and right-wing opposition parties criticized deficits, taxes, and the government's failure to alleviate economic problems with equal inconsistency and vehemence. For the German Nationalists and the Nazis, the culprit was parliamentary democracy; for the Communists it was capitalism. Only the final demise of the "system" would end the country's political and economic crisis.

Prussia's Attempt to Deal with the Depression, 1930–1932

More than forty years after one of the worst disasters in Western history, the debate about the causes and consequences of the great Depression has not ended. Economists and historians have illuminated many aspects of the disaster, and we now realize that the Reich and Prussian leaders concentrated far too long on the fiscal dimensions of the Depression because they feared a return of the hyperinflation of the early 1920s.

While fixated on the imaginary dangers of countercyclical measures, Germany's leaders clearly could not ignore the social consequences of the Depression. For some groups, such as the members of the old *Mittelstand* and farmers, the Depression compounded difficulties caused earlier by hyperinflation. As a result, their problems assumed greater importance, until quite late in the Depression, than the relatively new problem of mass blue-collar and white-collar unemployment. It was assumed that the rationalization procedures of the mid-1920s and the revival of world trade had solved the major structural problems in industry and manufacturing. Symptomatic of this thinking were the actuarial projections on which contributions to the national unemployment insurance were based. The system could support no more than 800,000 unemployed in any given year; however, the average number for 1928 was 1.3 million, and by February 1929 the number had risen to 3.2 million.[26]

Nevertheless, the concerns for agriculture were warranted. While the acute problems of industry and commerce seemed to emerge with a sudden fury following the New York stock market crash of October 1929, the difficulties of German farmers had been obvious for years. In Prussia the crisis was the subject of increasingly bitter Landtag debates. Although the problem was general, East Elbian agriculture in particular was too inefficient to compete with imports from areas such as the United States, Canada, and Argentina. However, few analysts and spokesmen for farm groups acknowledged this fundamental structural difficulty. They pointed instead to agricultural credit problems, reparations, and the Versailles Treaty that (until 1925) had banned agricultural tariffs. As remedies they called for an end to reparations, massive infusions of cheap credit, and protective tariffs.[27]

As agricultural prices declined precipitously, the farmers' political disaffection increased. They used various means of political activism to publicize their plight as they struggled desperately against mortgage foreclosures and falling prices. In East Elbia and Schleswig-Holstein, violent protests were on the increase. Led by charismatic agitators, farmers set fire to buildings holding tax records or forcibly prevented auctions of foreclosed farm property. Farmers' organizations, like the Landbund, aligned themselves even more closely with antirepublican opposition parties. At first the main beneficiaries were Alfred Hugenberg and the DNVP, but after 1929 the largest traditional farm organizations were increasingly headed by officials sympathetic to the Nazis.[28]

Discontent among the old *Mittelstand* was also expressed in political radicalization, although more peacefully. It is no longer argued that the old *Mittelstand* bear primary responsibility for bringing the Nazis to power, but the majority of *Mittelstand* voters did desert the moderate parties for a variety of radical, antirepublican groups that promised quick panaceas for the *Mittelstand's* economic problems, finally turning to the Nazis.[29]

But all was not well in the industrial sector, either. As employers forced the pace of rationalization measures after the currency stabilization, relations between management and labor became increasingly polarized. Collective bargaining agreements became more difficult to negotiate, and strikes increased. In the fall of 1928 a massive lockout in the Ruhr steel industry embittered labor-management relations for months. Even before the Depression, then, tension in the industrial sector was high.[30]

In defending fiscal responsibility, the federal authorities routinely argued as long as Germany had to pay reparations, any activist policy would be inflationary. Such arguments served the neoconservatives' economic and political agenda well, but the SPD's cooperation with such faulty reasoning and ineffective policies is more surprising. After all, the Social Democrats were not only ideologically committed to state intervention in the economic process, but also had been the main force behind the *soziale Volkstaat* (social welfare state), that net of social services and public insurance schemes that remains one of the Weimar Republic's most lasting legacies. Nevertheless, for different reasons the economic experts in the SPD's national leadership believed that short-run interventionism had no future. They not only accepted the reparations argument, but also contended that while socialism would eventually require profound structural changes in the economy, until capitalism had lost its grip, little could be done to change the situation.[31]

To their credit, Prussia's leaders were not content to simply wait for the arrival of socialism. The clear evidence of social destabilization persuaded them that something had to be done. Yet their fiscal orthodoxy placed them between the Scylla of political discontent and the imagined Charybdis of renewed inflation. Otto Braun expressed this dilemma in addressing the national convention of the Socialist unions (ADGB) in April 1932: "We can't continue to live with six million unemployed," but he also warned against opening the floodgates of inflation.[32]

Although constrained by fiscal orthodoxy, the leaders of the Prussian Weimar coalition parties were willing to intervene to prevent further social destabilization. However, they disagreed on a fundamental question: was political stability the prerequisite for economic recovery, or was concern for those most severely affected by the Depression the key to preserving democracy? If the first were true, as Ernst Heilmann argued, it was important to maintain the coalition and to preserve law and order in the face of the destabilizing efforts by the Nazis and other political extremists. If, on the other hand, reducing the misery index would preserve the democratic consensus, the state should concentrate on supporting countercyclical measures and making sure that the already frayed social net did not deteriorate further. Prussia's contradictory policies ultimately failed. The government vacillated between preserving order and well-meaning, but unsuccessful attempts to intervene on behalf of those most seriously affected by the Depression.[33]

In Prussia, a long tradition of public paternalism went back to the time of enlightened despotism. This tradition, now coupled with the republic's social welfare programs, mostly took the form of reemphasizing the state's role as economic arbiter and watchdog. For example, in the face of employers' efforts to cut production costs by whatever means, the government vigorously enforced safety rules and prohibited pricing cartels.[34]

But such activities failed to restimulate business activity. Here the government's insistence on a balanced budget was an insurmountable barrier. The public works programs the cabinet discussed were poorly worked out, superficial public relations efforts. The state did not even attempt to use its many state-owned enterprises, primarily in mining and utilities, to create jobs. Prussia's interventionist policies were minimal. The state attempted to persuade the Reich to maintain the postrevolutionary social net, but beyond that Prussia followed the principle that activism had to be "fiscally responsible." This was a fatal error. For the average German the foremost symbol of the crisis was the seemingly infinite number of unemployed. Here, above all, the federal and state governments should be active. Failure to address unemployment seemed to be the Weimar Republic's most glaring failure.[35]

According to Brüning, foreign policy considerations took precedence over unemployment.[36] The Prussian leaders did not share the chancellor's priorities, but their attitude toward the growing army of unemployed Germans was curiously ambivalent and a little dishonest. True, as early as November 1929 unemployment was identified as a major cause of political unrest. In the war of memoirs about the end of the Weimar Republic, Otto Braun later claimed that he repeatedly and publicly decried the massive unemployment problem. But Braun's proposals were vague and predicated on impossible preconditions, such as suggesting that private foreign investment should finance public works programs. Similarly, the Prussian government, despite its trumpeted concern about unemployed, did little to back the so-called WTB-Plan, the only full-scale public works program developed by the Socialist unions during the Depression. In effect, Prussia's attitude on interventionist, countercyclical measures was essentially the same as Brüning's: the problem was real, but the available cures would make matters worse.[37]

Prussia attacked the social disasters caused by the Depression with more vigor, recognizing the close connection between destitution and political radicalism. Several times since the revolution of 1918 an upswing in political radicalism could be linked to intolerable social conditions. In the past, Prussia had also not been afraid to go against the Reich to alleviate obvious social injustices, particularly during the bitter labor dispute in the iron and steel industry in 1928.

Unable to agree on a new national contract, employers had used a nation-wide lockout to force workers to accept their terms.[38] The Prussian government was not concerned about the agreement itself—arbitration was the Reich's responsibility—but it took immediate and vigorous action to help the locked-out workers. Led by the prime minister and the welfare minister, Heinrich Hirtsiefer, the state cabinet determined that Prussian locked-out workers (the overwhelming majority) were unemployed and thus entitled to unemployment benefits. Employers fumed at what they regarded as Prussia's deliberate intervention on the unions' side.

However, the ministers were not taking sides in a labor dispute, but seeking to forestall political radicalization among socially desperate men and women. Specifically, the government was afraid Socialist and Catholic union members, the political backbone of Prussia's SPD and the Center party's left wings, might turn to the KPD. The activities of the Communist "Red Army" in the Ruhr area in 1920 gave ample reason for such concern, and it was no secret that in 1928 the Communists were again campaigning strenuously among the metalworkers.[39]

The iron and steel industry conflict was eventually settled, and it would seem that Prussia would repeat its activist tactics to alleviate the social distress caused by unemployment during the Great Depression. After all, workers were again suffering through no fault of the own. Public statements seemed to support this view. In October, 1931 Severing noted that helping welfare recipients to survive the next few weeks was "the *one* [sic] problem that needs to be solved."[40]

But the solutions that had worked in 1928 were now inadequate. In 1928 there had been money to continue social services, now there was not. Confronting mounting budget deficits on the one hand and vast social misery on the other, the coalition parties pursued contradictory priorities. Their differing proposals for increases in the 1931 welfare budget was symptomatic of the widely divergent approaches to the social problems. The Center party proposed increases of 965,000 RM, the SPD 11.5 million RM.[41]

Following a pattern apparent since 1929, the coalition party leaders determined that preserving the coalition was more important than taking action. In 1930, although Otto Braun was distressed to see the Reich's grand coalition heading for disaster, he refused to accede to Hermann Müller's request to use the state's influence to help keep the Reich coalition in office. He decided that the cohesion of his own government was more important than preventing the fall of the Müller cabinet.[42] That decision set the tone for the crisis years.

Faced with intracoalition disagreements on social policies, the cabinet took extraordinary care to prevent leaks to the press about cabinet or intraparty disagreements,[43] and hid behind the overriding concern for fiscal solvency.

The Prussians became determined minimalists. Typical was Braun's statement in May 1932, in the depths of the crisis, that because of growing budget deficits social services would have to be further reduced. Joseph Hess had seen the light even earlier. Brüning, who was no admirer of the Prussian Catholic leader, noted that at the end of 1931 Hess had recognized the errors of fiscal irresponsibility, and backed without reservation even Brüning's most unpopular fiscal measures. Actually, Hess's top priority was not support for Brüning, but maintaining the Prussian coalition—for both Braun and Hess an end in itself. The Prussian leaders succeeded in realizing their major goal, but it was a Pyrrhic victory.[44]

Even more than social policies, the state's agricultural problems were a political minefield. Agricultural interest groups had their spokesmen both in the coalition parties and in the opposition groups. The Social Democrats and the Center party's left wing formed a rather coherent consumer bloc, but the Center party also had a powerful farmers' wing that was sharply opposed to the Social Democrats' consumerism. The Catholic farmers' lobby shared many points of view with the German Nationalists, and the latter was traditionally closely linked to the largest German farmers' organization, the Landbund. Finally, the agricultural problems of East Elbia, and notably those of East Prussia and Posen-Grenzmark, formed part of the ethnic conflict in the east. Virtually all of Prussia's politicians claimed to protect the interests of ethnic Germans in these border areas against the Poles—whatever the cost.

Prussia's agricultural problems originated in longstanding structural difficulties that had been aggravated by the worldwide agricultural depression since the mid-1920s. Earlier attempts at far-reaching structural reforms had failed. This was particularly true for the controversial idea to "secure the German East," the so-called settlement policy *(Siedlungspolitik)*, a term covering various schemes designed to increase the number of family farms in East Elbia. The land to be settled was uncultivated, mostly state-owned property, and some of the debt-ridden, largely Junker-owned latifundia. Not surprisingly, the idea was immediately and passionately opposed by the large landowners, who labeled any settlement policy the "Bolshevization" of East Elbia. Little land had been turned over by 1930, but the controversy flared up again during the Depression since the head of the Preussenkasse (and later minister of finance), Otto Klepper, was known to be an enthusiastic supporter of the settlement policy.

Agricultural interest groups saw two policies they had advocated as panaceas since the 1890s, protective tariffs and easy credit, as the only remedies for the farmers' difficulties. Their lobby placed especially unrealistic hopes in

tariffs as a form of short-term relief because the Treaty of Versailles had prohibited protective tariffs against goods imported from Allied countries before
January 1, 1925. In practice, this meant that Germany could not impose levies
against any nation, since under the most favored nation principle, the best terms
of trade offered to one nation had to apply to all of Germany's trading partners.

Then as now Germany's prosperity depended primarily on exports of
manufactured goods, so the enforced low tariff structure actually benefited the
economy as a whole, but spokesmen for agriculture insisted that it had ruined
Germany's farmers. These arguments, exploiting the widespread resentment
against the Treaty of Versailles, ignored the fact that tariffs had done little to
help German farmers before World War I, and as a postwar instrument of
national policy, agricultural tariffs made even less sense. In the 1920s the
balance of the German economy had shifted significantly in favor of industry.
A wall of protective tariffs would not only result in retaliatory measures by
foreign countries against German industrial goods, but would also dramatically increase labor costs by raising the cost of basic foodstuffs. Inevitably,
then, the agricultural tariff issue sharply polarized the German political spectrum. The Social Democrats and the left wing of the Center party, as well as
the spokesmen for export-oriented industries allied to the DDP and the DVP,
argued against them. The German Nationalists, the Center party's right wing,
parts of the DVP, and the Nazis took the side of the farmers.[45]

Because most of Germany's farmers lived in Prussia, the Reich's agricultural problems were of direct concern to the state. Generally speaking, the
cabinet, reflecting the left-of-center orientation of the Weimar coalition parties, was less sympathetic to the farm lobbies' demands than was the Reich
government. Cabinet members disagreed on agricultural policies, but on institutional rather than ideological and political grounds. The minister of commerce sided with the interests of industry and urban consumers against the
minister of agriculture. The coalition parties were similarly divided. The SPD
and the DDP, for example, were sharply critical of the right wing of the
Center party, in which western agricultural interests, especially the powerful
wine-making lobby, were influential. As always, the leaders of all the coalition parties placed harmony within the coalition above all else.[46]

Negotiating international trade pacts was the Reich's responsibility, but
Prussia was directly involved in the ratification process since under the
Weimar constitution international treaties had to be ratified by both houses of
the national legislature. The first of the new trade agreements negotiated after
Germany regained its tariff autonomy was a 1925 commercial treaty with
Spain. Setting a precedent, the treaty raised all the vexing issues that continued to confront Germany's trade negotiators. Spain was a virtually under-
developed country that promised to become a major market for German
industrial goods, but Spain's primary export to Germany was an agricultural

product, cheap wine. The result was a clash between the Reich's industrial interests, who wanted a low tariff treaty to facilitate their exports, and the West German vineyard owners along the Rhine and Mosel—political allies of the Center party—who demanded tariff protection against the import of Spanish wine.

The Reich cabinet, at the time dominated by the DNVP and the Center party's right wing, yielded to the winemakers' protests and negotiated a stiff tariff against Spanish wine imports as part of the commercial treaty. Prussia took the side of consumers and the industrial interests, and introduced amendments designed to lower the wine tariff when the treaty came before the Reichsrat for ratification. For public consumption the full cabinet favored the amendments, but the ministers of agriculture and welfare, both from the Center party, had abstained during the cabinet vote. However, neither minister pressed his objections to the point of creating a cabinet crisis.

Prussia lost this round. In the Reichsrat the Prussian amendments were easily defeated by an alliance of the delegates from the Prussia's agricultural provinces and representatives from the southern and western *Länder*. Except for the delegate from Berlin, the Prussian provincial delegates voted for the draft treaty as presented by the Reich and against the amendments. Nevertheless, the battle over the Spanish treaty demonstrated yet again that at the state level the Weimar coalition functioned well even in the face of extraordinary pressures from its constituent members.[47]

Agricultural tariffs on pork were a controversial part of a 1928 trade treaty with Poland. East Elbian farmers regarded Polish pork as unfair competition for their own products. Under pressure from the SPD, now the largest party in the federal coalition, the draft treaty negotiated by the Reich government contained low tariffs on Polish agricultural products.

Lead by the DNVP and the Center party, the Prussian Landtag passed a resolution instructing the cabinet to oppose the treaty when it came before the Reichsrat. But, in firm support of consumers' interests, the cabinet voted to support the Reich's draft treaty. Once again the Center party would not sacrifice the coalition to the tariff question. Center party leaders hastened to assure the cabinet that their joint vote with the German Nationalists in the Landtag was not intended as a vote of no confidence in the Prussian cabinet. Various other commercial treaties that came before the Reichsrat evoked similar reactions. Even while appeasing special interest groups, the Prussian coalition parties made sure that tariff issues did not endanger the cohesion of the state's governing coalition.[48]

The issue of direct aid to agriculture was even more controversial than agricultural tariffs. All agreed that aid of some sort was required, and that the need was greatest in East Elbia. All blamed the Treaty of Versailles for whatever problems existed, an unwarranted but politically popular view. But here the consensus ended. Fierce debates raged as to whether aid programs should be earmarked for East Elbia as a region, or targeted to the farmers within that area. Nor were all parts of East Elbia equal. Spokesmen for East Prussia, including its longtime governor, Otto Siehr, argued that since it was cut off from the rest of Germany by the Polish Corridor, East Prussia was particularly disadvantaged and therefore entitled to the lion's share of any *Osthilfe*. The other provinces in the region pointed out, however, that their structural problems were no less severe, and eventually the border areas of western Germany discovered that they, too, labored under extraordinary difficulties.[49]

The Conservatives and their allies in the farmers' lobbies contended that the solution to the difficulties in the east lay in helping East Elbia's farmers. The *Osthilfe* should therefore provide help directly to them. Financial aid in the form of cheap credit should be provided by the Reich and state governments, but the farmers' organizations insisted they were best qualified to determine who should receive the aid.[50]

The Junkers' thesis that agricultural problems could be solved by credit and tariffs was sharply contested by a number of less partisan experts. Prominent among them was Otto Klepper, from 1928 until his appointment as Prussian finance minister in 1931 the president of the Preussenkasse. Klepper contended that data gathered by his bank's field offices revealed no general crisis in the east, but that problems were concentrated in certain areas and specific types of agricultural holdings. Klepper showed that the debt problem was far less severe for medium-sized farms (less than 400 hectares) than for large estates. Smaller farms with diversified products, worked by family members and a few hired hands, were generally in much better shape than the large estates specializing in a single crop and worked by migrant labor. The president of the Preussenkasse also suggested that the major reason for the debt problem was not the worldwide fall of prices (although this was certainly a contributing factor), but the massive land speculation by many Junkers during the good years of 1924 to 1926.

Klepper rejected blanket subsidies and proposed a much cheaper aid program limited to those who demonstrated convincingly that a loan could save their property. For Klepper and his allies, the solution to the agricultural crisis was to foreclose a large number of estates and divide them into medium-sized family farms—in other words, a form of *Siedlungspolitik*. In essence, Klepper argued, the Junkers and their estates were the problem, not the solution to the crisis; therefore, Prussian authorities had no intention of letting the farmers' organizations in East Elbia, dominated by large estate owners, control the distribution of aid. They were increasingly convinced that East Elbian agriculture required massive restructuring, and that a credit policy should accomplish this purpose.[51] The leaders of the Prussian coalition parties also insisted that while farming formed the backbone of the East Elbian economy, the region's problems were not limited to a single economic group, but involved the entire economic infrastructure. The battle lines were drawn: on one side the Prussian banking experts, on the other the Junkers, represented by their lobbying groups, the Agrarian League, and the DNVP.[52]

The *Osthilfe* occasioned fierce battles, but it was much ado about relatively little. The aid program remained a rather modest effort. Between 1920 and 1930 perhaps 100 million RM was allocated for the East Elbian aid program. Nor was there much difficulty about its administration. Most of the money came from the Reich (24 million RM in 1926), but its distribution was handled by Prussian officials, and they treated the *Osthilfe* as a regional aid program. Although the bulk of the money did go to the farmers, some was spent on improving the overall infrastructure.[53]

Until 1927 the federal role in the *Osthilfe* was quite limited. The situation began to change with the appointment of Martin Schiele, a German Nationalist and former head of the Landbund as Reich minister of the interior. As self-appointed cabinet spokesman for the East Elbian agricultural lobby, Schiele proposed a vast expansion of the annual *Osthilfe* budget to 500 million RM. Schiele also complained that the Prussian administration of the *Osthilfe* was insensitive to the needs of the East Elbian farmers, and called on the Reich government to take a more direct role in its administration.

Schiele's efforts came to little. He succeeded in establishing an office for East Prussia in his ministry as a bridgehead for a future federal administration of the *Osthilfe*, but since he left office after a few months, the new agency (which Prussia had opposed) remained stillborn. But Schiele left a more lasting legacy. He persuaded Reich president von Hindenburg—a Junker, an East Prussian, and shortly to become a large estate owner—to become involved in the controversy. Presiding at a meeting of Reich and Prussian ministers in December 1927, Hindenburg took the side of the farmers. The Prussian cabinet defended its point of view, and the meeting ended inconclusively, but the stage was set for future confrontations.[54]

Beginning in 1928, discussions between the east Elbian farmers' organizations, the Reich cabinet, and the Prussian government over the future of the *Osthilfe* became increasingly acrimonious. The debt burden of East Elbian farmers rose alarmingly; their spokesmen, vigorously supported by Hugenberg's DNVP, clamored for more government credit and tax relief to prevent mass foreclosures resulting from mortgage defaults. They also demanded that the agricultural cooperatives (dominated, as we have seen, by the Junkers) should control the activities of the Preussenkasse. The pleas were addressed primarily to President von Hindenburg and the Reich government. But the Junkers were in an impossible situation. In the winter of 1928–29 the Reich cabinet developed serious cash flow problems, foreshadowing the fiscal disasters ahead. At about the same time, Klepper intensified Prussia's efforts to use the *Osthilfe* to bring about what he regarded as long overdue structural changes in East Elbia. To avoid throwing good money after bad, the Preussenkasse would loan money to small farms and relatively debt-free large estates, in while refusing credit to many hopelessly indebted Junker estates.[55]

When Heinrich Brüning took office as Reich chancellor, there was little agreement on either the past or the future course of the *Osthilfe*. The East Elbian Junkers claimed that it had been vastly underfunded and had done little to help the farmers. The Prussian government, on the other hand, pointed with pride to improvements in the overall infrastructure of the east. All sides agreed that only the Reich, not Prussia, could provide the funds necessary to make the *Osthilfe* more effective. And the political stakes were becoming higher; Nazi influence among the German farmers grew rapidly after the onset of the Depression.[56]

Initially, Brüning had no clear ideas about the future of the *Osthilfe*. As a Westphalian, a Catholic labor union functionary, and chairman of the Reichstag's Ways and Means Committee, he had never taken much interest in the problems of East Elbia. But the *Osthilfe* issue was politically volatile. To appease the political right, he appointed Martin Schiele, the former interior minister and powerful champion of the Landbund, minister of agriculture in his first cabinet. Before becoming Reich chancellor, Brüning also promised the Reich president and his entourage that the new cabinet would pay more attention to the complaints of large estate owners in East Elbia, and that his government would take steps to reduce Prussia's administrative control of the aid program.[57]

Still, for some time after becoming chancellor, Brüning did little to change the *Osthilfe*. Deficit spending in any form, even to aid Hindenburg's friends, ran counter to the chancellor's fiscal conservatism. In addition, Brüning soon recognized that Prussia's policy of not extending credit to hopelessly indebted estates was the only fiscally sound way of administering the program.[58] But that did not solve the chancellor's political problems. When the Junker estate owners and their political allies realized that Brüning was not going to change the *Osthilfe*, he became the target of venomous criticism.

Nevertheless, the Junkers continued to concentrate their attacks on the Prussian officials responsible for administering the *Osthilfe:* Klepper, Hans Krüger, the state secretary in the ministry of agriculture and the coauthor of the SPD's 1927 agricultural program, and Franz Rönneburg, head of the ministry's field office in Königsberg. Rönneburg's position was particularly pivotal, since all applications for credit from East Prussian landowners had to pass through his office for evaluation and approval. (Minister of Agriculture Steiger did not play a major role in the politics of the *Osthilfe*.)

The chancellor, aware of Hindenburg's sympathies, was determined to appease the Landbund and its allies in the DNVP by forcing Prussia out of the *Osthilfe* program. Using the Reich's strong financial lever, the federal cabinet relieved Prussia of formal responsibility and placed the aid program under a special Reich commissioner. But the change was more cosmetic than real. The first Reich commissioner, Brüning's friend, Gottfried Treviranus, left the field administration pretty much in the hands of the old Prussian administrators, although they now acted in the name of the Reich. Especially Franz Rönneburg retained a dominant position as chief of staff in the Reich office for the *Osthilfe* and federal commissioner for East Prussia, Prussia fully expected a continuation of the state's efforts to advance the controversial rural settlement program, and even earmarked a portion of the BIT for loans to new settlers.[59]

In October 1931, Brüning reshuffled his cabinet, and Treviranus became Reich minister without portfolio. He was succeeded as *Osthilfe* commissioner by Franz von Schlange-Schöningen, a quintessential Junker who had been a prominent DNVP member of the Landtag and longtime chairman of the party's provincial organization in Pommerania. But by 1931 Schlange-Schöningen was neither a political reactionary nor very sympathetic to the plight of his fellow Junkers. As we saw earlier, he left the DNVP in protest over Hugenberg's pro-Nazi line, and despite hard times Schlange-Schöningen had been able to manage his own estates at a profit.

At the end of 1931, when Schlange-Schöningen took over, the *Osthilfe* was in a deep crisis, but its failures were no longer Prussia's responsibility. Shortly before, Prussia had transferred control of the Bank for Rural Settlement (Siedlungsbank) to the Reich in return for RM 100,000,000 in cash. Two months later Schlange-Schöningen insisted that all provincial offices be subordinated to the Reich office and that Prussia give up its traditional power to veto Reich directives in this policy area. By 1932 control of all agricultural credit measures rested in the hands of the Reich government.[60]

Brüning had won the *Osthilfe* battle, but it was a hollow triumph. Although the newly established Reich administration spent additional millions on the *Osthilfe* (much of it, Prussian critics claimed, wasted on unnecessary administrative costs and bankrupt estates), the program neither solved East Elbia's problems nor satisfied the Junkers and their allies, who claimed that the spirit of former Prussian officials continued to permeate its administration. Like Klepper and Rönneburg, Schlange-Schöningen soon became a hated symbol of Prussia's continuing influence. Junker opposition to Schlange-Schöningen became one of the factors that alienated Hindenburg from Brüning, a development that eventually led to the chancellor's fall in the spring of 1932.[61]

Brüning was also unsuccessful in forging a permanent alliance of industrial and agricultural interests. One of the chancellor's enthusiastic supporters, Paul Silverberg, a leading Ruhr entrepreneur, proposed in 1931 that a number of industrialists provide funds for a new bank, the Bank for Industrial Obligations (Bank für Industrieobligationen), whose sole purpose would be to help underwrite credit for eastern agriculture. The expected political benefits were obvious: industrialists would be able to form an alliance with the rural Conservatives that, much like the *Sammlungspolitik* during the Wilhelminian years, would exclude the Social Democrats permanently from political power in Germany. But while the industrialists were willing to help some Junkers keep their property, as businessmen they were as opposed as any Prussian civil servant to granting further credit for obviously mismanaged property. In addition, the Junkers were not content with monetary subsidies; as noted above, they also demanded prohibitive tariffs on agricultural imports. That policy, however, created a direct conflict of interest between the export-oriented industrialists and the domestic market–oriented Junkers.[62]

Prussia was unfairly blamed for the *Osthilfe's* failures, but in other respects the state's record in dealing with the socioeconomic effects of the Depression was poor. While they understood the political consequences of the Depression, the state's leaders essentially accepted the orthodox economic arguments that put monetary stability ahead of all other considerations. Even more disappointing was their unwillingness to use the strength of their intact political system to implement those policies which they did recognize to be necessary. Time after time, the leaders of the Weimar coalition parties in Prussia—and that included the prime minister—abandoned interventionist measures without a struggle rather than oppose some of the Reich's most disastrous social and economic policies. In effect, coalition harmony became not a means to achieve policy goals, but an end in itself. As a result, Prussia increasingly had to use police and security measures to combat the symptoms of the crisis, rather than relying on social and economic policies to soften the Depression's impact.

Prussian Crisis Management at the End of the Weimar Era: Personnel Appointments and Security Matters

The state's republican leaders recognized that the most visible symptoms of the breakdown of consensual politics were the bands of political extremists hoping to further their aims by attacking each other in Prussia's cities and villages. To combat this acute danger the state needed above all reliable territorial administrators and an effective and loyal police. Prussia's leaders were economic and fiscal minimalists, but in administration and security matters they pursued more activist policies.

The importance of Prussia's personnel and security policies was also obvious to the opposition parties. In strident tones the DNVP and the Nazis claimed that under the rule of the "Marxists" party membership in one of the coalition parties rather than professional competence determined appointments to the senior ranks of the state's civil service. Count von Garnier-Turawa, the DNVP's spokesman on security affairs, saw a link between the state's "failed" *Innenpolitik* and parliamentary democracy. He demanded "men, or, even better *one man* [*sic*] at the head of the government who placed the good of the state [*Staatswohl*] . . . above party interests and a specific constitutional form of government."[63] On the other side, the Communists raised their perennial cry that under republican administrations Prussia's civil servants and police forces remained lackeys of the capitalists and Junkers.

During the crisis years, administering Prussia's provinces and maintaining law and order required strong nerves and considerable political acumen. When security problems first became acute, the head of the state's territorial administration was the hapless Hermann Waentig. Although a disappointment in many respects, Waentig did attempt to do something about the crisis of law and order before it became uncontrollable. In March 1930, just after Brüning was named Reich chancellor, the Prussian government replaced a number of governors and district directors in politically sensitive areas. The new men, all prominent and public supporters of parliamentary democracy, had still been recommended by Grzesinski, but Waentig agreed that they would strengthen the territorial civil service in the face of challenges by political extremists.

The cabinet named three new governors (a quarter of the total) and six new district directors in areas where either the Nazis or the Communists had recently scored notable gains. August Haas, a longtime Social Democratic union functionary and member of the Landtag, became governor of Hessen-Nassau; von Halfern, a member of the DVP, but a loyal supporter of the republic, was appointed governor of Pommerania, long a stronghold of the German Nationalists; and Falck, another prominent SPD leader, went to Saxony. Simultaneously, a number of new district directors were sent to the same provinces. Thus, Hans Simons, who later had a distinguished career as vice president of the New School for Social Research in New York, became district director of Stettin (Pommerania), while Weber was appointed to the same position in Magdeburg (Saxony). Additional district director appointments followed in April and May.[64]

In a parallel move, the cabinet took steps to prevent the infiltration of the state's civil service by political extremists. This campaign culminated in a June 1930 decree prohibiting the appointment of NSDAP and KPD members to the Prussian civil service. The decree also forbade incumbent Prussian civil servants from joining or actively supporting these political parties. Communists and Nazis, aided by the DNVP, venomously attacked the measures, but the state's disciplinary court (Disziplinarhof) upheld the constitutionality.[65]

But active enforcement of the decree was difficult. Waentig made a good start by dismissing three county commissioners in the province of Hanover who as members of the provincial diet had voted for a Nazi-sponsored resolution against the governor, but when he left office a few months later, it fell to Carl Severing to put additional teeth into the document. Severing's record was unimpressive. Only a few weeks after the decree had been issued, prohibitions against Nazis and Communists were lifted in cases of civil servants who were candidates in the 1930 Reichstag election. To be sure, there were some good reasons for this decision: Severing argued that making martyrs of a number of Nazi officials (no Communists were involved) who were candidates for the Reichstag on the NSDAP ticket would increase the sympathy vote for these candidates.[66]

More important than this tactical decision was Prussia's unwillingness—once again—to insist on implementing its policies in the face of objections from the Reich. Although Joseph Wirth, the Reich minister of the interior in Brüning's first cabinet, had originally indicated that he would not oppose Prussia's moves against the Nazis, the government's overall strategy soon ended cooperation between Reich and state in this area. Anxious to cultivate Hitler and the Nazis, Brüning rejected Severing's suggestion that the Reich follow Prussia's lead and emphasized that the Reich would not exclude Nazi sympathizers from the federal civil service.

Because Severing was unwilling to risk a Reich-state clash, the June 1930 decree became a far less incisive instrument than it might have been. The problem was most severe among the lower ranks of Prussia's territorial administrators. In October 1930, 75 percent of the state's governors, 71 percent of the district directors, and 83 percent of the municipal police chiefs were members of one of the Weimar coalition parties, as against less than half of Prussia's county commissioners.[67] Moreover, reports reached the cabinet that among the lower ranks of the civil service the number of opponents of the republic was growing alarmingly.[68]

A far more immediate cause of the declining morale and increasing unreliability of the state's corps of administrators, however, was the policy of salary cuts that gave credibility to a steady stream of antirepublican propaganda by the Nazis and other groups of the self-styled "national opposition." Prussia's cuts in personnel costs were coordinated with those of the Reich, but this did not make them any less onerous. In October 1930 the cabinet announced a 6 percent across-the-board pay cut for all civil servants. Both Braun and Severing feared the political consequences, but did not dispute the need for budget cuts. The cabinet soon recognized that the October cuts were insufficient and that further drastic reductions were unavoidable. Prussia continued to coordinate its policies with those of the Reich and the other *Länder* to reduce the political fallout, but the consequences were nevertheless devastating. The cabinet debates in August and September 1931 over a new wave of cuts were some of the most dramatic in the history of Weimar Prussia.

Höpker-Aschoff, the most enthusiastic champion of fiscal orthodoxy, proposed cuts that included freezing the civil servants' already meager salaries, while significantly cutting the housing and cost-of-living allowances that made up a major part of these salaries. Those hardest hit included Prussia's public schoolteachers, especially those teaching in elementary schools.[69]

The finance minister's original proposals met with sharp criticism. Especially Severing and Hirtsiefer warned of the political consequences of these measures; some weeks later Severing called Höpker-Aschoff's proposals "the stupidest thing that could be done." The leaders of the Weimar coalition parties in the Landtag, including Höpker-Aschoff's own DDP, were unwilling to back the finance minister. (These attacks undoubtedly contributed to Höpker-Aschoff's decision to resign.) Surprisingly, Otto Braun both during the cabinet meeting and later seemed to take neither side, although a year earlier he had vigorously supported Severing's position. The reason once again was Braun's almost pathological fear of a coalition crisis, as well as his desire to avoid controversy with the Reich cabinet—also pressing for further cuts—so as not to weaken Brüning's already precarious position. Ironically, although the cabinet rejected Höpker-Aschoff's proposals as too excessive, a few months later the Reich government, using the authority of the Dietramszeller emergency decree, forced the *Länder* to implement even more drastic cuts.[70]

Braun was also concerned that the actions and attitudes of the new minister of education would further strain the coalition. Adolf Grimme, for all his conciliatory manner, was "an even more republican minister" than his predecessor.[71] He was also an activist who was determined to advance the "democratization" of the state's schools and teachers.[72] Braun was not surprised that Grimme's policies evoked bitter attacks from the opposition parties, but even the Center party disagreed with him, especially over personnel policies. The Catholics criticized the minister's decision that so-called dissident teachers—who were neither practicing Christians nor Jews—could teach in Prussia's public schools. This decision mattered little in the crisis years, since teachers were being laid off, but it went against the Catholic opposition to atheists and agnostics as public schoolteachers. A more immediate problem, however, was the Center party's charge that in implementing the personnel cuts, Grimme dismissed disproportionately more Catholic than Protestant teachers. The minister denied the charge, but distrust remained between him and the Catholic education lobby.[73]

Unable to secure the love of Prussia's citizens by providing them with better services performed by enthusiastic public officials, the cabinet was at least determined to obtain their respect by demonstrating the strength of the constitutional system. In the Braun cabinet's last major wave of appointments to the territorial service, in April 1932 the cabinet sent a number of newly appointed or transferred judicial and police administrators to the Rhineland, Pommerania, and Schleswig-Holstein, where political violence was particularly severe. The April appointments were the Prussian government's last line of defense in the battle with political extremism. In effect, Prussia hoped to weather the crisis by relying upon its police and territorial administrators to prevent the Nazis and Communists from controlling the streets of Prussia.[74]

Political violence was a very serious problem. Although violence had been endemic throughout the Weimar years, beginning in 1930 the number of clashes and serious injuries increased rapidly. In June 1932, almost 40,000 cases involving political violence were pending before the Prussian courts, and 525 defendants were indicted for murder or manslaughter. (In the last years of the republic the democratic forces had high praise for the performance of the Prussian judiciary.)[75]

State and federal authorities deplored what amounted to an undeclared civil war, but Prussia and the Reich disagreed sharply on causes and solutions. While acknowledging that both right-wing and left-wing extremists were responsible, Prussia's security experts increasingly saw the Nazis as the more dangerous threat to law and order. They noted that after the May 1929 Communist-inspired riots in Berlin, the left-wing extremists were relatively quiescent until provoked to new levels of activism by the rise of the Nazis.

Reich authorities, however, continued to look upon a Communist coup as a genuine and acute danger. Brüning and his close advisor General Kurt von Schleicher wanted to retain the good will of what the general once called the "good human material" among the Nazi storm troopers. And Schleicher had another nightmare: that Germany's neighbors, Poland and France, would use the Reich's domestic difficulties as an opportunity to invade the German homeland. Schleicher wanted to have the right-wing paramilitary groups, including the storm troopers, available as auxiliary defense units.[76] Prussia's task, then, was not easy. The state either had to persuade the Reich interior ministry that the Nazis were a real danger to law and order, or pursue its own policies in the face of indifference or even opposition from the federal cabinets.

The Prussian administrators responsible for maintaining law and order were apparently particularly well qualified. After Heinrich Waentig's obvious failure, Braun and Ernst Heilmann immediately thought of Grzesinski as his successor (so did Grzesinski), but there were two insurmountable problems. One was the continuing resentment among rank-and-file Center party delegates; Joseph Hess, who was personally not opposed to Grzesinski's returning to office, informed the SPD leaders in the Landtag that he could not guarantee the unanimous support of the Catholic party delegates. Paradoxically, the other difficulty was Grzesinski's excellent record as police chief of Berlin, a difficult and important post. For this reason, Braun, Heilmann, and eventually

Grzesinski himself agreed that he should not leave this position and that Carl Severing should return to the cabinet as Prussian minister of the interior. Severing was available, having lost his job as Reich minister of the interior when Brüning became federal chancellor. He remained exceedingly popular among rank-and-file Social Democrats, while the enemies of the republic both feared and respected him. Finally, Severing's consensus-oriented administrative style would be useful in preserving harmony among the Prussian coalition parties.[77]

Nevertheless, Severing was not without critics. After they were forced into exile, Brüning, Grzesinski, and the state secretary in the Prussian ministry of the interior, Wilhelm Abegg, all sharply attacked their former colleague. No doubt Brüning's claim that Severing retained a number of incompetent officials in his ministry was influenced by personal pique, since these included some Center party officials whom Brüning regarded as his personal enemies, but his criticism that Severing lacked toughness was echoed by some of the minister's closest associates in the ministry.[78]

Abegg, the number two man in the Prussian interior ministry, was to become one of Severing's most bitter critics. It was typical of Severing's conciliatory manner that he did not replace Abegg as state secretary, although he knew that Abegg had been particularly close to Albert Grezinski. (As we saw, Grezinski himself had been less generous. When he came into office, he had immediately dismissed Severing's state secretary, and appointed Abegg.) The choleric Abegg was an activist and "confrontationalist" who became increasingly impatient with Severing's defensive and "soft" tactics. Abegg argued that the Prussian authorities should move aggressively against political extremism, concentrating their efforts on the Nazis, not the Communists. Although in retrospect this was clearly the right approach, Abegg vastly exaggerated his ability to lead the crusade against Hitler and his followers.[79]

Severing's relationship with Albert Grzesinski was similarly strained. There is little doubt that in October 1930 Grzesinski would have been a better choice as minister than Severing. He was more energetic and had a much clearer appreciation of the acute danger presented by the Nazi menace. Grzesinski also was willing to take effective measures to combat Nazi violence, even if they were politically unpopular. However, from his position as Berlin police chief (in which he reported to Severing) he could do little but fume and recommend measures which the minister of the interior for the most part rejected.[80] Severing felt Reich and state needed to cooperate in combating political extremism and that Grzesinski's "dog whip" approach (during a political speech in Leipzig in February 1932, Grzesinski had exclaimed, Hitler should be chased out of Germany with a dog whip [*Hundepeitsche*]) was politically unrealistic.[81]

It is fair to conclude that Severing's view of the security crisis of the 1930s was too much influenced by his successful handling of the Kapp putsch and its aftermath. In agreement with most Prussian officials, the minister was convinced that the Nazis would attempt to seize power through a second Beer Hall–type coup.[82] The Prussian government was not particularly concerned with what turned out to be the extremists' primary extraparliamentary tactic, the progressive destabilization of political life by chronic and often unfocused violence.

After the fall of 1931 there was no real basis for cooperation between Prussia and the Reich on security policy. Joseph Wirth was succeeded as Reich minister of the interior by Wilhelm Groener, a professional military man in the Seeckt and Schleicher mold. Groener (who also held the defense portfolio) was a political conservative and nationalist who looked upon all of the "national opposition parties," including the Nazis, as potential allies of the Reich government. Like most career army officers, he believed it possible to transform the storm troopers from political hooligans into something like an auxiliary military force. On the other hand, Groener, like Schleicher, was convinced that physical force and legal suppression were the only ways of dealing with the Communists.[83]

Actually, Groener's attitudes merely confirmed differing views among Reich and Prussian authorities on how to forestall a coup by extremists. The Prussians classified three groups as potential organizers of a putsch: the Nazis, the Stahlhelm, and the Communists. They saw the Nazis as the most violent, while federal officials thought only the Communists were dangerous. The Prussians had good reason to fear the Nazis. The NSDAP's paramilitary wing, the storm troopers (SA; the SS was still in its formative stages) was well organized under the command of former professional officers. It was also known that the Nazis had succeeded in infiltrating many Prussian police units with their sympathizers.

Interior ministry officials in Prussia had two options. One was to mobilize the prorepublican, extraparliamentary forces as a sort of auxiliary police against the Nazis; the other was to take bold executive action. The first course meant essentially deputizing the members of the Reichsbanner Schwarz-Rot-Gold, much as the Nazis were to do with the SA after they came to power in 1933. But Prussian leaders rejected this idea as contrary to democratic principles. Despite later claims by the right-wing officials in the Reich interior ministry, there was never any serious consideration of using the Reichsbanner as an auxiliary police force.[84]

The second option, executive action, received careful consideration in the summer of 1930. In August, three officials of the Prussian ministry of the interior submitted a lengthy memorandum to the minister and the cabinet proposing the prohibition of the Nazi party. To justify such a move, they cited first-hand evidence, including speeches and writings by Hitler and other leading Nazis, that the Nazis intended to overthrow Germany's and Prussia's constitutional government. (The August memorandum was hardly an isolated piece of documentation. Much of the same material had been used—successfully—to justify the June 1930 decree against Nazis in the civil service.)[85] The cabinet's failure to act upon this recommendation was to have disastrous consequences. The ministers failed to act for several reasons. Some officials in the interior ministry were opposed to using strong measures against the Nazis. They included ideological sympathizers of the "national opposition" parties as well as political opportunists, several of whom were promoted under the Papen regime. The natural tendency of high-level administrators to think in legal, rather than political terms also played a role. One ministry official peppered a list of cases of Nazi-provoked violence which Waentig sent to the cabinet in October 1930 with marginal comments like "not proved" and "some doubts remain" *(nicht zu unzweifelhaft).*[86] In addition, Severing and Heilmann contended that vigorous action by the Prussian police (which the Nazis grudgingly acknowledged)[87] had significantly reduced the danger of a Nazi putsch. Indeed, the minister went so far as to argue in April 1931 that the NSDAP was in the process of disintegration, and that further action by the government might actually halt its decline.[88]

After the defeat of the extremists' initiative and referendum campaign in October 1931, the Prussian authorities again considered various measures to hinder the Nazis' political activities. In addition to dissolving the NSDAP, the state also gave serious thought to prohibiting Goebbels from speaking in public and arresting Hitler and expelling him as an unwanted alien. (Until the spring of 1932 Hitler did not hold German citizenship.) In the face of the Reich government's continuing appeasement of Hitler, none of these steps were put into practice by the Prussian authorities. Severing insisted upon delay and caution. Prussia did indict Goebbels for high treason *(Hochverrat),* but even that action became moot after the Berlin *Gauleiter* (regional leader) acquired parliamentary immunity as a member of the Landtag in April 1932.[89]

In the end, Prussia put all blame for the failure of its activist policies against the extremists on the Reich. In the words of Robert Kempner, one of the authors of the August memorandum, Brüning "torpedoed Prussia's moves to take energetic steps against Hitler and the Nazis" and "sealed the fate of the Weimar Republic."[90] In dismissing the danger of a Nazi coup, the chancellor cited Hitler's promise to pursue his party's aims exclusively by legal means. The Nazi leader had taken an "oath of legality" as part of his sworn testimony at the trial of two former Reichswehr officers who were accused of fomenting Nazi propaganda in the army.[91] Brüning was unpersuaded by Prussian arguments that such Nazi promises of legality, like similar ones made by the Communists, were worthless.[92] In fact, we now know, the Reich government went much further; it actively sought Hitler's cooperation.

Legally, the Reich cabinet's differing assessment of the Nazis did not prevent Prussia from taking vigorous action of its own, but there is little doubt that Brüning's appeasement policies seriously discouraged those in Prussia (and some other *Länder*) who wanted to move against the Nazis. The state officials lamented that since the Nazis were organized throughout the country, prohibiting the party in one state would simply mean that Hitler's movement would transfer its operations to other *Länder*. But there was a persuasive counterargument: if, as the Prussians had always argued, control of Prussia meant control of Germany, then making things difficult in Germany's largest state would have meant a serious weakening of the Nazi movement. Instead, after the summer of 1930 Prussia allowed the initiative in the battle against political extremism to slip out of its hands.[93]

Prussian interior ministry officials were concerned with the threat posed by the Nazi storm troopers, but they were almost as worried about another far right paramilitary group, the Stahlhelm. For many contemporaries, the Stahlhelm seemed both ready and able to stage a putsch of its own. It had a membership of almost 5 million, its leadership corps was composed primarily of former career military officers, and it was closely linked to the DNVP, the Reichswehr, and the Nazis. In retrospect, fears of the Stahlhelm putsch appear groundless; despite its impressive numbers, and combat-simulating activities (including nighttime "maneuvers"), the Stahlhelm, like the Communists' paramilitary organization, was a paper tiger.[94]

Even more than in the case of the Nazis, Reich and state took entirely different approaches to Stahlhelm activities. The veterans' organization had powerful friends in high places, notably the Reich president, its honorary national chairman. Moreover, Hindenburg interpreted his *Schirmherr* (protector) role quite literally: at the request of the Stahlhelm's leaders he intervened openly to protest Prussia's moves against "his" organization. Since it was virtually impossible to coordinate actions with the Reich government, Prussian authorities once again watered down their planned moves against the organization (which included a total prohibition of the Stahlhelm's paramilitary activities and uniformed demonstrations) in order to avoid friction with the Reich government.[95]

The Prussian and Reich governments also had far different views of the threat from the extreme left, the Roter Frontkämpferbund (Red Front Fighters' Association, RFB). Prussian authorities certainly recognized the RFB's violent character. According to Prussian statistics, it was involved in about as many instances of political violence as the Nazi storm troopers, since the two organizations often attacked each other. Severing and Abegg, however, doubted (accurately) that the RFB was capable of staging a coup or starting the "revolution" that was a constant theme of the organization's rhetoric. The Reich government, however, argued as it had since the 1920s: the RFB was a far more serious threat to law and order than the storm troopers or the Stahlhelm. The result was more friction between Reich and state. Federal authorities again urged the Prussian government to order the dissolution of the RFB. (As we saw, Prussia had prohibited the RFB for a time after the May 1929 Berlin riots.) When the state refused, the Reich cabinet accused Prussia of being soft on Communism.[96]

The destabilization efforts by Germany's political extremists were not limited to violent and illegal activities. Actually, legal actions by anti-republican groups played a far greater role in undermining consensus politics in the last years of Weimar Germany. Early on, the Nazis sought to gain influence among Germany's university and high school students. Spearheaded by Austrian Nazi students leaders, the German Student Association (Deutsche Studentenschaft, DStS), encompassing student organizations at Austrian and German universities, adopted what was later called the "Aryan paragraph": it barred Jewish students from membership. Although Prussian authorities took strong countermeasures, severing all relations between the DStB and the state in 1927, these moves were unable to halt the growing number of Nazis elected to the student councils of Prussia's educational institutions. As early as 1928, the NS-Studentenbund (National Socialist Student Association) was the largest political organization among German university students, and by 1931 the Nazi student affiliate virtually controlled student life on many campuses.[97]

While Prussia failed to prevent the Nazi takeover of student organizations, the government felt it had defeated another major legal effort by extremists to destabilize its political system: the campaign in the fall of 1931 to force an early dissolution of the Prussian Landtag. As pointed out earlier, the Stahlhelm, the Nazis, and after some hesitation, the Communists, took advantage of the initiative and recall provisions of the Prussian constitution to sponsor jointly a plebiscite to force early Landtag elections.

The campaign pitted the media and political resources of the Prussian government and the Weimar coalition parties against the financial resources of big business, Alfred Hugenberg's press empire, and the formidable propaganda of the Nazis and the other sponsoring organizations. Prussian authorities vigorously fought the dissolution initiative by alerting Prussian voters to the destabilizing intentions of its sponsors, and, equally important, demonstrating the state's ability to control the situation. As noted, the government's media measures ranged from a statewide radio address by the prime minister to threats that newspapers supporting the initiative would be barred from publicizing official government announcements. (The state's payment for the publication of such notices was a major source of income for many rural and small-town weeklies.) Using the authority of one of Brüning's emergency decrees, on the eve of the plebiscite the state also forced all Prussian papers to publish a front-page proclamation in bold print opposing the plebiscite. The Prussian interior ministry notified all civil servants that it would discipline any government employee who signed a petition or in any other way publicly supported the extremists' efforts.[98]

Prussia regarded the outcome of the Landtag recall effort—supported by fewer than 40 percent of the voters—as a victory for democracy and a clear sign that the extremists were on the defensive. The vote for the recall motion was significantly lower than the sponsoring organizations had obtained in the September 1930 Reichstag election.[99]

News of the decline of the Nazis was, of course, highly premature. In fact, confronted with the failure of its appeasement policy and growing political violence, at the beginning of 1932 even the chancellor and the Reich cabinet acknowledged that the situation was getting out of hand. Federal authorities had long demanded the dissolution of the RFB, but now the Reich interior minister admitted that there was no place for the storm troopers in the German political system either. The only questions were how and when to move against them. Both Groener and Schleicher rejected an immediate dissolution of paramilitary organizations, demanded by the *Länder*, led by Prussia and Bavaria, to avoid alienating the thousands of men with a "superb attitude" *(bester Gesinnung)* who were active in the SA. Groener and Schleicher wanted to keep the states out of the decision making. Schleicher argued that only the Reich government, and not state government "party hacks," had the finesse *(Fingerspitzengefühl)* to handle the storm troopers.[100] Brüning, for his part, wanted a foreign policy triumph before acting; as late as March he argued that the prohibition of the storm troopers was "premature."[101]

Immediately after Hitler's defeat in the first round of the Reich presidential elections, the Prussian government ordered a surprise raid on a number of storm trooper command posts. This action, which Prussia initiated primarily to force the Reich's hand, left no doubt that, anticipating Hitler's victory over Hindenburg, the storm troopers had been preparing for violent action against the federal and state governments. When the seized material was placed before the Reich authorities, Brüning and Groener still refused to take immediate action, but even they could not ignore the mounting evidence that the storm troopers were restless for action. (Incidentally, this also worried the Nazis' political leadership.)[102]

As violence continued unabated during the second presidential campaign, all of the larger *Länder*, not just Prussia, urged concerted action against the Nazis' and Communists' paramilitary organizations. The pressure from the states became so overwhelming that on April 13, 1932, Hindenburg signed a decree prohibiting the storm troopers, the Nazi SS, and the RFB in all parts of the Reich. But the action came too late. Most of the SA and SS leaders had been warned by sympathizers among the police and local officials.

The Nazis and Communists raised a howl of protest against the dissolution order which they blamed—correctly—on their enemies in the Prussian interior ministry. The Communists' criticism had no effect, but the Nazis' protests found a ready ear in the Reich president. Knowing Hindenburg's distrust and dislike of all "Marxists," the "national opposition" groups flooded his office with telegrams conveying the message that the Reich had prohibited a "nationalist" organization like the SA, while the "Marxist" Reichsbanner Schwarz-Rot-Gold was free to roam the streets.[103]

Despite the April decree, there were few who favored vigorous action among the Reich's security experts. A number of high-ranking officials in the Reich interior and the justice ministries argued that prohibiting the Nazis' paramilitary organization would push the Nazis further into the twilight of illegal activities. (These officials had no qualms about banning Communist organizations.) Groener went out of his way to apologize to his friends on the right for supporting an unpopular decision.[104]

The dissolution decree revealed Prussia's weakness in its relationship with the Reich. In a few short months the euphoria that followed the extremists' failure in the Landtag recall campaign had been replaced by defensiveness on the part of the Prussian government. Evidence was also mounting that leading officials in the Reich bureaucracy regarded Prussia, not the Nazis, as the real obstacle to achieving their goals. At the end of May, Schlange-Schöningen, hardly a flaming leftist, urged Severing and Abegg to regain the initiative. He proposed that the Prussian authorities simply arrest Hitler and his "clique" at the Kaiserhof Hotel, Hitler's Berlin headquarters. Abegg was enthusiastic, but Severing voiced "constitutional qualms."[105]

Conclusion

Historians and contemporaries alike have given Prussia a decidedly mixed report card for its actions during the Weimar Republic's final years. Heinrich Brüning, who during his long years in exile became increasingly bitter about most of his earlier colleagues and associates, presented a picture of a Prussian government under Otto Braun that had lost control of the situation, paralyzed by corruption, dominated by "politics" and "self-interest." "One had become tired, indifferent, and lazy [bequem]. . . . The consequences of being in office too long"—criticisms that fell right in line with the attacks of the "national opposition."[106]

A less biased observer, however, concluded that at least until the April 1932 Landtag elections Prussian authorities vigorously attempted to preserve parliamentary democracy. Only when the voters themselves abandoned hope in democracy did the minister of the interior essentially give up the struggle and resigned himself to following the Reich's lead. Others put the watershed date earlier, arguing that the state's mission to save democracy in Germany by preserving democracy in Prussia was hopeless after the advent of the regime of the presidential chancellors in the Reich.[107]

When the Nazis came to power in January 1933, they quickly destroyed not only Prussian democracy, but for all practical purposes, Prussia itself. But the question remains: could the Prussians have done more to prevent this outcome? In one sense, the answer is clearly yes. Few would disagree that hard-headed measures such as dissolving the SA and SS, prohibiting the Nazi party, or expelling Adolf Hitler would have seriously hampered the Nazis on their road to power.

The problem was partly that Prussia lacked the courage of its convictions. Its leaders recognized the Nazi menace far more accurately than their Reich colleagues, but they refused seriously to challenge the Reich's appeasement policies. But the advent of the presidential chancellors' regime after 1930 placed the Prussians in an entirely new relationship to the Reich. After all, political extremism was hardly a new phenomenon. From the Spartacus uprising of 1919 and the Kapp Putsch of 1920, the Weimar Republic was under siege by its enemies. In each case, the constitutional system was saved by firm measures by the Prussian cabinet and close cooperation between Prussia and the Reich in implementing these measures.

After March 1930, cooperation with the Reich became increasingly difficult as the two entities developed completely different views of the nation's political future. For Prussia to proceed on its own would have meant open confrontation with the Reich, a course of action for which Prussia's democratic leaders had neither the constitutional authority nor the political will; in their eyes, it would have destroyed a fundamental pillar upon which the success of Weimar democracy rested.

Prussia's leaders might be credited with a correct evaluation of the Nazi challenge, but it is difficult to praise their fiscal, economic, and social policies. Obsessed with fiscal orthodoxy, the Prussians failed to see that their lack of interventionist, countercyclical measures irrevocably destroyed the political system they were attempting to save. Their fall-back position, at least preserving the state's Weimar coalition government, represented less a tower of strength than an admission of failed policies.

Here, perhaps, also lay the ultimate failure of Otto Braun. It was, to be sure, understandable. As a master of coalition politics who had steered a steady course for almost a dozen years, the prime minister, like most of his colleagues, did not see that the challenges of the Depression called for bolder, riskier, and above all more active policies.

Prussian Coalition Politics and the Regime of the Presidential Chancellors, 1930–1933

In the final years of the Weimar Republic, the political dichotomy between Reich and state, the so-called Reich-Prussian dualism, again dominated political discussions in the state. As at the beginning of the republican era, spokesmen from every political camp insisted that only by establishing parallel government coalitions in Prussia and the Reich could Germany weather the political and economic crisis facing the country. But by the late Weimar years, the relationship between Reich and state had changed profoundly. Earlier, the strength and stability of its parliamentary democracy enabled Prussia to chart its own course and in many ways dominate its relationship with the Reich. In sharp contrast, after 1930 the Reich cabinets, backed by the authority of the president and free from parliamentary control, took the initiative, putting Prussia on the defensive. The rock was to become a sand castle.

Reich president von Hindenburg and his entourage as well as the neoconservative chancellors who led the Reich between 1930 and 1933—Brüning, von Papen, and von Schleicher—were all convinced they had an historic mandate to bring about major changes in Germany's political and constitutional makeup. Abolishing the Reich-Prussian dualism was an important part of their program. Beginning with Brüning, the Reich chancellors and their backers in and around the Reich president's office expected that the "socialist-free" Reich cabinets would soon be followed by a similar government coalition in Germany's largest state. To this end, Brüning's own party, the Center party, was expected to break off its longtime coalition with Prussia's Social Democrats and become the kingpin of a *Bürgerblock* cabinet in the state.[1]

Heinrich Brüning's silence about his ultimate political aims during his long years of exile did much to nurture the myth that despite his reliance on the president's decree powers, his ultimate goal had been to save Weimar Germany's constitutional system. With the posthumous publication of his memoirs and letters, the former chancellor himself demolished the pedestal upon which his postwar admirers had put him. No champion of parliamentary

197

democracy, he had sought to use the opportunities provided by the country's economic and political crisis to return Germany to a modified Prusso-German authoritarianism. In constitutional terms, the chancellor wanted to rectify what he regarded as an unworkable democratic system by shifting power from parliament to the executive. Politically, Brüning was determined to exclude the Social Democrats permanently from power while he did not reject the Nazis as potential coalition partners. Although opposed to giving Hitler's movement a dominant role in either the Reich or Prussian cabinets, Brüning's political scenario included a place for the Nazis as junior in right-of-center coalitions at either or both levels of government.[2]

The chancellor had never approved of the coalition that had governed Prussia a dozen years. In his memoirs Brüning sadly recalled that long before becoming chancellor he had tried unsuccessfully to bring about a *Bürgerblock* coalition in Prussia, blaming the DNVP's and his own party's intransigence for the failure of these efforts. Despite his disappointments with the DNVP, a few weeks after his appointment as chancellor Brüning promised Alfred Hugenberg, the DNVP leader, that in return for support for the Reich cabinet's program, the DNVP could replace the SPD as the Center party's coalition partner in Prussia.[3] It is true that after he became chancellor for tactical reasons Brüning valued the Braun government's support for the implementation of the chancellor's crisis-management policies, but in the long run Brüning had little respect for the leaders of the Weimar coalition parties in Prussia. Brüning regarded the Social Democrats as well as his own party colleagues as a group of self-serving politicians of little distinction.

Brüning insisted on delaying a cabinet crisis in Prussia until the fall of 1930 because he recognized that he needed the SPD to continue its "policy of toleration" in the Reichstag until he had achieved his principal foreign policy aim: the end of reparations. Forcing the Social Democrats out of the Prussian cabinet would have led the socialists' to abandon their "policy of toleration" and join Brüning's opponents. The German Nationalists, however, held to their obstructionist line. Hugenberg refused to cooperate with Brüning's plans; he demanded an immediate coalition change in Prussia.[4]

In discussing future political scenarios with the DNVP leader and others, Brüning rather naively assumed that he could persuade the leaders of the Prussian center party to go along with his plans. The Prussian Catholics, that is to say, could be treated as pawns in the chancellor's grand political game. Actually, neither the state's Center party nor the other Weimar coalition parties were willing to become a mere object of Reich politics. Although the leaders of the Prussian coalition parties were not fully aware of Brüning's long-range political agenda, they had no illusions about the seriousness of the threat he posed to Prussia's coalition government. With the advent of the presidential chancellors' regime in the Reich, Prussia had become the last bastion of the Weimar coalition parties.[5]

Although increasingly pessimistic, Otto Braun and most of the Prussian Social Democrats were still determined to preserve the state as the "rock of democracy." To be sure, some argued that the SPD should resign from the state government and resume its favorite position on the opposition benches in both state and Reich, leaving the Nazis and the bourgeois parties to "wear themselves out" coping with the Depression. However, the prime minister, Ernst Heilmann, and the vast majority of Prussia's Social Democrats saw clear political parallels between the spring of 1930 and the Ruhr crisis in 1923. As before, Prussia had to balance the rightward drift of the Reich government by continuing the left-of-center orientation in the state to save democracy in Germany. This did not preclude a continuation of the SPD's "policy of toleration" at the federal level, by which Prussian Social Democrats supported the Reich government's efforts to cope with a temporary national crisis.[6]

To be workable this scenario needed the continued cooperation of the Prussian Center party. (The third Weimar coalition party, the DStP, had by now been reduced to negligible factor in any future coalition discussions.) Prussia's Catholics did not disappoint the Social Democrats. Much to the surprise and annoyance of Heinrich Brüning, the Prussian Center party leaders remained true to the left-of-center course which they had pursued virtually without interruption since 1918. True, there were some mavericks who wanted to end the alliance with the Social Democrats, but they were in the minority. In contrast to Brüning, who worked for a permanent alliance of the Center party and the rightist groups, the Center party's Prussian leaders remained deeply suspicious of the right.[7]

The mood of quiet, albeit defensive, determination among the Weimar coalition parties in 1930 contrasted sharply with the aggressive optimism of the opposition groups. All of Prussia's bourgeois opposition parties from the DVP to the German Nationalists initially welcomed Brüning's appointment in the expectation that the chancellor would use the power of the Reich government to force the election of a *Bürgerblock* cabinet in Prussia.[8]

While the Nazis were part of the opposition, their role in any future right-wing coalition was uncertain. At the Reich level Hugenberg treated Hitler practically as an equal, but, as we saw earlier, the situation was different in Prussia. Not only had Hitler and the Nazis shown little interest, but the strength of the Hitler movement in the Prussian legislature was negligible; the eight-member delegation was not even large enough to form a caucus. Moreover, they were not a very distinguished group. Joseph Goebbels, the Nazi leader of Berlin, had little respect for his future comrades in the legislature. Heinrich Haake, the Nazi representative from Cologne, was an "ass"; Hans

Kerrl, who would become speaker of the Landtag in May 1932, a "philosophical babbler, really into Kant [*philosophischer Quatschkopf in Kant*]." Only Wilhelm Kube, an old-line *völkisch* politician and the Nazi leader in the Landtag, received some grudging praise from Goebbels: "A real loudmouth . . . but a good guy. One just had to know how to treat him right."[9]

The Nazis would remain an unimportant force in the Landtag until April 1932, but their phenomenal successes in local, regional, and national elections throughout this period gave them far greater political clout in Prussian coalition politics than one of the smallest groups in the legislature would normally have had. The Prussian policies of the Nazis suddenly mattered. For this reason it was significant that all of the Nazi Landtag delegates belonged to the "socialist" and "moderate" wing of the party. Especially Kube was a strong supporter of Gregor Strasser, the NSDAP's national executive secretary who consistently advocated that the Nazis should join a *Bürgerblock* coalition as a step toward total power. Like Strasser, the Nazi leader in the Landtag worked hard to create a parliamentarily elected Prussian coalition that would include the Nazis—albeit on the party's own terms.[10]

Not all Prussian opposition parties, of course, were on the right. The Communists were as noisy and often as violent as the Nazis, but in terms of coalition politics they mattered far less. The KPD had no interest in joining any coalition. The prevailing party line of opposing "social fascism" at any cost led the Communists to concentrate their attacks on the Social Democrats as disguised fascists whose policies, the Communists claimed, were not markedly different from either those of the "Brüning fascists" or the Nazis themselves. The KPD actually welcomed a *Bürgerblock* government in Prussia, since it was convinced that such a development would lead the SPD's rank and file to desert their "proto-fascist leaders" and flock to the Communists instead, thereby fulfilling the KPD's dream of "proletarian unity from below."[11]

When Brüning was appointed Reich chancellor, he did not face a hostile Reichstag. It was still dominated by the moderate parties, and the chancellor's decision to call for new elections in September 1930 was neither politically nor constitutionally necessary. In retrospect, of course, calling new elections was a disastrous tactical move that enabled the Nazis to increase their delegate strength in the Reichstag from 12 to 107. Since the national campaign pitted all parties against each other, the Reichstag election also put additional strains on consensual politics in Prussia. Nevertheless, the Prussian coalition held. The leaders of the Prussian SPD and the state's Catholics not only firmly rejected calls to dissolve the Landtag in order to stage parallel contests at the federal and state levels, but also made it clear that they expected the Prussian coalition to continue regardless of the outcome of the Reichstag contest.[12]

Although the September elections did not formally affect the Prussian balance of power, the results certainly changed the atmosphere. Fresh from their triumphs in the Reichstag, the antidemocratic forces now eyed Prussia as the last major obstacle to restoring authoritarianism or propelling Germany toward either Nazi totalitarianism or Communist proletarian dictatorship.

In the afterglow of his election triumph, Hitler seems to have expected that the Nazis would now become part of both the Reich and Prussian coalitions. At the federal level the NSDAP wanted control of the foreign, interior, and defense ministries, while for the state Goebbels talked more vaguely about his "taking control of Prussia for the time being." However, he added cautiously (and with a sense of realism), "I don't believe it until it happens. There is a lot of resistance to overcome in the Center party."[13]

Goebbels was right: Prussia's democratic forces had by no means been defeated. In fact, with the Weimar coalition government still firmly in control, the state's leaders launched some far-reaching proposals designed to solve the problem of the Reich-Prussia dualism without changing the letter or spirit of the Weimar constitution. In October 1930 the Prussian prime minister implored Brüning to reestablish the pre-World War I "personal unions" between federal and state executives. Under Braun's proposal he would resign as Prussian prime minister but remain a member of the state's cabinet as minister without portfolio. In addition, Braun would join the Reich cabinet as vice chancellor. The way would then be free for Brüning, who would remain Reich chancellor, to be elected the state's prime minister with the support of the Weimar coalition parties in Prussia.

For a variety of reasons Brüning refused the offer. He had his own plans for overcoming the Reich-Prussian dualism: by establishing parallel *Bürgerblock* coalitions in both the Reich and Prussia. Brüning also knew that Hindenburg would reject any proposal that left the SPD a dominant force in Prussia, and Braun's scenario did not envision a change in the composition of the two cabinets. Finally, as Prussian prime minister, the chancellor would be subject to parliamentary control, and Brüning saw parliamentary democracy as a cause of, rather than a solution for Germany's political difficulties.[14]

With the failure of Braun's plan, the two cabinets continued on their separate ways, although they remained somewhat tenuously linked by the Social Democrats' "policy of toleration" for the Brüning government, which Prussia's Social Democratic leaders strongly supported. Unable to offer any alternatives to Brüning's deflationary program, the Prussian government had no interest in creating difficulties for the chancellor. In the meantime, the "policy of toleration" gained time for both Brüning and the Social Democrats. The only question was who benefited more. The Prussian Social Democrats naively assumed that time was on their side. "If . . . there is a six months long breathing space, something really significant will have been accomplished against the threat of fascism," Heilmann concluded. Above all, however, the Prussian Social Democrats were convinced the "policy of toleration" was necessary to preserve the state's Weimar coalition. If the SPD intensified its opposition in the Reich, the Prussian Center party would be put in an impossible position. In all likelihood the state's Catholics would yield to pressure from their national leaders and abandon the coalition. In other words, the "policy of toleration" was the only way to preserve parliamentary democracy in the state and harbor realistic hopes for restoring it in the Reich.[15]

Although the Prussian SPD leaders tried to make a virtue out of a necessity, the "policy of toleration" was clearly a defensive tactic that left political initiative in the hands of the Reich cabinet. This was certainly Brüning's view; he was convinced he was operating from a position of strength. Disdainful of the now politically impotent Prussian *Sozen,* whom he still despised for "overthrowing" the Hohenzollern monarchy to which the chancellor remained emotionally and politically attached, Brüning at the end of 1930 set out forcefully to realize his political agenda. (Incidentally, Albert Grezesinski was one of the few Prussian SPD leaders who recognized the tactical weakness of the "policy of toleration," and consequently expressed serious doubts about the party's political strategy.)[16]

The chancellor's aims in Prussia were straightforward, but his tactics were convoluted, risky, and ultimately politically fatal to him. Assuming that his political position would be secure for a long time, Brüning worked systematically to persuade the Prussian Center party to sever its ties to the SPD and form a coalition with the DVP, DNVP, and the Nazis instead. Such a coalition, Brüning argued, would be able to enlist the Nazis' anti-Bolshevik fervor in the battle against the Communists, whom he always regarded as a "more dangerous" threat to domestic political stability than Hitler's followers.[17]

However, the potential partners in a *Bürgerblock* coalition in Prussia pursued their own agendas, and these did not necessarily include playing the parts which the chancellor had assigned to them. The "national opposition" parties were deeply divided. The Prussian DVP, admittedly no longer a significant political factor, increasingly aligned itself with the right, but some of the party's prominent national leaders, such as Reich foreign minister Robert Curtius, not only favored a return of the grand coalition, but were passionately opposed to including the Nazis in any *Länder* coalitions. All of the state's DNVP leaders wanted to eliminate the Weimar coalition government in Prussia, but many also had little use for Brüning. Instead of cooperating with the chancellor, a number of German Nationalists hoped to force the Prussian government to schedule early state elections that would presumably result in a Nazi-DNVP majority in the Landtag. The result would be a rightist dictatorship—independent of the Center party and Brüning. Others, less confident of the outcome of any new elections and uneasy about tying the DNVP's fate completely to the Nazis, urged the German Nationalists to agree to the formation of a *Bürgerblock* coalition in Prussia that would be dominated by the state's Center party and the DNVP. Harboring no illusions about the Prussian Catholics' reluctance to enter into a coalition with the Conservatives, these elements in the DNVP welcomed Brüning's help in persuading the Center party to drive the SPD from its last major stronghold.[18]

The Nazis, too, spoke with forked tongues. Some were willing to cooperate with Brüning in transforming the Prussian coalition. Hermann Göring established early contacts with the chancellor to gain influence with the Center party. These Nazis recognized that the Prussian Center party leadership was fundamentally opposed to cooperating with Hitler and that without Brüning's persuasive power it would reject a *Bürgerblock* coalition that included the Nazis.

Others, like Goebbels, rejected both parliamentary politics and any cooperation with the Center party. Goebbels complained bitterly about Göring's "friendship" with Brüning and the policy of "legality that makes you puke [*zum Kotzen*]!" Instead of welcoming the possibility of a coalition with the Center party, Goebbels sharply attacked the Catholics in his Berlin newspaper, *Der Angriff*, and wrote in his diary, "You have to expose these hypocrites [*diesen Heuchlern muss man die Maske von der Fratze reissen*]." It is difficult to determine where Hitler stood. Still unable to persuade the Nazi leader to take any real interest in Prussia, Goebbels complained that Hitler was too "soft" and "anxious to compromise at any price [*kompromisswütig*]." On the other hand, in the Reich Hitler supported the tactics of the antiparliamentary radicals. In mid-February 1931, the newly elected Nazi delegates stormed out of the Reichstag, and for the next several months they boycotted the sessions of the national legislature.[19]

In the face of pressures from both the jubilant opposition parties in the Landtag and the Brüning government in the Reich, the Weimar coalition in Prussia weathered the storm that followed the September Reichstag elections remarkably well. It was true that the volatile atmosphere that polarized Germany's politics also increased friction among the Prussian coalition partners. The Center party complained that the emphasis which the left wing of the Social Democrats put on the SPD's Marxist heritage, alienated the party from its bourgeois allies in Prussia. The Catholics also grumbled about Braun's high-handed style of making appointments. They noted with displeasure that he had chosen replacements for both Höpker-Aschoff and Becker with little or no consultation with his coalition partners. The Social Democrats for their part accused the national leaders of the Center party of appeasing the antidemocratic right. Still, neither the SPD nor the Center party seriously considered dissolving the coalition. For all their grumbling, the Prussian Catholic leaders also recognized that Braun did not choose König as Becker's successor precisely because the prime minister knew König was extremely unpopular among the state's Catholics. Standing together the Weimar coalition parties easily rebuffed the seemingly unending series of votes of no confidence and other obstructionist tactics pursued by the opposition parties.[20]

Long years of cooperation had benefited all partners, but intransigence and lack of finesse by the opposition parties also strengthened the Weimar coalition's cohesion even in these difficult times. No one was surprised by the DNVP's well-worn litany that the solution for all of Prussia's problems was the return of the Hohenzollern monarchy, but surely while wooing the Center party, it was tactical folly to evoke old *Kulturkampf* memories by emphasizing the DNVP's decidedly anti-Catholic sentiments. The same was true for Goebbels's vicious attacks on the Center party.[21]

Instead of engaging in parliamentary bargaining, radicals in the opposition parties gained the upper hand and pinned their hopes on early Landtag elections. The opposition parties calculated that if Landtag elections had been held along with the September 1930 Reichstag elections, they would have won 312 seats to the Weimar coalition's 228. As a result, they were understandably impatient for a statewide contest and unwilling to wait until the regularly scheduled Landtag elections in April 1932. But in October 1930 the Landtag decisively voted down a motion to dissolve the Landtag and schedule early elections.[22]

Defeated in the Landtag, the opposition, as we saw earlier, turned to the hyperdemocratic provisions in the Prussian constitution to hasten the downfall of democracy, a drive spearheaded by the Stahlhelm. Citing the reappointment of Severing as Prussian interior minister as evidence that Marxism was solidifying its hold on Prussia, Stahlhelm leaders contemplated an initiative and referendum campaign to realize two aims: in addition to early state elections, the Stahlhelm also hoped to amend the Prussian constitution so as to make the Reich president simultaneously president of Prussia with authority to appoint the state's prime minister and cabinet.[23] Although the "national opposition" parties were uninterested in the Stahlhelm's effort to force constitutional changes, they were enthusiastic about early Landtag elections. Consequently, the Stahlhelm dropped the constitutional amendment idea and concentrated instead on a campaign to dissolve the Landtag.[24]

Throughout the campaign the partners remained distrustful of each other. Stahlhelm organizers recognized that little united the sponsors of the initiative and referendum campaign except opposition to the Weimar coalition and parliamentary democracy. The Nazis, for example, were careful to stage a parallel, not a joint campaign with the other organizations. They refused to subordinate themselves to the Stahlhelm leaders and emphasized their differences from their "bourgeois" partners. To preserve the ad hoc partnership, Stahlhelm leaders pleaded with the other party leaders to emphasize that a successful initiative and referendum would end "Marxist rule" in Germany's heartland and to avoid discussing the makeup of any future coalition in the state.[25]

Even though the initiative campaign succeeded, privately its sponsors were severely disappointed with the results. The more realistic among them doubted that the subsequent referendum would be successful.[26] But its chances seemed to improve when the Communists decided for tactical reasons to join the "national opposition" in supporting the referendum. Like the Nazis, the Communists welcomed constant campaigns because they afforded opportunities for agitation and political violence. Campaigning not only prevented internal dissent, but helped to destabilize the country and increase difficulties for the Brüning and Braun cabinets. Party leaders were also rushing after their followers; some rightist leaders suspected that if the KPD did not endorse the referendum, much of the Communist rank and file would ignore the party and vote for the referendum to bring down the hated Weimar coalition in Prussia.[27]

As we saw, even with the Communists' help, the referendum was a dismal failure. The outcome demonstrated the residual strength of the state's Weimar coalition, seemingly leaving the opposition no alternatives except to wait for the state elections scheduled for April 1932, or lure the Center party away from its alliance with the Social Democrats. In fact, in the fall of 1931 extremists' frontal assaults on the constitutional system of the Weimar Republic were rebuffed on several fronts. The Reichstag boycott by the "national opposition" removed the national arena for parliamentary maneuvers, and in Thuringia the state government, the first *Bürgerblock* coalition that included a Nazi minister (Wilhelm Frick as minister of the interior) lost a vote of confidence after only a few months in office. Looking about them, the leaders of the Prussian coalition parties concluded that the tide had turned in their favor.[28]

The failure of the referendum left coalition politics in an uneasy balance. Either an open feud between the Reich and state cabinets or escalating tensions among the coalition parties in Prussia might enable the chancellor to draw the state's Center party away from the SPD and toward cooperation with the DNVP and the Nazis. Conversely, good relations among the coalition parties and a relative absence of friction between the Reich and Prussian cabinets kept the state's Catholics from drifting to the right and preserved the Weimar coalition. Brüning worked hard to break up the Weimar coalition in Prussia. According to some contemporaries, in the fall of 1931 he proposed a deal of his own whereby Braun and Severing would become members of the Reich cabinet in return for resigning from the Prussian cabinet and making way for a *Bürgerblock* government. The plan was rejected by Kurt von Schleicher before the Social Democrats could even take a position.[29]

Even if the chancellor's friends had been more enthusiastic about his

Prussian plans, it is unlikely that he would have succeeded in breaking up the state's Weimar coalition. In the fall of 1931 the coalition was not beset by serious internal dissension. Major personnel changes did not lead to feuds. When Friedrich Bartels (SPD) died in November 1931 after serving as speaker of the Landtag for almost a dozen years, Ernst Wittmack, another Social Democrat, was easily elected as new speaker by all of the Weimar coalition parties. The resignations and replacements of two liberal ministers, Höpker-Aschoff and Becker, embittered some left-wing members of the DStP, but their anger was of no political consequence, and especially Höpker-Aschoff's resignation actually assuaged conflicts; Höpker-Aschoff had been a particularly abrasive personality in the cabinet.

It is true that the coalition partners, besieged by attacks from all sides, emphasized to their constituents what set them apart from all other groups, but the opposition's hope for a breakup of the coalition was wishful thinking. So was Kurt von Schleicher's view that both the Center party and the Nazis were about to split and that the Adenauer-Papen wing of the Center party would join in a coalition with the "moderate" Prussian Nazis. Severing well described the atmosphere among the Prussian coalition parties: they were in complete agreement on the major issues of both Prussian and Reich politics.[30]

It could be argued that Severing and the SPD had no alternative: preserving the Weimar coalition was their only means of staying in power. This was not true for the Center party, which was in the enviable position of being courted by several suitors. The Catholic party could remain in partnership with the Social Democrats, but it could also join with the right-wing parties to form a *Bürgerblock* coalition. But despite a public show of support for Brüning's policies at the federal level, Hess and the leaders of political Catholicism in Prussia resolutely kept to the left-of-center course they had followed since 1920.[31]

There were good political reasons for this stand. The Center party's options on the right were not very attractive. Despite the referendum debacle, the right-wing opposition groups were unwilling to accept parliamentary democracy as the foundation of coalition politics. The DVP, at one time the champion of a grand coalition, but now deeply divided, appeared increasingly eager to join the *Harzburger Front* alongside the Nazis and German Nationalists. The DNVP still insisted that the *Bürgerblock* coalition also had to mean the end of parliamentary democracy in Prussia.

As for the Prussian Nazis, they were certainly talking to the Center party. Informal discussions continued off and on from August 1931 until the Nazis came to power in January 1933. However, most of the time the negotiators talked at cross purposes. The Catholics were exploring the possibility of a new parliamentary coalition that would lead the Prussian Nazis to cease their obstructionist and violent tactics in the state, but few (if any) of the Nazis shared this goal. Even if "moderates" had wanted to join a parliamentary coalition—and the evidence here is dubious at best—Nazi "radicals" would have rejected the idea. Joseph Goebbels, who remained deeply suspicious of any contacts with the Center party and fearful of parliamentary constraints, described the alternatives as, "Either strongest opposition or . . . total power." "Toleration," the Berlin *Gauleiter* concluded, "means death." No wonder Joseph Hess all but precluded an alliance between the Center party and the Nazis. The Catholic leader promised Ernst Heilmann there could be no pact with Hitler's men unless they accepted parliamentary democracy—a most unlikely scenario.[32]

Unable to dislodge the Weimar coalition by extraparliamentary maneuvers or political violence, the parties of the "national opposition" had to rely on their campaign skills and the ballot box. Their first opportunity after the 1931 referendum campaign was the Reich presidential election in the spring of 1932. Although, like the September 1930 Reichstag contest, the election of the federal president had no immediate bearing on the state, it was important to the state for both symbolic and political reasons. Brüning worked hard for Hindenburg's reelection because he expected the president's stay in power would solidify the chancellor's hold on national power and give him additional time to pursue his political and constitutional goals. Despite considerable misgivings about Hindenburg's person and politics, the Prussian coalition parties also vigorously supported his reelection, although their motivations were rather different from Brüning's. They feared the election of Adolf Hitler. (The other two candidates, Ernst Thälmann for the KPD, and Theodor Düsterberg for the Stahlhelm and the DNVP, had no chance of success.) Nevertheless, the presidential campaign was one of the few occasions of genuine cooperation between the Reich and Prussian governments. At the request of the federal cabinet, the Prussian government even agreed to use secret state funds to subsidize newspaper coverage favorable to Hindenburg.[33]

After two bitter and violent campaigns, Hindenburg was the clear winner over Hitler. The state's coalition leaders were relieved and delighted; they were convinced that the president's reelection meant that the fascist danger in Germany had been beaten back. The political fallout did indeed give some cause for optimism. Not only was the size of Hindenburg's victory in the runoff impressive, but it was clear that the maneuvering in the rightist camp before and during the two campaigns had considerably cooled relations between the Nazis and the German Nationalists. Hitler seemed to have gone for broke and lost.[34]

The feeling that the Weimar coalition had—once again—won some breathing room provided the background for a controversial and perhaps ill-considered attempt to prevent the future election of an extremist prime minister in Prussia.[35] The Prussian constitution provided that the state's chief executive was to be elected by the Landtag, but details of the election were spelled out only in the legislature's bylaws. From 1920 until 1932 the Landtag's bylaws provided that to be elected on the first ballot, a candidate had to obtain a majority. On all subsequent ballots a plurality sufficed.

In the spring of 1932, the Weimar coalition parties became acutely concerned about a worst-possible-case situation that might emerge after the Landtag elections scheduled for April 24. There was a real possibility that the opposition would control a majority of the seats in the new Landtag. Under the bylaws, the opposition could then put together a plurality to elect a prime minister, in all likelihood a Nazi. The new prime minister would probably not obtain a vote of confidence for his cabinet (for which a majority of Landtag votes was always required), but once elected he would have full executive powers as head of a provisional government as long as the crisis continued.

To prevent this scenario, the legislative leaders of the Weimar coalition parties decided to change the Landtag's bylaws before the election so that a majority vote was necessary to elect a prime minister on all ballots. The net effect might well be to keep the Weimar coalition in office, since under the Prussian constitution a cabinet remained in power, even if it had lost the confidence of the Landtag, until the legislature succeeded in electing a new prime minister.

Although most of the Weimar coalition delegates eventually supported this procedural attempt to prevent the "accidental" election of a Nazi prime minister, the driving force behind the initiative came from the Social Democrats, notably Ernst Heilmann and his young protegé, Ernst Hamburger. The two leaders argued that changing the bylaws was the only way to force the NSDAP to abide by the parliamentary rules in any subsequent coalition talks. Other leaders were less sure. The right wing of the Center party objected to the change. Konrad Adenauer, for example, felt the move was unconstitutional. Franz von Papen refused to vote for the change because it would bind the Center party even closer to the SPD and help block the formation of a *Bürgerblock* coalition. Others, including some DStP delegates, argued that any tactical advantages were offset by the political fallout from the image of the Weimar parties trying to hold onto power at all costs.[36]

The Prussian government took little part in the affair. The cabinet was not consulted by the Landtag leaders, and there is no evidence that the plan was ever discussed in a cabinet meeting. Otto Braun attended a caucus meeting of the Weimar party leaders, but he apparently did not speak. The ministry of the interior eventually commissioned a legal brief on the constitutionality of the move, but the results did not become available until after the Landtag had voted on the resolution.[37]

The resolution to change the bylaws was introduced at a special session on

April 12, 1932, three weeks after the legislators had recessed to prepare for the election. The delegates certainly did not anticipate a special session on changing the bylaws of a Landtag that was about to end. The opposition parties were stunned and reacted furiously to what they described as a parliamentary "deception." They refused to participate in the debate and, after failing to pass a resolution tabling the initiative, voted stoically, but impotently, against the motion.[38]

The political impact of the initiative was unclear. Some analysts argued that the change in the bylaws significantly reduced the prestige of democracy because it showed that the Weimar parties themselves had lost faith in the system. After the election, the "national opposition" also pointed out that the new bylaws paralyzed the Landtag and essentially made the election of a new prime minister all but impossible. The de facto paralysis of parliamentary politics in the state in turn facilitated the federal takeover of Prussia some months later. The Weimar coalition parties pointed out that the new Landtag was free to change the bylaws that it had inherited. The new Landtag never mustered the necessary majority to pass such a resolution largely because the Communists refused to vote for it, also recognizing that this would mean the election of a Nazi prime minister.[39]

None of this maneuvering mattered very much. While the change in the Landtag's bylaws occasioned a great deal of discussion after the fact, at the time it was completely overshadowed by the statewide election campaign. The 1932 Landtag contest was not a campaign to which the Weimar coalition parties looked forward; that the opposition parties would score massive gains was a foregone conclusion. As a result, the Weimar coalition faced the election with pessimism and despair. The prime minister, already in poor health, later wrote that despite his upbeat campaign speeches, he knew the Prussian bastion could no longer be held. Earlier he had characterized his last appearance before the old Landtag as his "farewell speech." But Braun also told the legislature the coalition partners were determined to preserve Prussia's democratic stability until the present "political apparition [*politischer Spuk*]" had passed.[40]

Between the 1930 Reichstag contest and the March 1933 national elections, Germany was subjected to a series of increasingly violent election campaigns. The Prussian contest was an important milestone: it came just two weeks after the runoff election for Reich president and only a few weeks before the July Reichstag elections. As expected, the result of the Landtag election was a severe blow for all of the moderate groups. The Weimar coalition parties lost control of the Prussian legislature, and moderate conservative groups, like the DVP and the VKP, virtually disappeared. (Incidentally, the election effectively ended the political career of Count von Westarp, the longtime DNVP leader whom Hugenberg had ousted. Westarp attempted but failed to make a political comeback on the VKP ticket.) The big winners were the extremist groups: Communists and Nazis together controlled 52 percent of the legislature, and the NSDAP had the largest block of delegates. For once Goebbels's hyperbole ("a fantastic victory") was fully justified.[41]

All groups on the right expected the Prussian elections to signal major changes in the state's governing coalition. Hindenburg, no doubt reflecting Brüning's views, had expressed hope as early as February that after the elections negotiations would begin to create a government of "national concentration." Goebbels put it more succinctly: "Prussia has to fall."[42]

Initially, all seemed to go well for the right-wing opposition. Two days after the election, the Braun cabinet formally resigned,[43] although it continued to govern until the Landtag elected a new prime minister and cabinet. Nevertheless, the ailing Otto Braun saw his role in Prussian politics as coming to an end and spent much of his subsequent time either in his house in the Berlin suburb of Zehlendorf or in his vacation home in Ascona, Switzerland. Because of his senior status in the cabinet, Heinrich Hirtsiefer, the Center party minister of welfare, became de facto prime minister.[44]

Much as they savored their triumph, the right-wing opposition groups also recognized that they lacked the votes to form a government of their own. Plans for an inaugural session of the new Landtag in early May were dropped when it became clear that the legislature could not agree on a new prime minister. The first working meeting of the new Landtag did not take place until May 25, a month after the election. Goebbels's diary reflected the extreme right's frustration and confusion. He wrote, "Something has to happen. We have to get power soon. Otherwise we will win ourselves to death electioneering. . . . We have to make some sharp calculations [*eiskalt kalkulieren*]. . . . The most important thing is to keep one's nerves."[45]

At its inaugural session the legislature did manage to elect a new speaker. Hanns Kerrl, the number two man in the Nazi delegation, received the support of all of the bourgeois parties, including the Center party. Kerrl's election certainly symbolized the passing of an era; he was the first speaker of the Landtag since 1919 who was not a Social Democrat. But imediately after Kerrl's triumph, showing utter disrespect for the prestige of the house, the Nazis initiated an attack on the Communist members that led to a massive brawl. Kerrl had to call police into the chamber to separate the combatants and restore order.[46]

In the meantime, events in the Reich had taken an unexpected and dramatic turn. On May 10, Hindenburg refused to grant Brüning further authority to continue governing by decree, thereby forcing his resignation. The new Reich chancellor was Franz von Papen. Hindenburg was disappointed with Brüning for a variety of reasons, but the failure of the chancellor's Prussian policies ranked high on the list. Despite the outcome of the Landtag election, Brüning had been unable to persuade the leaders of his own party in Prussia to leave the Social Democrats and join a *Bürgerblock* coalition instead.

Since it was well known that Brüning supported a *Bürgerblock* coalition with Nazi participation in Prussia, it is surprising that he did not move more forcefully to advance this goal. Brüning badly misjudged his political power. Convinced the outcome of the presidential election had strengthened his hand with Hindenburg and that he continued to have the president's full confidence, Brüning did not force the Prussian issue. He wanted a Prussian *Bürgerblock* cabinet on his own terms, which meant that neither the prime minister's office nor the ministry of the interior should be headed by a Nazi. His hesitation contributed to his political downfall. Much to his surprise, he was "tripped up a hundred meters before the goal."

At the beginning of May the chancellor suggested a Prussian *Bürgerblock* coalition with Nazi participation headed by Carl Goerdeler, the conservative mayor of Leipzig. To reduce the Nazis' influence in the new cabinet, the chancellor also wanted Hindenburg to appoint Goerdeler vice chancellor in the Reich cabinet and to appoint federal commissioners for the Prussian ministry of justice and the state's police. However, both Hitler and Goebbels rejected a coalition with the Center party if this meant subjecting the Nazis to the rules of parliamentary democracy. The Prussian Center party was still reluctant to break up it alliance with the SPD. At Brüning's request Hirtsiefer seems to have approached Severing with a proposal that the Social Democratic ministers might resign from the cabinet to facilitate the formation of a new government, but as Severing wrote later, Hirtsiefer was clearly unenthusiastic about the plan and readily acknowledged the force of Severing's objections.[47]

Aside from rejecting parliamentary democracy as such, a number of Nazi leaders, including Hitler himself, also showed little interest in joining a Prussian cabinet because they thought they were getting a better offer from the new regime in the Reich. Although some segments of the business community and the agrarian sector initially welcomed the new chancellor's appointment, without the Nazis' good will Papen had virtually no support in the Reichstag; his cabinet would overwhelmingly lose any vote of confidence.[48]

The deal between the Nazis and the new Reich leaders was struck in a series of secret conversations between Hitler, Papen, and Schleicher at the beginning of May. The key terms of the agreement are known. In return for initial Nazi support of Papen's government, Kurt von Schleicher (who continued in his role as *eminence grise* of Reich politics under Papen) and the new chancellor agreed to two Nazi demands: the storm troopers (as well as the Communist RFB) would be allowed back on the streets, and there would be new Reichstag elections at the end of July. Both decisions, of course, would allow the Nazis ample opportunity for new waves of agitation and political violence.

Prussia's role in these conversations remains unclear. Both Friedrich von Gayl, the new Reich minister of the interior in Papen's cabinet, and Schleicher later claimed that the Nazi leader had agreed to the federal take-over of Prussia as part of a long-range program for bringing domestic peace and stability to the Reich. In return, Schleicher and Papen offered the Nazis a power-sharing arrangement in Prussia. Hitler denied that any such agreement existed, and for once the evidence seems to suggest he was right: Prussia was not part of the deal. The Nazis remained deeply suspicious of Papen's future intentions in Prussia, and they had good reasons for their distrust. Papen had his own agenda for Prussia. The new chancellor was already planning to appoint a Reich commissioner for Prussia, and his scenario did not envision a Nazi role in the federal takeover of the state.[49]

While dramatic changes were taking place at the Reich level, efforts by the Prussian parties to create a new coalition in Prussia remained deadlocked. The key to electing any *Bürgerblock* cabinet, of course, was an agreement between the Nazis and the Center party. The other parties were condemned to remain on the sidelines, or, at best, attempt to act as catalysts. Among the Weimar coalition parties, the SPD wavered between trying to hold onto Prussia as long as possible and simply resigning from the cabinet in the hope that a new *Bügerblock* cabinet would be blamed for the problems facing the state. In the end both the legislative and executive leaders of the Prussian SPD, men like Heilmann, Severing, and Grzesinski, concluded that the party should not desert the cabinet and drive the Center party into the arms of the Nazis. Instead, the SPD would continue its efforts to keep the Center party on its left-of-center course.[50]

Strengthening the Weimar coalition as the last bulwark against Nazism was also the goal of a bizarre effort by the ubiquitous Wilhelm Abegg. He convinced himself (and some historians) that after the Nazi triumph in the April elections, the KPD was ready to work with the SPD, and that he, Abegg, could bring the estranged brothers together again. What was needed was bold action, which was sadly lacking among the state's Social Democratic leaders.[51] In a much overvalued conversation between Abegg and two leaders of the Communist delegations in the Reichstag and Landtag, Ernst Torgler and Wilhelm Kasper, the state secretary sharply criticized both Braun and Severing. According to Abegg, instead of "seizing hold of the wheel they sat there with their hands in their laps." Abegg and his visitors discussed possible parliamentary cooperation between the KPD and the parties of the Weimar coalition. Abegg, who had initiated the meeting, suggested that the KPD help solve the Prussian cabinet crisis by voting for a Center party candidate for prime minister. The state secretary specifically mentioned

Johannes Gronowski, the *Oberpräsident* of Westphalia. The Communist delegates listened with interest but made no commitments.[52]

There is very little evidence that the Communists were willing to tolerate,
much less support, any parliamentary government that included the Social
Democrats. The KPD central committee's analysis of the results on the day
after the Landtag election did call for the union of all forces opposed to
fascism and Nazism, but unity still had to be on the Communists' terms:
"from below." They continued to insist that Social Democratic workers had to
desert their party and union leaders before working-class unity could be
accomplished. Braun, Severing, and Zörgiebel (the police chief of Berlin at
the time of the May 1929 riots) were singled out as SPD leaders with whom
the Communists would never work.[53]

The Communists' actions also spoke with a loud and unmistakable
voice. With a few exceptions, the KPD formed a solid bloc with the DNVP
and the Nazis in the Landtag, routinely voting against both the Weimar
coalition and parliamentary democracy itself.[54] As long as the KPD saw the
Prussian government as the primary obstacle to proletarian revolution, the
party had no interest in cooperating with the Prussian defenders of political
pluralism. Finally, the Communists felt there was no risk involved in their
obstructionist policy. The Comintern leaders were apparently convinced as
early as mid-May that there would be no *Bürgerblock* cabinet in Prussia; the
Nazis and the Catholics were too far apart to make a coalition agreement
possible.

On the surface this seemed a hasty conclusion. The Center and right-wing
parties had a comfortable majority in the Landtag, and none of the potential
partners in a *Bürgerblock* coalition rejected such a partnership on principle.
However, they were far apart on a large number of issues, ranging from
fundamental constitutional questions to personnel appointments. To begin
with, the neoconservatives were slow to recognize that the Nazis were now
the largest bully on the block. Schleicher's decision to strike Kube's name
from the guest list for a dinner of leading right-wing politicians on January 4,
1932, with the notation, "not important enough [*zu klein*]" indicated the
neoconservatives' feelings about the Prussian Nazis. Alfred Hugenberg, the
DNVP leader and now an enthusiastic supporter of Franz von Papen, exhibited similar arrogance and naiveté. He envisioned a Prussian cabinet composed of ministers from the DNVP, the Center party, and the Nazis, headed
by a German Nationalist prime minister. However, once elected, the government would not be bound by the rules of parliamentary democracy or collegiality. Hugenberg proposed that the Reich president should then appoint
the prime minister as federal commissioner for Prussia, and that the chief
executive should be independent of both the Landtag and the cabinet and
responsible only to the Reich president. Hugenberg's plans were rejected as

unconstitutional by the Center party and as politically insulting by the NSDAP.[55]

Ironically, elements in both the Catholic party and the NSDAP seemed less intransigent than the German Nationalists on the question of a parliamentary *Bürgerblock* coalition. Heinrich Brüning no longer held executive office, but he was deeply involved in the ongoing discussions about a new Prussian coalition. He continued to press for a Prussian *Bürgerblock* cabinet that included the Center party and the Nazis. Some Prussian right-wing Catholic leaders, including Adenauer and the prominent Landtag members Lauscher and Grass, also agreed that the experiment should be tried. Papen, the new Reich chancellor, joined the chorus. At the beginning of June he met several times with representatives of the DNVP, the Center party, and the NSDAP, ostensibly to act as midwife for the Prussian *Bürgerblock* coalition.[56]

Brüning's conclusion that most of the Prussian Center party was prepared "virtually without conditions" to form a government with the Nazis and that he had to restrain his colleagues from giving away all of their bargaining chips, was a vast exaggeration. Even he had difficulty characterizing the stand of Hirtsiefer, the de facto leader of the Prussian Center party. Brüning described Hirtsiefer alternately as the only member of the Landtag delegation with sound political instincts (in other words, willing to follow Brüning's lead) and as a product of the "Hess system," which had committed the Prussian Center party to an unbreakable alliance with the Social Democrats. Above all, in assessing the position of his Prussian colleagues the former chancellor tended to forget that he and the Prussian Center party leaders had sharply differing priorities. Brüning wanted to bind the Nazis to neoconservatism, but most of the Prussian Catholics were willing to enter into an alliance with the Nazis only if Hitler's men accepted the state's system of parliamentary democracy. All of the Prussian Center party spokesmen thought in terms of a parliamentary *Bürgerblock,* not a cabinet independent of the legislature and the rules of parliamentary democracy.[57]

The Nazis were not divided on systemic issues—they all wanted to destroy parliamentary democracy—but in the second half of 1932 the NSDAP was torn by massive internal debates over tactics. Prussian coalition politics lay at the center of this struggle. The so-called Strasser wing, which included the Prussian NSDAP leaders Kube and Kerrl, argued joining a *Bürgerblock* cabinet in the state would give the Nazis a foothold on executive power and prevent the party from "winning itself to death with electioneering," as Goebbels put it. While recognizing the pitfalls of the party's obstructionist course, Goebbels himself opposed any parliamentary deal, even for tactical reasons. He feared that once the party had executive responsibility without possessing a monopoly of power, the Nazis would wear themselves out coping with the details of governing, and lose their "fighting spirit." Goebbels also acknowledged, however, that at least for a time Hitler wavered between the two positions.[58]

Since the Nazis and the Prussian Center party started with clearly incompatible ideological positions, a number of historians have questioned whether the potential partners ever really engaged in serious coalition talks. Were the numerous contacts not all parts of elaborate schemes of bluff and counterbluff in which the two parties sought to use the Prussian coalition negotiations to increase their leverage in the perennial struggles over power in the Reich? The answer seems to be, not entirely. Certainly for Goebbels and probably for Hitler the Prussian coalition was indeed part of a game of bluff. They had no real interest in forming a new parliamentary government in the state. On the other hand, for their own (often contradictory) reasons, men like Göring, Strasser, Kube, and Kerrl did think that forming a *Bürgerblock* coalition in Prussia was in the interest of the NSDAP. Brüning and some Prussian Center party leaders also expected political benefits from the experiment. Potential junior partners in a *Bürgerblock* coalition, like the DVP, similarly hoped and expected the negotiations to succeed.[59]

Negotiations between Nazi and Center party representatives began almost immediately after the elections and continued with varying degrees of intensity virtually until Hitler's appointment as Reich chancellor. The talks reached a first impasse at the beginning of June. At the Reich level, Brüning and the Center party's national chairman, Monsignor Ludwig Kaas, insisted on linking the formation of a Prussian *Bürgerblock* coalition with their (and Papen's) foreign policy agenda. Brüning argued that since the formation of a *Bürgerblock* government in Prussia would undoubtedly lead the national SPD to abandon its "policy of toleration" on foreign policy matters, dissolving the Weimar coalition in Prussia should be delayed until the Reich government had achieved arms parity at the Lausanne disarmament conference.[60]

Paralleling the discussion between Brüning, Kaas, and the Nazis, two leaders of the Prussian Landtag delegation, Lauscher and Grass, held a series of talks with Kube and Kerrl. Hovering in the background were Hirtsiefer, Strasser—and Hitler. Apparently acting on orders from the Nazi leader, Kube and Kerrl demanded that in addition to the prime minister, Nazis should fill two to four other cabinet posts, including that of minister of the interior. No wonder Goebbels, who was opposed to any deal with the Catholics, noted gleefully, "In Prussia . . . we are insisting on conditions which the Center party cannot accept."[61] At the same time, the NSDAP's negotiators refused even to divulge the names of their candidates for any of these posts. Not until after the August 13 crisis in the Reich did it become clear that Hitler himself was to have become Prussian prime minister. In contrast, the Center party Landtag leaders, acting in concert with the Social Democrats, insisted on keeping both the position of prime minister and that of minister of the interior out of Nazi hands. Drawing an analogy with the fascist takeover in Italy, the Prussian Center party boasted of a strength it did not have. A Center party delegate told the NSDAP, "You are not dealing with the Popolari here, you know."[62]

The Reich-Prussian linkage remained a complicating factor. At the beginning of June, the new chancellor made public a letter to the speaker of the Landtag threatening a federal takeover of the state unless the Landtag elected a prime minister. Like so much else during these dramatic months, Papen's motivation remains unclear. Some historians have claimed that he was essentially seconding the Brüning line; the carrot of a Prussian *Bürgerblock* coalition was to entice Hitler to become a junior partner of the neoconservatives. It is more likely, however, that Papen was merely engaging in a public relations ploy. By this time everybody knew of the difficulties in the negotiations between the Prussian Nazis and the Center party. Virtually certain that the Prussians could not meet his conditions, Papen's initiative was part of his propaganda preparations for the planned federal takeover of Prussia. The leading men in the Reich government—Papen, Gayl, and Schleicher—did not want to elect a prime minister who had the support of the Prussian legislature. The cabal around Hindenburg feared that the neoauthoritarian agenda would be blocked or at least delayed if the Prussian parties actually succeeded in electing a parliamentary government in the state.[63]

Each side blamed the other for the failure of the negotiations. Brüning, who discovered a host of enemies after he went into exile, accused Kaas of maintaining secret contacts with Papen that enabled the chancellor to undermine Brüning's plans. Historians, however, have found no evidence to support this claim.[64] The Prussian Nazi delegates later insisted that they and the Center party representatives had come quite close to agreeing in principle and that the pact had been sabotaged by left-wing Catholics. After the failure of the talks, Kube, who had worked hard to persuade the Prussian Center party to agree to a coalition on the Nazis' terms, accused the Prussian Catholics of being "camouflaged Social Democrats" who preferred to govern "with Jews and atheists instead of German Christians."

But this charge was equally groundless. In fact, the Prussian talks failed because at least at this stage the potential partners were speaking different political languages. The Center party was not willing to give up Prussia's constitutional system in return for the Nazis' cooperation, and the Nazi "radicals" succeeded in sabotaging any Prussian agreement that included abiding by constitutional rules. Goebbels wrote that although the Strasser wing continued to press for a deal with the Center party, Hitler had decided, "We will accept no responsibility [in Prussia]." The Nazi leader seems to have lost interest in the Prussian negotiations—if he ever had much—after

Schleicher's and Papen's promise to schedule new Reichstag elections gave Hitler yet another chance to achieve total power at the Reich level.[65]

On July 18 Kerrl wrote Papen that efforts to form a parliamentary coalition government had failed.[66] Two days later the Reich cabinet invoked the emergency powers of Article 48 of the Reich constitution, dismissed the caretaker Prussian government, and assumed direct control of the state. Papen had solved the Prussian government crisis and the Reich-Prussian dualism in his own way. In one sense, the federal takeover made the search for a new coalition in Prussia largely irrelevant. The chancellor in his capacity as Reich commissioner for Prussia acted as de facto prime minister; he also appointed ministers *pro tem* to head all cabinet departments. The "old" Braun government remained in office, but it had no influence on decision making in the state.

At the same time, the dynamics of coalition politics went on. The Landtag continued to meet, and for reasons of their own, the major parties also went on with their efforts to put together a new coalition. In some ways the federal takeover actually led to intensified negotiations. At least some of the negotiators were genuinely interested in regaining Prussia's states' rights, and putting together a new government would go a long way toward restoring the state's autonomy. Since part of Papen's justification for his coup had been the legislature's inability to solve the state's cabinet crisis, after the selection of a constitutionally elected cabinet the Reich government would have had considerable difficulty justifying federal control of Prussia.

Precisely for these reasons, after July 20 the chancellor had no interest in facilitating the formation of a new coalition in Prussia. A parliamentary *Bürgerblock* cabinet would not only revive the Reich-Prussian dualism, which the neoconservatives had just eliminated, but also present a formidable political rival to Papen's own Reich cabinet, which had virtually no backing in the Reichstag.[67]

In the last ten days of July, negotiations were suspended as the parties concentrated on the Reichstag elections. During the campaign, another bitter and violent affair, the Nazis, following their usual pattern, viciously attacked all other political groups, including their potential *Bürgerblock* partners. The Nazis' campaign style would undoubtedly make future negotiations in Prussia more difficult, particularly since there were unmistakable signs that the DVP and the DNVP were beginning to be uneasy about further association with the Nazis. For the July election contest the People's party and the German Nationalists concluded a tactical pact designed to prevent both a return of the Weimar coalition and a Reich and Prussian cabinet dominated by the Nazis.[68]

The outcome of the Reichstag elections was a stunning defeat for the Reich government; less than 10 percent of the new legislature would support

Papen's cabinet. The Nazis more than doubled their representation in the Reichstag, but failed to achieve the majority they had hoped for.

As far as Prussia was concerned, the elections changed little. For the moment the chancellor was not in danger; as long as he retained the confidence of the Reich president, he could ignore his lack of popular and parliamentary support and continue to rule by decree in both the Reich and Prussia. The left-wing groups remained impotent spectators on the sidelines. There were some tentative attempts by the SPD to revive contacts with the KPD after the July 20 coup, but they came to little. The Communists were still dominated by ultraleftists, and "social fascism" remained the official party line. The Social Democrats continued to argue against a *Bürgerblock* cabinet that included the Nazis, by the party's leaders also recognized that they would have little influence over the future course of events. Especially Otto Braun was fatalistic, having all but lost hope now that the Center party would resist making a deal with the Nazis. He claimed that he had come to recognize that in its "innermost being" *(Grundwesen)* the Catholic party was "antidemocratic and authoritarian."[69]

The key to any *Bürgerblock* coalition was still an agreement between the Center party and the Nazis. The two parties resumed negotiations on a variety of levels. Brüning continued his contacts with Nazi leaders, while in the Landtag Prussian Center party representatives met with their Nazi counterparts, notably Kube and Kerrl. At the same time, there were ongoing the talks between Papen, Schleicher, and the Nazis.

Center party leaders pursued parallel but not identical aims. Brüning and the party's national leaders agreed that the Catholics should attempt to form coalitions with the Nazis in states where only a caretaker government held office, Prussia foremost among them. The object was not only to give these states stable governments, but also to undermine or at least weaken Papen's position. There was a great deal of bitterness among members of the Center party against their former colleague who, many Catholics felt, was personally responsible for Brüning's fall. The Prussian Center party leaders shared these sentiments—after all, Papen had been a right-wing maverick in the Prussian Center party long before he became chancellor—but they had a specifically Prussian agenda as well. Contrary to Braun's pessimistic conclusion, Prussia's Catholics remained true to their political principles and were determined to preserve parliamentary democracy in the state.[70]

The Nazis recognized that under the parliamentary rules only an agreement with the Center party would give them a share of power in the state. For many this prospect remained unenticing. They preferred to deal with Papen and Schleicher, and at the beginning of August the Nazi "radicals" thought they had achieved their goal. The Prussian negotiations were put on hold;

Kerrl was "ordered" not to call the Landtag into session. Goebbels wrote on August 7, two day after Hitler had met with Schleicher, "All is set for next week. Chief [Hitler] will be Reich chancellor and Prussian prime minister. Strasser Reich and Prussian prime minister of the interior. Goebbels Prussian and Reich minister of education. . . . Göring air [ministry]. [Ministry of] justice for us. . . . I still can't believe it. At the gates of power. . . . Just a few days more."[71]

The Nazis' euphoria was premature. A week later the Nazi leader had been rebuffed, the party's hopes dashed. On August 13, 1932, the Reich president, obviously acting on Papen's advice, refused Hitler's demand for plenipotentiary power. As a consolation prize, Hindenburg offered the Nazi leader the post of vice chancellor in Papen's cabinet. There was no mention of any Prussian posts. Hitler refused.[72]

The August setback precipitated not only a severe crisis in the NSDAP, but also moved the Prussian negotiations off dead center. All along, the Prussian Nazi negotiators had taken the talks with the Center party much more seriously than did the party's national leaders. This was particularly true after it became clear how little the commissioners' regime benefited the Nazis. True, Papen's appointees instituted a wholesale purge of democratic officials from the Prussian ministries and territorial administrative offices, but they also systematically blocked the appointment of Nazis to influential posts. Members of the Weimar coalition parties were replaced by men close to the neoconservatives. Papen's rule in Prussia prevented the Nazis from taking their place at the patronage trough, and Kerrl and Kube hoped to rectify this situation by becoming part of a Prussian *Bürgerblock* coalition.[73]

As the Prussian negotiations intensified in the second half of August, the talks alternately raised fears and hopes that the negotiations might actually succeed. Stung by the setback of August 13, Hitler seemed briefly to permit Strasser and the Prussian Nazis to play the Prussian card in earnest. As a result, the Nazis suddenly appeared quite accommodating, and all of the negotiators later remembered that the talks had reached a stage at which agreement no longer seemed impossible. The Nazis reduced their demands for ministerial posts to two of those previously held by Social Democrats: the offices of prime minister and interior minister. The Nazis also agreed to a Center party demand for Catholic state secretaries (deputy ministers) in all Nazi-controlled ministries. Above all, Kerrl assured his potential partners that the NSDAP would abide by parliamentary rules in running Prussia. Kerrl was so confident that the Landtag could elect a prime minister that he suggested to Papen and Hindenburg the new Prussian chief executive should also be appointed Reich commissioner. Papen was sufficiently worried about the chances of a constitutionally elected *Bürgerblock* cabinet in the state that he not only refused Kerrl's request, but also asked the Reich president for contingent authority to federalize the Prussian police if a new Prussian parliamentary government took office.[74]

In the end, the talks failed again. This was not the fault of the Prussian negotiators, but of the Reich government and the national leaders of the Nazi and Center parties. Papen continued to work against the election of a parliamentary government in Prussia. Among the Nazis Goebbels feverishly stoked the fires against Strasser and a deal with the Catholics. As far as the Center party was concerned, Brüning seems to have gotten cold feet, fearing that if the Prussian Center party negotiated a *Bürgerblock* coalition on its own, this would reduce his options for influencing the political dynamics in the Reich. Brüning still hoped for a return to power together with simultaneous *Bürgerblock* cabinets in the Reich and state. At the end of August, the parties tabled their Prussian proposals, and the political focus again shifted to the Reich. A final summit meeting between Hitler and the Prussian Center party leaders on September 10 was little more than a face-saving exercise for both sides.[75]

But, like a jack-in-the-box, the prospect of a Prussian *Bürgerblock* cabinet quickly reemerged. On several occasions the Prussian negotiators came close to agreement on specific Prussian aspects of a coalition deal, only to be thwarted by the Nazis's insistence on a Reich-Prussian linkage. They attempted to persuade Hindenburg that he should use his authority to revoke the changes in the Landtag bylaws voted in April. This would make it possible to elect a Prussian prime minister, who—according to this scenario—would be Hitler. Hindenburg would then appoint the Prussian prime minister as Reich chancellor, and eliminate the Reich-Prussian dualism. At the beginning of November Goebbels allowed himself another brief moment of euphoria as he contemplated the future. "If it works, I get power in Prussia. Then we'll clean up." But he added cautiously, "I still can't believe it, and I don't believe it." Again guided by Papen, Hindenburg refused to accept the Nazi plans for a Reich-Prussian linkage, although the Reich cabinet now agreed that it would recognize a constitutionally elected Prussian government. It could make this promise because such a development was highly unlikely: by now neither the Nazis (nor, for that matter, the national Center party leaders) had any interest in a coalition agreement limited to Prussia.[76]

In the last two months of 1932, the political ground shifted considerably. Papen's power eroded, and Schleicher emerged as the Reich cabinet's strongman. The November Reichstag elections brought major setbacks for the Nazis, demonstrating that their popularity had peaked. This gave additional ammunition to the Strasser wing of the party, which had long argued that the NSDAP could not achieve power through the ballot box alone.

There was movement on other sides as well. Otto Braun stirred himself

out of his lethargy and met with Papen and Hindenburg in an effort to persuade the Reich president to withdraw the regime of the commissioners. As
expected, the Reich leaders refused, but the effort itself was sufficient to
alarm the Nazi hard-liners. Since the Prussian Nazis, too, were anxious to
rescind the federal takeover, a symbiosis of sorts existed between the Prussian
Nazis and the state's caretaker government. Goebbels warned his party comrades not to be "roped in [einspannen]" by Braun.[77]

Papen was also sufficiently concerned to buttress the powers of the commissioners's regime. Determined "not to permit interference by the former
[sic] Prussian cabinet in the workings of the executive," the chancellor obtained another presidential decree giving the commissioners exclusive power
to issue decrees in the names of the Reich or Prussian governments. Yet,
while taking further steps to prevent the restoration of parliamentary democracy in Prussia, Papen also began a series of talks with national party leaders
to increase his support in the Reichstag. Tutored by Papen, Hindenburg
offered to appoint Hitler as head of a parliamentary national cabinet, provided
that he, Hindenburg, had final control of the choice of cabinet members and
the Reich-Prussian dualism was permanently eliminated. Hitler refused to
accept the rules of parliamentary democracy for any cabinet he headed.

Parallel negotiations between Prussian Nazi and Center party representatives also resumed. The Nazis gave up proposing Hitler as prime minister
and nominated the "moderate" Göring instead. (Goebbels once called Göring,
who was now speaker of the Reichstag, "Brüning's friend.") In addition to the
office of prime minister, the Nazis demanded the ministries of education and
interior. The negotiations faltered again on the issue of the Reich-Prussian
dualism. The Catholics insisted that the Nazis should not control both the
office of Reich chancellor and Prussian prime minister. The Center party
resurrected the candidacy of Carl Goerdeler as prime minister, but he was
rejected by the Nazis.[78]

In the meantime, the penultimate plot of these intrigue-rich final months
of the Weimar era was taking place in the president's office. Kurt von
Schleicher had decided to move from behind the scenes to center stage. At the
heart of the general's plans for bringing political stability to Germany lay the
illusion that he could gain a parliamentary majority in the Reichstag through
an ad hoc coalition composed primarily or right-wing SPD delegates and
"moderates" in the Nazi party. Schleicher was able to persuade Hindenburg
(or, more precisely, the president's son, Oskar von Hindenburg, who in turn
brought his father around) that he could obtain a vote of confidence in the
Reichstag on this basis, and at the beginning of December 1932 Papen was
forced out of office.

Prussia played a major role in Schleicher's tactical plans, although his
views on the Reich-state relationship and the future of democracy were little

different from those of Papen. Long before his appointment as Reich chancellor, as *eminence grise* of Weimar politics, the general had worked hard to destroy parliamentary democracy in the state. Schleicher had also been one of the driving forces behind the federal takeover of Prussia.

At the beginning of December, Schleicher offered the Nazis a deal. In return for their votes of confidence for his cabinet in the Reichstag, he would appoint some Nazis to the Reich cabinet, and most important, accept Gregor Strasser as Prussian prime minister. Schleicher specifically rejected Göring, insisting on Strasser. It was unclear whether Schleicher's offer included lifting the federal takeover. The general seems to have suggested to Strasser that with his election the commissioners's regime would come to an end, but he made it equally clear to Braun and the provisional Prussian ministers that the Reich cabinet had no intention of restoring Prussia's rights as a state.[79]

The leaders of a potential Prussian *Bürgerblock* coalition were divided on the offer. Since Schleicher's proposals essentially followed the lines already tentatively worked out by Center party and Nazi negotiators in the Prussian Landtag, the Catholics would have accepted the offer. Strasser himself was also willing to go along with the proposal; it corresponded to his "salami slice" concept of gaining power. Others in the NSDAP immediately rejected Schleicher's scheme, notably Goebbels, who argued, "If we had power in Prussia, we probably wouldn't know what to do with it." In the end, the Nazi hard-liners won. Hitler refused Schleicher's proposal, and Strasser resigned his party posts, precipitating a major, if brief, crisis in the NSDAP.[80]

Actually, Schleicher's scheme would have failed even if Hitler had accepted Strasser's advice and cooperated with the general. The Social Democrats, the second leg of Schleicher's as hoc coalition, resolutely rejected the new chancellor's Machiavellian scheme. Although Schleicher attempted to persuade the SPD that selecting Gregor Strasser as Prussian prime minister was a diabolically clever move that would lead to the disintegration of the NSDAP (he claimed Strasser and Hitler were bitter political rivals and personal enemies, which was not true), for the Social Democrats the issue was not personality, but constitutionality. Schleicher's discussions with Leipart, the head of the Socialist unions, and Rudolf Breitscheid, chairman of the SPD's caucus in the Reichstag, made it clear that the chancellor's hopes of splitting the Socialists were completely illusory. The Social Democrats rejected out of hand Schleicher's tentative suggestion that the SPD would look the other way if the Reich government acted unconstitutionally, if this were the only way of keeping the Nazis from achieving total power.[81]

The Schleicher episode—and it was hardly more than that—had a curious epilogue. The Nazi hard-liners finally triumphed. Goebbels celebrated his victory: Strasser's resignation meant "no more negotiations with the Center party." There was no exodus of "moderates" when Strasser left the NSDAP, but all of his associates remained under a cloud. This was certainly true of Wilhelm Kube, until the December crisis one of Strasser's closest political allies. "Kube is a marked man [*gestellt*]," wrote Goebbels. "He is going to stay with us. But [I] don't trust him." The Prussian Nazi leaders were completely excluded from the future negotiations, and when the Nazis came to power at the end of January, the new Prussian prime minister was Göring, not Kerrl or Kube.[82]

More significant was a last-ditch effort by Otto Braun at the beginning of January to strike a deal with Schleicher. For obvious reasons, the prime minister and the "old" ministers had rejected cooperation with Papen, but unlike the SPD's national leaders, both Severing and Braun felt that the new chancellor's ideas should be explored further. Severing criticized Breitscheid's proud statement that the SPD would call the masses to the streets if Schleicher acted unconstitutionally to stop Hitler. His prophetic words were: "You will bitterly regret and perhaps even curse this hour."[83]

In a clear departure from the SPD's policy of not dealing with Schleicher, Braun met secretly with the chancellor (the SPD's national chairman, Otto Wels, knew nothing about the contacts) on January 6 and offered to support Schleicher's attempt to rule by decree at the Reich level—the chancellor's plan for an ad hoc coalition in the Reichstag having collapsed in the meantime—if Schleicher would withdraw the commissioners' regime and permit the restoration of constitutional, parliamentary government in Prussia. The Prussian government would then dissolve the Landtag and schedule new elections for late spring—by that time Braun expected the Nazis to have lost much of their electoral appeal. The purpose of Braun's "coup d'état of the center" was to return Prussia to its status as the rock of democracy. Once that had been secured, the restoration of democracy for the whole Reich would follow in due course—as it had in 1923.[84]

Schleicher rejected Braun's offer and thereby revealed his true authoritarian colors. Although now desperately searching for allies, the chancellor was unwilling to restore democratic government to Prussia as the price for Braun's support. His insistence that the commissioners' regime would have to stay demonstrated above all else that the destruction of parliamentary democracy in Prussia lay at the heart of the neoconservative agenda. Schleicher categorically refused to cooperate with Otto Braun and the "old" government. In fact, he also rejected removing the federal commissioners to make way for any other parliamentarily elected Prussian government.[85]

It all came to nothing, of course. While Schleicher thought he was still operating from a position of strength, his authority was being actively undermined by Papen's intrigues. In the first days of January, Hitler and the former chancellor worked out a deal that would put the Nazi leader in the chancellor's office and inaugurate the nightmare of the Third Reich.

Was there ever a realistic alternative to the neoconservative authoritarian regime or the continuation of the Weimar coalition cabinet? Probably not. Otto Braun's rejection of the DVP as a potential coalition partner and the DVP's choice to link its fortunes to the "national opposition" parties blocked any chance of reviving the grand coalition, undoubtedly the best hope for long-term stability in the state. As for a *Bürgerblock* coalition in Prussia, although the Center party insisted it was open to all offers, there were major systemic barriers to its cooperation with the "national opposition." Despite frequent disclaimers, the Weimar coalition parties were bound in more than a tactical alliance. They were convinced their cooperation represented the key to preserving parliamentary democracy in Prussia and ultimately in the Reich.

The gap between the two camps was unbridgeable. The coalition parties insisted that the neoconservative chancellors remove the federal commissioners' regime while attempting to force the Nazis to obey the rules of parliamentary democracy. They failed on both counts. The neoconservatives, for their part, failed to realize that in making a pact with Hitler they also signed their own political death warrants.

CHAPTER 8

The Coup of July 20, 1932

No single event in the twisted story of the last years of the Weimar Republic has been debated so passionately as the federal takeover of Prussia in July 1932. The coup not only effectively ended the state's autonomy and its political system, but also, many argued, was instrumental in bringing the Nazis to power only a few months later. The result was a flood of mutual recriminations, especially after World War II when the surviving participants in the drama sought to justify their responses to the coup. Braun, Severing, Abegg, Grzesinski, and Klepper accused each other of lacking the courage to act or of unrealistically recommending that the Prussian leaders should have "actively resisted" the federal takeover. Historians have joined the fray, liberally passing out blame and praise and pronouncing one or the other of the contemporary camps to be "right" in its reaction to the coup.

The historiography of Papen's Prussian coup has concentrated on two issues: the motivation of those in the Reich government who initiated the federal takeover and the reasons and appropriateness of Prussia's response. Any discussion of the motivation issue has to begin not with Papen, but with Brüning. The first of the neoconservative presidential chancellors had considered a partial federal takeover of Prussia as early as December 1930. The plan was part of the chancellors' complicated scenario for coopting the Nazis into the neoconservative camp. Without yielding to Hitler's ambitions for total power, Brüning intended to obtain the Nazis' support for his national government by offering them seats in the Prussian cabinet. From Brüning's point of view, such a scenario achieved two of the neoconservative's long-sought goals: to destroy the Weimar coalition and to establish a *Bürgerblock* cabinet in Prussia. At the same time, Brüning did not want the Nazis to exercise decisive control. To prevent Hitler and his followers from monopolizing power in Prussia, the chancellor intended to place the Prussian police forces as well as those of the other northern German *Länder* under federal control.[1]

Brüning's plans failed. The Nazis were unwilling to accept a junior partnership, and the Prussian Weimar coalition leaders vigorously opposed both the dissolution of the state's longtime coalition and the chancellor's plans for a partial federal takeover. In the face of strenuous objections, Brüning did not actively pursue his goals. Papen resurrected the idea of federalizing the Prussian police after the Nazi victory in the April 1932 Landtag elections increased the likelihood that the NSDAP would become part of a right-of-center cabinet in Prussia. In fact, much to Brüning's annoyance, after World War II Papen claimed that his actions on July 20, 1932, were simply a continuation of Brüning's earlier plans to contain the Nazis' influence in Prussia. In retrospect, then, the neoconservative apologists portrayed the coup of July 20 as primarily a bold step to prevent the Nazi seizure of power.

Brüning's explanation was at least subjectively honest, but his successor's account was a wholly self-serving distortion. As we shall see, Papen was pursuing his own agenda, and his claim that the federal takeover was primarily directed against the Nazis was an afterthought that has no support in contemporary documentation.[2]

Many contemporaries, as well as later historians, charged that far from intending to stop the Nazis, Papen acted in close consultation with them. According to this view Papen, the chancellor who was "beholden to Hitler [hitlerhörig]," staged his Prussian coup as part of the secret agreement worked out between Schleicher, Papen, and Hitler.[3] This claim relies heavily on *cui bono* considerations. The Nazis were the ultimate beneficiaries of the coup when they came to power a few months later, so that it appeared likely that they also participated in its planning and implementation. There is no doubt that all Nazis—hard-liners and moderates alike—supported any course of action that would put the Prussian police under federal control. Right-wing extremists insisted that as long as the Prussian minister of the interior was a "Marxist," the state would systematically harass the Nazis and other right-wing groups and prevent them from exercizing their rights of free speech and assembly. Moreover, the Nazi campaign against the Prussian police grew increasingly strident as the 1932 Reichstag election campaign heated up, with attacks culminating on July 18 and 19. Hitler sent Papen a strongly worded telegram complaining about the handling of a Nazi rally in Königsberg by the Prussian police on July 18. A day later Hans Kerrl, the Nazi speaker of the Landtag, seconded his *Führer*'s complaints in a letter to Papen. Surely, then, it was no coincidence that on July 20 the Reich government took over the state. (Incidentally, an investigation by Papen's appointees in the interior ministry showed that Hitler's charges were groundless. The Königsberg police had acted correctly at all times.)[4]

The neoconservatives and the Nazis remained uneasy partners. As we shall see in more detail in the next chapter, Papen and Schleicher had plans of their own for Prussia, and it is not certain that Hitler and other National Socialists either knew of the Reich government's intentions or that they shared Papen's and Schleicher's desire for a complete federal takeover of the state. There is no record of what was said in the secret discussions between Hitler, Papen, and Schleicher that led to Brüning's dismissal and Papen's appointment as Reich chancellor in May 1932. In fact, the uneasy partnership between the Nazis and the neoconservatives dissolved into bitter animosity soon after the coup. Finally, there is a danger in arguing *prae hoc ergo post hoc*. The agreement between Hitler and Papen in January 1933, which did indeed lead to the Nazi seizure of power, does not mean that a similar deal had been struck six months earlier. In July 1932, the Reich government and Papen himself were convinced they held a full suit of trump cards and did not need the Nazis.[5]

The Nazis were agreed on the police issue, but Hitler and his followers were divided on virtually all other aspects of Prussia's role in their drive for total power. "Hard-liners" like Goebbels and Hitler and "moderates" like Strasser and the Nazi leaders in the Prussian Landtag differed sharply on the advantages or disadvantages of a federal takeover in Prussia. For the most part, the "moderates" opposed it. They distrusted Papen and the Reich minister of the interior, Baron Wilhelm von Gayl, and they argued (correctly) that while the takeover would solve the NSDAP's problems with the Prussian police, it would also preclude a parliamentary *Bürgerblock* cabinet in Prussia, thus delaying further the party's achieving a share of executive power. Goebbels and Hitler welcomed the federal takeover for its short-term benefits. With Severing and the republican officials in the interior ministry out of the way, the Nazis were free to unleash the wave of political terror that Goebbels and Hitler felt would assure them an absolute majority in the upcoming Reichstag elections and consequently pave the way for gaining total power in all of Germany.[6]

Politics aside, Germany in 1932 was still a *Rechtsstaat,* and any takeover of a state by the Reich government had to be justified by invoking Article 48 of the Weimar constitution. This emergency clause gave the Reich president authority to suspend the rights of self-government in a state if, in his judgment, the *Land* had either violated its constitutional duty to preserve republican government or it was demonstrably unable to maintain law and order. The Papen government argued that both applied to Prussia.

The claim that Prussia had neglected to maintain the republican form of government was a piece of blatant political cynicism. Ostensibly the state's offense was its failure to control political extremism. As we saw earlier, the Reich and Prussian governments had repeatedly clashed over the issue. Since the mid-1920s, the right-of-center Reich cabinets had argued that the Communists posed an acute revolutionary threat, while the Nazis and other extreme right-wing groups were either harmless or could be useful as auxiliary forces to contain the Communist danger. The Prussian government, especially after 1930, was convinced the KPD was a paper tiger, while the Nazis represented a real danger to parliamentary democracy.

The Papen government insisted that leading Prussian officials not only refused to take the Communist threat seriously, but also were clandestinely cooperating with left-wing extremists to sabotage the Reich's security policies and to increase the Communists influence in Prussia.[7] As proof, the Reich cabinet cited the conversation between Abegg and the Communist leaders Torgler and Kasper in June 1932. Actually, the contacts revealed much about Abegg's ambition to put himself in the limelight. They were certainly not a conspiracy against the Weimar constitution. (Heilmann dismissed them as "highly superfluous jabbering.")[8] Moreover, the initiative for the meeting seems to have been the work of an agent provocateur. Abegg contacted the two Communists at the suggestion of Rudolf Diels, head of the police desk in the Prussian interior ministry. Diels was also present at the talks, and it was he who reported the substance of the conversation to Papen. News of Abegg's discussions immediately leaked to the press, convinced the Reich interior minister that he had enough evidence to persuade Hindenburg that the Prussian government was conspiring with the Bolsheviks.[9] (Diels was a witness for the Reich cabinet in the later legal altercations between Prussia and the Reich. As a reward he not only survived Papen's purge of most senior officials in the Prussian interior ministry, but also went on to become the first head of the Gestapo after the Nazis took over.)[10]

The charge that the Prussian government was unable to maintain law and order was also related to the "soft on Communism" theme. The Papen cabinet claimed that political violence in the state had risen primarily because the Prussian police failed to react to Communist provocations. Of course, the Reich government itself was largely responsible for the increased number of bloody clashes. At Hitler's insistence, Papen not only revoked the federal ban on demonstrations by uniformed Nazi storm troopers and Communist Red Front Fighters, but also prevented the states from prohibiting them within their own borders. The Prussian government acted vigorously to contain the consequent explosion of political violence between Nazis and Communists, but the problem simply exceeded the state's authority and resources.[11]

Seemingly unaware of the contradictions in their arguments, the neoconservatives also charged that the Prussian interior ministry was hampered in its efforts to maintain law and order because the state's police forces contained a growing number of Nazi sympathizers. Even on its face, the charge did not ring true. If the Prussian police was full of Nazi sympathizers—especially in its senior ranks, as Brüning, for example, claimed—Hitler would hardly have looked upon the state police as the primary barrier to his rise to power.[12]

As when it charged that Prussian officials were conspiring with Communists, the Reich government needed another smoking gun to claim that Prussia was unable to maintain law and order. It was provided by the so-called Bloody Sunday of Altona. The town is now part of the city-state of Hamburg, but in 1932 it was still part of Prussia. On July 17 a large force of uniformed Nazi storm troopers paraded through Altona's working-class districts, where they knew large numbers of Communist sympathizers lived. Not surprisingly, the Nazi demonstration led to a violent clash. The police underestimated the volatility of the situation. At the time, Altona's police chief was meeting with Severing in Lübeck. For several hours the police lost control of the situation, and when order was restored, more than a dozen Nazis and Communists lay dead. The Prussian authorities protested that the tragedy would not have happened if the Papen cabinet had not lifted the restrictions on demonstrations by political extremists, but the Reich government ignored this point. The cabinet claimed the Bloody Sunday of Altona demonstrated the Prussian police's impotence. The federal government had found a second smoking gun.[13]

There is no doubt that the ostensible justifications for the federal takeover were public relations pretenses. The real motivation for the coup was the neoconservatives' determination to change fundamentally the political and constitutional landscape of Germany: abolish the Reich-Prussian dualism, eliminate parliamentary democracy in Prussia, and incorporate Nazis into a right-of-center national coalition that would permanently exclude the Social Democrats and other leftist forces from political power.[14]

The constitutional aspects of the federal takeover had a long history. As noted earlier, suggestions that eliminating the Prussian superstate would solve the problem of Germany's lopsided federal structure could be found in commission and conference reports going back to the nineteenth century. The political goals, too, were not new. They essentially involved the Conservatives' long-pursued aim of reversing the results of the 1918 revolution. The Prussian government would later point to the "obvious" parallels between Papen's coup and the putsch plans drafted by the leader of the Pan-German Association in 1926.[15] The only new features were the rise of the Nazis and the weakness of the Prussian government. Hitler's strong showing in the Reich presidential elections and the defeat of the Weimar coalition parties in the April 1932 Landtag contest led to the de facto collapse of parliamentary democracy in Prussia. Otto Braun presided over his last cabinet meeting on April 21; the next day he all but withdrew from public life and retired to his home in Zehlendorf.[16] The Reich government, for its part, increasingly ignored the Prussian cabinet and conferred directly with leading members of the Landtag.

While many of the state's leaders despaired, others, such as Grzesinski, Abegg, and Klepper, urged the cabinet and the democratic forces to take steps to regain the initiative. They argued that despite the Nazis' electoral triumphs, the state should move forcefully against the NSDAP. Such a step would either force the Reich to cooperate with Prussia in controlling political extremism or put the national cabinet on the defensive when the ties between the Reich government and Hitler's forces were exposed. But the state's senior leaders did not act, attempting instead to gain time by not giving the neoconservatives any reason to implement a federal takeover. Appeasement was precisely the wrong strategy. Prussia's accommodating stance merely confirmed the Reich authorities' belief that the state was ripe for the taking.[17]

It is ironic that the last barrier standing in the way of the neoconservatives was not the Prussian government or its supporters in the Weimar coalition parties, but certain traditional Prussian Conservatives. These champions of states' rights and especially of Prussia's position as *primus inter pares* among the German *Länder* included a number of Prussian DNVP leaders and the Reich president. Wolfgang von Kries, one of the oldest and most respected members of the German Nationalists's Landtag delegation, warned the Prussian cabinet in 1931 against relying on the president's authority under Article 48 of the Weimar constitution to implement the Reich government's austerity program in the state by issuing Prussian decrees. He feared that this would be a precedent for subordinating the state to Reich control. Some traditional Conservatives in the office for constitutional affairs in Prussia's interior ministry went even further, concluding in June 1932 that the appointment of a Reich commissioner for Prussia under Article 48 would be unconstitutional.[18]

Such considerations were also a problem for the Reich president. Hindenburg had sworn to uphold the Reich constitution, and he was very reluctant to authorize a federal takeover of Prussia. Hindenburg was also concerned about the reactions of the southern German *Länder*. Their fears of the growing power of the Reich government were not assuaged by Gayl's assurances that any federal takeover of Prussia would not affect the constitutional rights of the other states.[19] However, Hindenburg was also impressed by Papen's and Gayl's "evidence" that Prussia's Social Democratic leaders were conspiring with the Bolsheviks. Similarly, for a man who had spent his entire professional life surrounded by military discipline, the apparent breakdown of law and order in Altona was a powerful argument that the time had come for action. On July 11 Hindenburg had authorized the cabinet to initiate the federal takeover, but not until the Bloody Sunday riots six days later did he allow Papen to implement the decree.[20]

Nevertheless, rumors that a takeover was imminent had been in the air since February, and they thickened noticeably after Papen was named Reich chancellor. The reasons were obvious. Papen's appointment ushered in a new chapter in the political dynamics of the Weimar Republic. Unlike Brüning, who for tactical reasons attempted to preserve a consensus between the government and the SPD at least on foreign policy issues, Papen made no secret of his desire to destroy the Social Democrats. Since the Prussian Landtag elections had created a power vacuum in Prussia, leaving the caretaker government without parliamentary support, Papen felt he could move with impunity against his longtime political rivals.[21]

Even so, it appears that just before the actual takeover, Schleicher and Gayl, rather than the chancellor, were behind the decision to appoint a Reich commissioner for Prussia.[22] Especially the Reich minister of the interior urged the chancellor to seize the opportunity and destroy the last major bulwark of parliamentary democracy in Germany. For Gayl the coup would bring personal as well as political satisfaction. As the longtime chairman of the DNVP caucus in the Prussian Staatsrat, he had been a fierce opponent of the Weimar coalition parties and Prussia's parliamentary system for many years. Now he was determined to use his powers as Reich minister to destroy it.[23]

Did the Prussian political leaders know about the maneuvering by the Reich authorities? Not in detail, perhaps, but they were certainly aware of the neoconservatives overall goals and the pressure Gayl, Papen, and Schleicher were exerting on Hindenburg. Thus it seems remarkable that the Prussian leaders had no contingency plans to counteract a federal takeover. In fact, no scenario for dealing with a potential coup by the Reich government was ever discussed in a cabinet meeting, and Severing, who was most directly concerned, discouraged officials in his ministry from considering countermeasures.[24]

Instead, the Prussian cabinet intensified its strategy of appeasement. The government imposed a new and highly unpopular animal slaughter tax to balance the state budget and not give the Reich cabinet an additional opportunity for financial blackmail. In the days before July 20, the interior ministry issued a series of decrees giving the police forces wide-ranging powers to take whatever steps they considered necessary to contain political violence. Severing was convinced this would eliminate any grounds for a federal takeover, but it seems merely to have delayed the federal takeover for a few days. Hindenburg had already signed the undated decree, and the Reichswehr commander of the Berlin military district was making preparations for enforcing a state of emergency. Perhaps the only significant consequence of the delay was to increase the Nazis' distrust of Gayl. Hitler authorized Goebbels to attack the Reich minister of the interior for his "irresponsible procrastination [*Saumseligkeit*]."[25]

The only last-minute problems involved personnel, not policy issues. The Reich cabinet had considerable trouble finding a willing candidate as de facto federal commissioner. Nominally the chancellor would function in this capacity, with a lower-level official handling the actual administration of the state under federal control. Gayl's first choice was Wilhelm Peters, a long-time DNVP member who in 1925 had been that party's candidate for Prussian prime minister. However, Peters declined, expressing serious doubts about the constitutionality of the takeover. After looking briefly at another DNVP leader, Friedrich von Winterfeld, the Reich cabinet settled on Fritz Bracht, like Papen a right-wing Center party man with political views close to those of Gayl and the chancellor. Bracht had been a senior official in the Prussian ministry of the interior during the 1920s, but, realizing that his ministerial ambition was thwarted by the stability of the Weimar coalition in the state, had turned to municipal politics. In July 1932 Bracht was lord mayor of Essen.[26] He accepted the appointment as commissioner sometime between July 14 and 17.[27]

The Reich government took over Prussia on July 20. Without stating a reason for his request, Papen asked Severing, Hirtsiefer, and Klepper to meet with him at the Reich chancellery at 9:30 A.M. At Papen's side was Ludwig Nobis, a high official in Braun's office who turned out to have been the chancellor's "mole" among the prime minister's staff. The chancellor informed the assembled ministers of the takeover and announced that he was dismissing Severing and Braun from their posts. Also fired were some prominent Social Democratic and prorepublican ministerial officials: Abegg, Robert Weismann (Braun's chief of staff), as well as Hans Krüger and Hans Staudinger, the state secretaries in the ministries of finance and commerce. Papen asked the other ministers to stay on for the time being, and invited them to attend a cabinet meeting with Papen as Reich commissioner presiding. When they refused, the chancellor dismissed them as well.[28]

Papen took immediate steps to play down the significance of the takeover and to reassure the other Länder that his coup did not threaten their state's rights. Later in the morning the Reich chancellery telephoned the prime ministers of Bavaria, Württemberg, and Baden to inform them that Braun and Severing had been dismissed, but that the other Prussian ministers were cooperating with the Reich commissioner. Since this scenario proved illusory, Papen three days later met with all the Länder prime ministers and reiterated that the Reich president's decree involved only Prussia. As far as the Reich government was concerned, eliminating the Reich-Prussian dualism had solved the major problem of German federalism.[29]

In Prussia the takeover decree was first carried out by the Reichswehr. The Reich president imposed a state of emergency in the city of Berlin, putting Colonel von Rundstedt, commander of the Berlin garrison, in charge of all security measures in the city. Rundstedt in his capacity as the new security chief of Berlin, immediately discharged the city's police chief, Grzesinski, his deputy Berhard Weiss, and Colonel Magnus Heimannsberg, the chief of the state's uniformed police forces. The Reichswehr commander asked Kurt Melcher to replace Grzesinski. Melcher and Bracht had teamed up earlier; before taking up his position in Berlin Melcher had been police chief in Essen.

The state of emergency remained in force until July 26. Outside the capital, the commanders of the Reichswehr units stationed in Prussia contacted the civilian administrators in their areas to assure that orders by the civilian forces of law and order did not conflict with those of the military authorities. On the first day of the state of emergency, all of the state's territorial administrative offices down to the county commissioners were ordered to appoint someone who could receive and implement orders from the military at a moment's notice. District directors had to radio situation reports to the ministry of the interior three times a day.[30]

Reaction to the federal takeover was contradictory and confusing. Politicians of every stripe and pundits from every camp expressed opinions along a spectrum ranging from shock and indignation to enthusiastic approval. All eyes, of course, were on the Prussian government and the Weimar coalition parties that backed the cabinet. They remained largely passive. In fact, the coup was received calmly throughout the state. Reports reaching the *Reichswehr*'s crisis center in Berlin from the provinces all read "nothing unusual to report."[31]

What about the Nazis and the Communists? For the Nazis, the coup raised questions about the future relationship to the neoconservatives, while the KPD had to decide if in the face of Papen's takeover the party should consider a reconciliation between Communists and Social Democrats in order to prevent the final triumph of neoauthoritarianism or fascism in Germany.

The Nazis initially reacted to the coup with cautious approval. The party press praised the Reich government's decision to dismiss Grzesinski and Severing, noting that the Nazis had urged this step for weeks, but Hitler's movement also expressed doubts that Papen and Bracht were the "right personalities" for the job that lay ahead. The Nazi newspaper in Hamburg wrote the NSDAP's number two man, Gregor Strasser, would have been a better choice as Reich commissioner. Goebbels confided in his diary that the Nazis were a little like children at Christmas: they had a long gift list, but they probably would not get much and what they would get was not what they wanted. In any case, as far as the Nazis were concerned, the regime of Papen's Reich commissioners was an interim solution. The "permanent new order [*endgültige Neuordnung*]" would come only after the NSDAP had won a majority in the upcoming Reichstag elections.[32]

The Nazis' wish list involved primarily personnel changes. So did Papen's. Both agreed that a large-scale purge of Prussia's territorial and ministerial administrators was necessary and for the most part they even agreed on whom to remove. However, they seldom picked the same replacements.[33] In addition, the Prussian Nazis urged the new regime to repeal many of the Braun government's fiscal austerity decrees, but here, too, the new Prussian masters refused.

When the Nazis, in spite of the Prussian police's new benevolent neutrality toward their campaign practices, fell far short of winning a majority in the Reichstag elections, the Papen-Hitler honeymoon was over. To the delight of the Nazi "radicals," all talk to "tolerating" the Reich cabinet was soon ended. The Nazi press and speakers attacked Papen and his government much as they had heaped scorn on Brüning or Severing earlier. By August rumors of a planned coup by the storm troopers against the Reich government began circulating. As far as the Nazis were concerned, Papen's takeover of Prussia had failed to accomplish its purpose. In the Prussian Landtag the NSDAP introduced a motion of no confidence in the Reich commissioners.[34]

The Communists' initial reaction was rather similar to that of the Nazis. The Prussian KPD had long insisted that the Social Democratic officials in charge of the interior ministry's police forces had singled out the Communists for special persecution, so they welcomed the removal of the party's arch-enemies Braun, Severing and Grzesinski with gleeful *Schadenfreude*. In addition, the prevailing party line interpreted Papen's coup as an important escalation in the continuing crisis of German capitalism. For the Communists, Papen's action was a "fascist coup," one of a series of increasingly desperate measures by which the Reich's rulers were attempting to halt the collapse of capitalism. The party predicted further and more violent measures, including possibly the Nazis' coming to power, but it saw no reason to defend parliamentary democracy, since these developments were necessary preludes to the coming Communist revolution. Although KPD leaders had some advance warning of the takeover, they took no steps to organize any sort of active resistance.[35]

There is some evidence that this "ultraleft" stance of the Communist leadership, which essentially condemned the party to inaction and had the full backing of the Comintern, was opposed by the party's rank and file. In Berlin and other Prussian cities there were spontaneous moves for joint action with the Social Democrats to oppose the federal takeover. Seemingly in response to such sentiments, Communist leaders eventually invited the SPD to join them in calling for a general strike to protest Papen's coup. But a closer look at the call to united action showed that the KPD's ultraleft line had not changed. Addressed to "all German workers," the strike call again urged proletarian unity "from below," the Communists' code phrase asking the workers to turn their backs on their Social Democratic political and union leaders, "the Brauns, the Severings, and the Grzesinskis." The SPD saw the KPD's offer as a public relations gesture, and most historians agree with this assessment.[36]

The Communists' official version of their role in the events following the July 20 coup was that they were the only organized political force willing to "take action" against Papen.[37] This interpretation continues to have some plausibility because the SPD never called the KPD's bluff, having themselves decided against active resistance. That decision surprised and angered many contemporaries. It also inaugurated a debate among historians that still continues: why did the Social Democrats refuse to join in a general strike or other forms of resistance? They had not been afraid to associate with the Communists on other occasions, such as the 1920 general strike and the national referenda on the expropriation of the property of the former ruling houses and the navy's battle cruiser.

Moreover, at first glance the chances for a successful resistance seemed promising. On paper the Prussian Social Democrats had superiority. Social Democracy was still the best-organized political and economic force in the state. The SPD also dominated the Reichsbanner Schwarz-Rot-Gold, the largest prorepublican paramilitary organization. Social Democratic leaders controlled pivotal positions in the state's executive branch, notably the prime minister's office, the ministry of the interior, and the Prussian police. In spite of all these apparent assets, party leaders, rather than mobilizing the political and governmental forces at their disposal to resist Papen's clear violation of the spirit of the Weimar constitution, merely joined their Weimar coalition partners in an appeal to the judiciary, which had a long tradition of opposing parliamentary democracy. The SPD's only direct challenge to Papen's coup was a court case before the federal court *(Reichsgericht)* charging that the Reich president's invocation of Article 48 was unconstitutional.

The Social Democrats' decision to remain passive in the face of Papen's coup resulted from a careful evaluation of a complex set of "what if" scenarios. Plans for active resistance always involved three possible courses of action; they were not mutually exclusive, and indeed could be used in combination. One was political action—that is, mobilizing public opinion against the Reich government—by means ranging from editorial comments in the prorepublican press to mass demonstrations in the streets. A second possibility was executive action. Under this scenario the cabinet ministers would first defy Papen's orders by refusing to yield their posts, and then order the Prussian police, perhaps in cooperation with the Reichsbanner, to resist the federal takeover as illegal and unconstitutional. Finally, there was the labor movement's time-honored and (at least in theory) most powerful weapon, the general strike. In July 1932, as in March 1920, the general strike would be used to achieve a political end, the preservation of parliamentary democracy, to whose support the Socialist movement was committed.

Before analyzing why the Prussian SPD leaders and their coalition partners rejected all of these scenarios, it might be useful to sketch the arguments advanced by the supporters of active resistance. Spearheading the drive to mobilize public opinion would be the responsibility of Carl Severing and Otto Braun, generally acknowledged to be the most charismatic figures among the supporters of the republic. In the eyes of many, Braun and Severing personified parliamentary democracy, and a public outcry by them would mobilize the still numerous supporters of democracy in Prussia. An upsurge of public opinion would lead the moderate governments in southern Germany to take a firm stand against Papen, thereby isolating the federal government. Seeing the growing cleavage between the Reich and the states, the Reichswehr, which since 1920 feared above all becoming involved in domestic political controversy, would put pressure on the Reich president and cabinet, forcing them to abandon their attempt to subject Prussia to federal control.[38]

Far more dramatic, but also considerably riskier, was to use the Prussian police and the Reichsbanner. Nevertheless, a number of Prussian political leaders, including Grzesinski, Abegg, and Minister of Finance Klepper, vigorously advocated armed defense of parliamentary democracy by the Prussian police in conjunction with the prorepublican paramilitary forces. The assumption here was that the Prussian police, which under a succession of Social Democratic interior ministers had become a reliable prorepublican force, and the Reichsbanner, which was ready and eager to defend the republic, would have obeyed an order by the interior minister to oppose a clear threat to Prussia's constitutional government. (In fact, evidence later surfaced that a number of policemen were deeply disappointed that they had not been permitted to defend the republic.) The result, according to this scenario, would be a hasty retreat by Papen, at heart a coward, and the Reichswehr, because of its well-known fear of becoming involved in a civil war.[39]

Finally, the general strike. There was strong evidence that a political general strike could work. No one doubted that swift action by the united labor movement had been decisive in the defeat of the Kapp Putsch. A general strike could also be put into effect at very short notice; at the time of the Kapp putsch it took only a few hours to organize a nationwide strike. Again using the experience of 1920, proponents argued that a general strike was precisely the sort of resistance activity the Reichswehr feared; unless the military was willing to risk civil war, it was powerless against a general strike. The only new element in 1932 was the strength of the Nazis, but advocates of a general strike argued that the NSDAP's strong working-class contingent, especially among the storm troopers, would force the Nazi leaders to abandon any thought of using the SA as strikebreakers.[40]

The entire debate over the feasibility of active resistance on July 20 had an element of unreality. Actually, a decision not to engage in active resistance was made before the Reich government's takeover. The SPD's national leaders rejected all proposals for active resistance on July 16, two days before the Bloody Sunday of Altona. The SPD's national executive committee, which included a large number of Socialist union leaders, decided that the party and the Socialist unions would not oppose a potential coup either by calling for extraparliamentary action or by organizing a general strike. The committee reasoned that mobilizing public opinion to take extraparliamentary action in favor of a government that had been rejected by the voters was futile; "Save the republic" was not a slogan that would encourage mass participation.

Calling a general strike when more than one-third of the labor force was out of work would demonstrate organized labor's weakness, not its strength. (The issue of using the Prussian police was not discussed, since this decision could be made only by the Prussian government.)[41]

But a decision by the national leaders was not the same as a verdict by the Prussians. Reflecting the Prussian Social Democrats' desire to stay out of the national limelight throughout the Weimar years, few prominent Prussians served on the SPD's national executive committee. Severing attended the July 16 meeting, but most of the party's Prussian leaders, including Braun, Grzesinski, and Heilmann, were not present. Would they go along with the national body's decision? After all, the Prussians had argued for years that the state was not like the rest of Germany, that Prussia had a political spirit and dynamic all its own. Politically, the state in the past had dominated the Reich.

The Prussian leaders' initial reaction to the actual coup was hardly a credible manifestation of their often voiced conviction that a strong and autonomous Prussia safeguarded democracy in the rest of the Reich. The pattern was set in the meeting between the Prussian ministers and the Reich chancellor on the morning of July 20. That meeting, or rather the ministers' performance during the session, was to become the subject of a bitter postwar debate among the participants. To begin with, the prime minister was not even present when the cabinet members were asked to assemble in Papen's office. Otto Braun decided to remain at home in Zehlendorf, not formally responding to Papen's move until two days later. In a brief letter to the chancellor, Braun disputed any constitutional basis for the federal takeover and requested air time on national radio to respond to the Reich chancellor's address to the nation on the evening of July 20.[42]

The rump cabinet, led by Severing and Hirtsiefer, protested the federal takeover during its meeting with Papen and noted for the record that it was leaving office "under duress," but the ministers issued no call to resistance. Subsequently, the minister of the interior, the key official in any Prussian counteraction against the coup, made sure that he would not become the rallying point for any officially sanctioned resistance activities. Despite repeated attempts by hard-liners like Grzesinski to contact Severing, the minister was "unavailable" for the rest of the day.[43]

The hard-liners attributed this response to a combination of political naiveté and a failure of nerves. Leading the pack of critics was Otto Klepper, the Prussian minister of finance. After the Second World War Klepper wrote a scathing account of the dramatic encounter between Papen and the Prussian cabinet. In an article published in the journal *Die Gegenwart,* Klepper claimed that Severing was primarily responsible for sabotaging any plans for resistance. Both he, Klepper, and Hirtsiefer had vigorously urged forceful resistance to the takeover. Klepper also claimed that Heilmann agreed with the tough stance. Additional support came from the southern German *Länder* and from Konrad Adenauer, president of the Staatsrat.

In fact, according to Klepper, except for Severing virtually all of the Prussian leaders were determined to take action to counter the federal takeover. The finance minister mentioned specifically deploying the Prussian police and arming the Reichsbanner as an auxiliary force. Severing's attitude during the confrontation with Papen, Klepper claimed, sabotaged all of these possibilities. After the chancellor, whom Klepper described as "obviously nervous," had read Hindenburg's decree, Klepper, supported by Hirtsiefer, suggested that the Prussian ministers withdraw to confer among themselves. Severing, however, remained seated, noting that there was nothing further to be done. "Now Papen realized that his coup had succeeded," was Klepper's conclusion.[44]

Supporters of the interior minister were not slow to come to his defense. They attacked both Klepper's character and the truthfulness of his account. "Political lightweight" and "pathological desire to show off [*Geltungsbedürfnis*]" were among the milder characterizations of the former finance minister.[45] While such assessments might be dismissed, the question of Klepper's veracity is indeed troublesome. The finance minister's picture of nearly unanimous backing for any sort of active resistance—including armed resistance—is not supported by other contemporary evidence. Among prominent politicians in Prussia only Abegg, Grzesinski, and Klepper are known to have urged a call for active protest; the positions of Hirtsiefer and Heilmann are at best doubtful. Adenauer was certainly not a hard-liner.[46]

The question remains, why were the democratic leaders of the state so reluctant to consider active resistance? There is no doubt that the "soft" approach was supported not only by the SPD's national leaders, but also by most of the Prussian leaders, including a majority of the state's provincial governors.[47] The reasons were political, tactical, and psychological.

As far as mobilizing public opinion was concerned, the Prussian leaders felt there was neither enough time nor sufficient consensus among those opposed to Papen's coup to mount a convincing campaign. In addition, they argued that the undoubted charisma of the state's political leaders owed less to personal popularity than to their *Amtscharisma*, and Papen, by removing the state's leaders from office, had also destroyed their *Amtscharisma*. A call to action by Prussia's deposed leaders would have met with little positive response. Finally, contrary to Klepper's and the hard-liners' belief, the Prussian leaders were convinced the southern German states would not support any action on behalf of democracy in Prussia.[48]

After more than fifty years of argument and counterargument, most historians agree that the Prussian leaders were probably right. It is difficult to imagine mass demonstrations like those of November 1918 in July 1932, demanding the reinstatement of a government that the voters had rejected a few months earlier. On the other hand, in their desire to remain cool-headed and pragmatic, the Prussians overlooked an important psychological factor. By not attempting to mobilize public opinion in support of the Prussian constitutional system, they severely demoralized the thousands of rank-and-file supporters of democracy who were convinced that *something* ought to be done and who were anxiously awaiting a call to action. Too late, many Prussian leaders, including Severing, seem to have recognized that their inaction on July 20 severely disappointed many of their supporters and contributed to the massive feeling of resignation that characterized the political atmosphere in January 1933, when the enemy was not Papen, but Hitler.[49]

The argument that there was insufficient time did not apply to mounting a general strike, but there was no doubt that such a step was risky. It was an accepted axiom in the German labor movement that a failed general strike represented a particularly severe setback. The Prussian leaders decided in July 1932 that the risks of failure were too high. Obviously, the large number of unemployed counted against the success of a general strike. Moreover, many of the unemployed sympathized with either the Communists or the Nazis. The Social Democratic leaders were convinced that left-wing extremists wanted the SPD to call a general strike, because its failure would have destroyed the moderate unions. And in sharp contrast to the hard-liners's view, the Prussian leaders were convinced that the Nazis were looking for an opportunity to act as strikebreakers. Ernst Heilmann quoted Hitler as promising his followers on the evening of July 20, "Tomorrow there will be no more unemployed storm troopers."[50]

Instead of calling for a general strike, the union leaders decided to adopt the tactic that they would also follow—to their peril—at the beginning of the Third Reich. At the meeting of the SPD's national executive committee on July 16, the union leaders announced that in the event of a federal takeover they would take no action that would violate "constitutional legality." Their reasoning, which the political leaders endorsed, was that if the Papen government was determined to destroy the left-wing political parties, the unions would be the only refuge of the organized labor movement. For this reason, it was important not to give the government an excuse for moving against the unions as well. Refraining from calling a general strike would demonstrate that the unions had not involved themselves in overt political activity. The German unions, in other words, were not a political threat to the Reich government.[51]

Deciding who was right means venturing onto the murky terrain of "what if," but in retrospect, the arguments against the general strike seem like a smoke screen designed to hide the union leaders' fatalism about the future of parliamentary democracy. Calling a general strike was clearly legal. In fact, the Reich government was concerned that the Reich president might refuse to proclaim a national state of emergency to counter a general strike, precisely because Hindenburg might doubt his constitutional authority to do so. As for the storm troopers acting as strikebreakers, this, too, was at best doubtful. A few weeks later, the political leaders of the NSDAP in Berlin were virtually forced by rank-and-file pressure to support a strike against the municipal transportation authority called by the Communists and Social Democrats. There is also no doubt that in July 1932 the Nazis were both surprised and delighted by the political inactivity of their archenemies. The quotation Heilmann cited was apocryphal; Hitler did not mention any possible Nazi reaction to a general strike in the speech which the SPD leader quoted.[52]

The Nazis' relief said something about the Communists' attitude as well. It is true, of course, that the KPD opposed cooperation with the Social Democratic union leaders, but this had also been the Communists' initial decision in 1920. At that time pressure from rank-and-file members had forced the Communist leaders to join in the general strike proclaimed by the non-Communist unions. Is it really likely that the KPD rank-and-file would have permitted their leaders to stand aside in 1932, thereby supporting the Reichswehr, Schleicher, and Papen, while the Social Democrats were leading a general strike against these forces of Prusso-German authoritarianism? On balance, then, it would appear that a general strike might well have regained the initiative for the republican forces, or, at least prevented the demonstration of weakness that was the most demoralizing aspect of the drama of July 20.[53]

The accusation that those calling for active resistance lacked a sense of political realism and were willing to risk useless bloodshed applied particularly to plans that included ordering the Prussian police and the prorepublican paramilitary organizations to engage in armed conflict with the Reichswehr to prevent Papen from taking over the state. The Prussian leaders advanced a number of practical considerations for not even considering this form of resistance. Hampered by interrupted lines of command and inferior armaments, the Prussian police were no match for the Reichswehr—especially if, as the Prussian leaders expected, the storm troopers and other right-wing extremist groups enthusiastically joined the fray on the side of the Reichswehr. And even if the outcome of the battle had not been a foregone conclusion, the state's decision makers were afraid that once armed resistance started, the Communists as the better street fighters would seize the initiative and subvert the defense of democracy into a Bolshevik revolution.[54]

The Prussian leaders certainly made a good case against using armed force to oppose the federal takeover. History shows that police forces, no matter how well motivated, are no match for regular army troops. But this argument did not address the psychological dimension. The hard-liners contended that the threat of armed resistance alone would have dissuaded the Reich government from continuing the takeover attempt, and even in hindsight it is impossible to determine if they were right.

But in a larger sense, the debate about what might have been possible if the Prussian leaders had only seized the moment, misses the central point. Any course of action that risked an open and violent confrontation between Reich and state really called into question Prussia's political raison d'être. The possibility that physical resistance would lead to civil war conjured up the nightmare of the disintegration of the Reich. All Prussian political leaders, regardless of their ideology, were convinced that Prussia's primary historic service to Germany had been to create a unified nation and to guarantee its territorial integrity. Faced with a choice between national unity and defense of a political system, the Prussian leaders chose unity. In addition, using the police and paramilitary groups to defend Prussia's constitutional system itself violated the principles of parliamentary democracy. Not only was the action of doubtful constitutional legality—Papen's coup, after all, followed the letter of the Weimar constitution—but the Prussian government had always taken great care to separate the state's official forces of coercion from any political paramilitary groups, even those supporting the republic. In the eyes of the Prussian leaders, armed resistance against federal authority in the form of joint action by the police and the Reichsbanner betrayed everything that republican Prussia had created and stood for. As Braun put it, "I have been a democrat for forty years; I will not now become the leader of a band of brigands [Bandenführer]."[55]

In the end, then, the Prussian leaders, albeit for somewhat different reasons, took the same position as the SPD's national executive committee. Contrary to what Papen might have expected, there would be no call to active resistance to counter the federal takeover. The Prussian leaders remained convinced that this was the only decision consistent with their political beliefs and Prussia's past and future role in a united Germany. In their eyes, active resistance against the Reich government was itself a violation of their political credo.[56]

Instead, the Prussian cabinet and the Weimar coalition parties went to court. This decision has often been described as a futile gesture, a poor substitute for real action. It is certainly true that the legal proceedings had little effect upon developments in the last months of the Weimar Republic. But it must also be remembered that Papen and Schleicher were not Hitler. In 1932 Germany was still a Rechtsstaat, and Prussia's republican leaders felt they had an open-and-shut case. Under the Weimar constitution, the Reich president's invocation of Article 48 was restricted to the specific conditions cited earlier. The Prussian leaders were convinced there was overwhelming prima facie evidence that the state's government had neither neglected its constitutional duties, nor failed to maintain law and order. They had no doubts that after examining the evidence, the Reich court would declare Papen's coup unconstitutional. Consequently, the Reich president would have to withdraw his authorization for a federal takeover. The judicial setback for the Reich in turn would have an immediate political advantage for the plaintiffs, since it was expected to give a significant uplift to the prorepublican forces in the July 1932 Reichstag election campaign.[57]

The legal challenge which the Braun government and the Weimar coalition parties expected would vindicate their policies and reinstate the old Prussian government in office turned out to be an anticlimax. Prussia's republican leaders, as plaintiffs, the Reich government as defendant, and the court itself all had quite different agendas in mind as they began the legal proceedings. The Prussians set out to prove that they had not violated their constitutional duties. The Papen cabinet wanted to gain time. As we shall see in the next chapter, while the case was before the court, the Reich commissioners worked feverishly to "create facts" in Prussia. The neoconservative Reich leaders were also anxious to discredit the constitutional system of parliamentary democracy by showing that the foremost champion of that system, republican Prussia, by its policies had created a *Verfassungsnotstand* (state of constitutional emergency), forcing the Reich government to intervene. The Reich court, finally, hoped to steer clear of the case. The judges were fully aware of the political volatility inherent in a fundamental confrontation between Reich cabinet and the government of Germany's largest state, and the court was anxious to avoid becoming an issue of controversy at a time when political tensions in Germany were already rising to a fever pitch.

The legal doctrine of the *Verfassungsnotstand* surfaced at various times in modern German history, but never more insistently than in the last years of the Weimar Republic. A large number of jurists, politicians, and academics contributed to the debate, but it was the conservative legal theorist Carl Schmitt who was most closely identified with the neoauthoritarian view of Weimar Germany's constitutional dilemma. Deriving his ideas from the principles of natural law embodied in Roman legal tradition, Schmitt argued that the survival of a societal organism always took precedence over the maintenance of a particular constitutional system. If a specific political system had demonstrably "failed" because it was unable to preserve law and order to keep the society viable, it was necessary to eliminate or at least suspend the rules for political interaction during the "constitutional emergency." In that case, power devolved to the executive authority or the "state" as the final repository of authority in the society.

Applying this doctrine to the Weimar Republic, Schmitt contended that the cabinet crisis of March 1930 demonstrated the failure of parliamentary democracy as a constitutional system. The Reichstag (and after April 1932, the Prussian Landtag) had de facto relinquished their constitutional authority to the "state" or more specifically, to the Reich president as the personification of executive power. The Reich's highest official now had the right and duty to take whatever action he regarded as necessary to save the body politic from disintegration. In making his decisions he was not bound by the formal rules of the "failed" constitution.

It will be readily appreciated that Schmitt's ideas were enthusiastically endorsed by the presidential chancellors. They also served the Nazis well in carrying out their *Gleichschaltung* when they came to power, although the Nazis' subsequent creation of a totalitarian, one-party state was not to Schmitt's liking. As an authoritarian rather than a totalitarian, his role as "theorist for the Reich" (to use the title of a recent biography) was short-lived.[58]

Schmitt's role in Papen's coup and the subsequent court proceedings went beyond supplying theoretical arguments for the Reich government. He is credited with removing Hindenburg's doubts about the constitutionality of the takeover, and he served as one of the Reich government's legal consultants in the later court case. As far as Schmitt was concerned, the case of Prussia versus Reich was a welcome opportunity to apply his doctrines in practise: In July 1932 a state of constitutional emergency existed, and the federal president and cabinet had acted correctly in order to preserve the viability of the Reich.[59]

The Prussians' legal team was headed by Arnold Brecht, since 1927 the state's chief delegate to the Reichsrat. One of the best known constitutional lawyers of the Weimar era and a fervent supporter of parliamentary democracy, Brecht regarded his appearance before the Reich court as a high point of his career. The Prussian lawyer refused to be drawn into the debate on the legal existence of a state of constitutional emergency and its implications. Rejecting the entire concept of a constitutional emergency, he insisted the Weimar and Prussian constitutions remained the highest law of the land. Consequently, Brecht set out to present a point-by-point refutation of the Papen government's claim that the state had violated its obligations under the Weimar constitution. Since the Reich's claims were indeed factitious, Brecht had a relatively easy time in proving his case.[60]

Unfortunately, proving the case was not the central issue as the Reich court saw it. To begin with, the court worked hard for an out-of-court settlement. The chief justice, Erwin Bumke, approached both parties with a proposal for an out-of-court settlement along lines that had originally been suggested by Hermann Höpker-Aschoff, the former Prussian minister of finance. Under this plan, Otto Braun and the other Social Democratic ministers would resign from the cabinet, and the Landtag could then elect a

Bürgerblock government. Satisfied that it had destroyed the "Marxists'" hold in Prussia, the Reich government in turn would rescind its federal takeover order.

Bumke's efforts failed completely. On the Prussian side the state's Center party and the SPD adamantly refused to compromise: the Catholic leaders were willing to risk defeat rather than agree to a deal with Papen. Braun was certainly anxious to be relieved as head of the caretaker cabinet, but he insisted that the Reich government simultaneously withdraw its accusation that Prussia had violated its constitutional duties. The chancellor also refused to yield. He was convinced that time, if not the constitution, was on his side.[61]

The Reich court issued its judgment in October. The judges found that Prussia had not violated its constitutional duties; the federal takeover could not be justified by invoking Article 48. At first glance the ruling represented a complete Prussian victory. Arnold Brecht celebrated the verdict as a triumphal vindication of his efforts; he went so far as to claim that the setbacks for the right in the November Reichstag election were in part a consequence of the state's legal victory in October.[62]

Politically, however, the judgment was a complete triumph for the Reich government. The court's decision that the federal authorities did not have the right to remove the state cabinet from office and that the Prussian government retained all of the rights *specifically* assigned to it in the Prussian constitution, was an empty grant of power, because the court also determined that the Reich president had the right to invoke Article 48 to take control of a state if he was convinced the well-being of the Reich required such a step. In other words, the Reich court accepted Schmitt's argument that the Reich president had the authority to determine when a constitutional emergency superseded the constitution. As far as the Reich court was concerned, both sides were right. Joseph Goebbels described the legal confusion in graphic terms: "Total chaos reigns in Prussia after the decision. . . . One cabinet competes with the other."[63]

In reality, of course, there was not much competition. The verdict gave the Braun government the illusion of authority and Papen the reality of power, leaving the chancellor in de facto control of the state. Papen lost no time in savoring his victory. Three days after the court handed down its judgment, he "interpreted" in unequivocal terms the significance of the verdict in a letter to the "provisional" Prussian ministers: "All powers of government [*Regierungsgewalt*] have remained in the hands of the appointed Reich commissioner."[64] In the weeks and months that followed, the Reich cabinet "implemented" the court decision by curtailing even further the rights of the parliamentary Prussian government. Presiding at a meeting of the "provisional" Prussian cabinet at the beginning of November, Papen dropped all pretense of a short-term federal takeover. The chancellor noted that the Reich commissioner and the team of officials he had appointed in Prussia were not a temporary institution. Together with the Reich cabinet they formed a "fighting community [*Kampfgemeinschaft*]" whose accomplishments "would be proved right by history."[65]

Among the accomplishments for which Papen praised himself on the eve of his fall from power (less than a month later he had been replaced by Kurt von Schleicher) was cutting the Gordian knot of the elusive *Reichsreform*. Both Papen and Reich Minister of the Interior Gayl were convinced the court's verdict had given them the authority to abolish the Reich-Prussian dualism. Ignoring the elaborate discussions and proposals by the 1928 Reich Conference, Gayl in a series of speeches and meetings with representatives of the non-Prussian states outlined a far-reaching program of constitutional changes that were intended to return Germany to the traditions of the Bismarck constitution. Gayl argued that the elimination of Prussia as an autonomous *Land* and its takeover by the Reich solved the "Prussian problem." Moreover, this was best for all concerned: strengthened by its new authority over Prussia, the Reich government could yield additional states' rights to the southern German *Länder*.[66] Papen and Gayl left unsaid the political consequences of their *Reichsreform:* Their "solution" to the "Prussian problem" meant that a strong, democratic Prussia could no longer block the triumphant return of neoauthoritarianism as the Reich's political and constitutional system. For the neoconservatives, the federal takeover represented the culmination of long years of trying to undo the results of the revolution of 1918.

Prussia celebrated a Pyrrhic victory at the Reich court, but the vision of a return to Bismarckian authoritarianism nurtured by Papen, Schleicher, and Gayl was no less illusory. The coup of July 20 was not a portent of things to come, but the last battle between two contestants both of whom were about to become irrelevant. The federal takeover was possible only because Prussia had lost its position as the rock of German democracy. Buffeted by the financial and economic problems of the Depression on the one hand, and the erosion of its political mandate on the other, Prussia in the summer of 1932 was easy prey for Papen and the New Conservatives. It did not take a great deal of courage to implement the coup. As Joseph Goebbels wrote at the time, "If something is about to fall, it should be pushed."[67]

The triumph of the neoconservatives lasted only a few months before the Nazis' seizure of power replaced parliamentary democracy, neoconservatism, and the resurrected Bismarck constitution with something far different and far worse. This was not the intention of the neoconservatives—and in this sense it is a misnomer to speak of Papen's coup as a forerunner of Hitler's *Machtergreifung*—but the coup of July 20 served the Nazis well.

The series of emergency decrees signed by Hindenburg that formed the constitutional and legal foundation for the Nazi *Gleichschaltung* and the creation of Hitler's totalitarian society, continued the doctrine of unlimited presidential authority.[68]

Equally important, the failure to call for any form of political resistance in July 1932 severely demoralized the forces in German society that continued to support parliamentary democracy, while it buoyed the elements ranged against the republic. In this sense, arguing that the failure to resist Papen's coup presaged the collapse of opposition to the Nazi seizure of power six months later is sadly valid.

CHAPTER 9

Reichsreform and the Neoconservatives, 1930–1933

D ebates on the *Reichsreform* had been a feature of German politics for decades, but the advent of the neoconservative regime in the Reich marked a watershed in the perennial discussions. The presidential chancellors put particular stress on the political dimension of the reform efforts; the *Reichsreform* was an important component of their long-range program for restoring an authoritarian political system in Germany. Moreover, the fall of the Müller cabinet and the beginning of government by decree meant that after March 1930 Prussia was increasingly the object of, rather than a participant in, the decision-making process.[1]

During the republic's final crisis years, discussion focused increasingly on the two essentials of the Weimar Constitution. The first was Germany's federal structure, specifically Prussia's disproportionate size and population among the German *Länder*. This made the state a strong potential partner (or rival) of the Reich, rather than a simple unit of the federation. The second was the parliamentary system, and here, too, Prussia's role was pivotal. Since 1918 parliamentary democracy had found its most reliable pillar among Prussian leaders.

Although at heart the *Reichsreform* debate concerned the foundations of the Germany's constitutional system and territorial structure, the issue also had its nonpolitical dimensions. Few disputed that Prussia's relationship to the Reich and the other *Länder* involved numerous anomalies and paradoxes. Many of Prussia's twelve provinces were considerably larger and more populous than most of the Reich's twenty-six states. Administrative boundaries represented a jungle of overlapping Prussian and federal jurisdictions. Not only were the federal jurisdictional boundaries inconsistent with each other (the army divided the Reich into seven territorial command areas, the Reich Ministry of Finance supervised twenty-six regional offices, the Federal Railroad Administration was divided into thirty districts, and the postal service into forty-six),[2] but they were often completely uncoordinated with the state's administrative districts.

The onset of the Depression and the subsequent fiscal problems at all levels of government gave additional impetus to the need to eliminate duplication of effort. The Reich's control of the purse strings also gave the central authorities a powerful lever for implementing reform. It was particularly irksome to the ambitious presidential chancellors that the central government for the most part still depended upon the states, and especially Prussia, to implement federal legislation and decrees. In practice, the Reich legislated, but Prussia administered.

Nevertheless, politics, not administrative efficiency, was the real subject of the debate. The presidential chancellors, vigorously supported by Prussian Conservatives, argued that reform was necessary above all to eliminate what they saw as the excessively democratic features of the Weimar Constitution. For them the "Prussian problem" was not federalism, but parliamentarism. Most of their plans for dealing with the "problem" were variations on the theme that the Reich would govern Prussia directly or indirectly as a *Reichsland* (federal district). The former leader of the DNVP, Count Kuno von Westarp, for example, proposed that the Reich president should also serve as Prussian head of state. In his dual capacity he would have the power to name the members of the Reich and Prussian cabinets. Both governments would serve at the pleasure of the president; neither the Reichstag nor the Prussian Landtag could force the resignation of the government by a vote of no confidence.[3]

The Prussian government and the Weimar coalition parties refused either to limit discussions of the *Reichsreform* to the "Prussian problem," or to endorse proposals that would strengthen the powers of the Reich president at the expense of parliamentary democracy. The state's leaders welcomed discussion of a comprehensive *Reichsreform*, but only if it involved all units of the federation. Prussia rejected any plan that tampered with its territorial integrity or political autonomy, while leaving the status of other states unchanged.[4] Prussia's republican leaders also consistently argued that reform should not subvert the rules of parliamentary democracy and rejected the "authoritarian" use of Article 48 (the Reich president's decree powers). When the ambitious Prussian minister of finance, Hermann Höpker-Aschoff, advocated the use of Article 48, his cabinet colleagues issued public disclaimers, a rare event in the usually very collegial cabinet group. Not until the very end of 1932, when the only choice for Germany seemed to be a Nazi dictatorship or the continuation of the presidential regime, were some of Prussia's republican leaders willing to consider bending the rules of parliamentary democracy to prevent Hitler from coming to power.[5]

The widely disparate political agendas of the neoconservatives and Prussia's democratic leaders meant that between 1930 and 1933 Prussia and the Reich were more often antagonists than partners in their attempts to advance the *Reichsreform*. But it was an unequal contest. As the Depression deepened, the Reich cabinet acquired increasingly greater leverage over Prussia. All of the German *Länder*, including Prussia, could remain solvent only with the help of federal credits and grants-in-aid. In addition, the Prussian cabinet tied its own hands. It determined quite soon after Brüning's appointment as chancellor that the state government would "place no obstacles in the path of the new Reich cabinet." The Prussians persisted in this policy even after it became obvious that the Reich government's long-range goals were antithetical to the political principles of Prussia's republican leaders.[6]

The Presidential Chancellors and the *Reichsreform*

All three presidential chancellors were convinced that the political constellation during their terms of office gave them unique opportunities to cut through the conflicts of interest that had blocked the *Reichsreform*. The authority of the Reich president, they felt, now enabled them to ignore the role of the states in the *Reichsreform* debate. Typically, federal initiatives were now drafted without either consultation or discussion with the states, including Prussia.[7]

The presidential Reich cabinets never developed a coherent set of specific *Reichsreform* proposals, but the contours of their program were clear at the outset of their regime, and they remained remarkably unchanged. Beginning with Heinrich Brüning, the presidential chancellors worked toward constitutional reforms that would have restored Germany to its pre-1918 status. Brüning was determined to liberate the Reich executive from the restrictions imposed upon it by what he regarded as excessive parliamentary controls and runaway states' rights. As the culmination of his constitutional reform efforts, Brüning envisioned the restoration of the monarchy under a Hohenzollern emperor.[8]

When the first neoconservative chancellor was forced out of office in May 1932, he was no nearer to realizing his *Reichsreform* goals than he had been when he became chancellor. He failed in part because the rise of the Nazis forced him to shelve his reform plans. In addition, Brüning's secrecy about his ultimate plans also prevented him from generating support from those forces who clearly agreed with his authoritarian and restorationist aims.[9]

Franz von Papen's ideal political system for Germany was also the Bismarck constitution, and in some ways Papen's style of government was even more reminiscent of the imperial days than his predecessor's. While Brüning's cabinets had been drawn from both the moderate and right-of-center parties, Papen chose a politically homogenous "cabinet of barons" (the majority of the ministers were aristocrats) from the Conservative and neoconservative side of the political spectrum. Papen and his cabinet colleagues also had far fewer scruples about violating the spirit of the Weimar constitution than Brüning. The first presidential chancellor for the most part used indirect,

financial pressure to advance his program, while Papen and Gayl quite deliberately relied solely on the authority of the Reich president, the *Ersatzkaiser*
in their eyes, to implement their *Reichsreform* plans.[10] Brüning and Papen
also differed in tactics. Brüning did not object to cooperating with parties and
parliamentary bodies if this advanced his long-range aims, but Papen and his
associates rejected working with popularly elected parliaments as a matter of
principle.[11]

An intellectual lightweight himself, Papen left reform initiatives to the
minister of the interior, Baron Wilhelm von Gayl, who had joined Papen's
cabinet only on condition that the government was committed to destroying parliamentary democracy as the basis of Germany's constitutional system. Following the Bismarck constitution, Gayl proposed to strengthen the
powers of the Reichsrat (whose members were appointed) at the expense of
the popularly elected national and state legislatures. He had analogous plans
for Prussia. To reduce the powers of Prussia's elected assemblies, Gayl
wanted to convert its indirectly elected Staatsrat into an appointed House of
Lords.[12]

Kurt von Schleicher stood somewhere between his two predecessors. A
man of intrigue with a well-earned reputation for behind-the-scenes ma-
nipulation, Schleicher was not averse to striking deals with party leaders if it
suited his purpose. At the same time, he was no greater friend of parliamentary democracy than Brüning or Papen. He, too, wanted to head a Reich
cabinet that would be independent of parties, parliaments, and the *Länder*.
Schleicher was similarly determined to retain federal control of the state.
The Weimar Republic's last chancellor fully endorsed Papen's "solution"
to what all three of the presidential chancellors saw as the "Prussian
problem."[13]

Finally, we should note the contrast between the aims and tactics of the
presidential chancellors and those of Adolf Hitler. Brüning, Papen, and
Schleicher all worked for Conservative restorationism, but they respected the
fundamentals of the *Rechtsstaat*. Hitler, on the other hand, had no scruples
about destroying all vestiges of the *Rechtsstaat*. Less than two weeks after
becoming chancellor, he let it be known not only that he regarded the Weimar
Constitution as antiquated, but also that his cabinet would not hesitate to
violate its provisions in order to achieve the government's aims.[14]

The neoconservatives's regime also opened a new chapter in the ongoing
discussions about territorial reform—or rather, a section of that chapter, since
the neoconservatives were interested in territorial restructuring only insofar as
it concerned Prussia. When Brüning came into office, the Reich-Länder Conference had just adjourned, with inconclusive results; as we saw.[15] It seemed
like a golden opportunity for the new government to persuade the Reich
president to invoke Article 48 to advance territorial reform. Brüning was

known to favor greater autonomy and possibly statehood for the Prussian provinces, and he could legitimately point out that the "democratic" approach to reform had failed.

Nevertheless, Brüning did not use the president's decree powers to effect the territorial *Reichsreform* with a stroke of the pen, later giving contradictory reasons for his inaction. He claimed that Hindenburg had refused to consider breaking up Prussia as the Reich-Länder Conference report had recommended. But the chancellor also did not want to implement the *Reichsreform* by decree power, since this would have meant by-passing the Reichstag and the Reichsrat. The first reason sounds plausible; as a Prussian *Junker,* Hindenburg was emotionally attached to Prussia as both a *Land* and a concept. The chancellor's respect for parliamentarism was a belated postwar development. The real reason for Brüning's inaction, as we shall see, was tactical. Brüning felt he could shift the contours of the Reich-Prussian relationship by destroying the state's financial and political autonomy, and so avoid entering the controversies over territorial changes.[16]

The Prussian government also maintained its low profile on the issue of territorial changes, although some leaders suggested that Prussia should absorb some of the smaller *Länder* in northern Germany to prevent the Nazis, whose strength was growing there, from gaining additional influence in the Reichsrat. The danger was acute, since the votes in the second chamber were disproportionately weighted in favor of small states. The Prussian coalition, however, remained paralyzed by sharp differences of opinion on the issue of territorial reform among Center party leaders. The Prussian wing of the party was quite content to retain the status quo or even to let Prussia annex the smaller north German states. They insisted only that the cultural and education autonomy of the Catholic provinces be safeguarded. The national leaders of the Center party, on the other hand, favored dissolving Prussia and converting the state's provinces into new *Länder*. With the Center party unable to take a clear stand, the Prussian cabinet was limited to rejecting restructuring proposals as they surfaced, rather than furthering the *Reichsreform* discussion with concrete initiatives of its own.[17]

Finding a solution to another aspect of the Reich-state relationship, the overlapping administrative jurisdictions between the Reich and Prussia, initially seemed much more promising. As Germany's political crisis worsened, there were increasing demands for a return of the prewar custom of the *Personalunionen,* whereby a single incumbent occupied the same office in both the Reich and Prussian cabinets. In this area the Prussians did come forward with concrete suggestions. Several times during 1931 Braun proposed that the Reich chancellor should in *Personalunion* become Prussian prime minister. (Braun, himself in ill health for much of the year, intended to resign from the cabinet.) The prime minister also suggested that whenever the

Reich and Prussian administrative offices performed overlapping functions, they should be merged.

For a number of reasons Brüning was unreceptive to these overtures. He clearly did not want to be bound by the rules of parliamentary democracy in Prussia, which he would have been if he had become Prussian prime minister, and in view of the greater depth and experience of the Prussian civil service, merging state and federal offices would have meant strengthening Prussia's position in Reich affairs. Instead, the chancellor revived an earlier idea that the Prussian prime minister join the Reich government as vice chancellor. Now it was Braun's turn to be unenthusiastic: the Prussian prime minister did not want to be the only Prussian voice in a group of Reich ministers selected by and responsible only to the chancellor and the Reich president.[18]

Brüning and Braun put their proposals in the form of interoffice memoranda, but the Prussian minister of finance, Hermann Höpker-Aschoff, went public with his contributions to the *Reichsreform* debate. Like most supporters of the republic, Höpker-Aschoff feared that the scheduled Landtag elections in April 1932 would give the Nazis a dominant position in the Landtag and decisive influence in a new Prussian government. To prevent Hitler's party from gaining control of Prussia, the minister of finance in August 1931 proposed that the separate Reich and Prussian ministries of interior, finance, and justice be merged into single ministries under the control of the appropriate federal cabinet officer. In addition, he supported Brüning's proposal that the Prussian prime minister should become vice chancellor. The minister suggested the entire package of reforms should be implemented under the Reich president's decree powers.[19]

Brüning found much merit in Höpker-Aschoff's plans; the chancellor was particularly anxious for a union of the two finance ministries. But in Prussia the minister's suggestions met with a storm of protest. Among his political friends, Höpker-Aschoff was criticized not only for airing in public plans that were more suitable for private discussions, but above all for using Satan to drive out Beelzebub—that is to say, advocating the use of Article 48 to save parliamentary democracy. Here he touched upon a bedrock item in the Prussian coalition contract. His colleagues issued a formal statement that Höpker-Aschoff's proposals did not have the endorsement of the full cabinet. The finance minister was deeply disappointed by this reaction, and his hurt feelings undoubtedly contributed to his resignation from the cabinet a few weeks later.[20]

Personalunionen made little headway during Brüning's term of office, but the situation changed dramatically under Papen. The chancellor claimed the coup of July 20, 1932, had once again fused the Reich and Prussian cabinet into a "union of combatants" *(Kampfgemeinschaft)*. Papen noted proudly that in his capacity as Reich commissioner for Prussia he was responsible only to the Reich president, but he had the authority to act as the state's prime minister. In reality matters were more complicated. The singularly sibylline judgment of the *Reichsgericht* was particularly important regarding relations between the Reich and Prussian executives and the relevant parliamentary bodies.

Among the three bodies concerned—the Reichsrat, the Landtag, and the Staatsrat—the Reichsrat was undoubtedly the most significant for advancing Papen's ultimate aims. The second chamber of the national legislature became increasingly important as Weimar Germany's political crisis reached its climax. With the Reichstag and (after April 1932) the Prussian Landtag unable to fulfill their constitutional functions, the Reichsrat remained the sole parliamentary check on the Reich executive. As long as the Weimar constitution remained in effect, the representatives of the *Länder* had to approve any proposed constitutional or territorial changes. As we saw earlier, of the twenty-six votes allotted to Prussia in the Reichsrat, thirteen delegates voted as instructed by the cabinet, while the other thirteen represented the provinces.

Brüning did not attempt to change the balance of voting power in the Reichsrat, although he discontinued the tradition of consulting with the Prussian government before presenting initiatives in the Reichsrat.[21] Despite this affront, the Prussian cabinet, in line with its decision not to put obstacles in the path of the Reich government, usually supported Brüning's proposals when they reached the second chamber. Only when Prussia perceived a threat to its fundamental state's rights or basic democratic values did the Prussian government instruct its delegates to vote against the Reich government. One such case was Brüning's submission of a national amnesty law that would have pardoned persons convicted of political murders.[22]

Papen and Gayl were determined to gain control of the Prussian government's votes in the Reichsrat. However, their efforts were blocked by the ruling of the *Reichsgericht*. The otherwise murky judgment was unequivocal on one point: only the "old" Braun cabinet had the right to represent the state's executive in the Reichsrat. Papen had to wait for the Nazi era before he could savor a revenge of sorts. In February 1933 another presidential decree assigned the power to cast all of Prussia's Reichsrat votes to the Reich commissioner for Prussia. As a result, Papen, who was vice chancellor and federal commissioner for Prussia at the time, nominally controlled Prussia's representation in the Reichsrat. But it was a short-lived triumph. The decree of February was simply another step in the Nazi *Gleichschaltung;* a few months later, Hitler abolished the Reichsrat altogether. [23]

Relations between the Reich cabinet and the two Prussian legislative bodies, the Landtag and the Staatsrat, were not in dispute until the spring of 1932. As long as parliamentary democracy functioned in the state and the cabinet had the confidence of the Landtag, the Reich government had neither reason nor occasion to establish direct relations with the Prussian legislative houses. The situation changed abruptly in April 1932. Unable to obtain a vote of confidence in the new Landtag, the Braun cabinet resigned. Even before the July coup, Papen attempted to take advantage of the new power vacuum in the state. Soon after he became chancellor, he appealed directly to the leaders of the rightist parties in the Landtag to compromise their differences and facilitate the election of a new right-of-center government. The move was unsuccessful; not only the Weimar coalition parties and the caretaker government vigorously protested the Reich's interference in internal Prussian affairs.[24]

The federal takeover complicated the situation even further. Spokesmen for the Landtag, led by the Nazis and the German Nationalists, insisted that under the terms of the Prussian constitution the federal commissioner was responsible to the Landtag, just as had been true for the democratically elected prime minister. The groups that had heaped scorn on the state's democratic constitution for years now demanded that Papen govern Prussia in consultation with the rightist parties in the legislature.[25]

To the consternation of his political allies, the Reich chancellor rejected all demands for ministerial responsibility. For Papen, the Landtag was a negligible quantity. The chancellor and the Reich minister of the interior insisted that Hindenburg's July 1932 decree had created the best of all possible worlds for them. The Reich commissioner and his appointees possessed the powers assigned to the state cabinet by the Reich and Prussian constitutions, but they were accountable only to the Reich president. The Landtag leaders protested Papen's constitutional reasoning, but neither their objections nor the judgment of the *Reichsgericht* changed the political power relationship between the Landtag and the commissioner's regime. Papen and Gayl could essentially ignore a legislature that was incapable of electing a constitutional government or even passing legislation.[26]

Papen and his minister of the interior had an entirely different feel for the Staatsrat. While the Landtag symbolized democracy and popular representation, the Staatsrat evoked images of the prewar House of Lords. Unlike the Landtag, the Staatsrat had a firm place in the commissioner's long- and short-range constitutional plans. As part of their long-range reform plans, the federal leaders intended to remove the state's second chamber even further from popular control, converting it into an unelected house composed of notables appointed by the executive.[27]

The neoconservative rulers of the Reich anticipated that their constitutional reform plans would get a more sympathetic hearing in the Staatsrat, a much more conservative body than the Landtag. Moreover, as longtime chairman of the informal DVP-DNVP caucus, Gayl had close personal and political connections to the Staatsrat. For this reason, the Reich cabinet was severely disappointed by the reaction of the second chamber to its offer to consult with the Staatsrat on executive measures and its constitutional plans. Regardless of their political differences, most Staatsrat members resented the federalization of Prussia no less than their colleagues in the Landtag. The Staatsrat repeatedly passed resolutions denying Papen's claim that he represented the Prussian cabinet. Within a short time, relations between the Reich commissioners and the Staatsrat were as acrimonious as those with the Landtag. Politically, of course, none of this mattered. The Staatsrat had neither the constitutional authority nor the political will to challenge the regime of the commissioners.[28]

Kurt von Schleicher fully supported Papen's views on the relationship of the Reich commissioners and the Prussian legislative bodies. Before his appointment as chancellor, the general had favored dismissing the Landtag on trumped-up charges, but once in office he, too, refrained from such high-handed action. However, unlike Papen, who could ignore the legislature's pointless debates, Schleicher was confronted with a genuine constitutional dilemma. In mid-December 1932, the Landtag on its own initiative actually passed a law. It was not an important measure (the legislation permitted certain categories of debtors to delay repayment of their mortgages), but, except for the Communists, it had the support of all parties in the Landtag. Schleicher's regime had no substantive objections to the law; the problem was the constitutional issue of proclamation and implementation. Were the commissioners obligated to enforce a law passed by the Landtag? Or could they ignore Landtag's actions, even if the legislation had the backing of the majority of Prussia's elected representatives? Schleicher and his associates eventually reached a Solomonic decision: both the old government and the commissioner's regime would proclaim the law.[29]

Politically unimportant, the episode nevertheless demonstrated the gulf that separated the neoconservative restorationists from their Nazi successors, who had no such scruples. A Nazi *Gauleiter,* confronted with the claim that as Reich chancellor Hitler could not simply abolish parliamentary bodies provided for in the Prussian constitution, replied, "The time for such legal niceties has passed."[30]

The coming to power of the neoconservatives meant significant qualitative changes in the financial relationship between Reich and state. Heinrich Brüning's successors continued his practice of deliberately using the Reich's financial powers to destroy Prussia's political and constitutional autonomy.[31] Since 1927 financial relations between the Reich and the states had been governed by the National Financial Equity Law *(Reichsfinanzausgleichsgesetz)*. As the Depression worsened, the distribution key for federal revenue sharing, which Prussia had long claimed favored Bavaria and the southern states as well as the smaller northern states at the expense of Prussia,[32] left the state in a severely weakened financial position and highly vulnerable to the Reich's financial blackmail. Prussia's decision to balance its budget at any cost meant that as the economic and fiscal crisis grew progressively worse, the state's government had to pay the political price the Reich government demanded for financial aid from its treasury.[33]

To avoid becoming a permanent ward of the Reich, Prussia proposed a long-term compromise. In return for a commitment from the Reich to transfer specific, agreed-upon sums for unrestricted use by the state, Prussia was willing to grant the Reich the right to be consulted in the formulation of the Prussia state budget. Brüning refused any cooperative plans, and insisted on exacting a heavy price for the infusion of federal aid. When the Prussian budget revealed an unanticipated shortfall of RM 100 million in February 1932, for example, the Reich forced the state to transfer its shares in the Bank for Rural Settlement to the Reich in return for financial aid.[34]

Brüning's rejection of Prussia's ideas for a contractual agreement on finances was not a capricious act, but part of a long-range pursuit of concrete political objectives. By emasculating Prussia's financial autonomy, the chancellor intended to strengthen the powers of the federal government and those of the Prussian provinces.[35] Brüning came very close to realizing his financial *Reichsreform*. By the time he left office, the Prussian government readily acknowledged that control of the state's economic and financial policies had passed almost entirely to the Reich. Papen and Schleicher were the beneficiaries of Brüning's single-minded efforts to erode Prussia's financial autonomy. Even before imposing direct federal control over the state, Papen, for example, used the simple device of ten-day renewable credits to keep a tight rein on Prussia's finances. Without offering a quid pro quo, Johannes von Popitz, the Reich minister of finance under Papen (he went on to serve Schleicher and Hitler in the same capacity) insisted on active involvement in all stages of the Prussian budget-drafting process.[36]

Administrative Reforms: The Final Chapter

The history of administrative reforms in Prussia was largely the story of failed initiatives and paper proposals. This was true for the Weimar era no less than for the years before the First World War. The ubiquitous Bill Drews, the last royal minister of the interior and a walking encyclopedia of Prussian administrative history, blamed "the stubbornness of the Prussian privy councillor" for the lack of progress before 1918, and the "idiosyncracies of the parties" for the failures during the republican years.[37] There was something to Drews' analysis. Until the spring of 1930, the Landtag had played a major role in shaping—and more often blocking—the cabinet's initiatives for administrative reforms.

The era of the presidential chancellors with its policy of government by decree brought new opportunities for meaningful changes in Prussia's antiquated administrative structure. The *Dietramszeller Notverordnung* authorized the state to implement the comprehensive administrative reform packages which the cabinet complained the Landtag had consistently failed to enact. Even so, the Prussian government remained true to its democratic convictions, and did not attempt to impose reforms by decree. Instead, it tried to adhere to at least the spirit of parliamentary democracy as long as possible. Even when it was clearly impossible to work with the full Landtag, the cabinet consulted with the committee of the coalition parties (Interfraktioneller Ausschuss) and the legislature's rules committee (Ältestenausschuss).[38]

The framers of the Weimar constitution had clearly erred on the side of excessive democracy in specifying Prussia's representation in the Reichsrat. Over the years all efforts had failed to have Prussia's provincial delegates and those appointed by the state cabinet cast their votes as a single block. The new political situation in the spring of 1930 heightened the dilemma. Many Conservative provincial delegates, like Freiherr von Gayl, were more determined than ever to use the Reichsrat to sabotage the state's prorepublican policies. Yet the Prussian government also recognized the future significance of the Reichsrat. It was the key to Prussia's remaining ability to influence policy decisions by the presidential cabinets—at least as long as the chancellors still presented budgets and austerity measures for its approval.

In February 1930, the cabinet instructed the Prussian interior minister to search again for a formula that would assure that Prussia's Reichsrat votes were cast as a bloc. Waentig took his time responding, not answering until July, after prodding by the Landtag rules committee. Much like the DVP's proposal earlier, Waentig's plan called for casting Prussia's votes as a unit in accord with the wishes of the majority of the state's governmental and provincial delegates. To assure an equal distribution of influence, he called for a complicated set of weighted votes and mandatory discussions of the issues on the Reichsrat's agenda among all state delegates before any votes were taken.[39]

Waentig's mathematically cumbersome formula for weighting votes did not arouse much enthusiasm among either his cabinet colleagues or the provincial delegates. The prime minister, reluctant to become involved in the dispute, provided little leadership on this important issue, ostensibly because he regarded all Prussian attempts to find a solution to the problem as futile; the debate over Prussia's Reichsrat votes, he believed, could be settled only by an amendment to the Reich constitution—a most unlikely development. Experts in the Prussian ministry of justice agreed, but Braun's attitude also reflected his belief that doing nothing was generally preferable to taking a stand that endangered the coalition.[40]

The same sense of fatalism prevailed (although it was far less justified) when the cabinet turned to the problem of state administrative reforms. This time Otto Braun and his cabinet colleagues agreed that a comprehensive administrative reform package, the so-called *grosse Verwaltungsreform,* had to be linked to the overall *Reichsreform.* Prussia, that is to say, would have to wait for initiatives from the federal cabinet.[41] After the neoconservatives came to power in the Reich, this was politically contradictory and ultimately counterproductive. Since for the neoconservatives the *Reichsreform* was synonymous with fundamental changes in Germany's democratic system, leaving the initiative to the Reich meant abandoning the effort to use administrative reforms as a way of strengthening German democracy.

Somewhat belatedly, the cabinet seems to have recognized its mistake. In February 1932, when the neoconservative agenda had become abundantly clear, the ministers naively decided that bills for comprehensive administrative reforms should be ready for submission to the Landtag by September. But Prussia would coordinate its reform activities with the Reich. The decision came far too late. Realizing the futility of the effort, the cabinet abandoned the project after the April elections.[42]

Comprehensive administrative reforms were probably doomed in any case. As we saw earlier, comprehensive reform efforts had failed in the best of times, and the politically turbulent years after 1930 hardly increased chances for success.[43] On the other hand, the crisis atmosphere did provide additional impetus for tackling the "little" administrative reform *(kleine Verwaltungsreform),* a number of specific, but not necessarily interdependent, measures to deal with the administrative inefficiencies that had plagued the state for years. The proposals ranged from abolishing at least one of Prussia's six ministries to reducing the number of counties and judicial districts in the state. And, of course, there still remained the most vexing problem of all, the overlapping jurisdictions of provincial governors and district directors.[44]

Over the years, the combination of parochial interests, bureaucratic infighting, legislative pork barreling and ideological disagreements among the coalition parties had prevented much progress on any of the longstanding issues. The obstacles had hardly disappeared in 1930, but the desperate need to cut costs gave new urgency to many administrative reform projects. Calls for "simplifying" the state's government came from all sides. At the beginning of November 1931, the ministry of the interior promised to present to the cabinet proposals for the "little" reform. Three months later, Severing told a meeting of provincial governors and district directors that county and district boundaries would be "streamlined [*rationalisiert*] in the not too distant future." Even the opposition parties urged the cabinet to take some action. In March the Staatsrat passed a resolution introduced by the DNVP, DVP, and

Center party calling upon the cabinet to seize the initiative: "History teaches
[us] the most important administrative innovations have often been the product of the most difficult times."[45]

Unfortunately, the plans promised by the interior ministry never materialized, and even if they had it would not have mattered. The cabinet members took the position that all significant reforms would have to await the
unlikely return of politically less turbulent times or the passage of specific
legislation by the Landtag giving the government unlimited decree powers.
The Braun government's achievements in the area of administrative reforms
remained unimpressive, the government doing little more than react to crises.
This was the case, for example, when a massive scandal in Berlin rocked the
municipal administration in 1929, leading to the resignation of the city's
longtime mayor, Gustav Böss. As a consequence, the cabinet amended a 1920
law to permit increased state control over the city's administration.[46]

The primary reason for the cabinet's disappointing record on administrative reforms was the seeming lack of interest by the prime minister and, to
a somewhat lesser degree, the minister of the interior. Once again, Braun and
Severing felt that preserving peace among the coalition parties took priority
over administrative reform. In doing so, they thought they had public opinion,
or at least the supporters of the coalition parties, on their side. They noted, for
example, that before and during the 1932 Landtag election campaign, territorial administrators were anxious to announce that counties in their election
districts would not be redistricted. The provincial governors and district directors feared a massive voter backlash if the government were to stir up the
hornet's net of territorial reform. Still, in the long run the Prussian leaders'
decision to follow the "people" was probably counterproductive. Whatever
short-term benefits passivity bought, it also demonstrated the paralysis of
the democratic system and provided more ammunition for the republic's
enemies.[47]

When Papen and Gayl seized control of the Prussian executive, they had
no qualms about ignoring the wishes of the people, nor did they intend to
submit their proposals to the legislature. They were determined to use their
decree authority to effect both specific Prussian administrative reforms and a
comprehensive *Reichsreform*. Especially Gayl regarded himself as something
of an expert on administrative reforms. In fact, he argued that one reason for
the federal takeover was that the needed reforms could not be implemented in
any other way.[48]

The new regime set to work with an impressive display of energy. An
interagency committee composed of Reich officials, high-level bureaucrats in
the Prussian interior ministry, and some members of the Staatsrat drafted
position papers and reform proposals on a large variety of subjects. Included

were such thorny issues as collegial decision making in the cabinet, the overlapping functions of provincial governors and district directors, changes in the rights of municipal self-government, and county redistricting.[49]

Despite a plenitude of presidential power, however, all was not smooth sailing for Papen and his associates. The chancellor had little knowledge of the detailed problems involved in tackling Prussian administrative reforms, and even less inclination to learn the intricacies. Moreover, Papen quickly found that implementing reforms was far more difficult than drafting proposals. Like the parliamentary cabinets before them, the federal commissioners were confronted with conflicts among a wide variety of vested interests, both inside and outside government. Reich and Prussian offices were very reluctant to "simplify" their operations if that involved reducing their personnel or the scope of their functions. It also did not take the federal commissioners long to develop a parochial Prussian mentality. Bracht's complaints about the federal revenue-sharing key echoed those of Otto Braun, and Bracht, too, soon insisted Prussia had to preserve its financial autonomy in relations with the Reich. A grandiosely entitled "Decree Regarding the Simplification and Cost Reduction of the Administration" was stillborn.[50]

Eliminating one of the six cabinet posts had long been the subject of animated debate. (The old Braun government would later claim that only Papen's coup had prevented it from eliminating a ministry.)[51] Disagreement over which cabinet post was superfluous had blocked action in the past, but Papen and his Conservative allies had no doubts about their target: the ministry for social services. Although this particular ministry had been headed by a member of the Center party since 1920, the neoconservatives were convinced it was a bastion of Marxist social engineering. At the end of October, the Reich commissioners abolished the ministry, transferring its functions to other ministries.[52]

The elimination of the social services ministry essentially ended Papen's cost-cutting efforts at the ministerial level. The attempt to introduce a new code of ministerial procedures, although ostensibly motivated by considerations of efficiency, actually reflected the neoconservative ideological agenda. Bracht and especially Gayl wanted to replace the time-honored tradition of collegial decision making in the cabinet with a more bureaucratic model. By *collegiality* Prussian administrative practice meant that the department heads were not subordinated to the prime minister or to each other, but had equal authority, so that decisions affecting two or more ministries could be reached only after discussion among all of the cabinet members. Under the "bureaucratic" alternative, the prime minister would be the final decision-making authority. But principle is not the same as practice, and the plan to impose "bureaucratic" administrative practices in Prussia was quickly buried in intra-cabinet discussions.[53]

Bureaucratic and collegial traditions of governance also affected the state's territorial administration. The proper relationship among the provincial governors, district directors, and county executives raised as many controversies for the authoritarian reformers as it had for their parliamentary predecessors. At first glance, the introduction of bureaucratic administration seemed to provide a clear answer. Presumably, officials at each level of the territorial administration would be superior to officials at lower jurisdictional levels in the same province. County commissioners, that is to say, would report to the district directors, and the district chiefs to the provincial governors.[54]

In practice, things were much less clear-cut. Various interest groups, many of them with close ties to the neoconservatives, protested vigorously against subordinating "their" governmental service organization to offices they regarded as inappropriate and incompetent. Each side in turn had its champion at the cabinet table. Papen's appointees for the ministries of finance and education pleaded for strengthening the provincial governors and the eventual elimination of the district directors, while other commissioners supported stronger district directors. The arguments between those who wanted to strengthen the governors versus the district directors were familiar for the most part, although those favoring strong governors did add to their argument the prospect of the supposedly imminent *Reichsreform*. They pointed out that if the provinces were to become "Reich provinces," that is, federal districts directly subordinated to the control of the Reich cabinet, they would clearly need strong territorial administrators who could effectively carry out federal orders.[55]

In contrast to Severing, Papen's choice for the ministry of the interior, Fritz Bracht, made his position clear. On the difficult relationship of governors and district directors, he generally followed Grzesinski in leaving day-to-day administration to the district directors, while assigning to the governors general oversight and ceremonial functions. As if to underscore the continuity of views on this point between the parliamentary cabinet and the commissioners's regime, Bracht suggested that Arnold Brecht, whom Grzesinski had brought in to head the interior ministry's office for constitutional affairs, should be asked to submit additional concrete proposals.[56]

If Bracht had expected his proposals to be accepted without debate by his fellow commissioners, he was soon disappointed. He too experienced the frustrations of collegial decision making, and despite the constant talk of efficiency and authoritarianism, Papen provided no more leadership on this issue than Braun had. He agreed with the general tenor of Bracht's proposals, but in the face of fierce opposition from a number of vested interests, he, too, retreated. By the time the authoritarian regime ended in Prussia, little progress had been made on reallocating the functions of the two middle levels of the territorial administration. Both continued much as they had since 1918. Two weeks before Hitler became chancellor, the cabinet still could not agree whether the directors of the agricultural extension service should report to the governors or the district directors.[57]

The new rulers seemed to have more success when they turned to county and local government. Deciding which of Prussia's 450 counties and 1,000 local judicial districts should be eliminated was very controversial, but unlike the democratic cabinet, Papen used the authority granted the states under the *Dietramszeller Notverordnung* and acted swiftly to restructure Prussia's rural government. At the end of August, 58 counties were merged with their larger neighbors and 60 (out of a total of 1,006) local court districts disappeared. But this was also Papen's last and only significant piece of administrative reform. The solution of the commisssioners' regime to the problems of municipal self-government was to continue to appoint state receivers for Prussia's growing number of bankrupt cities. By the end of the Weimar years, more than 500 municipalities were in the hands of state receivers.[58]

The administrative reform record of the federal commissioners (which really meant the rule of Papen and Gayl; there were no new initiatives during Schleicher's term of office) certainly did not support the neoconservatives' claim that only the system of democracy and the pork-barrel mentality of the republican parties had prevented significant administrative reforms in the past. Papen's elimination of one of the six cabinet positions was a largely meaningless gesture. The financial savings were negligible; most of the civil servants in the ministry for social services were transferred to other offices. Nor were Papen and Gayl able to challenge the principle of collegial decision making in either the cabinet or in the territorial administration. Papen failed as completely as any of his predecessors in streamlining the overlapping jurisdictions of the offices of provincial governors and district directors. In the end, the Papen regime, too, substituted vague generalities for genuine administrative reforms. Only the reduction of the number of counties and judicial districts could be credited to the commissioners. But compared to such democratic accomplishments as the 1927 abolition of the *Gutsbezirke* and the reforms of municipal government in Western Germany under the terms of the Ruhr Settlement Act of 1920, Papen's and Gayl's reforms were minor triumphs at best.[59]

Personnel Policies and Appointments

Appointments to the corps of political administrators—which included the top positions in the ministries, the provincial governors, the district directors, the municipal police chiefs, and the county executives—had long been the subject of impassioned debates. Supporters of parliamentary democracy complained for years that the republican governments were too slow in saturating the ranks of the political administrators with men of genuine democratic convictions, while the opposition parties insisted that the Weimar coalition cabinets had staffed the state's corps of administrators with appointees whose only professional qualification was membership in one of the republican parties.

Brüning's appointment as Reich chancellor coincided with the forced resignation of Albert Grzesinski, the energetic Prussian minister of the interior whose name was synonymous with a policy of active "democratization" of the Prussian political civil service.[60] His departure in March 1930 left the state without a firm leader at the head of its most important ministry. As we saw, Grzesinski's immediate successor, Heinrich Waentig, was unequal to the job. In October 1930, Waentig in turn was succeeded by a familiar name in Prussian politics, Carl Severing.

Whatever Severing's shortcomings,[61] even his detractors acknowledged that he was a master politician. During his previous term of office the minister had already demonstrated an unusual capacity for working together with the leaders of the Center party in Prussia, a quality that was more important than ever now that Brüning was pulling the national Center party toward a decidedly rightist course in the Reich. Under Severing personnel decisions in Prussia largely became a bipartisan effort by the Social Democrats and the Center party, with the third coalition party, the left-wing Liberals, complaining that its partners tended to monopolize appointments. (In earlier years the Catholics and the Social Democrats had claimed a disproportionate share of the appointments went to the Liberals. Both sides were right.)[62]

In the past, efforts to "democratize" the political civil service had taken the form of brief gusts of extraordinary activity in response to specific political crises. The Kapp Putsch had led to a major purge earlier, and now the growing threat of antirepublican activity by political extremists inaugurated a similar wave of new appointments. In the spring of 1930, the cabinet replaced a number of governors and district directors in areas of the state where the cabinet excepted increased levels of political unrest. A second wave of appointments followed in July 1931, this time in response to the agitation in connection with the referendum to force early elections of the Prussian Landtag. A third cluster of appointments came just before the crucial April 1932 Landtag elections.[63]

The cabinet expected that intensified political campaigning and increased levels of street violence would constitute the prelude to a putsch attempt by one or more of the extremists's paramilitary formations. Consequently, the appointments were concentrated at the provincial and district levels; the ministers wanted strong and reliable officials in the territorial administration to keep a close eye especially on the activities of the Nazis' storm troopers and the Stahlhelm. In effect, the personnel policies were an attempt to apply the lessons of the Kapp Putsch. Unfortunately, the greatest danger to democracy in Prussia and Germany was not street violence provoked by the political extremists, but the plans coming from the offices of the Reich chancellor and the Reich president.[64]

Concern for the maintenance of law and order was also evident in the cabinet's choices of police chiefs in the major Prussian cities. As they had ever since 1918, the Weimar coalition parties tended to entrust prominent Social Democrats and especially former labor union leaders to head the police forces in pivotal urban centers. The government was convinced that for the most part Prussia's police forces were loyal to the republic, and Adolf Hitler's bitter complaints about police harassment of the Nazis would tend to support the government's claims. On the other hand, there was also some evidence (and even more rumors) that Nazi influence was growing rapidly—especially among younger police officers.[65]

Fear of infiltration by political extremists was not limited to the police. With the full support of the coalition parties (in the Landtag the left-wing Liberal delegate Grzimek urged Severing, "Mr. Minister, remain tough; in fact, get much tougher"), the cabinet responded with both policy and appointment decisions to counter the threat that card-carrying members of extremist groups would undermine the reliability of the corps of administrators. The Prussian cabinet responded immediately to the Nazis' surprising strength in the Prussian local elections of December 1929 with new rules making it more difficult for Nazis and Communists (the latter were added for reasons of symmetry) to serve in municipal government agencies. A few months later, in June 1930 the cabinet issued a decree prohibiting all members of the NSDAP, the KPD, or the Stahlhelm from being appointed to the civil service, Simultaneously, all incumbent civil servants were ordered not to be active in any of the Nazi or Communist front organizations, or to support the extremists' political efforts. As we saw, in a decision that was a pleasant surprise to many of the republic's supporters, the state's disciplinary court (Disziplinarhof) upheld the constitutionality of the Prussian decrees. Armed with the ruling of the court, the ministers moved swiftly to punish political insubordination. At the end of 1931, the cabinet dismissed five county executives because they had not taken a clear stand against the initiative and referendum campaign to force the early dissolution of the Landtag.[66]

It was certainly important to staff key offices with politically reliable and energetic officials. Equally significant, however, was the state's ability to maintain a high level of morale among its entire corps of civil servants. Here the Prussians were considerably less successful. The civil service was the primary victim of the clash between the competing principles of effective public administration and fiscal austerity. Since personnel costs constituted some 70 percent of the Prussian state budget, they were also prime targets for

the budget-slashing efforts. Reluctantly but persistently, the state cut personnel costs by a series of measures ranging from promotion stops to major
reductions in salaries and benefits. The measures affected all ranks—cabinet
ministers included—but the hardships were obviously greatest among the
already poorly paid lower ranks, especially Prussia's thousands of public
schoolteachers. Only the police were exempted from the most severe effects
of the austerity program.[67]

What, then, was the condition of the corps of political administrators on
the eve of Papen's coup? Was the civil service riddled with Nazi and Conservative sympathizers as some contemporaries and later analysts have claimed?
Or, conversely, was the extent of Papen's purge evidence that the "democratization" of the Prussian civil service had made great strides before the federal
takeover? The truth, as usual, lay somewhere in the middle. Pivotal positions
in the territorial administration, including the offices of all governors and
district directors, as well as many county executives, were filled with men
who were active supporters of the coalition parties and the constitutional
system of parliamentary democracy. In addition, the June, 1930 decree
successfully kept active, card-carrying Nazis and Communists out of the
civil service. But it is also true that especially in the lower ranks of the
administrators, there were sympathizers and "moles" of the extremist
groups; by mid-1932 the number of Nazi sympathizers was growing rapidly.
The state's fiscal measures had left many frustrated officials easy prey for
Nazi propaganda.[68]

Brüning had much to criticize about Prussia's personnel policies and
appointments, but except for the administration of the *Osthilfe*, he did not
attempt to interfere in individual Prussian appointments. In contrast, Papen
took immediate measures to transform the Prussian political civil service from
a bulwark of republicanism into a bastion of neoconservatism. Claiming all
republican appointments to the civil service had been motivated solely by
party politics, the men who engineered the July coup left no doubt that they
hoped to permeate the state's civil service once again with men committed to
the ideals of prerevolutionary Prussia. Positions in the political civil service
were to be filled by men who were "free" from party ties, but who had
demonstrated their adherence to "Christian"—that is to say, Protestant and
Conservative—principles. The new functionaries were also expected to welcome the restoration of the traditionally close ties between the civil service
and the military. In late August the commissioners urged all Prussian civil
services to make a point of attending public functions sponsored by the
Reichswehr.[69]

Although Papen, Gayl, and later Schleicher moved rapidly to impose their
imprint on Prussia's political administrators, the federal commissioners kept
within the bounds of the *Rechtsstaat* as they understood it. They did not

dismiss any judicial personnel (including the members of the Disziplinarhof) and, while working with feverish haste to dismiss republican officials and fill vacancies on an interim basis from what were obviously prepared lists (a week before the coup the Reich cabinet discussed Prussian appointments), until the judgment of the constitutional court confirmed Papen's powers as head of the Prussian executive, the Reich commissioner's appointments in Prussia were officially on an acting rather than permanent basis. As the legal base for their purge, the federal commissioners used the decree of February 1919, which the revolutionary Prussian government had employed (albeit very sparingly), to dismiss some of the most reactionary of the former royal officials immediately after the revolution. Once the Reich constitutional court had confirmed the Reich commissioner's authority to make permanent appointments, the appointment process became collegial and institutionalized. The Papen regime returned to the traditional practice of discussing potential appointments to the political civil service in full cabinet sessions on the basis of dossiers prepared by the interim minister of the interior.[70]

The federal commissioners instituted a large-scale purge of political administrators almost immediately after seizing control of the state. Within hours, the federal regime dismissed four governors (Kürbis, Lüdemann, Haas, and Falck), six district directors, and eight chiefs of police. Geographically, the commissioners's regime concentrated its attention on the politically volatile areas of northern and western Germany, precisely the regions where the parliamentary government had taken care to appoint stalwart prorepublican administrators.[71]

The purge continued unabated in the following weeks. At one cabinet meeting in mid-August, the commissioners confirmed the dismissals and replacements of over sixty county commissioners. The purge also included the board of directors of the Prussian Central Bank for Agricultural Cooperatives (Preussenkasse), who in the eyes of Papen's political friends were "agrarian Bolsheviks." By the end of the year, depending on whether transfers are counted as part of the purge, somewhere between 94 and 250 political administrators had been affected.[72]

There has been some debate as to who influenced the selection of those to be purged. Especially interesting is whether Nazis and neoconservatives cooperated in the purge and appointment process. It is certainly true that the Nazis had their "hit list" of Prussian administrators, notably police chiefs. After World War II, some of those dismissed claimed that their removal had been the result of specific demands by Nazi leaders. Arguing that the NSDAP and the Stahlhelm were nationalist groups, the Reich commissioners within a week after seizing power amended the June 1930 decree as far as the Nazis and the Stahlhelm were concerned. Membership in right-wing extremist groups was no longer a barrier to appointment to the Prussian civil service. Communists, however, remained barred from government jobs.[73]

Nevertheless, it is difficult to sustain the charge of full-scale Nazi-neoconservative collaboration. A far more persuasive case can be made for the influence of the Prussian DNVP and the Reichswehr. Hugenberg's press secretary, Herbert von Bose, was a major figure in the federal commissioner's office for public relations after the coup. The DNVP's Landtag spokesman on civil service and police matters, Eldor Borck, became an influential consultant on political civil service appointments. And traces of Schleicher's role are everywhere. One of the general's close confidantes, Carlowitz, became Papen's press spokesman for Prussia. There is also considerable evidence that the list of republican officials to be dismissed immediately after the July coup had been prepared in the Reich defense ministry.[74]

Proof that the NSDAP played a key role in Papen's and Gayl's personnel decisions is much harder to find. Except for rescinding the June 1930 decree, the commissioners' policies and appointments did not give the Nazis a favored status in the months after the coup. Although Nazis were no longer excluded from the civil service, no Nazis were named to a major position. The Papen regime also did not permit Prussian administrators to participate in any party-sponsored political activities, including those of the Nazis. Members of the Nazi unions were placed on the same potential enemies list as activists in the Reichsbanner Schwarz-Rot-Gold and the Communist party.[75]

Instead, the federal commissioners restored a distinctly pre-1914 flavor to the Prussian political civil service: the new appointees were academically trained and qualified, with a heavy sprinkling of aristocratic titles. Politically, the new administrators were members or sympathizers of the DNVP, the DVP, or the extreme right wing of the Center party. By the end of the commissioners' regime there were no members of the SPD and DDP among the top ranks of the political civil service, with one significant and symbolic exception. Gustav Noske, a darling of the Conservatives since his bloody suppression of the Communist uprising in 1919, remained governor of the province of Hanover until he was removed from office after the Nazi *Machtergreifung*.[76]

A comparison of the personnel policies and appointments initiated by the federal commissioners under Papen, Gayl, and Schleicher with those of that followed under the Nazi regime shows the fundamental differences between neoconservative restorationism and Nazi totalitarianism. Papen, Gayl, and Schleicher dismissed committed republicans from the political civil service and replaced them with men of Conservative hue, but they did not establish a one-party dictatorship. The July 1932 coup did not become the breakthrough some Nazis had hoped for. Moreover, none of the purged officials was actually thrown out of the Prussian corps of administrators. They were offered politically "less sensitive" positions in the administrative hierarchy (for example, Herbert Weichmann, Otto Braun's personal assistant and after World War II mayor of Hamburg, was transferred from the prime minister's office to the ministry of commerce), or sent into "temporary" retirement (*einstweiliger Ruhestand*) with their pension rights kept intact.[77]

In sharp contrast, the Nazis within a few weeks after coming to power had replaced virtually all of Papen's and Schleicher's Conservative provincial governors with Nazi party *Gauleiters,* while SA leaders became chiefs of police in most of the Prussian cities. (Similar developments were taking place in the Reich chancellor's office.) Finally, unlike the restorationists, the Nazis were not concerned with even the letter of the law in their handling of the state's personnel policies. In making appointments they ignored the rules on formal qualifications for membership in the Prussian civil service, just as they disdained the vested pension rights of the officials they purged. Many of the latter not only had their pensions stopped, but spent time in concentration camps as well. Ironically, these included men who a few months earlier had symbolized Papen's attempt to restore Conservative authoritarianism to Prussia.[78]

The battle between republicans and neoconservatives over the *Reichsreform* and the "Prussian problem" was a conflict over illusory goals. The ultimate aim of the presidential chancellors was to undo the results of the revolution of 1918; the democratic leaders of Prussia wanted to preserve the state's integrity as the guarantor of Germany's political transformation. Could the democratic leaders of Prussia have done anything to prevent what in the short term was a clear victory of the neoconservatives? Probably, at least until April 1932. The decision by the state's democratic leaders in the spring of 1930 to avoid conflicts with the presidential chancellors's regimes left virtually all trump cards in the relationship between the neoconservatives and the state's democratic leaders in the hands of the Reich cabinet. As a result, Prussia lost the initiative and was unable to use the remaining strength of its intact political system during the final crisis years of the Weimar era. In retrospect, it would have been far better if the state's leaders had insisted upon pursuing their own policies, especially in the area of combating the extremists and dealing with administrative reforms. Such a course of action might have led to tensions with the Reich leaders, but the image that Prussian democracy was "militant" rather than passive and fatalistic might well have prevented the short-lived victory of neoconservatives and the ultimate triumph of the Nazis.

CHAPTER 10

Conclusion

In his memoirs Otto Braun wrote that after the July 1932 coup it was obvious to him that the cause of democracy in Germany was lost. He remained in office only because he felt he could not disappoint his colleagues. It was, however, a case of the weak holding up the infirm. Some of Braun's colleagues remembered that they stayed on only because they felt they could not disappoint Braun. In the end, what the Prussian leaders seemed to want most was private and public assurances that, like good captains, they had remained on their sinking ship to the last.[1]

That the Nazis would take particular pleasure in destroying the flagship of German democracy once they came to power was a foregone conclusion. The Nazis and their fellow travelers had long complained that Papen and Schleicher "had not advanced the art of truly *völkisch* statesmanship." Although Papen nominally remained federal commissioner for Prussia after Hitler's appointment as Reich chancellor, the real strongman in the state was now Hermann Göring, the Nazi Reich and Prussian minister of the interior.[2]

Göring quickly revealed himself to be a master of the "art of *völkisch* statesmanship." Unlike the Papen regime, which had purged democratic officials, but also worried about the professional qualifications of their conservative successors, the Nazis' immediate concern was the creation of a terror machine that served the NSDAP. Göring's first appointments in Prussia named storm trooper leaders as police chiefs in the state's major cities. A short time later, Nazi *Gauleiters* became *Oberpräsidenten* and district directors, often replacing the men Papen's regime had appointmented only a few months before. The arrival of the Nazis also meant the end of the time-honored tradition of executive colleagiality in Prussia. To the consternation of his German Nationalist partners, Göring made personnel appointments without consulting Papen, Hugenberg, or anyone else, for that matter.[3]

But the Nazis were not content with establishing a de facto dictatorship. They also wanted to eliminate the last vestiges of pro forma and de jure democracy mandated by the October judgment of the Reich court. Immediately after Hitler's appointment, rumors circulated that the Reich cabinet intended simply to dismiss the Braun government and dissolve the Prussian Landtag in preparation for new elections. The object was obviously to elect a new state legislature under the same conditions of semiterror which the government had decreed for the election of a new Reichstag. Such a move by the Reich cabinet was blatantly unconstitutional—it will be recalled that the

Reich court had specifically prohibited the federal government from interfering in the workings of the state's legislature.

The lame-duck Braun government roused itself for the last time in order to prevent Hindenburg from issuing the necessary presidential decree. The Landtag itself on February 4, 1933, also rejected new elections. The Reich cabinet tried another route. Under the terms of the Prussian constitution a so-called three-man committee *(Dreimännerkollegium)*—the speaker of the Landtag, the prime minister, and the president of the *Staatsrat*—were authorized to act for the legislature in times of extreme emergency. Insisting this was such a time, the Reich cabinet asked the committee to dissolve the Landtag. But the *Dreimännerkollegium* voted 2 to 1 against the measure. Only Hans Kerrl, the Nazi speaker of the Landtag supported the move; the prime minister (Braun) and the president of the Staatsrat (Adenauer) cast dissenting votes.

All to no avail. On February 6 Hindenburg invoked Article 48 again and stripped the parliamentary government of its remaining powers. Papen became de facto and de jure prime minister. With its reconstituted personnel, that is to say, Papen replacing Braun, the three-man committee lost no time voting 2 to 1 for the dissolution of the Landtag. "We are the masters of the Reich and Prussia," wrote Goebbels triumphantly.[4]

Events now quickly took their course. After initially protesting the decree of February 6, the head of the Prussian Center party changed tactics and began appeasing the Nazis. Fritz Grass, the chairman of the Center party's Landtag caucus, offered to "cooperate" with Göring if the minister of the interior would put a stop to the purge of Center party members in the corps of Prussian officials. The Nazis ignored the offer.[5]

As expected, with most of the Communists and Social Democrats in concentration camps and storm troopers acting as "auxiliary police" throughout the state, the Nazis won the elections of March 1933. At the beginning of April, Hitler, again invoking the authority of the Reich president, appointed Göring prime minister in place of Papen. (Göring also remained minister of the interior.) In a final, ironic move, the new Landtag just before it was permanently abolished along with all of the other *Länder* parliaments formally ended the commissioners's regime. In June the legislature elected—or better, rubberstamped—the government already appointed by Hitler.

In the meantime, Otto Braun had fled Germany and gone into exile in Switzerland. Correctly anticipating that the Nazi government would use the Reichstag fire of February 28, 1933, to unleash a reign of terror throughout Germany, that same night the prime minister used the cover of darkness to drive to his home in Ascona, Switzerland. There was considerable criticism of Braun's precipitous action, and the Nazis' propaganda certainly made much of the prime minister's "cowardice," but given the hatred with which the Nazis looked upon the prime minister as the personification of everything they wanted to destroy, there is little doubt that only his flight prevented Braun from coming to bodily harm. The fate of Ernst Thälmann, the KPD's leader whom the Nazis murdered in a concentration camp, is instructive in this respect.[6]

What has remained of Prussia's historic legacy? There has never been a unanimity of views on this subject. The republican leaders saw themselves as the only legitimate authority in the state. Eleven years after he left Germany, Braun still claimed that only "Göring and his accomplices" prevented him from carrying out his duties as prime minister. In his reminiscences, written in exile, Albert Grzesinski quoted with approval the assessment that "Prussia and only Prussia had saved Germany from the almost inevitable fall into the abyss." For the Nazis, on the other hand, Weimar Prussia was an uninteresting interlude, a historic anachronism. When he first read Braun's memoirs, originally published in Zurich in 1940, Goebbels commented, "Senile mutterings. Totally uninteresting for our times." Ironically, in World War II the views of the victorious Allies were closer to the Nazis' than to those of Prussia's republican leaders. The heads of the anti-Hitler coalition preferred to see an ongoing history of Prussian aggression and militarism inevitably culminating in Adolf Hitler and the Nazis. Ignoring Weimar Prussia altogether, they insisted that Prussianism, German militarism, and Nazism were essentially the same thing.[7]

Undoubtedly, most historians would agree with E. J. Feuchtwanger's assessment that while the history of Weimar Prussia turned out to be an epilogue, it looked for a while as if it might have been a renaissance.[8] Nevertheless, however one might be tempted to celebrate what republican Prussia might have been, in the final analysis democracy in Weimar Prussia was a failure. Numerous explanations have been offered for the ultimate failure of parliamentarism in Weimar Germany, and while most focus on the shortcomings of federal politics, at least some are applicable to the state as well.

Many authors have pointed to the lack of real revolutionary changes brought about by the revolution of 1918. Most of the responsibility for treating the antirepublican, monarchical, restorationist forces with unexpected and unwarranted leniency lies with Friedrich Ebert and the leaders of the Reich, but the Prussians' long delay in enacting meaningful administrative and personnel reforms must bear some of the blame as well. The absence of any real give and take between the government coalition and a loyal opposition applies equally to Reich and state. Throughout the republican years, the consensual base for parliamentary democracy was so small that all of the prorepublican parties had to become part of the government coalition. With a few notable exceptions, the opposition forces, for their part, were antisystemic parties whose aim was not just to replace the governing coalition, but to destroy the constitutional system itself.[9]

Concentrating on the lack of consensual politics in Weimar Germany has an element of fatalism about it. After all, it was the responsibility of the republican parties to create mass support for the constitutional system they had created. Particularly the two largest democratic groups, the SPD and the Center party, did too little in this respect. As Otto Braun and other right-wing Social Democrats lamented about the national SPD just before the Nazis came to power, the SPD had allowed itself to be "maneuvered into playing the part of a sterile opposition."[10] As for the Center party, here the criticism focuses on the Catholics's political schizophrenia and especially during the last months of the republican years on the party's relationship to the Nazis. Contemporary and postwar critics pointed out that the Catholics were simply no match for the tactical machinations of Hitler and the Nazis. In the end, even the Prussian Center party became a collaborator of the Nazis for a variety of opportunistic, legalistic, and illusory reasons. Hoping to safeguard their cultural if not their political independence, Germany's Catholics sold out to the Nazis.[11]

All of these factors played a role in the final demise of the Weimar Republic, but (as noted earlier) they apply far more to politics at the Reich than at the state level. Parliamentary democracy in Prussia failed for different reasons. Ironically, they were the same reasons that had earlier provided the state with political strength and made it the much vaunted "rock of democracy."

The contrast between the weak and vacillating men who led the Reich, and the strong, effective, pragmatic Prussian leaders, genuine masters at the game of democratic politics, was a staple of Weimar history. And this was no mere rhetoric. There is no doubt that the quality of Prussia's democratic leaders was a decisive factor in providing the state years of political stability. On more than one occasion they prevented the Weimar Republic from collapsing much earlier than it did. These leaders also persuaded the major prorepublican parties in Prussia not to waste their time in sterile opposition, but to accept responsibility for governing the state for fifteen years. It was a conscious decision by the former outsiders to become insiders: The political forces that had been systematically excluded from power before 1918 both created and cooperatively sustained the new democratic system in the state. In effect, the Prussian leaders attempted to apply what they read as the lessons of history. They recognized and accepted that it was Prussia's "mission" both to impose its political system on the Reich and to guarantee its preservation. The state's republican leaders attempted to apply that lesson in the republican era. They established parliamentary democracy in Prussia and in turn were determined to have Prussia guarantee democracy in Germany. For this reason, too, they resolutely and successfully rejected any reforms of the German federal structure that would have destroyed Prussia's preeminent position among the

German *Länder*. Almost to the bitter end they fully recognized they had no alternative. Unless they remained insiders, they would again become outsiders—as Papen's coup aptly demonstrated.

Another major difference between Reich and state was the quality of the two constitutions. Specifically, the framers of the Prussian constitution seemed to have avoided many of the mistakes for which the creators of the national constitution were criticized. Avoiding the excesses of plebiscitory democracy, the Prussian document effectively balanced legislative and executive power, so that in contrast to the Reich, the state's executive did not have to invoke its decree powers to maintain either law and order or systemic viability.[12]

All of these factors were important and positive, but paradoxically, they also had their negative side. Prussia's leaders, for example, were a static and aging group. With remarkably few exceptions, the republican leaders of Prussia in 1932 were the same men who rose to power and prominence in 1918. Among the cabinet ministers only Adolf Grimme had not already reached late middle age at the end of World War I. Increasingly convinced they were indispensable and that no one could take their places, their very success precluded personnel changes within their ranks. Ernst Heilmann was one of the rare Prussian leaders who not only permitted, but encouraged, younger men to rise to positions of real power. Not surprisingly, after fifteen years of struggle and constant personal abuse these men suffered from burnout when the state's democracy faced its greatest challenge.

The successful cooperation of the republican parties in Prussia was also a mixed blessing. Their ability to create a long-term viable political alliance in the state led them to ignore developments within their own parties at the national level. For too long they persuaded themselves that as long as they continued their coalition in Prussia, it did not matter much that leaders of the same parties were unable to form alliances at the Reich level. Moreover, because their coalition in Prussia worked so well for so long, the insiders tended to want to remain an exclusive club. Nothing illustrated this better than the seemingly endless negotiations over enlarging the Weimar coalition in Prussia by including the DVP. While the right-wing Liberals were certainly not blameless in blocking the road to the grand coalition, it is equally true that the Weimar parties were very reluctant to risk abandoning the comfort of their cozy club even though enlarging the coalition was clearly in the interest of securing the political system as a whole.

Finally, perhaps decisively, Prussia's democracy fell victim to what was essentially a nineteenth-century mentality, which insisted that Prussia could impose its political system on the Reich. Much as was true of the state's leaders in the final years of the Wilhelminian era,[13] Prussia's republican leaders ignored the developments in Germany that continued to weaken the state's position in its relations with the Reich. The decline of Prussia's influence and power in the German federal structure was hastened by the decisions of those who created the Weimar constitution. Fearful of a resurrected Prussian authoritarianism, Hugo Preuss and his colleagues strengthened the central government at the expense of the states and especially Prussia. The state's leaders were unable to reverse that trend. As a result, as Gordon Craig has noted, in the twentieth century Prussia was simply not strong enough to play the stabilizing role that it had assumed in the nineteenth century. Prussia's republican leaders were unwilling either to recognize this development or to create new avenues to assert Prussia's influence under changed circumstances. The Weimar coalition parties in Prussia were neither willing to risk their political capital in support of the republican governments in the Reich, nor did they take the lead in advancing the *Reichsreform* as a way of creating a new federal contract.[14]

Did Weimar Prussia leave any legacy, then? Certainly not in the sense in which Otto Braun and some of the other republican leaders had hoped and expected. When the prime minister wrote his memoirs, he was confident his "political testament" would provide a detailed guide for rebuilding a future democratic Germany. He was severely disappointed that the publisher forced him to leave out long passages.[15] He was also sad that, like Brüning, he was to play no significant part in German history after 1945. The same is true of virtually all of the major leaders of Weimar Prussia.

On the other hand, a number of less prominent Prussian politicians of the Weimar era quickly rose to leadership positions after 1945, becoming "men of the first hour" in what was until recently East and West Germany. They included above all Konrad Adenauer. The former president of the Staatsrat was to dominate politics in the Federal Republic for many years. And there were others. Two former provincial governors, Rudolf Amelunxen, and Johannes Gronowski, as well as a former minister of education, Otto Boelitz, and a former prime minister, Adam Stegerwald, were among the founding members of the Christian Democratic Union.[16] Much to the chagrin of Otto Braun, Kurt Schumacher became the undisputed leader of the West German Social Democrats after 1945. Another SPD leader, Adolf Grimme, was instrumental in rebuilding a democratic system of public education in the Federal Republic.

Still, there was relatively little personnel and even less institutional continuity between Weimar Prussia and the two German states that emerged after 1945. But there was an aura, a sense that Weimar Prussia provided a model for a successful democracy in Germany that remained pervasive long after the leaders of the Weimar era had passed from the scene. Twenty years after the end of World War II, the Federal Republic was contemplating the possibility of a grand coalition between the Social Democrats and the Christian Democrats. The man who would be responsible for nominating the members of such a cabinet, Wilhelm Lübke, the president of the Federal Republic in 1965, had been a young Center party member of the Landtag in 1932. He later recalled that his memories of the good relations between Catholics and Social Democrats in Weimar Prussia were instrumental in removing whatever unease he might have had about endorsing the cooperation of the Christian Democrats under Kurt Kiesinger and the Social Democrats under Willy Brandt.[17]

NOTES

BIBLIOGRAPHY

INDEX

Abbreviations Used in Notes

ArchdSD	Archiv der sozialen Demokratie, Bonn–Bad Godesberg
BA	Bundesarchiv, Koblenz
Braun, *Weimar*	Otto Braun, *Von Weimar zu Hitler* (New York, 1940)
Braun, "Weimar-Ms."	Otto Braun, "Von Weimar zu Hitler," typescript, Braun papers, Rep. 92a/68 (PrGstAB)
DDP-PA	Sitzungen des DDP-Parteiausschusses, R 45 III (BA)
DrPrLT, [date]	*Sammlung der Drucksachen des Preussischen Landtages*
DVP-PV	Sitzungen des DVP-Parteivorstandes, R 45 II (BA)
DVPRTFrV.	Sitzungen des DVP-Reichstagsfraktionsvorstandes, R 45 II (BA)
ForHbg.	Forschungsstelle für die Geschichte des Nationalsozialismus, Hamburg
HiKo	Historische Kommission, Berlin
IISG	Internationaal Instituut voor Sociaal Geschiedenis, Amsterdam
LASH	Landesarchiv Schleswig-Holstein, Schleswig
LBI	Leo Baeck Institute, New York
NSStAH	Niedersächsisches Staatsarchiv, Hanover
PrGS	*Preussische Gesetzsammlung*
PrGStAB	Preussisches Geheimes Staatsarchiv, Berlin
SBPrLT, [date]	*Sitzungsberichte des Preussischen Lantages*
SitzPrStMin	Sitzungsberichte des Preussischen Staatsministeriums
SitzPrStMin (commissioners)	Sitzungsberichte des Preussischen Staatsministeriums (Kommissare des Reiches)
SitzPrStMin (Parl.)	Sitzungsberichte des Preussischen Staatsministeriums (Parlamentarische Regierung) (after July 20, 1932)
SPD Parteitag, [date]	*Protokoll über die Verhandlungen des Parteitages der SPD*
SPD Preussentag	*Protokoll über die Verhandlungen des Preussentages der SPD* (Berlin, 1928)
Z-Prot.	*Die Protokolle der Reichstagsfraktion und des Fraktionsvorstandes der Deutschen Zentrumspartei 1926–1933,* ed. Rudolf Morsey (Mainz, 1969)
ZStAM	Zentrales Staatsarchiv, Merseburg
ZStAP	Zentrales Staatsarchiv, Potsdam

Notes

Introduction

1. Hans-Ulrich Wehler, "Preussen ist wieder chic . . . ," in *Preussen ist wieder chic . . . Politik und Polemik in zwanzig Essays,* ed. Wehler (Frankfurt a.M., 1983), pp. 11–18. For a good critical survey of some recent publications, see Francis Carsten, "The *Preussenwelle,*" *German Historical Institute London Bulletin* 8 (Autumn 1981), 14–19. Some typical "wave" contributions include Kurt Forstreuter, *Wirkungen des Preussenlandes* (Cologne, 1982); Karl Dietrich Erdmann et al., *Preussen—Seine Wirkungen auf die Deutsche Geschichte* (Stuttgart, 1982); Otto Büsch and Wolfgang Neugebauer, eds., *Moderne Preussische Geschichte, 1648– 1947* (Berlin, 1982).

2. Carsten, *"Preussenwelle,"* p. 14.

3. Wehler, "Chic," and "Nicht verstehen—der Preussennostalgie widerstehen," in *Preussen,* ed. Wehler, pp. 67–71; Bernt Engelmann, *Preussen—Land der unbegrenzten Möglichkeiten* (Munich, 1979).

4. Such major collections as Hans-Jürgen Puhle and Hans-Ulrich Wehler, eds., *Preussen im Rückblick* (Göttingen, 1980); Oswald Hauser, *Zur Problematik "Preussen und das Reich"* (Cologne, 1984); Karl Dietrich Erdmann and Hagen Schulze, eds., *Weimar—Selbstpreisgabe einer Demokratie—Eine Bilanz heute* (Düsseldorf, 1980) contain no significant discussions of Weimar Prussia. For the link between Prussia and the Nazis see Wehler, "Nicht."

5. Gordon A. Craig, "Prussianism and Democracy: Otto Braun and Konrad Adenauer," in *The End of Prussia* (Madison, Wis., 1984), p. 71; and Horst Möller, "Das Ende Preussens," in *Preussen—Eine Herausforderung,* ed. Wolfgang Böhme (Karlsruhe, 1981), p. 109.

6. Dietrich Orlow, *Weimar Prussia, 1918–1925: The Unlikely Rock of Democracy* (Pittsburgh, Pa., 1986).

7. See, for example, Abegg to Severing, 31 May 1947, Abegg papers; Werner Conze, "Die Krise des Parteienstaates in Deutschland 1929/30," *Historische Zeitschrift* 178 (Aug. 1954), 75; Möller, "Ende," pp. 103–04.

8. See especially Horst Möller, *Parlamentarismus in Preussen 1919–1932* (Düsseldorf, 1985).

9. Erich Kuttner, *Otto Braun* (Berlin [1932]); Hagen Schulze, *Otto Braun oder Preussens demokratische Sendung* (Berlin, 1977); Craig, "Braun"; and Horst Möller, "Ernst Heilmann—Ein Socialdemokrat in der Weimarer Republik," *Jahrbuch des Instituts für Deutsche Geschichte an der Universität Tel Aviv* 11 (1982), 261–64.

10. Braun, "Weimar-Ms.," p. 390. See also Craig, "Braun," p. 72; Möller, "Ende," p. 109.

11. Braun, "Weimar-Ms.," p. 383.

Chapter 1. Prussia and the German Political Parties, 1925–1930

1. See, for example, Hermann Müller, *Die November-Revolution* (Berlin, 1928), pp. 285–86; Harry Graf Kessler, *Tagebücher 1918–1937,* ed. Wolfgang Pfeiffer-Belli (Frankfurt a.M., 1961), p. 566 (12 Aug. 1928).

2. See the section Election Results, later in this chapter.

3. Anton Erkelenz, "Parlamentarismus und Parteiwesen," *Demokratischer Zeitungsdienst,* 10 Feb. 1926. The best overall history of German liberalism during the Weimar Republic is Larry E. Jones, *German Liberalism and the Dissolution of the Weimar Party System, 1918–1933* (Chapel Hill, N.C., 1988).

4. Dieter Fricke et al. eds., *Die bürgerlichen Parteien in Deutschland, 1830–1945* (Leipzig, 1968, 1970), 1:195–200.

5. The best analysis of paramilitary politics during the Weimar Republic is James M. Diehl, *Paramilitary Politics in Weimar Germany* (Bloomington, Ind., 1977).

6. For details of the organization's history, see Karl Rohe, *Das Reichsbanner Schwarz-Rot-Gold* (Düsseldorf, 1966).

7. Wilhelm Marx, the national chairman of the Catholic party, joined the executive committee of the new organization, and Joseph Hess, the leader of the Center party delegation in the Prussian Landtag, described the Reichsbanner as the "defender of healthy nationalism." See *SBPrLT 1925–1928,* 15 Oct. 1925, vol. 3, col. 4417.

8. Josef Becker, "Joseph Wirth and die Krise des Zentrums . . . 1927–28," *Zeitschrift für die Geschichte des Oberrheins* 109 (1961), 453.

9. See chapter 3, below.

10. For a detailed history, see Kurt G. P. Schuster, *Der Rote Frontkämpferbund* (Düsseldorf, 1975).

11. For a detailed analysis of the Stahlhelm, see Volker R. Berghahn, *Der Stahlhelm—Bund der Frontsoldaten 1918–1935* (Düsseldorf, 1966). For a treatment highly sympathetic to the RFB by an East German historian, see Kurt Finker, *Geschichte des Roten Frontkämpferbundes* (Berlin, 1982).

12. For critical analyses of the SPD's history in the Weimar years, see Richard N. Hunt, *German Social Democracy 1918–1933,* (New Haven, Conn.: 1964); Richard Breitman, *German Socialism and Weimar Democracy* (Chapel Hill, N.C., 1981).

13. Wilhelm Keil, *Erlebnisse eines Sozialdemokraten* (Stuttgart, 1947–48), 2:337.

14. See, for example, Sollmann to Severing, 10 Sept. 1925, Severing papers/01/101; Hilferding to Kautsky, 8 Jan. 1926, Kautsky papers/D XII/642; Grzesinski to Noske, 19 March 1929, Grzesinski papers/283; Werner Conze, "Die Krise des Parteienstaates in Deutschland 1929/30," *Historische Zeitschrift* 178 (Aug. 1954), 61; Kurt Koszyk, *Zwischen Kaiserreich und Diktatur—Die sozialdemokratische Presse von 1914–1933* (Heidelberg, 1958), p. 182; Schöpflin to Keil, 30 May 1925, Keil papers/Briefe/20.

15. See, for example, Paul Kampffmeyer to Karl Kautsky, 20 and 25 Nov. 1925, Kautsky papers/D XIV/64–65.

16. For contemporary reflections on this state of affairs, see the exchange of letters on the issues before the 1927 Kiel congress between Sinzheimer and Müller, 12 and 14 March 1927, Müller papers/P; Georg Decker, "Katholizismus und Sozialismus,"

Gesellschaft 5 (1928), 289. Cf. Arno Scholz, *Null vier—ein Jahrgang zwischen den Fronten* (Berlin-Grunewald, 1962), pp. 94–95, 108.

17. *SPD Parteitag 1925,* pp. 93, 317. The vote against the resolutions opposing coalitions with the Center party was 285:81. The resolutions themselves are in ibid., pp. 309–10, 316–17.

18. Karl Kautsky, "Die moderne Nationalität," *Neue Zeit* 5 (1887), 392–405, 442–51; Braun, "Weimar-Ms.," pp. 286–87.

19. For a detailed analysis of the battle cruiser controversy, see Wolfgang Wacker, *Der Bau des Panzerschiffes "A" und der Reichstag* (Tübingen, 1959).

20. SitzPrStMin, 6 and 13 Dec. 1927, PrGStAB, Rep. 90a/16.

21. See the correspondence between Hermann Müller and Arnold Brecht, June–July, 1928, Müller papers/II/133. See also Braun, "Weimar-Ms.," p. 406.

22. See the handwritten notes of the SPD district leader in Hanover, Lau, on a joint meeting of the party's national executive committee and the Reichstag delegation, 18 Aug. 1928, and Lau's report to his district committee, 23 Aug. 1928, NSStAH, 310 II/A 19. See also Wacker, *Panzerschiff,* pp. 100, 108; *Sozialdemokratische Parteikorrespondenz (Ergänzungsband),* July 1930, pp. 359–63; correspondence of H. Müller and Otto Wels, 24 and 27 Aug. 1928, Müller papers, I/113, IV/555.

23. For the left-wing position, see Kurt Rosenfeld, "Die Kreuzerkrisis," *Klassenkampf* 2 (1 Sept. 1928), 517–20. See also Paul Herz to Karl Kautsky, n.d. [ca. early 1929], Kautsky papers/D XII/411; Ludwig Haas, "Wahrer oder falscher Parlamentarismus," *Deutsche Republik* 3 (1929), 807; Alfred Milatz, *Wähler und Wahlen in der Weimarer Republik,* 2d ed. (Bonn, 1968), p. 89.

24. Braun to Müller and Müller to Braun, 16 and 20 Aug. 1928, Müller papers, I/6, and IV/60. See also Braun, "Weimar-Ms.," p. 402.

25. Rosenfeld, "Kreuzerkrisis," p. 517.

26. For a list of members, see Wacker, *Panzerschiff,* p. 121, n. 51. On Heilmann's political career, see Horst Möller, "Ernst Heilmann—Ein Sozialdemokrat in der Weimarer Republik," *Jahrbuch des Instituts für Deutsche Geschichte an der Universität Tel Aviv* 11 (1982), 261–64; Dietrich Orlow, *Weimar Prussia 1918–1925: The Unlikely Rock of Democracy* (Pittsburgh, Pa., 1986), pp. 34–35.

27. Günther Grünthal, *Reichsschulgesetz und Zentrumspartei in der Weimarer Republik* (Düsseldorf, 1968), p. 218. The concordat is discussed in chap. 3, below.

28. *SPD Parteitag 1927,* pp. 69–70, 267; *SPD-Preussentag 1928.*

29. See *Schleswig-Holsteinische Volkszeitung,* no. 120a (24 May 1927); Otto Braun, *Von Weimar zu Hitler,* 2d ed. (Hamburg, 1949), p. 131; Braun, "Weimar-Ms.," p. 389.

30. Hagen Schulze, interview with Ernest Hamburger, 5 Oct. 1972 (hereafter: "Schulze-Hamburger Interview"). I am grateful to Prof. Schulze for providing me with a copy of the interview.

31. See Braun, "Weimar-Ms.," p. 384. On Braun's relationship to Severing, see the first edition of *Von Weimar zu Hitler* (New York, 1940), pp. 237–39, 265–70; Braun to Benedikt Kautsky, 11 Oct. 1946, Braun papers/B/B/I/133 (ArchdSD).

32. See Ernst Eckstein, "Die Preussenkoalition," *Klassenkampf* 2 (1 June 1928), 335–39; *SPD Parteitag 1927,* pp. 75, 189–90, 215; *Klassenkampf* 3 (15 July 1929);

Ernst Heilmann, "Ein Jahr 'Das Freie Wort,'" *Das Freie Wort* 2 (5 Oct. 1930), 1–2. See also *SPD Preussentag 1928,* pp. 4–24 (Grzesinski); Victor Schiff, "Das österreichische Beispiel," *Das Freie Wort* 2 (30 Nov. 1930), 8.

33. Michael Stürmer, *Koalition und Opposition in der Weimarer Republik 1924–1928* (Düsseldorf, 1967), pp. 263–64; Rudolf Morsey, *Der Untergang des politischen Katholizismus—die Zentrumspartei zwischen christlichem Selbstverständnis und 'Nationaler Erhebung' 1932/33* (Stuttgart, 1977), pp. 15–16; Becker, "Wirth," pp. 423–24, 453. See also SPD, *Der Bürgerblock—Wie er wurde und was er ist,* ed. Parteivorstand (Berlin, 1927), p. 11. For a full-scale history of the Prussian Center party, see Herbert Hömig, *Das preussische Zentrum in der Weimarer Republik* (Mainz, 1979).

34. Oswald Wachtling, *Josef Joos* (Mainz, 1974), pp. 66, 121, 130–31; *Sozialdemokratische Parteikorrespondenz* 1–2 (Feb. 1929), 51.

35. See Stresemann's remarks to the DVP executive committee, 19 March 1927, p. 10, R 45 II/42 (BA).

36. Braun, "Weimar-Ms.," p. 434. See also Severing to Braun, 28 July 1925, Severing papers/25/4; Keil, *Erlebnisse* 2:339–40.

37. Orlow, *Weimar Prussia,* pp. 173–74, 210.

38. Detlef Junker, *Die Deutsche Zentrumspartei und Hitler 1932–33* (Stuttgart, 1969), pp. 150–51; *SBPrLT 1928–1932* 9 July 1929, vol. 6, cols. 8064–65 (Hess).

39. See Max von Stockhausen, *6 Jahre Reichskanzlei,* ed. Walter Görlitz (Bonn, 1954), p. 251.

40. Braun, "Weimar-Ms.," pp. 434–35; Braun, *Weimar,* p. 151; Hömig, *Zentrum,* p. 152.

41. For a detailed analysis of the party's decline, especially at the national level, see Werner Schneider, *Die Deutsche Demokratische Partei in der Weimarer Republik 1924–1930* (Munich, 1978).

42. See Koch-Weser's remarks at the DDP-PA, 28 Nov. 1926; Erich Koch-Weser, "Sieben Ziele für den neuen Reichstag," *Demokratischer Zeitungsdienst,* 30 May 1928. See also Gustav Noske, *Erlebtes aus Aufstieg und Niedergang einer Demokratie* (Offenbach a.M., 1947), p. 286; Otto Nuschke, "DDP," in *10 Jahre Deutsche Republik,* ed. Anton Erkelenz (Berlin, 1928), p. 41.

43. See Eugen Schiffer, *Ein Leben für den Liberalismus* (Berlin, 1951), p. 235; minutes of the DDP-ZV, 10 March 1926.

44. Bernhard Falk, "Aufzeichnungen," p. 78, Kleine Erwerbungen (BA). The "Aufzeichnungen" is the typescript of Falk's unpublished autobiography. On Nuschke, see the detailed but also completely uncritical biography by a historian from the former GDR, Gerhard Fischer, *Otto Nuschke* (Berlin, 1983).

45. *SBPrLT 1925–1928,* 16 Dec. 1927, vol. 15, col. 22754. See also Falk, "Aufzeichnungen," p. 177; *SBPrLT 1925–1928,* 29 March 1928, vol. 17, col. 26366.

46. Stresemann to Scholz, 19 July 1928, in R 45 II/69 (BA). See also "Stenographische Niederschrift der Verhandlungen des 8. Parteitages der Deutschen Volkspartei in Mannheim . . . März 1930" (hereafter: "DVP Parteitag 1930"), p. 102, R 45 II/31 (BA).

47. For details, see Henry A. Turner, *Stresemann and the Politics of the Weimar Republic* (Princeton, N.J. 1963).

48. *SBPrLT 1925–1928,* 27 June 1925, vol. 2, cols. 2789–90 (Graf zu Stolberg-Wernigerode); *SBPrLT 1928–1932,* 13 Dec. 1929, vol. 7, col. 9475 (Leidig).

49. Hömig, *Zentrum,* p. 140, n. 14; *SBPrLT 1928–1932,* 23 April 1929, vol. 5, col. 6507; Fritz Rathenau, "Als Jude im Dienst von Reich und Staat," pp. 101ff., unpublished (Leo Baeck Institute, N.Y.). See also Orlow, *Weimar Prussia,* pp. 207–08.

50. See his statement in the meeting of the DVP national executive committee, DVP-ZV, 1 Oct. 1926, pp. 31–32. The stenographic protocol indicates expressions of skepticism and doubt from other members of the executive committee at this point.

51. For details on the controversy, see DVP-ZV, 1 Oct. 1926, pp. 6, 27–28, 39–42, 66.

52. Erich Koch-Weser, "Republikanische Einigung," *Hilfe* 32 (1 Sept. 1926), 348–52; DVP-ZV, 1 Oct. 1926, pp. 14, 33; "DVP Parteitag 1930," p. 47 (Scholz); *SBPrLT 1928–1932,* 5 July 1929, vol. 6, cols. 7710–17.

53. Martin Schumacher, *Mittelstandsfront und Republik* (Düsseldorf, 1972), p. 113. Schumacher's work is the most detailed analysis of the WiP.

54. *SBPrLT 1928–1932,* 19 Feb. 1930, vol. 8, cols. 10918–19 (O. Braun), col. 10972 (Rhode [WiP]).

55. *SBPrLT 1925–1928,* 13 June 1925, and 19 Feb. 1930, vol 2, cols. 2233–34, vol. 8, cols. 11908–11. See also Schumacher, *Mittelstandsfront,* p. 125.

56. The best account of the DNVP's disintegration is Manfred Dörr, "Die Deutschnationale Volkspartei 1925 bis 1928," Ph.D. diss., University of Marburg, 1964. The best history of the VKP is, Erasmus Jonas, *Die Volkskonservativen 1928–1933* (Düsseldorf, 1965).

57. Georg Schreiber, "Innenpolitik," *Politisches Jahrbuch* 2 (1926), 77; Georg Decker, "1912–1928," *Die Gesellschaft* 4 (1927), 120; Schlange-Schönigen's summary of the DNVP's campaign issues, *SBPrLT 1925–1928,* 27 March 1928, vol. 17, cols. 26146–58; minutes of meeting, Alldeutscher Verband—Geschäftsführender Ausschuss (hereafter: ADV-GA), 4 and 5 July 1925, ADV-papers/412 (ForHbg); DVP-ZV, 1 Oct. 1926. See also Stürmer, *Koalition,* p. 133; Karl-Dietrich Bracher, *Die Auflösung der Weimarer Republik,* 5th ed. (Düsseldorf, 1978), p. 501.

58. See *Angestelltenstimme* 8 (June 1928), 3–4.

59. On Hugenberg's political career and ideas, see John A. Leopold, *Alfred Hugenberg: the Radical Nationalist Campaign Against the Weimar Republic* (New Haven, Conn., 1977); D. Guratzsch, *Macht durch Organisation: Die Grundlegung des Hugenbergschen Presseimperiums* (Düsseldorf, 1974).

60. *Der Tag,* no. 207 (28 Aug. 1928), rpt. in Dörr, "DNVP," pp. 587–89.

61. Stürmer, *Koalition,* p. 191; Axel Freiherr von Freytag-Loringhoven, *DNVP* (Berlin, 1931), pp. 44ff.; and Heidrun Holzbach, *Das "System Hugenberg"* (Stuttgart, 1980), pp. 99ff. See also Jonas, *Volkskonservativen,* pp. 33–39; *SBPrLT 1928–1932,* 13 Dec. 1929, vol. 7, col. 9439.

62. Hans Schlange-Schönigen, *Am Tage Danach* (Hamburg, 1946), p. 26.

63. *SBPrLT 1928–1932,* 6 Feb. 1929, vol. 3, cols. 3108–26 (Lindner); 5 March 1929, vol. 4, cols. 4647ff. (Steuer); 22 April 1929, vol. 5, cols. 6345–57 (Rohr). Hilferding had been Reich finance minister in the first Stresemann cabinet in 1923.

64. Ibid., 15 Dec. 1928, vol. 2, cols, 1567–68 (Hess); ibid., 13 Dec. 1929, vol. 7, cols. 9942–54 (Hess).

65. Ibid., 22 April 1929, vol. 5, col. 6403 (Riedel).

66. Ibid., 17 Oct., 11 Nov., and 13 Dec. 1929, vol. 6, col. 8552, vol. 7, cols. 9269–70 (Steinhoff), vol. 7, cols. 9438–40 (Jaspert).

67. Ibid., 20 and 21 Feb. 1929, vol. 3, col. 3604 (Haake), col. 3707–16 (Kube). For a detailed description of the Nazis' urban plan, see Dietrich Orlow, *The History of the Nazi Party 1919–1933* (Pittsburgh, Pa., 1969), pp. 128ff.

68. Rudolf Rietzler, "Kampf in der Nordmark—Das Aufkommen des Nationalsozialismus in Schleswig-Holstein (1919–1928)," Ph.D. diss., University of Hamburg, 1980, p. 392.

69. *SBPrLT 1928–1932*, 13 Dec. 1929, vol. 7, col. 9450 (Hess). The Nazis' opponents were also singularly ill-informed about the NSDAP. Joseph Hess was convinced that the real power in the NSDAP was exercized not by Hitler, but by Joseph Goebbels, the Nazi leader in Berlin. See ibid., col. 9449.

70. Orlow, *The History of the Nazi Party*, pp. 138ff.; Sabine Höner, *Der nationalisozialistische Zugriff auf Preussen* (Bochum, 1984), pp. 102–05. In addition to Kube, the Nazi Landtag delegation included six regional party leaders (Hinrich Lohse, Schleswig-Holstein; Karl Kaufmann, Hamburg; Heinrich Haake, Cologne; Robert Ley, Rhineland; Paul Hinkler, Hanover; Wilhelm Brückner, Silesia) and a renegade Catholic abbot, Alois Münchmeyer. On the NSDAP's left wing, see Reinhard Kühnl, *Die nationalsozialistische Linke 1925–1930* (Meisenheim am Glan, 1966). For the activities of Robert Ley in this period, see Ronald Smelser, *Robert Ley* (New York, 1988), pp. 75ff.

71. Hermann Weber, *Die Wandlung des deutschen Kommunismus: Die Stalinisierung der KPD in der Weimarer Republik* (Frankfurt a.M., 1969), 1:199–205. See also *Sozialdemokratische Parteikorrespondenz (Ergänzungsband)*, July, 1930, 440–43.

72. Weber, *Wandlung* 1:186ff., 234–35; *SBPrLT 1928–1932*, 28 Dec. 1928, vol. 2, col. 1957.

73. *SBPrLT 1928–1932*, 9 July 1929, vol. 6, cols. 8111–12.

74. Weber, *Wandlung* 1:235.

75. A good comprehensive discussion of election results in the Weimar years is *Wahlen und Abstimmungen in der Weimarer Republik*, ed. Jürgen Falter et al. (Munich, 1986).

76. Wilhelm Matull, *Ostdeutschlands Arbeiterbewegung* (Würzburg, 1973), p. 90.

77. See the report on the election, LASH/309/17650. Admittedly, the Center party was not a major factor in this overwhelmingly Protestant province.

78. See W. Krüger, "Der Grosswahltag in Preussen," *Das Freie Wort* 1 (1 Dec. 1929), 7–8; *SBPrLT 1928–1932*, 9 June 1928, vol. 1, col. 27.

79. The foregoing analysis is based upon the detailed election returns in *Handbuch für den Preussischen Landtag 1928*, ed. E. Kienast (Berlin, 1928), pp. 470–77.

80. Ernst Heilmann, "Unser Gemeindewahlsieg," *Das Freie Wort* 1 (24 Nov. 1929), 1–2.

81. *Das Freie Wort* 1 (1 Dec. 1929).

82. See the election analysis in "Preussische Referentenschrift, Mai 1930," in *Staat und NSDAP 1930–1932: Quellen zur Ära Brüning*, ed. Ilse Maurer and Udo Wengst (Düsseldorf, 1977), pp. 68ff. See also Karl-Dietrich Bracher, "Probleme der Wahlentwicklung in der Weimarer Republik," in *Wählerbewegung in der deutschen Geschichte*, ed. Otto Büsch et al. (Berlin, 1978), p. 641.

Chapter 2. Coalitions and Cabinets, 1925–1930

1. See Dietrich Orlow, *Weimar Prussia: The Unlikely Rock of Democracy* (Pittsburgh, Pa., 1986), pp. 207ff.

2. *SBPrLT 1925–1928*, 29 April 1925, vol. 1, col. 1489 (Campe).

3. *SPD Parteitag 1927*, p. 197; *SBPrLT 1928–1932*, 22 April 1929, vol. 5, col. 6343 (Burghahn).

4. Bernhard Falk, "Aufzeichnungen" (typescript), p. 179, Kleine Erwerbungen/385 (BA). See also Hans-Peter Ehni, *Bollwerk Preussen: Preussen Regierung, Reich-Länderproblem und Sozialdemokratie, 1928–1932* (Bonn–Bad Godesberg, 1975), p. 31.

5. See Herbert Hömig, *Das preussische Zentrum in der Weimarer Republik* (Mainz, 1979), p. 147.

6. See, for example, Braun to cabinet, 7 June 1928, Grzesinski papers/18.

7. Braun to Ritzel, 14 Dec. 1949, Braun papers/Teil 2/C/I/233 (PrGStAB); Herbert Weichmann, interview with Hagen Schulze, 19 April 1972. I am grateful to Prof. Schulze for providing me with a copy of this interview. From 1930 to 1932 Weichmann was Braun's personal assistant.

8. See minister of finance to prime minister, 28 Jan. 1927, ZStAM, Rep. 120c B I Nr. 2a, Bd. 2; SitzPrStMin, 11 Feb. 1927, ibid.

9. The most detailed, albeit rather uncritical, account of Braun's life is Hagen Schulze, *Otto Braun oder Preussens demokratische Sendung: Eine Biographie* (Berlin, 1977).

10. Ehni, *Bollwerk*, p. 35; Gerhard Schulz, *Zwischen Demokratie und Diktatur: Verfassungspolitik und Reichsreform in der Weimarer Republik* (Berlin, 1963), 1:490–94. See also Braun, "Weimar-Ms.," p. 384; and Heilmann's almost lyrical remarks in *SBPrLT 1925–1928*, 30 Jan. 1926, vol. 6, cols. 8338–39.

11. See *SBPrLT 1925–1928*, 30 June 1926, vol. 9, cols. 13181–82 (Schwarzhaupt, DVP). This will be discussed more fully in chapter 3, below.

12. Michael Stürmer, *Koalition und Opposition in der Weimarer Republik 1924–1928* (Düsseldorf, 1967), p. 94.

13. *SBPrLT 1925–1928*, 24 and 26 June, 3 July and 30 Sept. 1925, vol. 2, cols. 2548–49, 2769–70, 3187–3203, 3209–16, vol. 3, col. 3814, quotation in col. 3814.

14. Stürmer, *Koalition*, pp. 100–06; Braun to Severing, 3 July and 1 Aug. 1925, Severing papers/01/10, 01/12. Cf. also Schulze, *Braun*, p. 476.

15. Stürmer, *Koalition*, pp. 112ff., 134.

16. Manfred Dörr, "Die Deutschnationale Volkspartei 1925 bis 1928," Ph.D. diss., University of Marburg, 1964, pp. 191–92.

17. *SBPrLT 1925–1928*, 15 Oct. 1925, vol. 3, col. 4404 (Maretzky).

18. On this episode, see the letter from the DNVP member of the Landtag, Bachem, to the party's executive office, 14 July 1925. The letter was leaked to the Berlin liberal paper *Vossische Zeitung* and read to the Landtag by Joseph Hess. See *SBPrLT 1925–1928*, 15 Oct. 1925, vol. 3, cols. 4409–11, 4441.

19. See Stresemann's remarks at the DVP-ZV meeting, 22 Nov. 1925, ibid., pp. 40–42; and those of Dr. Becker (Görlitz), ibid., 26 Feb. 1929, p. 51. See also Braun to Weismann, 8 Sept. 1925, O. Braun papers/Teil 2/B/I/45 (PrGStAB).

20. Hömig, *Zentrum*, pp. 139, 142. See also *SBPrLT 1925–1928*, 15 Oct. 1925 and 23 March 1927, vol. 3, col. 4424 (Hess), vol. 13, col. 18472.

21. *SBPrLT 1925–1928*, 2 July 1925, vol. 2, cols. 3070–71; Stürmer, *Koalition*, p. 128.

22. See the astute comment in H. Müller to Remmele, 8 April 1927, Müller papers/P3/1.

23. *SBPrLT 1925–1928*, 14 Oct. 1925, vol. 3, cols. 4301–06. The left-liberal periodical *Die Hilfe* 30 (15 Oct. 1925), 435, commented, "At least the DVP had the decency to abstain."

24. *SBPrLT 1925–1928*, 30 Oct. 1925, vol. 4, col. 5496 (Gressler); and Meissner's "Denkschrift," 2 Dec. 1925, cited in Stürmer, *Koalition*, p. 288.

25. Stürmer, *Koalition*, pp. 106–07, 125; Pünder to Luther, 29 Dec. 1925, ibid., pp. 288–91. See also Severing, "Und wieder für die Grosse Koalition," *Sozialistische Monatshefte* 62 (10 Dec. 1925), 730.

26. *SBPrLT 1925–1928*, 11 Dec. 1925, vol. 5, cols. 7109–10.

27. See *Kölnische Volkszeitung*, 19 Dec. 1925. Braun's marginalia is in PrGStAB, Rep. 90/237. The settlement of the princes's property claims is discussed in chap. 3, below.

28. See Scholz, remarks in DVP RTFrV, 9 Dec. 1925, pp. 61–62.

29. Orlow, *Weimar Prussia*, chap. 2.

30. *SBPrLT 1925–1928*, 11 Dec. 1925, vol. 5, cols. 7109–10 (Campe).

31. Hilferding to Karl Kautsky, 8 Jan. 1926, Kautsky papers/D XII/642.

32. Stürmer, *Koalition*, pp. 135–40, 292–93.

33. For developments on the federal side of the flag dispute, see *Die Akten der Reichskanzlei: Die Kabinette Luther I und II*, ed. Karl-Heinz Minuth (Boppard a.Rh., 1977), 2:1287ff. The Prussian protest is discussed in chap. 4, below.

34. Stürmer, *Koalition*, p. 148; see also the editorial comment in *Hilfe* 32 (1 May 1926), 178.

35. Hugo Stehkämper, "Konrad Adenauer und das Reichskanzleramt während der Weimarer Zeit," in *Konrad Adenauer, Oberbügermeister von Köln*, ed. Hugo Stehkämper (Cologne, 1976), pp. 413–17; Z-Prot. 15 May 1926, p. 40; Stürmer, *Koalition*, pp. 152–54.

36. Severing to Leinert, 16 July 1926 (strictly confidential), Severing papers 31/69.

37. Paul Herz to Luise Kautsky, 5 May 1926, Kautsky papers/D-XII/416; Stehkämper, "Reichskanzler," p. 416; and Georg Schreiber, "Innenpolitik des Reiches," *Politisches Jahrbuch*, 1926, p. 63.

38. Wolfgang Heine, "Die Beamten der Republik," *Sozialistische Monatshefte* 63

(20 Sept. 1926), 610–14; Albert Grzesinski, "Im Kampf um die deutsche Republik— Lebensweg eines Staatenlosen," Grzesinski papers/2457, pp. 181–82.

39. See *SBPrLT 1925–1928,* 7 July and 15 Oct 1926, vol. 9, cols. 13906–07, vol. 10, cols. 14698–700; DVP-ZV, 1 Oct. 1926, pp. 6–7, 10. See also Hömig, *Zentrum,* pp. 141, 147, 148, n. 27.

40. Braun to Weismann, 7 and 11 Aug. 1926, Braun papers/Teil 2/B/I/45 (PrGStAB).

41. See DVP-ZV, 19 March 1927, pp. 4–32; Schreiber, "Innenpolitik," pp. 78–80. The Jarres-Gayl plan is discussed in chap. 2, above.

42. DVP-ZV, 1 Oct. 1926, p. 10.

43. For details, see the section on Church-State Relations in chap. 3.

44. See Heinrich Brüning, *Memoiren* (Stuttgart, 1970), pp. 123–24.

45. See interview between Hagen Schulze and Ernest Hamburger, 5 Oct. 1972 (hereafter "Schulze-Hamburger Interview").

46. *Deutsche Allgemeine Zeitung,* no. 470 (8 Oct. 1926); *SBPrLT 1925–1928,* 10 Nov. 1926, vol. 10, col. 15232.

47. DVP RTFrProt, 15 Dec. 1926, p. 28; DVP-ZV, 19 March 1927, p. 4; Stürmer, *Koalition,* p. 176.

48. On the developments in the Reich at the end of 1926, see Stürmer, *Koalition,* pp. 171–76; Z-Prot., 15 Dec. 1926, p. 78; *Politisches Jahrbuch,* 1927/28, pp. 69–73.

49. Hermann Müller to Gustav Radbruch, 13 Jan. 1927, Müller papers/(P)/1.

50. Stürmer, *Koalition,* pp. 180–85; Pünder to Marx, 28 Dec. 1926, ibid., p. 299; Grzesinski notes for a conference with Braun on 23 Dec. 1926, Grzesinski papers/1327.

51. *Berliner Tageblatt,* no. 40 (25 Jan. 1927).On Marx, see the rather uncritical biography, Ulrich von Hehl, *Wilhelm Marx, 1863–1946: Eine politische Biographie* (Mainz, 1987).

52. The agreement is reprinted in *Politisches Jahrbuch,* 1927/28, pp. 88–89. See also Josef Becker, ed., "Zur Politik der Wehrmachtabteilung in der Regierungskrise 1926/27," *Vierteljahrshefte für Zeitgeschichte* 14 (Jan. 1966), 69–78; Dörr, "DNVP," pp. 268-69, 288.

53. For details of the complicated negotiations, see Stürmer, *Koalition,* pp. 190, 201–02; Z-Prot., 11–12 Jan. 1927, pp. 80–83; *Politisches Jahrbuch,* 1927/28, pp. 79–80; Günther Grünthal, *Reichsschulgesetz und Zentrumspartei in der Weimarer Republik* (Düsseldorf, 1968). The DDP's statement is reprinted in *Politisches Jahrbuch,* 1927/28, p. 88, n. 1.

54. Axel Freiherr von Freytag-Loringhoven, *DNVP* (Berlin, 1931), pp. 42–43; meeting of the DNVP's national executive committee, 2 June 1927, Diller papers.

55. *SPD Parteitag 1927,* pp. 180–81, 200–01. See also Braun, "Weimar-Ms.," p. 369.

56. Braun, "Weimar-Ms.," p. 368; SPD, Parteivorstand, ed., *Der Bürgerblock: Wie er wurde- und was er ist* (Berlin, 1927), p. 16; *SPD Parteitag 1927,* p. 11 (Müller); and Hömig, *Zentrum,* pp. 150. Prussia's role in the legislative battle over the Reich education law is discussed in chap. 4, below.

57. Freytag-Loringhoven, *DNVP,* pp. 57–59.

58. *SBPrLT 1925–1928*, 20 May 1927, vol. 14, cols. 20915–28.

59. See the section Personnel Policies in chap. 3, below.

60. Count Westarp to Count Seidlitz, 20 Oct. 1927, quoted in Stürmer, *Koalition*, p. 254; Scholz, remarks to the DVP Reichstag delegation, DVP RTFrProt, 15 Feb. 1928, p. 75.

61. Weismann to Braun, 4 Sept. 1927, Braun papers/Teil 2/B-2/27 (PrGStAB); *SBPrLT 1925–1928*, 16 Dec. 1927, vol. 15, col. 22755; Stürmer, *Koalition*, p. 244.

62. *SBPrLT 1925–1928*, 17 Dec. 1927 and 29 March 1928, vol. 15, col. 22851 (Hess), vol. 17, cols. 23368–70 (Campe), vol. 17, cols. 23383–86 (Hess); and Stürmer, *Koalition*, pp. 243–44.

63. *SBPrLT 1928–1932*, 9 June 1928, vol. 1, cols. 21, 28.

64. See Ernst Eckstein, "Die Preussenkoalition," *Klassenkampf* 2 (1 June 1928), 335–39.

65. Grzesinski to Braun, 3 May 1928, Grzesinski papers/204; Braun, "Weimar-Ms.," pp. 374, 399; Braun, *Weimar*, p. 135; Grzesinski, "Besprechung Severing," n.d. (ca. April 1928); *SBPrLT 1928–1932*, 8 June 1928, vol. 1, cols. 6–7. See also Möller, *Parlamentarismus*, pp. 376–77.

66. On the negotiations in the Reich, see *Akten der Reichskanzlei: Das Kabinett Müller II*, ed. Martin Vogt (Boppard a.Rh., 1970), 1:1ff. See also Grzesinski, "Besprechung mit Braun," 23 May 1928, Grzesinski papers/1327; list of cabinet members, n.d. [ca. 13 June 1928], Müller papers, II/17; Möller, *Parlamentarismus*, p. 377.

67. Müller to Karl Renner, 13 July 1928, Müller papers/IV/408.

68. Wachenheim to Braun, 1 March 1940, Braun papers/B/Teil 2/C/I/316 (PrGStAB). See also Wilhelm Abegg, "Die Preussische Verwaltung und ihre Reform, Länder und Reich," in *Zehn Jahre Deutsche Republik: Ein Handbuch für republikanische Politik*, ed. Anton Erkelenz (Berlin, 1928), p. 504.

69. Braun, "Weimar-Ms.," pp. 295–96; Braun, *Weimar*, pp. 132–33; Julius Leber, "Gedanken zum Verbot der deutschen Sozialdemokratie, Juni 1933," in *Ein Mann geht seinen Weg* (Berlin, 1952), pp. 227–28.

70. DVP RTFrProt, 5 and 13 June 1928; Erich Wende, *C. H. Becker, Mensch und Politiker: Ein biographischer Beitrag zur Kulturgeschichte der Weimarer Republik* (Stuttgart, 1959), p. 289; Wolfgang Wacker, *Der Bau des Panzerschiffes "A" und der Reichstag* (Tübingen, 1959), p. 79.

71. Grzesinski, "Besprechungen mit Braun," 21 May 1928, Grzesinski papers/1327; Grzesinski to Braun, 7 June 1928, ibid., 204; *SBPrLT 1928–1932*, 9 and 11 June 1928, vol. 1, cols. 31, 37; Möller, *Parlamentarismus*, p. 377.

72. Alex Möller (then a member of the Prussian Landtag and after World War II finance minister of the German Federal Republic), unpublished oral reminiscenses expressed in a round-table discussion on the July 1932 coup against Prussia, sponsored by the Friedrich Ebert Stiftung, Berlin, 17 July 1982. See also Müller papers/II/16, 24, 28; Leber, "Gedanken," pp. 227–28.

73. Braun, "Weimar-Ms.," pp. 295–96.

74. The concordat negotiations will be discussed in chap. 3, below.

75. See Müller's notes, Müller papers/II/22, 26, 29. See also *Vorwärts*, no. 293 (23 June 1928).

76. Stresemann to Müller, 23 June 1928, Müller papers, II/32.

77. DVP RTFrProt, 26 June 1928, p. 117; Scholz to Stresemann, 2 July 1928, ibid.; *Deutsche Tageszeitung,* no. 296 (26 June 1928). See also Stresemann to Weismann, 14 June 1928, Braun papers/247 (IISG).

78. DVP RTFrProt, 27 June 1928; Möller, *Parlamentarismus,* p. 378.

79. The following analysis is based on a variety of sources. In chronological order, see DVP RTFrProt, 14 June 1928, p. 87 (Curtius); Müller to Radbruch, 6 July 1928, and to Karl Renner, 13 July 1928, Müller papers/II/370, II/408; Grzesinski to Friedensburg, 24 Aug. 1928, Grzesinski papers/215; *SBPrLT 1928–1932,* 4 Oct. 1928, vol. 1, cols. 669–70; Breitscheid, notes on a meeting of SPD and Center party Reichstag leaders, 24 Oct. 1928, Müller papers, II/61; *Kölnische Zeitung,* no. 649a (25 Nov. 1928); DVP ZV, 26 Feb. 1929, p. 97 (Böhm). See also Wacker, *Panzerschiff,* p. 108.

80. *Vossische Zeitung,* 4 July 1928.

81. Ehni, *Bollwerk,* p. 124; Braun, "Weimar-Ms.," pp. 397–98; Braun, *Weimar,* p. 133; Gerhard Schulz, *Zwischen Demokratie und Diktatur: Verfassungspolitik und Reichsreform in der Weimarer Republik* (Berlin, 1963), 1:587; Wilhelm Keil, *Erlebnisse eines Sozialdemokraten* (Stuttgart, 1947–48), 2:336.

82. This analysis is based upon the retrospective assessment of the failure of the fall negotiations by a meeting of the DVP executive committee. See DVP ZV, 26 Feb. 1929, pp. 27–30. On the SPD's plans, see Koch to Grimme, 25 May 1928, Grimme papers/76/4.

83. DVP RTFrProt, 20 Oct. and 27 Nov. 1928, pp. 131, 148–53.

84. DVP ZV, 26 Feb. 1929, pp. 4–5, 30. Dieter Golombek, *Die politische Vorgeschichte des Preussenkonkordats* (Mainz, 1970), p. 112, is sharply critical of the DVP's decision.

85. On the Reich negotiations, see Müller's handwritten notes, n.d. [Oct. 1928] and 26 Nov. 1928, Müller papers, II/62, II/66; Hermann Pünder (state secretary in the Reich chancellery), "Niederschrift über eine politische Aussprache betreffend Schaffung der Grossen Koalition am 27. November 1928," 28 Nov. 1928, Müller papers II/67. See also Helga Timm, *Die deutsche Sozialpolitik und der Bruch der Grossen Koalition im März 1930* (Düsseldorf, 1952), p. 120.

86. DVP RTFrProt, 2 Oct. 1928, p. 131; Johannes Linneborn, "Konkordat," in *Nationale Arbeit: Das Zentrum und sein Wirken in der deutschen Republik,* ed. Karl Anton Schulte (Berlin, [1929]), p. 233.

87. DVP ZV, 26 Feb. 1929, pp. 9, 36. See also Möller, *Parlamentarismus,* p. 381.

88. The foregoing is again based on a variety of sources, including: Braun, "Notiz für die Koalitionsakte," 20 Feb. 1929, Braun papers/Teil 2/B-2/93 (PrGStAB); Müller, marginalia on Pünder, "Vermerk," 26 Jan. 1929; Pünder, "Vermerk," 30 Jan. 1929; Müller, notes, 30 Jan. 1929, Müller papers/II/77, II/80; Pünder, "Vermerk," 21 Feb. 1929, Müller papers/II/82; DVP RTFrProt, 25 Feb. 1929, pp. 130–33; Joseph Wirth, "Ende des Vertrauens"? *Deutsche Republik* 3 (15 Feb. 1929), 611; DVP ZV, 26 Feb. 1929, pp. 32ff.; *Vorwärts,* no. 103 (2 March 1929); SPD, *Sozialdemokratische Parteikorrespondenz* 1–2 (1929), 69–70. See also Möller, *Parlamentarismus,* pp. 381–82; Ehni, *Bollwerk,* pp. 131–32.

89. *Berliner Börsen-Zeitung,* no. 132 (19 March 1929).

90. DVP ZV, 26 Feb. 1929, pp. 32–33; Wirth, "Ende," p. 612; *SBPrLT 1928–1932*, 22 and 23 April, and 15 May 1929, vol. 4, col. 6344 (Burghahn), vol. 4, cols. 6425–26 (Stendel), vol. 5, col. 7093 (Hess). See also Brüning, *Memoiren*, p. 137.

91. Pünder, "Vermerk," 24 and 30 Jan. 1929, Müller papers/II/75, II/78; Müller, notes on a meeting with Braun, 29 Jan. 1929, ibid./II/79; Müller to Wels, 12 Feb. 1929, ibid./IV/558 (italics are Müller's). See also Golombek, *Konkordat*, pp. 105–06; Falk, "Aufzeichnungen," p. 192.

92. See the extended discussion in DVP ZV, 26 Feb. 1929, pp. 33ff.; Braun, "Notiz."

93. *SBPrLT 1928–1932*, 23 April 1929, vol. 5, cols. 6417–30; DVP Landtag delegation (Stendel) to Braun, 10 June 1929, Braun papers/246 (IISG).

94. Josepf Goebbels, *Die Tagebücher von Joseph Goebbels, Teil I: Aufzeichnungen, 1924–1941*, ed. Elke Fröhlich (Munich, 1987), 1:349, 358, 365, 395 (28 March, 12 and 28 April, and 5 July 1929).

95. *SBPrLT 1928–1932*, 19 Feb. 1930, vol. 8, cols. 10960–62; Golombek, *Konkordat*, p. 106, n. 56. On the Berlin affair, see Christian Engeli, *Gustav Böss: Oberbürgermeister von Berlin 1921–1930* (Stuttgart, 1971), pp. 226ff. Grzesinski's problems will be discussed below.

96. *SBPrLT 1928–1932*, 26 Feb. 1930, vol. 8, col. 11506 (Johanssen); Braun, Weimar-Ms.," p. 456; Braun, *Weimar*, p. 162; Braun, "Akten-Notiz," 14 Nov. 1929; Grzesinski to Braun, 6 Jan. 1930, and Goslar, "Aufzeichnung über die interfraktionelle Sitzung . . . ," 27 Jan. 1930, Braun papers/257, 259, 299 (IISG). See also Möller, *Parlamentarismus*, p. 383.

97. On Becker's resignation, see Möller, *Parlamentarismus*, pp. 388–89; Wende, *Becker*, pp. 187, 195–97; Braun, "Weimar-Ms.," pp. 457–59. For one of Heilmann's attacks on Becker, see "Minister Becker und die Kunst," *Das Freie Wort* 2 (16 Feb. 1930), 19–22. See also Goslar's report to Braun, "Aufzeichnung . . . 27. Januar," n.d., Braun papers/259 (IISG).

98. "Die Partei der Bildung und Preussens Kultusminister," *Tagebuch* 10 (8 June 1929), 934–38; collection of letters to Braun protesting the dismissal, Braun papers/242ff. (IISG).

99. *SBPrLT 1928–1932*, 19 Feb. 1930, vol. 8, cols. 10960–61, 10915; Grimme to Wende, 10 Oct. 1958, Grimme, *Briefe*, ed. Dieter Sauberzweig (Heidelberg, 1967), pp. 142–45. See also Braun, "Weimar-Ms.," p. 458; Gaede, note in Grimme, *Briefe*, p. 33.

100. Grimme to Becker, 11 Feb. 1930, Grimme, *Briefe*, p. 35; *SBPrLT 1928–1932*, 2 April 1930, vol. 9, col. 13226 (Kube); Grimme to König, 24 Nov. 1930, Ernst Heilmann's son to Grimme, 30 Aug. 1949, Grimme papers/59/41, 79/63.

101. See Grimme, *Briefe*, pp. 22–25; Heinrich Mann to Grimme, 14 Feb. 1932, Grimme to Association of Religious Socialists, 15 Feb. 1930, Grimme papers/P 79/M 103, P 65/M 35.

102. See Müller's handwritten notes, 3 March 1930, Müller papers/II/277; Dieter Gessner, *Agrarverbände in der Weimarer Republik* (Düsseldorf, 1976), p. 177. For a good discussion of the problem of parliamentary democracy in Germany at the beginning of 1930, see Werner Conze, "Die Krise des Parteienstaates in Deutschland 1929/30," *Historische Zeitschrift* 178 (Aug. 1954), 47–83.

103. For contemporary analyses, see Ludwig Quessel, "Neue Lage im Reich," *Sozialistische Monatshefte* 70 (14 April 1930), 315–20; *SBPrLT 1928–1932*, 28 March 1930, vol. 9, cols. 12838–39. See also Braun, Weimar- Ms.," p. 464; Richard Breitman, *German Socialism and Weimar Democracy* (Chapel Hill, N.C. 1981), p. 163.

104. Erich Matthias and Rudolf Morsey, eds., *Das Ende der Parteien 1933* (Düsseldorf, 1960), p. 112.

Chapter 3. *Innenpolitik:* Security Matters, Personnel Policies, Administration, and Church-State Relations

1. Hirtsiefer to prime minister, 28 May 1924, PrGStAB, Rep. 90/740; Schleusener, "Gutachten," 30 Dec. 1927, ibid./2302.

2. The administrative reforms and the treaties with the churches will be discussed below.

3. *SBPrLT 1925–1928*, 15 Oct. 1925, vol. 3, cols. 4406–24 (Hess), 1 March 1926, vol. 6, col. 9211 (Baecker).

4. See the formal correspondence between Severing and Braun, 6 Oct. 1926, Severing papers/01/14. See also Braun, *Weimar*, pp. 129, 384–86. On Severing's reaction to Mehlich's death, see Severing papers/29/33. See also Ferdinand Friedensburg, *Lebenserinnerungen* (Frankfurt a.M., 1969), p. 176; Horst Möller, *Parlamentarismus in Preussen 1919–1932* (Düsseldorf, 1985), p. 388.

5. See *Königsberger Hartungsche Zeitung*, no. 468 (6 Oct. 1926); *Berliner Lokal-Anzeiger*, no. 472 (6 Oct. 1926).

6. Albert Grzesinski, "Im Kampf um die deutsche Republik—Lebensweg eines Staatenlosen," p. 62, Grzesinski papers/2457; *Germania*, no. 266 (7 Oct. 1926). For the background of Grzesinski's appointment, see his note, 17 Oct. 1926, Grzesinski papers/2017; Möller, *Parlamentarismus*, p. 389.

7. *SBPrLT 1928–1932*, 3 Oct. 1928, vol. 1, col. 586. On the differences between Grzesinski and Severing, see Hans-Karl Behrend, "Zur Personalpolitik des Preussischen Ministeriums des Innern—Die Besetzung der Landratsstellen in den östlichen Provinzen 1919–1933," *Jahrbuch für die Geschichte Mittel- und Ostdeutschlands* 6 (1957), 186–87. For Grzesinski's criticism of Severing, see Grzesinski, "Kampf-Ms.," pp. 179–80; Grzesinski to Tejessy, 8 Nov. 1926, Grzesinski papers/322.

8. See their letters to him in Grzesinski papers/55, 84. See also Grzesinski, "Kampf-Ms.," p. 231.

9. See Grzesinski, "Ausscheiden 1930," Grzesinski papers/1332. On the altercation between Hörsing and Grezesinski, discussed below, see Hörsing to Grzesinski, 15 Nov. 1927, Grzesinski papers/73.

10. Braun, *Weimar*, pp. 124–30; Friedensburg, *Lebenserinnerungen*, p. 154; the interview between Hagen Schulze and Ernest Hamburger, 5 Oct. 1972 (hereafter: "Schulze-Hamburger Interview"); Anthony Glees, "Albert C. Grzesinski and the Politics of Prussia 1926–1930," *English Historical Review* 89 (Oct. 1974), 815, 823–24.

11. For a veiled reference to Grzesinski's "marital mistakes," see *SBPrLT 1925–1928*, 19 May 1927, vol. 14, col. 20758 (Wiedemann, DNVP).

12. On the "affair," see Grzesinski, "Kampf-Ms., pp. 225–26, 235; "Aus-

scheiden," p. 8; "Schulze-Hamburger Interview"; Joseph Goebbels, *Die Tagebücher von Joseph Goebbels, Teil I: Aufzeichnungen 1924–1941*, ed. Elke Fröhlich (Munich, 1987), 1:512 (9 and 10 March 1930); Möller, *Parlamentarismus*, p. 390. On Grützner's career, see also "Aktennotiz" [1 June 1929], Rep. 90/407 (PrGStAB).

13. On Grzesinski's resignation and new appointment, see "Ausscheiden," pp. 2–7; "Kampf-Ms.," pp. 229–30; "Schulze-Hamburger Interview." See also Albert Grzesinski, "Zweimal Polizeipräsident von Berlin," pp. 3, 11, Grzesinski papers/2456.

14. Braun, "Weimar-Ms.," pp. 460–61; Grzesinski, "Kampf-Ms.," pp. 230–32; "Ausscheiden," p. 10; "Schulze-Hamburger Interview." On Waentig's early political career, see *Freiheit*, no. 27 (11 Feb. 1920).

15. *SBPrLT 1928–1932*, 4 Oct. 1930, vol. 11, col. 15392 (Bachem); Braun, "Weimar-Ms.," pp. 485c [*sic*], 485–86. For criticism of Waentig, see also Abegg to Severing, 31 May 1947, Abegg papers; Möller, *Parlamentarismus*, p. 390.

16. Michael Stürmer, *Koalition und Opposition in der Weimarer Republik 1924–1928* (Düsseldorf: 1967), p. 155. See also *SBPrLT 1925–1928*, 5 July 1926, vol. 9, cols. 13583–84 (Bartels, KPD).

17. See the documentation in Rep. 90/237 (PrGStAB); Schulte, "Fürsten," *Politisches Jahrbuch*, 1926, pp. 491–93.

18. The most detailed analysis of the referendum is Ulrich Schüren, *Der Volksentscheid zur Fürstenenteignung 1926* (Düsseldorf, 1978). See also Franklin C. West, *A Crisis of the Weimar Republic: A Study of the German Referendum of 20 June 1926* (Philadelphia, 1985); Braun, "Weimar-Ms.," pp. 348–50; Alfred Milatz, *Wähler und Wahlen in der Weimarer Republik*, 2d ed. (Bonn, 1968), p. 121. For criticism of the SPD's stand by the other Weimar coalition parties, see Schulte, "Fürsten," pp. 501ff., 530; DDP-PA, 10 March 1926. For a balanced contemporary view, see Alfred Brodauf, "Der Todeskampf des monarchischen Gedankens—Die Auseinandersetzung mit den Fürstenhäusern," *Hilfe* 32 (1 and 15 Feb. 1926), 46–47, 61–63.

19. *SPD Parteitag 1927*, p. 30; Braun, "Weimar-Ms.," p. 350; DDP-PA, 28 Nov. 1926; Schulte, "Fürsten," pp. 518ff.; Werner Schneider, *Die Deutsche Demokratische Partei in der Weimarer Republik 1924–1930* (Munich, 1978), pp. 94–97; Bernhard Falk, "Aufzeichnungen," pp. 94–97 (typescript) Kleine Erwerbungen/385 (BA).

20. Braun, "Weimar-Ms.," p. 350; *SPD Parteitag 1927*, pp. 74–75.

21. Grzesinski, "Notizen zum einleitenden Vortrag anlässlich der Ob [erpräsidenten] und Reg. Präs. Konferenz am 18.7.1927," Grzesinski papers/1329.

22. On the incidence of political violence, cf. documentation in Rep. 15.01/25901 (ZStAP). For Braun's assessment of Keudell, see "Weimar-Ms.," pp. 365–66.

23. Grzsinski to Braun, 3 May 1928, Grzesinski papers/204; Prussian ministry of the interior to the governors, district directors, and the police chief of Berlin, 17 April 1928, LASH/301/4497. See also Stürmer, *Koalition*, pp. 213–15. The best treatment of the paramilitary scene in Weimar Germany is James M. Diehl, *Paramilitary Politics in Weimar Germany* (Bloomington, Ind., 1977).

24. See Kurt Rosenfeld, "Das Ende des Republikschutzgesetzes," *Klassenkampf* 3 (15 July 1929), 425.

25. Grzesinski to Braun, 6 Jan. 1930, Braun papers/299 (IISG); and SitzPrStMin, 18 Aug. 1929, ZStAM, Rep. 90a III 2b Nr. 6, Bd. 178.

26. *SBPrLT 1928–1932*, 9 July 1929, vol 6, cols. 8043–44. See also Manfred

Dörr, "Die Deutschnationale Volkspartei 1925 bis 1928," Ph.D. diss., University of Marburg, 1964, p. 305.

27. On Höpker-Aschoff's complaints about the police chiefs, see his letter to Grzesinski, 15 March 1929, Grzesinski papers/72.

28. See the documentation on the *Polizeibeamtengesetz*, 6 April 1927, *Sammlung der Drucksachen des preussischen Landtages, 2. Wahlperiode 1925–1928* (hereafter: *DrSPrLT 1925–1928*) (Berlin, 1928), no. 6217, 13:7009–20. See also Carl Severing, *1919/1920 im Wetter- und Watterwinkel* (Bielefeld, 1920), p. 100; Albert Grzesinski, "Aufzeichnungen über den 20. Juli 1932," p. 12, Grzesinski papers/2456.

29. *SBPrLT 1928–1932*, 7 Feb. 1929, vol. 3, col. 3227.

30. Cf. *SBPrLT 1925–1928*, 15 Jan. 1926, vol. 6, cols. 8019–20 (Schwenk).

31. The best history of the RFB is Kurt G. P. Schuster, *Der Rote Frontkämpferbund* (Düsseldorf, 1975). The following account of the RFB's role is based primarily on this book. See also the much less satisfactory work, Kurt Finker, *Geschichte des Roten Frontkämpferbundes* (Berlin, 1982).

32. See Hermann Weber, *Die Wandlung des deutschen Kommunismus: Die Stalinisierung der KPD in der Weimarer Republik* (Frankfurt a.M., 1969), 1:223–24; Schuster, *RFB*, pp. 216–24.

33. *SBPrLT 1928–1932*, 14 May 1929, vol. 5, col. 6987; *Rote Fahne*, no. 66, 19 March 1929.

34. *SPD Parteitag 1929*, pp. 15–16; Hermann Weber, ed., *Der deutsche Kommunismus: Dokumente 1915–1945*, 3d ed. (Cologne, 1973), p. 103; *SBPrLT 1928–1932*, 13 May 1929, vol. 5, col. 6866; Schuster, *RFB*, p. 237. The official KPD version of the May events is Werner Hirsch, *Blutige Maitage in Berlin* (Berlin, 1929).

35. Thomas Kurz, *Blutmai—Sozialdemokraten und Kommunisten im Brennpunkt der Berliner Ereignisse von 1929* (Bonn, 1988). See also Hans-Peter Ehni, *Bollwerk Preussen: Preussen Regierung, Reich-Länderproblem und Sozialdemokratie, 1928–1932* (Bonn–Bad Godesberg, 1975), p. 152.

36. Prussian ministry of the interior (Abegg) to all Oberpräsidenten, district directors, and the chief of police of Berlin (personally), 17 April 1928, LASH/301/4497.

37. Möller, *Parlamentarismus*, pp. 552–53.

38. Michael Geyer, *Aufrüstung oder Sicherheit: Die Reichswehr in der Krise der Machtpolitik 1924–1936* (Wiesbaden, 1980), pp. 198ff; Otto Gessler, *Reichswehrpolitik in der Weimarer Zeit*, ed. Kurt Sendtner (Stuttgart, 1958), p. 174; Braun's speech of 24 Feb. 1927, *Deutsche Tageszeitung*, no. 106 (4 March 1927); Thilo Vogelsang, *Kurt von Schleicher—Ein General als Politiker* (Göttingen, 1965), pp. 48ff.; DDP-PA, 4 Dec. 1925; Grzesinski, "Kampf," pp. 108–09.

39. Quoted in Josef Becker, ed., "Zur Politik der Wehrmachtabteilung in der Regierungskrise 1926/27," *Vierteljahreshefte für Zeitgeschichte* 14 (Jan. 1966), 72, n. 6.

40. Severing to Braun, 15 April 1926, Braun papers/11/B-2/14 (ForHbg).

41. On the Black Reichswehr, see Vogelsang, *Reichswehr* pp. 33ff.; John W. Wheeler-Bennett, *The Nemesis of Power: The German Army in Politics* (New York, 1964), pp. 92–93. For a defense of the Reich's actions, see Gessler, *Reichswehr*, p. 302. For the Prussian proposals, see Grzesinski to Braun, 6 Nov. 1926, Braun papers/11/B-2/14 (ForHbg); documentation in ibid./502–05 (IISG). The entire issue

was so sensitive that Landtag committees routinely discussed "Eastern questions" in executive session.

42. Dörr, "DNVP," p. 222; Braun, "Weimar-MS.," pp. 313–16.

43. Braun, "Weimar-Ms.," pp. 313–16; Becker, "Politik," 72–73; and Alfred Kruck, *Geschichte des Alldeutschen Verbandes 1890–1939* (Wiesbaden, 1954), p. 174.

44. *SBPrLT 1925–1928,* 17 May 1926, vol. 8, cols. 11876–77, 11901–02.

45. Dörr, "DNVP," p. 222; Kruck, *ADV,* p. 169; Becker, "Politik," pp. 72–73; *Sozialdemokratische Parteikorrespondenz (Ergänzungsband)* 1 (July, 1930), pp. 225–27.

46. *SBPrLT 1925–1928,* 4 Dec. 1926, vol. 11, col. 15671. See also Braun to Severing, 27 May 1926, Severing papers/01/13; Friedensburg, *Lebenserinnerungen,* p. 166.

47. Severing to president of the Landtag, 27 July 1925; and Braun to Prussian liaison office in Munich, 3 June 1929, PrGStAB, Rep. 90/478; *SBPrLT 1928–1932,* 15 May and 29 Oct. 1929, vol. 5, col. 7092 (Hess); vol. 6, cols. 8671–88; Möller, *Parlamentarismus,* p. 525.

48. Prussian Ministry of the Interior to Prussian Ministry of Education et al., 20 Nov. 1929, PrGStAB, Rep. 90/478; *SBPrLT 1928–1932,* 16 Oct. 1929, vol. 6, cols. 8438–45. On the conflict with the Reich, see Prussian prime minister to Reich Ministry of Defense, 3 Feb. 1930, PrGStAB, Rep. 90/478; Volker R. Berghahn, *Der Stahlhelm—Bund der Frontsoldaten 1918–1935* (Düsseldorf, 1966), p. 142.

49. *SBPrLT 1925–1928,* 17 May 1926, vol. 8, col. 11877 (Porsch).

50. See Carl Stoll, "Der Kampf um die Macht in den Rathäusern," *Freies Wort* 1 (3 Nov. 1929), 4–8; *SBPrLT 1925–1928,* 23 March 1928, vol. 13, col. 18350 (Grzesinski); "Anlageheft zu der Gegenerklärung der Reichsregierung vom 5.8.1932" (hereafter: "Anlageheft Rei. 5.8.1932"), p. 27, Braun papers 11/B-4/54 (ForHbg); Grzesinski, "Besprechung mit Braun," 15 March 1929, Grzesinski papers/705.

51. Grzesinski to Braun, 21 March 1930, Grzesinski papers/204.

52. Wolfgang Runge, *Politik und Beamtentum im Parteienstaat—Die Demokratisierung der politischen Beamten in Preussen zwischen 1918 und 1933* (Stuttgart, 1965), p. 247. On the spirit of the pre-1918 Prussian bureaucracy, see Tibor Süle, *Preussische Bürokratietradition: Zur Entwicklung von Verwaltung und Beamtenschaft in Deutschland, 1871–1918* (Göttingen, 1988).

53. Schlange-Schöningen (DNVP) told Severing, "The day on which you will vacate your office will be the Prussian state's first real day of recovery," *SBPrLT 1925–1928,* 16 Oct. 1925, vol. 3, col. 4507.

54. See the statistics presented by Paul Hirsch (SPD), ibid., 13 Oct. 1925, vol. 3, cols. 4239–42; and the article in *Die Hilfe* 31 (1 June 1925), 275. Statistics in the *Hilfe* piece were supplied by the official Prussian Press Service.

55. Prussian minister of finance to cabinet, 6 Sept. 1924, Prussian minister of agriculture to prime minister, 25 Feb. 1925; president of the Landtag to cabinet, 1 April 1925, PrGStAB, Rep. 90/741.

56. On the tug of war between the minister of finance and his colleagues, see SitzPrStMin, 25 March 1927 and 23 Oct. 1928, PrGStAB, Reps. 90a/7, 90/743; minister of justice to minister to finance, 17 May 1927, PrGStAB, Rep. 90/742.

57. See minister of the interior to members of the cabinet, 20 Oct. 1928, PrGStAB, Rep. 90a/20.

58. For the details of the Reich salary reform, see *Reichsgesetzblatt*, pt. 1 (19 Dec. 1927). Cf. also Stürmer, *Koalition*, pp. 236–39; Gerhard Schulz, *Zwischen Demokratie und Diktatur: Verfassungspolitik und Reichsreform in der Weimarer Republik* (Berlin, 1963), 1:551–52; Heinrich Köhler, *Lebenserinnerungen des Politikers und Staatsmannes 1878–1949*, ed. Josef Becker (Stuttgart, 1964), p. 186. Among those who foresaw the coming difficulties was the American reparations agent in Germany, Parker Gilbert. See Arno Panzer, *Das Ringen um die deutsche Agrarpolitik von der Währungsstabilisierung bis zur Agrardebatte im Reichstag im Dezember 1928* (Kiel, 1970), p. 110.

59. Prussian ministry of finance to Reich ministry of finance, 11 and 19 May 1928, PrGStAB, Reps. 90/742–43; Braun, "Weimar-Ms.," pp. 375–76. Panzer, *Ringen*, p. 117, estimates that of the RM 1.25 billion which the 1927 Salary Reform Act required in additional monies, the Reich paid only RM 300 million.

60. Köhler, *Lebenserinnerungen*, p. 264; *SBPrLT 1925–1928*, 13 Dec. 1927, vol. 15, cols. 20252, 22463–64, 22575–92.

61. *SBPrLT 1928–1932*, 22 March 1929, vol. 4, col. 5399. See also Braun, "Weimar-Ms.," pp. 376–77.

62. Albert C. Grzesinski, *Inside Germany*, tr. Alexander S. Lipschitz (New York, 1939), pp. 112–13. See also Grzesinski to president of the Landtag and members of the cabinet, 24 Dec. 1927 and their replies, PrGStAB, Rep. 90/478.

63. Grzesinski, "Notizen" [3 April 1928], Grzesinski papers/732.

64. Grzesinski, ["Besprechung mit Braun,"] 25 May 1929, Grzesinski papers/705; Ministry of the Interior to prime minister, 21 Oct. 1929, PrGStAB, Rep. 90/2415. See also Goslar (Official Prussian Press Service) to cabinet and press officers of the ministries, 17 Feb. 1927 and 30 May 1928, ibid.

65. The text of Braun's radio address is in Braun papers/539 (IISG). See also his remarks in *SBPrLT 1928–1932*, 16 Oct. 1929, vol. 6, col. 8437; SitzPrStMin, 16 Oct. 1929, ZStAM, Rep. 90, B III, 2b, Nr. 6, Bd. 178. On the DVP's position, see *SBPrLT 1928–1932*, 17 Oct. 1929, vol. 6, cols. 8506–07. It is interesting to note that the in-house jurists in the ministry of the interior were not at all sure the government's decrees would stand up in court. See Hartwig, "Vermerk," 15 Oct. 1929, Rep. 84a/3153 (PrGStAB).

66. Grzesinski to Braun, 6 Jan. 1930 (personally), Braun papers/299 (IISG); Runge, *Politik*, pp. 149–54, 267–72; SitzPrStMin, 21 Nov. 1929, ZStAM, Rep. 90a, B III, 2b, Nr. 6, Bd. 178; *SBPrLT 1928–1932*, 29 Oct. 1929 and 27 March 1930, vol. 6, cols, 8671–88, vol. 9, col. 12738; Ehni, *Bollwerk*, p. 146.

67. See *Berliner Tageblatt*, no. 412 (1 Sept. 1925).

68. *Welt am Abend*, no. 237, 11 Oct. 1926; Abegg to Braun, 23 Sept. 1943, Braun papers/92/Teil 1/C/1 (PrGStAB).

69. Höpker-Aschoff to Grzesinski, 15 March 1928, Grzesinski papers/72; Sabine Höner, *Der nationalsozialistische Zugriff auf Preussen: Preussischer Staat und nationalsozialistische Machteroberungsstrategie* (Bochum, 1984), p. 473.

70. Hess to Severing, 3 Oct. 1925, Severing papers/85/31; *SBPrLT 1928–1932*, 11 June 1928, vol. 1, col. 88; Grzesinski to Hirtsiefer, 5 Aug. 1927, Grzesinski

papers/734. See also Gerhard Schulz, "Staatsschutz und Nationalsozialismus in der Ära Brüning," in *Staat und NSDAP 1930–32: Quellen zur Ära Brüning* ed. Ilse Maurer and Udo Wengst (Düsseldorf, 1977), p. xxi; Behrend, "Personalpolitik," p. 195.

71. On Grzesinski's criticism of the DDP, see Grzesinski to Braun, 21 March 1930, Grzesinski papers/204; "Kampf," p. 234. In the manuscript of his memoirs, the minister crossed out a reference to the DDP "as a small group of politicians and braggarts *(Gernegrossen)*" ("Kampf," p. 234). The quotation is from Behrend, "Personalpolitik," p. 187.

72. See Grzesinski's remarks to the *Preussentag der Sozialdemokratischen Partei Deutschlands am 14. Februar 1928 in Berlin* (Berlin, 1928), p. 15; Runge, *Politik*, pp. 98–99, 194; Möller, *Parlamentarismus*, p. 531.

73. Grzesinski to Braun, 21 March 1930, Grzesinski papers/204. On Hörsing's career as *Oberpräsident* and his dismissal, see Hörsing papers/19–22; Hörsing to Grzesinski, 21 July 1927, Grzesinski papers/73; Karl Rohe, *Das Reichsbanner Schwarz-Rot-Gold* (Düsseldorf, 1966), p. 319.

74. See the documentation in Grzesinski papers/97, 193, 204, 310, 763. For a more detailed analysis of the corps of provincial governors, see Horst Möller, "Die preussischen Oberpräsidenten der Weimarer Republik als Verwaltungselite," *Vierteljahrshefte für Zeitgeschichte* 30 (Jan. 1982), 1–26; Klaus Schwabe, ed., *Die preussischen Oberpräsidenten 1815–1945* (Boppard a.Rh., 1985). At the end of 1928, eleven of the twelve *Oberpräsidenten* were *Aussenseiter*. See Grzesinski papers/763.

75. Runge, *Politik*, pp. 146–47; Grzesinski papers/763.

76. Behrend, "Personalpolitik," p. 207; Schulz, "Staatsschutz," p. xxi.

77. SPD, *Preussentag*, p. 15; Runge, *Politik*, p. 147; Möller, *Parlamentarismus*, pp. 530–31.

78. Behrend, "Personalpolitik," p. 191; SPD, *Sozialdemokratische Parteikorrespondenz* 1–2 (Feb. 1929), 28–29; Grzesinski to Eyhern, 2 Feb. 1928, Grzesinski papers/733.

79. Behrend, "Personalpolitik," p. 191.

80. Grzesinski, *Inside*, p. 79.

81. *SBPrLT 1928–1932*, 23 April 1929, vol. 5, cols. 6422–23; *SBPrLT 1932–1933*, 2 June 1933, vol. 1, cols. 201–02; Noske to Grimme, 23 March 1930, Grimme papers/M 79/M 114.

82. Grzesinski to district directors, 26 Feb. 1929, NSStAH/122a/VII/17.

83. See the figures in Grzesinski papers/738.

84. Runge, *Politik*, pp. 185–86, 202. See also Grzesinski's remarks to the SPD *Preussentag*, p. 18.

85. Wilhelm Abegg, "Die preussische Verwaltung und ihre Reform, Länder und Reich," in *Zehn Jahre Deutsche Republik: Ein Handbuch für republikanische Politik,* ed. Anton Erkelenz (Berlin, 1928), pp. 467–512; Grzesinski, "Vorschlag für eine Verwaltungsreform" (hereafter: "Vorschlag, Juli, 1928"), 24 July 1928, Rep. 90/2302 (PrGStAB), p. 3.

86. Drews's proposals as well as some of the reactions to them are found in PrGStAB, Rep. 90/2300. See also Horst Romeyk, "Der preussische Regierungspräsident im NS-Herrschaftssystem—Am Beispiel der Regierung Düsseldorf," in

Verwaltung contra Menschenführung im Staat Hitlers—Studien zum politisch-administrativen System, ed. Dieter Rebentisch and Karl Teppe (Göttingen, 1986), p. 121.

87. See Richter to prime minister, 30 Jan. 1922, PrGStAB, Rep. 90/2300.

88. SitzPrStMin, 14 Nov. 1923, and additional documentation in ibid.

89. SitzPrStMin, 31 Jan. 1924, minister of the interior to prime minister, 9 April 1924; see also additional documentation in ibid.

90. *SBPrLT 1921–1924,* 2 July 1924, vol. 16, cols. 22937ff. (Dominicus); *SBPrLT 1925–1928,* 14 Oct. 1925, vol. 3, col. 4340 (Severing). See also Dietrich Orlow, *Weimar Prussia 1918–1925: The Unlikely Rock of Democracy* (Pittsburgh, Pa., 1986), chap. 4.

91. Severing, "Die preussische Verwaltungsreform," 31 Dec. 1925, Rep. 90/2302 (PrGStAB).

92. *SBPrLT 1925–1928,* 3 Feb. 1926, vol. 6, cols. 8499–8500. For the Center party's objections to Severing's proposals, see ibid., vol. 3, col. 4407; for objections within the cabinet, see minister of agriculture to minister of the interior, 18 Nov. 1925, Rep. 90/2301 (PrGStAB)

93. *SBPrLT 1925–1928,* 14 May 1927, vol. 14, col. 20532 (Richter); Grzesinski to prime minister, 10 May 1927, Rep. 90/2302 (PrGStAB); Grzesinski to Abegg, 28 Jan. 1928, Grzesinski papers/193.

94. "Vorschlag, Juli 1928," pp. 9–18.

95. SitzPrStMin, 18 Oct. 1927, Rep. 90/742 (PrGStAB); Grzesinski to Abegg, 20 Jan. 1928, Grzesinski papers/193. For evidence of repeated postponement of the agenda item, see SitzPrStMin, 18 Jan., 11 and 21 Feb. 1928, Rep. 90/2302 (PrGStAB). The reaction of the cabinet members can be found in ibid., Rep. 84a/4277 (PrGStAB), Rep. 77, tit. 2025, Nr. 12, Bd. 5 (ZStAM). Grzesinski summed up the points of disagreement in a letter to the cabinet members, 9 Nov. 1928, Rep. 90/2302 (PrGStAB). For the vote, see Reschke, "Auszugsweise Abschrift aus Z.B. 2746," 20 Nov. 1928, ibid., Rep. 84a/4277.

96. See minister of education to members of the cabinet, 11 July 1928, Becker papers/1810; documentation in PrGStAB, Rep. 90/2302; Ministry of the Interior, "Vermerk," 7 Jan. 1929, Rep. 84a/4278 (PrGStAB); minister of commerce and trade to members of the cabinet, 19 Feb. 1929, ibid.

97. "Vorschlag, Juli 1928," pp. 26ff. See also SitzPrStMin, 13 Jan. 1926, PrGStAB, Rep. 90a/6; Braun, "Weimar-Ms.," pp. 386–87; Grzesinski to Braun, 1 Aug. 1928, O. Braun papers/475 (IISG).

98. See Drews, "Entwurf einer Landgemeindeordnung," 14 July 1919, Rep. 90/2300 (PrGStAB); *SBPrLT 1925–1928,* 22 June 1927, vol. 14, cols. 21133–34; Grzesinski, "Kampf," p. 193.

99. On the position of the parties in the Landtag, see *SBPrLT 1925–1928,* 11 Dec. 1925, and 6 and 12 Dec. 1927, vol. 5 cols. 7069–70, 7076–78, vol. 15, cols, 22231–32, 22411; *SPD Preussentag,* p. 4.

100. *SBPrLT 1925–1928,* 12 Dec. 1928, vol. 15, col. 22429; *SBPrLT 1928–1932,* 2 Oct. 1928, vol. 1, col. 506 (Grzesinski). See also Möller, *Parlamentarismus,* p. 490.

101. See, Abegg, "Verwaltung," p. 491; *SBPrLT 1925–1928,* 11 Dec. 1925, vol. 5, cols. 7123–7212.

102. *SBPrLT 1928–1932,* vol. 3, col. 3181; Braun, "Weimar-Ms.," p. 387. See also Möller, *Parlamentarismus,* pp. 528–29.

103. "Vorschlag, Juli 1927," pp. 18–30, 34–35; Christian Engeli, *Gustav Böss Oberbürgermeister von Berlin 1921 bis 1930* (Stuttgart, 1971), pp. 129–30. Grzesinski, "Das neue Selbstverwaltungsgesetz für die Hauptstadt Berlin," *Das Freie Wort* 2 (25 May 1930), 1–7; Ernst Hamburger, "Zum Selbstverwaltungsgesetz für Berlin," ibid. (15 June 1930), 12–17; Möller, *Parlamentarismus,* pp. 490ff. On the debate and passage of the Ruhr Law, see *SBPrLT 1928–1932,* 24 April and 8 and 10 July 1929, vol. 5, cols. 6733ff., vol. 6, cols. 7820ff., 8142ff. Grzesinski's comment is in "Kampf," p. 199. See also Braun, Weimar-Ms.," p. 387.

104. Grzesinski, *Inside,* p. 118.

105. The process is well documented in Rep. 90/2303 (PrGStAB). See also Falk, "Aufzeichnungen," p. 186; Friedensburg to Grzesinski, 1 March 1930, Grzesinski papers/32; *SBPrLT 1925–1928,* 3 March 1928, vol. 17, col. 25214 (Ritter); Ehni, *Bollwerk,* p. 120.

106. The best analysis of the subject is Dieter Golombek, *Die politische Vorgeschichte des Preussenkonkordats* (Mainz, 1970).

107. Ibid., pp. 13–14, 49–52; Marx to Braun, 28 Nov. 1926, PrGStAB, Rep. 90/2385; Conzing, "Vermerk über Besprechung Reich-Preussen, 8 Okt. 1926," 13 Oct. 1926, ibid. See also Stewart A. Stehlin, *Weimar and the Vatican, 1919–1933* (Princeton, N.J. 1983), pp. 412–29; Erich Wende, *C. H. Becker, Mensch und Politiker: Ein biographischer Beitrag zur Kulturgeschichte der Weimarer Republik* (Stuttgart, 1959), p. 188.

108. Braun, *Weimar,* p. 158. A good analysis of the political problems involved is provided by Trendelenburg, in ["Anlage"], May 1926, Becker papers/1300 (PrGStAB).

109. Porsch to Braun, 1 July 1925, PrGStAB, Rep. 90/2385.

110. Golombek, *Kondordat,* pp. 58–87. The best contemporary collection of materials on the negotiations are in the Becker papers, Sachakten/1300; Trendelenburg papers/7–10.

111. Golombek, *Kondordat,* pp. 54–56; Köhler, *Lebenserinnerungen,* p. 287.

112. Braun to Becker, 3 July 1928; Trendelenburg, "Vermerk," 7 Aug. 1928, Trendelenburg papers/7.

113. Trendelenburg, "Vermerk," 10 Aug. 1928, Trendelenburg papers/7.

114. Pope Pius XI to Cardinal Faulhaber, 23 Nov. 1923, Braun papers/B-2/Mappe 90 (ForHbg); Braun, "Weimar-Ms.," p. 445; Golombek, *Konkordat,* pp. 20, 23. The battle over the Reich Education Law is discussed in chap. 4, below.

115. Becker, "Niederschrift," 27 March 1926, Becker papers/Sachakten/1300; Becker, "Aktennotiz," 27 Dec. 1928, Pacelli to Braun 5 Aug. 1929, Trendelenburg papers/8; Golombek, *Konkordat,* p. 85.

116. On the final negotiations, see Trendelenburg papers/7–8. The details of the concordat are discussed in Golombek, *Konkordat.*

117. Hermann Höpker-Aschoff, *Unser Weg durch die Zeit* (Berlin, 1936), pp. 138, 142; Golombek, *Kondordat,* pp. 60, 63; Falk, "Aufzeichnungen," p. 194; Höpker-Aschoff to Becker, 10 Nov. 1927, Becker papers/Sachakten/1300; Trendelenburg, "Vermerk," 15 Aug. 1928, "Notiz," 12 Oct. 1928, Trendelenburg papers/7;

Theodor Eschenburg, "Carl Sonnenschein," *Vierteljahrshefte für Zeitgeschichte* 11 (Oct. 1963), 361.

118. *SBPrLT 1928–1932*, 31 March 1930, vol. 9, col. 13039 (Ausländer).

119. "DDP-PA," 21 Oct. 1928; Falk, "Aufzeichnungen," p. 194.

120. DVP-ZV, 19 March 1927 and 26 Feb. 1929; Golombek, *Kondordat*, pp. 31, 39; *SBPrLT 1925–1928*, 19 May 1927, vol. 14, cols. 20772–74 (Kähler).

121. Weismann, "Aufzeichnung," 25 Aug. 1928, PrGStAB, Rep. 90/2385; Trendelenburg to Heckel (strictly confidential), 6 May 1929; Trendelenburg, "In den Geschäftsgang," 10 May 1929, Trendelenburg papers/8. The quotation is from Trendelenburg's letter to Heckel.

122. See the documentation in Trendelenburg papers/8; *SBPrLT 1928–1932*, 1 and 5 July 1929, vol. 6, cols. 7564–70, 7625–28; Golombek, *Konkordat*, pp. 87–88; Weismann to caucus leaders and Adenauer, 4 June 1929, PrGStAB, Rep. 90/2386.

123. See the parties' statements, *SBPrLT 1928–1932*, 1, 5, and 9 July 1929, vol. 6, cols. 7604ff. See also Braun, "Weimar-Ms.," p. 446; Golombek, *Konkordat*, pp. 110, 113; and Erich Kuttner, *Otto Braun* (Berlin 1932), p. 89.

124. *SBPrLT 1928–1932*, 1 July 1929, vol. 6, cols. 7590–7604 (Ausländer), vol. 6, 7610–16 (Kube); Johann Victor Bredt, *Erinnerungen und Dokumente 1914 bis 1933*, ed. Martin Schumacher (Düsseldorf, 1970), p. 189. See also Jonathan R. C. Wright, *"Über den Parteien": Die politische Haltung der evangelischen Kirchenführern 1918–1933* (Göttingen, 1977), p. 55; Daniel R. Borg, *The Old-Prussian Church and the Weimar Republic: A Study in Political Adjustment, 1917–1927* (Hanover, N.H. 1984).

125. *SBPrLT 1928–1932*, 5 July 1929, cols. 7573–87 (Stendel), 7664 (Kriege), 7698–99 (Braun); Golombek, *Konkordat*, pp. 110–11; and Johannes Linneborn, "Kondordat," in *Nationale Arbeit: Das Zentrum und sein Wirken in der deutschen Republik* ed. Karl Anton Schulte, (Berlin [1929]), p. 230.

126. *SBPrLT 1928–1932*, 1 and 5 July 1929, vol. 6, cols. 7572, 7709–10, 7744.

127. See the roll-call vote, *SBPrLT 1928–1932*, 9 July 1929, vol. 6, cols. 8118–30.

128. *SBPrLT 1928–1932*, 17 April and 5 July 1929, vol. 5, col. 5923 (Wellmann), vol. 6, cols. 7684–85 (Bohner); DVP-ZV, 26 Feb. 1929; Wright, *Parteien*, p. 82; Braun, "Weimar-Ms.," p. 524; and Golombek, *Konkordat*, pp. 102–03.

129. For a general summary of the negotiation, see Wright, *Parteien*, pp. 48–65.

130. Golombek, *Konkordat*, pp. 44, 57–58; Becker, "Niederschrift über Verhandlungen mit der evangelischen Kirche," 5 Oct. 1927, Becker papers/Sachakten 1307; Senate of the Evangelical church of the "Old Prussian Union" to ministry of education, 24 Nov. 1930, PrGStAB, Rep. 84a/11954.

131. *SBPrLT 1928–1932*, 8 June 1931, vol. 15, cols. 21072ff. The final roll-call vote is in ibid., 13 June 1931, cols. 21415–32.

132. *SBPrLT 1925–1928*, 27 March 1928, vol. 17, cols. 26189ff. (Hirtsiefer). The minister's speech was later published as a separate pamphlet and used in the 1928 election campaign. See Heinrich Hirtsiefer, *Die preussische Regierungskoalition von 1925 bis 1928—Leistungen und Erfolge* ([Berlin, 1928]). See also Wright, *Parteien*, p. 65.

Chapter 4. The "Prussian Problem": State and Reich, 1925–1930

1. Prussian state cabinet, "Aufzeichnungen über die hauptsächlichsten zurzeit [sic] bestehenden Meinungsverschiedenheiten zwischen Reich und Preussen" (hereafter cited: "Aufz. Reich-Preussen"), 16 May 1927, *DrPrLT 1925–1928*, no. 6478, vol. 13, pp. 7468, 7470; Prussian minister of the interior to prime minister and members of the cabinet, 19 Aug. 1927, ZStAM, Rep. 77, tit. 253a, Nr. 45, Bd. 1; Brecht to Müller, 1 July 1928, Müller papers/II/115; and Lachs [?] to Grzesinski, 3 July 1928, Grzesinski papers/310. For a perceptive general discussion of Reich-Prussian relations until 1927, see Gerhard Schulz, *Deutschland am Vorabend der grossen Krise: Die Periode der Konsolidierung und der Revision des Bismarckschen Reichsaufbaus, 1919–1930* (Berlin, 1963), pp. 486–515.

2. See Braun, "Weimar-Ms.," pp. 292, 416, and 420; and Ernst Heilmann, "Erwiderung," *Das Freie Wort* 2 (21 Sept. 1930), 14–17.

3. Wilhelm Abegg, "Die preussische Verwaltung und ihre Reform, Länder und Reich," in *Zehn Jahre Deutsche Republik*, ed. Anton Erkelenz (Berlin, 1928), p. 500; Braun, "Weimar-Ms.," pp. 366–67.

4. See documentation in PrGStAB, Rep. 90 H/2, 390.

5. *SBPrLT 1925–1928*, 29 Jan. 1926, vol. 6, col. 8206; Georg Schreiber, "Innenpolitik," *Politisches Jahrbuch*, 1926, pp. 73–74, n. 5; Braun, "Weimar-Ms.," p. 353.

6. Braun, "Weimar-Ms.," pp. 294–95; Schreiber, "Innenpolitik," p. 61; Braun's notes for a speech in Altona, 7 Sept. 1927, Braun papers/611 (IISG).

7. Prussian prime minister to Reich chancellor, 10 May 1926, Braun papers/11/B-2/54 (ForHbg).

8. See the text of the decree in Braun papers/619 (IISG). See also Braun, "Weimar-Ms.," p. 298; *SBPrLT 1925–1928*, 13 Oct. 1927, vol. 15, cols. 21730–808; and *SBPrLT 1928–1932*, 4 Oct. 1928, vol. 1, cols. 630–44.

9. The best overall analysis of the entire controversy is Günther Grünthal, *Reichsschulgesetz und Zentrumspartei in der Weimarer Republik* (Düsseldorf, 1968). See also DDP-PA, 28 Nov. 1926.

10. Rainer Bölling, *Volksschullehrer und Politik* (Göttingen, 1978), pp. 155–56; Michael Stürmer, *Koalition und Opposition in der Weimarer Republik* (Düsseldorf, 1967), pp. 232–33.

11. Grünthal, *Reichsschulgesetz*, p. 221; Manfred Dörr, "Die Deutschnationale Volkspartei 1925 bis 1928," Ph.D. diss., University of Marburg, 1964, pp. 355–56. For a full-scale discussion of the political and constitutional issues involved, see Heinrich Schulz, *Der Leidensweg des Reichsschulgesetzes* (Berlin, 1926); Christoph Führ, *Zur Schulpolitik der Weimarer Republik* (Weinheim, 1970).

12. Grünthal, *Reichschulgesetz*, pp. 188, 217; *SPD-Parteitag 1927*, pp. 164, 261–64, 304–05.

13. Werner Schneider, *Die Deutsche Demokratische Partei in der Weimarer Republik, 1924–1930* (Munich, 1978), p. 108; Stürmer, *Koalition*, pp. 197–99; Grünthal, *Reichsschulgesetz*, pp. 221, 246; *SBPrLT 1925–1928*, 20 May 1927, vol. 14, cols. 20915–28.

14. See Becker to Braun, 28 Aug. and 2 Sept. 1927, Braun papers/519 (IISG); the

documentation in Becker papers/1181; and Grünthal, *Reichsschulgesetz*, pp. 196, 225, 226, n. 208.

15. See Braun, "Weimar-Ms.," pp. 370–72; report of Reichsrat session, 14 Oct. 1927, Becker papers/1168; documentation in PrGStAB, Rep. 90a/14; Prussian prime minister to members of the cabinet and provincial delegates, 19 Oct. 1927, PrGStAB, Rep. 84a/6369; Grünthal, *Reichschulgesetz*, pp. 228–29; Bölling *Lehrer*, pp. 161–62; Stürmer, *Koalition*, p. 234; Josef Becker, "Josef Wirth und die Krise des Zentrums . . . 1927–28," *Zeitschrift für die Geschichte des Oberrheins* 109 (1961), 402, 411–12. On the history of the constitutional provisions dividing the Prussian *Reichsrat* votes, see Dietrich Orlow, *Weimar Prussia 1918–1925: The Unlikely Rock of Democracy* (Pittsburgh, Pa., 1986), chap. 3; and Horst Möller, *Parlamentarismus in Preussen, 1919–1932* (Düsseldorf, 1985), pp. 497ff.

16. In February 1930, the DNVP Landtag delegate Lothar Steuer was still convinced there would have been a national education law if only the Center party had broken off its alliance with the Weimar coalition parties in Prussia. See *SBPrLT 1928–1932*, 19 Feb. 1930, vol. 8, col. 10944.

17. *SBPrLT 1925–1928*, 14 March 1928, vol. 17, cols. 25316–18 (Lauscher); Bölling, *Lehrer*, pp. 157–58; Braun, "Weimar-Ms.," p. 372; Stürmer, *Koalition*, p. 235.

18. SitzPrStMin, 16 Sept. 1925 and 5 Feb. 1929. PrGStAB, Rep. 90a/4 and ZStAM, Rep. 90a/III/2b/Nr. 6, Bd. 178; *SBPrLT 1928–1932*, 24 April 1929, vol. 5, col. 6370 (Braun); "Aufz. Reich-Preussen," p. 7469; Braun, "Weimar-Ms.," pp. 421–23. See also Herbert Hömig, *Das preussische Zentrum in der Weimarer Republik* (Mainz, 1979), p. 150; Hans-Peter Ehni, *Bollwerk Preussen: Preussen Regierung, Reich-Länderproblem und Sozialdemokratie, 1928–1932* (Bonn–Bad Godesberg, 1975), p. 105; Franz Menges, *Reichsreform und Finanzpolitik* (Berlin, 1971), pp. 173–74; Gerhard Schulz, *Zwischen Demokratie und Diktatur: Verfassungspolitik und Reichsreform in der Weimarer Republik* (Berlin, 1963), 1:547–49.

19. See the documentation in PrGStAB, Rep. 84a/1321; "Aufz. Reich-Preussen," pp. 7466–68.

20. Lachs [?] to Grzesinski, 3 July 1928, Grzesinski papers/310; *SBPrLT 1928–1932*, 11 July 1929 and 22 May 1930, vol. 6, cols. 8237–38, vol. 10, col. 14170; Prussian prime minister to minister of finance, 1 March 1930, PrGStAB, Rep. 90a/1077. The *Osthilfe* controversy after 1930 is discussed in chap. 6, below.

21. Ehni, *Bollwerk*, pp. 289–91. For a Prussian view of the problem, see "Aufz. Reich-Preussen," pp. 7465–66.

22. Möller, *Parlamentarismus*, pp. 151–67. The documentation is in PrGStAB, Rep. 90/193. See also *SBPrLT 1925–1928*, 19 Oct. 1925, vol. 3, cols. 4764–68 (Berten [SPD] and Leidig [DVP]).

23. *Kölnische Zeitung*, no. 440, 20 June 1925. For statistics on the votes of the Prussian cabinet and provincial delegates from 1921 to Oct. 1927, see "Zusammenstellung," in Grzesinski to Braun, 22 Nov. 1927, PrGStAB, Rep. 90/108. On the constitutional and legal aspects of the problem, see *SBPrLT 1925–1928*, 16 Dec. 1925, vol. 5, cols. 7579–80.

24. *Montag-Morgen*, no. 25 (22 June 1926); *Deutsche Tageszeitung*, no. 452 (25 Sept. 1925); *Germania*, no. 595 (21 Dec. 1925). See also DVP–ZV, 26 Feb. 1929.

25. *SBPrLT 1925–1928*, 13 Jan. 1926, vol. 5, cols. 7919–24.

26. See the documentation in PrGStAB, Rep. 90/109. See also *Berliner Tageblatt*, no. 26, 16 Jan. 1926.

27. Braun, "Weimar-Ms.," p. 291. See also Campe's remarks as cited in *Magdeburgische Zeitung*, no. 338 (7 July 1927).

28. See Weismann to Bredt, 20 April 1927; Prussian prime minister to provincial delegates, 19 Oct. 1927, PrGStAB, Rep. 90/108; *SBPrLT 1925–1928*, 12 May 1927, vol. 14, cols. 20085–86 (Braun). See also Braun's clash with Keudell in the *Reichsrat*, 21 July 1927, PrGStAB Rep. 84a/6369.

29. Prussian minister of the interior to prime minister, 22 Nov. 1927, PrGStAB, Rep. 90a/108; *Vossische Zeitung*, no. 590 (14 Dec. 1927); Braun to Adenauer (draft), 14 Feb. 1928, PrGStAB, Rep. 90/193. On the attitude of the DVP, see *Tägliche Rundschau*, nos. 59, 70 (5 and 11 Feb. 1926).

30. *SBPrLT 1925–1928*, 17 May 1927, vol. 14, col. 20520 (Richter).

31. SitzPrStMin, 18 Jan. 1927 and 20 Jan. 1928, PrGStAB, Rep. 90a/11 and 17; *SBPrLT 1928–1932*, 10 July 1928, vol. 1, cols. 369–82. See also Möller, *Parlamentarismus*, p. 497.

32. For the background on the negotiations between Prussia, Brunswick, and Thuringia, see Grzesinski to Noske, 19 March 1929 and Noske to Grzesinski, 22 March 1929, Grzesinski papers/283, 121; Höpker-Aschoff to Braun, 27 March 1939; Waentig to Braun, 2 May 1929, Braun papers/476, 479 (IISG).

33. Prussian ministry of finance to prime minister [draft], Dec. 1927 [sic], PrGStAB, Rep. 90/2302; Thomas Trumpp, "Franz von Papen, der preussisch-deutsche Dualismus und die NSDAP in Preussen," Ph.D. Diss. University of Tübingen, 1963, p. 25; Severing, "Vermerk," 26 March 1926, PrGStAB, Rep. 90/108; *SBPrLT 1928–1932*, 13 June 1928, vol. 1, cols. 200–03; Osterroth to Braun and Severing, 18 Oct. and 17 Dec. 1928 Braun papers/571–72 (IISG).

34. Braun papers/611 (IISG). Ironically, the mayor, Max Brauer, became mayor of Hamburg after World War II. In the meantime, Altona had become part of the larger city.

35. On the background of these longstanding issues, see documentation in PrGStAB, Rep. 90/2505. See also SitzPrStMin, 19 Feb. 1929, ibid., Rep. 90a/23; Gustav Noske, *Erlebtes aus Aufstieg und Niedergang einer Demokratie* (Offenbach a.M., 1947), p. 295; *SBPrLT 1925–1928*, 21 and 29 June 1927, vol. 14, cols. 20961ff., 21446; *SBPrLT 1928–1932*, 24 and 27 June 1930, vol. 10, cols. 14506ff, vol. 11, cols. 14744ff.

36. Horst Möller, "Das Ende Preussens," in *Preussen—eine Herausforderung*, ed. Wolfgang Böhme (Karlsruhe, 1981), p. 106.

37. Hugo Preuss to Paul Herz, 20 July 1925, Herz papers/62; SitzPrStMin, 10 Sept. 1927, ZStAM, Rep. 77, tit. 253a, Nr. 45, Bd. 1; Erwin Widder, "Reich und Preussen vom Regierungsantritt Brünings bis zum Reichsstatthaltergesetz Hitlers," Ph.D. Diss., University of Frankfurt a.M., 1959, pp. 31–32.

38. *SPD Parteitag 1925*, pp. 7, 276; *SPD Parteitag 1927*, pp. 177ff.; *SPD-Preussentag 1928*, pp. 11–13. See also SPD-Vorstand, ed., *Der Weg zum Einheitsstaat* (Berlin, 1929); Ehni, *Bollwerk*, p. 116.

39. DDP-PA, 4 Dec. 1927; *SBPrLT 1928–1932*, 22 April 1929, vol. 5, cols,

6405–06. See also Erich Koch-Weser, "Vom Kleinstaat zum Reich und zum Grossdeutschen Einheitsstaat," in *Zehn Jahre*, ed. Erkelenz, p. 91.

40. Gerhard Senger, *Die Politik der Zentrumspartei zur Frage Reich und Länder von 1918–1929* (Hamburg, 1932), pp. 84; *SBPrLT 1925–1928*, 2 Dec. 1925 and 17 Dec. 1927, vol. 5, cols. 6837ff., vol. 15, col. 22849; *SBPrLT 1928–1932*, 15 May 1929, vol. 5, col. 7094. See also Erich Kosthorst et al., *Jakob Kaiser* (Stuttgart, 1967), 1:132; Ehni, *Bollwerk*, p. 102.

41. Otto Braun, *Deutscher Einheitsstaat oder Föderativstaat* (Berlin, 1927); Braun, Weimar-Ms.," pp. 545–47. See also Sabine Höner, *Der nationalsozialistische Zugriff auf Preussen* (Bochum, 1984), p. 29; Schulz, *Zwischen*, pp. 598–99; Schneider, *DDP*, p. 156; *SBPrLT 1925–1928*, 1 Dec. 1925, vol. 5, cols, 6767–68 (Höpker-Aschoff); Hermann Höpker-Aschoff, *Deutscher Einheitsstaat* (Berlin, 1928).

42. Arnold Brecht, *Federalism and Regionalism in Germany—The Division of Prussia* (New York, 1945), pp. 22, 133, 136. See also Braun, Weimar-Ms.," pp. 362–63; Albert Grzesinski, "Im Kampf um die deutsche Republik—Lebensweg eines Staatenlosen," Grzesinski papers/2457 (IISG), p. 197; Schulz, *Zwischen*, pp. 508–09. For a variation on the decentralized unitary state, see Wilhelm Abegg, "Die preussische Verwaltung und ihre Reform, Länder und Reich," in *Zehn Jahre*, ed. Erkelenz, p. 503.

43. DVP-RTFrProt, 5 Feb. 1926; DVP-ZV, 26 Feb. 1929; *SBPrLT 1925–1928*, 17 May 1927, vol. 14, cols. 20522–23. For the SPD's comments on the DVP's proposals, see SPD, *Sozialdemokratische Parteikorrespondenz*, nos. 1–2 (Feb. 1929).

44. *SBPrLT 1925–1928*, 17 May 1927 and 28 March 1928, vol. 14, col. 20517, vol. 17, col. 26307; *SBPrLT 1928–1932*, 13 Dec. 1929, vol. 7, cols. 9433–34. See also Georg Schreiber, "Innenpolitik," *Politisches Jahrbuch*, 1927/1928, p. 137; *Kreuzzeitung*, 23 and 24 Jan. 1929 (Westarp); Dörr, "DNVP," p. 253.

45. Reich Press Office, ed., *Länderkonferenz am 16., 17. und 18. Januar 1928* . . . (Berlin, 1928). See also Walther Vogel, *Deutsche Reichsgliederung und Reichsreform in Vergangenheit und Gegenwart* (Leipzig, 1932), pp. 100–10. For a perceptive overall appraisal of the Federal Conference, see Schulz, *Vorabend*, pp. 486–515.

46. *SBPrLT 1925–1928*, 16 Dec. 1927, vol. 15, col. 22753; Höner, *Zugriff*, pp. 26–27; Schulz, *Vorabend*, p. 588. Ironically, the former German Nationalist Reich minister of the interior, Keudell, feared that Prussia would attempt to use the Federal Conference to seize the initiative in the *Reichsreform* (Schulz, *Vorabend*, pp. 577–78).

47. On the background of the affair, see H. Müller [?] "Zur Personalpolitik 1927," 10 Oct. 1927, Müller papers/Nr. 1, B1. 176–78 (ZStAP). See also Brecht's memoirs, *Vorspiel zum Schweigen—Das Ende der Deutschen Republik* (Vienna, 1948), pp. 84–86.

48. See Brecht, "Vorschläge."

49. Kurt Gossweiler, "Bund zur Erneuerung des Reiches (Lutherbund)," in *Die bürgerlichen Parteien in Deutschland 1830–1945*, ed. Dieter Fricke et al. (Leipzig, 1968, 1970), 1:195–200; and Thilo Freiherr von Wilmovsky, *Rückblickend möchte ich sagen* . . . (Oldenburg, 1961), pp. 117–18.

50. The final communique is reprinted in Hermann Pünder, "Das Reich und die Länder," in *Zehn Jahre deutsche Geschichte 1918–1928*, 2d ed., ed. Hermann Müller et al. (Berlin, 1928), pp. 83–84.

51. Braun to Hess, 9 Dec. 1929, Braun papers/Teil 2/B/I/13 (ForHbg). See also Möller, *Parlamentarismus*, p. 323. For an example of a committee's deliberations, see *Stenographische Niederschrift über die Sitzung des Ausschusses der Länderkonferenz* (Berlin, 1928).

52. Braun, "Weimar-Ms.," p. 550.

53. *SBPrLT 1928–1932*, 14 Dec. 1928, 15 May 1928, 22 April 1929, 24 Feb. 1930, vol. 2, cols, 1519–22 (Braun), vol. 5, cols. 6372–73, 7094–95 (Hess), vol. 8, col. 11308 (Heilmann). See also Carl Severing, "Der Weg der Reichsreform," *Sozialistische Monatshefte* 70 (17 Feb. 1930), 118–22; Werner Conze, "Die Krise des Parteienstaates in Deutschland 1929/30," *Historische Zeitschrift* 178 (Aug. 1954), 80; Trumpp, "Papen," p. 26; Ehni, *Bollwerk*, 109.

54. Widder, *Reich*, pp. 35–37.

Chapter 5. The German Parties and Prussia, 1930–1933

1. Heinz O. Ziegler, *Autoritärer oder Totaler Staat* (Tübingen, 1932).

2. Among contemporary reflections about the symptoms and causes of the crisis, see Grzesinski to Braun, Heilmann, and SPD Landtag caucus, 14 and 17 Feb., 18 Oct., 1 Nov., and 4 Dec. 1929, Grzesinski papers/701, 697, 700, 698, 699; Albert Grzesinski, "Im Kampf um die deutsche Republik—Lebensweg eines Staatenlosen," Grzesinski papers/2457 (IISG), p. 139; Braun, *Weimar*, p. 232; Gustav Noske, *Erlebtes aus Aufstieg und Niedergang einer Demokratie* (Offenbach a.M., 1947), pp. 309–11; and Harry Graf Kessler, *Tagebücher 1918–1937*, ed. Wolfgang Pfeiffer-Belli (Frankfurt a.M., 1961), entry for 25 April 1932, pp. 611–12. Among the voluminous secondary literature, see esp. Werner Conze and Hans Raupach, eds. *Die Staats-und Wirtschaftskrise 1929/33* (Stuttgart, 1967); Ilse Maurer and Udo Wengst, eds., *Staat und NSDAP, 1930–32: Quellen zur Ära Brüning* (Düsseldorf, 1977); Karl Dietrich Bracher, *Die Auflösung der Weimarer Republik*, 5th ed. (Düsseldorf, 1978); Gerhard Schulz, *Deutschland am Vorabend der grossen Krise: Zwischen Demokratie und Diktatur* (Düsseldorf, 1987).

3. Larry E. Jones, "Sammlung oder Zersplitterung? Die Bestrebungen zur Bildung einer neuen Mittelpartei in der Endphase der Weimarer Republik 1930–1933," *Vierteljahrshefte für Zeitgeschichte* 25 (July 1977), 265–304; *German Liberalism and the Dissolution of the Weimar Party System, 1918–1933* (Chapel Hill, N.C. 1988); Kurt Gossweiler, "Bund zur Erneuerung des Reiches (Lutherbund)," in *Die bürgerlichen Parteien in Deutschland 1830–1945*, ed. Dieter Fricke et al., (Leipzig, 1968, 1970), 1:195–200; Thilo Freiherr von Wilmovsky, *Rückblickend möchte ich sagen . . .* (Oldenburg, 1961), pp. 117–18; Ferdinand Friedensburg, *Lebenserinnerungen* (Frankfurt a.M., 1969), pp. 199–206; Henry A. Turner, "The *Ruhrlade*, Secret Cabinet of Heavy Industry in the Weimar Republic," *Central European History* 3 (Sept. 1970), 209; Heinrich August Winkler, *Mittelstand, Demokratie und Nationalsozialismus* (Cologne, 1972), p. 151.

4. See "Richtlinien zur Abwehr des Faschismus unter Berücksichtigung der be-vorstehenden [Preussen] -Wahlen," n.d. 1932, Severing papers/50/34.

5. See the detailed discussion in chap. 8, below.

6. Braun, *Weimar*, p. 483.

7. Richard Breitman, "German Social Democracy and General Schleicher 1932–1933," *Central European History* 9 (Dec. 1976), 354. On Heilmann's public and private position after 1930, see Albert Grzesinski, "Mein Ausscheiden als Minister," p. 25 (typescript diary), Grzesinski papers/1332; *SBPrLT 1928–1932*, 24 Nov. 1931, vol. 16, col. 22794 (Hilger-Spiegelberg [DNVP]; and Heilmann to Grimme, 3 May 1931, Grimme papers/P-79/63. The information that Heilmann wanted Hamburger as his successor was given to the author by Dr. Hamburger in an interview, 8 June 1976.

8. Jonathan R. C. Wright, *"Über den Parteien" Die politische Haltung der evangelischen Kirchenführern 1918–1933* (Göttingen, 1977), p. 72; Grzesinski to Severing, 22 Dec. 1931, Grzesinski papers/310.

9. See Hilferding to Kautsky, 15 April 1931, Kautsky papers/D/XII/652.

10. For general analyses of the SPD at the end of the Weimar Republic, see Erich Matthias and Rudolf Morsey, eds., *Das Ende der Parteien 1933* (Düsseldorf, 1960); Richard Breitman, *German Socialism and Weimar Democracy* (Chapel Hill, N.C., 1981); Richard N. Hunt, *German Social Democracy 1918–1933* (New Haven, Conn., 1964), p. 237; Heinrich August Winkler, *Der Weg in die Katastrophe: Arbeiter und Arbeiterbewegung in der Weimarer Republik 1930 bis 1933* (Bonn, 1987), pp. 584–95.

11. See Braun, "Weimar-Ms.," p. 468; Hörsing to party executive, 9 Dec. 1930, Hörsing papers/19; Braun to Höltermann, 31 Dec. 1932, Braun papers/415 (IISG); Braun to Ritzel, 18 Oct. 1949, Braun papers/C/1/233 (PrGStAB); Heilmann's article in *Das Freie Wort* 2 (29 June 1930), 8–11.

12. Hilferding to Kautsky, 2 Oct. 1931, Kautsky papers/D-XII/653. See also Michael Schneider, *Das Arbeitsbeschaffungsprogramm des ADGB* (Bonn–Bad Godesberg, 1975), pp. 119ff.; Kurt Koszyk, *Zwischen Kaiserreich und Diktatur—Die sozialdemokratische Presse von 1914–1933* (Heidelberg, 1958), pp. 183–84.

13. For a detailed history of the SAPD, see Hanno Drechsler, *Die Sozialistische Arbeiterpartei Deutschlands (SAPD)* (Meisenheim am Glan, 1965), esp. pp. 101–03, 253–56. See also *SBPrLT 1928–1932*, 17 March 1932, vol. 17, cols. 24710–19 (Marckwald); Stampfer to Kautsky, 6 Oct. 1931, Kautsky papers/D-XXI/310.

14. Karl Rohe, *Das Reichsbanner Schwarz-Rot-Gold* (Düsseldorf, 1966), pp. 380–82; Koszyk, *Zwischen*, p. 249, n. 18.

15. Illo [i.e., Ernst Heilmann], "Gegen die Nazis," *Das Freie Wort* 2 (6 April 1930), 17; ibid. 2 (7 Dec. 1930), 4; Carl Severing, "20. Juli 1932," *Die Gegenwart* 2 (31 July 1947), 14ff. The SPD's changing assessment of the Nazis can be followed particularly well in *Das Freie Wort* for 1930. See also Rohe, *Reichsbanner*, pp. 360ff.

16. Rohe, *Reichsbanner*, pp. 399, 416, 439. See also Carl Severing, "20. Juli 1932," 14 [Ernst Heilmann], "Entscheidungstag: 31. Juli," *Das Freie Wort* 4 (31 July 1932), 4–5.

17. Schneider, *ADGB*, p. 117.

18. On the overall development of the DDP, see Werner Schneider, *Die Deutsche Demokratische Partei in der Weimarer Republik, 1924–1930* (Munich, 1978), p. 256; Werner Stephan, *Aufstieg und Verfall des Linksliberalismus in der Weimarer Republik* (Göttingen, 1973), pp. 399ff.; Bruce B. Frye, *Liberal Democrats in the Weimar Republic—The History of the German Democratic Party and the German State Party*

(Carbondale, Ill., 1985), p. 159. See also DNVP, "Mitteilungen der Parteizentrale," no. 1 (1 Jan. 1930), 3–4.

19. For details on the founding of the DStP, see Frye, *Liberal,* pp. 155ff. See also DDP-PA, 30 July 1930; DDP-PV, 27 Sept. and 16 Oct. 1930.

20. On the rivalry of Koch-Weser and Höpker-Aschoff, see Frye, *Liberal,* pp. 164–65, 172–73; Schneider, *DDP,* pp. 136–37; Stephan, *Aufstieg,* p. 486; Alexander Kessler, *Der Jungdeutsche Orden auf dem Wege zur Deutschen Staatpartei* (Munich, 1980), pp. 16–18; DDP-PA, 28 Nov. 1926. Höpker-Aschoff's resignation is discussed below.

21. For—quite contrasting—views of the Center party's path in the years from 1930 to 1933, see Heinrich Brüning, *Memoiren* (Stuttgart, 1970), pp. 154ff.; Rudolf Morsey, *Der Untergang des politischen Katholizismus—die Zentrumspartei zwischen christlichem Selbstverständnis und "Nationaler Erhebung" 1932/33* (Stuttgart, 1977); Detlef Junker, *Die Deutsche Zentrumspartei und Hitler 1932/33* (Stuttgart, 1969). An interesting contemporary document is the Center party's handbook for the September 1930 Reichstag election, *Zentrum und Reichspolitik—Ein politisches Handbuch in Frage und Antwort,* ed. Georg Schreiber (Cologne, 1930).

22. *SBPrLT 1928–1932,* 2 March, 4 May, and 14 Oct. 1931, vol. 14, cols. 19433, 20029, vol. 16, col. 22087; Franz von Papen, *Der Wahrheit eine Gasse* (Munich, 1952), p. 134; Victor Schiff, "Brünings Kabale und Pleite," *Das Freie Wort* 2 (27 July 1930), 9; Thomas Trumpp, "Franz von Papen, der preussisch-deutsche Dualismus und die NSDAP in Preussen," Ph.D. Diss., University of Tübingen, 1963, p. 62. See also Braun, "Weimar-Ms.," p. 399.

23. See Hess's remarks at the congress of the Prussian Center party, 11 May 1930, as distributed by the party's press office, Braun papers/11/B-2/43 (ForHbg), quotation on p. 7. See also the sharp attacks on the DNVP by Hess (*SBPrLT 1928–1932,* 17 Dec. 1930, vol. 12, cols. 16381–91) and Letterhaus (ibid., 24 and 26 March 1931, vol. 14, cols. 19529, 19705–12).

24. *SBPrLT 1928–1932,* 16 April 1929, vol. 5, cols. 5823ff. See also ibid., 18 March 1932, vol. 17, col. 24857; Morsey, *Untergang,* p. 21.

25. Braun, "Weimar-Ms.," pp. 467–68, 645.

26. On Hirtsiefer's strong prorepublican sentiments and good relations with the Social Democrats, see Otto Klepper, "Das Ende der Republik," *Die Gegenwart* 2 (30 Sept. 1947), 20–22; "Hamburger-Schulze Interview."

27. Morsey, *Untergang,* pp. 48, 218–19.

28. DVP-ZV, 4 July 1930. For criticism of the dominant role of the Reichstag caucus, see ibid., 14 Dec. 1929.

29. See the debates in ibid., 28 April 1930; DVP-RTFrProt, 18 Feb. 1929, 8 Nov. 1930, 13 Dec. 1931, and 22 Feb. 1932. See also Kessler, *Orden,* p. 7.

30. DVP-ZV, 4 July and 24 Aug. 1930 (Curtius and Stendel); Hans Booms, "Die Deutsche Volkspartei (DVP)," in *Ende,* ed. Matthias and Morsey, p. 529. Prussian affairs were almost never discussed in the meetings of the DVP's Reichstag delegation.

31. *SBPrLT 1928–1932,* 22 Jan. 1932, vol. 17, col. 23759.

32. Ibid., 23 Jan. 1932, cols. 23834–36, 24784–812. See also *Das Freie Wort* 4 (10 July 1932), 29.

33. Alfred Milatz, *Wähler und Wahlen in der Weimarer Republik*, 2 ed. (Bonn, 1968), p. 133; Martin Schumacher, *Mittelstandsfront und Republik* (Düsseldorf, 1972), pp. 177, 183. See also Sabine Höner, *Der nationalsozialistische Zugriff auf Preussen* (Bochum, 1984), p. 134; *SBPrLT 1928–1932*, 22 Jan. 1932, vol. 17, cols. 23776–92.

34. Alfred Kruck, *Geschichte des Alldeutschen Verbandes 1890–1939* (Wiesbaden, 1954), p. 169; Dieter Gessner, *Agrarverbände in der Weimarer Republik* (Düsseldorf, 1976), p. 111. See also Hess's ironic commentary on the DNVP's troubles in *SBPrLT 1928–1932*, 13 Dec. 1929, vol. 7, cols. 9442–44. For Hugenberg's version of the failure of the moderates' "coalition strategy," see "Mitteilungen der Parteizentrale," no. 1 (1 Jan. 1930). A copy of this document, intended only for distribution within the DNVP, is in the Diller papers.

35. For intraparty explanations of these developments, see DNVP-Parteivorstandssitzung (hereafter: DNVP-PV), 18 Sept. 1930, DNVP papers/7533/3 (ForHbg); "Mitteilungen," 1 Jan. 1930. See also *Angestelltenstimme und Arbeiterstimme* 10 (Jan. 1930), 1, 7.

36. See Count Friedrich von der Schulenburg to Schleicher, 2 June 1928, quoted in Erasmus Jonas, *Die Volkskonservativen 1928–1933* (Düsseldorf, 1965), p. 185.

37. Günter J. Trittel, "Hans Schlange-Schöningen: Ein vergessener Politiker der 'Ersten Stunde,'" *Vierteljahrshefte für Zeitgeschichte* 35 (Jan. 1987), 28ff.; Dieter Gessner, *Agrarverbände in der Weimarer Republik*, (Düsseldorf, 1976), pp. 119–20; *SBPrLT 1928–1932*, 23 Jan. 1932, vol. 17, cols. 23885–86 (Posadowsky-Wehner).

38. On the VKP, see Jonas, *VKP*, esp. p. 102. See also Gessner, *Agrarverbände*, p. 236.

39. On the CSVD see *SBPrLT 1928–1932*, 14 Oct., 4 Nov. 1930, 24 March, and 15 Oct. 1931, vol. 11, cols. 14900–01, vol. 14, cols. 15442–44, vol. 16, cols. 19461–64, 19475, 22187.

40. For comments on the DNVP's new leaders, see *SBPrLT 1928–1932*, 15 May 1929, vol. 5, col. 7101 (Hess), and 23 March 1931, vol. 14, cols. 19380–81 (Buchert [SPD]).

41. Ibid., 15 Oct. 1931, vol. 16, col. 22344 (Steuer).

42. Ibid., 26 March 1931, vol. 14, col. 19689 (Borck), 6 May 1931, vol. 14, cols. 20277–78 (Morsch). See also Dieter Golombek, *Die politische Vorgeschichte des Preussenkonkordats* (Mainz, 1970), p. 109.

43. Braun, "Weimar-Ms.," p. 510; *SBPrLT 1928–1932*, 23 March 1931, vol. 14, col. 19367 (Rohr), and 17 March 1932, vol. 17, col. 24745 (Oelze).

44. Goslar to Braun, 15 Dec. 1930, Braun papers/551 (IISG); *Waldeckischer Landbund*, no. 29 (19 July 1931).

45. For the history of the NSDAP in the last year of the Weimar Republic, see esp. Dietrich Orlow, *The History of the Nazi Party 1919–1933*, (Pittsburgh, Pa., 1969), pp. 185ff.; Bracher, *Auflösung*. On the NSDAP's left wing, see Peter D. Stachura, *Gregor Strasser and the Rise of Nazism* (London, 1983); and Udo Kissenkötter, *Gregor Strasser und die NSDAP* (Stuttgart, 1978). The best study specifically of the Prussian NSDAP is Höner, *Zugriff*. For the the political attitude of Kube and the Landtag delegation, see ibid., pp. 115ff., 155, 286, 434; *SBPrLT 1928–1932*, 14 June 1928, 31 Jan. 1930, vol. 1, col. 291 (Kaufmann), vol. 8, cols. 10411–20 (Kube).

46. The quotation is from a speech by Karl Kaufmann, ibid., 16 April 1929, vol. 5, col. 5833. Kaufmann was a member of the Landtag and the Nazi *Gauleiter* of Hamburg.

47. Anselm Faust, *Der Nationalsozalistische Deutsche Studentenbund* (Düsseldorf, 1973); Michael Kater, *Studentenschaft und Rechtsradikalismus in Deutschland, 1918–1933*, (Hamburg, 1975).

48. *SBPrLT 1928–1932*, 26 Nov. 1929, vol. 7, col. 8911.

49. Joseph Goebbels, *Die Tagebücher von Joseph Goebbels*, vol. 1: *Aufzeichnungen 1924–1941*, ed. Elke Fröhlich (Munich, 1987), 2:66, 74 (19 May and 5 June 1931); Joseph Goebbels, *Vom Kaiserhof zur Reichskanzlei*, 28th ed. (Berlin, 1940), pp. 36, 78 (entries for 2 Feb. and 10 April 1932); Höner, *Zugriff*, pp. 200–01.

50. Goebbels, *Tagebücher* 2:105, 149 (5 Jan., 1 April 1932).

51. Höner, *Zugriff*, pp. 11, 195, 245.

52. See, Orlow, *Nazi Party*, 1:180ff.; Stachura, *Strasser*, pp. 82ff. For Goebbels's derisive comments on Strasser's effort, see *Tagebücher* 2:181 (9 June 1932).

53. See chaps. 8 and 9, below.

54. Höner, *Zugriff*, pp. 171ff., 290; Goebbels, *Kaiserhof*, pp. 154–56 (31 Aug.–3 Sept. 1932); Goebbels, *Tagebücher* 2:162, 236 (30 April and 3 Sept. 1932).

55. Goebbels, *Tagebücher* 1:273 (6 Oct. 1928); 2:105 (6 Jan. 1932).

56. Goebbels, *Kaiserhof*, pp. 100–01 (entry for 28 May 1932). Goebbels wrote that Hitler, too, was "just delighted" (ibid., p. 101).

57. Ibid., pp. 73, 100, 107–08 (1 April, 24 May, and 6 June 1932); Höner, *Zugriff*, p. 377. On the party's financial problems, see Orlow, *Nazi Party* 1:284–88; and documentation in Bracht papers/2.

58. Major analyses of the KPD's history in this period, all of which stress the importance of the party's relationship to the Soviet Union and the Comintern, include Hermann Weber, *Die Wandlung des deutschen Kommunismus: Die Stalinisierung der KPD in der Weimarer Republik*, 2 vols. (Frankfurt a.M., 1969); *Hauptfeind Sozialdemokratie: Strategie und Taktik der KPD 1929–1933* (Düsseldorf, 1981); Siegfried Bahne, *Die KPD und das Ende von Weimar* (Frankfurt a.M., 1976); Ossip K. Flechtheim, *Die KPD in der Weimarer Republik* (Frankfurt a.M., 1969); Winkler, *Katastrophe*, pp. 595ff. For an interesting "revisionist" view that emphasizes German domestic factors in the evolution of the KPD's political line, see Eric D. Weitz, "State Power, Class Fragmentation, and the Shaping of German Communist Politics," *Journal of Modern History*, 62 (June 1990), 253–97.

59. On the evolution of the doctrine of social fascism, see Siegfried Bahne, "Sozialfaschismus," *International Review of Social History* 10 (1965), 233–34; "KPD," p. 669 Weber, *Wandlung*, 1:220ff., *Hauptfeind*, pp. 15, 27ff., 64 ff. 86ff.; Weber, ed., *Der deutsche Kommunismus: Dokumente 1915–1945*, 3d ed. (Cologne, 1973), p. 103, n. 29; James J. Ward, " 'Smash the fascists' . . . German Communist Efforts to Counter the Nazis, 1930–31," *Central European History* 14 (March 1981), 40ff., 60–61; Leonid Luks, *Entstehung der kommunistischen Faschismustheorie* (Stuttgart, 1984).

60. Weber, *Hauptfeind*, pp. 26ff., 68–69, 101.

61. Among the numerous examples, see *SBPrLT 1928–1932*, 16 Oct. 1930, vol. 11, cols. 15033–34, 4 May 1931, vol. 14, cols. 20065–76, 20 Jan. 1932, vol. 17, col.

23550, 18 March 1932, vol. 17, cols. 24819–37; *SBPrLT 1932–1933*, 2 June 1932, vol. 1, cols. 139, 145. See also Ernst Thälmann's address to the KPD's central committee, 19 Feb. 1932, in *Kommunismus*, ed. Weber, p. 185. On the Communists' use of political violence, see esp. Eve Rosenhaft, *Beating the Fascists? The German Communists and Political Violence, 1929–1933* (Cambridge, Mass., 1983).

62. Joachim Petzold, "Der Staatsstreich vom 20. Juli 1932 in Preussen," *Zeitschrift für Geschichtswissenschaft* 4 (1956), p. 1147 n. 5. See also Wilhelm Pieck's statement quoted in ibid., p. 1161; Ward, "Smash," p. 239; Möller, *Parlamentarismus*, p. 320, n. 192.

63. For the steps that led to the decision, see Weber, *Hauptfeind*, pp. 36ff., 87–88. For the KPD's abrupt about-face, see also *SBPrLT 1928–1932*, 8 July and 14 Oct. 1931, vol. 15, cols. 21568, vol. 16, col. 22106.

64. District director of Cologne to members of the cabinet, 11 Aug. 1931, ZStAM, Rep. 120a C B I Nr. 8a, Bd. 3; Thomas Weingartner, *Stalin und der Aufstieg Hitlers* (Berlin, 1970), pp. 85–88; Ward, "Smash," pp. 57–59; Bahne, *KPD*, p. 13; Weber, *Wandlung* 1:239–42.

65. Aviva Aviv, "The SPD and the KPD at the End of Weimar: Similarity within Contrast," *Internationale Wissenschaftliche Korrespondenz* 14 (June 1978), 184; *SBPrLT 1928–1932*, 17 Feb. and 17 March 1932, vol. 17, cols. 24261–62 (Kasper), 24753–54; *SBPrLT 1932–1933*, 2 June 1932, vol. 1, col. 148 (Pieck); Ernst Heilmann, "Der Umschwung," *Das Freie Wort* 3 (9 Aug. 1931), 2; Weingartner, *Stalin*, pp. 133, 137; Ward, "Smash," p. 59; Weber, *Hauptfeind*, pp. 48–49.

66. Weber, *Hauptfeind*, pp. 49ff. The Torgler-Kasper episode will be discussed in chap. 8, below.

67. Bahne, *KPD*, pp. 23–24; and Weber, *Hauptfeind*, pp. 55ff. For views more sympathetic to the KPD, see Petzold, "Staatsstreich," p. 1152, nn. 31, 32; Hans-Peter Ehni, *Bollwerk Preussen: Preussen Regierung, Reich-Länderproblem und Sozialdemokratie, 1928–1932* (Bonn–Bad Godesberg, 1975), p. 260.

68. *SBPrLT 1928–1932*, 24 March 1931, vol. 14, col. 19508 (Steuer [DNVP]).

69. The sources of the exploding Nazi vote have been the subject of numerous and detailed analyses. Karl Dietrich Bracher's account (*Auflösung*, pp. 106ff.) remains valuable. See also Richard F. Hamilton, *Who Voted for Hitler* (Princeton, N.J., 1982); Thomas Childers, *The Nazi Voter: The Social Foundations of Fascism in Germany, 1919–1933* (Chapel Hill, N.C., 1983). Hamilton and Childers reach rather different conclusions on the basis of the same statistical material.

70. Milatz, *Wähler*, p. 131; Hans Neisser, "Statistische Analyse des Wahlergebnisses," *Die Arbeit* 7 (1930), 658–59.

71. *SBPrLT 1928–1932*, 23 March 1931, vol. 14, col. 19375 (Rohr).

72. See the interesting report by the district director of Cologne (Elfgen) to members of the cabinet and provincial governors, 11 Aug. 1931, ZStAM, Rep. 120a B I Nr. 8a, Bd. 3.

73. The percentages are extrapolated from the figures in *Statistisches Jahrbuch für das Deutsche Reich, 1932* (Berlin, 1932), pp. 546–47. They are slightly distorted, since some of the electoral districts included both Prussian and non-Prussian territory.

74. See chap. 7, below.

75. *SBPrLT 1928–1932*, 18 March 1932, vol. 17, cols. 24885–90. See also Höner, *Zugriff*, p. 222.

76. The foregoing analysis is based upon the statistical information contained in *Handbuch für den Preussischen Landtag 1932*, ed. E. Kienast (Berlin, 1932), pp. 388–95. See also Bracher *Auflösung*, p. 568; Milatz, *Wähler*, p. 140; and Möller, *Parlamentarismus*, pp. 241–43.

77. Hans Schlange-Schöningen, *Am Tage Danach* (Hamburg, 1946), p. 80.

78. Golo Mann, "Das Ende Preussens," in *Preussen: Portrait einer politischen Kultur*, ed. Hans-Joachim Netzer (Munich, 1968), p. 160.

Chapter 6. Prussia and the Depression: *Innenpolitik* During the Republic's Final Years, 1930–1933

1. The most detailed political history of the Weimar Republic's final years is still Karl Dietrich Bracher, *Die Auflösung der Weimarer Republik*, 5th ed. (Düsseldorf, 1978). See also Werner Conze, "Die Krise des Parteienstaates in Deutschland 1929/30," *Historische Zeitschrift* 178 (Aug. 1954), 47–48; Thilo Vogelsang, *Reichswehr, Staat und NSDAP*, (Stuttgart, 1962); Werner Conze and Hans Raupach, eds., *Die Staats- und Wirtschaftskrise 1929/33* (Stuttgart, 1967); Ilse Maurer and Udo Wengst, eds., *Staat und NSDAP 1930–32: Quellen zur Ära Brüning*, (Düsseldorf, 1977); Dieter Gessner, *Das Ende der Weimarer Republik: Fragen, Methoden und Ergebnisse interdisziplinärer Forschung* (Darmstadt, 1978); Karl Holl, ed., *Wirtschaftskrise und liberale Demokratie* (Göttingen, 1978); Karl-Dietrich Erdmann and Hagen Schulze, eds., *Selbstpreisgabe einer Demokratie: Eine Bilanz heute* (Düsseldorf, 1980); Gerhard Schulz, *Deutschland am Vorabend der Grossen Krise: Verfassungspolitik und Reichsreform in der Weimarer Republik* (Berlin, 1987); Ursula Büttner, "Politische Alternativen zum Brüningschen Deflationskurs," *Vierteljahrshefte für Zeitgeschichte* 37 (April 1989), 229–51.

2. Joseph Goebbels, *Die Tagebücher von Joseph Goebbels Teil I: Aufzeichnungen 1924–1941*, ed. Elke Fröhlich (Munich, 1987), 2:41 (31 March 1931).

3. Sabine Höner, *Der nationalsozialistische Zugriff auf Preussen* (Bochum, 1984), p. 254, stresses the long-range political consequences of the decree.

4. Braun, *Weimar*, pp. 131, 209; Braun, "Weimar-Ms.," pp. 388, 541; Carl Severing, *Mein Lebensweg* (Cologne, 1950), 2:42; and Theodor Heuss, *Erinnerungen 1905–1933* (Tübingen, 1963), p. 319. See also Horst Möller, *Parlamentarismus in Preussen 1919–1932* (Düsseldorf, 1985), p. 391.

5. Braun to Severing, 3 and 13 July 1925, Severing papers/01/10; Grzesinski to Braun, 3 May 1928, Grzesinski papers/204; Bruce B. Frye, *Liberal Democrats in the Weimar Republic—The History of the German Democratic Party and the German State Party* (Carbondale, Ill., 1985), p. 115.

6. See especially Weismann to Braun, 13 Oct. 1931, Braun papers/11/B–2/93 (ForHbg); *SBPrLT 1928–1932*, 17 March 1932, vol. 17, cols. 24741, 24749–50. Heinrich Brüning, *Memoiren 1918–1934* (Stuttgart, 1970), p. 176.

7. Braun, "Weimar-Ms.," p. 544. The prime minister did not include this passage in the published version of his memoirs. See *Weimar*, pp. 209–11. On Braun's health problems, see Hagen Schulze, *Otto Braun* (Berlin, 1977), pp. 709ff.

8. See Weismann to Braun, 23 Oct. 1931, Braun papers/11/B–2/93 (ForHbg). For

the DNVP's attacks on Klepper, see *SBPrLT 1925–1928*, 26 March 1928, vol. 17, col. 26082; *SBPrLT 1928–1932*, 18 Dec. 1928, vol. 2, cols. 1812–14, and 16 March 1932, vol. 17, col. 24597. See also Winfried Steffani, *Die Untersuchungsschüsse des Preussischen Landtages zur Zeit der Weimar Republik* (Düsseldorf, 1960), pp. 210–24; Möller, *Parlamentarismus*, p. 391.

9. Braun, "Weimar-Ms.," pp. 542–45; Brüning to Rudolf Olden, 28 Aug. 1935, in Heinrich Brüning, *Briefe und Gespräche 1934–1945*, ed. Claire Nix et al. (Stuttgart, 1974), p. 85; Prussian ministry of agriculture to ministry of finance and prime minister, 25 April 1932, PrGStAB Rep. 90/1367.

10. *SBPrLT 1928–1932*, 12 Dec. 1928 and 10 Dec. 1929, vol. 1, cols. 1383–88, vol. 7, col. 9222 (Höpker-Aschoff); minister of finance to members of the cabinet, 22 Oct. 1929, PrGStAB, Rep. 90a/26.

11. See the complaints by Höpker-Aschoff and the spokesmen for the coalition parties, *SBPrLT 1925–1928*, 8 Feb. 1926, vol. 6, cols. 8777ff.; *SBPrLT 1928–1932*, 22 April 1929, vol. 5, col. 6369. See also Braun, "Weimar-Ms.," pp. 408–10.

12. Pünder (state secretary in the Reich chancellery), "Betrifft: Kassenlage des Reiches," 22 April 1929, Müller papers/Kasette II/84.

13. See *SBPrLT 1925–1928*, 17 May 1927, vol. 10, cols. 20564–67 (Ladendorff); Pfeiffer (office of the prime minister), "Vermerk," 22 Oct. 1928, PrGStAB, Rep. 90a/20; Prussian Ministry of Finance to prime minister, 31 May 1930, PrGStAB, Rep. 90a/1367.

14. *SBPrLT 1928–1932*, 19 May 1930, 16 Dec. 1930, and 15 March 1932, vol. 10, col. 13945, vol. 12, cols. 16311–50, vol. 17, col. 24571; *PrGS*, no. 22 (11 July 1930), p. 195; SitzPrStMin, 5 Feb. 1932, PrGStAB, Rep. 90a/40; minister of finance to members of the cabinet, 17 May 1932, PrGStAB, Rep. 90/1367; Braun, "Weimar-Ms.," p. 541.

15. On the plight of the Prussian municipalities, see Helga Timm, *Die deutsche Sozialpolitik und der Bruch der Grossen Koalition im März 1930* (Düsseldorf, 1952), p. 163; Otto Büsch, *Geschichte der Berliner Kommunalwirtschaft in der Weimarer Epoche* (Berlin, 1960), pp. 157ff. For Brüning's praise of Prussia's handling of the crisis in the cities and the chancellor's criticism of the actions taken by Konrad Adenauer, the lord mayor of Cologne, see *Memoiren*, pp. 208, 214. For the state's law on foreign municipal credit, see *PrGS*, no. 19 (18 July 1925), p. 89. For a contemporary view "from below" of the financial problems facing the municipalities, see Hess to Herbst, 19 Dec. 1930, NSStAH/310/B/30. Hess was the head of the local government section of the SPD's district organization in Hanover; Herbst the district director of Lüneburg. Hess was describing the situation in Harburg, then a small industrial city just south of Hamburg.

16. Höpker-Aschoff, "Denkschrift über die Lage der Preussischen Finanzen," 18 Sept. 1931, Braun papers/476 (IISG); Bernhard Falk, "Aufzeichnungen" (typescript), Kleine Erwerbungen/385 (BA), p. 182; Timm, *Sozialpolitik*, pp. 121–23; Höner, *Zugriff*, p. 255.

17. SitzPrStMin, 14 July 1932, ZStAM, Rep. 90a B III 2b Nr. 6, Bd. 181. See also Möller, *Parlamentarismus*, p. 446.

18. *SBPrLT 1928–1932*, 19 May 1930, 11 Feb. and 16 March 1932, vol. 10, cols. 13906–07, vol. 17, cols. 23946ff., 24608. For an early and perceptive analysis of the

political dimensions of the crisis, see Stampfer to Müller, 4 Sept. 1929, Müller papers/178.

19. See SitzPrStMin, 21 June 1932, ZStAM, Rep. 90a, B III 2b Nr. 6, Bd. 181; Möller, *Parlamentarismus,* pp. 447–48.

20. See SitzPrStMin, 5 Nov. 1929, ZStAM, Rep. 90a, B III 2b Nr. 6, Bd. 178; Reich minister of finance to state secretary of the Reich chancellery, 3 Feb. 1930, Müller papers/254; *SPD Parteitag 1925,* p. 302; SitzPrStMin, 8 Oct. 1931, PrGStAB, Rep. 90a/39.

21. The Reich minister of finance argued along these lines as early as February 1930. See Moldenhauer to state secretary of the Reich chancellery, 25 Feb. 1930, Müller papers/268; Höpker-Aschoff to members of the Prussian cabinet, 8 March 1930, PrGStAB, Rep. 90/1667.

22. SitzPrStMin, 9 May, 16 Sept. 1930, and 7 June 1932, PrGStAB, Rep. 90a/32, 33, 40.

23. For consideration of tax matters in the Landtag and the cabinet, see for example, *SBPrLT 1928–1932,* 19 and 23 May, 7 and 13 Nov. 1930, and 4 March 1931, vol. 10, cols. 13912–13, 14413–30, vol. 11, cols. 15636–38, 15907–18, vol. 13, cols. 18648–53; and SitzPrStMin, 7 June 1932, PrGStAB, Rep. 90a/40. For the cabinet's invoking of its decree powers, see SitzPrStMin, 24 Feb. 1931, PrGStAB, Rep. 90a/37.

24. SitzPrStMin, 12 Nov. 1930, and 10 March 1931, PrGStAB, Rep. 90a/35, 38; marginalia in SitzPrStMin, 29 April 1932, ZStAM, Rep. 90a/B III 2b Nr. 6, Bd. 181.

25. *SBPrLT 1928–1932,* 25 Feb. and 13 Nov. 1930, vol. 8, col. 11435 (Abegg), vol. 11, cols. 15811–13; SitzPrStMin, 7 June 1932, PrGStAB, Rep. 90a/40.

26. See the contemporary analysis of Germany's economic problems by the Prussian minister of commerce, *SBPrLT 1928–1932,* 11 March 1930, vol. 9, cols. 11825–26. See also Michael Schneider, *Das Arbeitsbeschaffungsprogramm des ADGB* (Bonn–Bad Godesberg, 1975), p. 168. The best analysis of the historiographic debate on ways of coping with the Depression is Büttner, "Alternativen."

27. The best analyses of the problems of German agriculture during the Weimar years are two works by Dieter Gessner, *Agrarverbände in der Weimarer Republik* (Düsseldorf, 1976) and *Agrardepression, Agrarideologie und konservative Politik in der Weimarer Republik* (Wiesbaden, 1976). See also Grzesinski to prime minister et al., 23 June 1927, PrGStAB, Rep. 90/237.

28. Gessner, *Agrarverbände,* pp. 115ff.; Arno Panzer, *Das Ringen um die deutsche Agrarpolitik von der Währungsstabilisierung bis zur Agrardebatte im Reichstag im Dezember 1928* (Kiel, 1970), pp. 77, 129–30. For a contemporary report on farmers' protests and the Nazis' role in these activities in East Prussia, see *Oberpräsident* of East Prussia to ministry of the interior, 21 Jan. 1930, ZStAP, RMdI Nr. 25730, Bl. 84–87.

29. See Heinrich August Winkler, *Mittelstand, Demokratie und Nationalsozialismus* (Cologne, 1972). For a perceptive, early analysis of the political radicalization process among the *Mittelstand,* see Goslar (chief of the Prussian press office) to Stegermann, 15 Feb. 1929, PrGStAB, Rep. 90/2415.

30. The Ruhr strike is discussed in this section, below. On the rationalization of German industry in the 1920s, see Bernd Weisbrod, *Schwerindustrie in der Weimarer*

Republik (Wuppertal, 1978); and the classic study, Robert Brady, *The Rationalization Movement in German Industry* (Berkeley, Calif., 1933). On the Ruhr conflict, see also Ernst Fraenkel, "Ruhreisenstreit," in *Staat, Wirtschaft und Politik in der Weimarer Republik—Festschrift für Heinrich Brüning,* ed. Ferdinand A. Hermens and Theodor Schieder (Berlin, 1967), pp. 108–10; Weisbrod, *Schwerindustrie,* pp. 393–457; Timm, *Sozialpolitik,* pp. 99–104.

31. Schneider, *ADGB,* pp. 33, 43, 118, 130–31; Braun, "Weimar-Ms.," p. 496; Richard N. Hunt, *German Social Democracy 1918–1933* (New Haven, Conn., 1964), p. 35; Hermann Höpker-Aschoff, *Geld und Währungen* (Stuttgart, 1948), pp. 105–06.

32. Quoted in Schneider, *ADGB,* p. 95.

33. Ernst Heilmann, "Internationale Planwirtschaft," *Das Freie Wort* 3 (23 Aug. 1931), 1. See also Heilmann, "Die Krise—nach einem Jahr," ibid. 3 (20 Sept. 1931), 1–6; *PrGS,* no. 35 (7 Nov. 1930), 280.

34. Schneider, *ADGB,* pp. 194–95, 199–201; Hans-Joachim Winkler, *Preussen als Unternehmer 1923–1932* (Berlin, 1965). See also Hans Staudinger, *Wirtschafts- politik im Weimarer Staat: Lebenserinnerungen eines Politischen Beamten im Reich und in Preussen 1898–1934,* ed. Hagen Schulze (Bonn, 1982). Until he was dismissed by Papen, Staudinger was state secretary in the Prussian Ministry of Commerce.

35. Ursula Büttner, *Hamburg in der Staats- und Wirtschaftskrise 1928–1931* (Hamburg, 1982), pp. 310–12. On the relations between unemployment and politics during the crisis years, see also Helmut Marcon, *Arbeitsbeschaffungspolitik der Re- gierungen Papen und Schleicher* (Frankfurt a.M., 1974); and Peter D. Stachura, *Unemployment and the Great Depression in Weimar Germany* (New York, 1986).

36. Brüning, *Memoiren,* p. 225.

37. See Braun, "Weimar-Ms.," pp. 492–96; Braun to Brüning, 30 April 1932, Braun papers/563 (IISG); SitzPrStMin, 29 April 1932, PrGStAB, Rep. 90a/40. On the Society for Public Works and the WTB Program, see Schneider *ADGB,* pp. 97ff., 123–25, 186ff., 225–34; and Büttner, *Hamburg,* pp. 282ff. See also Brüning, *Memoiren,* p. 198.

38. On the 1928 lockout, see Weisbrod, *Schwerindustrie,* pp. 420ff.; Henry A. Turner, "The *Ruhrlade," Central European History* 3 (Sept. 1970), 201.

39. SitzPrStMin, 6 Nov. 1928, PrGStAB, Rep. 90a/21; *SBPrLT 1928–1932,* 6–7 Nov. 1928, vol. 1, cols. 942ff.

40. *SBPrLT 1928–1932,* 14 Oct. 1931, vol. 16, col. 22089.

41. See *SBPrLT 1928–1932,* 30 Jan. 1931, vol. 12, cols. 17168–69.

42. Pünder to Müller, 10 Sept. 1929, Müller papers/33.

43. SitzPrStMin, 18 June and 10 July 1929, ZStAM, Rep. 90a III 2b Nr. 6, Bd. 178.

44. SitzPrStMin, 29 April 1932, PrGStAB, Rep. 90a/40; Brüning, *Memoiren,* pp. 214–15; and Wilhelm Keil, *Erlebnisse eines Sozialdemokraten* (Stuttgart, 1947–48), 2:440. For an example of a concrete and far-reaching proposal by an individual minister to reduce unemployment, see Prussian minister of commerce to members of the cabinet, 16 Oct. 1930, PrGStAB, Rep. 90a/34.

45. See Baade to Müller, 4 Jan. 1930, Müller papers/173; Panzer, *Ringen,* pp. 38ff., 137; Michael Stürmer, *Koalition und Opposition in der Weimarer Republik 1924–1928* (Düsseldorf, 1967), pp. 219–24.

46. SitzPrStMin, 15 April 1926, 8 Nov. 1927, and 9 Dec. 1929, PrGStAB, Rep. 90a/7, 15, and ZStAM, Rep. 90a B III 2b Nr. 6, Bd. 178; *SBPrLT 1925–1928*, 13 and 15 June 1926, vol. 2, cols. 2244, 2307ff.; *SPD-Parteitag 1925*, p. 221. See also Gessner, *Agrarverbände*, p. 215; Panzer, *Ringen*, pp. 45–47, 74–75; Hermann Höpker-Aschoff, *Unser Weg durch die Zeit* (Berlin, 1936), pp. 221–22.

47. Nobis, "Notiz," 18 June 1925, PrGStAB, Rep. 90/109. See also Panzer, *Ringen*, pp. 83, 87; Stürmer, *Koalition*, p. 101; *Berliner Tageblatt*, 20 June 1925.

48. *SBPrLT 1928–1932*, 19 Feb. 1930, vol. 8, col. 10922 (Braun); Timm, *Sozialpolitik*, pp. 167, 167, n. 301; Gessner, *Agrarverbände*, pp. 138–39, 144–45.

49. Otto Siehr, "Das neue Ostpreussenprogramm, 16 Feb. 1926, PrGStAB, Rep. 90/1068ff.; Weichmann, "Vermerk," 22 Oct. 1928, PrGStAB, Rep. 90a/20; SitzPrStMin, 11 Feb. 1930, Rep. 90a/30; *SBPrLT 1928–1932*, 21 Oct. 1930, vol. 11, col. 15320.

50. Von Zitzewitz und von Knebel, "Vorschläge für eine anderweitige Gestaltung der Osthilfe," (n.d.) [Fall 1930], ZStAM, Rep. 90a D II 1 Nr. 53. See also Gessner, *Agrarverbände*, pp. 201ff.; Friedrich Martin Fiederlein, "Der deutsche Osten und die Regierungen Brüning, Papen, Schleicher," Ph.D. diss., University of Würzburg, 1966, pp. 154ff., 206.

51. Gessner, *Agrarverbände*, pp. 94–95; Fiederlein, "Osten," pp. 324–25 424ff.

52. *SBPrLT 1928–1932*, 28 Jan. 1931, vol. 12, cols. 16813–26; Panzer, *Ringen*, p. 144.

53. Gerhard Schulz, "Staatliche Stützungsmassnahmen in den Ostgebieten," in *Staat*, ed. Hermens et al., pp. 167–70; SitzPrStMin, 27 Sept. 1926, PrGStAB, Rep. 90a/9; Gessner, *Agrarverbände*, pp. 216–17; Widder, "Reich," pp. 71ff. See also von Zitzewitz, "Vorschläge," p. 11.

54. On the 1927 disagreements, see minister of the interior, "Denkschrift," 7 July 1927, PrGStAB, Rep. 90a/15; Strunden, "Vermerk," 2 Nov. 1927, ibid.; SitzPrStMin, 25 Oct., 29 Nov. 1927, ibid., 14–15. On the meeting with Hindenburg, see "Niederschrift der Ministerbesprechung," 21 Dec. 1927, Braun papers/11/B–2/69 (ForHbg). See also Schulz, "Ostgebiete," pp. 141–204; Panzer, *Ringen*, p. 116; Hans-Peter Ehni, *Bollwerk Preussen: Preussen Regierung, Reich-Länderproblem und Sozialdemokratie, 1928–1932* (Bonn–Bad Godesberg, 1975), pp. 65–66.

55. For Klepper's, the farmers' lobbies', and the Prussian cabinet's positions, see minister of agriculture to members of the cabinet, 15 Feb. 1928, PrGStAB Rep. 90/2302; documentation ibid., 1073; Prussian minister of agriculture to members of the cabinet, 20 Jan. 1930, PrGStAB Rep. 90a/29; *SBPrLT 1928–1932*, 14 Dec. 1928, vol. 2, col. 1559 (Braun); Höpker-Aschoff, *Weg*, pp. 221–22. See also Gessner, *Agrarverbände*, pp. 225, 231. Karl von Plehwe, "Ostpreussenhilfe" (Braun papers, clippings file [IISG]); Panzer, *Ringen*, pp. 131–32, 149, are sharply critical of the head of the Preussenkasse. Among the secondary accounts, Panzer's book provides the most vigorous defense of the East Elbian farmers' points of view.

56. See the debate in *SBPrLT 1928–1932*, 11 July 1929, vol. 6, cols. 8255–56, 8260–62, 8275–78; see also minister of agriculture to prime minister, 14 Feb. 1930, and Braun's marginalia on this document, PrGStAB Rep. 90/1076; Gessner, *Agrarverbände*, pp. 248–49.

57. Brüning, *Memoiren,* pp. 172–73; Fiederlein, "Osten," pp. 3, 38–46, 253ff.; Gessner, *Agrarverbände,* pp. 106–08, 155–56, 198–99, 220–21.

58. On Brüning's and Treviranus's agreement with Prussia's policies, see Krüger (state secretary in the Prussian Ministry of Agriculture) to prime minister, 15 Jan. 1931, Braun papers/332 (IISG); Treviranus to state secretary in the Reich chancellery, 12 June 1931, Braun papers/11/B-2/69 (ForHbg); documentation in PrGStAB Rep. 90/1667. For Hindenburg's support of the Junker position, see the president's letter to Brüning, 13 May 1931, Braun papers/11/B-2/2 (ForHbg). See also Gessner, *Agrarverbände,* pp. 217–18; Hans-Peter Ehni, *Bollwerk,* p. 73.

59. SitzPrStMin, 3 and 26 March 1931, ZStAM, Rep. 90a B III 2b Nr. 6, Bd. 180; PrGStAB Rep. 90a/38; Brüning, *Memoiren,* p. 215. For the chancellor's later bitter criticism of Prussia's *Osthilfe* administration, see also Brüning to Sollmann, 29 Sept. 1940, in Thomas A. Knapp, ed., "Heinrich Brüning im Exil: Briefe an Wilhelm Sollmann 1940–1946," *Vierteljahrshefte für Zeitgeschichte* 22 (Jan. 1974), 108–09.

60. Fiederlein, "Osten," pp. 212ff., 312–13. See also Heinrich Muth, "Agrarpolitik und Parteipolitik im Frühjahr 1932," in *Staat,* ed. Hermens and Schieder, p. 326.

61. The wasted funds became something of a cause célèbre which the Nazis later used to attack the Papen government. See Rudolf Morsey, *Der Untergang des politischen Katholizismus: die Zentrumspartei zwischen christlichem Selbstverständnis und "Nationaler Erhebung" 1932/33* (Stuttgart, 1977), p. 82; Fiederlein, "Osten," pp. 344ff., 434 ff.; Albert Grzesinski, "Reichskanzler Dr. Brünings Sturz," in "Eine politische Artikelserie" (typescript), Grzesinski papers/2456, p. 5.

62. SitzPrStMin, 3 March 1931, PrGStAB, Rep. 90a/38; Freiherr von Wilmovsky to Bracht, 14 Jan. 1933, Bracht papers/2 (ZStAP); Gessner, *Agrarverbände,* p. 197.

63. *SBPrLT 1928–1932,* 4 Feb. 1929, vol. 3, col. 2916.

64. SitzPrStMin, 25 March, 8 April, and 17 May 1930, ZStAM, Rep. 90a B III 2b Nr. 6, Bd. 179. See also Horst Möller, "Die preussischen Oberpräsidenten der Weimarer Republik als Verwaltungselite," *Vierteljahrshefte für Zeitgeschichte* 30 (Jan. 1982), 1–26.

65. SitzPrStMin, 16, 21, and 25 June 1930, Rep. 90/477–478 (PrGStAB); Grzesinski, "Kampf-Ms.," p. 241; documentation in PrGStAB, Rep. 90/477–78; Gerhard Schulz, "Staatsschutz und Nationalsozialismus in der Ära Brüning," in *Staat,* ed. Maurer and Wengst, pp. xxiii–xxviii, and doc. 3, p. 6. See also Möller, *Parlamentarismus,* p. 318; Höner, *Zugriff,* pp. 36ff., 61. For the verdict of the state court, see Staatsgerichtshof, "Urteil," 27 April 1931, Rep. 90/477 (PrGStAB).

66. *SBPrLT 1928–1932,* 23 May 1930, vol. 10, cols. 14346–47; and the documentation in Schulz, "Staatsschutz," p. xxxii, n. 45.

67. See documentation in Grzesinski papers/743.

68. Waentig to Braun, 14 June 1930, Braun papers/11/B-2/49 (ForHbg); Höner, *Zugriff,* pp. 57ff.; Schulz, "Staatsschutz," pp. xxiv–xxv. For a comprehensive (and pessimistic) report on the Nazi infiltration of the territorial administration, see district director of Lüneburg to Ministry of the Interior, 7 Nov. 1931, PrGStAB, Rep. 90/478.

69. For the effects of the budget cuts on teachers' salaries, see Rainer Bölling,

Volksschullehrer und Politik: Der Deutsche Lehrerverein 1918–1933 (Göttingen, 1978), pp. 200–03.

70. SitzPrStMin, 16 Oct. 1930, 18 Aug. and 2 Sept. 1931, PrGStAB, Rep. 90a/34, 39. For an account of the dramatic meeting with the Landtag leaders that confirmed Höpker-Aschoff in his decision to resign, see Weismann to Braun, 13 Oct. 1931, Braun papers/11/B-2/93 (ForHbg). See also Möller, *Parlamentarismus*, p. 447.

71. *SBPrLT 1928–1932*, 19 Feb. 1930, vol. 8, col. 10924.

72. Ibid., 17 March 1931, vol. 13, col. 18818; Braun, "Weimar-Ms.," p. 374; "Hamburger Interview," 8 July 1976.

73. See [Ministry of Education], "Zur Frage der Anstellung dissidentischer Schulamtsbewerber" [1931], Braun papers/528 (IISG); Lauscher to Grimme, 17 Dec. 1931, Trendelenburg papers/10; documentation in Grimme papers/56/9, 61/17.

74. SitzPrStMin 29 April 1932, PrGStAB, Rep. 90a/40.

75. *SBPrLT 1932–1933*, 15 June 1932, vol. 1, col. 372 (Schmidt, minister of justice). See also the documentation in PrGStAB, Rep. 84a/11770. On the Social Democratic praise for the judiciary see "Ratgeber für Wahlredner," *Das Freie Wort* 4 (28 Feb. 1932), 8–12.

76. Heinrich Brüning, "Ein Brief," *Deutsche Rundschau* 70 (July 1947), 2.

77. On the change of ministers in the fall of 1930, see Grzesinski, "Notiz," 17, 20, and 21 Oct. 1930, Grzesinski papers/2017; Braun, *Weimar*, p. 182; Braun, "Weimar-Ms.," p. 486. For the Nazis' view of the minister, see Goebbels, *Tagebücher*, p. 297 (30 Nov. 1928).

78. Brüning to Sollmann, 29 Sept. 1940, quoted in Knapp, ed., "Brüning," p. 108; Schulz, "Staatsschutz," p. xxiii; Höner, *Zugriff*, p. 70.

79. Abegg to Severing, 31 May 1947, Severing papers/60/12. After Papen's July 1932 coup, federal authorities blamed Abegg for Severing's unwillingness to move forcefully against the Communists. Prussian cabinet, "Anlageheft zu der Gegenerklärung der Reichsregierung," 5 Aug. 1932 (hereafter: "Anlageheft ReiReg. 5.8.32"), pp. 21, 270, Braun papers/11/B-4/54 (ForHbg).

80. Albert Grzesinski, "Im Kampf um die deutsche Republik," p. 237, Grzesinski papers/2457; Grzesinski to Braun, 4 Nov. 1930, Grzesinski papers/2017. For criticism of Grzesinski's performance as police chief from the extreme right, see Prussian cabinet, "Anlageheft zu der Erwiderung der Reichsregierung," 25 Aug. 1932 (hereafter: "Anlageheft ReiReg. 25.8.32"), pp. 11–21, Braun papers/11/B-4/54 (ForHbg); Joseph Goebbels, *Vom Kaiserhof zur Reichskanzlei*, 28th ed., (Berlin, 1940), p. 22 (9 Jan. 1932).

81. For the Nazis' reaction, see Goebbels, *Kaiserhof*, p. 44 (10 Feb. 1932).

82. See Höner, *Zugriff*, pp. 9, 72ff.

83. Schulz, "Staatsschutz," p. xlvii, n. 81; Höner, *Zugriff*, p. 66.

84. See Quaatz to Brüning, 17 Sept. 1931, ZStAP, 1501/25705; Karl Rohe, *Das Reichsbanner Schwarz-Rot-Gold* (Düsseldorf, 1966), pp. 371–78.

85. The memorandum was first published by Robert M. W. Kempner in an English translation, "Blueprint of the Nazi Underground—Past and Future Subversive Activities," *Research Studies of the State College of Washington* 13 (1945), 51–153. In 1930 Kempner was a junior official in the Prussian Ministry of the Interior; he later became one of the prosecuting attorneys at the Nuremberg International Military

Tribunal. The original version is now available in *Staat*, ed. Maurer and Wengst, doc. 13, pp. 96–155, and *Der Verpasste Nazi-Stop: Die NSDAP als staats- und republik-feindliche hochverräterische Verbindung*, ed. Robert Kempner (Frankfurt, 1983). See also *Staat*, ed. Maurer and Wengst, doc. 7, p. 64.

86. PrGStAB, Rep. 84a/3157/1.

87. Goebbels, *Tagebücher* 2:51 (18 April 1931).

88. See *Staat*, ed. Maurer, p. 199, n. 2; E [rnst] H [eilmann], "Sieg durch Fehler," and Wengst, *Das Freie Wort* 3 (22 Feb. 1931), 1; Prussian ministry of the interior to Reich ministry of the Interior, 9 April 1931, in *Staat*, ed. Maurer and Wengst, doc. 30, pp. 192–93.

89. Richard Breitman, *German Socialism and Weimar Democracy* (Chapel Hill, N.C. 1981), pp. 176–78; Maurer and Wengst, eds., *Staat*, pp. 266–68; Schulz, "Staatsschutz," ibid., p. liv; Arnold Brecht, *Vorspiel zum Schweigen—Das Ende der Deutschen Republik* (Vienna, 1948), pp. 178–79; Goebbels, *Kaiserhof*, pp. 4, 34, 40, 59–60, 90 (entries for 30 Jan., 4 Feb., 11 March, 4 and 29 April 1932).

90. Kempner, ed., *Verpasster Nazi-Stop*, p. 10. See also Schulz, "Staatsschutz," pp. xxxix–xl.

91. For a detailed analysis of the Reichswehr trial, see Peter Bucher, *Der Reichswehrprozess—Der Hochverrat der Ulmer Reichswehroffiziere 1929/1930* (Boppard a.Rh., 1967).

92. See "Die Nationalsozialistische Deutsche Arbeiterpartei . . . ," ca. May 1930, PrGStAB, Rep. 90/477.

93. Höner, *Zugriff*, p. 36. See also Schulz, "Staatsschutz," p. lxix.

94. James M. Diehl, *Paramilitary Politics in Weimar Germany* (Bloomington, Ind., 1977); Volker R. Berghahn, *Der Stahlhelm* (Düsseldorf, 1966); Schulz, "Staatsschutz," pp. xlvi–xlvii. On the Stahlhelm's involvement in political clashes, see Severing to Reich ministry of the interior, 14 Jan. 1932, ZStAP, 1501/25706.

95. Braun, "Weimar-Ms.," pp. 472–75; Schulz, "Staatsschutz," p. xli; and *Staat*, ed. Maurer and Wengst, doc. 22a, pp. 175, 175–76, n. 3; Brüning, *Memoiren*, p.177; Ehni, *Bollwerk*, p. 159.

96. See the documentation in ZStAP, Rep. 30.01/22074; "Anlageheft ReiReg. 5.8.32," pp. 21, 27; Höner, *Zugriff*, pp. 194–95. On the RFB's verbal grandstanding, much of which was a form on self-deception, see Hermann Weber, *Die Wandlung des deutschen Kommunismus: Die Stalinisierung der KPD in der Weimarer Republik* (Frankfurt a.M., 1969); Eve Rosenhaft, *Beating the Fascists? The German Communists and Political Violence, 1929–1933* (Cambridge, Mass., 1983).

97. Hans Peter Bleuel and Ernst Klinnert, *Deutsche Studenten auf dem Weg ins Dritte Reich—Ideologie—Programme—Aktionen, 1918–1935* (Gütersloh, 1967), p. 192; Schulz, "Staatsschutz," p. xxxii.

98. See the documentation in ZStAP, 15.01/25705, 25706; ZStAM, Rep. 120 C B I Nr. 8a, Bd. 3; SitzPrStMin, 30 June 1931, Rep. 90a/39 (PrGStAB); Grzesinski to Braun, 26 May 1931, Grzesinski papers/204. See also Möller, *Parlamentarismus*, p. 321; Henry A. Turner, Jr., *German Big Business and the Rise of Hitler* (New York, 1985), p. 169.

99. Georg Decker, "Nach einem Jahr," *Die Gesellschaft* 8 (Oct. 1931), 292–97; Möller, *Parlamentarismus*, pp. 320–22.

100. Maurer and Wengst, eds., *Staat*, pp. 283, 299–300, n. 6; Rohe, *Reichsbanner*, p. 420; *Blätter des Deutschland-Bundes* 2 (18 April 1932).

101. Brüning, "Brief," p. 4; Maurer and Wengst, eds., *Staat*, pp. 301, n. 2, 305–08. See also Goebbels, *Kaiserhof*, p. 71 (27 March 1932); Ehni, *Bollwerk*, p. 241.

102. See documentation in ZStAP, 15.01/25901; Maurer and Wengst, eds., *Staat*, pp. 279ff. See also Schulz, "Staatsschutz," pp. lviff.

103. Maurer and Wengst, eds., *Staat*, p. 319. See also Goebbels, *Kaiserhof*, pp. 79–80 (11 April 1932). For the implementation of the decree in Prussia, see documentation in ZStAP, Rep. 15.01/25900. For a left-wing analysis of the Nazis' infiltration of local government offices, see Florian Geyer, "Kampf um Preussen," *Neue Blätter für den Sozialismus* 3 (May, 1932), 225–32.

104. See his article, "Ein Staat im Staat," *Blätter des Deutschlandbundes* 2 (18 April 1932), 1 (special edition).

105. Hans Schlange-Schönigen, *Am Tage Danach* (Hamburg, 1946), p. 75; documentation in ZStAP, 15.01/25730, 30.01/22074. See also Erbe to Dingeldey, 9 April 1932, in *Staat*, ed. Maurer and Wengst, pp. 310–11; Jürgen Bay, "Der Preussenkonflikt 1932/33: Ein Kapitel aus der Verfassungsgeschichte der Weimarer Republik," Ph.D. diss., University of Erlangen, 1965, p. 127.

106. Brüning to Sollmann, 20 Sept. 1940.

107. Höner, *Zugriff*, p. 212; Gordon A. Craig, "Prussianism and Democracy: Otto Braun and Konrad Adenauer," in *The End of Prussia*, ed. Craig, (Madison, Wis., 1984), p. 87.

Chapter 7. Prussian Coalition Politics and the Regime of the Presidential Chancellors, 1930–1933

1. Magnus Freiherr von Braun, *Von Ostpreussen bis Texas* (Stollhamm, Oldenburg, 1955), pp. 212, 250; Werner Conze, "Die Krise des Parteienstaates in Deutschland 1929/30," *Historische Zeitschrift* 178 (Aug. 1954), 79–80.

2. Heinrich Brüning, *Memoiren* (Stuttgart, 1970); Brüning to Hans Peters, 17 Oct. 1947, and to Josef Bollig, 30 Jan. 1953, in Heinrich Brüning, *Briefe und Gespräche 1934–1945*, ed. Claire Nix (Stuttgart, 1974), pp. 98, 482–83; Rudolf Morsey, *Zur Entstehung, Authenzität und Kritik von Brünings "Memoiren 1918–1934"* (Cologne, 1975), p. 35; Rudolf Morsey, *Der Untergang des politischen Katholizismus—die Zentrumspartei zwischen christlichem Selbstverständnis und "Nationaler Erhebung" 1932/33* (Stuttgart, 1977), pp. 24, 51; Josef Becker, "Brüning, Prälat Kaas und das Problem einer Regierungsbeteiligung der NSDAP, 1930–1932," *Historische Zeitschrift* 196 (Feb. 1963), 86; Sabine Höner, *Der nationalsozialistische Zugriff auf Preussen* (Bochum, 1984), pp. 138–39.

3. Brüning, *Memoiren*, pp. 178–80; Brüning to Sollmann, 29 Sept. 1940, in Thomas A. Knapp, ed., "Heinrich Brüning im Exil: Briefe an Wilhelm Sollmann 1940–1946," *Vierteljahrshefte für Zeitgeschichte* 22 (Jan. 1974), 109; Conze, "Krise," pp. 79–80; Friedrich Martin Fiederlein, "Der deutsche Osten und die Regierungen Brüning, Papen, Schleicher," Ph.D. diss., University of Würzburg, 1966, p. 394; Ernest Hamburger, "Betrachtungen über Heinrich Brünings Memoiren," *Inter-*

nationale Wissenschaftliche Korrespondenz, no. 15 (April, 1972), 28; Rudolf Morsey, "Neue Quellen zur Vorgeschichte der Reichskanzlerschaft Brünings," in *Staat, Wirtschaft und Politik in der Weimarer Republik—Festschrift für Heinrich Brüning,* ed. Ferdinand A. Hermens and Theodor Schieder (Berlin, 1967), pp. 213–15.

4. Brüning, *Memoiren,* pp. 179–80. See also Horst Möller, *Parlamentarismus in Preussen 1919–1932* (Düsseldorf, 1985), p. 589.

5. Morsey, *Untergang,* p. 21; Erwin Widder, "Reich und Preussen vom Regierungsantritt Brünings bis zum Reichsstatthaltergesetz Hitlers," Ph.D. diss., University of Frankfurt a.M., 1959, pp. 44, 49; Braun, *Weimar,* pp. 166, 245; Braun, "Weimar-Ms.," pp. 464, 599; Herbert Weichmann, "Reply," in ed. Knapp, "Brüning," p. 460.

6. Grzesinski, "La Tragi-Comédie de la République allemande," cited in Becker, "Kaas," p. 74; Paul Crohn, "Vertrauen vertan," *Das Freie Wort* 2 (9 Feb. 1930), 31–32; E[rnst] H[eilmann], "Die Tatsachen," ibid. (31 Aug. 1930), 3. See also Sitz-PrStMin., 8 April 1930, ZStAM, Rep. 90a, B III, 2b Nr. 6, Bd. 179; Richard Breitman, *German Socialism and Weimar Democracy* (Chapel Hill, N.C., 1981), p. 165; Ludwig Quessel, "Die neue Lage im Reich," *Sozialistische Monatshefte* 70 (14 April 1930), 315–20; Eberhard Kolb, "Die sozialdemokratische Strategie in der Ära des Präsidialkabinetts Brüning—Strategie ohne Alternative?" in *Das Unrechtsregime,* ed. Ursula Büttner (Hamburg, 1986), 1:157–76; Hans-Peter Ehni, *Bollwerk Preussen: Preussen Regierung, Reich-Länderproblem und Sozialdemokratie, 1928–1932* (Bonn–Bad Godesberg, 1975), p. 182.

7. *SBPrLT 1928–1932,* 8 May 1930, vol. 10, col. 13716 (Grebe); Höner, *Zugriff,* p. 147; Fiederlein, "Osten," p. 207. For criticism of the Prussian Center party's stand, see Franz von Papen, *Der Wahrheit eine Gasse* (Munich, 1952), p. 131; Georg Schreiber, ed., *Zentrum und Reichspolitik—Ein politisches Handbuch in Frage und Antwort* (Cologne, 1930), pp. 35–36, 167–69.

8. *DNVP- Mitteilungen,* no. 16 (18 July 1930), 4; Braun, "Weimar-Ms.," 480; E[rnst] H[eilmann], "Im Wirwarr," *Das Freie Wort* 2 (16 March 1930), 1–6.

9. Joseph Goebbels, *Die Tagebücher von Joseph Goebbels Teil I: Aufzeichnungen 1924–1941,* ed. Elke Fröhlich (Munich, 1987), 1:140, 161, 271, 293 (6 Nov. 1925, 15 Feb. 1926, 1 Oct., and 22 Nov. 1928).

10. For Kube's analysis of Prussia's political situation, see *SBPrLT 1928—1932,* 9 May and 14 Oct. 1930, vol. 10, cols. 13790–94, vol. 11, col. 14847. Cf. also Höner, *Zugriff,* pp. 141ff.

11. For a typical Communist attack on the "social fascists," see *SBPrLT 1928–1932,* 31 March 1930, vol. 9, col. 13041 (Ausländer).

12. For Braun's later criticism of Brüning's decision, see his letter to Rudolf Pechel (editor of the *Deutsche Rundschau),* 25 May 1948, Braun papers/Teil 2/C/III/7 (PrGStAB). For Brüning's own justification of the decision, see *Memoiren,* pp. 181ff. On the Center party's complaints about the SPD's campaign attacks, see Hess to Braun, 20 July 1930, Braun papers/241 (IISG). For Braun's and Hess's expectations of continuing cooperation, see their statements, *SBPrLT 1928–1932,* 15 and 16 Oct. 1930, vol. 11, cols. 14937–40, 15013–15.

13. E[rnst] H[eilmann], "Im Sturm der Ereignisse," *Das Freie Wort* 2 (19 Oct.

42.21930), 3; Goebbels, *Tagebücher* 1:606–07 (23 Sept. 1930). See also the DNVP's arguments for introducing a resolution of no confidence against Severing, *SBPrLT 1928–1932*, 4 Nov. 1930, vol. 11, col. 15374.

14. On this episode, see Braun, "Weimar-Ms.," p. 484; Becker, "Kaas," p. 78; Reinhard Neebe, *Grossindustrie, Staat und NSDAP 1930–1933* (Göttingen, 1981), p. 77; Knapp, "Brüning," p. 107; Breitman, *German,* p. 167.

15. See, E[rnst] H[eilmann], "Freiheit der Entscheidung," *Das Freie Wort* 3 (15 March 1931), 4; Braun, "Weimar-Ms.," pp. 483–84; Breitman, *German,* p. 167; *SBPrLT 1928–1932*, 16 Oct. 1930, vol. 11, col. 15050; Michael Schneider, *Das Arbeitsbeschaffungsprogramm des ADGB* (Bonn–Bad Godesberg, 1975), p. 137. For a good summary of the arguments used by the opponents of the "policy of toleration," see Kolb, "Strategie," pp. 161ff.

16. For an assessment of Prussia's political weakness as well as Brüning's attitude toward the SPD, see Grzesinski to Braun, 26 Jan. 1931, O. Braun papers/204 (IISG); Brüning to Sollmann, 29 Sept. 1940, in Knapp, "Brüning," p. 110; Brüning to Treviranus, 17 Sept. 1945, in Brüning, *Briefe,* p. 436; and Johann Victor Bredt, *Erinnerungen und Dokumente, 1914 bis 1933,* ed. Martin Schumacher (Düsseldorf, 1970), p. 230; Becker, "Kaas," p. 81; Höner, *Zugriff,* p. 153. For Grzesinski's objections, see Albert Grzesinski, "Im Kampf um die deutsche Republik—Lebensweg eines Staatenlosen," Grzesinski papers/2457 (IISG), p. 186.

17. Höner, *Zugriff,* p. 194; Becker, "Kaas," pp. 79–80.

18. DVP-ZV, 4 July 1930, pp. Z–69, Z–121, Z–153–54 [*sic*]; Januschau, letter of April 1931, cited in Fiederlein, "Osten," pp. 393–94; Meissner's memorandum of a meeting between Hugenberg and Hindenburg, 1 August 1931, cited in Friedrich Freiherr Hiller von Gaertringen, "Die Deutschnationale Volkspartei," in *Das Ende der Parteien 1933,* ed. Erich Matthias and Rudolf Morsey (Düsseldorf, 1960), p. 624; *SBPrLT 1928–1932*, 4 May 1931, vol. 14, col. 20032 (Oelze).

19. Goebbels, *Tagebücher,* 2:14, 30, 41, 53, 67 (30 Jan., 6 Mar., 21 April, and 20 May 1931); *SBPrLT 1928–1932*, 17 Oct. 1932, vol. 11, col. 15092 (Haake); Höner, *Zugriff,* p. 167; and Becker, "Kaas," p. 82.

20. *SBPrLT 1928–1932*, 16 Oct. 1930, vol. 11, cols. 15012–14 (Hess); Bernhard Falk, "Aufzeichnungen" (typescript), Kleine Erwerbungen/385 (BA), pp. 208–09; Morsey, *Untergang,* p. 24; Georg Schreiber, *Brüning und Hitler-Schleicher—Das Zentrum in der Opposition* (Cologne, 1932), pp. 189–90; Illo [i.e., Ernst Heilmann], "Was ist Marxismus?" *Das Freie Wort* 2 (16 Nov. 1930), 1–5; and Grimme to Wende, 22 Oct. 1958 in Adolf Grimme, *Briefe,* ed. Dieter Sauberzweig (Heidelberg, 1967), p. 247.

21. *SBPrLT 1928–1932*, 14 and 15 Oct. 1930, vol. 11, cols. 14869 (Keukel), 14962–67 (Borck). See also "Notizen," *Das Freie Wort* 2 (30 Nov. 1930), 30.

22. On the opposition parties' calculations, see *SBPrLT 1928–1932*, 15 Oct. 1930, vol. 11, col. 14896 (Kube). The vote rejecting the motion for an early dissolution of the Landtag was 237 to 185 (ibid., cols. 15325–64).

23. Stahlhelm executive office to regional leaders, 24 and 31 Oct. 1930, BA R45 II/22, and ZStAM, Rep. 77, Tit. 496a, Nr. 197, Beiakte 1, Bd. 1.

24. Wagner (Stahlhelm executive secretary) to regional leaders, 31 Oct. 1930, BA

R45 II/22; Gilsa to Stendel, 20 Feb. 1931; DVP, press release, 4 March 1931, ibid. See also Ehni, *Bollwerk*, pp. 198–99.

25. Goebbels, *Tagebücher* 2:18, 100–01 (8 Feb. and 15 Aug. 1931); *SBPrLT 1928–1932*, 24 March 1931, vol. 14, col. 19527; Jochmus to Mahnke, 14 March 1931, BA 45 II/22.

26. *SBPrLT 1928–1932*, 28 April and 5 May 1931, vol. 14, cols. 19751, 20122, 20130–31; Goebbels, *Tagebücher* 2:98 (5 Aug. 1931).

27. "Sitzungsbericht," 12 Nov. 1930, pp. 16–17, BA, R 45 II/22; Höner, *Zugriff*, pp. 132–33. A Communist offer not to support the referendum if the Prussian government would rescind its prohibition of the RFB was summarily rejected by Severing. See "Erklärung des Preussischen Staatsministeriums vom 10. August 1932 auf die Gegenerklärung der Reichsregierung vom 5. August 1932," p. 27, Braun papers/11/B-4/54 (ForHbg).

28. E[rnst] H[eilmann], "Der Umschwung," *Das Freie Wort* 3 (9 Aug., 1931), 1–3; "Verbrechen und Sühne," ibid. 3 (16 Aug. 1931), 1–4; Kolb, "Strategie," pp. 168–69.

29. Morsey, *Untergang*, p. 23; Breitman, *German*, pp. 172–73; Trumpp, "Papen," pp. 34–35; Wilhelm Gerviens [i.e., Carl Severing], *Der 20. Juli 1932 in Wahrheit und Dichtung* (Bielefeld, 1946), p. 6; *SBPrLT 1928–1932*, 17 March 1932, vol. 17, col. 24756. See also Becker, "Kaas," p. 98.

30. *SBPrLT 1928–1932*, 23 Jan. and 17 Mar. 1932, vol. 17, cols 23857 (Barteld), 24742 (Oelze); Severing to Braun, 20 Jan. 1932, Severing papers/53/39; see the exchange of letters between Riedel (DDP) and Grimme, 20 and 21 April 1932, Grimme papers/M65/M50; Goebbels, *Tagebücher* 2:130 (20 Feb. 1932).

31. Becker, "Kass," p. 101. See also Trumpp, "Papen," p. 84; Brüning, *Briefe*, p. 540; Gerhard Schulz, "Erinnerungen an eine misslungene Restoration, Heinrich Brüning und seine Memoiren," *Der Staat* 11 (1972), 70.

32. Höner, *Zugriff*, pp. 235–36, 242; Trumpp, "Papen," pp. 65, 68, 76; Goebbels, *Tagebücher* 2:213 (2 Aug. 1932); Severing, interview with UPI correspondent, 26 April 1932, Severing papers, 54/90.

33. See Brecht, "Notiz," Braun papers/641 (IISG); Brecht to Nobis, 8 Feb. 1933, Braun papers/11/54-II/B2 (ForHbg).

34. See E[rnst] H[eilmann]'s anticipatory article, "Die letzte [*sic*] Notverordnung," *Das Freie Wort* 3 (20 Dec. 1931), 1–6; Goebbels, *Tagebücher* 2:122, 130, 149 (4 and 21 Feb. and 31 Mar. 1932).

35. The account that follows is based primarily upon the detailed analysis in Jürgen Bay, "Der Preussenkonflikt 1932/33: Ein Kapitel aus der Verfassungsgeschichte der Weimarer Republik," Ph.D. diss., University of Erlangen, 1965, pp. 20ff.; Horst Möller, *Parlamentarismus in Preussen 1919–1932* (Düsseldorf, 1985), pp. 386–88. See also Ehni, *Bollwerk*, pp. 244–45; Höner, *Zugriff*, pp. 223ff.

36. [Ernst Heilmann], "Der Staatsgerichtshof für Preussen," *Das Freie Wort* 5 (1 Jan. 1933), 28. For Adenauer's doubts on the constitutionality of the change, see Adenauer to Braun, 7 April 1932, PrGStAB, Rep. 90/129; Prussian State Cabinet, "Denkschrift über die Vorgänge vom 20. Juli 1932," *Drucksachen des Staatsrates* (Berlin, 1932), no. 313 (7 Nov. 1932), cols. 73–74. Papen ostentatiously abstained

from voting on the resolution in the Landtag. See Papen, *Gasse,* p. 135; Trumpp, "Papen," pp. 60–62. See also Möller, *Parlamentarismus,* pp. 387, n. 253, 388.

37. Bay, "Preussen," p. 22. See also "Anlageheft zu der Erklärung des Preussischen Staatsministeriums" (hereafter: "Anlageheft Pr. 10.8.32"), pp. 57–58, Braun papers/11/B-4/54 (ForHbg); Möller, *Parlamentarismus,* p. 387, n. 253. For the legal brief of the ministry of the interior, see Severing to prime minister, 21 May 1932, PrGStAB, Rep. 90a/40.

38. See the remarks by the speaker, *SBPrLT 1928–1932,* 18 March 1932, vol. 17, col. 24884. For the opposition's objections, see ibid., 12 April 1932, vol. 17, cols. 24891ff.; for the roll-call vote, see ibid., 24916–20. Incidentally, a similar change was voted by the Württemberg Landtag. See Erwin Widder, "Reich und Preussen vom Regierungsantritt Brünings bis zum Reichsstatthaltergesetz Hitlers," Ph.D. diss., Frankfurt a.M., 1959, p. 98.

39. Cuno Graf Westarp, *Am Grabe der Parteiherrschaft* (Berlin, 1932), p. 114; Ludwig Dierske, "War eine Abwehr des 'Preussenschlages' vom 20. Juli 1932 möglich?" *Zeitschrift für Politik* 17 (1970), 216–17; Ehni, *Bollwerk,* pp. 244–45. See also Braun, "Weimar-Ms.," p. 579; Papen, *Gasse,* p. 135; Bay, "Preussen," pp. 27, 40. The federal takeover is discussed in chap. 8, below.

40. Braun, "Weimar-Ms.," pp. 571, 574. See also Friedrich Stampfer, *Die vierzehn Jahre der ersten deutschen Republik,* 3d ed. (Hamburg, 1953), pp. 617–18; *SBPrLT 1928–1932,* 17 March 1932, vol. 17, cols 24679–94 (Braun).

41. Goebbels, *Tagebücher,* 2:160 (23 [*sic*] April 1932). For the flavor of the campaign, see Braun, "Weimar-Ms.," p. 577; Erasmus Jonas, *Die Volkskonservativen 1928–1933* (Düsseldorf, 1965), p. 116. For a sense of the moderates' feelings of impotence and frustration, see DVP-RTFr.Prot., 9 May 1932, pp. 372–73.

42. Hindenburg to Berg, 25 Feb. 1932, in Erich Matthias, ed., "Hindenburg zwischen den Fronten—zur Vorgeschichte der Reichspräsidentenwahlen von 1932," *Vierteljahrshefte für Zeitgeschichte* 8 (Jan. 1960), 80; Henning Grund, "Preussenschlag und Staatsgerichtshof im Jahre 1932," Ph.D. diss., University of Göttingen, 1976, pp. 53–54; Goebbels, *Tagebücher* 2:153 (10 April 1932).

43. SitzPrStMin., 26 April 1932, ZStAM, Rep. 90a, B III, 2b Nr. 6, Bd. 181. See also Bay, "Preussen," pp. 18–19.

44. Braun, "Weimar-Ms.," p. 600; Trumpp, "Papen," p. 85; Abegg to Severing, 31 May 1947, Severing papers/60/12; Bay, "Preussen," pp. 24, 46; Grzesinski, "Kampf," p. 185.

45. Prussian ministry of the interior to prime minister, 6 June 1932, ZStAM, Rep. 120, C B I Nr. 8a, Bd. 3; Goebbels, *Tagebücher* 2:160, 174 (23 April and 28 May 1932); Möller, *Parlamentarismus,* p. 556.

46. *SBPrLT 1932–1933,* 25 May 1932, vol. 1, cols. 25–26, 34.

47. Becker, "Kaas," pp. 101–04; Grund, "Preussenschlag," pp. 53–54; Höner, *Zugriff,* p. 279; Ehni, *Bollwerk,* p. 247; Bay, "Preussen," p. 31; Morsey, *Untergang,* pp. 24, 51, 56–57; Schulz, "Brüning Erinnerungen," p. 78; Morsey, *Entstehung,* p. 41; and Goebbels, *Kaiserhof,* p. 108. See also Detlef Junker, *Die Deutsche Zentrumspartei und Hitler 1932/33* (Stuttgart, 1969), p. 56; Gerviens, *20. Juli,* pp. 5, 16; Goebbels, *Tagebücher* 2:162, 164 (29 April, 3 and 4 May 1932).

48. Henry A. Turner, "The *Ruhrlade:* Secret Cabinet of Heavy Industry in the Weimar Republic," *Central European History* 3 (Sept. 1970), p. 220.

49. Gayl, "Niederschrift," n.d., quoted in Trumpp, "Papen," pp. 213–16; "Denkschrift . . . 7.11.32," p. 44; Bay "Preussen," p. 95; *SBPrLT 1932–1933,* 2 June 1932, vol. 1, col. 148 (Kube); Goebbels, *Tagebücher* 2:164–73 (4–24 May 1932).

50. E[rnst] H[eilmann], "Das Spiel der Generäle; "Nach Brünings Sturz—das Faustrecht?" *Das Freie Wort* 4 (22 May and 5 June 1932), 1–5. See also Breitmann, *German,* pp. 179–80; Ehni, *Bollwerk,* pp. 246–47, 249.

51. Ehni, *Bollwerk,* p. 248. See also Harry Graf Kessler, *Tagebücher 1918–1937,* ed. Wolfgang Pfeiffer-Belli (Frankfurt a.M., 1961) pp. 652, 657 (8 Dec. 1931 and 23 March 1932).

52. Differing (and somewhat contradictory) accounts of the conversation are in Prussian cabinet, "Anlageheft zu der Erklärung des Preussischen Staatsministeriums vom 10.8.1932," pp. 46–51; "Anlageheft zu der Gegenerklärung der Reichsregierung vom 5.8.1932," pp. 35–39; "Anlageheft zu der Erwiderung der Reichsregierung vom 25. August 1932," pp. 6–8, 45, Braun papers/11/B-4/54 (ForHbg). On other SPD-KPD contacts, see Erich Matthias, "Die Sozialdemokratische Partei Deutschlands," in *Ende,* p. 155.

53. Siegfried Bahne, "Die Kommunistische Partei Deutschlands," in *Ende,* pp. 670–71; Bahne, "Sozialfaschismus," *International Review of Social History* 10 (1965), 211–45; and Thomas Weingartner, *Stalin und der Aufstieg Hitlers* (Berlin, 1970), pp. 123ff. See also, *Pravda*'s comments on the election results quoted in Florian Geyer, "Kampf um Preussen," *Neue Blätter für den Sozialismus* 3 (May 1932), 228, n.1; Höner, *Zugriff,* pp. 336–38; Hermann Weber, ed., *Der deutsche Kommunismus: Dokumente 1915–1945,* 3d ed. (Cologne, 1973), pp. 194–95; Gerviens, *20. Juli,* p. 16; *SBPrLT 1932–1933,* 2 and 16 June 1932, vol. 1, cols. 163, 645–50; Henning Grund, "Preussenschlag," p. 34.

54. For an example of the bitter memories left by the 1932 feud between the two parties, see Friedrich Stampfer, letter to editors of *Die Zeit,* no. 24 (15 June 1950).

55. Höner, *Zugriff,* pp. 261–67, quotation on p. 266. The Nazis were equally contemptuous of their German Nationalist "allies." See Goebbels, *Tagebücher* 2:189ff. (20 June 1932ff.).

56. Morsey, *Untergang,* pp. 67, 79; Bay, "Preussen," pp. 30ff.; Severing to Keil, 9 Sept. 1946, Keil papers, Briefe/17; Konrad Adenauer, "Adenauer als Präsident des Preussischen Staatsrates," in *Konrad Adenauer, Oberbürgermeister von Köln,* ed. Hugo Stehkämper (Cologne, 1976), pp. 389–91; Ehni, *Bollwerk,* pp. 254–55; Joachim Petzold, "Der Staatsstreich vom 20. Juli 1932 in Preussen," *Zeitschrift für Geschichtswissenschaft* 4 (1956), 1157.

57. Brüning, *Memoiren,* p. 570; Brüning to Sollmann, 29 Sept. 1940, in Knapp, "Brüning," p. 109. On Hirtsiefer's role, see also Mende to Severing, 25 Feb. 1948, Severing papers/58/56; Breitman, *SPD,* p. 181; Fiederlein, "Osten," p. 394.

58. Höner, *Zugriff,* pp. 270, 287; Bay, "Preussen," p. 39; Goebbels, *Tagebücher* 2:170, 179–80 (19 May, 4 and 6 June 1932). See also *SBPrLT 1932–1933,* 2 June 1932, vol. 1, col. 250 (Lohse).

59. Bay, "Preussen," pp. 39, 100–01; Braun, "Weimar-Ms.," pp. 656–57; Höner, *Zugriff,* pp. 272–73, 287–88; Trumpp, "Papen," pp.78, 86; *SBPrLT 1932–1933,* 2 June 1932, vol. 1, col. 218 (Stendel).

60. Becker, "Kaas," pp. 101–04; Höner, *Zugriff,* p. 279; Ehni, *Bollwerk,* p. 247; Bay, Preussen," p. 31; Morsey, *Untergang,* pp. 24, 51, 56-57; Schulz, "Brüning Erinnerungen," p. 78.

61. Goebbels, *Tagebücher* 2:181 (9 June 1932); Höner, *Zugriff,* pp. 237–38, 272–73; Gottfried Treviranus, "Schleicher," in *Staat,* pp. 378–79; Morsey, *Untergang,* p. 51; See also Prussian cabinet, "Anlageheft zu der Erklärung des Preussischen Staatsministeriums vom 29. August 1932," pp. 14–15, Braun papers/11/B-4/54 (ForHbg). The August crisis is discussed below.

62. Gerviens, *20. Juli,* pp. 5, 15–16; Trumpp, "Papen," pp. 77–78; Morsey, *Untergang,* p. 219; Widder, "Reich," p. 99. The quotation is in *SBPrLT 1932–1933,* 16 June 1932, vol. 1, col. 593 (Wester).

63. Dierske, "Abwehr," p. 236; Trumpp, "Papen," pp. 46ff.; and Grund, "Preussenschlag," pp. 55ff., all insist that Papen had a sincere interest in a parliamentary *Bürgerblock* in Prussia. For a different interpretation, see Severing, "Der 20. Juli 1932. Eine Richtigstellung," Severing papers/58/66; Petzold, "Staatsstreich," p. 1050; Möller, *Parlamentarismus,* pp. 566–67. The exchange of letters between Papen, Kerrl, and Hirtsiefer is reprinted in Trumpp, "Papen," pp. 181–93.

64. See Brüning's 1947 letter to Esser, quoted in Becker, "Kaas," p. 103; Morsey, *Untergang,* p. 25. For a ringing statement of the Center party's continuing commitment to democracy, see *SBPrLT 1932–1933,* 2 June 1932, vol. 1, cols. 181–95 (Letterhaus).

65. On the June negotiation, see Bay, "Preussen," pp. 33ff.; Morsey, *Untergang,* pp. 5, 61, 235, n. 6; Trumpp, "Papen," p. 105; Bracher, *Auflösung,* pp. 544–45; Goebbels, *Tagebücher* 2:189–90 (22 June 1932); *SBPrLT 1932–1933,* 16 June 1932, vol. 1, cols 525, 533. The most detailed treatments of Gregor Strasser's role in the coalition talks are in Udo Kissenkötter, *Gregor Strasser und die NSDAP* (Stuttgart, 1978) and Peter D. Stachura, *Gregor Strasser and the Rise of Nazism* (London, 1983). See also Kerrl's speech in Altona, 23 July 1932, as reported in *Hamburger Tageblatt,* no. 169 (25 July 1932).

66. Kerrl to Papen, 18 July 1932, quoted in Trumpp, "Papen," pp. 187–93. See also Möller, *Parlamentarismus,* pp. 568–69.

67. See Papen's speech in Münster, 28 Aug. 1932. A copy of the WTB news agency's report on the speech is in ZStAP, 15.01/25706.

68. For Nazi attacks on both the Center party and Papen's initial moves in Prussia after the coup, see *Hamburger Tageblatt,* nos. 168 and 172 (24 and 28 July 1932). A copy of the DNVP-DVP pact is in BA R 45/11/16. The agreement was renewed for the November contest (see ibid., 17). See also Bracher, *Auflösung,* p. 531.

69. Braun, "Weimar-Ms.," p. 646; Friedrich Stampfer, *Erfahrungen und Erkenntnisse* (Cologne, 1957), pp. 264–65; Emigratus, "Kriegserklärung an den Faschismus," *Das Freie Wort* 4 (28 Aug. 1932), 7–11; Siegfried Bahne, *Die KPD und das Ende von Weimar* (Frankfurt a.M., 1976), pp. 29ff.

70. Morsey, *Untergang,* p. 58; Junker, *Zentrum,* pp. 78, 86–88, 94, 127. For

Braun's postwar bitterness toward Papen, see letter to Severing, 3 Feb. 1947, Braun papers/Rep. 92/B/C/I/276 (PrGStAB).

71. Goebbels, *Tagebücher* 2:211, 214–15, 217 (31 July, 3, 5, and 7 Aug. 1932).

72. Ibid. 2:224–25 (13 Aug. 1932). See also documentation in ZStAP, 15.01/ 25706.

73. Bay, "Preussen," pp. 168–73.

74. Junker, *Zentrum*, pp. 95–96; Grund, "Preussenschlag," p. 78; Bay, "Preussen," p. 263; Petzold, "Staatsstreich," p. 1183; Braun, "Weimar-Ms.," p. 645; Morsey, *Untergang*, pp. 58–63; Junker, *Zentrum*, pp. 99–101; Hermann Pünder, *Politik in der Reichskanzlei—Aufzeichnungen aus den Jahren 1929–1932*, ed. Thilo Vogelsang (Stuttgart, 1961), p. 143 (19 Aug. 1932); Höner, *Zugriff*, pp. 361–62.

75. Junker, *Zentrum*, pp. 96–97, 105; Höner, *Zugriff*, p. 362; Morsey, *Untergang*, pp. 60, 237, n. 16; Goebbels, *Tagebücher* 2:231, 233, 240 (25 and 28 Aug., 10 Sept. 1932).

76. Adenauer, "Staatsrat," pp. 389–90, 399; Höner, *Zugriff*, p. 366. See also "Gefährlicher Unsinn," *Das Freie Wort* 4 (18 Sept. 1932), 31; Goebbels, *Tagebücher* 2:272 (6 Nov. 1932); Goebbels, *Kaiserhof*, p. 210 (25 Nov. 1932).

77. See the official press release on the meeting and Braun's handwritten comments in Braun papers/11/54/II/B 2 (ForHbg). See also Hagen Schulze, *Otto Braun* (Frankfurt a.M., 1977), p. 766. Goebbel's comment is in *Tagebücher* 2:274 (9 Nov. 1932).

78. SitzPrStMin (commissioners), 27 Oct. 1932, ZStAM, Rep. 90a, B III 2b Nr. 6, Bd. 181; Hindenburg to Braun, 18 Nov. 1932, Braun papers/11/B-2/54 II (ForHbg); Holtzendorff, "Bericht," 15 Nov. 1932, p. 14; WTB report no. 2520, 24 Nov. 1932, ZStAP, 15.01/25706; Junker, *Zentrum*, p. 112; Morsey, *Untergang*, pp. 76–77.

79. Prussian ministry of justice (commissioners), "Vermerk," 7 Jan. 1933, PrGStAB, Rep. 84a/4388; SitzPrStMin (commissioners), 23 Jan. 1933, PrGStAB, Rep. 90a/41; Morsey, *Untergang*, p. 79; Goebbels, *Tagebücher* 2:304 (13 Dec. 1932); Braun, "Weimar-Ms.," p. 652; Bay, "Preussen," p. 250; Thilo Vogelsang, *Reichswehr, Staat und NSDAP* (Stuttgart, 1962), p. 342.

80. Höner, *Zugriff*, p. 380; Friedrich-Karl von Plehwe, *Reichskanzler Kurt von Schleicher: Weimars letzte Chance gegen Hitler* (Esslingen, 1983), p. 251; Neebe, *Grossindustrie*, p. 170; Goebbels, *Tagebücher* 2:292–93, 306 (5 and 15 Dec. 1932); Goebbels, *Kaiserhof*, p. 199 (8 Nov. 1932).

81. Braun, "Weimar-Ms.," p. 65; Richard Breitman, "German Social Democracy and General Schleicher, 1932–33," *Central European History* 9 (Dec. 1976), 353; Morsey, *Untergang*, p. 79; Plehwe, *Schleicher*, pp. 237, 259; Gustav Noske, *Erlebtes aus Aufstieg und Niedergang einer Demokratie* (Offenbach a.M., 1947), p. 311; E[rnst] H[eilmann], "Was fordert der Verfassungseid," *Das Freie Wort* 4 (20 Nov. 1932), 3.

82. Goebbels, *Tagebücher* 2:340, 362 (17 and 30 Jan. 1933). For Göring's earlier ideas on the future of Prussia, see Vogelsang, *Reichswehr*, p. 343.

83. Severing, "Aufzeichnung," Severing papers/52/32.

84. Braun to Schleicher, 8 Dec. 1932, PrGStAB, Rep. 84a/4388; Breitman, "Schleicher," pp. 371, 374; Willy Brandt, *Links und frei: Mein Weg 1930–1950* (Hamburg, 1982), p. 53; and Plehwe, *Schleicher*, pp. 270–71; Schulze, *Braun*,

p. 774. In his report to the (old) cabinet, Braun ignored the key points of his talk with Schleicher and talked only about some peripheral items. See SitzPrStMin, 6 Jan. 1933, Braun papers/11/B-2/ 54/11 (ForHbg).

85. Arnold Brecht, *Mit der Kraft des Geistes: Lebenserinnerungen 1927–1967* (Stuttgart, 1967), p. 240; Rudolf Morsey, ed., "Der Beginn der 'Gleichschaltung' in Preussen: Adenauers Haltung in der Sitzung des 'Dreimännerkollegiums' am 6. Februar 1933," *Vierteljahrshefte für Zeitgeschichte* 11 (Jan. 1963), 91–93; Morsey, *Untergang,* pp. 98, 101; Adenauer to Kaas, 12 Dec. 1932, quoted in Adenauer, "Staatsrat," p. 395. See also Schleicher's remarks to the commissioners in the only cabinet meeting at which he presided (ZStAM, Rep. 90a, B III, 2b, Nr. 6, Bd. 182).

Chapter 8. The Coup of July 20, 1932

1. Josef Becker, "Brüning, Prälat Kaas und das Problem einer Regierungsbeteiligung der NSDAP, 1930–1932," *Historische Zeitschrift* 196 (Feb. 1963), 100–01; Hans-Peter Ehni, *Bollwerk Preussen: Preussen Regierung, Reich-Länderproblem und Sozialdemokratie, 1928–1932* (Bonn–Bad Godesberg, 1975), pp. 254, 257; Werner Stephan, *Aufstieg und Verfall des Linksliberalismus 1918–1933* (Göttingen, 1973), p. 486. Sabine Höner, *Der nationalsozialistische Zugriff auf Preussen* (Bochum, 1984), pp. 205–07; Thilo Vogelsang, *Reichswehr, Staat und NSDAP* (Stuttgart, 1962), pp. 127–28. Brüning's apologists, such as Hermann Pünder, the chancellor's state secretary (chief of staff), denied as late as 1965 that the chancellor "'had for one moment thought of a federal commissioner for Prussia.'" (quoted in Jürgen Bay, "Der Preussenkonflikt 1932/33: Ein Kapitel aus der Verfassungsgeschichte der Weimarer Republik," Ph.D. diss., University of Erlangen, 1965, p. 67, n. 353).

2. Rudolf Morsey, *Der Untergang des politischen Katholizismus—die Zentrumspartei zwischen christlichem Selbstverständnis und 'Nationaler Erhebung' 1932/33* (Stuttgart, 1977), p. 54; Papen's letter to the editor of *Die Zeit,* no. 22 (1 June 1950). See also Franz von Papen, *Der Wahrheit eine Gasse* (Munich, 1952), pp. 215–18. Nevertheless, Papen too retains his apologists. See the analysis of the July coup in Henry M. Adams and Robin K. Adams. *Rebel Patriot: A Biography of Franz von Papen* (Santa Barbara, Calif., 1987). p. 152.

3. Karl Rohe, *Das Reichsbanner Schwarz-Rot-Gold* (Düsseldorf, 1966), p. 424; Ernst Heilmann, "Der geschäftstüchtige und betriebsame Herr Papen," *Das Freie Wort* 4 (20 Oct. 1932), 5–9; Höner, *Zugriff,* p. 349; Abegg to Severing, 4 August 1932, Severing papers/60/4; Joachim Petzold, "Der Staatsstreich vom. 20. Juli 1932 in Preussen," *Zeitschrift für Geschichtswissenschaft* 4 (1956), 1150; Kurt Gossweiler, "Die Absetzung der Preussenregierung Braun-Severing durch Papen," in *Aufsätze zum Faschismus,* 2d ed. (Cologne, 1988), 1:1–18; Ulrike Hörster-Philipps, *Konservative Politik in der Endphase der Weimarer Republik: Die Regierung Franz von Papen* (Cologne, 1982), p. 279.

4. For earlier complaints along this line, see Quaatz to Brüning, 29 Oct. 1931, ZStAP, Rep. 15.01/25706. For Hitler's telegram from Königsberg, see ibid./25730. The report of the subsequent investigation is in Bracht to Reich ministry of the interior, 26 Aug. 1932, ibid; see also additional documentation in ibid./25731/1. The text of the

telegram is also reprinted in Thomas Trumpp, "Franz von Papen, der preussischdeutsche Dualismus und die NSDAP in Preussen," Ph.D. diss., University of Tübingen, 1963, pp. 195–97. For a discussion of Kerrl's letter, see Ludwig Dierske, "War eine Abwehr des 'Preussenschlages' vom 20. Juli 1932 möglich?" *Zeitschrift für Politik* 17 (1970), 204–07; Petzold, "Staatsstreich," p. 1165. See also Karl Dietrich Bracher, *Die Auflösung der Weimarer Republik,* 5th ed. (Düsseldorf, 1978), p. 510.

5. Ehni, *Bollwerk,* p. 257; Bay, "Preussen," pp. 73ff.; Gerhard Schulz, *Aufstieg des Nationalsozialismus—Krise und Revolution in Deutschland* (Frankfurt, a.M., 1975), pp. 728–29; Trumpp, "Papen," pp. 43–44; Papen, *Gasse,* p. 195; Karl Dietrich Bracher, "Der 20. Juli 1932," *Zeitschrift für Politik* 3 (Dec. 1956), 245–47; Henning Grund, "Preussenschlag und Staatsgerichtshof im Jahre 1932," Ph.D. diss., University of Göttingen, 1976, pp. 21, 23.

6. Joseph Goebbels, *Vom Kaiserhof zur Reichskanzlei,* 28th ed. (Berlin, 1940), pp. 106ff.; Trumpp, "Papen," p. 105.

7. Prussian State Cabinet, "Denkschrift über die Vorgänge vom 20. Juli 1932" (hereafter: "Denkschrift . . . 7.11.32"), Berlin, Drucksachen des Staatsrates, no. 313 (7 Nov. 1932), pp. 21–24; documentation in ZStAP, Rep. 30.01/22074; Prussian cabinet, "Anlageheft zu der Gegenerklärung der Reichsregierung vom 5.8.1932" (hereafter: "Anlageheft, 5.8.32"), pp. 21–22; Prussian cabinet, "Anlageheft zu der Erwiderung der Reichsregierung vom 25. August 1932" (hereafter: "Anlageheft, 25.8.32"), p. 27. See also Bay, "Preussen," p. 117.

8. [Heilmann], "Staatsstreich und Beamtencharaktere," *Das Freie Wort* 4 (21 Aug. 1932), 27.

9. Dierske, "Abwehr," pp. 202–03; "Anlageheft 5.8.32," p. 33. On Diels, see Heinz Höhne, *Mordsache Röhm* (Reinbek b. Hamburg, 1984), p. 163; Joseph Goebbels, *Die Tagebücher von Joseph Goebbels Teil I: Aufzeichnungen 1924–1941,* ed. Elke Fröhlich (Munich, 1987), 2:383, 431; and his own account, *Lucifer ante Portas . . . Es spricht der erste Chef der Gestapo* (Stuttgart, 1950).

10. Trumpp, "Papen," pp. 105–11, 211–12, 220–24.

11. Ibid., pp. 204–05; Gayl, "Besprechung mit 9 preussischen Landtagsabgeordneten der NSDAP . . . ," 24 June 1932, ZStAP, 15.01/25706; Prussian ministry of the interior to district directors and police president of Berlin, 1 June 1932, LASH, 301/4498.

12. Brüning to Sollmann, 29 Sept. 1940, in Thomas A. Knapp, ed., "Heinrich Brüning im Exil: Briefe an Wilhelm Sollmann 1940–1946," *Vierteljahrshefte für Zeitgeschichte* 22 (Jan. 1974), 108. See also Friedrich-Karl von Plehwe, *Reichskanzler Kurt von Schleicher: Weimars letzte Chance gegen Hitler* (Esslingen, 1983), pp. 216, 330.

13. See, Heinrich August Winkler, *Der Weg in die Katastrophe: Arbeiter und Arbeiterbewegung in der Weimarer Republik 1930 bis 1933* (Bonn, 1987), pp. 650–52; police chief of Altona to Severing, 1 Sept. 1932, Severing papers/52/23; "Anlageheft 25.8. 32," pp. 56–57; "Denkschrift . . . 7.11.32," p. 32. See also Höner, *Zugriff,* pp. 318ff.; for the Nazi version, *Hamburger Tageblatt,* no. 163 (18 July 1932); Goebbels, *Tagebücher* 2:206 (17 July 1932).

14. Horst Möller, *Parlamentarismus in Preussen 1919–1932* (Düsseldorf, 1985), pp. 565ff.

15. "Aun den Verhandlungen vor dem Staatsgerichtshof für das Deutsche Reich vom 10. bis 17. Oktober 1932" (hereafter: "Verhandlungen StGH, 10.–17.10.32") (typescript), Braun papers /11/B-2/54, p. 15 (ForHbg).

16. Reich ministry of the interior, "Notiz über eine Besprechung Gayl/Severing," 25 June 1932, ZStAP, 15.01/25706; Ferdinand Friedensburg, *Lebenserinnerungen* (Frankfurt a.M., 1969), p. 208; Braun to Kautsky, 19 Feb. 1932, in Erich Matthias, ed., "Hindenburg zwischen den Fronten—Zur Vorgeschichte der Reichspräsidenten-wahlen von 1932," *Vierteljahrshefte für Zeitgeschichte* 8 (Jan. 1960), 82–84; Ehni, *Bollwerk*, p. 247; Hagen Schulze, *Otto Braun* (Frankfurt, 1977), p. 737.

17. Prussian ministry of the interior to prime minister and members of the cabinet (secret), 6 June 1932, ZStAM, Rep. 120 C B I, Nr. 8a, Bd. 3; Albert Grzesinski, "Im Kampf um die deutsche Republik—Lebensweg eines Staatenlosen," Grzesinski papers/2457, pp. 233–34, 249, 286; Richard Breitman, *German Socialism and Weimar Democracy* (Chapel Hill, N.C., 1981), pp. 183, 187; Bay, "Preussen," pp. 88–90; Trumpp, "Papen," pp. 97–98, 103; Gerhard Schulz, "Staatsschutz und Nationalsozialismus in der Ära Brüning," in Ilse Maurer and Udo Wengst, eds., *Staat und NSDAP 1930–32: Quellen zur Ära Brüning* (Düsseldorf, 1977), pp. lxvii, 333; Wilhelm Gerviens [i.e., Carl Severing], *Der 20. Juli 1932 in Wahrheit und Dichtung* (Bielefeld, 1946), p. 7; Fritz Rathenau, "Als Jude im Dienste von Reich und Staat," (typescript), p. 114 (Rathenau papers).

18. *SBPrLT 1928–1932*, 13 and 14 Oct. 1931, vol. 16, cols. 21997–98, 22097–98; Bay, "Preussen," pp. 86–87.

19. Bracher, *Auflösung*, p. 506; Arnold Brecht, *Mit der Kraft des Geistes—Lebenserinnerungen* (Stuttgart, 1967), p. 216; Gerviens, *20. Juli*, p. 16; Ehni, *Bollwerk*, p. 264; Rohe, *Reichsbanner*, pp. 432–33; Albert Grzesinski, "Auf dem Wege zum 20. Juli 1932" (hereafter: "20.7.32"), p. 12, Grzesinski papers/2456; Hannes Heer, *Burgfrieden oder Klassenkampf* (Berlin, 1971), pp. 62–63.

20. Bracher, *Auflösung*, p. 509; Grund, "Preussenschlag," pp. 63–64; Trumpp, "Papen," p. 141.

21. *SBPrLT 1932–1933*, 2 June 1932, vol. 1, col. 186 (Letterhaus); Heinrich Pfeiffer, "Was wird aus Preussen," *Neue Blätter für den Sozialismus* 3 (July 1932), 384–86; Gerviens, *20. Juli*, p. 5; Bay, *Preussen*, pp. 57ff.; Ehni, *Bollwerk*, p. 239; Schulz, *Aufstieg*, p. 668; Goebbels, *Tagebücher* 2:181 (8 June 1932).

22. Trumpp, "Papen," pp. 103, 115–18. For a different view of Schleicher's role, see Thilo Vogelsang, *Kurt von Schleicher—Ein General als Politiker* (Göttingen, 1965), pp. 79–80.

23. Trumpp, "Papen," pp. 101–03, 128, 224–27; Maurer and Wengst, eds., *Staat und NSDAP*, pp. 329–30; Grund, "Preussenschlag," pp. 60ff.; Dierske, "Abwehr," p. 205; Rudolf Morsey, ed., "Zur Geschichte des 'Preussenschlags' am 20. Juli 1932," *Vierteljahrshefte für Zeitgeschichte* 9 (Oct. 1961), p. 431; Vogelsang, *Reichswehr*, pp. 239–41.

24. Prussian ministry of the interior to chiefs of police, 19 July 1932, LASH, 301/4498. See also Trumpp, "Papen," p. 139; Vogelsang, *Reichswehr*, p. 243; Bay, "Preussen," pp. 114–15.

25. Trumpp, "Papen," pp. 140ff.; Petzold, "Staatsstreich," p. 1163; Grzesinski, "20.7.32," p. 10; Gerviens, *20. Juli;* Goebbels, *Tagebücher* 2:201 (8 July 1932).

26. Trumpp, "Papen," pp. 136, 228; Grund, "Preussenschlag," p. 62; Petzold, "Staatsstreich," p. 1159; Grzesinski, "20.7.32," p. 9. See also Udo Wengst, "Unternehmerverbände und Gewerkschaften in Deutschland im Jahre 1930," *Vierteljahrshefte für Zeitgeschichte* 25 (Jan. 1977), 105.

27. Bay, "Preussen," p. 128. See also Goebbels, *Tagebücher* 2:207–08 (19 July 1932).

28. See Hirtsiefer's and Severing's account of the meeting, in Prussian cabinet, "Anlageheft zu der Erklärung des Preussischen Staatsministeriums vom 10.8.1932," Anlage 1, pp. 1–7. Klepper's version was published after the war in his article, Otto Klepper, "Das Ende der Republik," *Die Gegenwart* 2 (30 Sept. 1947), 20–22. See also Albert Grzesinski, "Mein Tagebuch—Aufzeichnungen über den 20. Juli 1932," pp. 2, 9–11 (typescript), Grzesinski papers/2456; Gerviens, *20. Juli*, p. 10; Morsey, "Preussenschlag," p. 433; Papen to Krüger and Staudinger, 20 and 23 July 1932, PrGStAB, Rep. 84a/4388; Rundstedt to Melcher, 20 July 1932, Grzesinski papers/2036. Among the numerous secondary accounts, see esp. Höner, *Zugriff*, pp. 334ff.; Winkler, *Katastrophe*, pp. 655ff.; Dierske, "Abwehr," pp. 198–200.

29. Morsey, "Preussenschlag," p. 432; Piper (representative of the city of Hamburg in Berlin) to Petersen (mayor of Hamburg), 25 July 1932, ForHbg/344223.

30. On the contacts between the Reichswehr and provincial administrators, see Prussian ministry of the interior (commissioners) to governors, districts directors, and police chiefs, 20, 21 and 29 July 1932, LASH, 301/5649. The "(commissioners)" indicates that this was the ministry acting under Papen's orders as federal commissioner.

31. See for example, the series of reports from the governor's office in the province of Schleswig-Holstein, 20 July–1 Aug. 1932, LASH, 301/5649.

32. *Hamburger Tageblatt*, nos. 165 and 166 (20 and 21 July 1932); Goebbel's *Tagebücher* 2:207, 209.

33. See chap. 9, below.

34. Kerrl to Papen, 27 July 1932, quoted in Trumpp, "Papen," pp. 197–98; DNVP, local organization of Nowawes (a section of Berlin) to Bracht, 29 July 1932, Bracht papers/4; Wels to Bracht, 10 Aug. 1932, ibid/2; *Das Freie Wort* 5 (19 Feb. 1933), 251.

35. Siegfried Bahne, "Die Kommunistische Partei Deutschlands," in *Das Ende der Parteien 1933*, ed. Erich Matthias and Rudolf Morsey (Düsseldorf, 1960), pp. 671ff.; Hermann Weber, *Hauptfeind Sozialdemokratie: Strategie und Taktik der KPD 1929–1933* (Düsseldorf, 1981), pp. 55–56; Thomas Weingartner, *Stalin und der Aufstieg Hitlers* (Berlin, 1970), p. 144; Bahne, *Die KPD und das Ende von Weimar* (Frankfurt a.M., 1976), p. 25.

36. The KPD's proclamation is reprinted in Petzold, "Staatsstreich," p. 1169. See also police chief of Berlin to Prussian chiefs of police, 21 July 1932, LASH, 301/5649; Weingarten, *Stalin*, p. 144; Weber, *Hauptfeind SD*, pp. 55–56; Winkler, *Katastrophe*, p. 625.

37. Petzold, "Staatsstreich," pp. 1168–70. See also Aviva Aviv, "The SPD and the KPD at the End of Weimar: Similarity within Contrast," *Internationale Wissenschaftliche Korrespondenz* 14 (June 1978), 184.

38. Ehni, *Bollwerk*, pp. 46, 268; Richard Breitman, "German Social Democracy

and General Schleicher, 1932–33," *Central European History* 9 (Dec. 1976), 356ff.; Ferdinand Friedensburg, *Lebenserinnerungen* (Frankfurt a.M., 1969), p. 96.

39. See Grzesinski to Severing, 21 Nov. 1932, Grzesinski papers/310; Abegg to Severing, 31 May 1947, Abegg papers; Gelpke to Braun, 20 Sept. 1949, Braun papers/92/Teil 1/C/75 (PrGStAB); Grzesinski, "Kampf," pp. 303–10; Ernst Lemmer, *Manches war doch anders—Erinnerungen eines deutschen Demokraten* (Frankfurt a.M., 1968), p. 161; Willy Brandt, *Links und frei: Mein Weg 1930–1950* (Hamburg, 1982), p. 51; Erich Matthias, "Die Sozialdemokratische Partei Deutschlands," in *Ende*, ed. Matthias and Morsey, pp. 139ff.; Bay, "Preussen," pp. 14–17, 127; Rohe, *Reichsbanner*, pp. 415, 427–29; Bracher, *Auflösung*, p. 508; Winkler, *Katastrophe*, pp. 592, 671–73; Dierske, "Abwehr," p. 208.

40. Petzold, "Staatsstreich," p. 1172.

41. Hans J. L. Adolph, *Otto Wels und die Politik der deutschen Sozialdemokratie 1894–1939* (Berlin, 1970), p. 246; Höner, *Zugriff*, p. 352; ADGB, "Ausschuss-Protokoll" (hereafter: "ADGB-Ptotokolle"), 21 July 1932, pp. 115–16 (Hiko, Berlin); Gerviens, *20. Juli*.

42. Braun to Papen, 22 July 1932, Braun papers/11/B-4/52 (ForHbg).

43. On the meeting with Papen and the subsequent events of the day, see Grzesinski, "Tagebuch 20.7.32" (manuscript), pp.1–7; Harry Graf Kessler, *Tagebücher 1918–1937*, ed. Wolfgang Pfeiffer-Belli (Frankfurt, a.M., 1961), pp. 690–91 (21 Sept. 1932); Carl Severing, *Mein Lebensweg* (Cologne, 1950), 2:349; Ehni, *Bollwerk*, pp. 264, 270; Bay, "Preussen," pp. 131–32.

44. Klepper, "Ende," pp. 20–22. Severing's rejoinder is in Severing to editor of *Die Gegenwart*, 13 Nov. 1947, Severing papers/58/76. Friedensburg, Lebenserinnerungen, p. 96; and Grzesinski, "20.7.32," pp. 7–8, are equally critical of Severing.

45. See Severing and Braun to editor of *Die Gegenwart*, 13 Nov. 1947 and 24 Jan. 1948, Severing papers/58/76; Braun papers/Teil 2/C/III/11 (PrGStAB); Dietrich Mende to Severing, 25 Feb. 1948, Severing papers/58/86.

46. Mende to Severing, 25 Feb. 1948; Severing, *Lebensweg* 2:350–51; Kessler, *Tagebücher*, pp. 690–91 (21 Sept. 1932); Grzesinski, "20.7.32," pp. 7–8. See also Bay, "Preussen," pp. 120–21, 134; Adolph, *Wels*, pp. 247–49.

47. Gerviens, *20. Juli*, pp. 8, 14–17; *DrPrStR* (1932), Nr. 313, p. 54; Bay, "Preussen," pp. 119–22; Willy Hellpach, *Der deutsche Charakter* (Bonn, 1954), p. 232; Walter Menzel, "Carl Severing und der 20. Juli 1932," *Die Gegenwart* 7 (8 Nov. 1952), 734. (Menzel was Severing's son-in-law.)

48. Braun, "Weimar-Ms.," 623–26; Arnold Brecht, "Die Auflösung der Weimarer Republik und die politische Wissenschaft," *Zeitschrift für Politik* 2 (Dec. 1955), 302; Dierske, "Abwehr," pp. 209, 221, 238; Gerviens, *20. Juli*, p. 11; Grzesinski's *advocatus diaboli* article, "Warum blieb die Sozialdemokratie am 20. Juli passiv?" Article Series 7, pp. 1–5, Grzesinski papers, 2456.

49. See Dierske, "Abwehr," p. 218; Höner, *Zugriff*, pp. 354–55; Schulze, *Braun*, pp. 746ff.; Julius Leber, "Gedanken zum Verbot der deutschen Sozialdemokratie, Juni 1933," in *Ein Mann geht seinen Weg* (Berlin, 1952), p. 190; and Matthias, "SPD," in *Ende*, p. 145; Winkler, *Katastrophe*, p. 657.

50. "Immer noch der 20. Juli," *Das Freie Wort* 4 (23 Oct. 1932), 27; Gerviens, *20. Juli*, p. 16.

51. "ADGB-Protokolle," 21 July 1932, p. 116. See also Dierske, "Abwehr," pp. 237–38; Braun, "Weimar-Ms.," p. 613; Gerviens, *20. Juli*, p. 13; Menzel, "Carl Severing," p. 734; Heer, *Burgfrieden*, pp. 67ff.

52. Morsey, "Preussenschlag," p. 434. On the Nazis' reaction, see *Hamburger Tageblatt*, no. 166 (21 July 1932); Goebbels, *Tagebücher* 2:207–08.

53. Leipert to Keil, 30 Dec. 1940, Keil papers, Briefe/11; Rohe, *Reichsbanner*, pp. 427–29, 435–37.

54. "Denkschrift . . . 7.11.32," col. 27; Gerviens, *20. Juli*, pp. 10–11, 16; Brecht, *Kraft*, pp. 210–14; Arnold Brecht, *Vorspiel zum Schweigen—Das Ende der Deutschen Republik* (Vienna, 1948), pp. 99–100; Dierske, "Abwehr," pp. 210–12, 225ff.; Bracher, *Auflösung*, pp. 521–23; Ehni, *Bollwerk*, pp. 265–67, 271; Rohe, *Reichsbanner*, pp. 427–31; Mende to Severing, 25 Feb. 1948.

55. Cited in Dierske, "Abwehr," p. 208.

56. The Reich cabinet seems to have initially expected active resistance of some sort. See Dierske, "Abwehr," p. 206; Ehni, *Bollwerk*, p. 270; Petzold, "Staatsstreich," p. 1166.

57. Grund, "Preussenschlag," pp. 72–73; Horst Möller, "Das Ende Preussens, in *Preussen—eine Herausforderung*, ed. Wolfgang Böhme (Karlsruhe, 1981), p. 113; Bay, "Preussen," pp. 10–11; Morsey, *Untergang*, p. 54.

58. For Schmitt's general criticism of parliamentary democracy see his *Die geistesgeschichtliche Lage des heutigen Parlamentarismus*, 2d ed. (Berlin, 1926); for his justification of the use of Article 48 in 1932, see *Legalität und Legitimität* (Berlin, 1932). The best analysis of Schmitt's political ideas is Joseph W. Bendersky, *Carl Schmitt—Theorist for the Reich* (Princeton, N.J., 1982).

59. Brandt to Nicolai, 30 Sept. 1932, PrGStAB, Rep. 90/129; Bracher, *Auflösung*, p. 509; Brecht, *Kraft*, p. 180.

60. Brecht reprinted his oral presentation of the case before the Reich court in his memoirs. See Brecht, *Kraft*, pp. 181–201.

61. On the compromise proposals, see Brecht's handwritten marginalia on the title page of "Verhandlungen StGH 10.–17.10.32"), (typescript), Braun papers/11/B-2/54 (ForHbg); Brecht, *Kraft*, p. 222; Bay, "Preussen," pp. 182–85.

62. Brecht, "Auflösung," p. 303; Heilmann, "Bracht mit Syrup," *Das Freie Wort* 4 (11 Dec. 193), 3.

63. Goebbels, *Tagebücher* 2:265–66 (29 Oct. 1932).

64. See Reich commissioner (Papen) to Prussian ministers (commissioners), 28 Oct. 1932, PrGStAB, Rep. 84a/4388. See also Brecht, *Kraft*, p. 229; Bay, "Preussen," p. 155.

65. SitzPrStMin (commissioners), 1 Nov. 1932, ZStAM, Rep. 90a A III 2b Nr. 6, Bd. 181. See also Rudolf Morsey, ed., "Der Beginn der 'Gleichschaltung' in Preussen: Adenauers Haltung in der Sitzung des Dreimännerkollegiums am 6. Februar 1933," *Vierteljahrshefte für Zeitgeschichte* 11 (Jan. 1963), 86; Bay, "Preussen," pp. 210–12, 222–25.

66. See the report of Gayl's speech to the Verein Berliner Presse, 28 Oct. 1932, ZStAP, 15.01/75076; report of Holtzendorff (head of the Saxon interest section in Berlin) on meetings between Gayl and representatives of the *Länder*, 13 and 15 Nov. 1932, PrGStAB, Rep. 216/139; Brecht, draft of a letter from Braun to the cabi-

net, 7 Dec. 1932, Braun papers/11/B-2/54 II (ForHbg). See also Bay, "Preussen," pp. 207–09.

67. Goebbels, *Tagebücher* 2:206 (18 July 1932).

68. Bay, "Preussen," p. 283; Höner, *Zugriff*, p. 429.

Chapter 9. Reichsreform, and the Neoconservatives 1930–1933

1. Arnold Brecht, "Die Auflösung der Weimarer Republik und die politische Wissenschaft," *Zeitschrift für Politik* 2 (Dec. 1955), 305–06.

2. Arnold Brecht, "Vorschläge für eine geschäftstechnische Beratungsunterlage zur Frage einer Änderung des Verhältnisses des Reiches zu den Ländern—Vorentwurf Juli 1928," Müller papers/II/117.

3. *SPBrLT 1928–1932*, 14 Oct. 1931, vol. 16, col. 22055 (Kries); Count Cuno Westarp, *Am Grabe der Parteiherrschaft—Bilanz des deutschen Parlamentarismus 1918–1932* (Berlin, 1932), pp. 125–27.

4. See the articles by Hermann Höpker-Aschoff, *Volkswirt*, 21 Aug. 1931. See also Braun, "Weimar—Ms.," pp. 552–53; Jürgen Bay, "Der Preussenkonflikt 1932/33: Ein Kapitel aus der Verfassungsgeschichte der Weimarer Republik," Ph.D. diss., University of Erlangen, 1965, p. 181, n. 964; Hans-Peter Ehni, *Bollwerk Preussen: Preussen Regierung, Reich-Länderproblem und Sozialdemokratie, 1928–1932* (Bonn–Bad Godesberg, 1975), p. 224.

5. Westarp, *Grabe*, pp. 35–36; Otto Meisner, "Aufzeichnung über eine Besprechung Hindenburg, Papen, Braun 29.10.1932," 29 Oct. 1932, pp. 13–19, ZStAP, 30.01/22075; *SBPrLT 1928–1932*, 14 Oct. 1931, vol. 16, col. 22092 (Severing). Even Höpker-Aschoff eventually returned to the parliamentary fold. See his letter to Poetzsch-Heffter, 21 Aug. 1932, Braun papers/ 626 (IISG).

6. SitzPrStMin, 8 Apr. 1930, PrGStAB, Rep. 90a/31; Ernst Heilmann, "Hindenburg gegen die Nazidiktatur," *Das Freie Wort* 4 (21 Aug. 1932), 1–4.

7. See the documentation in ZStAM, Rep.90a B III 2 b Nr. 6, Bde. 179–180. See also Braun, "Weimar-Ms.," p. 535; Erwin Widder, "Reich und Preussen vom Regierungsantritt Brünings bis zum Reichsstatthaltergesetz Hitlers," Ph.D. diss., University of Frankfurt a.M., 1959, p. 89.

8. Dieter Gessner, *Agrarverbände in der Weimarer Republik* (Düsseldorf, 1976), p. 184; Rudolf Morsey, *Zur Entstehung, Authenzität und Kritik von Brünings "Memoiren 1918–1934"* (Cologne, 1975), pp. 33–34.

9. Gessner, *Agrarverbände*, pp. 186–87; Ehni, *Bollwerk*, p. 226.

10. SitzPrStMin (commissioners), 4 Aug. 1932, PrGStAB, Rep. 90a/40; Arndt von Holtzendorff, "Bericht über die Sitzung der vereinigten Reichsratsausschüsse," 15 Nov. 1932, p. 3, PrGStAB, Rep. 216/139; Thomas Trumpp, "Franz von Papen, der preussisch-deutsche Dualismus und die NSDAP in Preussen," Ph.D. diss., University of Tübingen, 1963, pp. 124–25. Holtzendorff was the head of the Saxon interest section in Berlin.

11. See SitzPrStMin (commissioners) 13 Dec. 1932, ZStAM. Rep. 90a B III 2b Nr. 6, Bd. 181; Hugenberg's memoranda to prime minister and members of the cabinet, 5 and 25 Apr. 1933, PrGStAB, Rep. 84a/2056. See also Braun, "Weimar-

Ms.," p. 634; Heinrich Class, "Lebenserinnerungen," vol. 2, Heft 8, Class paper/11/C 2, 3 (ForHbg); Bay, "Preussen," p. 179; Trumpp, "Papen," pp. 96–97, 151.

12. Bay, "Preussen," p. 201; Trumpp, "Papen," pp. 97, 121. See also Spahn to Bracht, n.d. [ca. Oct. 1932], Bracht papers, no. 2; editorial in *Vossische Zeitung*, no. 420 (1 Sept. 1932).

13. Pünder to Severing, 1 Aug. 1946, Severing papers/128/44; Gottfried Treivranus, "Schleicher," in *Staat, Wirtschaft und Politik in der Weimarer Republik— Festschrift für Heinrich Brüning*, ed. Ferdinand A. Hermens and Theodor Schieder (Berlin, 1967), pp. 370–75; SitzPrStMin (commissioners), 23 Jan. 1933, ZStAM, Rep. 90a B III 2b Nr. 6, Bd. 181. See also Gessner, *Agrarverbände*, p. 185; Friedrich Schäfer, "Wahlrecht und Wählerverhalten in der Weimarer Republik," in *Wähler- bewegung in der deutschen Geschichte*, ed. Otto Büsch et al. (Berlin, 1978), p. 626.

14. State secretary of the Reich chancellery (Lammers) to Reich minister of the interior, 11 Feb. 1933, ZStAP, 30.01/22075.

15. See chap. 4, above.

16. Heinrich Brüning, "Ein Brief," *Deutsche Rundschau* 70 (July 1947), 9; Braun's response, 21 Feb. 1948, Braun papers/2/C/III/7 (ForHbg). Braun had intended his response to be printed in the *Deutsche Rundschau*, but differences with the editor over wording prevented a publication in full.

17. SitzPrStMin, 26 Mar. 1931, PrGStAB, Rep. 90a/38, and 13 Dec. 1932, Braun papers/11/B-2/54/II (ForHbg). See also Gerhart Seger, "Politischer Brief aus Anhalt," *Das Freie Wort* 3 (12 July 1931), 14–17; "Aus den Verhandlungen vor dem Staatsgerichtshof für das Deutsche Reich vom 10 bis 17. Oktober 1932," p. 42 (type- script) Braun papers/11/B-2/54 (ForHbg); Rudolf Morsey, *Der Untergang des poli- tischen Katholizismus—Die Zentrumspartei Zwischen christlichem Selbstverständnis und "Nationaler Erhebung" 1932/33* (Stuttgart, 1977), pp. 72–73.

18. Braun, "Weimar-Ms.," pp. 546, 551; Erich Matthias, "Die Sozialdemokrati- sche Partei Deutschlands," in *Das Ende der Parteien 1933*, ed. Matthias and Rudolf Morsey (Düsseldorf, 1960), pp. 113–16; Wilhelm Gerviens [i.e., Carl Severing], *Der 20. Juli 1932 in Wahrheit und Dichtung* (Bielefeld, 1946), p. 6; Horst Möller, "Das Ende Preussens," in *Preussen—eine Herausforderung*, ed. Wolfgang Böhme (Karls- ruhe, 1981), pp. 110–11. For a different interpretation of this episode, see Herbert Weichmann, "Kritische Bemerkungen Herbert Weichmanns zu den Briefen Brünings an Sollmann," *Vierteljahrshefte für Zeitgeschichte* 22 (Oct. 1974), 458–60. For even more outlandish proposals to solve the Reich's "leadership crisis," see Hans Menzel, "Carl Severing und der 20. Juli 1932," *Die Gegenwart* 7 (8 Nov. 1952), 734. Menzel was Severing's son-in-law.

19. Walther Vogel, *Deutsche Reichsgliederung und Reichsreform in Vergangen- heit und Gegenwart* (Leipzig, 1932), p. 184, n. 1; Trumpp, "Papen," pp. 41–42; Erich Matthias and Rudolf Morsey, "Die Deutsche Staatspartei," in *Ende*, ed. Matthias and Morsey, pp. 43–45.

20. Pünder to Weismann, 20 Oct. 1931, Braun papers/11/B-2/93 (ForHbg); Braun, "Weimar-Ms.," pp. 545–46; Breitscheid to Grimme, 26 Aug. 1931, Grimme papers/P 49/M-53 (PrGStAB). See also Ehni, *Bollwerk*, pp. 223–28.

21. See documentation in ZStAM, Rep. 90a B III 2b Nr. 6, Bd. 179. For a

different view, see Gerhard Schulz, *Aufstieg des Nationalsozialismus—Krise und Revolution in Deutschland* (Frankfurt, a.M., 1975), p. 544.

22. SitzPrStMin, 3 July 1930, PrGStAB, Rep. 90a/36a; Braun, "Weimar-Ms.," p. 502.

23. Prussian State Cabinet, "Denkschrift über die Vorgänge vom 20. Juli 1932," 7 Nov. 1932, *Drucksachen des Staatsrates*, no. 313 (Berlin, 1932), pp. 28, 54; Bracht to prime minister and members of the cabinet (commissioners), 24 Sept. 1932; Prussian prime minister to Reich minister of the interior et al., 3 May 1933, PrGStAB, Rep. 84a/6370; SitzPrStMin (commissioners), 6 Dec. 1932, ZStAM, Rep. 90a B III 2b Nr. 6, Bd. 181; Arnold Brecht, *Mit der Kraft des Geistes—Lebenserinnerungen* (Stuttgart, 1967), p. 280.

24. See the correspondence between Hirtsiefer and Papen, June 1932, in Trumpp, "Papen", pp. 182–83, 186.

25. See Kerrl to Papen 27 July 1932, ibid., p. 197. See also Winterfeldt to Bracht, 20 Oct. 1932, Bracht papers, no. 2.

26. Bay, "Preussen," p. 171; SitzPrStMin (commissioners), 12 Aug. 1932, ZStAM, Rep. 90a B III 2b Nr. 6, Bd. 181; Papen to Kerrl, 27 Aug. 1932, ZStAP, Rep. 30.01/22074. See also Ehni, *Bollwerk*, p. 274; Holtzendorff, "Bericht," 15 Nov. 1932.

27. See Popitz's remarks in, SitzPrStMin (commissioners), 29 May 1933, PrGStAB, Rep. 90a/41; ministry of the interior (commissioners) to Staatsrat, 26 Sept. 1932, PrGStAB, Rep. 90/2303.

28. *Sitzung des Preussischen Staatsrates*, 24 Nov. 1932 (Berlin, 1932), cols. 680–82; resolution of the Center party caucus, 22 Nov. 1932, Braun papers/637 (IISG). See also the comment in *Deutsche Allgemeine Zeitung*, 24 Nov. 1932.

29. Ministry of justice (commissioners), "Vermerk," 30 Oct. 1932, PrGStAB, Rep. 84a/2056; SitzPrStMin (commissioners), 8 March 1933, PrGStAB, Rep. 90a/41; file note cited by Schäfer, "Wahlrecht," p. 626. For comments on the constitutional niceties of this question by the Reich commissioners and their aides, see the documentation in PrGStAB, Rep. 84a/4388; ZStAM, Rep. 120c B I Nr. 8a, Bd. 3, 90a B III, 2b Nr. 6, Bd. 181. For Schleicher's decision, see SitzPrStMin (commissioners), 23 Jan. 1933, PrGStAB, Rep. 90a/41.

30. See the remarks of *Gauleiter* Sprenger (Hessen-Nassau-Süd) in the Staatsrat, 26 April 1933, PrGStAB, Rep. 84a/4388.

31. Werner Conze, "Die Reichsverfassungsreform als Ziel der Politik Brünings," *Der Staat* 11 (1972), 212.

32. Prussian minister of the interior to members of the cabinet, 2 May 1930, ZStAM, Rep. 77, tit. 253a Nr. 45, Bd. 1.

33. Prussian minister of finance to prime minister, 9 Sept. 1931, ZStAM, Rep. 90a B III 2b Nr. 6, Bd. 180; SitzPrStMin, 19 Dec. 1931, PrGStAB, Rep. 90a/39. For Prussia's ideas on the future of Reich-state financial relations, see documentation in PrGStAB, Rep. 90a/31.

34. SitzPrStMin, 21 Oct. 1930, ZStAM, Rep. 90a B III 2b Nr. 6, Bd. 179. See also SitzPrStMin, 12 and 13 Feb. 1932, PrGStAB, Reps. 90a/40, 90/2303.

35. Morsey, *Untergang*, p. 21; Braun, "Weimar-Ms.," p. 591; Widder, "Reich,"

pp. 39–41; Conze, "Die Reichsverfassungsreform," p. 212; Holtzendorff, "Bericht," 15 Nov. 1932, pp. 3–4.

36. SitzPrStMin (commissioners), 13 Sept. 1932, ZStAM, Rep. 90a, B III 2b Nr. 6, Bd. 181; ibid., 1 Nov. 1932 and 23 Jan. 1933, PrGStAB, Rep. 90a/40–41. On Popitz, see also Sabine Höner, *Der nationalsozialistische Zugriff auf Preussen* (Bochum, 1984), p. 393.

37. See his unpublished "Vortrag" at the Deutsche Hochschule für Politik, 1 Nov. 1932, PrGStAB, Rep. 90/2303; *SBPrLT 1928–1932*, 24 March 1931, vol. 14; cols. 19487–88. See also resolution of the DVP and Deutsche Fraktion in the Landtag, 2 and 6 Nov. 1931, PrGStAB, Rep. 90/2303.

38. SitzPrStMin, 8 Oct. 1931, ZStAM, Rep. 90a B III 2b Nr. 6, Bd. 180.

39. See SitzPrStMin, 4 Feb. 1930, PrGStAB, Rep. 90/108; Waentig's proposal in ibid.; Severing to minister of finance et al., 26 Feb. 1931, PrGStAB, Rep.84a/6370. See also resolution of the Landtag Rules Committee, 5 May 1930, PrGStAB, Rep.90/108; Waentig to members of the cabinet, 12 Aug. 1930, PrGStAB, Rep.84a/6370.

40. Ministry of justice, "Vermerk," 14 July 1930, PrGStAB, Reb. 84a/6370. See also Drews, "Vortrag."

41. See Ministry of the interior, draft answer to a Landtag interpellation, 1 March 1931, ZStAM, Rep. 77, tit. 2025 Nr. 12, Bd. 5.

42. SitzPrStMin, 13 Feb. 1932, PrGStAB, Rep. 90/2303; prime minister to chairman of the Landtag Ways and Means Committee, 30 June 1932, ibid. See also documentation in PrGStAB, Rep. 84a/4275; Höner, *Zugriff*, pp. 28–29.

43. *SBPrLT 1928–1932*, 26 March 1931, vol. 14, cols. 19700–01 (Severing).

44. SitzPrStMin, 14 and 18 Dec. 1931, ZStAM, Rep. 90a B III 2b Nr. 6, Bd. 180.

45. Ministry of the interior, "Vermerk," n.d. [ca. March–April 1932], ZStAM, Rep. 77 tit. 2025 Nr. 12, Bd. 6. See also Severing's remarks to a meeting of governors and district directors, 27 Feb. 1932, Severing papers/54/78. The historical reference was to the Stein-Hardenberg reform era after Prussia's defeat by Napoleon.

46. SitzPrStMin, 6 May 1930, PrGStAB, Rep. 90a/32. See also Waentig's presentation of the legislation and the subsequent Landtag debate in *SBPrLT 1928–1932*, 17 Oct. 1930ff., vol. 11, cols. 15238ff. For the problems of the Berlin city administration at this time, see also Christian Engeli, *Gustav Böss* (Stuttgart, 1971).

47. See Graf Hardenberg, "Vermerk," 27 July 1931, PrGStAB, Rep. 90/2303; Ilse Maurer and Udo Wengst, eds., *Staat und NSDAP 1930–1932: Quellen zur Ära Brüning* (Düsseldorf, 1977), doc. 58, p. 285.

48. See SitzPrStMin (commissioners), 19 Aug. and 2 Sept. 1932, PrGStAB, Reps. 90a/40, 90/2303; Bracht to Gayl, 31 July 1932; Bracht to Planck, 22 Oct. 1932, Bracht papers/2, 4; Thilo Vogelsang, *Reichswehr, Staat und NSDAP* (Stuttgart, 1962), p. 240; Bay, "Preussen," pp. 175ff.

49. See documentation in PrGStAB, Rep. 84a/4275.

50. See SitzPrStMin (commissioners), 2 Sept. 1932, ZStAM, Rep. 90a B III 2 b Nr. 6, Bd. 181; "Verordnung zur Vereinfachung und Verbilligung der Verwaltung," *PrGS*, no. 283/85 (3 Sept. 1932). See also documentation in PrGStAB, Reps. 90/2303, 90a/40–41.

51. *Berliner Tageblatt*, no. 516 (10 Oct. 1932). On earlier efforts to abolish the ministry, see Hirtsiefer to members of the cabinet, 13 Jan. 1928, ZStAM, Rep. 77 tit. 2025, Nr. 12, Bd. 4.

52. For Conservative attacks on the ministry, see *SBPrLT 1928–1932*, 15 Aug. 1931, vol. 17, col. 24740; *Deutsche Zeitung*, no. 255 (29 Oct. 1932); Braun to Amelunxen, 4 Jan. 1950, Braun papers/Teil 2/C/I/5 (PrGStAB). For the transfer of its functions, see ministry of welfare to cabinet (commissioners), 6 Oct. 1932, PrGStAB, Rep. 84a/2056. For Bracht's justification of this measure see Bracht to Cardinal Bertram, 1 Nov. 1932, Bracht papers, no. 4. See also Bay, "Preussen," p. 155.

53. SitzPrStMin (commissioners), 2 Sept. 1932, PrGStAB, Rep. 90a/40; ministry of finance (commissioners) and ministry of social services (commissioners) to members of the cabinet (commissioners), 29 July 1932, PrGStAB, Rep. 90/2303.

54. SitzPrStMin (commissioners), 28/29 [*sic*] Oct. 1932, ZStAM, Rep. 90a B III 2b Nr. 6, Bd. 181; SitzPrStMin (commissioners), 2 Sept. 1932, PrGStAB, Rep. 90a/40.

55. Minister of finance to prime minister, 29 July and 8 Aug. 1932; SitzPrStMin (commissioners), 24 Aug. 1932, PrGStAB, Rep. 90a/2303. See also ministry of agriculture to members of the cabinet, 25 March 1933, PrGStAB, Rep. 84a/2056; *Deutsche Zeitung*, no. 258b (2 Dec. 1932).

56. SitzPrStMin (commissioners), 2 Sept. 1932, PrGStAB, Rep. 90a/40. This folder also contains much additional documentation on the positions taken by various commissioners. For the critical view of an outsider, see Ernst Hamburger, "Verwaltungsreform, Verfassungsreform, Reichsreform," *Das Freie Wort* 4 (20 Nov. 1932), 5–12. For some of Brecht's ideas, see documentation in Braun papers/626 (IISG).

57. SitzPrStMin (commissioners) 19 Aug. 1932, 10 Jan. and 10 Mar. 1933, PrGStAB, Rep.90a/40–41. Ministry of finance (commissioners) to prime minister (commissioners), 8 Aug. 1932, and ministry of education (commissioners) to prime minister (commissioners), 15 Aug. 1932, PrGStAB, Rep. 90/2302; Holtzendorff, "Bericht," p. 15. See also Bay, "Preussen," p. 156–57.

58. SitzPrStMin (commissioners), 12 and 27 Aug., 2 Sept. 1932, and 10 Jan. 1933; PrGStAB, Rep.90a/40–41; minister of the interior (commissioners) to Oberpräsidenten, 30 Aug. 1932, LASH/310/4950; SitzPrStMin (commissioners) 27 July 1932, ZStAM, Rep.90a B III 2b Nr. 6 Bd. 181; and ministry of justice (commissioners), "Ressortbesprechung," 23 Oct. 1932, PrGStAB, Rep. 84a/2056. See also Bay, "Preussen," p. 155.

59. SitzPrStMin (commissioners), 13 Dec. 1932, and 23 Jan. 1933, ZStAM, Rep.90a B III 2b Nr. 6, Bd. 181–82. See also Drews, "Vortrag." On the 1927 abolition of the *Gutsbezirke* see chap. 3, above.

60. Grzesinski to Braun, 27 June 1931, Grzesinski papers/204 (IISG). The letter bears the notation "not sent."

61. Grzesinski, "Im Kampf um die deutsche Republik" (hereafter: "Kampf-Ms.), 31 Aug. 1932, p. 235.

62. Theodor Heuss, *Erinnerungen 1905–1933* (Tübingen, 1963), p. 394.

63. See the documentation in PrGStAB, Rep.90a/31, 39–40; Rep. 90/407.

64. See documentation in Braun papers/300, 304 (IISG); and the official commu-

nique issued after a meeting of Oberpräsidenten and Regierungspräsidenten, 27 Feb. 1932, Severing papers/54/78.

65. SitzPrStMin, 4 Nov. 1930 and 27 Nov. 1931, ZStAM, Rep. 90a B III 2b Nr. 6, Bd. 179; Hitler to Papen, 18 July 1932, quoted in Trumpp, "Papen," p. 195. On the loyalty of the police forces, see documentation in ZStAP, Rep. 15.01/25730. For contrasting views of the reliability of the state's police forces, see *SBPrLT 1928–1932*, 18 Dec. 1930, 20 and 21 Jan. and 14 Oct. 1932, vol. 12, cols. 16456–62, vol. 16, col. 22065, vol. 17, cols. 23553, 23699.

66. SitzPrStMin, 23 Jan., 16 and 25 June 1930, PrGStAB, Rep. 90a/29, 32; ZStAM, Rep. 90a B III 2b Nr. 6, Bd. 179; Wolfgang Runge, *Politik und Beamtentum im Parteienstaat—Die Demokratisierung der politischen Beamten in Preussen zwischen 1918 und 1933* (Stuttgart, 1965), p. 155; Brecht, *Vorspiel*, p. 70. For the disciplinary court's judgment, see president of the Disziplinarhof to prime minister, 11 Mar. 1931, PrGStAB, Rep. 90/478. For a favorable comment, see *Das Freie Wort* 4 (28 Feb. 1932), 8–12. Grzimek's remarks are in *SBPrLT 1928–1932*, 25 Mar. 1931, vol. 14, col. 19640.

67. SitzPrStMin, 1 Sept. 1931, ZStAM, Rep. 90a B III 2b Nr. 6, Bd. 180. See also Grzesinski's pleading of the case of the Prussian police in Grzesinski to Braun, 26 May 1931, Grzesinski papers/204 (IISG).

68. See minister of the interior to Oberpräsidenten and Regierungspräsidenten, 10 Mar. 1931, NSStAH/122a/VIII/17; relevant statistics in Grzesinski papers/743 (IISG); Runge, *Politik*, p. 237.

69. SitzPrStMin (commissioners), 18, 19, and 30 Aug., 2 Sept., 29 Nov. 1932, PrGStAB, Rep. 90/2303, ZStAM, Rep. 90a B III 2b Nr. 6, Bd. 181; PrGStAB, Rep. 90a/40. See also Trumpp, "Papen," p. 126.

70. SitzPrStMin (commissioners) 12 and 19 Aug., 4 and 28/29 [*sic*] Oct., and 4 and 10 Nov. 1932, PrGStAB, Rep. 90a/40; "Auskunft," 24 Aug. 1932, ZStAP, Rep. 30.01/22074; Gayl to state secretary of the Reich chancellery, 5 Sept. 1932, ZStAM, Rep. 90a B III 2b Nr. 6, Bd. 181. See also Bay, "Preussen," pp. 206–07, 215; Höner, *Zugriff*, p. 348.

71. SitzPrStMin (commissioners), 21 and 22 July 1932, PrGStAB, 90a/40; ibid., 19 Aug. 1932, ZStAM, Rep. 90a B III 2b Nr. 6, Bd. 181; ibid., 24 Aug. 1932, PrGStAB, Rep. 90/2303; "Denkschrift . . . 7.11.1932," pp. 26–27; Braun to Hindenburg, 7 Nov. 1932, ZStAP/30.01/22075. See also Hindenburg's executive order, 18 Nov. 1932, Braun papers/11/54-II/B 2 (ForHbg); Ehni, *Bollwerk*, p. 421; Trumpp, "Papen," pp. 38–39; Rudolf Morsey, ed. "Zur Geschichte des 'Preussenschlages' am 20. Juli 1932," *Vierteljahrshefte für Zeitgeschichte* 9 (Oct. 1961), doc. 3, p. 439; Rudolf Amelunxen, *Ehrenmänner und Hexenmeister* (Munich, 1960), p. 108; Höner, *Zugriff*, pp. 340–41; Bay, "Preussen," pp. 136–37.

72. SitzPrStMin (commissioners), 19 Aug. and 27 Sept. 1932, PrGStAB, Rep. 90a/40; notes (n.a.), Jan. 1933, O. Braun papers/640 (IISG); Albert Grzesinski, "Die Futterkrippe," *Das Freie Wort* 5 (19 Feb. 1933), 229–36; Prussian cabinet, "Denkschrift über die Vorgänge vom 20. Juli 1932," 7 Nov. 1932, PrGStAB, Rep. 84a/4388.

73. SitzPrStMin (commissioners), 27 July 1932, PrGStAB, Rep. 90a/40; "Ausführungsbestimmungen," PrGStAB, Rep. 90/478; Maurer and Wengst, eds., *Staat*, doc. 74, p. 334; Amelunxen, *Ehrenmännner*, p. 108. See also Hitler to Papen,

18 July 1932, cited in Trumpp, "Papen," p. 195; Bay, "Preussen," p. 138; Michael Schneider, *Das Arbeitsbeschaffungsprogramm des ADGB* (Bonn–Bad Godesberg, 1975), p. 189; Morsey, *Entstehung*, p. 39.

74. Bay, "Preussen," pp. 138, 152–53; Ehni, *Bollwerk*, p. 278; Thilo Vogelsang, *Kurt von Schleicher—Ein General als Politiker* (Göttingen, 1965), p. 75; Höner *Zugriff*, pp. 340–41; Heinz Höhne, *Mordsache Röhm* (Reinbek bei Hamburg, 1984), p. 232.

75. SitzPrStMin (commissioners), 30 Aug. 1932, PrGStAB, Rep. 90a/40; *ADGB-Protokolle*, 9 and 10 Sept. 1932, p. 125.

76. SitzPrStMin (commissioners), 28 July and 4 Oct. 1932, PrGStAB, Rep. 90a/40; Morsey, ed., "Preussenschlag," p. 435. See also Bay, "Preussen," p. 150; Möller, "Ende," p. 114; Höner, *Zugriff*, p. 391. The most recent full-scale biography of Gustav Noske is Wolfram Wette, *Gustav Noske: Eine politische Biographie* (Düsseldorf, 1987).

77. See Popitz's remarks in SitzPrStMin (commissioners), 1 Nov. 1932, PrGStAB, Rep. 90a/40; ibid., Aug. 1932; Höner, *Zugriff*, p. 348.

78. SitzPrStMin (commissioners), 23 Jan., 15 Feb., 25 Mar. 1933, PrGStAB, Rep. 90a/41. See also Prussian prime minister to members of the cabinet, 21 June 1933, PrGStAB, Rep. 84a/6370; Dieter Rebentisch, "Hitlers Reichskanzlei zwischen Politik und Verwaltung," in *Verwaltung contra Menschenführung im Staat Hilters*, ed. Rebentisch and Karl Teppe (Göttingen, 1986), pp. 76–77.

Chapter 10. Conclusion

1. Braun, "Weimar-Ms.," pp. 640–41. See also Albert Grzesinski, "Im Kampf um die deutsche Republik—Lebensweg eines Staatenlosen" (hereafter: Grzesinski, "Kampf"), p. 184, Grzesinski papers, 2457; Hildebrandt to Grimme, 18 May 1946, Adolf Grimme papers/56; *Das Freie Wort* 5 (15 Jan. 1933), 95–96; Werner Freiherr von Rheinbaben, *Kaiser, Kanzler, Präsidenten—Erinnerungen* (Mainz, 1968), pp. 280–81; Hirtsiefer and members of the Prussian cabinet to Reich commissioner for Prussia, 25 March 1933, PrGStAB, Rep. 84a/4388.

2. Heinrich Class, "Lebenserinnerungen" (typescript), 2:923–24, ADV papers, 11/C2, 3 (ForHbg).

3. SitzPrStMin (commissioners) 4 and 15 Feb., 8 and 25 March, 1933, PrGStAB, Rep. 90a/41. On the immediate consequences of Göring's rule, see also Sabine Höner, *Der nationalsozialistische Zugriff auf Preussen: Preussischer Staat und nationalsozialistische Machteroberungsstrategie* (Bochum, 1984), pp. 409ff., 450ff. For complaints by the DNVP on the Nazis' personnel policies, see Friedrich Freiherr Hiller von Gaertringen, "Die Deutschnationale Volkspartei," in *Das Ende der Parteien 1933*, ed. Erich Matthias and Rudolf Morsey (Düsseldorf, 1960), pp. 640–41.

4. See Papen to Braun and enclosure, 6 Feb. 1933, Braun papers/11/54II/B2 (ForHbg); "Anlage zum Antrag des Preussischen Staatsministeriums auf Ausführung der Verordnung v. 6.2.1933," 6 Feb. 1933, ZStAP, 30.01/22075; Joseph Goebbels, *Vom Kaiserhof zur Reichskanzlei*, 28th ed. (Berlin, 1940), pp. 258–59 (9 Feb. 1933). See also Jürgen Bay, "Der Preussenkonflikt 1932/33: Ein Kapitel aus der Ver-

fassungsgeschichte der Weimarer Republik," Ph.D. diss., University of Erlangen, 1965, pp. 267–68.

5. For the Center party's protest against the decree of Feb. 6, see *Germania*, no. 42 (11 Feb. 1933). For the party's appeasement policy, which included voting for a Prussian Enabling Law granting Göring decree powers, see Rudolf Morsey, *Der Untergang des politischen Katholizismus—die Zentrumspartei zwischen christlichem Selbstverständnis und 'Nationaler Erhebung' 1932/33* (Stuttgart, 1977), pp. 111–12, 185, 197.

6. Braun, "Weimar-Ms.," pp. 680–81; Arnold Brecht, *Mit der Kraft des Geistes—Lebenserinnerungen* (Stuttgart, 1967), pp. 295–96; "Hamburger Interview," 6 Oct. 1976.

7. Albert C. Grzesinski, *Inside Germany*, tr. Alexander S. Lipschitz (New York, 1939), p. 119; Braun to Cerf, 26 Sept. 1944, Braun papers, Rep. 92, Teil 2/C/I/41 (PrGStAB); Joseph Goebbels, *Die Tagebücher von Joseph Goebbels, Teil I: Aufzeichnungen, 1924–1941*, ed. Elke Fröhlich (Munich, 1987), 4:77 (17 March, 1940); Henning Köhler, *Das Ende Preussens in französischer Sicht* (Berlin, 1982), pp. 13, 75.

8. *German Historical Institute London Bulletin* 10 (Feb. 1988), 24.

9. Walter Tormin, *Geschichte der deutschen Parteien seit 1848*, 3d ed. (Stuttgart, 1968), pp. 128–29; Michael Stürmer, *Koalition und Opposition in der Weimar Republik 1924–1928* (Düsseldorf, 1967), p. 278.

10. Höltermann to Braun, 3 Jan. 1933, Braun papers/Rep. 92, Teil 2/C/1/46 (PrGStAB).

11. Braun to Hoegner, 5 Jan. 1948, ibid., 120; Detlef Junker, *Die Deutsche Zentrumspartei und Hitler 1932/33* (Stuttgart, 1969), pp. 127ff., 156ff., 179ff.; Morsey, *Untergang*, pp. 19, 95, 116, 185, 197.

12. Horst Möller, *Parlamentarismus in Preussen 1919–1932* (Düsseldorf, 1985) provides the most detailed discussion of the Prussian constitution.

13. On this development, see esp. Manfred Rauh, *Die Parlamentarisierung des deutschen Reiches* (Düsseldorf, 1977).

14. Gordon Craig, "Prussianism and Democracy: Otto Braun and Konrad Adenauer," in *The End of Prussia* (Madison, Wis., 1984), p. 72.

15. Braun to Ritzel, 9 Feb. 1950, Braun papers/Rep. 92, Teil 2/C/I/233 (PrGStAB).

16. Winfried Becker, *CDU und CSU, 1945–1950: Vorläufe, Gründung und Regionalentwicklung bis zum Entstehen der Bundespartei* (Mainz, 1987), pp. 77, 107–08, 123.

17. Arnulf Baring, *Machtwechsel: Die Ära Brandt-Scheel* (Stuttgart, 1982), p. 32.

Bibliography

Unpublished and Archival Sources

Amsterdam. International Institute for Social History (IISG)
Otto Braun papers
Albert Grzesinski papers
Paul Herz papers
Karl Kautsky papers
Erich Kuttner papers

Berlin. Preussisches Geheimes Staatsarchiv (PrGStAB)
Akten des Finanzministeriums (Rep. 151)
Akten des Innenministeriums (Rep. 77)
Akten des Justizministeriums (Rep. 84a)
Akten des Ministeriums für Handel und Gewerbe (Rep. 120)
Akten des Ministeriums für öffentliche Arbeiten (Rep. 93)
Akten des Staatsministeriums (Rep. 90)
Carl Heinrich Becker papers (Rep. 92)
Otto Braun papers (Rep. 92)
Adolf Grimme papers (Rep. 92)
Friedrich Trendelenburg papers (Rep. 92)

Berlin. Archiv der Historischen Kommission zu Berlin (HiKo) Restakten des Allge-
meinen Deutschen Gewerkschaftsbundes (NB 65/0053)
Otto Hörsing papers

Bonn–Bad Godesberg. Archiv der sozialen Demokratie (ArchdSD)
Otto Braun papers
Karl Giebel papers
Ernst Heilmann papers
Wilhelm Keil papers
Hermann Molkenbuhr papers
Hermann Müller papers
Gustav Noske papers
Carl Severing papers

Cologne. Historisches Archiv der Stadt Köln
Wilhelm Marx papers

341

Hamburg. Forschungsstelle für die Geschichte des Nationalsozialismus in Hamburg (ForHbg)
    Akten des Alldeutschen Verbandes (412)
    Akten der Parteien (740)
    Akten der Verbände (7533)
    Heinrich Class papers
    Alfred Diller papers

Hamburg. Staatsarchiv
    Carl Petersen papers

Hanover. Niedersächsisches Hauptstaatsarchiv (NSStAH)
    Akten der SPD. Bezirk Hannover (Rep. 310 II)
    Akten des Oberpräsidiums Hannover (Rep. 122a)
    Akten des Regierungspräsidiums Lüneburg (Rep. 80)

Koblenz. Bundesarchiv (BA)
    Akten der Reichskanzlei (R 43 I and II)
    Bestand DDP (R 45 III)
    Bestand DVP (R 45 II)
    Bestand Kleine Erwerbungen
    Bestand Parteien-und Verbandsdrucksachen (ZSg 1)
    Bestand Stahlhelm (R 72)
    Hermann Dietrich papers
    Eduard Dingeldey papers
    Anton Erkelenz papers
    Georg Gothein papers
    Rudolf ten Hompel papers
    Wolf Jaenicke papers
    Erich Koch-Weser papers
    Wilhelm Külz papers
    Friedrich von Loebell papers
    Paul Moldenhauer papers
    Friedrich Saemisch papers
    Gustav Stresemann papers
    Gottfried Traub papers

Merseburg. Zentrales Staatsarchiv (ZStAM)
    Akten des Staatsministeriums (Rep. 90a)
    Akten des Ministeriums des Innern (Rep. 77)
    Akten des Ministeriums für Handel und Gewerbe (Rep. 120)

New York. Leo Baeck Institute (LBI)
    Ernst Feder papers
    Paul Hirsch papers
    Kurt Kersten papers

Philipp Loewenfeld papers
Fritz Mauthner papers
Fritz Rathenau papers

Potsdam. Zentrales Staatsarchiv (ZStAP)
Hermann Müller papers
Gustav Noske papers
Fritz Bracht papers

Schleswig. Landesarchiv Schleswig-Holstein (LASH)
Akten des Oberpräsidiums Schleswig-Holstein (Rep. 301)
Akten des Provinzial-Schulkollegiums (Rep. 302)
Akten des Regierungspräsidiums Schleswig (Rep. 309)

Significant Individual Unpublished Documents

Braun, Otto. "Aus den Verhandlungen vor dem Staatsgerichtshof für das Deutsche Reich vom 10. bis 17. Oktober 1932." Typescript. Braun papers/11/B-2/54 (ForHbg).

Brecht, Arnold. "Vorschläge für eine geschäftstechnische Beratungsunterlage zur Frage einer Änderung des Verhältnisses des Reiches zu den Ländern—Vorentwurf Juli 1928." Hermann Müller papers/II/117 (AdSD).

Class, Heinrich. "Lebenserinnerungen." Class papers/11/C 2-3 (ForHbg).

Falk, Bernhard. "Aufzeichnungen." Typescript. Kleine Erwerbungen/385 (BA).

Grzesinski, Albert. "Aug dem Wege zum Zwanzigsten Juli 1932." Grzesinski papers/2456.

———. "Im Kampf um die deutsche Republik—Lebensweg eines Staatenlosen." Grzesinski papers/2457.

———. "'Reichskanzler Dr. Brünings Sturz.'" In Eine politische Artikelserie. Typescript. Grzesinski papers/2456.

———. "Warum blieb die Sozialdemokratie am 20. Juli passiv?" Artikelserie 7. Grzesinski papers/2456.

Holtzendorff, Arndt von. "Bericht über die Sitzung der vereinigten Reichsratsausschüsse, 15 Nov. 1932." PrGStAB, Rep.216/139.

Prussian cabinet. "Anlageheft zu der Erklärung des Preussischen Staatsministeriums vom 10.8.1932." Braun papers/11/B-2/54 (ForHbg).

———. "Anlageheft zu der Erklärung des Preussischen Staatsministeriums vom 29. August 1932." Braun papers/11/B-2/54 (ForHbg).

———. "Anlageheft zu der Erwiderung der Reichsregierung vom 25. August 1932." Braun papers/11/B-2/54 (ForHbg).

———. "Anlageheft zu der Gegenerklärung der Reichsregierung vom 5.8.1932." Braun papers/11/B-2/54 (ForHbg).

———. "Denkschrift über Vorgänge vom 20. Juli 1932." Berlin: Drucksachen des Staatsrates, no. 313, 7 Nov. 1932.

Rathenau, Fritz. "Als Jude im Dienste von Reich und Staat." Typescript. Rathenau papers.

Primary Sources

Documentary, Legal, and Parliamentary Publications

Die Akten der Reichskanzlei: Die Kabinette Brüning I und II. Ed. Tilmann Koops. 2 vols. Boppard a.Rh., 1982, 1988.

———. *Die Regierung Hitler, Teil I: 1933/1934.* Ed. Karl-Heinz Minuth. 2 vols. Boppard a.Rh., 1983.

———. *Die Kabinette Luther I und II.* Ed. Karl-Heinz Minuth. 2 vols. Boppard a.Rh., 1977.

———. *Die Kabinette Marx I und II.* Ed. Günter Abramovski. 2 vols. Boppard a.Rh., 1973.

———. *Die Kabinette Müller I und II.* Ed. Martin Vogel. 2 vols. Boppard a.Rh., 1970.

———. *Die Regierung Schleicher.* Ed. Anton Golecki. Boppard a. Rh., 1986.

Aktenstücke zum Reichsvolksschulgesetz. Ed. Walter Landé. Leipzig, 1928.

Allgemeiner Deutscher Gewerkschaftsbund. *Protokolle der Verhandlungen der Kongresse der Gewerkschaften Deutschlands.* Berlin, 1925– .

Handbuch für den Preussischen Landtag 1925–1933. Ed. E. Kienast. 4 vols. Berlin, 1925–33.

Handbuch über den Preussischen Staat. Ed. Preussisches Staatsministerium. 7 vols. Berlin, 1925–31.

Hannover, Heinrich, and Elisabeth Hannover-Drück, eds. *Politische Justiz, 1918–1933.* Frankfurt a.M., 1966.

Hirtsiefer, Heinrich. *Die Preussische Regierungskoalition von 1925–1928: Leistungen und Erfolge.* Berlin, 1928.

Kempner, Robert, ed. *Der Verpasste Nazi-Stop: Die NSDAP als Staats- und republikfeindliche, hochverräterische Verbindung.* Frankfurt, 1983.

Länderkonferenz am 16., 17. und 18. Januar 1928. Ed. Reich Press office. Berlin, 1928.

Maurer, Ilse, and Udo Wengst, eds. *Staat und NSDAP 1930–32: Quellen zur Ära Brüning.* Düsseldorf, 1977.

Ministerial-Blatt für die preussische innere Verwaltung. Berlin, 1925– .

Preussen contra Reich: Stenogrammbericht der Verhandlungen vor dem Staatsgerichtshof in Leipzig . . . Oktober, 1932. Pref. by Arnold Brecht. Berlin, 1933.

Preussen 1932: Politik in Stichworten. Ed. Prussian Press Office. 2d ed. Berlin, 1932.

Preussische Gesetzsammlung. Berlin, 1925– .

Quellen zur deutschen Schulgeschichte seit 1800. Ed. Gerhardt Giese. Göttingen, 1961.

Sammlung der Drucksachen des preussischen Landtages, 1925–1933. Berlin, 1925–33.

Sitzungsberichte des preussischen Landtages, 1924–1933. Berlin, 1924–33.

Statistisches Jahrbuch für das Deutsche Reich, 1925–1933. Ed. Reich Statistical Office. Berlin, 1925–33.

Statistisches Jahrbuch für den Preussischen Staat, 1925–1933. Ed. Prussian Statistical Office. Berlin, 1925–33.

Weber, Hermann, ed. *Der deutsche Kommunismus: Dokumente 1915–1945*. 3d ed. Cologne, 1973.

Handbooks

Biographisches Lexikon des Sozialismus. Ed. Franz Osterroth. Hanover, 1960.
Biographisches Staatshandbuch. Ed. Wilhelm Kosch and Eugen Kuri. 2 vols. Bern, 1963.
Chronik der deutschen Sozialdemokratie. Ed. Franz Osterroth and Dieter Schuster. 3 vols. Bonn–Bad Godesberg, 1971.
Die bürgerlichen Parteien in Deutschland, 1930–1945, 2 vols. Ed. Dieter Fricke et al. Leipzig, 1968, 1970.
Dittman, Wilhelm. *Das politische Deutschland vor Hitler*. Zurich, 1945.
MdR—Biographisches Handbuch der Reichstage 1848–1933. Ed. Max Schwarz. Hanover, 1965.
Reichshandbuch der deutschen Gesellschaft. Ed. Robert Volz. 2 vols. Berlin, 1930.
Schulthess' Europäischer Geschichtskalender. Munich, 1929– .
Wähler und Wahlen in der Weimarer Republik. Ed. Alfred Milatz. 2d ed. Bonn, 1968.
Wahlen und Abstimmungen in der Weimarer Republik. Ed. Jürgen Falter et al. Munich, 1986.
Wahlen in Deutschland. Ed. Bernhard Vogel et al. Berlin, 1971.

Memoirs and Diaries

Amelunxen, Rudolf. *Ehrenmänner und Hexenmeister—Erlebnisse und Betrachtungen*. Munich, 1960.
Brandt, Willy. *Begegnungen und Einsichten*. Hamburg, 1976.
————. *Links und frei: Mein Weg 1930–1950*. Hamburg, 1982.
Braun, Magnus Freiherr von. *Von Ostpreussen bis Texas*. Stollhamm (Oldenburg), 1955.
Braun, Otto. *Von Weimar zu Hitler*. New York, 1940. 2d ed. Hamburg, 1949.
————. "Rückblick auf Weimar: Ein Briefwechsel zwischen Otto Braun und Joseph Wirth im Exil." Ed. Hagen Schulze. *Vierteljahrshefte für Zeitgeschichte* 26 (Jan. 1978), 144–85.
Brecht, Arnold. *Lebenserinnerungen*. 2 vols. Stuttgart, 1966, 1967.
————. *Vorspiel zum Schweigen—Das Ende der Deutschen Republik*. Vienna, 1948.
Bredt, Johann Victor. *Erinnerungen und Dokumente 1914 bis 1933*. Ed. Martin Schumacher. Düsseldorf, 1970.
Brüning, Heinrich. *Briefe und Gespräche 1934–1945*. Ed. Claire Nix et al. Stuttgart, 1974.
————. *Briefe 1946–1960*. Ed. Claire Nix et al. Stuttgart, 1974.
————. *Memoiren*. Stuttgart, 1970.
————. "Ein Brief." *Deutsche Rundschau* 70 (July 1947), 1–22.
Buchwitz, Otto. *50 Jahre Funktionär der deutschen Arbeiterbewegung*. 2d ed. Berlin, 1973.
Curtius, Julius. *Sechs Jahre Minister der Deutschen Republik*. Heidelberg, 1948.
Feder, Ernst. *Heute sprach ich mit . . . Tagebücher eines Berliner Publizisten 1926–1932*. Ed. Cécile Lowenthal-Hensel and Arnold Paucker. Frankfurt a.M., 1971.

Friedensburg, Ferdinand. *Lebenserinnerungen.* Frankfurt a.M., 1969.

Gerviens, Wilhelm [Carl Severing]. *Der 20. Juli 1932 in Wahrheit und Dichtung.* Bielefeld, [1946].

Gessler, Otto. *Reichswehrpolitik in der Weimarer Zeit.* Ed. Kurt Sendtner. Stuttgart, 1958.

Goebbels, Joseph. *Vom Kaiserhof zur Reichskanzlei.* 28th ed. Berlin, 1940.

―――. *Die Tagebücher von Joseph Goebbels,* Teil I: *Aufzeichnungen, 1924–1941.* Ed. Elke Fröhlich. 4 vols. Munich, 1987.

Grimme, Adolf. *Briefe.* Ed. Dieter Sauberzweig. Heidelberg, 1967.

Grzesinski, Albert C. *Inside Germany.* Trans. Alexander S. Lipschitz. New York, 1939.

Heimann, Hugo. *Vom tätigen Leben.* Berlin, 1949.

Hellpach, Willy. *Der deutsche Charakter.* Bonn, 1954.

Heuss, Theodor. *Erinnerungen 1905–1933.* Tübingen, 1963.

Hoffman, Josef. *Journalist in Republik, Diktatur und Besatzungszeit—Erinnerungen 1916–1947.* Ed. Rudolf Morsey. Mainz, 1977.

Höpker—Aschoff, Hermann. *Unser Weg durch die Zeit.* Berlin, 1936.

Keil, Wilhelm. *Erlebnisse eines Sozialdemokraten.* 2 vols. Stuttgart, 1947–48.

Kessler, Harry Graf. *Tagebücher 1918–1937.* Ed. Wolfgang Pfeiffer-Belli. Frankfurt a.M., 1961.

Klepper, Otto. "Das Ende der Republik." *Die Gegenwart* 2 (30 Sept. 1947), 20–22.

Knapp, Thomas A., ed. "Heinrich Brüning im Exil: Briefe an Wilhelm Sollmann 1940–1946." *Vierteljahreshefte für Zeitgeschichte* 22 (Jan. 1974), 93–120.

Köhler, Heinrich. *Lebenserinnerungen des Politikers und Staatsmannes 1878–1949.* Ed. Josef Becker. Stuttgart, 1964.

Lange, Friedrich C. A. *Gross-Berliner Tagebuch 1920–1933.* Berlin-Lichtenrade, 1951.

Leber, Julius. *Ein Mann geht seinen Weg.* Berlin, 1952.

Lemmer, Ernst. *Manches war doch anders—Erinnerungen eines deutschen Demokraten.* Frankfurt a.M., 1968.

Levi, Paul. *Zwischen Spartakus und Sozialdemokratie—Schriften, Aufsätze, Reden und Briefe.* Ed. Charlotte Beradt. Frankfurt a.M., 1969.

Löbe, Paul. *Der Weg war lang.* 3d ed. Berlin, 1954.

Luppe, Hermann. *Mein Leben.* Ed. Stadtarchiv Nuremberg et al. Nuremberg, 1977.

Luther, Hans. *Politiker ohne Partei.* Stuttgart, 1960.

Matull, Wilhelm. *Ostdeutschlands Arbeiterbewegung.* Würzburg, 1973.

Mayer, Eugen. *Skizzen aus dem Leben der Weimarer Republik.* Berlin, 1962.

Mayer, Gustav. *Erinnerungen.* Zurich, 1949.

Niekisch, Ernst. *Politische Schriften.* 2d ed. Cologne, 1966.

Noske, Gustav. *Erlebtes aus Aufstieg und Niedergang einer Demokratie.* Offenbach a.M., 1947.

Papen, Franz von. *Vom Scheitern einer Demokratie, 1930–1933.* Mainz, 1968.

―――. *Der Wahrheit eine Gasse.* Munich, 1952.

Pünder, Hermann. *Von Preussen nach Europa—Lebenserinnerungen.* Stuttgart, 1968.

———. *Politik in der Reichskanzlei—Aufzeichnungen aus den Jahren 1929–1932*. Ed. Thilo Vogelsang. Stuttgart, 1961.

Radbruch, Gustav. *Der innere Weg—Aufriss meines Lebens*. Stuttgart, 1951.

Rheinbaben, Werner Freiherr von. *Kaiser, Kanzler, Präsidenten—Erinnerungen*. Mainz, 1968.

Schiffer, Eugen. *Ein Leben für den Liberalismus*. Berlin, 1951.

Schlange-Schönigen, Hans. *Am Tage Danach*. Hamburg, 1946.

Scholz, Arno. *Null vier—ein Jahrgang zwischen den Fronten*. Berlin-Grunewald, 1962.

Schreiber, Georg. *Zwischen Demokratie und Diktatur—Persönliche Erinnerungen . . . 1919–1944*. Regensberg-Münster, 1949.

Sender, Toni. *The Autobiography of a German Rebel*. London, 1940.

Severing, Carl. *Mein Lebensweg*. 2 vols. Cologne, 1950.

Stampfer, Friedrich. *Erfahrungen und Erkenntnisse*. Cologne, 1957.

———. *Mit dem Gesicht nach Deutschland—Aus dem Nachlass Friedrich Stampfers*. Ed. Erich Matthias. Düsseldorf, 1968.

Staudinger, Hans. *Wirtschaftspolitik im Weimarer Staat—Lebenserinnerungen . . . 1889–1934*. Ed. Hagen Schulze. Bonn, 1982.

Stegerwald, Adam. "Aus meinem Leben." In *25 Jahre christliche Gewerkschaftsbewegung 1899–1924*, 132–52. Berlin, 1924.

Stockhausen, Max von. *6 Jahre Reichskanzlei*. Ed. Walter Görlitz. Bonn, 1954.

Stresemann, Gustav. *Reden und Schriften 1897–1926*. Ed. Rochus Freiherr von Rheinbaben. 2 vols. Dresden, 1926.

———. *Vermächtnis—Der Nachlass in drei Bänden*. Ed. Henry Bernhard et al. 3 vols. Berlin, 1932.

Treviranus, Gottfried R. *Für Deutschland im Exil*. Düsseldorf, 1973.

Wachenheim, Hedwig. *Vom Grossbürgertum zur Sozialdemokratie*. Ed. Susanne Miller. Berlin, 1973.

Westarp, Cuno Graf. *Am Grabe der Parteiherrschaft*. Berlin, 1932.

Wilmovsky, Thilo Freiherr von. *Rückblickend möchte ich sagen*. Oldenburg, 1961.

Official and Semioffical Party Publications

SOCIAL DEMOCRATIC PARTY (SPD)

Die Arbeit, Zeitschrift für Gewerkschaftspolitik und Wirtschaftskunde. 1925– .

Das Freie Wort. 1929– .

Die Gesellschaft. 1925– .

Kampffmeyer, Paul, ed. *Das Heidelberger Programm*. Rpt. Offenbach a.M., 1947.

Heimann, Hugo. *Der Reichshaushalt*. Berlin, 1929.

Jahrbuch der deutschen Sozialdemokratie. 1926– .

Der Klassenkampf. 1928– .

Krüger, Hans and Fritz Baade, eds. *Sozialdemokratische Agrarpolitik*. Berlin, 1927.

Mitteilungsblatt der SPD. 1924– .

Neue Blätter für den Sozialismus. 1925– .

Die Neue Zeit. 1925– .

Protokoll über die Verhandlungen des Parteitages der SPD, Heidelberg, 1925. Berlin, 1925.

Protokoll über die Verhandlungen des Parteitages der SPD, Kiel, 1927. Berlin, 1927.

Protokoll über die Verhandlungen des Parteitages der SPD, Magdeburg, 1929. Berlin, 1929.

Protokoll über die Verhandlungen des Parteitages der SPD, Leipzig, 1931. Berlin, 1931.

Protokoll über die Verhandlungen des Preussentages der SPD, Berlin, 1928. Berlin, 1928.

Raiffeisen—ein deutschnationaler Finanz- und Korruptionsskankal. Ed. Richard Hauschild. Berlin, 1930.

Rundschreiben des Parteivorstandes der SPD. 1925– .

Sozialistische Monatshefte. 1925– .

Sozialdemokratische Parteikorrespondenz. 1925– .

Sozialdemokratische Parteikorrespondenz (Ergänzungsband). 1930.

Sozialistische Politik und Wirtschaft. 1925–1928.

SPD, Parteivorstand, ed. *Der Bürgerblock: Wie er wurde- und was er ist.* Berlin, 1927.

———. *Es geht um Preussen! Referenten-Material zum Stahlhelm-Volksbegehren.* Berlin, 1931.

———. *Gegen die Parteispaltung.* Berlin, 1931.

———. *Materialien zur Landtagswahl 1928.* Berlin, 1928.

———. *Materialien zur Landtagswahl 1932.* Berlin, 1932.

———. *Der Weg zum Einheitsstaat—Gutachten zur Frage der Vereinheitlichung des Reiches.* Berlin, 1929.

———. *Vorwärts.* 1925– .

CENTER PARTY (Z)

Bericht des 4. Reichsparteitages der Deutschen Zentrumspartei, Kassel, 1925. Berlin [1925].

Bericht des 5. Reichsparteitages der Deutschen Zentrumspartei, Köln, 1928. Berlin [1929].

Deutsche Republik. 1926– .

Die Einheit der nationalen Politik. Ed. Alfred Bozi and Alfred Niemann. Berlin, 1925.

Germania. 1925– .

Mitteilungen der Deutschen Zentrumspartei. 1925– .

Politisches Jahrbuch. 1925– .

Die Protokolle der Reichstagsfraktion und des Fraktionsvorstandes der Deutschen Zentrumspartei 1926–1933. Ed. Rudolf Morsey. Mainz, 1969.

Schreiber, Georg. *Brüning und Hitler-Schleicher—Das Zentrum in der Opposition.* Cologne, 1932.

———. *Regierung ohne Volk.* Cologne, 1932.

Schreiber, Georg, ed. *Zentrum und Reichspolitik—Ein politisches Handbuch in Frage und Antwort.* Cologne, 1930.

Schulte, Karl Anton, ed. *Nationale Arbeit: Das Zentrum und sein Wirken in der deutschen Republik.* Berlin, [1929].

Teipel, Heinrich. *Wir müssen aus dem Turm heraus! Gedanken zur Krise des deutschen Parteiwesens.* Berlin, 1925.
Das Zentrum. 1930– .

GERMAN DEMOCRATIC PARTY (DDP) AND GERMAN STATE
PARTY (DStP)
Bäumer, Gertrud.*Grundlagen demokratischer Politik.* Berlin, 1928.
DDP-Jahresberichte. 1926– .
Der Demokrat—Mitteilungen aus der DDP. 1925– .
Demokratischer Zeitungsdienst. 1925– .
Erkelenz, Anton, ed. *Zehn Jahre Deutsche Republik—Ein Handbuch für republikanische Politik.* Berlin, 1928.
Die Hilfe. 1925– .

GERMAN NATIONALIST PEOPLE'S PARTY (DNVP)
Der Deutschen-Spiegel—Politische Wochenschrift. 1925– .
DNVP Mitteilungen/Mitteilungen der Parteizentrale. 1929– .
Freytag-Loringhoven, Axel Freiherr von. *DNVP.* Berlin, 1931.
Lambach, Walther, ed. *Politische Praxis 1926.* Hamburg, 1926.
Mitteilungen aus dem Büro Lambach. 1923–1927.
Quaatz, R. G., and Paul Bang. *Das Freiheitsprogramm der DNVP.* Berlin, [1932].
Weiss, Max, ed. *Der nationale Wille.* Berlin, 1928.
Zentrum—Steigbügelhalter der Sozialdemokratie. Berlin, 1932.

GERMAN PEOPLE'S PARTY (DVP)
Deutsche Stimmen. 1925– .
Kempkes, Adolf, ed. *Deutscher Aufbau—Nationalliberale Arbeit der DVP.* Berlin, 1927.
Nationalliberale Correspondenz. 1925– .
Die Reichsgemeinschaft—Blätter der Reichsgemeinschaft junger Volksparteiler. 1930– .
Stenographische Niederschrift der Verhandlungen des 8. Parteitages der Deutschen Volkspartei . . . 1930. Berlin, 1930.
Wahlhandbuch 1928. Ed. Reichsgeschäftsstelle der DVP. Berlin, 1928.

NATIONAL SOCIALIST GERMAN WORKERS'S PARTY (NSDAP)
Franke, Heinz. *Korruptionssumpf Preussen.* Munich, 1932.
Hamburger Tageblatt. 1928– .
Völkischer Beobachter. 1925– .

COMMUNIST PARTY (KPD)
Die Generallinie—Rundschreiben des Zentralkomitees der KPD 1929–1933. Ed. Hermann Weber, Düsseldorf, 1981.
Remmele, H. *Kommunismus die einzige Rettung.* Berlin, 1931.
Thälmann, Ernst. *Volksrevolution über Deutschland.* Berlin, 1931.
_____. *Roter Sturm über Preussen.* Berlin, 1932.

————. *Wie schaffen wir die rote Einheitsfront? Antwort auf 21 Fragen von SPD-Arbeitern.* Berlin, 1932.

Die Wahrheit über Preussen. Ed. KPD Landtagsfraktion. Berlin, 1932.

Secondary Sources

Abegg, Wilhelm. "Die Preussische Verwaltung and ihre Reform, Länder und Reich." In *Zehn Jahre Deutsche Republik: Ein Handbuch für republikanische Politik,* ed. Anton Erkelenz, 467–512. Berlin, 1928.

Adams, Henry M., and Robin K. Adams. *Rebel Patriot: A Biography of Franz von Papen.* Santa Barbara, Calif., 1987.

Adenauer, Konrad. "Konrad Adenauer als Präsident des Preussischen Staatsrates." In *Konrad Adenauer, Oberbürgermeister von Köln,* ed. Hugo Stehkämper, 355–404. Cologne, 1976.

Adolph, Hans J. L. *Otto Wels und die Politik der deutschen Sozialdemokratie 1894–1939.* Berlin, 1970.

Anschütz, Gerhard. *Das preussisch-deutsche Problem.* Berlin, 1932.

Apelt, Willipalt. *Geschichte der Weimarer Verfassung.* 2d ed. Munich, 1964.

Aviv, Aviva. "The SPD and the KPD at the End of Weimar: Similarity within Contrast." *Internationale Wissenschaftliche Korrespondenz* 14 (June 1978), 171–86.

Bach, Jürgen A. *Franz von Papen in der Weimarer Republik.* Düsseldorf, 1977.

Bahne, Siegfried. *Die KPD und das Ende von Weimar.* Frankfurt a.M., 1976.

————. "Die Kommunistische Partei Deutschlands." In *Das Ende der Parteien 1933,* ed. Erich Matthias and Rudolf Morsey, 655–739. Düsseldorf, 1960.

————. "Sozialfaschismus." *International Review of Social History* 10 (1965), 211–45.

Baring, Arnulf. *Machtwechsel: Die Ära Brandt-Scheel.* Stuttgart, 1982.

Barmeyer, Heide. *Andreas Hermes und die Organisation der deutschen Landwirtschaft.* Stuttgart, 1971.

Bay, Jürgen. "Der Preussenkonflikt 1932/33: Ein Kapitel aus der Verfassungsgeschichte der Weimarer Republik." Ph.D. diss., University of Erlangen, 1965.

Becker, Carl H. *Die Pädagogische Akademie im Aufbau unseres nationalen Bildungswesens.* Leipzig, 1926.

Becker, Josef. "Brüning, Prälat Kaas und das Problem einer Regierungsbeteiligung der NSDAP, 1930–1932." *Historische Zeitschrift* 196 (Feb. 1963), 74–111.

————. "Joseph Wirth und die Krise des Zentrums . . . 1927–28." *Zeitschrift für die Geschichte des Oberrheins* 109 (1961), 361–482.

Becker, Josef, ed. "Zur Politik der Wehrmachtabteilung in der Regierungskrise 1926/27." *Vierteljahrshefte für Zeitgeschichte* 14 (Jan. 1966), 69–78.

Becker, Winfried. *CDU und CSU, 1945–1950: Vorläufe, Gründung und Regionalentwicklung bis zun Entstehen der Bundespartei.* Mainz, 1987.

Behrend, Hans-Karl. "Zur Personalpolitik des Preussischen Ministeriums des Innern—Die Besetzung der Landratsstellen in den Östlichen Provinzen 1919–1933." *Jahrbuch für die Geschichte Mittel- und Ostdeutschlands* 6 (1957), 173–214.

Bendersky, Joseph W. *Carl Schmitt—Theorist for the Reich.* Princeton, N.J., 1983.

Berghahn, Volker R. *Der Stahlhelm—Bund der Frontsoldaten 1918–1935*. Düsseldorf, 1966.

Bergsträsser, Ludwig. *Geschichte der politischen Parteien in Deutschland*. 6th ed. Mannheim, 1932.

Berlau, Abraham Joseph. *The German Social Democratic Party*. New York, 1949. Rpt. New York, 1970.

Bieberstein, Johannes Rogalla von. *Preussen als deutsches Schicksal: Ein dokumentarischer Essay über Preussentum, Militarismus, Junkertum und Preussenfeindschaft*. Munich, 1981.

Bleuel, Hans Peter, and Ernst Klinnert. *Deutsche Studenten auf dem Weg ins Dritte Reich—Ideologie—Programme—Aktionen, 1918–1935*. Gütersloh, 1967.

————. *Deutschlands Bekenner—Professoren zwischen Kaiserreich und Diktatur*. Bern, 1968.

Böhme, Wolfgang, ed. *Preussen—Eine Herausforderung*. Karlsruhe, 1981.

Bölling, Rainer. *Volksschullehrer und Politik—Der deutsche Lehrerverein 1918–1933*. Göttingen, 1978.

Booms, Hans. "Die Deutsche Volkspartei (DVP)" in *Das Ende der Parteien 1933*. Ed. Erich Matthias and Rudolf Morsey, 523–39. Düsseldorf, 1960.

Borg, Daniel R. *The Old-Prussian Church and the Weimar Republic: A Study in Political Adjustment, 1917–1927*. Hanover, N.H., 1984.

Born, Karl Erich. *Staat und Sozialpolitik seit Bismarcks Sturz*. Wiesbaden, 1957.

Bracher, Karl Dietrich. "Der 20. Juli 1932." *Zeitschrift für Politik* 3 (Dec. 1956), 243–49.

————. *Die Auflösung der Weimarer Republik*. 5th ed. Düsseldorf, 1978.

————. "Probleme der Wahlentwicklung in der Weimarer Republik." In *Wählerbewegung in der deutschen Geschichte*, ed. Otto Büsch et al., 627–48. Berlin, 1978.

Brady, Robert. *The Rationalization Movement in German Industry*. Berkeley, Calif., 1933.

Braun, Otto. *Deutscher Einheitsstaat oder Föderativstaat*. Berlin, 1927.

Brecht, Arnold. *Federalism and Regionalism in Germany—The Division of Prussia*. New York, 1945.

————. *"Die Auflösung der Weimarer Republik und die politische Wissenschaft." In Zeitschrift für Politik* 2 (Dec. 1955), 291–308.

Breitman, Richard. "German Social Democracy and General Schleicher 1932–1933." *Central European History* 9 (Dec. 1976), 352–78.

————. *German Socialism and Weimar Democracy*. Chapel Hill, N.C., 1981.

Bridenthal, Renate. "Beyond *Kinder, Küche, Kirche:* Weimar Women at Work." *Central European History* 6 (June 1973), 148–66.

Bucher, Peter. *Der Reichswehrprozess—Der Hochverrat der Ulmer Reichswehroffiziere 1929/1930*, Boppard a.Rh., 1967.

Büsch, Otto. *Gechichte der Berliner Kommunalwirtschaft in der Weimarer Epoche*. Berlin, 1960.

Büsch, Otto, ed. *Das Preussenbild in der Geschichte*. Berlin, 1980/81.

Büsch, Otto, and Wolfgang Haus, eds. *Berlin als Hauptstadt der Weimarer Republik 1919–1933*. Berlin, 1987.

Büsch, Otto, and Wolfgang Neugebauer, eds. *Moderne Preussische Geschichte, 1648–1947*. Berlin, 1982. 3 vols.

Büsch, Otto, et al., eds. *Wählerbewegung in der deutschen Geschichte—Analysen und Berichte zu den Reichstagswahlen 1871–1933*. Berlin, 1978.

Büttner, Ursula. *Hamburg in der Staats- und Wirtschaftskrise 1928–1931*. Hamburg, 1982.

———. "Politische Alternativen zum Brüningschen Deflationskurs." *Vierteljahrshefte für Zeitgeschichte* 37 (April 1989), 229–51.

Büttner, Ursula, ed. *Das Unrechtsregime: Internationale Forschung über den Nationalsozialismus*. 2 vols. Hamburg, 1986.

Caspar, Gustav Adolf. *Die sozialdemokratische Partei und das deutsche Wehrproblem in den Jahren der Weimarer Republik*. Frankfurt a.M., 1959.

Chanady, Attila. "The Disintegration of the German National People's Party, 1924–1930." *Journal of Modern History* 39 (March 1967), 65–91.

Childers, Thomas. *The Nazi Voter: The Social Foundations of Fascism in Germany, 1919–1933*. Chapel Hill, N.C., 1983.

Conway, John S. *The Nazi Persecution of the Churches, 1933–1945*. New York, 1968.

———. "Die Reichsverfassungsreform als Ziel der Politik Brünings." *Der Staat* 11 (1972), 209–17.

Conze, Werner. "Die Krise des Parteienstaates in Deutschland 1929/30." *Historische Zeitschrift* 178 (Aug. 1954), 47–83.

Conze, Werner, and Hans Raupach, eds. *Die Staats- und Wirtschaftskrise 1929/33*. Stuttgart, 1967.

Craig, Gordon A. "Prussianism and Democracy: Otto Braun and Konrad Adenauer." In *The End of Prussia*, ed. Craig, 70–91. Madison, Wis., 1984.

Czisnik, Ulrich. *Gustav Noske*. Göttingen, 1969.

Deak, Istvan. *Weimar Germany's Left-Wing Intellectuals: A Political History of the Weltbühne and Its Circle*. Berkeley, Calif., 1968.

Deutz, Josef. *Adam Stegerwald*. Cologne, 1952.

Diehl, James M. *Paramilitary Politics in Weimar Germany*. Bloomington, Ind., 1977.

Dierske, Ludwig. "War eine Abwehr des 'Preussenschlages' vom 20. Juli 1932 Möglich?" *Zeitschrift für Politik* 17 (1970), 197–245.

Döhn, Lothar. *Politik und Interesse—Die Interessenstruktur der Deutschen Volkspartei*. Meisenheim am Glan, 1970.

Dörr, Manfred. "Die Deutschnationale Volkspartei 1925 bis 1928." Ph.D. diss., University of Marburg, 1964.

Dona Westfalica—Georg Schreiber zum 80. Geburtstag. Ed. Historische Kommission Westfalen. Münster, 1963.

Drechsler, Hanno. *Die Sozialistische Arbeiterpartei Deutschlands (SAPD)*. Meisenheim am Glan, 1965.

Ehni, Hans-Peter. *Bollwerk Preussen: Preussen Regierung, Reich-Länderproblem und Sozialdemokratie, 1928–1932*. Bonn-Bad Godesberg, 1975.

———. "Zum Parteienverhältnis in Preussen 1918–1932." *Archiv für Sozialgeschichte* 11 (1971), 241–88.

Eisner, Freya. *Das Verhältnis der KPD zu den Gewerkschaften in der Weimarer Republik*. Frankfurt a.M., 1977.

Engeli, Christian. *Gustav Böss: Oberbürgermeister von Berlin 1921–1930.* Stuttgart, 1971.

Engelmann, Bernt. *Preussen—Land der unbegrenzten Möglichkeiten.* Munich, 1979.

Erdmann, Karl Dietrich, and Hagen Schulze, eds. *Weimar—Selbstpreisgabe einer Demokratie—Eine Bilanz heute.* Düsseldorf, 1980.

Erdmann, Karl Dietrich, et al. *Preussen—Seine Wirkungen auf die Deutsche Geschichte.* Stuttgart, 1982.

Eschenburg, Theodor. "Carl Sonnenschein." *Vierteljahrshefte für Zeitgeschichte* 11 (Oct. 1963), 333–61.

Falter, Jürgen, et al., eds. *Wahlen und Abstimmungen in der Weimarer Republik.* Munich, 1986.

Faust, Anselm. *Der Nationalsozalistische Deutsche Studentenbund. 2 vols.* Düsseldorf, 1973.

Fiederlein, Friedrich Martin. "Der Deutsche Osten und die Regierungen Brüning, Papen, Schleicher." Ph.D. diss., University of Wärzburg, 1966.

Fijalkowski, Jürgen. *Die Wendung zum Führerstaat: Ideologische Komponenten in der politischen Philosophie Carl Schmitts.* Cologne, 1958.

Finker, Kurt. *Geschichte des Roten Frontkämpferbundes.* Berlin, 1982.

Fischer, Gerhard. *Otto Nuschke.* Berlin, 1983.

Flechtheim, Ossip K. *Die KPD in der Weimarer Republik.* Frankfurt a.M., 1969.

Forstreuter, Kurt. *Wirkungen des Preussenlandes.* Cologne, 1982.

Frye, Bruce B. *Liberal Democrats in the Weimar Republic—The History of the German Democratic Party and the German State Party.* Carbondale, Ill., 1985.

Führ, Christoph. *Zur Schulpolitik der Weimarer Republik: Darstellung und Quellen.* Weinheim, 1970.

Gaertringen, Friedrich Freiherr Hiller von. "Die Deutschnationale Volkspartei." In *Das Ende der Parteien 1933*, ed. Erich Matthias and Rudolf Morsey. Düsseldorf, 1960.

Gamm, Hans-Jochen. "Politisches Fehlverhalten als Problem des Geschichtsunterrichts." *Frankfurter Hefte* 23 (1968), 390–402.

Gay, Peter. *Das Dilemma des demokratischen Sozialismus.* Nuremberg, 1954.

Gessner, Dieter. *Agrardepression, Agrarideologie und konservative Politik in der Weimarer Republik.* Wiesbaden, 1976.

_____. *Agrarverbände in der Weimarer Republik.* Düsseldorf, 1976.

_____. *Das Ende der Weimarer Republik: Fragen, Methoden und Ergebnisse interdisziplinärer Forschung.* Darmstadt, 1978.

Geyer, Michael. *Aufrüstung oder Sicherheit: Die Reichswehr in der Krise der Machtpolitik 1924–1936.* Wiesbaden, 1980.

Giesecke, Hermann. "Zur Schulpolitik der Sozialdemokraten in Preussen und im Reich." *Vierteljahrshefte für Zeitgeschichte* 13 (April 1965), 162–77.

Glees, Anthony. "Albert C. Grzesinski and the Politics of Prussia 1926–1930." *English Historical Review* 89 (Oct. 1974), 814–34.

Golombek, Dieter. *Die politische Vorgeschichte des Preussenkonkordats.* Mainz, 1970.

Gossweiler, Kurt. *Aufsätze zum Faschismus.* 2d ed. 2 vols. Cologne, 1988.

Grebing, Helga. "Die Linke in der Weimarer Republik." *Politische Studien* 18 (1967), 334–40.

────. "Weimarer Portraits." *Politische Studien* 6 (1956), 17–35.

Grund, Henning. "Preussenschlag und Staatsgerichtshof im Jahre 1932." Ph.D. diss., University of Göttingen, 1976.

Grünthal, Günther. *Reichsschulgesetz und Zentrumspartei in der Weimarer Republik.* Düsseldorf, 1968.

Guratzsch, D. *Macht durch Organisation: Die Grundlegung des Hugenbergschen Presseimperiums.* Düsseldorf, 1974.

Gurland, Arkadij R., ed. *Faktoren der Machtbildung.* Berlin, 1952.

Haas, Ludwig. "Wahrer oder falscher Parlamentarismus." *Deutsche Republik* 3 (1929), 807.

Haffner, Sebastian. *Preussische Profile.* Frankfurt a.M., 1986.

Hamburger, Ernest. "Betrachtungen über Heinrich Brünings Memoiren." *Internationale Wissenschaftliche Korrespondenz* (April 1972), 18–39.

Hamel, Iris. *Völkischer Verband und nationale Gewerkschaft—Der Deutschnationale Handlungsgehilfen-Verband 1893–1933.* Frankfurt a.M., 1967.

Hamilton, Richard F. *Who Voted for Hitler?* Princeton, N.J., 1982.

Hauser, Oswald. *Zur Problematik "Preussen und das Reich."* Cologne, 1984.

Heberle, Rudolf. *Landbevölkerung und Nationalsozialismus.* Munich, 1963.

Heer, Hannes. *Burgfrieden oder Klassenkampf.* Berlin, 1971.

Hehl, Ulrich von. *Wilhelm Marx, 1863—1946: Eine politische Biographie.* Mainz, 1987.

Heinemann, Manfred, ed. *Der Lehrer und seine Organisation.* Stuttgart, 1977.

Heller, Hermann. "Genie und Funktionär in der Politik." *Neue Rundschau* 41 (1930), 721–31.

Herlemann, Beatrix. *Kommunalpolitik der KPD im Ruhrgebiet 1924–1933.* Wuppertal, 1977.

Hermens, Ferdinand A., and Theodor Schieder, eds. *Staat, Wirtschaft und Politik in der Weimarer Republik—Festschrift für Heinrich Brüning.* Berlin, 1967.

Herzfeld, Hans, and Gerd Heinrich, eds. *Berlin und die Provinz Brandenburg im 19. und 20. Jahrhundert.* Berlin, 1968.

Höhne, Heinz. *Mordsache Röhm.* Reinbek b. Hamburg, 1984.

Holl, Karl, ed. *Wirtschaftskrise und liberale Demokratie.* Göttingen, 1978.

Holzbach, Heidrun. *Das "System Hugenberg."* Stuttgart, 1980.

Hömig, Herbert. *Das preussische Zentrum in der Weimarer Republik.* Mainz, 1979.

Höner, Sabine. *Der nationalsozialistische Zugriff auf Preussen.* Bochum, 1984.

Höpker-Aschoff, Hermann. *Deutscher Einheitsstaat.* Berlin, 1928.

────. *Geld und Währungen.* Stuttgart, 1948.

Hörster-Philipps, Ulrike. *Konservative Politik in der Endphase der Weimarer Republik: Die Regierung Franz von Papen.* Cologne, 1982.

Hunt, Richard N. *German Social Democracy 1918–1933.* New Haven, Conn., 1964.

Jasper, Gotthard. *Der Schutz der Republik—Studien zur staatlichen Sicherung der Demokratie in der Weimarer Republik 1922–1930.* Tübingen, 1963.

Jonas, Erasmus. *Die Volkskonservativen 1928–1933.* Düsseldorf, 1965.

Jones, Larry E. "Adam Stegerwald." *Vierteljahreshefte für Zeitgeschichte* 27 (March 1979), 1–29.

_____. *German Liberalism and the Dissolution of the Weimar Party System, 1918–1933*. Chapel Hill, N.C., 1988.

_____. "Sammlung oder Zersplitterung? Die Bestrebungen zur Bildung einer neuen Mittelpartei in der Endphase der Weimarer Republik 1930–1933." *Vierteljahrshefte für Zeitgeschichte* 25 (July 1977), 265–304.

Junker, Detlef. *Die Deutsche Zentrumspartei und Hitler 1932/33*. Stuttgart, 1969.

Kaeble, Hartmut, ed. *Zur Sozialgeschichte der Modernisierung in Deutschland im 19. und 20. Jahrhundert*. Opladen, 1977.

Kaltefleiter, Werner. *Wirtschaft und Politik in Deutschland—Konjunktur als Bestimmungsfaktor des Parteiensystems*. 2d ed. Cologne, 1968.

Kater, Michael H. *Studentenschaft und Rechtsradikalismus in Deutschland, 1918–1933*. Hamburg, 1975.

Kehr, Eckart. In *Der Primat der Innenpolitik*, ed. Hans-Ulrich Wehler. Berlin, 1965.

Kessler, Alexander. *Der Jungdeutsche Orden auf dem Wege zur Deutschen Staatpartei*. München, 1980.

Kissenkötter, Udo. *Gregor Strasser und die NSDAP*. Stuttgart, 1978.

Kittel, Helmuth. *Die Entwicklung der pädagogischen Hochschulen 1926–1932*. Berlin, 1957.

Kittel, Helmuth, ed. *Die pädagogischen Hochschulen: Dokumente ihrer Entwicklung 1920–1932*. Weinheim, 1965.

Knapp, Thomas A. "The German Center Party and the Reichsbanner." *International Review of Social History* 14 (1969), 159–79.

Knütter, Hans-Helmuth. *Die Juden und die deutsche Linke in der Weimarer Republik 1918–1933*. Düsseldorf, 1971.

Köhler, Henning. *Arbeitsdienst in Deutschland*. Berlin, 1967.

_____. *Das Ende Preussens in französicher Sicht*. Berlin, 1982.

Kosthorst, Erich, et al. *Jakob Kaiser*. 3 vols. Stuttgart, 1967.

Koszyk, Kurt. *Zwischen Kaiserreich und Diktatur—Die sozialdemokratische Presse von 1914–1933*. Heidelberg, 1958.

Koza, Ingeborg. *Die erste deutsche Republik im Spiegel des politischen Memoirenschrifttums*. Wuppertal, 1971.

Krohn, Claus-Dieter. *Stabilisierung und Ökonomische Interessen—Die Finanzpolitik des Deutschen Reiches 1923–1927*. Düsseldorf, 1974.

Kruck, Alfred. *Geschichte des Alldeutschen Verbandes 1890–1939*. Wiesbaden, 1954.

Küppers, Heinrich. "Weimarer Schulpolitik in der Wirtschafts- und Staatskrise der Republik." *Vierteljahrshefte für Zeitgeschichte* 28 (Jan. 1980), 20-46.

Kurz, Thomas. *Blutmai—Sozialdemokraten und Kommunisten im Brennpunkt der Berliner Ereignisse von 1929*. Bonn, 1988.

Lebovics, Herman. *Social Conservatism and the Middle Classes in Germany, 1914–1933*. Princeton, N.J., 1969.

Leopold, John A. *Alfred Hugenberg: The Radical Nationalist Campaign Against the Weimar Republic*. New Haven, Conn., 1977.

Luks, Leonid. *Entstehung der kommunistischen Faschismustheorie*. Stuttgart, 1984.

Mann, Golo. *Geschichte und Geschichten*. Frankfurt a.M., 1961.

Manstein, Peter. *Die Mitglieder und Wähler der NSDAP 1919–1933*. Frankfurt a.M., 1988.

Marcon, Helmut. *Arbeitsbeschaffungspolitik der Regierungen Papen und Schleicher*. Frankfurt a.M., 1974.

Matthias, Erich. *Die deutsche Sozialdemokratie und der Osten 1914–1945*. Tübingen, 1954.

Matthias, Erich. "Die Sozialdemokratische Partei Deutschlands." In *Das Ende der Parteien 1933*, ed. Matthias and Rudolf Morsey, 101–278.

———. "German Social Democracy in the Weimar Republic." In *German Democracy and the Triumph of Hitler*, ed. Anthony Nicholls and Matthias, 47–57. London, 1971.

Matthias, Erich, ed. "Hindenburg zwischen den Fronten—zur Vorgeschichte der Reichspräsidentenwahlen von 1932." *Vierteljahrshefte für Zeitgeschichte* 8 (Jan. 1960), 75–84.

Matthias, Erich, and Rudolf Morsey, eds. *Das Ende der Parteien 1933*. Düsseldorf, 1960.

Matull, Wilhelm, ed. *Ostdeutschlands Arbeiterbewegung*. Würzburg, 1973.

Menges, Franz. *Reichsreform und Finanzpolitik*. Berlin, 1971.

Menzel, Hans. *Carl Severing*. Berlin, 1932.

Menzel, Walter. "Carl Severing und der 20. Juli 1932." *Die Gegenwart* 7 (8 Nov. 1952), 734–35.

Möller, Horst. "Das Ende Preussens." In *Preussen—eine Herausforderung*, ed. Wolfgang Böhme, 100–14. Karlsruhe, 1981.

———. "Die preussischen Oberpräsidenten der Weimarer Republik als Verwaltungselite." *Vierteljahrshefte für Zeitgeschichte* 30 (Jan. 1982), 1–26.

———. "Ernst Heilmann—Ein Sozialdemokrat in der Weimarer Republik." *Jahrbuch des Instituts für Deutsche Geschichte an der Universität Tel Aviv* 11 (1982), 261–64.

———. *Parlamentarismus in Preussen 1919–1932*. Düsseldorf, 1985.

Mommsen, Hans. *Arbeiterbewegung und nationale Frage*. Göttingen, 1979.

Mommsen, Hans, et al. eds. *Industrielles System und politische Entwicklung in der Weimarer Republik*. Düsseldorf, 1974.

Morsey, Rudolf. *Der Untergang des politischen Katholizismus—die Zentrumspartei zwischen christlichem Selbstverständnis und 'Nationaler Erhebung' 1932/33*. Stuttgart, 1977.

———. *Zur Entstehung, Authenzität und Kritik von Brünings "Memoiren 1918–1934."* Cologne, 1975.

Morsey, Rudolf, ed. "Der Beginn der 'Gleichschaltung' in Preussen: Adenauers Haltung in der Sitzung des 'Dreimännerkollegiums' am 6. Februar 1933." *Vierteljahrshefte für Zeitgeschichte* 11 (Jan. 1963), 85–97.

Morsey, Rudolf, ed. *Zeitgeschichte in Lebensbildern—Aus dem politischen Katholizismus des 20. Jahrhunderts*. Mainz, 1973.

Morsey, Rudolf, ed. "Zur Geschichte des 'Preussenschlags' am 20. Juli 1932." *Vierteljahrshefte für Zeitgeschichte* 9 (Oct. 1961), 430–39.

Mosse, George L. "German Socialists and the Jewish Question in the Weimar Republic." In *Yearbook of the Leo Baeck Institute*, 123–51. London, 1971.

Müller, Hermann, et al. *Zehn Jahre deutsche Geschichte 1918–1928*. 2d ed. Berlin, 1928.

Muth, Heinrich. "Agrarpolitik und Parteipolitik im Frühjahr 1932." In *Staat*, ed. Ferdinand A. Hermens and Theodor Schieder, 317–60. Berlin, 1967.

Naphtali, Fritz, ed. *Wirtschaftsdemokratie: Ihr Wesen, Weg und Ziel*. Berlin, 1928.

Neebe, Reinhard. *Grossindustrie, Staat und NSDAP 1930–1933*. Göttingen, 1981.

Netzer, Hans-Joachim, ed. *Preussen: Portrait einer politischen Kultur*. Munich, 1968.

Neumann, Sigmund. *Die Parteien der Weimarer Republik*. Stuttgart, 1965.

Niewyk, Donald L. *Socialist, Anti-Semite, and Jew: German Social Democracy Confronts the Problem of Anti-Semitism, 1918–1933*. Baton Rouge, La., 1971.

Orlow, Dietrich. *The History of the Nazi Party 1919–1933*. Pittsburgh, Pa., 1969.

———. *Weimar Prussia 1918–1925: The Unlikely Rock of Democracy*. Pittsburgh, Pa., 1986.

Osterroth, Franz. "Der Hofgeismar Kreis der Jungsozialisten." *Archiv für Sozialgeschichte* 4 (1964), 525–69.

Panzer, Arno. *Das Ringen um die deutsche Agrarpolitik von der Währungsstabilisierung bis zur Agrardebatte im Reichstag im Dezember 1928*. Kiel, 1970.

Petzold, Joachim. "Der Staatsstreich vom 20. Juli 1932 in Preussen." *Zeitschrift für Geschichtswissenschaft* 4 (1956), 1146–86.

Pikart, Eberhard. "Preussische Beamtenpolitik 1918–1933." *Vierteljahrshefte für Zeitgeschichte* 6 (April 1958), 119–37.

Petzina, Dietmar. *Die deutsche Wirtschaft in der Zwischenkriegszeit*. Wiesbaden, 1977.

Plehwe, Friedrich-Karl von. *Reichskanzler Kurt von Schleicher: Weimars letzte Chance gegen Hitler*. Esslingen, 1983.

Puhle, Hans-Jürgen. *Von der Agrarkrise zum Präfaschismus*. Wiesbaden, 1972.

Puhle, Hans-Jürgen, and Hans-Ulrich Wehler, eds. *Preussen im Rückblick*. Göttingen, 1980.

Rebentisch, Dieter. "Hitlers Reichskanzlei zwischen Politik und Verwaltung." In *Verwaltung contra Menschenführung im Staat Hitlers*, ed. Rebentisch and Karl Teppe, 65–99. Göttingen, 1986.

Reulecke, Jürgen, ed. *Arbeiterbewegung an Rhein und Ruhr*. Wuppertal, 1974.

Rietzler, Rudolf. "Kampf in der Nordmark—Das Aufkommen des Nationalsozialismus in Schleswig-Holstein (1919–1928)." Ph.D. diss., University of Hamburg, 1980.

Ritter, Gerhard A. *Arbeiterbewegung, Parteien und Parlamentarismus—Aufsätze zur deutschen Sozial- und Verfassungsgeschichte im 19. und 20. Jahrhundert*. Göttingen, 1976.

Ritter, Gerhard A., ed. *Entstehung und Wandel der modernen Gesellschaft*. Berlin, 1970.

Ritthaler, Anton, ed. "Eine Etappe auf Hitlers Weg zur ungeteilten Macht: Hugenbergs Rücktritt als Reichsminister." *Vierteljahrshefte für Zeitgeschichte* 8 (April 1960), 193–219.

Rohe, Karl. *Das Reichsbanner Schwarz-Rot-Gold*. Düsseldorf, 1966.

Rosenhaft, Eve. *Beating the Fascists? The German Communists and Political Violence, 1929–1933*. Cambridge, Mass., 1983.

Runge, Wolfgang. *Politik und Beamtentum im Parteienstaat—Die Demokratisierung der politischen Beamten in Preussen zwischen 1918 und 1933.* Stuttgart, 1965.

Schäfer, Friedrich. "Wahlrecht und Wählerverhalten in der Weimarer Republik." In *Wählerbewegung*, ed. Otto Büsch et al., 119–40.

Schauff, Johannes. *Die deutschen Katholiken und die Zentrumspartei.* Cologne, 1928.

Schmitt, Carl. *Die geistesgeschichtliche Lage des heutigen Parlamentarismus.* 2d ed. Berlin, 1926.

———. *Legalität und Legitimität.* Berlin, 1932.

Schneider, Michael. *Das Arbeitsbeschaffungsprogramm des ADGB.* Bonn–Bad Godesberg, 1975.

Schneider, Werner. *Die Deutsche Demokratische Partei in der Weimarer Republik 1924–1930.* Munich, 1978.

Schoeps, Hans Joachim. *Zeitgeist der Weimarer Republik.* Stuttgart, 1968.

Schönhoven, Klaus. *Die Bayerische Volkspartei, 1924–1932.* Düsseldorf, 1972.

Schorr, Helmut J. *Adam Stegerwald.* Recklinghausen, 1966.

Schulz, Gerhard. *Aufstieg des Nationalsozialismus—Krise und Revolution in Deutschland.* Frankfurt a.M., 1975.

———. *Deutschland am Vorabend der grossen Krise.* 2 vols. Berlin, 1986, 1987.

———. *Deutschland am Vorabend der grossen Krise: Die Periode der Konsolidierung und der Revision des Bismarckschen Reichsaufbaus, 1919–1930.* Berlin, 1963.

———. "Erinnerungen an eine misslungene Restoration, Heinrich Brüning und seine Memoiren." *Der Staat* 11 (1972), 61–81.

Schulz, Heinrich. *Der Leidensweg des Reichsschulgesetzes.* Berlin, 1926.

———. *Kirchenschule oder Volksschule? Ein Kampf gegen den Reichsschulgesetzentwurf der Rechtskoalition.* Berlin, 1927.

Schulze, Hagen. *Otto Braun oder Preussens demokratische Sendung: Eine Biographie.* Berlin, 1977.

Schumacher, Martin. *Mittelstandsfront und Republik.* Düsseldorf, 1972.

Schüren, Ulrich. *Der Volksentscheid zur Fürstenenteignung 1926.* Düsseldorf, 1978.

Schuster, Kurt G. P. *Der Rote Frontkämpferbund.* Düsseldorf, 1975.

Schustereit, Hartmut. *Linksliberalismus und Sozialdemokratie in der Weimarer Republik.* Düsseldorf, 1975.

Schützinger, Hermann. "Die 'Machtergreifung.'" *Deutsche Rundschau* 70 (Feb. 1947), 96–101.

Schwabe, Klaus, ed. *Die preussischen Oberpräsidenten 1815–1945.* Boppard a.Rh., 1985.

Schwarz, Gotthart. *Theodor Wolff und das "Berliner Tageblatt" . . . 1906–1933.* Tübingen, 1968.

Senger, Gerhard. *Die Politik der Zentrumspartei zur Frage Reich und Länder von 1918–1929.* Hamburg, 1932.

Sering, Max, et al. *Die deutsche Landwirtschaft.* Berlin, 1932.

Smelser, Ronald. *Robert Ley.* New York, 1988.

Stachura, Peter D. *Gregor Strasser and the Rise of Nazism.* London, 1983.

———. *Unemployment and the Great Depression in Weimar Germany.* New York, 1986.

Stampfer, Friedrich. *Die vierzehn Jahre der ersten deutschen Republik*. 3d ed. Hamburg, 1953.

Steffani, Winfried. *Die Untersuchungsausschüsse des Preussischen Landtages zur Zeit der Weimar Republik*. Düsseldorf, 1960.

Steffen, Hans. *Otto Braun*. Berlin, 1932.

Stehkämper, Hugo, ed. *Konrad Adenauer, Oberbügermeister von Köln*. Cologne, 1976.

――――. "Konrad Adenauer und das Reichskanzleramt während der Weimarer Zeit." In *Adenauer*, ed. Stehkämper, 405–31. Cologne, 1976.

Stehlin, Stewart A. *Weimar and the Vatican, 1919–1933*. Princeton, N.J., 1983.

Stephan, Werner. *Aufstieg und Verfall des Linksliberalismus in der Weimarer Republik*. Göttingen, 1973.

Stoltenberg, Gerhard. *Politische Strömungen im schleswig-holsteinischen Landvolk 1918–1933*. Düsseldorf, 1962.

Stump, Wolfgang. *Geschichte und Organisation der Zentrumspartei in Düsseldorf*. Düsseldorf, 1971.

Stürmer, Michael. *Koalition und Opposition in der Weimarer Republik 1924–1928*. Düsseldorf, 1967.

Thadden, Rudolf von. *Prussia: The History of a Lost State*. Cambridge, Mass., 1987.

Timm, Helga. *Die deutsche Sozialpolitik und der Bruch der Grossen Koalition im März 1930*. Düsseldorf, 1952.

Treviranus, Gottfried. *Das Ende von Weimar—Heinrich Brüning und seine Zeit*. Düsseldorf, 1968.

――――. "Zur Rolle und zur Person Kurt von Schleichers." In *Staat*, ed. Ferdinand A. Hermens and Theodor Schieder, 363–82.

Trittel, Günter J. "Hans Schlange-Schöningen: Ein vergessener Politiker der 'Ersten Stunde.'" *Vierteljahrshefte für Zeitgeschichte* 35 (Jan. 1987), 25–64.

Trumpp, Thomas. "Franz von Papen, der preussisch-deutsche Dualismus und die NSDAP in Preussen." Ph.D. diss., University of Tübingen, 1963.

Turner, Henry A., Jr. *German Big Business and the Rise of Hitler*. New York, 1985.

――――. "The *Ruhrlade*." *Central European History* 3 (Sept. 1970), 195–228.

――――. *Stresemann and the Politics of the Weimar Republic*. Princeton, N.J., 1963.

Turner, Henry A., Jr., ed. *Faschismus und Kapitalismus in Deutschland—Studien zum Verhältnis zwischen Nationalsozialismus und Wirtschaft*. Göttingen, 1972.

Vogel, Walther. *Deutsche Reichsgliederung und Reichsreform in Vergangenheit und Gegenwart*. Leipzig, 1932.

Vogelsang, Thilo. *Kurt von Schleicher—Ein General als Politiker*. Göttingen, 1965.

――――. *Reichswehr Staat und NSDAP*. Stuttgart, 1962.

Wachtling, Oswald. *Josef Joos*. Mainz, 1974.

Wacker, Wolfgang. *Der Bau des Panzerschiffes "A" und der Reichstag*. Tübingen, 1959.

Ward, James J. "'Smash the Fascists' . . . German Communist Efforts to Counter the Nazis, 1930–31." *Central European History* 14 (March 1981), 30–62.

Weber, Hermann. *Die Wandlung des deutschen Kommunismus: Die Stalinisierung der KPD in der Weimarer Republik*. 2 vols. Frankfurt a.M., 1969.

————. *Hauptfeind Sozialdemokratie Strategie und Taktik der KPD 1929–1933.* Düsseldorf, 1981.

Wehler, Hans-Ulrich, ed. *Preussen ist wieder chic . . . Politik und Polemik in zwanzig Essays.* Frankfurt a.M., 1983.

Weichmann, Herbert. "Kritische Bemerkungen Herbert Weichmanns zu den Briefen Brünings an Sollmann." *Vierteljahrshefte für Zeitgeschichte* 22 (Oct. 1974), 458–60.

Weingartner, Thomas. *Stalin und der Aufstieg Hitlers.* Berlin, 1970.

Weisbrod, Bernd. *Schwerindustrie in der Weimarer Republik.* Wuppertal, 1978.

Wende, Erich. *C.H. Becker, Mensch und Politiker: Ein biographischer Beitrag zur Kulturgeschichte der Weimarer Republik.* Stuttgart, 1959.

Wengst, Udo. "Unternehmerverbände und Gewerkschaften in Deutschland im Jahre 1930." *Vierteljahrshefte für Zeitgeschichte* 25 (Jan. 1977), 99–119.

West, Franklin C. *A Crisis of the Weimar Republic: A Study of the Referendum of 20 June 1926.* Philadelphia, 1985.

Wette, Wolfram. *Gustav Noske: Eine politische Biographie.* Düsseldorf, 1987.

Wheeler-Bennett, John W. *The Nemesis of Power: The German Army in Politics.* New York, 1964.

Widder, Erwin. "Reich und Preussen vom Regierungsantritt Brünings bis zum Reichsstatthaltergesetz Hitlers." Ph.D. diss., University of Frankfurt a.M., 1959.

Willoweit, Dietmar. "Preussische Vergangenheit und deutsche Gegenwart." *Jahrbuch für die Geschichte Mittel- und Ostdeutschlands* 19 (1978), 186–205.

Winkler, Hans-Joachim. *Preussen als Unternehmer 1923–1932.* Berlin, 1965.

Winkler, Heinrich August. *Mittelstand, Demokratie und Nationalsozialismus.* Cologne, 1972.

————. *Der Weg in die Katastrophe: Arbeiter und Arbeiterbewegung in der Weimarer Republik 1930 bis 1933.* Bonn, 1987.

Wright, Jonathan R. C. *"Über den Parteien"—Die politische Haltung der evangelischen Kirchenführern 1918–1933.* Göttingen, 1977.

Ziegler, Heinz O. *Autoritärer oder Totaler Staat.* Tübingen, 1932.

Index